THE JEW AS ALLY OF THE MUSLIM

The Jew As Ally of the Muslim
Medieval Roots of Anti-Semitism

ALLAN HARRIS CUTLER
and
HELEN ELMQUIST CUTLER

UNIVERSITY OF NOTRE DAME PRESS
NOTRE DAME, INDIANA 46556

Library of Congress Cataloging in Publication Data

Cutler, Allan Harris.
  The Jew as ally of the Muslim.

  Bibliography: p.
  Includes indexes.
  1. Christianity and antisemitism. 2. Christianity and
other religions—Islam. 3. Islam—Relations—Christianity.
4. Marranos—Spain—History. 5. Jews—Spain—History.
6. Spain—Ethnic relations. I. Cutler, Helen Elmquist.
II. Title.
BM535.C87   1985   305.6'09'02   84-40295
ISBN 0-268-01190-7

TO
JACOB AND RUTH CUTLER
HOMER AND MERCEDES ELMQUIST

May God grant them continued life, health, productivity, and happiness, until their proverbial 120th year (Deut. 34:7).

Contents

CONTENTS

Acknowledgments

We wish to thank the following scholars whose encouragement of our work over the years has played an especially important role in the evolution and completion of this book:

(1) Donald Queller, University of Illinois, Urbana (an authority on the Crusades and medieval/Renaissance diplomacy), who supervised Mr. Cutler's graduate training;

(2) Richard C. Dales, University of Southern California (an authority on medieval science and technology, as well as medieval intellectual and cultural history), who assisted Donald Queller in that supervision;

(3) Lynn T. White, Jr., emeritus, University of California at Los Angeles (an authority on medieval science and technology, as well as medieval relations between Asia and Europe), former director of his university's Center for Medieval and Renaissance Studies;

(4) Robert Ignatius Burns, S.J., University of California at Los Angeles (an authority on medieval Mediterranean Spain and the Christian-Islamic encounter), director, Institute of Medieval Mediterranean Spain;

(5) Edward Synan, Pontifical Institute of Mediaeval Studies, Toronto (an authority on medieval philosophy and Christian-Jewish relations), whose work is discussed in chapter one;

(6) James Kritzeck, University of Utah (an authority on medieval Christian-Islamic relations), whose work is discussed in chapter two; and

(7) Benzion Netanyahu, emeritus, Cornell University (an authority on medieval Christian-Jewish relations and Spanish Jewish history), whose work is discussed in chapter seven.[1]

To them we say what Boaz said to Ruth (Ruth 2:12): "May the Lord recompense you for your work and may you receive a full reward from the Lord God of Israel."

We would also like to acknowledge here, with gratitude, receipt of two postdoctoral fellowships and several grants-in-aid-of-research, without which the completion of this book would have been impossible. The postdoctoral fellowships were from the Danforth Foundation, 1963-1964, and the National Endowment for the Humanities, 1967-1968. The grants were from: (1) the American Philosophical Society, 1964-1965; (2) California State University at San Diego, 1964-1965; (3) Temple University, Philadelphia, two grants, summer 1966 and academic year 1966-1967; (4) University of California at Los Angeles, Center for Medieval and Renaissance Studies, 1967-1968; (5) Florida State University, Tallahassee, 1973-1974; and (6) American Council of Learned Societies, 1976-1977.

Our travels in Spain, southern Italy/Sicily, and Israel, between August 1968 and December 1971, and then in Spain, southern France, and Portugal in December 1979 and October 1981, were also of crucial importance in helping us develop the background necessary to interpret the multifarious and complex data in this book. The earlier travels, 1968 to 1971, were made possible in part via a Cross-Disciplinary Fellowship, Society for Religion in Higher Education (since renamed Society for Values in Higher Education), assisted by the Danforth Foundation, 1968–1969; and a visiting appointment, Florida State University's Florence, Italy, campus, June through December 1971.

Allan Harris Cutler
Helen Elmquist Cutler

Introduction

Judaism, Christianity, and Islam are not three separate religions but *three branches of the same religion*, the religion of Abraham. This is the teaching of Louis Massignon, the great twentieth-century French Islamologist.[1] Massignon has strongly influenced Pope John Paul II as evidenced by two historic pronouncements of this pope in August and September of 1983.

Concluding an historic pilgrimage to the southern French shrine of Lourdes, Pope John Paul II called for "harmony and collaboration among Christians, Jews and Moslems, in order to fight prejudice."[2] At the celebration of the third centennial of the Christian defeat of the Turks at the gates of Vienna, the pope gave thanks for the fact that the former Muslim enemies and the Jews now live at peace among the Christians of Austria. Their presence in Austria serves as a reminder "to use every opportunity to promote human and spiritual understanding."[3]

Hopefully, in the coming generations, the papacy will consider the struggle to achieve the Massignonian vision its primary mission. This vision looks forward to the day of total reconciliation between the three branches of the religion of Abraham: Judaism, Christianity, and Islam. It is to this same struggle to achieve the Massignonian vision that our book is dedicated.

*****

Bernhard Blumenkranz, a European Jewish authority on medieval Christian-Jewish relations, concludes his stimulating book *Le Juif Medieval au Miroir de l'Art Chretien* with the following statement on Christian-Jewish relations:

> A scientific and unprejudiced analysis of Jewish-Christian relations can lead to only one conclusion, which is the same as the conclusion

1

to which I have come after studying the image of the Jew in medieval Christian art. This conclusion is that the struggle of Christianity against Judaism is not inevitable, necessary, nor essential. Rather, it is a product of general conditions emerging out of internal and external politics and of sociological facts. In short, it is only contingent.

If a modest enterprise of a scholar can sometimes lead to action, my most ardent desire is that my study reinforce this conviction and contribute thus, even if only in a small way, to putting an end to this struggle.[4]

We could not agree more wholeheartedly with these sentiments. Our book, like Blumenkranz's, seeks to make a small but significant contribution to the study of the Middle Ages and to contemporary interreligious reconciliation by developing the following two theses.

(1) After the rise of Islam in the seventh century the study of the history of Christian-Jewish relations *cannot be understood apart* from the study of the history of *Christian-Islamic* relations.

(2) *Anti-Muslimism was the primary*, though not the only, factor in the revival of anti-Semitism during the High Middle Ages (1000-1300), the effects of which have been felt in all subsequent centuries, including our own.

*****

The title and subtitle of our book were suggested by Robert Ignatius Burns, S.J., professor of history, University of California at Los Angeles. Professor Burns is an authority on medieval Mediterranean Spain and the Christian-Islamic encounter, whose encouragement of our work we deeply appreciate.

"A Jew is not a Jew until he converts to Islam."[5] This paradoxical statement, found in Peter the Venerable's famed twelfth-century Toletano-Cluniac corpus (cf. chapter two infra), is one of the many pieces of evidence presented throughout our book, especially its pivotal fourth chapter. This evidence demonstrates that medieval Western European Christians tended, in their own minds, to associate Jew with Muslim, equating the two non-Christian groups, and to consider the Jew an *ally* of the Muslim as well as an Islamic fifth columnist in Christian territory. Hence, the title of the book, *The Jew as Ally of the Muslim*.

2

The subtitle of the book, *Medieval Roots of Anti-Semitism*, reflects our view, influenced by such scholars as Joshua Trachtenberg and Norman Cohn, that modern anti-Semitism, including that of the twentieth century, has deep roots in medieval anti-Semitism, which arose primarily out of medieval anti-*Muslimism*.

Chapter one, "Toward a New Comparative Approach to the History of Papal-Jewish Relations," presents six criteria for a new history of papal-Jewish relations. The most important of these is the comparative approach. "Each pope's general policy toward the Jews should be understood in the light of what we know, from the most recent research, about his policy toward other non-Catholics, whether pagans, Christians (medieval Western Christian heretical movements, Protestants, Eastern Orthodox, and Middle Eastern Christians), or Muslims, especially Muslims." The chapter then calls for an international Christian-Jewish scholarly effort to produce a history of papal-Jewish relations from Peter to John Paul II in accordance with these criteria.

Chapter two, "Peter the Venerable (1094–1156) and Islam: an Introduction to the Study of Medieval Christian-Islamic Relations," discusses recent developments in the field of medieval Christian-Islamic relations. The chapter focuses in detail on the Toletano-Cluniac corpus, a landmark in the history of Western Christian attempts to understand Islam by translating Arabic texts and refuting Islamic literature. This corpus was sponsored by Peter the Venerable, abbot of Cluny, during the early 1140s in connection with his trip to Spain. It consists of two types of documents: (1) Latin translations from Arabic texts written both by Muslims and Christians and (2) original Christian Latin texts.

Among the translations were two by Robert of Ketton: the Quran itself, the first of three medieval Latin Quran translations (the second was by Mark of Toledo, early thirteenth century; the third, now lost, by John of Segovia, midfifteenth century); and the *Fabulae Saracenorum*, a highly legendary chronicle beginnning with the creation of the world and ending with Caliph Yazid (680). Herman of Dalmatia contributed two translations: the *Liber Generationis Mahumet* and the *Doctrina Mahumet*. Both are based on material going back to early converts from Judaism to Islam circa 630, Kab al-Ahbar and Abdallah ibn Salam respectively.

Peter of Toledo (whom we suggest was Petrus Alphonsi) prepared one translation, the *Epistola Saraceni cum Rescripto Christiani*. It was based on al-Kindi's *Risalah*, a major anti-Islamic treatise written by a ninth-century Christian Iraqi Arab. Among the original texts in the Toletano-Cluniac corpus were two by Peter the Venerable himself: the more objective *Summa Totius Haeresis Saracenorum* and Peter's refutation of Islamic belief (but not Islamic practice), the *Liber contra Sectam sive Haeresim Saracenorum.*

This second chapter also issues a warm invitation to other scholars to edit, translate, and comment upon an extensive body of medieval Latin primary source materials, including the Toletano-Cluniac corpus, wherein Western Christian writers upheld their side of an important and fascinating dialogue with Islam.

Chapter three, "Petrus Alphonsi (1076-1146) and Peter the Venerable: the Anti-Islamo/Judaic Origins of the Twelfth-Century Renaissance," calls for a revival of research on Petrus Alphonsi (circa 1076-1146; Spain, England, and possibly France). A convert from Judaism to Christianity, he was one of the fathers of the Twelfth-Century Renaissance. Petrus Alphonsi made crucial contributions to the intellectual and cultural revival of Western Europe during the twelfth century in three closely related areas: polemics, fiction, and science.

Petrus Alphonsi's unusually well-informed *Dialogi* against the Jews and Muslims were of great importance in the history of Western Christian polemics against these two non-Christian monotheistic faiths. Such polemics played a major but hitherto relatively unappreciated role in the Twelfth-Century Renaissance.

His *Disciplina Clericalis*, based on Arabic materials, was of great influence in the history of Western European fiction, which itself experienced a major creative expansion during the Twelfth-Century Renaissance. This work also played a significant role in breaking down the anti-Islamic prejudices of the Western European educated class. Petrus Alphonsi probably reasoned as follows. The Islamic world was ahead of the Western Christian in science and technology. For this reason the knights of the successful First Crusade (1095-1099) could only provide Western Christendom with a temporary victory. Permanent Christian victory over Islam could not come until the Christians overtook and surpassed the Muslims in science and technology. The quickest way to accomplish that was for Western Christians to borrow Islamic science and technology in toto and then improve upon it. However, Western Christians would be pyschologically unable to begin that borrowing process unless and until their prejudices against

4

the Muslims were overcome and they could think more rationally about the Islamic challenge. To help overcome those prejudices Petrus Alphonsi wrote the *Disciplina Clericalis*.

Petrus Alphonsi's contribution to the development of medieval science (astronomy, mathematics, geography, etc.) was crucial. He played a major role in the transmission of Arabic scientific knowledge to Western Europe when the Twelfth-Century Renaissance was only in its infancy.

Chapter three also presents a preliminary case in favor of the high likelihood that Petrus Alphonsi played a leading role in the Toletano-Cluniac corpus, Peter the Venerable's project of the 1140s to translate and refute Islamic religious literature. It suggests that Petrus Alphonsi was Peter of Toledo, the person who translated al-Kindi's *Risalah* (the ninth-century Middle Eastern Christian anti-Islamic polemic), probably planned which works were to be translated for the Toletano-Cluniac corpus, and annotated the corpus, especially the Quran and *Risalah*. If this hypothesis should prove correct, it would further confirm the crucial role which Petrus Alphonsi played in the intellectual and cultural life of the twelfth century. It would also charge us to ponder whether indeed the Twelfth-Century Renaissance grew more out of an attempt to solve the problem of Christianity's relations with Islam and Judaism than out of an attempt to recover the classical heritage of Greece and Rome.

Chapter four, "The Association of Jew with Muslim by Medieval Christians: A New Comparative Approach to the Origins of Modern Anti-Semitism," presents a challenging theory which we have been developing during a program of research, pursued since 1960, on medieval Christian attitudes toward *Islam*. This theory is influenced by Blumenkranz and other scholars. It suggests that the great outburst of anti-Semitism in Western Europe in the High Middle Ages (1000-1300), continuing into the Later Middle Ages (1300-1500) and modern times (after 1500), was *not* due primarily to the deicide charge (the charge that the Jews killed Christ) nor to socioeconomic rivalry between Christians and Jews. Of course, we do not deny that these and other factors did play a role. Rather, this great outburst of anti-Semitism was due *primarily* (though by no means exclusively) to the dynamic expansion of medieval civilization between 900 and 1100. This expansion resulted in the centuries-long clash between Christianity and Islam known as the Crusades, which has not ended yet.

The Jews were caught in the middle. *Because of their similarities to the Muslims*, the Jews were viewed by Christians *as allies of the Muslims*, Islamic fifth columnists in Christian territory and agents of the dangerous foreign Islamic conspiracy. As such, the Jews had to be degraded, converted, exiled, or killed. Had there been no great outburst of Christian hatred against the Muslims in the Crusades, there might well have been no great outburst of anti-Semitism in Western Europe during the High Middle Ages. Indeed, had there been no such outburst of Christian hatred against the Muslims, anti-Semitism might well have died out altogether in Western society,[6] for anti-Semitism was dormant during most of the previous period in Western European history, the Carolingian-Ottonian (circa 700-1000). With the developing Christian-Jewish dialogue of today, stimulated greatly by Pope John XXIII and Vatican II, we finally have a significant opportunity to move toward overcoming the terrible legacy of anti-Semitism born out of medieval *anti-Muslimism*.

Minority groups often contribute unwittingly to their own persecution. Thus, chapter five, "The Association of Jew with Muslim by Medieval *Jews*: A Crucial Factor in the Association of Jew with Muslim by Medieval Christians," attempts to demonstrate that *medieval Hebrew literature itself* often closely associated Jew with Muslim. When this aspect of medieval Hebrew literature became known to Western Christians, as almost certainly was the case during the ninth through the eleventh centuries, it would have tended to reconfirm Western Christian suspicions that the Jews were in league with the Muslims.

There are five major Jewish historical works circa 600 to 1100 which tend to associate Jew with Muslim. We refer, in chronological order, to the following: (1) the "life" of Bustanai (circa 650–900); (2) the travel narrative of Eldad the Danite (ninth century); (3) the chronicle of Nathan the Babylonian (tenth century); (4) the exchange of letters between Hasdai the son of Shaprut, the Jewish foreign minister of the caliphate of Cordova, and Joseph, the Jewish khan of the Khazars (tenth century); and (5) the chronicle of Ahima'atz (eleventh century).

Of these five works the chronicle of Ahima'atz offers the best illustration of the point we are trying to make. It was written in southeastern Italy and tells in rhymed prose (influenced by Arabic models) the unique story of a remarkable and powerful Jewish family.

After wavering between pro- and anti-Arab sentiments, this chronicle concludes by clearly embracing the pro-Arab position. Its favorable Italian Jewish attitude toward the Arabs in the mideleventh century sharply contrasts with the increasingly hostile Western Christian attitude toward the Arabs during this very same period. Such a dichotomy may help explain in part why the crusading movement, which began primarily as an attempt to solve the problem of Islam, rapidly developed into an attack on the Jews as well.

One area in which we have attempted to develop this new comparative approach to medieval anti-Semitism *via medieval anti-Muslimism* is in interpreting Pope Innocent III's decision at the Fourth Lateran Council of 1215 to impose a "badge of shame" on the Jews. This decision is generally considered by Jewish historians to have been of crucial importance in the history of anti-Semitism, as well as one of the most infamous things any pope has ever done to the Jewish people. However, to Pope Innocent III (1198–1216) Christian-Islamic relations (and the Crusades) were undoubtedly far more important than Christian-Jewish relations, and the decree of the Fourth Lateran Council imposing the Jewish badge *also imposes a Muslim badge*. Yet, to our knowledge, these facts have been largely ignored; and no one has ever attempted to interpret Pope Innocent III's Jewish policy in terms of his Muslim policy.

It seemed to us that such a new comparative approach was long overdue. In attempting to relate the pope's Jewish policy to his Muslim policy with regard to the badge we came across evidence, presented in chapter six, "Why Did Pope Innocent III Want the Fourth Lateran Council (1215) to Impose a Distinction in Clothing on *Muslims* and Jews?" to support the following revisionary conclusions.

During the latter part of his pontificate (certainly from April 1213 on) Pope Innocent III came to hold the following beliefs.

(1) The Second Coming of Christ would take place in 1284.

(2) In order to pave the way for this eschatological event, the Muslims of the Middle East would have to be converted to Christianity.

(3) To achieve the conversion of the Muslims of the Middle East, missionaries would have to be sent among them.

In order to facilitate the work of these missionaries,

(4) a great (Fifth) Crusade would have to be launched that would conquer and occupy the Islamic lands in the Middle East; and

(5) the conquered Muslims in these lands would have to be degraded socially by means of a distinction in clothing imposed upon them by their Christian conquerors.

Concomitant with this, the pope believed, the Jews living in Western Europe, who were equated with the Muslims and considered an Islamic "fifth column" in Christian territory, would also have to be degraded socially by means of a distinction in clothing. The purpose was to facilitate their conversion en masse as part of the same preparation for the Second Coming of Christ.

Thus, uppermost in the mind of Pope Innocent III was the conversion of the Muslims, not the Jews. The Jews were brought into the picture primarily because of their link with the Muslims. The main thrust of the requirement for a distinction in clothing, as conceived by Pope Innocent III, was directed against the Muslims he hoped to conquer in the Middle East, not the Jews of Western Europe. Hence, it was Christian-Islamic relations which determined Christian-Jewish relations in one of the most crucial episodes in the history of the Jewish people in Western Europe.

From Pope Innocent III and the early thirteenth century we move on to the highly controversial problem of the Marranos of fifteenth—century Spain. Chapter seven, "The Netanyahu Thesis on the Marranos: A New Ethnic Approach to the Origins of the Spanish Inquisition," is based upon the researches of Benzion Netanyahu, as presented in two books. They are as follows: *Don Isaac Abravanel, Statesman and Philosopher* (Philadelphia: Jewish Publication Society of America, 1st edition, 1953; 2nd edition, 1968; 3rd edition, 1972); and especially *The Marranos of Spain, from the Late XIVth to the Early XVIth Century, According to Contemporary Hebrew Sources* (New York: American Academy for Jewish Research, 1st edition, 1966; 2nd edition, 1973). The Marranos were the thousands of Spanish Jews who converted to Christianity in the late fourteenth and early fifteenth centuries.

Contrary to regnant scholarly opinion, Netanyahu demonstrates that the overwhelming majority of the Marranos were sincere Christians, not secret Jews. The fifteenth-century Marranos wanted nothing other than to participate fully and completely, on an equal basis with the Old Christians, in the exciting and dynamic Spanish Christian civilization which in the sixteenth century spilled over its borders, colonized the New World, and became the leading power in the Old. The Marranos despised Judaism as much as did the Old Christians. Both

8

groups wanted no relationships whatsoever with the unconverted Jews still residing in Iberia.

The Marranos were permitted to assimilate fully into Spanish Christian society during the first two-thirds of the fifteenth century. However, the establishment of the Inquisition circa 1480 halted and began to reverse partially that movement. Given the sincere Christianity of the Marranos, the Spanish Inquisition could not have been established for religious reasons, *i.e.*, to suppress the alleged secret Judaism of the Marranos. Rather, according to Netanyahu, the Inquisition was a product of "racial [ethnic] hatred and political considerations."

The Inquisition persecuted the Marranos essentially because of their race, *i.e.*, their Jewish ethnic background. The "political considerations" included the desire of the monarchy to use the Inquisition to forge a unified modern nation state in Spain by suppressing regionalism and the nobility (with whom the Marranos were generally allied). The alleged secret Judaism of the Marranos was not the motivating factor behind the Inquisition but did provide this institution with a convenient pretext to mask its true motives. The establishment of the Inquisition represented a decision by Spanish Christian society to reject the Marranos as converts to Christianity, even though their conversion was sincere, because such rejection satisfied ethnic emotions and served political considerations which seemed overwhelmingly more important than the true teaching of the church at the time.

In shocked and bewildered response to the sudden turn of events in the 1480s—their persecution by the Inquisition and rejection by Christian society—*some* (but not most) of the Marranos did as follows. They attempted, as a form of defiance and protest, to rediscover their origins—the Jewish heritage of their grandparents of the late fourteenth and early fifteenth centuries. To accomplish this they either fled Spain in order to return to Judaism in a more tolerant foreign land or else remained in Spain but began to practice Judaism in secret. Hence, the secret Judaism of the Marranos did not produce the Spanish Inquisition. Quite the contrary. The Spanish Inquisition produced the secret Judaism of the Marranos!

Netanyahu's work, thus, requires us to ask and attempt to answer the following question. Why did Spanish Christian society through the Inquisition established circa 1480, decide to reject the Marranos, despite their sincere conversion, when it had accepted them during the first two-thirds of that century? In short, why did Spanish Christian society refuse to permit total Jewish assimilation and disappearance? Netanyahu's response is "race" and "politics." This chapter of our book develops eight possible additional explanations for the refusal, the last of which is the following. The Christian world requires the continued existence of the Jews as Jews in order to maintain the delicate balance between Christianity's Semitic/Judaic heritage and its Indo-European/Greco-Roman heritage. Without that balance Christianity could not survive as a world religion.

Netanyahu's work has paved the way for a complete reappraisal of the history of the Jewish people in the Iberian peninsula. One way of continuing the momentum of the advance introduced by Netanyahu into the study of Christian-Jewish relations in late medieval/early modern Spain is via the comparative method. We need a thorough comparative study of the problem of the Marranos with that of the Moriscos (forcible converts from Islam to Christianity) in sixteenth-century Spain; prior thereto, of the Jews with that of the Mudejars (Muslims) within Christian society in high medieval Spain; prior thereto, of the Jews with that of the Mozarabs (Arabic-speaking Christians) within Muslim Spain circa 711-1250; and prior thereto, of the Jews with that of the Arian heretics within Visigothic Spain circa 589 to 711. This kind of comparative approach of a future, ecumenically oriented scholarship on the Marranos may offer the best hope for a thorough modern understanding of the genuine dynamic of interreligious relations in Iberia throughout the centuries, especially during the Renaissance period (circa 1400 to 1600).

Once we accept the Netanyahu thesis, that the overwhelming majority of the Spanish Marranos of the fifteenth century were sincere Christians, we must confront the serious historiographical problem which Netanyahu has not yet addressed. That problem is what factors caused the unprecedented sincere mass conversion to Christianity of the Jews of Spain and southern Italy during the Later Middle Ages. Such is the topic of chapter eight of our book, "The Crucial Influence of *Islam* upon the Collapse of the Jewish Communities of Spain (circa 1400) and Southern Italy (circa 1300)." By "collapse" in the title of this chapter we mean "sincere mass Jewish conversion to Christianity." During the Middle Ages and the Renaissance, to our knowledge, this phenomenon of sincere mass Jewish conversion to another reli-

10

gion occurred uniquely in the Mediterranean, *i.e.*, in Spain and southern Italy. It was unknown north of the Pyrenees and Alps where the overwhelming majority of the Jews chose martyrdom or exile rather than forsake their ancestral faith.

This chapter of our book proceeds to consider the following factors as possible explanations of why the Jewish community of Spain collapsed so totally circa 1400 that it sincerely converted en masse to Christianity at that time:

(1) Spanish Jewry's especially strong power drive;

(2) the Spanish civil war circa 1350-1370 (between King Pedro the Cruel and his rebel half-brother Henry of Trastamara) in which the Jews chose to support the loser (Pedro);

(3) Spanish Jewry's excessive social sophistication (really pseudo-sophistication) which misled it into thinking that it could escape the law of "superfluous people" as well as the Jewish fate and destiny in general (*i.e.*, perpetual migration);

(4) Spanish Jewish desire for revenge upon the Muslims, the other and even larger non-Christian ethnoreligious minority in the Iberian peninsula, and the equally intense Spanish Jewish desire to refute, once and for all, the devastating Christian charge that the Jews were in league with the Muslims;

(5) Spain's geography and climate;

(6) ethnic tensions within the Spanish Jewish community itself;

(7) the geriatric factor and Spanish Jewry's desire for cultural rejuvenation;

(8) the role of philosophy;

(9) the role of mysticism;

(10) the economic interpretation, *i.e.*, Spanish Jewry's excessive wealth;

(11) the constant shifting of the majority culture within the Iberian peninsula; and, *perhaps most importantly*,

(12) the especial attraction of Spanish Christian culture as *a heavily Semiticized Christian culture*.

The primary effects of the sincere mass conversion of the Spanish Jews were as follows: to help generate (1) a major Spanish exploration and colonization effort in the New World, as well as (2) powerful currents of theological and philosophical liberalism and skepticism that would make intellectual and cultural freedom and individualism far

11

more possible in eighteenth- than in fifteenth-century Europe.

The Jews of southern Italy also converted to Christianity en masse and with relative sincerity circa 1290, about a century earlier than their Spanish Jewish brethren. The same factors which may well have been operative in Spain circa 1400 would also seem to have been operative in southern Italy circa 1300.

But the crucial overarching factor which made the Spanish and south Italian Jewish communities so uniquely susceptible to the desire for mass conversion and complete assimilation was undoubtedly the same factor which made both Spain and southern Italy in general so unique in Western Europe. This factor cuts across most of the tentative explanations suggested above. We refer to *the overpowering presence of the Muslims* and the centuries-long threat, implicit as well as explicit, which Islam posed to Christian religious and social values within both the Iberian and the Italian peninsulas.

Thus, once again it was Christian-Islamic relations which crucially determined Christian-Jewish relations in one of the most tragic episodes of Jewish history and Western civilization. The Iberian Inquisition and its demonic attack upon thousands of innocent people in Europe and the New World circa 1480-1825 must ultimately be traced to the Islamic conquest of Spain in 711!

Chapter nine, "Louis Massignon (1883-1962) and the Contemporary Ramifications of the Thesis about the Anti-Islamic Origins of Modern Anti-Semitism," discusses the implications of the thesis developed in this book that Christian anti-Muslimism was the primary (though not the only) factor in medieval Christian anti-Semitism. We maintain that medieval anti-Muslimism was a crucial factor in medieval anti-Semitism. According to Joshua Trachtenberg and Norman Cohn medieval anti-Semitism is a crucial factor in modern anti-Semitism. Therefore, medieval anti-Muslimism may also be a crucial factor in modern anti-Semitism.

If this is true, then by solving the problem of anti-Muslimism we would go a long way toward solving the problem of anti-Semitism. The best way to solve the problem of anti-Muslimism is to accept the Massignonian teaching that Judaism, Christianity, and Islam are not three separate religions but rather *three branches of the same religion, the religion of Abraham.* Until Christians and Muslims embrace the Massignonian vision and end the states of war and belligerency which

12

have prevailed between them for the past fourteen centuries, we may not see the end of the long nightmare of Christian anti-Semitism in the West.

*****

We hope our book can also help people attain a greater awareness of the following important consideration relative to the contemporary and future struggle against anti-Semitism.

The book argues that the medieval roots of modern anti-Semitism are to be sought, not primarily in Christian theology (the deicide charge), but rather in other factors. These factors include the equation of Jew with Muslim by medieval Christians and the accompanying charge that the Jew was an ally of the Muslim planning the destruction of Christendom (our thesis influenced by Blumenkranz and others), as well as racial, ethnic, and political motivations (in common with Netanyahu). By so arguing we are not apologizing for anti-Semitism, as some may claim in reacting to this book. Rather, we are actually exposing anti-Semitism for what it is, thus helping to combat and eliminate it. If we hold that anti-Semitism arises primarily out of Christian theology, we make it much easier for people to come to the following dangerous conclusion. Because Christian theology is dead and/or has revised its traditional anti-Jewish stereotypes, we have cured the anti-Semitic disease and, hence, can relax our vigilance against it.

However, if we correctly recognize that modern anti-Semitism arises, not primarily out of Christian theology, but rather out of anti-Muslimism and ethnopolitical tensions, we make it much more difficult for people to come to the dangerous conclusion that in our post-Christian and post-Vatican II world we have cured the anti-Semitic disease, hence can relax our struggle against it. Anti-Muslimism (whether Christian, Communist, or Hindu), as well as racial, ethnic, and political passions and enmities, remain very powerful forces in the late twentieth century. If anti-Semitism is viewed as arising primarily out of these powerful forces which make daily headlines in contemporary Western society, people will quickly comprehend that we are nowhere near curing the anti-Semitic disease, hence cannot relax our vigilance. This approach to the history of anti-Semitism via anti-Muslimism and ethnopolitical tensions makes a far greater contribution to modern efforts to fight and cure the chronic and pernicious social disease which is anti-Semitism than the approach via Christian theology and the deicide charge!

Allan Harris Cutler
Helen Elmquist Cutler

Institute of Medieval Mediterranean Spain
Los Angeles, California
1984

1. Toward a New Comparative Approach to The History of Papal-Jewish Relations*

The Popes and the Jews in the Middle Ages by Edward Synan, informed by a genuinely sympathetic Roman Catholic attitude toward the Jewish people, is an excellent contribution to the highly important field of the history of papal-Jewish relations.[1] This field has become more exciting the past few years because of many commendable Roman Catholic initiatives (encouraged by Pope John XXIII and Vatican II) toward genuine Christian-Jewish dialogue and reconcilation. Of course, the church can still make additional progress in dealing with this highly sensitive question.[2] Since these Roman Catholic initiatives toward genuine Christian-Jewish dialogue and reconciliation will undoubtedly continue, hopefully at an accelerated pace, additional works on the history of papal-Jewish relations by both Christian and Jewish scholars are bound to follow Synan's book and be inspired by it. Hitherto, Jewish scholars have been almost the only serious students of this question; even though far more progress toward thoroughness and objectivity in this field could have been made if both Christians and Jews had shared equally in its development, which is our hope for the future. In view of the likely prospects for a contemporary revival of research on the history of papal-Jewish relations, we believe that a constructive purpose would be served by presenting several admittedly highly idealistic critieria for a new history of papal-Jewish relations and then by examining the extent to which Synan's book measures up to these criteria.

1. Each and every pope's policy toward the Jews should be understood in the light of what we know, from the most recent research, about his total personality and his total program for the church, the state, Western Christian society, and the world at large. His biography and his writings, before and after becoming pope, with emphasis upon his prepapal life and thought, are especially important. An attempt must be made to compare each pope's Jewish policy with his general

15

policy and to relate the one to the other as integrally as possible.

2. The views of modern Christian and Jewish scholars on each specific policy with regard to the Jews promoted by a given pope should be presented side by side, as should the views of Christians and Jews who were contemporaries of the pope in question, if these views are known. Thereby, the prejudices of one scholarly and religious community and of time past can balance the prejudices of the other scholarly and religious community and of time present, hopefully leading us closer to the ultimate truth of the matter.

3. It is not really the task of the historian to judge the past, to praise or condemn it, to defend or apologize for it. The historian is called upon primarily to attempt to discover what happened in the past and why it seems to have happened. However, many laymen and even some scholars who are especially sensitive to the particular needs and wishes of the general public expect the historian to judge as well as merely to endeavor to understand. If specific papal policies with regard to the Jews must be judged, these policies should be judged (a) not only in terms of the highest possible ethical standards but also in terms of the ethical standards actually prevailing today among the majority of people; also (b) not only in terms of the highest possible ethical standards according to contemporary opinion but also in terms of the highest ethical standards according to the understanding of those who lived at the time of the pope in question. These various sets of standards are by no means always the same.

4. If a specific policy of an individual pope with regard to the Jews must be judged (and, we repeat, this is not really the historian's obligation), it should always be judged in comparison with the attitudes and practices, on the same question at the same period of time, of the following: (a) the leaders of other Christian churches, i.e., heretical movements within Roman Catholic territory like the Waldensians and the Albigensians; the four major tendencies within Protestantism and their various denominational subdivisions: Anglicans, Lutherans, Calvinists and Anabaptists; the Eastern Orthodox ethnic churches: Greeks, Slavs, Rumanians, and Georgians; and the Middle Eastern Christian communities: the Monophysites of Armenia, Syria, Egypt, and Ethiopia, and the Nestorians of Iraq; (b) the leaders of Islam, whether the Sunni Islam of the Arabs and Turks or the Shii Islam of the Iranians; (c) the leaders of the non-Abrahamitic faiths: those of the Middle East, e.g., Zoroastrianism and Manicheanism, and those of South

16

and East Asia, *e.g.*, Hinduism, Buddhism, Jainism, Sikhism (though with a strong Islamic and therefore Abrahamitic admixture), Confucianism, Taoism, and Shintoism; and (d) of the rabbis themselves.

What we are saying is simply that in judging a given pope's attempt to prevent intermarriage between Christians and Jews, for example, it undoubtedly makes a considerable difference if at the same period of time the leaders of heretical movements within Roman Catholic territory and of the various Protestant, Eastern Orthodox, and Middle Eastern Christian communities, along with the Islamic *fuqaha* (legists), the Zoroastrian magi, the Manichean elect or *perfecti*, and the rabbis themselves, were all trying simultaneously to prevent intermarriage between non-Jews (Christians, Muslims, Zoroastrians, or Manicheans) and Jews. Indeed, most of the very same Jewish historians who so harshly condemn papal attempts to prevent intermarriage between Christians and Jews would condemn with equal vigor any Jew who dared take advantage of a more liberal papal policy allowing Christians and Jews to marry.

But let us remember that Hillel the Elder (circa 37–4 B.C.), the founder of rabbinic Judaism and one of the inspirations of Jesus, taught us: "Do not judge your fellow until you have put yourself in his place" (Mishnah Avot 2:5).[3] This sentiment was powerfully echoed by Jesus, who urged us: "First take the log out of your own eye and then you will see clearly enough to be able to take the speck out of your brother's eye" (Matthew 7:5). What we do not need in evaluating the highly complex issues of papal-Jewish relations is self-righteousness. What we do need is candor, sincerity, honesty, and genuine self-deprecation. Needless to say, these virtues are not foreign to the hearts and minds of both true Christians and true Jews. Both sides need them in equally strong doses if we are to overcome the misunderstandings and hatreds of past centuries which have assuredly been reflected in both the history of papal-Jewish relations and in the historiography thereof. A critical comparative study (similarities and differences) of papal attitudes and practices toward the Jews with the same attitudes and practices of modern bourgeois liberals (both committed and uncommitted Christians), socialists, communists, and fascists would also be in order and might lead to some rather startling conclusions which we never thought we could draw before.

5. If a specific policy of a given pope with regard to the Jews must be judged after all, the motives and the results of this policy, not

17

merely the policy itself, must also be taken into consideration in evaluating it. For example, it makes a significant difference if a given papal policy with regard to the Jews, which is adjudged to be evil, sinister, vicious, or cruel (*e.g.*, papal attempts to segregate the Jews from Christian society through a special badge and then a special place of enforced residence, the ghetto) (a) was motivated by a desire to destroy the Jews physically or simply by a desire to bring about their conversion; (b) had results which, in the short or the long term, harmed or benefited the Jews, decreased or increased their chances for survival. On the whole, we would conclude from our own studies of this question that papal segregationist policies were motivated primarily by a desire to convert the Jews to Christianity rather than to destroy them physically. This desire to convert the Jews was based upon love rather than hatred and was therefore a desire which true and believing Christians could not help but consider holy and pure. Precisely because such papal segregationist policies were motivated primarily by a desire to convert the Jews to Christianity rather than destroy them physically, these policies had the distinctly opposite effect of insuring the survival of the Jews *as Jews*. As ironic as life and history can both be, papal segregationist policies directed at hastening Jewish assimilation encouraged precisely the opposite, the continued existence of Jewish distinctiveness. Such is the work of Providence within history!

6. Each pope's general policy toward the Jews should be understood in the light of what we know, from the most recent research, about his policy toward other non-Catholics, whether pagans, Christians (medieval Western Christian heretical movements, Protestants, Eastern Orthodox, and Middle Eastern Christians), or Muslims, *especially Muslims*. To a great extent, medieval Christians tended, as we shall see, to equate Jew with Muslim and to consider the Jews, among other things, as Islamic fifth columnists in Christian territory. For this reason a simultaneous comparison of papal attitudes toward and dealings with both Jews and Muslims, pope by pope, decade by decade, generation by generation, century by century, is an especially great *desideratum*.

Thus, in evaluating Synan's work we should note that he has made a worthy and creditable start in the direction of fulfilling most of these admittedly highly idealistic criteria. For example, Synan attempts to understand papal policy toward the Jews in the light of general papal policy, *e.g.*, in the case of Pope Innocent III (1198–1216), the greatest medieval pope. Also, Synan knows some of the major secondary works relevant to this subject written by nineteenth- and twentieth-century Jewish historians (*e.g.*, Graetz, Baron, Grayzel) and some of the major Jewish chronicles contemporary with the popes whose policies he describes (*e.g.*, the three Hebrew chronicles, by Solomon bar Simson, Eliezer bar Nathan, and the Mainz Anonymous, which describe the persecutions of the Jews during the First Crusade). However, the book might have been improved by more extensive use of these same medieval and modern Jewish historical works.

Occasionally, however, in addition to telling us what happened and why (to do this well is achievement enough!), Synan (along with Edward Flannery, author of *The Anguish of the Jews*),[4] seems to feel compelled to apologize for papal actions with regard to the Jews. These apologies do show that the author's conscience as a learned and sensitive modern post-Vatican II Catholic is troubled by the papal-Jewish relations which prevailed in the past. For this no person of good will can possibly condemn him. Yet the apologies do not really seem necessary, because the enlightened reader, whether Protestant, Catholic, Jew, or otherwise, knows that no *human* institution, even if divinely inspired or guided, can ever be perfect.

The comparative approach to papal-Jewish relations (criteria numbers 4 and 6 supra, especially number 6) does not seem to have exerted sufficient influence upon Synan's work, though he does at times cite the rabbinic view on a given issue, *e.g.*, intermarriage between Christians and Jews, which was just as negative about this phenomenon as was the papal view, if not more so. The comparative approach is, perhaps, the primary approach upon which future, ecumenically oriented scholarship on the question should concentrate and the approach which may offer us the best hope for a thorough modern understanding of the genuine dynamics of papal-Jewish relations throughout the ages.

Finally, it should be noted that the author is a leading authority on medieval Western Christian philosophy and logic, a successor of Etienne Gilson.[5] However, though papal-Jewish relations have indeed been a highly meaningful personal and literary concern of Synan over the years, they have not hitherto been his major area of scholarly specialization. This distinction may help explain in part why Synan did not treat several important episodes in the history of papal-Jewish relations as thoroughly as some would have wanted him to do. For example, there is no discussion of the reaction of Popes John XVIII

19

(1003–1009) and Sergius IV (1009–1012) to the great persecution of the Jews of Western Europe during the early eleventh century, a persecution which may have been an even more crucial watershed in the history of Christian-Jewish relations than the First Crusade.[6] Nevertheless, Synan's book is a major literary landmark in the contemporary Christian-Jewish dialogue. It calls upon Christian and Jewish scholars to begin a new analysis of the history of papal-Jewish relations that will reflect Vatican II's attempt to inaugurate a new era of reconciliation and cooperation between the peoples of the church and the synagogue.

Perhaps Synan's work and the discussion it has provoked will provide the impetus for an international Christian-Jewish scholarly venture, enlisting the cooperation of distinguished authorities in the United States, Europe, and Israel, to produce a multivolume history of papal-Jewish relations from Peter to John-Paul II. Such a work should be inspired by the highest ideals of the great nineteenth- and twentieth-century Christian historians of the papacy and papal-Jewish relations, as well as by the highest ideals of the great nineteenth- and twentieth-century Jewish historians of the Jewish people and of papal-Jewish relations.[7]

This joint effort would approach the problem of the history of papal-Jewish relations in terms of the criteria outlined above, especially the comparative approach; and, within this approach, in terms of papal-Islamic relations. It would do so at least for the period circa 632–1683, i.e., from the death of the Prophet Muhammad to the failure of the second and last Ottoman Turkish siege of Vienna, the high-water mark of Islamic expansion against Western Europe in early modern times. The study of the history of relations between the peoples of the church and the mosque is an area of research that has taken on greatly increased significance in view of Vatican II's "Declaration on Islam" (paragraph no. 3 in the "Declaration on the Relationship of the Church to Non-Christian Religions," promulgated October 28, 1965.)[8] It has also taken on such significance in view of the vast transfer of wealth from the Christian countries of the West to the Islamic countries of OPEC, occasioned by the steep hike in oil prices for which the Yom Kippur War (October 1973) provided the convenient excuse. Finally, the study of Christian-Islamic relations has taken on increased significance in view of especially intensive recent American efforts, initiated by Secretary of State Henry Kissinger and pursued by both Presidents Carter and Reagan, to mediate the Arab-

Israeli dispute. These efforts led to President Anwar Sadat's historic visit to Prime Minister Menahem Begin in Jerusalem (1977), the awarding of the Nobel Peace Prize to the Egyptian and Israeli leaders (1978), the signing of the Egyptian-Israeli Peace Treaty in Washington, D.C. (1979); and the signing of the Lebanese-Israeli accord in the Middle East (1983). Such a new history of papal-Jewish relations would achieve best results if prepared in accordance with the comparative approach and informed at every step by a comprehensive knowledge of the history of *papal-Islamic* relations. Let us hope that work on such a project can begin in the not too distant future![9]

2. Peter the Venerable (1094-1156) and Islam: An Introduction to the Study of Medieval Christian-Islamic Relations*

Recent studies of medieval Christian attitudes toward Islam have been notable and fruitful.[1] Among the many contributors to this field, James Kritzeck is a leading North American Islamologist and authority on the past and present dialogue between the peoples of the church and the mosque.[2] Kritzeck's *Peter the Venerable and Islam* (Princeton: Princeton University Press, 1964), the fruit of many years of diligent study of challenging twelfth-century Latin texts, has benefited from the suggestions of numerous scholars of international repute both in the United States and Europe. It thus represents a very convenient and readable introduction to many of the epoch-making studies which have gone on since 1945 in the field of medieval Christian-Islamic relations. However, *Peter the Venerable and Islam* also issues a warm invitation to other scholars to edit, translate, and comment upon an extensive body of medieval Latin primary source materials, wherein Western Christian writers upheld their side of an important and fascinating dialogue with Islam.[3]

During the 1140s, the decade of the Second Crusade (1145-1150), Peter the Venerable (1094-1156) was abbot of the monastery of Cluny and head of a Western European monastic movement which profoundly influenced medieval religion and life. As abbot, Peter sponsored a project consisting of (1) Latin translations from Islamic, and Christian, Arabic texts and (2) original Christian Latin texts. To this project, a landmark in the history of medieval Western Christian attitudes toward Islam, Norman Daniel has given the name "the Toletano-Cluniac corpus." It is with this corpus that Kritzeck's book is concerned.

Peter the Venerable and Islam is composed of two separate sections. The first (pages 1-199) is an analytical summary of Peter the

22

Venerable's project, all of the translations and most of the original texts which form a part thereof. The second section (pages 201-291) is an annotated transcription from the manuscripts of several of the original Latin texts. Each section is valuable, but the first is of more immediate interest here.

*****

The preface (pages vii-xii) begins with a short description of the circumstances surrounding Theodore Bibliander's two sixteenth-century editions of much of the Toletano-Cluniac corpus (dated 1543 and 1550 respectively). Kritzeck states (page viii) that Bibliander published "the major source of informed European Christian knowledge of Islam since the twelfth century." This judgment may be a bit hasty. The major source of Western Christian knowledge of Islam during the Middle Ages probably was not the Toletano-Cluniac corpus, for all its importance, but rather the anti-Islamic (the fifth) chapter of Petrus Alphonsi's *Dialogi* against the Jews (circa 1110, Spain). Forty-two twelfth-through fifteenth-century manuscripts of the *Dialogi* have been listed; still more undoubtedly remain unlisted.[4] To our knowledge, the number of manuscripts of the Toletano-Cluniac corpus does not equal forty-two. Most medieval Christians interested in these matters probably would have preferred to derive their information about Islam from the shorter, more readable chapter in Alphonsi rather than the longer, more difficult Toletano-Cluniac corpus.

Kritzeck (page ix, note 5) sees no point in calling attention to the many misreadings and misinterpretations of the Toletano-Cluniac corpus in the numerous articles and books on this subject between a pioneering piece by Marcel Devic in 1883 and Marie Therese d'Alverny's epoch-making study of the late 1940s.[5] However, Kritzeck does praise (page ix, note 6) the "valuable preliminary work" of Pierre Mandonnet (1893), Moritz Steinschneider (1905), and Ugo Monneret de Villard (1944).

Peter the Venerable and Islam does not conclude with a separate bibliography. Kritzeck (page ix, note 13) states that the lengthy bibliography in Daniel's monumental *Islam and the West* (Edinburgh: Edinburgh University Press, 1960) "makes it unnecessary to append a special bibliography" to *Peter the Venerable and Islam*. However, the bibliographical footnotes within Kritzeck's book are excellent (the

23

scholars cited therein are found in the index to the book, pages 293–301) and cite many works not cited by Daniel, who attempted to cover a much broader field.[6] Thus, the fine bibliographical footnotes in *Peter the Venerable and Islam* have improved upon Daniel's bibliography.

Kritzeck (page xi) indicates that he is working on new editions of other texts relevant to the Toletano-Cluniac corpus and to "later projects of a similar nature." We hope that Kritzeck will soon publish a transcription of the Arsenal manuscript no. 1162, the autograph of the Toletano-Cluniac corpus, including a transcription of the important annotations to the Latin translations of the Quran and of al-Kindi's *Risalah* contained therein. We also hope that Kritzeck will soon publish a revised edition of *Peter the Venerable and Islam*, with a new prolegomenon discussing important studies of the history of Christian-Islamic relations and of Peter the Venerable's life and work as affecting his approach to Islam, which have appeared in print subsequent to the publication of the first edition in 1964.

*****

The first section of *Peter the Venerable and Islam*, the analytical summary, is divided into five chapters, each having from five to eight subdivisions. Chapter one (pages 1–47) deals with Peter the Venerable, the sponsor of the Toletano-Cluniac corpus. It presents a brief discussion of (1) Peter's trip to Spain, 1142–1143, during which he organized the translation part of the Toletano-Cluniac corpus (pages 3–14); (2) Peter's ambivalent attitude toward the Crusades, both approving and condemning them (pages 15–23); (3) the circumstances surrounding the inception of the Toletano-Cluniac corpus and the purposes which inspired Peter to undertake such a project in the first place (pages 24–36); (4) Peter's knowledge of patristic literature and his appeal to its example in defense of his right to attempt to solve the problem of Islam with the pen instead of the sword, a solution which was highly controversial (pages 37–41); and (5) the double purpose of Peter's project, to study Islam and to refute it (pages 42–47).

Kritzeck informs us (page 6) that Cluny changed its attitude from anti- to prointellectualistic during the eleventh century, a change which, of course, was of great significance in the origins of the Toletano-Cluniac corpus of the midtwelfth century. Kritzeck also points out (page 5) that when Peter the Venerable became abbot (circa 1122) Cluny was contributing more to the Twelfth-Century Renaissance of the arts and sciences than were most of the other contemporary monastic movements (some of which were its rivals), e.g., the Vallombrosans, Carthusians, Augustinian Canons, Premonstratensians, and Cistercians, as well as the Orders of Camaldoli, Grammont, Sempringham and Fontevrault.

Kritzeck may be a bit hasty when he states (page 14) that Peter the Venerable conceived the Toletano-Cluniac corpus during the course of his journey to Spain. Peter may have thought of this project even before and been influenced by the pioneering efforts of Pope Gregory VII, Abbot Hugh of Cluny, and the monk Anastasius of Cluny, to convert al-Muqtadir b. Hud (1046-1081), the Muslim ruler of Saragossa, in the 1070s.[7]

Kritzeck is fully aware (pages 15–16) of the importance of Middle Eastern Arabic and Byzantine Greek Christian anti-Islamic polemics. His book can serve as a stimulus to further research on these eastern Mediterranean Christian anti-Islamic polemics as well as their influence upon medieval Latin anti-Islamic polemics in general and those of Peter the Venerable and his Toletano-Cluniac corpus in particular.[8]

Kritzeck suggests (page 16) that had the Carolingian Empire survived there would probably have been many more friendly Western Christian contacts with the Islamic world circa 800–1050. One might add that if the West had been strong enough to prevent the Islamic incursions into northern Spain, southern France, and Sicily/southern Italy during the ninth and tenth centuries, there might have been far less Western hatred of Islam during the crucial eleventh century. On the other hand, Western European civilization's tremendous dynamism in all fields of human endeavor circa 900–1100 probably meant that this civilization had to overflow its borders in some direction. Of the three possible areas for expansion—the pagan (northeastern Europe), the Byzantine (southeastern Europe), and the Islamic—the Islamic was the area most likely to receive the overflow. It was the wealthiest of the three possible areas for expansion. It was also the only one of the three which had once been Christian but which had been seized by a religion which still posed a serious threat to Christianity. For these reasons the main thrust of Western European expansion circa 1000–1300 was directed primarily against Islamic territory.

Of course, the prevailing attitude which imperialists have toward people whose territory they are successfully conquering is contempt. What other attitude could serve as well to help absolve the guilty consciences of aggressors? However, when the crusading movement began to slow down considerably circa 1200, Western Christian attitudes toward Islam began to become more tolerant. From this point of view, the fall of the Carolingian Empire as a crucial factor in the development of Western Christian attitudes toward Islam becomes far less significant. The crucial factor now becomes the rapidity with which medieval Western Europe developed a truly dynamic civilization. Had Western Europe achieved such a civilization circa 800 under the Carolingians, the initial attitude toward Islam even at that relatively early date might well have been hatred born of expansionist desires, just as it was later circa 1100.[9]

Kritzeck commendably raises (page 16) the important question of why Western Christian missionaries (and Byzantine missionaries, one might add) largely ignored the Muslims circa 600–1000 in order to concentrate their energies on the pagan barbarians of northern and eastern Europe. Unfortunately, Kritzeck does not offer any specific and concrete answers to this question. Perhaps one can infer from his remarks (pages 16–17) the suggestion that the absence of any mass heretical movements in Western Europe circa 600–1000 was partly responsible for the disinterest in Islam (which probably was viewed by many Christians of these centuries as another Christian heresy). Favoring this suggestion is the consideration that Byzantium was racked by heresy problems (iconoclasm and neo-Manicheanism in the persons of the Paulicians and the Bogomils) during this period and would seem to have been much more interested in Islam than was Western Europe (of course, the main center of Islamic power was always much closer to Byzantium than to Western Europe). Opposing this suggestion is the consideration that perhaps the absence of any serious internal heresy problem should have set Western Europeans free to deal with the external religious problem of Islam. The fact that circa 600–1000 Western Europe, in the absence of any serious internal heresy problems, chose to attack the external religious problem of northern and eastern European paganism rather than Islam would then still remain to be explained.

Possible explanations are the following. Paganism was both an external and an internal danger (for at this early period the Christianity of the recently converted Germanic invaders was still rather super-

26

ficial and tentative). Islam, on the other hand, was purely an external danger. What is more, Christian missionary activity had been oriented toward northern and eastern Europe since the early fourth century (when the process by which the Goths were converted to Arian heterodox Christianity was initiated by Bishop Ulfilas, who came from the Greek rather than the Latin Mediterranean Christian sphere). Perhaps the habit of looking toward northern and eastern Europe for converts to Christianity was too strongly entrenched by the time Islam burst on the scene (three centuries later) to be easily uprooted. Also, the northern and eastern European pagan barbarians, who were scripture-less, were easier to convert to, and at the same time in far greater need of, Christianity and the Latin cultural heritage that went along with Christianity than were the monotheistic Muslims, who did indeed have a poetic and moving scripture of their own (the Quran) and who as heirs of the Greek, Persian, and Indian civilizations were culturally far in advance of Western Europe circa 600–1000.[10] Finally, the northern and eastern European pagans were Indo-European ethnolinguistic cousins of the Latin Christians of Western Europe, whereas the Muslims as Semites and Hamites (Egyptians, Berbers, etc.) were ethnolinguistically different. It may be that the Latin Christians preferred to bring what they considered the blessings of Christian civilization first to their own ethnolinguistic cousins, the northern and eastern European pagans, rather than to the Muslim Semites and Hamites who were ethnolinguistically alien from them.

Kritzeck is fully aware of the many medieval Christian "biographies" of the Prophet Muhammad (pages 17–19) but does not choose to discuss them in chronological order.[11] However, given Kritzeck's vast knowledge this is something which he could easily remedy in the eagerly awaited second edition of his book, so that we can obtain a fuller appreciation of how far indeed those earlier Christian accounts of the life and work of the Prophet Muhammad were transcended by Peter the Venerable's Toletano-Cluniac corpus.

Kritzeck tends to deemphasize the role played by Christian interest in the possibility of the conversion of the Muslims during the First Crusade (pages 19–20; page 19, note 53; page 20, note 55). However, elsewhere we have published a long article attempting to demonstrate that there was far more Christian interest in this possibility than has hitherto been realized by scholars.[12] Kritzeck also deemphasizes Cluny's role in the development of the crusading ideal (page 20, note 56). Yet, as he readily admits, Cluny strongly supported the Spanish *Reconquista*. However, the *Reconquista* of the eleventh century was a crucial stage in the evolution of the First Crusade. In general throughout the Middle Ages the Spanish *Reconquista* can easily be considered the western front of the crusading movement as a whole.

In dealing with Peter the Venerable's attitude toward the Crusades (pages 21–23), Kritzeck has pointed out that there are some statements by Peter which seem to approve the Crusades, others which seem to condemn them. Apparently Peter approved of the noble ideals which originally called forth the crusading movement (*e.g.*, the recapture of the Holy Land, the land of Christ). But he was appalled by the corruption (massacre, plunder, rape, internecine feuding, *etc.*) which characterized the various crusading enterprises. All things considered, Kritzeck holds that Peter's attitude toward the Crusades was more negative than positive. If so, it should be pointed out, Peter's attitude toward the Crusades would not have been too dissimilar from that of St. Francis of Assisi.

Some Franciscan scholars prefer to see St. Francis as a radical opponent of the Crusades when he was only a critic of them. Indeed, a position of radical opposition to the Crusades would have placed him within the camp of the heretics in general and the Albigensians in particular, when St. Francis struggled to avoid any and every possible association with heresy. St. Francis of Assisi *both approved and condemned* the Crusades at one and the same time in that he was only willing to give his enthusiastic approval to the crusading movement on four conditions: provided the soldiers (1) remained good Christians, ethically and ritually, loving one another as brothers and showing intense devotion to the sacraments (especially the eucharist); (2) saw their goal not as extermination of Muslims but merely their subjugation; (3) did not kill or abuse unarmed Muslim civilians; and (4) promised to allow him and his Franciscan disciples the freedom to work, by nonviolent means, for the mass conversion of the subjugated Muslims after the crusaders had accomplished the military victory.[13] To the student of history, with its manifold ironies and contradictions, St. Francis's ambivalent attitude toward the Crusades, like that of Peter the Venerable, offers no serious scholarly problems.

In his remarks on Peter the Venerable's attitude toward the Jews, Kritzeck tries to be fair to both sides. He states (page 25) that Peter's polemics against Judaism and Islam were "the first European books dealing with these faiths in which Talmudic and Koranic sources are cited verbatim." However, once again, the honor that Kritzeck claims here for Peter the Venerable probably should go instead to Petrus Alphonsi, whose *Dialogi*, approximately thirty years earlier in time than the writings of Peter on these same questions, were a major source of even Peter's own anti-Judaic and anti-Islamic polemics. Kritzeck holds that Peter the Venerable's anti-Judaic polemic possessed a goodly measure of originality (page 26). However, Kritzeck is aware (page 27, note 83) of the view of Saul Lieberman, one of the leading authorities on rabbinic literature, that the sources of Peter the Venerable's anti-Judaic polemic were "the Dialogue of Peter Alphonsi, which he used almost word for word," and a version of the *Alphabet of Ben Sira*, a Babylonian Jewish storybook compiled during the Gaonic period (circa 600–1000), one version of which reached the Jews of high medieval Franco-Germany. Kritzeck also believes that Peter the Venerable's anti-Judaic polemic abandoned "all the customary Christian invective" (page 26). However, Salo Baron, the great Jewish historian, whom Professor Kritzeck inadvertently overlooked, has expressed himself otherwise in his monumental *Social and Religious History of the Jews*.[14]

In considering Peter the Venerable's invitation to St. Bernard of Clairvaux to refute Islam (pages 43–46), Kritzeck holds that Peter properly recognized, respected, and actually liked St. Bernard more than was true vice versa and that Peter sincerely wanted Bernard, rather than himself, to write the refutation of Islam. The pope at the time was a Cistercian, and St. Bernard was the pope's official Crusade-preacher. Therefore, Peter probably felt that a refutation of Islam written by Bernard, which attacked but did so in a civilized manner, would carry far more weight in, and exercise a far more salutary effect upon, the Christian world than a refutation written by himself. Also, Peter may have hoped that his offer to permit St. Bernard to write the refutation would serve as a means of repairing the breach in their friendship which Peter especially regretted. Indeed, as Kritzeck points out (page 45, note 152), "a high point in the estrangement between Bernard and Peter was reached about this time, because of the rivalry between their orders," *i.e.*, Citeaux and Cluny. According to Kritzeck, St. Bernard's refusal to write the refutation of Islam was a "tragedy" (page 46) in that it set back both Peter the Venerable's hope to lend the prestige of St. Bernard's name to the Toletano-Cluniac corpus and his hope of healing thereby the breach which had developed between the two great monastic orders.

Yet one can not help but ask whether St. Bernard was really the right type of personality to do what Peter the Venerable hoped he would do. St. Bernard was more of a mystic than a rationalist.[15] It is unlikely that anyone who was not primarily a rationalist would have been sufficiently interested in, and sufficiently capable of, studying another faith in order to refute it. In this case it probably is fortunate that St. Bernard of Clairvaux left the refutation of Islam within the Toletano-Cluniac corpus exclusively to Peter the Venerable of Cluny.

Kritzeck rightly points out (pages 45, 158–159) the twofold purpose of Peter the Venerable's refutation of Islam, i.e., offensive and defensive, to convert Muslims to Christianity and dissuade Christians from converting to Islam. The subject of conversion from Christianity to Islam in the Middle Ages deserves a thorough modern study.[16] Such conversions may well have been taking place in significant numbers during Peter the Venerable's own lifetime. Sometimes they occurred for purely ideological or idealistic reasons, as in twelfth-century Sicily and Palestine which were then under Norman and Frankish-Crusader Christian domination respectively. More often they took place under the milder pressure of the desire for social advancement; or under the more extreme pressure of violent persecution as in Spain/Morocco circa 1140, due to the harsh anti-Christian policies of the last of the Almoravides followed by the first of the Almohades. For this reason, we should seriously consider the possibility that the defensive purpose may have been of slightly more importance to Peter the Venerable than the offensive.

Indeed, circa 1140 French Christian ecclesiastical circles (e.g., Hugh of St. Victor) were stunned by the news that Archbishop John of Seville, succumbing to threats of torture, had agreed to practice Islam in public (though he remained a Christian at heart).[17] French Christians may have reasoned that if the leader, the archbishop of Seville, could convert to Islam, how much the more so would the followers, the Christians (the Mozarabs) living within Muslim Spain, convert to Islam in imitation of his example. Perhaps it was Peter the Venerable's hope that through the Toletano-Cluniac corpus he would win Archbishop John of Seville and/or the many Christian followers who joined him in practicing Islam in public (while remaining Christians at heart) to confess Christianity publicly once again and die as heroic martyrs if necessary, or flee north to Christian territory.

*****

Chapter two of *Peter the Venerable and Islam* (pages 49–69) deals with the translators whom Peter the Venerable assembled in Spain to work on his project. It presents a brief discussion (by way of introduction) of the school of translators from Arabic into Latin who worked at Toledo under its great archbishop, Raimundo (1125–1151); this is followed by equally brief discussions of each of the five translators who worked on the Toletano-Cluniac corpus. Peter of Toledo (pages 56–58), an enigmatic figure, translated al-Kindi's *Risalah*, probably planned which works were to be translated for the project, and did the annotations thereto, especially to the Quran and the *Risalah*. Peter of Poitiers (pages 59–61), Peter the Venerable's Latin secretary and friend, polished the Latin of Peter of Toledo's translation of al-Kindi, may have assisted Peter of Toledo in planning the translation project, prepared a digest of information which Peter the Venerable relied upon in writing his *Summa*, and was the author of the *Capitula*, or proposed chapter headings, for Peter the Venerable's refutation of Islam. Robert of Ketton (pages 62–65), whose work as a translator from Arabic has long been known, translated the Quran and the *Fabulae Saracenorum*, writing significant prefaces to both translations. Herman of Dalmatia (pages 66–67), as well-known as Robert, translated the *Liber Generationis Mahumet* and the *Doctrina Mahumet*. Muhammad (pages 68–69), an otherwise unknown Spanish Muslim, was of general assistance to Peter of Toledo but especially aided Robert and Herman in their translations.

Little is known with certainty about the very important translator Peter of Toledo. Kritzeck aptly suggests (page 56) that the archives of the cathedrals of Toledo and of other Spanish cities through which Peter the Venerable's entourage passed may yield information about this translator. However, Kritzeck may well be acting a bit hastily when he rejects, without giving any reasons, what he calls the "tempting possibility" of identifying Peter of Toledo with Petrus Alphonsi.

Indeed, a good case can be developed in favor of the probability, though not the certainty, that these two persons, Peter of Toledo and Petrus Alphonsi, were one and the same. Aside from the argument that Peter was allegedly a common name in Spain at this time (which may not be the case), the chief argument against this identification has traditionally been that Petrus Alphonsi was allegedly born in 1062 and would thus have had to be circa eighty years old when Peter the Venerable came to Spain in 1142–1143. It is unlikely, so it has been argued, that Petrus Alphonsi could have lived to such a ripe old age (Peter the Venerable himself only lived sixty-two years, 1094–1156). However, as long ago as 1906 C. Nedelcou demonstrated that the belief that Petrus Alphonsi was born in 1062 was totally groundless and rested on a corrupt reading in the most widely used printed version of the *Dialogi, i.e.,* in Migne's nineteenth-century *Patrologia Latina*.[18] Thus, for all we know, Alphonsi could have been born five, ten, or even twenty years later than the mythical year 1062. Indeed, the younger we assume he was when he converted to Christianity in 1106, the easier it would seem to be to explain his conversion and his travels (to England, possibly also to France, then back to Spain), which can be documented for at least the following two decades.

Kritzeck's suggestion (pages 57–58 and note 31), reversing his earlier opinion, that Peter of Toledo was the person who annotated the Arsenal manuscript no. 1162 (cf. infra), especially the translations of the Quran and *Risalah* contained therein, is a definite advance over previous scholarship. D'Alverny had identified the Annotator with Peter of Poitiers, Peter the Venerable's Latin secretary, who almost certainly did not have as much knowledge of Islam as is shown by the Annotator. Daniel had suggested that the Annotator was an unknown Mozarab. However, basing ourselves on Kritzeck's conclusion, we would suggest the probability that Petrus Alphonsi = Peter of Toledo = the Annotator. What is badly needed is an edition of the annotations to the Toletano-Cluniac corpus, with translation and commentary, and a comparison of these annotations with Alphonsi's *Dialogi* and his other writings, both belletristic and scientific. Such a comparison might produce startling results that would revolutionize our understanding of Petrus Alphonsi's life and work and the Toletano-Cluniac corpus, as well as our knowledge of the history of Christian relations with Muslims and Jews and the Twelfth-Century Renaissance.

*****

Chapter three of *Peter the Venerable and Islam* (pages 71–112) deals with the five translations produced by the translators. It begins (pages 73–74) with an introductory section on the Arsenal manuscript no. 1162, probably the original twelfth-century collection transcribed by or for the translators in Spain and put together in final form at Cluny (page 74). We thus are very fortunate that we still possess the actual autograph copy of the Toletano-Cluniac corpus in this precious Arsenal manuscript.

Of the translations proper, the *Fabulae Saracenorum* (pages 75–83), translated by Ketton, is a highly legendary chronicle based on an Arabic original which has yet to be identified. It begins with the creation of the world and proceeds through the heroes and worthies of the Old and New Testaments, the birth, life, and death of the Prophet Muhammad, and the lives of the first six caliphs. It ends with Yazid I, who (in 680) quelled the rebellion of Husayn, son of Ali (Ali being Muhammad's cousin and son-in-law) and grandson of Muhammad. The *Liber Generationis Mahumet* (pages 84–88), translated by Herman of Dalmatia, is based on the *Kitab Nasab Rasul Allah*, going back, at least in theory, to Kab al-Ahbar, the Jew who converted to Islam in the 630s under the caliphate of either Abu-Bakr or Umar I. It is a highly legendary account of how the prophetic light (*nur* in Arabic) descended generation by generation from Adam to Muhammad, and of the numerous miracles which attended the prophet's birth. The *Doctrina Mahumet* (pages 89–96), also translated by Herman, is based on the *Masa'il Abdillah ibn Salam*, going back, at least in theory, to Abdallah ibn Salam, the Jew who converted to Islam during the late Medinan period of Muhammad's life (circa 629–630). It is an imaginary didactic dialogue between Muhammad and Abdallah in which Abdallah asks Muhammad an endless number of questions and Muhammad answers so successfully that Abdallah converts to Islam.

Kritzeck's discussion of Robert of Ketton's translation of the Quran (pages 97–100) is followed by a discussion of the *Epistola Saraceni cum Rescripto Christiani* (pages 101–107). This work was translated by Peter of Toledo, from the *Risalah* of al-Kindi, a major Middle Eastern Christian anti-Islamic polemic purporting to have been written in Iraq during the reign of Caliph al-Ma'mun (813–833). The chapter's concluding section (pages 108–112) deals with "the choice and accuracy of the translations."

Kritzeck's translations of the documents of the Toletano-Cluniac corpus are accurate. However, when he paraphrases these documents, his summaries are often too concise. Therefore, they omit details which might interest scholars seeking to compare the particulars of these documents with those of other documents of equal importance in the development of Western Christian attitudes toward Islam or in the development of medieval belles lettres. Kritzeck's annotations to the translations and summaries are commendable, as is his use (encouraged by d'Alverny's prior example) of illustrative material from Louis Ginzberg's monumental seven-volume *Legends of the Jews* (Philadelphia: Jewish Publication Society of America, 1946–1955). Commendable as well are Kritzeck's efforts to identify the Arabic original of the *Fabulae Saracenorum* and his utilization of the rich Arabic manuscript collection at Princeton University (cf. page 75 and note 12; page 76, note 14; page 89, note 75).

Kritzeck's discussion (page 99) of the Islamic prohibition against translating the Quran is well documented but all too brief. He points out that apparently no extensive medieval or modern monographs seem to exist on the subject. Therefore, no definitive conclusions can be reached regarding the various stages in the development of the prohibition or the strength of the prohibition and its persistence.[19]

Kritzeck (page 100) considers it an important responsibility to demonstrate that Ketton's was the first truly full-length translation of the Quran. However, Kritzeck gives the far more important question of the quality and peculiarities of Ketton's translation inadequate treatment. Here Kritzeck has been content to rely on the work of other outstanding scholars—*e.g.*, Cabanelas Rodriguez as well as d'Alverny and Vajda (pages 110–111, page 111, notes 162 and 165)—but has given us an all too brief summary of the conclusions of these other scholars in their analyses of this important question. All we learn from *Peter the Venerable and Islam* is that Ketton's translation style was more florid than that of his colleague Herman of Dalmatia but less accurate than that of Mark of Toledo, who translated the Quran into Latin in the early thirteenth century.[20] Hopefully in the second edition of his book Kritzeck will offer us a detailed, original comparison of the Latin Quran translations of Ketton and Mark of Toledo.

Professor Kritzeck's summary of the *Epistola Saraceni cum Rescripto Christiani* (pages 101–107) calls our attention to the great need for new critical editions, with translation and commentary, of both the Arabic and Latin texts of al-Kindi's *Risalah*, despite some previous efforts along these lines (pages 101–102). Kritzeck believes that the name of the Christian author of this work (al-Kindi) and his alleged high position at the court of Caliph al-Ma'mun (813–833) are fictional, despite some indications in the work which Kritzeck admits would support a contrary conclusion. Kritzeck follows those (*e.g.*, Louis Massignon) who prefer to ascribe the work to the early tenth century. However, the arguments of Kritzeck and the scholars he cites in the footnotes (page 102 with notes 132 and 134) against the traditional ninth-century dating of the work are not conclusive.[21]

The discussion of al-Kindi's *Risalah* (pages 101–107) could be greatly enriched in the second edition of Kritzeck's book by a list of the many Quranic passages which al-Kindi comments upon, as well as by more extensive discussions of how informed this polemic is, how fair, how violent, how persuasive. Much work on the *Risalah* remains to be done. It would be fruitful to compare al-Kindi's polemic with that of his two great Middle Eastern Christian predecessors, John of Damascus and Theodore Abu-Qurrah (circa 750–850); as well as with his two great successors Yahya ibn Adi (tenth century) and the anonymous author of the *Contrarietas Alpholica* (tenth, eleventh, or twelfth century, Spain);[22] and especially with the other great midninth = century Christian anti-Islamic polemics written by Nicetas of Byzantium and by Eulogius and Alvarus of Cordova (the two leaders of the ninth-century Spanish martyrs' movement). Indeed, a comparison of al-Kindi, Nicetas, and Eulogius/Alvarus with each other would make an especially fascinating study and would give us a panoramic view of midninth-century Christian attitudes toward Islam from the Tigris to the Guadalquivir.

Kritzeck suggests (page 109) that on the whole the selection of Islamic material for the translation project was not a bad one. Even the works which Herman of Dalmatia translated, though unrepresentative of normative Islam, nonetheless performed the positive function of giving a good picture of popular Islam. Kritzeck expresses regret that the historical works of ibn-Ishaq (died 768; author of the classic biography of the Prophet Muhammad) and al-Tabari (died 923; author of a monumental world history/Islamic history from the creation to

915), despite their great length, were not translated or paraphrased. Along these same lines we might also regret the absence from the project of a translation or paraphrase of al-Buhari (died 870; author of the most important collection of Hadith literature, the traditions of the Prophet Muhammad, second in authority within Islam after the Quran itself) or of a treatise on Islamic law as interpreted by the Malikites, the Sunni/Orthodox school of Islamic law that generally prevailed in Spain and North Africa from circa 800.

*****

Chapter four (pages 113–152), an analytical summary of Peter the Venerable's *Summa Totius Haeresis Saracenorum*, is divided into eight sections: (1) an introduction (pages 115–116) wherein Kritzeck informs us that the *Summa* was originally intended for the use of St. Bernard of Clairvaux and the French clergy in general. This is followed by Kritzeck's summaries of what the *Summa* offers us about the Islamic view of (2) God, Christ, and the last judgment (pages 117–123); (3) the Prophet Muhammad (pages 124–128); (4) the Quran and its sources (pages 129–134); (5) heaven, hell, and moral precepts (pages 135–138); (6) the spread of Islam (pages 139–140); and (7) Islam as a Christian heresy (pages 141–149). It concludes with (8) Kritzeck's discussion of the value of Peter the Venerable's summary of Islam (pages 150–152).

Kritzeck notes (page 116) Peter the Venerable's reliance upon Ketton's Quran translation, upon Peter of Toledo's translation of al-Kindi's *Risalah*, and upon the treatment of Muhammad in Anastasius Bibliothecarius's (otherwise known as Anastasius the Roman Librarian, circa 850) translation of the *Chronicon* of the Byzantine historian Theophanes (circa 800). However, Kritzeck inadvertently overlooked Peter's reliance upon the anti-Islamic (the fifth) chapter of Petrus Alphonsi's *Dialogi* as well. Alphonsi's chapter seems merely to be a summary of al-Kindi's *Risalah*, and thus what looks like al-Kindi in Peter's *Summa* and *Refutation* may really be al-Kindi via the summary thereof in Alphonsi. Kritzeck also overlooked Peter's possible use of the anti-Islamic writings of Eulogius and Alvarus, the leaders of the ninth-century Spanish martyrs' movement. Their writings were available in Spain during Peter the Venerable's lifetime. Peter's view of Muhammad (page 145) as the link between Arius (the founder of the fourth-century Arian heresy which tended to deemphasize Christ's divinity) and anti-Christ may owe something to Eulogius and Alvarus of Cordova, who already in the ninth century had stressed Muhammad's alleged link with anti-Christ.[23]

Kritzeck stresses the fact (page 117) that Peter the Venerable, at the very beginning of the *Summa*, notes the Islamic disbelief in the Christian trinity. It would be fruitful to contrast Peter's statement with the popular Christian belief, as seen, *e.g.*, in the French *chansons de geste*, that Muslims worship an infernal trinity of their own made up of three deities, Muhammad, Apollo, and Tervagant (Diana?). In general, the question of the relationship between Peter's attitudes and those in twelfth-century French, Spanish, and German belles lettres deserves more detailed study.

In chapter four the method followed by Kritzeck is first to present a quotation from the *Summa* in English translation, then to analyze it. The analyses concentrate especially on contrasting the authentic Islamic view on the particlar issue in question (1) with Peter the Venerable's description of the Islamic view and (2) with the Christian view on the same subject. In general Kritzeck's translations and analyses are quite good. However, the last translated quotation in each section of the chapter is usually left without adequate analysis, and sometimes this leaves important questions undiscussed, *e.g.*, Peter's charge that conquest by Islam equals (forced) conversion to Islam (page 140). At times Kritzeck's analysis fails to delve deeply enough, *e.g.*, on the question of the evolution of the legend of the monk (often called Bahira by the Muslims, Sergius by the Christians) who allegedly gave Muhammad indispensible help (page 130). The component parts of this important legend must be broken down more clearly by future scholarship and traced in the Middle Eastern Islamic and Christian sources, as well as in the Byzantine Western Christian sources, with greater care as to author, date, and place of origin of each particular in the legend.

Kritzeck points out (pages 143–144) that Peter the Venerable wavered between the less charitable view that Islam was paganism and the more charitable view that it was only a Christian heresy, usually preferring the latter view. Kritzeck was fully aware of the fact (though he inadvertently neglected to mention it in this context) that there was a third alternative view of Islam, more tolerant than either of the other two, *i.e.*, to classify Islam as a separate, non-Christian, monotheistic faith containing many of Christianity's truths (albeit in slightly different form), a faith definitely worthy of respectful study, sympathetic understanding, and even some degree of concerned love on the part of Christians. This seems to be the view expressed in Pope Gregory VII's letter of 1076 to "Anzir" (*i.e.*, Nasir ibn Alnas, the Hammadid ruler of Algeria, 1062–1088/89) and also may have been the view of St. Francis of Assisi.[24]

$$* * * * *$$

Chapter five (pages 153–199), an analytical summary of Peter the Venerable's great anti-Islamic polemic *Liber contra sectam sive haeresim Saracenorum*, called simply *Refutation* by Kritzeck, is divided into seven sections. (1) The introduction to the chapter (pages 155–156) deals with the Douai manuscript no. 381, the only surviving manuscript of the *Refutation*, which is the last item therein, folios 177r to 195r (this manuscript is in addition one of the three main manuscripts of Peter the Venerable's anti-Judaic polemic). The introduction also deals with the *Capitula*, or proposed chapter headings, which Peter of Poitiers, Peter the Venerable's Latin secretary and friend, wrote for his abbot's *Refutation*. (2) The prologue of the *Refutation* (pages 157–160) treats the origins of, and patristic authority for, Peter the Venerable's project to study Islam and compares the nature of Islam with that of Christianity. (3) In book one: I (pages 161–174) Peter pleads with the Muslims to abandon their traditional unwillingness even to listen to the arguments of Christian missionaries. Peter asks the Muslims to give him a fair hearing because he attacks them not "as some of us often do, by arms, but by words; not by force, but by reasons; not in hatred, but in love" (page 161). This highly Franciscan statement by Peter the Venerable, so often quoted in the secondary literature on the history of Christian-Islamic relations, justly deserves its place in the history of the development of the more sympathetic post-Vatican II Christian attitude toward Islam. (4) In book one: II (pages 175–184) Peter attempts to persuade the Muslims to accept as divinely inspired both Old and New Testaments *in toto*, as preserved by Jews and Christians. He attempts to refute the Islamic charge that Jews and Christians have lost, concealed, and/or corrupted (especially corrupted, the Islamic charge of *tahrif*) the original revelations given them. (5) In book two: I (pages 185–190) Peter attempts to demonstrate that Muhammad was not a true prophet, for he did not manifest "to mortals . . . unknown things about the past, or present or future" (page

187). (6) In book two: II (pages 191–194) Peter comes to a rather abrupt conclusion and summarizes his argument. Kritzeck's fifth chapter is concluded by (7) a very fine section on "the stature of the *Refutation*" (pages 195–199), which discusses its sources, main and incidental arguments, style, method of refutation, major weaknesses, and influence upon the development of Western Christian attitudes toward Islam.

Kritzeck admirably corrects (page 156) the traditional view that two of the original four books of the *Refutation* were lost. This view is based on a misunderstanding by the scribe who wrote the lone surviving manuscript. This scribe mistook Peter of Poitier's *Capitula*, which call for four books, as the actual table of contents of the *Refutation*. Instead, it probably was merely a suggested outline that Peter the Venerable chose in many cases not to follow. Kritzeck admits that the *Refutation* breaks off rather suddenly but argues convincingly that this was probably the way Peter wrote it and that it probably never went beyond this abrupt ending.

Kritzeck points out that Peter the Venerable noted the fact that the Muslims could not read his polemic in its original Latin and expressed the hope that it would be translated into Arabic. Several questions come immediately to mind here. How serious was Peter in this matter, considering that his work was probably directed mainly at Christians? Did Peter have in mind that the Arabic translation of his work would be read primarily by the decreasing number of Mozarabs who still remained behind in Muslim Spain or were exiled to Morocco, upon whom the Almoravides followed by the Almohades were putting increasingly heavy pressure in an attempt to force them into Islam? Whom did Peter have in mind to translate the work into Arabic? Was it Peter of Toledo?

Kritzeck presents (page 162) Peter the Venerable's noble statement that he was moved toward love for Muslims by two different factors: (1) Christ's commandment to love all people and (2) the natural kinship one member of a species, *i.e.*, the human race, has with other members of this same species. The second factor here is of relevance to the relatively unexplored question of the extent to which Greek philosophy (and Peter Abelard, who lived at Cluny from 1140 until his death in 1142) may have influenced Peter the Venerable and even the Toletano-Cluniac corpus.[25]

Kritzeck describes (pages 162–163) Peter the Venerable's enlightened view that philosophy could be of service to religion and his attempt to use philosophy to refute Islam. However, we should note that at this time religious Muslims were becoming increasingly suspicious of the rationalist movement, especially in Spain/Morocco (*viz.*, the persecution by the Islamic legists of two great twelfth-century Spanish Muslim philosophers who also went to Morocco, Ibn Bajja and Averroes). Islam was moving away from philosophical toward mystical theology (under the influence of al-Ghazzali, who wrote circa 1100).

Kritzeck presents (page 172) Peter the Venerable's appeal to Muslims to give Christians the freedom to attack Islam, for freedom of speech and decision are the only means by which people can discover truth, and, as Peter contended, Christians give freedom of speech to Jews (whom he must have considered the cousins of the Muslims) in Europe and to Muslim captives in Palestine. We should note here that Peter's claim concerning Muslim captives, though undoubtedly false, nonetheless reveals Peter's opposition to forced conversion of such captives. However, most of the Christians of Palestine in the twelfth and thirteenth centuries were also opposed to forced conversion of Muslims. Their reason for opposing forced conversion was not humanitarianism, as was Peter's. Rather, they preferred to accept ransom for Muslim captives and/or exploit them as slaves, as well as to place extraordinary taxes on free Muslims (farmers, craftsmen, merchants, professionals) in their territories, the Christian version of the Islamic *jizyah*, or poll tax on infidels, rather than permit these Muslims, let alone force them, to convert to Christianity.

Kritzeck points out (page 177) the incorrectness of Peter the Venerable's claim that he could not find any written Islamic source which charged Jews and Christians with *tahrif* (or the corruption of Scripture). Kritzeck shows that the Quran does indeed make such claim, but he fails to note that Peter's ignorance of the Quranic view on this point might mean that Peter did not really study Ketton's Quran as well as he should have.[26] A fuller footnote by Kritzeck on the Islamic charge of *tahrif* would also have been helpful here. We should note how shrewd but unfair were Peter's tactics in refuting this Islamic charge. What Peter did was to set up two straw persons, two relatively weak arguments, to summarize and stand for the entire Islamic case for *tahrif*, and then to destroy these arguments with ease (pages 175–184). Hopefully in the second edition of his *Peter the Venerable and Islam* Kritzeck will consider the fully developed case for *tahrif* which the great Spanish Islamic theologian Ali ibn Hazm (with whom Kritzeck is thoroughly familiar) made in his *Kitab al-Fisal fi-al-Milal w'al-Ahwa w'al-Nihal* about a century before Peter.[27]

Kritzeck presents (page 185) Peter the Venerable's unusual admission that Christians have erred in the past. Jews have erred; so have Muslims. Members of all religious traditions have erred. So, Peter argued, why do not Muslims allow Christian missionaries to come into their territory to help them correct their errors? Obviously a very shrewd argument, but would Peter the Venerable have been willing to give Islamic missionaries the same right to come into Christian territory to help correct errors there as well?

Kritzeck analyzes with sensitivity (pages 188–189) Peter the Venerable's mistaken notion that the Quran itself contains a statement to the effect that only what the Prophet Muhammad said in the Quran was to be accepted as genuinely Muhammad's. This alleged statement is not in the Quran at all but rather is in the Hadith (or post-Quranic Islamic tradition literature). Whence did Peter derive the idea that this statement was Quranic? Kritzeck shows that it probably came to Peter from al-Kindi, who had the same mistaken notion. Perhaps! Our own research, however, shows that Peter might have taken this idea from al-Kindi not directly but only indirectly, *i.e.*, via the anti-Islamic (the fifth) chapter of Petrus Alphonsi's *Dialogi*, where al-Kindi's mistake is repeated.[28]

Kritzeck presents (page 192) Peter the Venerable's contention that Muslims must accept Jewish (Old Testament) prophecies because both Jews and Muslims share physical descent from Abraham, cognate sacred languages (Hebrew and Arabic), and circumcision of the flesh as an initiation rite. We should note here this tremendously significant Western Christian tendency to equate Jews with Muslims. This factor, the theme of our book, was a primary influence upon the massacre of, and the imposition of a distinction in clothing upon, the Jews of Western Europe during the High Middle Ages and subsequent thereto.[29]

Kritzeck may well be correct when he states (page 195) that Peter the Venerable's polemic was the first systematic refutation of Islamic doctrine in the Latin language. However, Kritzeck could have given a bit more credit here to previous Spanish Christian efforts along these lines by Felix of Urgel and Speraindeo of Cordova (the former in the 790s and the latter circa 825; the work of the former no longer extant, of the latter extant only in fragments); by Speraindeo's two chief disciples who were the leaders of the ninth-century Spanish martyrs' movement (circa 850): Eulogius and Alvarus, both of Cordova; and by Petrus Alphonsi.[30]

Kritzeck points out (page 195) that Peter the Venerable's polemic differs greatly from al-Kindi's, avoiding the latter's mistakes and developing his arguments. But Kritzeck, alas, does not elaborate here on any of these very interesting and important points.

Kritzeck has admirably traced (pages 161-194 passim) Peter the Venerable's quotations from the Quran, the *Doctrina Mahumet*, and the Hadith literature.

Kritzeck's summary of the main arguments in the *Refutation* is quite good (pages 195-196). He points out that Peter the Venerable presents no exposition of Christian doctrine, but Kritzeck inadvertently fails to note that this may well be a serious defect if Peter's work was intended primarily for Muslims. Did Peter believe that the mere refutation of Islam would automatically entail conversion by Muslims to Christianity and that therefore no positive arguments had to be presented in favor of Christianity? Perhaps. More likely this failure to provide an exposition of Christian doctrine within the *Refutation* indicates that the work was directed more at Christians who, under intense Islamic pressure, were either wavering in their faith and seriously entertaining the thought of converting to Islam or had already converted to Islam in public while remaining Christians at heart (like Archbishop John of Seville circa 1140). Such Christians assuredly did not need an exposition of Christian doctrine, since they had already received one in their earlier lives from their own parents and priests.

We should also note Peter's failure to attack specific Islamic religious practices, *e.g.*, the "Five Pillars of Islam," the confession of faith, prayer, almsgiving, fasting, and pilgrimage. They were attacked by Petrus Alphonsi following the example of al-Kindi's *Risalah*. Both of these writers had lived among the Muslims for a considerable length of time—which was not the case with Peter the Venerable—and thus knew from personal experience how important these "Pillars" were to the Islamic faith. Perhaps Peter's failure to attack Islamic practice was a result of his desire to attempt to convert the Muslims without offending them. Did he reason that he would offend the Muslims less by attacking Islamic doctrine than by attacking both Islamic doctrine and Islamic practice, or by attacking Islamic practice alone? Or perhaps

Peter thought that theory (as the foundation) was more important than practice (which was the house). If the theory of Islam (the foundation) was undermined by his attack, the practice of Islam (the house) would come crashing down upon it. Of course, this is not always the case in religion, where practice often come first and theory is developed later to justify the practice. Or perhaps Peter simply did not know enough in detail about Islamic practices to feel confident enough of being able to attack them effectively. More likely this failure to attack Islamic practice within the *Refutation* once again indicates that the work was directed more at Christians who were wavering in their faith or had already gone over to Islam in public rather than at the Muslims. Peter would have reasoned that to reconvert such Christians away from Islam and back to Christianity would only require a successful attack on Islamic doctrine, but to convert Muslims away from the religion of their parents and legists would require a successful attack on both Islamic doctrine and Islamic practice.

Kritzeck points out (page 196) that occasionally Peter the Venerable would write as if he were speaking to the Prophet Muhammad himself rather than to twelfth-century Muslims, but Kritzeck does not comment on this peculiarity of Peter's style. It could merely have been poetic rhetoric (*i.e.*, the Prophet Muhammad standing for the average twelfth-century Muslim "person-in-the-street"). However, it could also have been influenced by a popular Christian belief that the Prophet Muhammad, as a diabolic/Satanic figure, was still alive and thus could be spoken to in direct address.

Kritzeck offers several criticisms of Peter the Venerable's *Refutation* (page 198). It is too rhetorical as well as too repetitious. More importantly, it abruptly breaks off before attempting to prove what its author said it was going to prove. Kritzeck suggests no reasons for the abrupt ending. Perhaps Peter the Venerable's interest in Islam never went deep enough to sustain the long hours of analysis of Islamic texts necessary for a complete and thorough refutation of the religious doctrines and practices of the mosque. If Peter was writing more for Christians, he may well have felt that he did not need to do as thorough a job with the *Refutation* as he would have had to do if he had been writing for Muslims. The moment other matters came along which seemed more urgent and compelling to him (*e.g.*, the continually pressing problem of the reform of the Cluniac Order and/or of straightening out the frightful financial muddle into which the order had fallen circa 1148), Peter probably dropped the work, perhaps with a combined sense of both sorrow and relief, never to resume it again.

Kritzeck's section on the influence of Peter the Venerable's *Refutation* (pages 198-199) is not quite adequate, and we look to a more extended treatment in a second edition. All Kritzeck does here is to state that the influence of the *Refutation* was not as great as that of the translations, a conclusion which seems to be correct even though Kritzeck himself would be the first to lament the fact that no one as yet has thoroughly traced even the influence of the translations, let alone the *Refutation*. Kritzeck does not attempt to offer any evidence for his conclusion. One could point out that only one manuscript of the *Refutation* seems to have survived, whereas many more manuscripts of the translations are extant. Also, Vincent of Beauvais, in his widely read encyclopedia *Speculum Historiale* (circa 1250), seems to have summarized material from the translations but not from the *Refutation*.[31]

Kritzeck has made no attempt to explain this apparent difference in influence. Possible explanations are the following. The translations contained material that was more exotic and thus more interesting to later generations than that contained in the *Refutation*. The translations dealt with actual Islamic religious practices as well as with the theory behind Islam. The *Refutation*, on the other hand, dealt only with the theory behind Islam. Most Christian readers probably preferred material that dealt with both practice and theory. Perhaps also the Christian readers of succeeding generations found Peter's arguments against Islam crude and unconvincing. Perhaps Peter's pre-Aristotelian philosophical terminology had little appeal in the increasingly Aristotelian-minded West. Perhaps Citeaux's victory over Cluny in their battle for prestige meant that Peter the Venerable's own writings in general, of which the *Refutation* was one, would be consigned to relative oblivion along with the memory of their author as far as succeeding generations were concerned. The problem of the comparative influence of the translations and the *Refutation* needs much further study.[32]

It would be very fruitful to compare Peter the Venerable's anti-Islamic writings with the similar writings of another great twelfth-century French scholar, Alan of Lille (who flourished circa 1175-1200). We refer specifically to the anti-Islamic (the fourth) section of Alan of Lille's *De Fide Catholica* and Alan's highly advanced treatise *Ars Catholicae Fidei*. The latter attempts to prove the truth of Christianity to the Muslims and Jews on the basis of reason alone, without the help of scripture (the New Testament), whose inspiration neither non-Christian monotheistic group accepted. This treatise, because of its attempt to use reason alone, is a connecting link between St. Anselm of Canterbury's *Cur Deus Homo*, essentially eleventh century, and St. Thomas Aquinas's *Summa contra Gentiles*, thirteenth century, both of which follow the same method and are great landmarks in the history of the Christian dialogue with Muslims and Jews.[33]

In the last paragraph of chapter five (pages 198-199) Kritzeck states that Peter the Venerable's work forces us to revise our general notions of European attitudes toward Islam during the period of the earlier Crusades. Peter's work does indeed show us that as early as the first half of the twelfth century (when the memory of the great victory won by the First Crusade in taking Antioch and Jerusalem from the Muslims was still fresh in the minds of Western Christians), one great Christian churchperson, blessed with broad vision and boundless energy, could fervently believe and argue that the Muslims were not to be approached in ignorant hatred but rather with intelligent love. For this reason Peter the Venerable occupies such a prominent place in the history of the Christian approach to the Muslim, and Kritzeck has seen fit to pay tribute to him, as it were, with the perceptive study that is his book.

*****

The final (the sixth) chapter of the book (pages 201-291) presents Kritzeck's selectively annotated transcription of five of the original texts (as opposed to the translations, none of which are transcribed here) in the Toletano-Cluniac corpus: (1) Peter the Venerable's *Summa* (pages 204–211; cf. pages 113–152); (2) his *Epistola Petri Cluniacensis ad Bernardum Claraevallis* (pages 212–214; cf. pages 27–29, 43–45) [(1) and (2) above being from the Arsenal manuscript no. 1162]; (3) Peter of Poitiers's letter to Peter the Venerable introducing the *Capitula* (pages 215–216; cf. pages 155–156); (4) Peter of Poitier's *Capitula* proper (pages 217–219; cf. pages 155–156); and (5) Peter the Venerable's *Refutation* (pages 220–291; cf. pages 153–199) [(3) to (5) above being from the Douai manuscript no. 381]. The texts are prefaced by a short note (page 203) explaining the method of transcription followed.

None of the texts presented here is taken from more than one manuscript, and thus none is equipped with a scientific *apparatus criticus*. This is because texts (1) and (2) above are transcribed from the Arsenal manuscript, the actual autograph; hence there is no *need* for an *apparatus criticus*. Texts (3)-(5) above are transcribed from the Douai manuscript, the only extant manuscript which contains these texts; hence the *impossibility* of an *apparatus criticus*.

The texts which Kritzeck presents are a significant improvement over the most accessible printed version, that in Migne's nineteenth-century *Patrologia Latina*, especially where Kritzeck restores to the text many paragraphs which are omitted by Migne, who relied upon the eighteenth-century edition by Martene-Durand. In general, however, where Migne's edition is not guilty of careless omissions, it does not really differ that often from the manuscripts transcribed and presented by Kritzeck. We have found the same thing to be true in comparing Migne's edition of Petrus Alphonsi's *Dialogi* with the twelfth-century manuscripts of the same work.

*****

To sum up, Kritzeck's book *Peter the Venerable and Islam* is a magnum opus of a leading American Christian authority in the field of the history of Christian-Islamic relations. We believe that it will remain a classic in its field, continuing to inform and inspire scholars for many years to come. Whatever criticisms have been offered above of the book cannot detract, either individually or collectively, from its importance. Kritzeck's *Peter the Venerable and Islam* is a valuable contribution to its field and an indispensable aid to any scholar interested in the developing, momentous, and captivating field of medieval Christian attitudes toward Islam, which we believe must henceforth determine our understanding of the closely related field of medieval Christian attitudes toward the Jews. If this proposed new comparative approach to the study of medieval Christian attitudes toward the Jews be sound, anyone wanting to pursue it will have to become thoroughly familiar with Kritzeck's *Peter the Venerable and Islam*.

Postscript

We have recently become aware of important artistic data from early twelfth-century France which has considerable bearing on the question of the Cluniac interest in Islam in general and Peter the Venerable's interest in Islam in particular. We refer to (1) the triforium of the surviving transept of the abbey church (circa 1088-1112) with its great, reconstructed semicircular door (circa 1115) at Cluny; (2) the Last Judgment tympanum over the doorway of the south porch of the Abbey Church of Saint-Pierre, Moissac (circa 1115); and (3) the Ascension combined with the Mission to the Apostles tympanum over the inner west doorway of the Abbey Church of Sainte-Madeleine, Vezelay (circa 1130). All of these great artistic monuments at Cluny, Moissac, and Vezelay are directly relevant to the Christian-Islamic encounter. At the same time they are also directly relevant to the Cluniac movement and to Peter the Venerable.

Peter became abbot of Cluny in 1122, only about a decade after the completion of the abbey church and its great door. "In the Cluniac Order, the Abbot of Moissac was second only to the Abbot of Cluny."[34] Kritzeck does mention Moissac as one stop on Peter's itinerary from France to Spain, between Le Puy and Roncevalles.[35] Peter the Venerable was prior of Vezelay before becoming abbot of Cluny in 1122 and may have been the theologian who drew up the plan for the sculpture in question at Vezelay.[36] Likewise, Kritzeck also mentions Vezelay and its role as a Cluniac center.[37] He tells us that Peter the Venerable spent twelve years there between circa 1110 and 1122 (during his sixteenth to twenty-eighth years), achieving the priorate of the abbey, and that Peter the Venerable's older brother, Pontius, was also at Vezelay with Peter, Pontius eventually being elected abbot of Vezelay. Thus, Kritzeck certainly seems to have been aware of the important place of such abbeys as Moissac and Vezelay in the Cluniac system and in Peter the Venerable's own life.

According to A.J. Denomy, writing in the early 1950s and relying upon the researches of such noted authorities as Emile Male and Joan Evans published between World Wars I and II,[38] we have at least two instances of Islamic influence on the artistic monuments at Cluny itself which date from the late eleventh and early twelfth centuries. (1) There is a typical Islamic great mosque motif in the triforium of the surviving transept of the abbey church (begun in 1088, consecrated in 1095, and completed in 1112), wherein a series of semicircles touch and form a scallop about each of the circular arches. (2) The Cathedral Mosque of Cordova influenced the reconstructed door of Cluny, which was enclosed within a rectangular frame with a line of arcading about (and joined to) it by a frieze of sculptured roundels, wherein the horizontal band of the frame forms an exact tangent to the door itself.

John Beckwith, the distinguished authority on medieval art, mentions several examples of Islamic influence on twelfth-century Western Christian art. These examples include the dome of the Cathedral of Pisa; the vaulting of the narthex of the Cathedral of Casale Monferrato in Piedmont; the polychrome walls of the Church of Saint-Michel d'Aiguilhe at Le Puy (which, Kritzeck points out, pages 12-13, was also closely linked with Peter the Venerable); and this church's doorway with lobed compartments and vegetable arabesque, showing the influence of the Great Mosque at Cordova or some similar Islamic building. However, says Beckwith:

> But in a sense the greatest monument to the recently expired Western Caliphate [of Cordova] is the superb doorway at Moissac . . . executed about 1120 and generally recognized as one of the supreme achievements of Romanesque sculpture.[39]

What particulars of the Moissac doorway indicate Islamic influence? According to Beckwith[40] Islamic influence is indicated by the decoration of the doorways with scalloped sides, by the foliated medallions on the lintel, and by the pairs of intercrossed lionesses. However, says Beckwith:

> But the scene on the tympanum at Moissac is a *diwan* of Divinity, Christ holding court like an Umayyad or Buwaiyid prince . . . surrounded by the elders playing lutes and viols, themselves derived from illustrations of Islamic musicians.[41]

Thus, in view of this striking Islamic influence in the artisitc monuments at Cluny and Moissac in the late eleventh and early twelfth centuries, it is likely that Spanish Christian artists with significant knowledge of Islam visited Cluny, Moissac, and other French Cluniac abbeys during the twilight years of Abbot Hugh (who died in 1109), Peter the Venerable's great uncle, and the early years of Abbot Pontius (1109–1122), Peter the Venerable's predecessor in office. It is highly possible that these artists encouraged the young Peter the Venerable to take a special interest in the problem of Islam, which interest would later come to full fruition in the Toletano-Cluniac corpus of the 1140s.

So much for Cluny and Moissac. Now for Vezelay. According to Beckwith the tensions and nervous expressiveness characteristic of Burgundian sculpture in the early twelfth century

> are carried to an extreme of virtuosity in the serene, majestic vision of the Ascension combined with the Mission to the Apostles, on the tympanum . . . of the inner door at Vezelay, about 1125–1130, where the structural stability of the overall scheme of the design emphasizes the ultracosmic nature of the vision in spite of the flurry and agitation of the component parts . . . the whole content of the tympanum has its sources in the Gospels, the Acts, in the prophecies of Isaiah and in geographical writings of antiquity and of the Middle Ages which describe the appearance of foreign and monstrous races [e.g., the way the Muslims, who are often equated with the Black Africans, are described in the *Chanson de Roland* of the late eleventh century]. The plan must have been drawn up by a theologian, possibly Peter the Venerable, once prior of Vezelay, then Abbot of Cluny in 1122, who took a great interest in the liberation of the Holy Land, at a time in Christian history when the crusaders seemed again to be accomplishing the tasks of the Apostles.[42]

The comments of H.W. and D.J. Janson, the noted authorities on the history of Western art, about the Vezelay tympanum are even more powerful and relevant than those of Beckwith. According to the Jansons:

> Perhaps the most beautiful of all Romanesque tympanums is that of Vezelay. . . . Its subject, the Mission of the Apostles, had a special meaning for this age of Crusades, since it proclaims the duty of every Christian to spread the Gospel to the ends of the earth. From the hands of the majestic ascending Christ we see the rays of the Holy Spirit pouring down upon the Apostles, all of them equipped with copies of the Scriptures in token of their mission. The lintel and the compartments around the central group are filled with representatives of the heathen world, a veritable encyclopedia of medieval anthropology which includes all sorts of legendary races (figure 355 [page 221, 'Pig-snouted Ethiopians']). On the archivolt (the arch framing the tympanum) we recognize the signs of the zodiac and the labors appropriate to every month of the year, to indicate that the preaching of the Faith is as unlimited in time as it is in space.[43]

If, as Beckwith suggests, Peter the Venerable was indeed the theologian who inspired the Ascension/Mission to the Apostles tympanum over the inner west doorway of the Abbey Church of Sainte-Madeleine at Vezelay, a suggestion which seems eminently plausible; if, further, this tympanum, in the Jansons' description, "proclaims the duty of every Christian to spread the Gospel to the ends of the earth," to the "representatives of the heathen world," presumably to the Muslims as much as to the "pig-snouted Ethiopians"; and if, finally, this tympanum dates from circa 1130, it would seem highly likely that Peter the Venerable's interest in the problem of Islam antedated his important work on the Toletano-Cluniac corpus (of the 1140s) by at least one decade, perhaps two.

Who could have influenced Peter the Venerable's interest in the conversion of the heathen world, presumably including the Muslims, at this relatively early date in his life? Could it have been the Spanish Christian artists with significant knowledge of Islam who executed the sculptures on the tympanum at Moissac circa 1115? Or could it have been Petrus Alphonsi who (as we shall see in the following chapter) was influential in England and France in the 1110s (perhaps also in the 1120s and 1130s)? Or was it the living memory of the intense interest in the conversion of the Muslims which developed at Cluny during the 1070s, the time of Pope Gregory VII, Abbot Hugh, and Anastasius of Cluny, "the Monk of France," as we have attempted to demonstrate.[44] Whatever or how many factors were involved we believe that the artistic evidence from Moissac and Vezelay presented above (from the treatments thereof by Beckwith and Janson) further confirms the strong likelihood that the intense interest in Christian-Islamic relations manifested by Peter the Venerable in the 1140s (the time of the Toletano-Cluniac corpus) did not arise overnight, as it were. Rather it was the culmination of one or more decades of interest in the problem of Islam and in the solution of that problem at Cluny in general and on the part of Peter the Venerable in particular.

In a sense, then, the tympana of Moissac and Vezelay, circa 1115–1130, are "missing links" between Anastasius of Cluny, who attempted to convert the Muslim ruler of Saragossa in the 1070s,[45] and Peter the Venerable's Toletano-Cluniac corpus of the 1140s.

Henry Kraus calls attention to two depictions of Muslims held in slavery by Christians, the first depiction at the Basses-Pyrenees Church of Oloron-Sainte-Marie, near Pau, in southern France; the second at

Santo Domingo de Silos, near Burgos, in northern Spain.[46] Kraus suggests that the Muslims depicted as caryatids at Oloron-Sainte-Marie could have been designed to help exorcise the feared enemy. On the other hand, the Muslims depicted at Santo Domingo de Silos reflect actual (much more so than magical) reality. They are runaway slaves shown being captured and returned to their work on the abbey lands by the patron saint, Santo Domingo de Silos himself. These two works of art may reflect the fact that, during the great expansion of the Spanish *Reconquista* (in which French knights played a major role) between circa 1085 (the fall of Toledo to the Castilians) and 1120 (the approximate time of the fall of Saragossa and the actual time of the fall of Tarragona to the Aragonians), many Muslims may well have been enslaved in Christian Spain, and some may have been taken by French knights back home across the Pyrenees to southern France. If so, Peter the Venerable's intense interest in the problem of Islam and his work on the Toletano-Cluniac corpus during the 1140s may well, in part, have been directed toward stimulating Christians who owned such Muslim slaves to allow them to accept baptism with a view toward their eventual manumission and absorption into the Christian population of Western Europe.[47]

3. Petrus Alphonsi (1076-1146) and Peter the Venerable: The Anti-Islamo/Judaic Origins of the Twelfth-Century Renaissance *

In view of recent developments in the significant and relevant field of medieval Christian attitudes toward Islam as outlined in chapter two, there has never been a greater need to prepare a scientific edition of Petrus Alphonsi's *Dialogi*, with full critical apparatus, utilizing all of the presently known Latin manuscripts. This edition should be prefaced by an introductory study, reflecting the latest research, of Alphonsi's life, work, and influence on Western European intellectual and cultural history during the High and Later Middle Ages (1000–1500). It should be supplemented by (1) an English translation, literal while adhering to good idiom; (2) a full commentary to explicate difficult phrases and arguments while tracing them to their sources in previous Christian (and non-Christian) writings on the Jews and Muslims; and (3) a copious bibliography.[1]

At present the text of Petrus Alphonsi's *Dialogi* is available primarily via the fairly satisfactory edition in Migne's nineteenth-century *Patrologia Latina*, CLVII: 535–672. However, this is not a critical edition, no more than are the earlier editions in *Maxima Bibliotheca Veterum Patrum* (Lyons: Anissonii, 1677), XXI: 172–221; *Magna Bibliotheca Veterum Patrum* (Cologne: A. Hieratus, 1618), XII:1: 358–404; and the first printed edition, *Dialogi Lectu Dignissimi* (Cologne: J. Gymnicus, 1536).[2] In the history of medieval Christian attitudes toward Jews the *Dialogi* had a bearing on many subsequent Christian anti-Judaic polemics, both outside and within Spain. For example, outside Spain, let us take only the twelfth (and very early thirteenth) century into consideration, the century in which they were composed and one of the critical centuries in the history of Christian anti-Judaic polemics. The *Dialogi* influenced England (where Petrus Alphonsi spent considerable time circa 1110–1120), *e.g.*, the anti-Judaic polemics written by Bartholomew, bishop of Exeter (circa 1180), and by Peter of Cornwall. The latter, flourishing in London circa 1197–1221, wrote his anti-Judaic polemic in the year 1208, only a few years before the anti-Jewish legislation of the Fourth Lateran Council, which may have been influenced, in part, by this anti-Judaic polemic. The *Dialogi* also influenced France (which Petrus Alphonsi may have visited circa 1110–1120), e.g., the *Liber adversus Judaeorum inveteratam duritiem* (1140s) of Peter the Venerable, a polemic of major importance; and Italy, e.g., the anti-Judaic polemics of Joachim of Flora (late twelfth century), one of the most revolutionary thinkers in the history of Western civilization, the Karl Marx of the Middle Ages, who may himself, like Petrus Alphonsi and Marx, have been born a Jew.[3]

Finally, the *Dialogi* had a bearing on Christian anti-Judaic polemics in Spain, Petrus Alphonsi's native country, during the High and Later Middle Ages. The possiblity that Christian anti-Judaic polemics played a significant role in the spiritual collapse and ultimate demise of the proud and wealthy Spanish Jewish community in the fourteenth and fifteenth centuries emerges from the fundamental researches of Ben-Zion Netanyahu. We refer to his *The Marranos of Spain, From the Late XIVth to the XVIth Century, According to the Contemporary Hebrew Sources* (New York: American Academy for Jewish Research, 1st edition, 1966; 2nd edition, 1973); as well as his earlier *Don Isaac Abravanel, Statesman, Financier and Philosopher* (Philadelphia: Jewish Publication Society of America, 1st edition, 1953; 2nd edition, 1968; 3rd edition, 1972), which have provoked considerable discussion.[4] Alphonsi's *Dialogi*, via their anti-Islamic fifth chapter, also were of great importance in the history of medieval Christian attitudes toward Islam. Indeed, the anti-Islamic chapter of the *Dialogi* may have been the single most influential medieval Western European description of Islam.[5]

Petrus Alphonsi was also crucial in the development of medieval science. We refer especially to his role in the transmission of Arabic scientific knowledge to Western Europe when the Twelfth-Century Renaissance was just beginning.[6] However, in order to gain a fuller understanding of Alphonsi's contribution to medieval science, we must first increase our knowledge of his work in the other, and related, major area which he developed earlier in life and in which he always retained an active interest: Christian polemics against other Abrahamitic faiths.

The first step in preparing an edition of the *Dialogi* is to consult

Manuel C. Diaz y Diaz's standard *Index Scriptorum Latinorum Medii Aevi Hispanorum* (Salamanca: Consejo Superior de Investigaciones Cientificas and Universidad de Salamanca, 1958), I: 202, no. 893, for a list of forty-two twelfth- through fifteenth-century manuscripts of the *Dialogi* found in twenty-seven European libraries. There are published catalogues of the Latin manuscript collections of many of these libraries, but these catalogues are not invariably accurate, and the data in them should always be checked against more up-to-date information supplied directly by the curator.[7] Some curators are quite slow in responding to inquiries from abroad, if they respond at all; but other curators will provide invaluable information which corrects and supplements Diaz y Diaz and otherwise helps the scholar in his research.[8] Blumenkranz has advised us that an article describing the various manuscript traditions of the *Dialogi* should be published first, before any actual edition of the work itself is prepared. This is what Blumenkranz did before publishing (as *Stromata patristica et mediaevalia*, number 3 [Utrecht: Spectrum, 1956]) the important *Disputatio Iudei et Christiani* by Gilbert Crispin, abbot of Westminster (circa 1085–1117). Crispin was an exact contemporary of Petrus Alphonsi who may have met Alphonsi when Alphonsi visited England in the second decade of the twelfth century.[9]

With regard to the English translation of the *Dialogi*, the more ponderous Latin theological prose of this text might perhaps more profitably be approached only after a thorough study of the same author's lighter and more readable story-book prose in the *Disciplina Clericalis*. Throughout Petrus Alphonsi's writings the translator is confronted by a Latin which was strongly influenced by Arabic and Hebrew, for it was almost certainly in these two Semitic languages that Alphonsi first learned how to express himself in writing and perhaps in speaking as well.[10]

For the Christian sources of Petrus Alphonsi's anti-Judaic polemic in the *Dialogi* three books by Blumenkranz are fundamental: (1) *Die Judenpredigt Augustins: Ein Beitrag zur Geschichte der Juedisch-christlichen Beziehungen in den Ersten Jahrhunderten* (Basel: Helbing and Lichtenhahn, 1946); (2) *Juifs et Chretiens dans le Monde Occidental 430-1096* (Paris-The Hague: Mouton, 1960); and (3) *Les Auteurs Chretiens Latins du Moyen Age sur les Juifs et le Judaisme* [circa 350-1100] (Paris-The Hague: Mouton, 1963). It is also possible that Alponsi's anti-Judaic polemic was influenced by the powerful attack on Judaism in the *Kitab al-Fisal*

54

fi-al Milal w'al-Ahwa w'al-Nihal by the great eleventh-century Spanish Muslim theologian Ali ibn Hazm.[11] Finally, Karaite (or Jewish sectarian) polemics against Rabbanite (or orthodox) Judaism may also have influenced Alphonsi's anti-Judaic polemic.[12]

D'Alverny, the distinguished medieval Latin paleographer and authority on the intellectual and cultural history of Western Europe during the Middle Ages, has recently pointed out that a major source of the anti-Islamic fifth chapter of Petrus Alphonsi's *Dialogi* was al-Kindi's *Risalah*, the great ninth-century Iraqi Christian anti-Islamic polemic written in Arabic (which language Alphonsi knew).[13] Another influence upon the anti-Islamic chapter of the *Dialogi* may have been the *Contrarietas Alpholica* (Refutation of the Legists), a major Spanish Christian anti-Islamic polemic written originally in Arabic during the tenth, eleventh, or twelfth centuries (the date is uncertain; of course, if this polemic was written in the twelfth century, as opposed to the tenth, or eleventh, it could not have influenced Alphonsi's *Dialogi*). This work is purportedly by a Muslim convert to Christianity.[14] Finally, it is also possible that Alphonsi was influenced by a highly effective anti-Quranic polemic written in Arabic by Samuel Ha-Nagid (*circa* 993-1056), the vizier of the Berber rulers of Granada and the most powerful Jewish scholar-prince in eleventh-century Spain.[15]

It is very important here to correct the *Jewish Encyclopedia*, whose mistaken birth and death dates for Petrus Alphonsi, as 1062 and 1110 respectively, have been widely repeated, though the *Jewish Encyclopedia* itself was probably repeating this error from an earlier source.[16] As long ago as 1906 C. Nedelcou demonstrated that the date 1062 rests on a corrupt reading in Migne's text of the *Dialogi*.[17] Migne, *Patrologia Latina*, CLVII: 537: C, reads

hoc [Alphonsi's baptism] autem factum est
anno a nativitate Domini
millesimo centesimo sexto [*i.e.*, 1106],
aetatis meae anno [italics ours]
quadragesimo quarto.

According to Migne's text Petrus Alphonsi says here that in the year 1106, when he was baptized, he was forty-four years old; *i.e.*, Alphonsi says that he was born in the year 1062. However, all of the

55

twelfth-century manuscripts of the *Dialogi* which we have been able to check read instead:

hoc autem factum est
anno a nativitate Domini
millesimo centesimo sexto
era millesima centesima [italics ours]
quadragesima quarta.

According to the manuscripts, what Petrus Alphonsi really was say-ing here was that the year 1106, the year of his baptism, was the year 1144 according to the Spanish era system of reckoning time, which was thirty-eight years ahead of the regular A.D. reckoning. Thus, Alphonsi was not saying anything at all about his birth date. For all we know he could have been born in the year 1072 or 1082.

Indeed, the younger we assume Alphonsi was in 1106, the year of his conversion to Christianity, the easier it becomes, or so it would seem, to explain his manifold activities which are documented for England and Spain (with the possibility that he also visited France) dur-ing the second and third decades of the twelfth century.[18] Jose Maria Millas-Vallicrosa, the great Spanish authority on medieval relations in the Iberian peninsula between all three communities—Christian, Mus-lim, and Jewish—held that a recently published document testifies to Petrus Alphonsi's presence in Saragossa in 1121, just three years after the city's reconquest from the Muslims by Alfonso I of Aragon, Al-phonsi's own godfather. Petrus Alphonsi's Saragossan presence in 1121 could even mean that he traveled between England and Spain perhaps more than once circa 1110-1130.[19] In any case, if we assume that Alphonsi was only thirty (not forty-four) years of age in 1106 and thus was born in 1076, which seems to make more sense in view of the added information we now have about him, and lived to a biblical age of seventy, an age which many intellectuals of the High Middle Ages reached[20]—this would mean that he did not die until circa 1146.[21]

If Petrus Alphonsi did indeed live to a biblical age of circa seventy years, it follows that Alphonsi certainly could have been identical with the Peter of Toledo who played such a crucial role in the Toletano-Cluniac corpus, Peter the Venerable's great project of the early 1140s to translate and refute Islamic religious literature (includ-ing the Quran, the bible of Islam). Peter of Toledo probably decided which Islamic texts would be translated for the corpus and certainly translated al-Kindi's *Risalah* into Latin for it. According to Kritzeck, whose *Peter the Venerable and Islam* remains the latest word on this subject, Peter of Toledo is the Annotator, who annotated the Islamic texts translated for the project, especially the Quran and al-Kindi's *Risalah*. Kritzeck is preparing an edition of these very interesting and important annotations, which are still found only in manuscript, the Arsenal manuscript no. 1162, the original autograph of the entire Toletano-Cluniac corpus. If Peter of Toledo is the Annotator, a detailed comparison of all the writings of Petrus Alphonsi—theological (*Dialogi*), belletristic (*Disciplina Clericalis*), and scientific (some of which still remain in manuscript)—with the work of the Annotator might well bear out the suggestion that Petrus Alphonsi = Peter of Toledo = the Annotator. If so, this would revolutionize our knowledge of Petrus Alphonsi; of Peter the Venerable and his Toletano-Cluniac corpus; of the history of Christian-Islamic and Christian-Jewish relations, both of which, as we once again can see, were inextricably interrelated in the Middle Ages; and finally our knowledge of the Twelfth-Century Renaissance.[22]

In the remaining portion of this chapter we present a preliminary case in favor of the strong possibility that Petrus Alphonsi is Peter of Toledo. In presenting this case we first refute several arguments against the identification of Alphonsi with Peter of Toledo and then present the arguments in favor of equating the two Peters.

Refutation of the Main Arguments against the
Equation of Petrus Alphonsi with Peter of Toledo

The two major arguments which have hitherto been presented against the equation of the two Peters are the argument from age and the argument from name.[23] Regarding the argument from age, it has been contended that Petrus Alphonsi, allegedly born in 1062, would have had to have lived until an impossibly old age in order to have had a share in the Toletano-Cluniac corpus circa 1142. This argument, which rests upon the mistaken notion that Alphonsi was born as early as 1062, has already been disposed of above.

Regarding the second argument, the argument from name, it has been maintained that Peter was simply too common a name at that time to allow us to identify Petrus Alphonsi with Peter of Toledo. However, in employing an argument of this kind, we must be very careful as to place and time. It is true that Peter (= Petrus, Pierre, Pietro, Pedro) was quite a common name throughout the Middle Ages, but that is not the real issue. Since we know that the popularity of names is cyclical, the real issue is whether Peter was a common name (1) in *Spain* in general and Aragon in particular, (2) in the generation of Petrus Alphonsi as well as in the generation immediately preceding and the generation immediately following.

The answer to this question seems to be more problematical. Pedro does not seem to have been an especially popular name in Spain at this time. The first Pedro among the rulers of Aragon was Pedro I (1094-1104), the very same generation as that of Petrus Alphonsi. The second Pedro was Pedro II of Aragon a century later (1196-1213). There were very few if any Pedros among the rulers of Portugal, Leon-Castile, or Navarre. Far more popular names were Alfonso, Bermudo, Garcia, Ordonyo, Pelayo, Ramiro, Ramon, and Sancho, even in Aragon itself.[24] Alfonso, the second part of Petrus Alphonsi's name, was more popular among the rulers of Spain at this time than was Pedro. Had the two men we wish to consider one and the same been named respectively Alfonsus Petri and Alfonso of Toledo, one could much more legitimately argue that the commonness of the name (Alfonso) would make it hazardous to equate them. But what can be argued for the more popular name Alfonso cannot be argued as easily for the less popular name Pedro.

It might be argued that the identification of Petrus Alphonsi with Peter of Toledo contradicts the available evidence regarding the geographical whereabouts of Petrus Alphonsi. We have two pieces of evidence which explicitly link him with Aragon: the statement in the preface to his *Dialogi* that he was baptized at Huesca in 1106 and a document which places him at Saragossa in 1121.[25] We have other evidence which seems to place him in England circa 1110-1120, where he is linked with Walcher of Malvern. Indeed, Petrus Alphonsi may have been invited to England by St. Anselm of Canterbury (died 1109) and/or by Gilbert Crispin of Westminster (died 1117), both of whom were seriously interested in Christian dialogue with non-Christians, the first area of endeavor wherein Alphonsi gained fame (with his *Dialogi* circa 1110).[26] Petrus Alphonsi may also have visited the great intellectual centers of France in the 1110s.[27] France was the philosophical, literary, and artistic center of Western Europe in the twelfth century. Petrus Alphonsi was interested in helping Western European civilization learn more about Islamic civilization in order some day to be able to defeat and convert the Arabs. Hence, it is difficult to see how he could possibly have avoided traveling through France and meeting its intellectual and cultural leaders, especially since France lay directly athwart the land route between Aragon and England which Alphonsi traveled twice, once from Aragon to England in the early 1110s and once from England to Aragon in 1121. Petrus Alphonsi may also have wanted to visit France in order to thank the French for their crucial military assistance to the Spanish *Reconquista* in the eleventh and early twelfth centuries and to encourage them to continue that assistance, perhaps at an intensified level.[28]

Thus, we have explicit evidence placing Petrus Alphonsi in northeastern Spain, 1106 and 1121, and in England in the 1110s, along with the serious possibility that he visited France as well in the 1110s. However, we have no piece of explicit evidence which would allow us to place Alphonsi in Castile or Toledo at any time prior to 1142.

In repy to this possible argument against the identification of Petrus Alphonsi with Peter of Toledo, we need only note the following. If Petrus Alphonsi was willing and able to leave his native Aragon and to travel hundreds of miles, by land and sea, to visit England and perhaps even France, he might also have crossed the border between Aragon and Castile in order to take up residence in Toledo. This might especially have been the case since Archbishop Raimundo (1125-1151) transformed Toledo into the "great city of the medieval Renaissance, the point of junction between the Muslim and Christian cultures."[29] In the second quarter of the twelfth century, Toledo boasted four distinct and autonomous communities—Christians, Muslims, Jews, and Karaites (sectarian Jews)—each of which had major libraries of religious and secular literature. Toledo more than any other city of the twelfth century reflected a cosmopolitan atmosphere reminiscent of Bagdad and Cordova of the ninth and tenth centuries respectively. Did not Petrus Alphonsi himself describe Bagdad in his *Disciplina Clericalis* in a way which showed that he too would have longed to have lived there during the days of its glory under Caliphs Harun ar-Rashid and al-Mamun, or else in a twelfth-century city that was more or less its equivalent, *i.e.*, Toledo?[30] Through the efforts of Archbishop Raimundo scholars from England, France, and Italy came to Toledo to help translate Arabic texts into Latin. Would it have been so improbable for a scholar who was actually born in Spain, but then went into a temporary (voluntary?) exile to England (and perhaps also to France), to have gone to Toledo as well? Castile and Aragon, despite a serious altercation during the early 1120s, were essentially at peace and allied in the period 1126-1146. Hence, no reasons of patriotism would have kept a native of the Aragonese area, like Petrus Alphonsi, from Toledo, the spiritual capital of Castile, during the time of Archbishop Raimundo.

Further, we do have a document which places Petrus Alphonsi in Saragossa in 1121, about 45 miles south of Huesca where he had been baptized in 1106. Saragossa is quite close to the frontier between Aragon and Castile. If Alphonsi had been born or raised in or near Barcelona or Gerona, one could argue that as a native of the coastal provinces, the farthest inland Alphonsi would have been inclined to venture would have been Huesca and/or Saragossa. However, since he was a native of the area around Huesca-Saragossa, he grew up in the Aragonese backcountry, its western frontier. It would then have been a matter of little if any physical and psychological difficulty for him to cross the frontier between the two kingdoms and proceed across Castile to Toledo. Indeed, the route Petrus Alphonsi traveled between Huesca/Saragossa (where we can document his presence in 1106 and 1121 respectively) and Toledo (where we believe he was present circa 1142) may well have been as follows: Saragossa to Tarrazona, to Burgo de Osma, to Toledo. Both Saragossa and Tarrazona were within Aragonese territory and are only about 45 miles apart, or roughly the same distance as between Huesca and Saragossa. Burgo de Osma, while not within the province of Aragon, is within the neighboring Castilian province of Soria bordering Aragon. Burgo de Osma is only about 80 miles from Tarrazona, with the provincial capital, Soria, roughly midway between Tarrazona and Burgo de Osma, a convenient stopping place between the two. Thus, Saragossa and Burgo de Osma are relatively close to each other (circa 120 miles apart) on a quite well-traveled commercial route between Saragossa and Valladolid.[31]

There were three main centers of translation from Arabic into Latin in twelfth-century Spain: (1) Barcelona, (2) Tarrazona, and (3) Toledo. The center at Tarrazona, midway between the other two, flourished during the time of Bishop Michael of Tarrazona (circa 1119-1151). Its most famous translator seems to have been Hugh of Santalla.[32] The center at Toledo began under Archbishop Raimundo of Toledo (circa 1125-1151). Its most famous personality, at least according to our present understanding of the work done there, would seem to have been Domenico Gundisalino (second half of the twelfth century).[33] However before Raimundo came to Toledo in 1125, he was bishop of Burgo de Osma. Thus, in the early 1120s Michael of Tarrazona and Raimundo of Toledo (then called Raimundo of Burgo de Osma) were neighbors geographically, only 80 miles apart via the town of Soria. What is more, Raimundo was of French Cluniac background, and it is highly possible that Michael of Tarrazona was of the same background.[34]

It is possible that Raimundo of Burgo de Osma first derived the idea of setting up a school of translators from his neighbor Michael of Tarrazona and that Michael of Tarrazona, in turn, derived this idea from Catalonia (especially the monastery of Ripoll and the city of Barcelona proper), a major translation center in the first half of the twelfth century. Its two leading personalities were Plato of Tivoli and the well-known Jewish scholar Abraham bar Hiyya (called Savasorda).[35] If Michael of Tarrazona was already interested in Latin translations from the Arabic in the early 1120s, it is possible that Petrus Alphonsi came from nearby Saragossa to meet with him in Tarrazona (circa 1121). It is also possible that through Michael of Tarrazona, Alphonsi met Raimundo of Burgo de Osma at this early date.

When Raimundo moved from Burgo de Osma to Toledo, did he then invite Alphonsi to become the head and chief teacher of the cathedral school of Toledo, charged with the responsibility of paying special attention to Latin translations from Arabic? Petrus Alphonsi was attractive because of unusual abilities with three classical languages—Arabic, Hebrew, and Latin—as well as the Romance dialects of northeastern Spain (perhaps also with Anglo-Norman and French acquired during the course of his stay in England and possible visit to France); his outstanding publication record (*Dialogi; Disciplina Clericalis; De Dracone; Epistola de Studio Artium Liberalium; Mappa Mundi;* chronological and astronomical tables; role in Adelard of Bath's translation of the astronomical tables of Majriti/Khwarizmi; *Humanum Proficuum,* etc.); his international contacts in England and France; and his fame. Hence, we regard it as highly likely that Petrus Alphonsi would have been the kind of person that Archbishop Raimundo would have chosen to head the cathedral school of Toledo, the cathedral school in the city of four religious communities: Christians, Muslims, Jews, and Karaites.

61

Did Petrus Alphonsi, in the employ of Archbishop Raimundo, summon both Robert of Ketton and Herman of Dalmatia to Toledo in the 1130s to assist in the translation work of the cathedral school? Was he also responsible for their participation in the Toletano-Cluniac corpus of the 1140s? Robert of Ketton was English. Petrus Alphonsi could have favored him for this reason alone since Alphonsi himself had spent considerable time in England. Both Robert of Ketton and Herman of Dalmatia had relationships with the school of Chartres in France (perhaps both were pupils of Thierry of Chartres). Petrus Alphonsi may have visited Chartres (possibly meeting Ivo of Chartres, Bernard of Chartres, and Gilbert of La Porree) during the 1110s.[36] When we examine the kinds of works Robert and Herman translated—works of astronomy, astrology, the astrolabe, mathematics (algebra, geometry), and alchemy rather than medicine or philosophy—we can see the clear influence of the popular scientific interests of Alphonsi rather than the more advanced scientific interests of Domenico Gundisalino, John of Seville, and the Jew Abraham ibn Daud, all of whom worked in Toledo from circa 1150. Like Robert and Herman, Petrus Alphonsi was also closely linked with the work of Arab astronomer-mathematicians like al-Khwarizmi and al-Majriti, and with the work of the Christian translator who took a special interest in them, Adelard of Bath.[37]

Thus, we consider it highly possible that Petrus Alphonsi was closely associated with Archbishop Raimundo of Toledo in the 1130s and that Alphonsi played a significant role in the general translation work of both Robert of Ketton and Herman of Dalmatia in Spain during the 1130s. He also probably invited both to join him in the Toletano-Cluniac corpus of the early 1140s.

It might be argued that if Peter of Toledo really is Petrus Alphonsi, why was he called Peter "of *Toledo*" rather than Petrus Alphonsi? After all, Petrus Alphonsi was called by the name Alphonsi in Spain upon his conversion to Christianity when he wrote the *Dialogi*. He was called by this same name in the prologue (line 1) of his *Disciplina Clericalis*; in the scientific and humanistic works which he composed while abroad in England (and perhaps also France) during the 1110s; and in Saragossa in 1121.[38] If so, why would he not have been called by this same name in connection with the Toletano-Cluniac corpus of the early 1140s?

There are several quite plausible answers to this legitimate question. Petrus Alphonsi's original name was *Mosheh* (in Hebrew) = *Musa* (in Arabic) = *Moyses* (in Latin) = Moses (in English). He is sometimes called "Rabbi Moses" or "Rabbi Moses the Spaniard."[39] However, upon being baptized in 1106, as the neophyte tells us in the preface to the *Dialogi*, he took two names: Petrus in honor of St. Peter, whose festival took place around the time of his baptism, and Alphonsus in honor of King Alfonso I of Aragon (1104-1134), his godfather at the baptism. His name Petrus may also have been partly in honor of the previous ruler of Aragon, Pedro I (1094-1104), with whom Moses/ Petrus may have been on good terms. Perhaps Petrus had even served as Pedro's physician.[40] However, conditions which may have impelled Moses to assume the name Petrus *Alphonsi* in 1106 might not have been the same as conditions which prevailed in Spain in the 1130s and 1140s, which indeed may well have impelled Petrus Alphonsi to drop "Alphonsi" from his name.

In 1106 Petrus Alphonsi was a resident of Aragon. If, as we argue, he participated in the Toletano-Cluniac corpus of the early 1140s, he would now have been a resident of Castile. The Alphonsi part of his name referred to King Alfonso I of Aragon. But in 1140 the ruler of Castile was also an Alfonso, Alfonso Raymond VII of Castile (1126-1157). This Alfonso Raymond VII of Castile had been at war with Alfonso I of Aragon, his own stepfather, during the early 1120s when both Alfonsos claimed the throne of Castile. It is true that their differences were settled completely by 1126 when Alfonso Raymond VII became ruler of Castile. Still, there once had been considerable enmity and strife between the two monarchs. Petrus Alphonsi might have considered it politic upon moving to Toledo in the 1130s to drop the Alphonsi part of his name lest the original Aragonese referent of his last name give the slightest modicum of offense to the Alfonso who was the ruler of Castile at this time.

Further, it is also possible that Petrus Alphonsi had a falling out with Alfonso I of Aragon and that perhaps this falling out was due to Petrus Alphonsi's deciding to move to Toledo, Castile, upon the invitation of Archbishop Raimundo of Toledo. Petrus Alphonsi's moving to Castile may also have been closely related, either as cause or effect, to Alfonso I's employment as a scholarly assistant of Abraham bar Hiyya (Savasorda), the great (unconverted) Jewish polymath of the first third of the twelfth century. Abraham's services may have included being secretary for Arabic correspondence, interpreter and diplomatic emissary in negotiations with the Arabs, royal astronomer and mathematician, as well as steward (and assistant in the subdivision) of the royal territory[41] Petrus Alphonsi's move to Castile may also have had something to do with Plato of Tivoli's coming to Barcelona circa 1130.[42] Perhaps Petrus Alphonsi and Alfonso I of Aragon quarreled as early as 1121 over a piece of property Petrus Alphonsi hoped to receive in Saragossa, reconquered from the Arabs in 1118.[43] Alternatively, the two may have quarreled as early as the first few years after Petrus Alphonsi's baptism in 1106, their falling out being a major reason why Petrus Alphonsi decided to go abroad to England (and perhaps also to France) in the 1110s.[44]

In any case, if Petrus Alphonsi and King Alfonso I of Aragon did fall out with each other, this would certainly explain why Petrus Alphonsi would have dropped the Alphonsi part of his name, especially after moving to Castile, and henceforth would have been called, by his own preference, Peter "*of Toledo.*" Of course, it is also possible that Petrus Alphonsi dropped the second part of his name not because of any quarrel with King Alfonso I of Aragon but rather because of the king's death in 1134. Was there any reason for him to be called Alphonsi after the great man this name was intended to honor had gone to heaven? In that blissful place the king surely had no further need of any of the earthly signs of honor and gratitude which his erstwhile subjects, for varying reasons, once felt compelled to lavish upon him when he ruled Aragon on earth!

Continuing on with the argument from the name, Petrus Alphonsi only took the name Alphonsi at baptism as a sign of his appreciation for the support of his godfather, the king of Aragon. What seemed right at the time of his transfer from one faith to another might well have seemed foolish thirty or forty years later, after he had already become well established in the faith which he had adopted in his younger days. Being called after a city, like Toledo, was common. Being called after a godfather was unusual and might have seemed immature to an older person and to those with whom he tended to associate.

Further, this name would have been a constant reminder to Christians that Petrus Alphonsi had not always been a member of their faith but had once been a Jew. The status of the Jew in both the Islamic and the Christian portions of Western Europe was in a serious state of decline during the first third of the twelfth century, circa 1100–1133.[45] Indeed, if, as we suggest, Petrus Alphonsi did move to Castile circa 1130, he would have had every reason to endeavor to conceal his Jewish origins as best he could, since King Alfonso Raymond of Castile was unfavorable to Jews and even to *converts* from Judaism to Christianity.[46] Archbishop Raimundo, on the other hand, was favorable to both. His position on the Jewish question would not have stood between him and Petrus Alphonsi. Indeed, it could even have brought the two closer together in view of their common disapproval (which, of course, could not be too open) of the king's anti-Jewish attitudes and policies.[47] However, Petrus Alphonsi, as an employee of the leading churchperson of Castile and indeed of all Spain (since Toledo was considered the main see of Spain and its archbishop the primate), might also have had some dealings with the king and/or his court. Hence, he might have felt it quite politic once again to change his name so as to deemphasize his Jewish origin as much as possible.

Finally, the name Petrus Alphonsi, with its indication of Jewish origin, represented Alphonsi's initial scholarly and literary interest, *i.e.*, the problem of Christian relations primarily with *Jews* and the justification of his conversion from *Judaism* to Christianity. However, Petrus Alphonsi rapidly transferred his interest from the problem of Christian-Jewish relations to the even more important problem of Christian-*Islamic* relations. The *Dialogi* of circa 1110 are primarily concerned with the problem of Christian-Jewish relations. Only one of the twelve chapters (chapter five) deals with the problem of Christian-Islamic relations. But all of Alphonsi's extant writings after the *Dialogi* seem to treat the problem of Christian-*Islamic* relations. These writings include *Disciplina Clericalis* and scientific treatises such as *De Dracone, Epistola de Studio Artium Liberalium, Mappa Mundi* based on Arabic models, chronological and astronomical tables, a role in Adelard of Bath's translation of the astronomical tables of Majriti/Khwarizmi (perhaps even Alphonsi's other works of which we only know the titles, *e.g., Humanum Proficuum*, and still other works which may lie buried in archives and libraries, their titles unknown to us at present).[48] Apparently, the problem of Christian-Jewish relations was of decreasing concern to Petrus Alphonsi after he wrote the *Dialogi*.

Indeed, the major thrust of Alphonsi's life and work *taken as a whole* was the attempt to solve the problem of Christian-*Islamic*, not

Christian-Jewish relations. He may well have writen the *Disciplina Clericalis* in order to break down Christian intolerance of Islam and to create a climate of opinion among Christian intellectuals in Western Europe that would be more receptive to Arabic culture.[49] Once this new climate of opinion was created, the Western Christian world could begin the task of overtaking and then surpassing the Islamic world in the crucial area of science and technology. For without doing that, the twofold crusading movement, *i.e.*, the *Reconquista* in Spain and the military struggle against Islam in the Middle East, was bound to fail. If the crusading movement failed, there would certainly be little if any hope for the conversion of the Islamic peoples to Christianity and the ultimate messianic redemption of mankind which was expected to follow their conversion. The translation movement, which Petrus Alphonsi so sedulously fostered, was the primary method, in his view, by which Western Europe could overtake and eventually surpass the Islamic world in the area of science and technology. The translation movement, thus, was not the result of the pure quest for knowledge. It was a weapon in the Christian struggle against Islam. In view of these considerations, if Alphonsi considered the problem of Christian-*Islamic* relations his main concern would he have wanted to retain a name which indicated precisely the opposite, *i.e.*, which indicated that he considered Christian-Jewish relations his major concern? The chances are that he would instead have dropped the Alphonsi part of his name upon moving to Toledo circa 1130.[50]

The Arguments in Favor of the Equation
Of Petrus Alphonsi with Peter of Toledo

Now that we have disposed of the major arguments against the identification of Petrus Alphonsi with Peter of Toledo, we can proceed to present the arguments in favor of the equation of the two Peters. In so doing we must carefully examine the admittedly meager data we have about Peter of Toledo and then compare it with what we know about Alphonsi. This comparison must be followed by a comparison of what we know about the Annotator of the Toletano-Cluniac corpus (who probably was identical with Peter of Toledo) with what we know about Alphonsi. A significant number of similarities between Peter of Toledo and Alphonsi, as well as between the Annotator and

Alphonsi, could establish a preliminary case in favor of the strong possibility that Petrus Alphonsi = Peter of Toledo = the Annotator.

Peter the Venerable called Peter of Toledo *magister Petrus*, "Master Peter." Jose Munyoz Sendino, the first editor (1949) of the Latin translation of al-Kindi's *Risalah* prepared by Peter of Toledo, suggested that Peter the Venerable called Peter of Toledo *magister* because Peter of Toledo had studied at one of the incipient universities of Western Europe, probably Paris. Kritzeck, while discounting this suggestion, believed that it was more likely that Peter the Venerable called Peter of Toledo *magister* because of what Peter of Toledo was then doing in Toledo.[51] If Kritzeck is correct, could not this title reflect the fact that Peter of Toledo was in the the service of the archbishop of Toledo and/or was headmaster of the cathedral school? Kritzeck also suggests that the title *magister* may refer to Peter of Toledo's great erudition and perhaps also his advanced age. In any case, when we combine all these possible implications of the title *magister*—i.e., studied at an incipient university such as Paris, erudition, advanced age—we find that we are dealing with a group of characteristics which certainly would have fit Petrus Alphonsi in the early 1140s. If, as we suggest, Archbishop Raimundo had brought Petrus Alphonsi to Toledo as headmaster of his cathedral school, to pay special attention to Latin translations from Arabic, this kind of position could easily be one of the possible implications of the title *magister Petrus*, "Master Peter."

Regis Blachere, the learned French translator of the Quran (1947), thought that Peter of Toledo was a convert from Islam to Christianity rather than a Mozarab (an Arabic-speaking Christian). Both possibilities, *i.e.*, Peter of Toledo's Islamic or Mozarabic origin, have something to recommend them, but Blachere thought his Islamic origin more probable.[52] We would agree with Blachere that Peter of Toledo was a *convert* to Christianity rather than a Mozarab, *i.e.*, rather than someone born a Christian. However, we would differ with Blachere on the religion which Peter of Toledo abandoned in order to embrace Christianity. We would argue that Peter of Toledo's former faith was Judaism, not Islam, because Peter of Toledo was Petrus Alphonsi.

Peter the Venerable stated that Peter of Toledo was skilled in both Arabic and Latin, but knew Arabic better. This certainly would apply to Petrus Alphonsi, a Jewish convert to Christianity whose original language was Arabic but who learned Latin after his conversion, and who therefore knew both Arabic and Latin, but Arabic better.[53] However, it might also apply to a Mozarab and/or to a convert from Islam to Christianity. The original language of both the Mozarab and the Muslim would have been Arabic. Both could have learnt Latin later, the Mozarab after moving from the Islamic south (e.g., Seville) to Christian Toledo, the Muslim after converting to Christianity. Thus, both the Mozarab and the convert from Islam, like Alphonsi, could have known Arabic and Latin, but Arabic better.

However, the question remains, Which kind of person—an Arabic-speaking Jewish convert to Christianity (like Petrus Alphonsi), an Arabic-speaking Christian Mozarab, or an Arabic-speaking Muslim convert to Christianity—would have felt the most pressure to learn Latin after either converting to Christianity and/or moving from Islamic to Christian territory? We would argue that the Arabic-speaking Jewish convert to Christianity (like Alphonsi) would have felt the most pressure to learn Latin. This argument assumes that a person converting from a minority to a majority religion (Judaism to Christianity) would be more greatly motivated to learn the sacred language of that majority religion (Latin) than a person not converting at all (the Mozarab) or a person converting from one majority religion to another (Islam to Christianity). This assumption itself rests upon the further assumption that a person converting from a minority to a majority religion (the Jew) is making a greater leap of faith and culture than a person not converting at all (the Mozarab) or a person converting from one majority religion to another (the Muslim). He therefore would feel a greater need to learn the sacred language of that majority religion (Latin) to provide crucial impetus for his greater leap and to cushion his harder fall when he reached the other side of the chasm after his greater leap. Therefore, while all three might have known Arabic better than Latin, the chances are greater that the Jewish convert (like Petrus Alphonsi) would have studied his Latin more assiduously than the Mozarab and/or the Muslim convert.

In short, the most likely possibility is that the person who knew both Arabic and Latin well, but Arabic better as his literary language, was a person of the religious middle. He was someone whose origins were in neither of the two religious extremes, neither in Christianity (a Mozarab) nor in Islam (a convert from Islam), but rather in Judaism. He was a Jew brought up among Muslims, then lived among Christians, converted to Christianity, and learned to write Latin, the religiocultural language of medieval Western Europe. He was someone like Petrus Alphonsi.

Further, an otherwise unknown unconverted Muslim named Muhammad participated in the Toletano-Cluniac corpus. This was an extremely rare phenomenon.[54] To our knowledge there is no other example of an unconverted Muslim participating in the translation movement from Arabic into Latin in twelfth-century Spain. It would seem that Peter of Toledo, who planned the translation portion of the Toletano-Cluniac corpus for Peter the Venerable, was responsible for including Muhammad in the project, especially as an assistant to Robert of Ketton and Herman of Dalmatia. Peter of Toledo himself did not really need Muhammad's help in translating al-Kindi's *Risalah* since Peter of Toledo knew Arabic well. Peter of Toledo also would seem to have worked closely with Muhammad on the annotations to the Latin translations of the Quran and al-Kindi's *Risalah*.

What kind of person would have been most likely to call upon an unconverted Muslim for assistance with this project? Would a Mozarab? The Mozarabs, as descendants of the former Christian rulers of Spain who were overwhelmed and conquered by the Arabs in the early eighth century, despised the Muslims. This feeling was reinforced during the unsuccessful attempt to overthrow Spanish Islam launched by the ninth-century Spanish martyrs' movement under the leadership of Eulogius and Alvarus, as well as during the persecutions which the Mozarabs suffered under waning Almoravide rule in early twelfth-century Spain. A Mozarab could never work with an unconverted Muslim in a project of this kind. Previous hatred too great to overcome would have stood in the way.

Likewise, would a convert from Islam to Christianity have called upon an unconverted Muslim for assistance? Would a convert from Islam have been willing to expose himself to the daily embarrassment he would have had to endure if one of his former coreligionists were to assist him in the project? The participation of the unconverted Muslim would have been a powerful reminder to both the converted Muslim and the born Christians involved in the project of the convert's former religious affiliation. Thus, the mere presence, the mere being and existence, of the unconverted Muslim assisting in the project (even if he kept strictly to his work and never discussed religion at all) would have been a perpetual consternation, perturbation, distress and reproach to the converted Muslim. A converted Muslim

69

(if we say that this is what Peter of Toledo was, following Blachere) and an unconverted Muslim (Muhammad) could never have cooperated successfully in the same project.

Therefore, neither if Peter of Toledo had been a Mozarab nor a converted Muslim would he have called upon an *unconverted* Muslim for assistance with the project. It would have been unthinkable. The only kind of person who would have been likely to call upon an unconverted Muslim for assistance would have been, once again, a person of the religious middle, *i.e.*, someone whose origins were in neither of the two religious extremes, in neither Christianity (the Mozarabs) nor Islam, but rather in Judaism. We refer to a Jew brought up among Muslims who then lived among Christians and converted to Christianity, someone like Petrus Alphonsi. After all, Alphonsi wrote the *Disciplina Clericalis* to break down anti-Islamic prejudices among Western Christians, so that Western Christians could learn enough from Islam eventually to be able to defeat it. Even the anti-Islamic fifth chapter of Petrus Alphonsi's *Dialogi* is relatively tolerant of Islam when compared with the anti-Islamic writings of his contemporaries.[55] Indeed, Alphonsi was probably the only person in all Spain at this time likely to call upon an unconverted Muslim for assistance with the project. Only Petrus Alphonsi would have been willing to use Muslims to aid the Christian effort eventually to overtake and defeat Islam. Only Alphonsi would have been willing to allow the unconverted Muslim Muhammad an opportunity to assist with the Toletano-Cluniac corpus. The seemingly unprecedented phenomenon of an unconverted Muslim aiding a project to translate Arabic works into Latin can only be understood if Petrus Alphonsi is Peter of Toledo.

Peter of Poitiers, Peter the Venerable's secretary, said that Peter of Toledo had a knowledge of Islamic customs in general and especially of Islamic sexual practices. Certainly, Petrus Alphonsi, who grew up among Muslims and was widely read in their belles-lettres, was acquainted with Islamic customs in general and makes constant reference to Islamic sexual practices in the fifth chapter of his *Dialogi* and in the *Disciplina Clericalis*.[56]

Peter of Toledo translated al-Kindi's *Risalah* for the Toletano-Cluniac corpus. Petrus Alphonsi knew al-Kindi's *Risalah*. Upon it he based the fifth chapter of his own *Dialogi*, written as early as circa 1110, *i.e.*, about thirty years before the *Risalah* was translated into

Latin by Peter of Toledo for the Toletano-Cluniac corpus. Indeed, to our knowledge Alphonsi was the only Latin author of his generation who knew the *Risalah* before it was authoritatively translated into Latin for the Toletano-Cluniac corpus. This would certainly seem to be a strong argument in favor of equating Petrus Alphonsi with Peter of Toledo.[57]

An even stronger argument in favor of equating Petrus Alphonsi with Peter of Toledo is the following. Not only was al-Kindi's *Risalah* chosen for translation from Arabic into Latin, but two other rather curious texts were also chosen. These were the *Liber Generationis Mahumet*, a highly legendary account of how the prophetic light (*nur*) descended generation by generation from Adam to Muhammad and of the numerous miracles which attended the Prophet Muhammad's birth, and the *Doctrina Mahumet*, and imaginary didactic dialogue in which the Prophet Muhammad is one of the two chief protagonists. But the interesting thing about both of these texts is that they are based on material which goes back to two Jewish converts to Islam circa 630, Kab al-Ahbar and Abdallah ibn Salam. Indeed, Abdallah ibn Salam is the second protagonist of the *Doctrina Mahumet*, and his conversion to Islam is described therein. Peter of Toledo was the person who planned the Toletano-Cluniac corpus. Peter of Toledo was also the person who chose to include these two peculiar texts, both of which involve converts from Judaism to another religion (*i.e.*, Judaism to Islam).

Would a Mozarab have chosen to translate such texts? Would the Mozarabs, who struggled for centuries to resist their own conversion to Islam, voluntary or forced, have been psychologically able to translate a text which went back to someone who did what to the Mozarabs would have been the unthinkable, *i.e.*, convert to Islam? Likewise, would a convert from Islam to Christianity have chosen to translate such texts? Would a convert from Islam to Christianity, who gave up the religion of the mosque, have been psychologically able to translate a text which went back to someone who did the exact opposite, gave up his own religion (Judaism) for the religion of the mosque? We would suggest that only a person of the religious middle whose origins were in neither of the two religious extremes, in neither Christianity (Mozarabs) nor Islam, but rather in Judaism; and only a Jew who himself had converted to another religion (*i.e.*, to Christian-

71

ity) but at the same time had a relatively favorable attitude toward Islam would have chosen to include such texts as the *Liber Generationis Mahumet* and the *Doctrina Mahumet*.

Indeed, when we examine the beginning of the anti-Islamic fifth chapter of Petrus Alphonsi's *Dialogi*, we find that his Jewish alter-ego or former self, Moyses, tells him that if he, Alphonsi, felt that he had to change his religion, had to abandon Judaism, he should not have become a Christian. Rather he should have become a *Muslim*, a member of another Semitic religion whose religious beliefs and practices are closer to pure monotheism and therefore closer to Judaism than are those of Christianity.[58] Moyses allowed that if the desire for self-aggrandizement was primary here, with the *Reconquista* reclaiming more and more territory for the church, then, of course, Petrus Alphonsi should have become a Christian. But if it really was his conscience, the pure search for truth, that had moved him to abandon Judaism, Alphonsi should definitely have become a Muslim. If Judaism could not be maintained, Islam was preferable to Christianity in a theoretical situation where choice was possible. This view probably reflected the sincere belief of many Spanish Jews circa 1110.

It undoubtedly made a deep impression upon Alphonsi, else he would not have cited it at the beginning of the fifth chapter of the *Dialogi* and have attempted to refute it. We suspect that within the deepest recesses of his psyche Petrus Alphonsi was forced to admit the cogency and relevance of this argument, which was one source of the relatively favorable attitude toward Islam which we find in his *Dialogi* (if we compare them to other anti-Islamic writings of the same generation) and especially in the *Disciplina Clericalis*. What is more, not only do we find the Jewish idea that conversion to Islam is preferable to conversion to Christianity in the fifth chapter of the *Dialogi*, but the same chapter also mentions none other than the two early converts from Judaism to Islam, Kab al-Ahbar and Abdallah ibn Salam.[59] Again this would seem to lend rather strong support to the thesis that Petrus Alphonsi is Peter of Toledo.

Kritzeck suggests that the inclusion in the Toletano-Cluniac corpus of two Islamic texts which contain material based upon the conversion of two Jews to Islam, Kab al-Ahbar and Abdallah ibn Salam, suggests Peter of Toledo's skilled polemical hand. If Kritzeck is correct, this would be even further proof that Petrus Alphonsi is Peter of Toledo. If the inclusion in the Toletano-Cluniac corpus of texts which go back to early converts from Judaism to Islam was indeed partly for polemical reasons, almost certainly the polemical reason involved was that these texts helped support the charge that there was strong heretical Jewish influence upon early Islam. This charge was presented by Petrus Alphonsi in the fifth chapter of his *Dialogi*, where he specifically mentions Kab al-Ahbar and Abdallah ibn Salam. It is also found in al-Kindi's *Risalah*, the source of the fifth chapter in general and no doubt the source of this particular charge as well.[60]

Thus, what seems to have transpired is the following. Petrus Alphonsi, who wrote his *Dialogi* circa 1110, knew al-Kindi's *Risalah* in its Arabic original, had it before him (obtained from Mozarabs in Aragon and not from Muslims, since it was a *Christian* Arabic text), and used it as the source of the fifth chapter of his *Dialogi*. From al-Kindi's *Risalah* Alphonsi learned of the importance of Kab al-Ahbar and Abdallah ibn Salam, who allegedly exerted heretical Jewish influence upon Muhammad. As a Jew who himself had converted out of Judaism, Petrus Alphonsi took an especial interest in Kab and Abdallah, mentioning both converts in his *Dialogi* along with the heretical Jewish influence upon Muhammad. But at this early date Alphonsi might well have not yet seen copies of the Arabic originals of the documents which were later translated in the Toletano-Cluniac corpus as the *Liber Generationis Mahumet* (Kab al-Ahbar) and the *Doctrina Mahumet* (Abdallah ibn Salam). Years later Peter the Venerable came to Petrus Alphonsi at Toledo in 1142 and put him in charge of the translations in the Toletano-Cluniac corpus. Thereupon Alphonsi decided, on the basis of what he had read and written circa 1110 at the time he composed his *Dialogi*, that al-Kindi's *Risalah* should be obtained once again from Mozarabs living in Toledo and translated into Latin for the Toletano-Cluniac corpus. At the same time Petrus Alphonsi would have decided that the Arabic texts dealing with Kab al-Ahbar and Abdallah ibn Salam should be obtained from Muslims living in Toledo (and not from Mozarabs since these were *Islamic* Arabic texts). Perhaps they were obtained from or through the good offices of the Muslim Muhammad who participated in the Toletano-Cluniac corpus. They were then translated into Latin to support *al-Kindi's* charge, repeated by Alphonsi in his *Dialogi*, that there was heretical Jewish influence upon Islam and that this influence was exerted upon Muhammad by these two early converts from Judaism to Islam, Kab al-Ahbar and Abdallah ibn Salam.

73

Going one step further, Peter the Venerable, in his major anti-Judaic polemic the *Liber adversus Judaeorum Inveteratam Duritiem*, was strongly influenced by the anti-Judaic polemic of Petrus Alphonsi's *Dialogi*. Was this pure coincidence? When and where did Peter the Venerable become acquainted with the *Dialogi*? It is possible that he became acquainted with them in France during the 1110s, 1120s, or 1130s. However, Peter the Venerable's anti-Judaic polemic was not completed until after he began the Toletano-Cluniac corpus in the early 1140s. Moreover, Peter the Venerable's other major document dealing with the Jewish question, his letter on the Jews to King Louis VII of France, dates from the late 1140s, *i.e.*, the Second Crusade. Hence, it seems likely that Peter the Venerable's interest in the problem of the Jews came *to full fruition* only after and was greatly stimulated by his interest in the problem of the Muslims which had given rise to the Toletano-Cluniac corpus. Peter the Venerable definitely felt that Judaism was an ally of Islam against Christianity but that Islam was clearly the greater danger. Therefore, any Christian attempt to solve the greater problem of Islam might also want to attempt to solve the lesser but closely related problem of Judaism. Thus, it is highly possible that Peter the Venerable's interest in the polemic against the Jews was more strongly influenced by his interest in the polemic against the Muslims than vice versa. If Peter of Toledo, whom Peter the Venerable put in charge of the Toletano-Cluniac corpus of the early 1140s, was Petrus Alphonsi, this would allow us to explain with ease the influence of Alphonsi's *Dialogi* upon Peter the Venerable's anti-Judaic polemic of the late 1140s.[61]

Allow us, then, to venture to suggest the following even more daring possibility. The conversion of the Muslims had been a subject of considerable interest at Cluny during the 1070s, the time of Abbot Hugh and Anastasius. Petrus Alphonsi may have come to Cluny in the 1110s, where he could have stirred up some interest in the problems of Judaism and Islam, perhaps influencing Peter the Venerable's plan for the Vezelay tympanum. Nevertheless, Peter the Venerable was not primarily interested in either the problem of Islam or Judaism during the 1110s, 1120s, or 1130s. He was primarily interested at this time in the problem of revitalizing the Clunic order after the disastrous administration of Abbot Pontius and in the face of the serious competition from the newly founded and highly dynamic Cistercian movement, as well as in the problem of combatting the heresy of the Neo-

Manicheans, or Petrobrusians, in France. The person who seriously moved Peter the Venerable to begin thinking about the problem of Christian-Islamic and Christian-Jewish relations in a very serious way was none other than Peter Abelard, who stayed with Peter the Venerable at Cluny for two years prior to Abelard's death in 1142. Abelard became interested in the problem of Islam and Judaism primarily under the influence of Petrus Alphonsi, whose *Dialogi* he had read (along with the *Disciplina Clericalis* and perhaps also Alphonsi's scientific writings). Indeed, Petrus Alphonsi may well have met Abelard in person in or near Paris in the 1110s and have kept in touch with him via correspondence thereafter. It is highly possible that Alphonsi was the person who supplied Abelard with information about the Islamic philosophers (especially the Spaniard ibn Bajja of Saragossa [which city also played a role in Petrus Alphonsi's life], Seville and Granada, who died at Fez in 1138), which Abelard utilized in his great dialogue between a philosopher (= a Muslim philosopher = ibn Bajja?), a Jew, and a Christian. Abelard would then have been the person who first mentioned Alphonsi to Peter the Venerable (and/or reminded him about Petrus Alphonsi if Peter the Venerable and Alphonsi had met at Cluny in the 1110s) and told Peter the Venerable that Petrus Alphonsi was now head of the cathedral school of Toledo. Peter the Venerable sought out Alphonsi on his trip to Spain in 1142 and put him in charge of the Toletano-Cluniac corpus. Petrus Alphonsi carried out this project masterfully and gave Peter the Venerable a copy of his *Dialogi* (or reminded him about a copy of the *Dialogi* which Alphonsi may already have presented to Cluny in the 1110s). They served as a major source of Peter the Venerable's own treatise against the Jews, finished in the late 1140s.

Peter the Venerable hoped that his anti-Islamic polemic, the *Liber contra Sectam sive Haeresim Saracenorum* (circa 1143 and thereafter), would be translated into Arabic so that it could serve as a means of evangelizing the Muslims and strengthening the faith of Arabic-speaking Christians, *i.e.*, the Mozarabs.[62] If this hope of Peter the Venerable was a serious one and not just a passing fancy (we would like to believe that it was at least moderately serious), it is highly likely that the person he had in mind to translate his *Liber contra Sectam sive Haeresim Saracenorum* was none other than Peter of Toledo. For of the four who worked on the Toletano-Cluniac corpus and knew Arabic, the two non-Spanish comrades, Robert of Ketton and Herman of

Dalmatia, knew Arabic only as a second language. They could do a fair job as translators from Arabic into Latin, but they almost certainly could not do the much more difficult job of working the other way around, translating from Latin into Arabic. Only someone whose original language was Arabic and who learned Latin later could work this way. Certainly the Muslim Muhammad would not have been able to translate a Latin treatise into Arabic. Moreover, even if he had had the ability to do so, would he, as a believing Muslim, have been willing to assume primary responsibility for, and expend considerable time and energy upon, translating into Arabic a polemic against his own faith and people? Indeed, even if Muhammad had been willing to betray his own faith and people in this way, would Peter the Venerable have been willing to trust an unconverted Muslim with such a major responsibility? Peter the Venerable might have been willing to allow Muhammad to assist Christians like Peter of Toledo, Robert of Ketton, and Herman of Dalmatia in their work. But would he have been willing to allow an unconverted Muslim to assume the primary responsibility for any individual project within the larger Toletano-Cluniac corpus?

Indeed, of those who worked on the Toletano-Cluniac corpus, the only person who could possibly have been intended by Peter the Venerable as the translator of his anti-Islamic polemic was Peter of Toledo. If so, this would also strengthen the possibility that Petrus Alphonsi was Peter of Toledo. Why would Peter the Venerable have believed that Peter of Toledo would be interested in taking the time to do the exceptional task of translating from Latin into Arabic unless Peter the Venerable knew that Peter of Toledo, like Peter the Venerable himself, was interested in the Christian polemic against Islam? But very few Christian intellectuals in Spain during the first half of the twelfth century who knew both Arabic and Latin, but Arabic a little better, had any sympathy with the attempt to develop a reasoned Christian polemic against Islam. Petrus Alphonsi was almost unique in this regard in Spain during the first half of the twelfth century. His *Dialogi* had been directed against both the Jews and the Muslims. The major concern of his life after circa 1110 had been the problem of Islam and of how Christendom could overtake and defeat the Islamic world. Thus, it seems likely that Petrus Alphonsi was Peter of Toledo and that this is why Peter the Venerable could entertain the hope that Peter of Toledo would translate Peter the Venerable's anti-Islamic polemic into Arabic.

*****

Now that we have concluded the arguments in favor of the equation of Petrus Alphonsi with Peter of Toledo, we are ready to take up, though only in the most preliminary way, the question of the relationship between Petrus Alphonsi and the Annotator. The annotations at issue are in the Arsenal manuscript no. 1162, the original autograph of the Toletano-Cluniac corpus, which Kritzeck has been preparing for publication. Prior to the publication of these annotations, with translation and commentary, we have had to rely upon the rather extensive, though selective, citations from the annotations in Daniel's *Islam and the West*.[63] Judging from these citations in the Daniel book, the Annotator may have been the first great, systematic Quranic commentator in Western Europe, and, to our knowledge, his work was not to be surpassed until that of Ludovico Maracci (Padua, 1698) and George Sale (London, 1734), who relied upon Maracci. Kritzeck has argued the strong likelihood that the Annotator was Peter of Toledo. If we can show a significant number of similarities between the Annotator and Alphonsi, this may well clinch the case in favor of the thesis that all three are one and the same and that Petrus Alphonsi = Peter of Toledo = the Annotator.

There are at least five points of similarity between the Annotator and Petrus Alphonsi, which, while important, cannot, of course, be decisive because the Annotator and Alphonsi both share these particulars with al-Kindi's *Risalah* and the *Contrarietas Alpholica* (tenth-, eleventh-, or twelfth-century Spain). These five points of similarity are (1) the role of the Angel Gabriel in the revelation of the Quran;[64] (2) that Islam puts its opponents to death without compunction;[65] (3) that Muhammad lusted after women and committed adultery;[66] (4) the numerous contradictions contained within the Quran;[67] and (5) the Jewish influence upon Muhammad and the Quran.[68] Since these five points are common not only to the Annotator and Petrus Alphonsi but to al-Kindi's *Risalah* as well, it is possible that the Annotator took them directly from the *Risalah* and that Alphonsi had nothing whatsoever to do with the matter. It is equally possible, however, that

Petrus Alphonsi was the Annotator and that he himself took these points from both the *Risalah* and the *Contrarietas Alpholica*. He would have then incorporated them first into the anti-Islamic fifth chapter of his own *Dialogi* circa 1110 and later into the annotations which he wrote to both Robert of Ketton's Quran translation and to his own translation of al-Kindi's *Risalah* in the Toletano-Cluniac corpus circa 1142.

Three of the Annotator's favorite adjectives for describing Muhammad and the Quran are *stultus* (foolish), *frivolus* (silly), and *mendax* (false); *mendax* especially where Muhammad seems to have retold the Old Testament stories in his own creative way as part of the Quran.[69] Petrus Alphonsi, likewise, in the anti-Islamic fifth chapter of his *Dialogi* uses these very same three adjectives on more than one occasion. The adjective *stultus* is used at least three times in the fifth chapter. The title of the chapter itself is "De Sarracenorum lege destruenda et sententiarum suarum *stultitia* confutanda." Abdallah ibn Salam and Kab al-Ahbar, the two heretical Arabian Jews, joined Muhammad and furnished him aid *ad complendam stultitiam ejus*. Hasan and Husayn, the great martyrs of the Shiite Muslims, were considered *stulti* by their own father Ali (though Ali is not mentioned by name here), because they almost killed themselves with fastings and vigils in mourning over the death of Muhammad, whom they considered the prophet.[70]

Alphonsi used *frivolus* to describe some of the miracles which the Prophet Muhammad is alleged to have performed. The word *mendax* is used at least four times in the concluding portion of the fifth chapter.[71] The Arabs discovered that Muhammad was a *mendax* when, contrary to what he had said before passing away, his body was not transported to heaven on the third day after his death. Muhammad was a *mendax* when he said that Jesus did not really die upon the Cross; rather, that Jesus only seemed to do so (Islamic Docetism). Petrus Alphonsi concludes the fifth chapter of his *Dialogi* by asking his Jewish opponent Moyses the following:

> How therefore can you urge me to believe [Muhammad], that *mendax*, when you find him deceitful [*fallax*] in everything. I pray the mercy [*pietatem*] of Almighty God to save me from his error.[72]

Four other adjectives were favorites of the Annotator in describing Muhammad and the Quran: *impius* (wicked), *delirus* (silly), *insanus* (mad), and *vanus* (meaningless).[73] To our knowledge none of these specific adjectives appear in the fifth chapter of Petrus Alphonsi's *Dialogi*. However, other adjectives do appear there which are fairly close to these in meaning. With regard to the adjective *impius*, Alphonsi speaks of Muhammad's *nequitia* (iniquity), which is not too far from *impius*.[74] Further, while Petrus Alphonsi does not use *delirus* and *insanus*, there do appear adjectives like *inconstans* and *irrationabile* to describe Judaism, and the *Dialogi* make it clear that they consider Judaism a sister religion of Islam which exerted significant influence upon Islam in its formative period.[75] Finally, though Alphonsi does not use the adjective *vanus* in the fifth chapter of the *Dialogi*, he does employ the adjective *inanis* to describe Muhammad's *doctrina*, and *inanis* is not too far from one of the meanings of *vanus*, i.e., empty.[76]

Finally, the Annotator castigated Muhammad's ignorance of physical science when the prophet stated in the Quran that birds flying in the air are upheld by the power of God. According to the Annotator the air supports the birds that fly through it, just as the water supports the fish that swim through it. God works no special miracle for the birds. This kind of comment, which Daniel calls "unusually unreasonable," seems to be the kind of comment which someone who was a popular scientist would make. This is what Petrus Alphonsi really was.[77]

It is our sincere and earnest view that these annotations are the work of Petrus Alphonsi (= Peter of Toledo) and therefore that Alphonsi was the first great systematic Quranic commentator of the Western Christian world.[78] However, before such a view can be fully substantiated, if it ever can, we will have to await not only the publication of the annotations, which are still in manuscript (Arsenal no. 1162), but also the publication of those of Petrus Alphonsi's writings, especially his scientific treatises, which are still in manuscript. It would also help greatly if we had an edition of the anonymous Spanish anti-Islamic polemic of the (tenth–twelfth centuries), the *Contrarietas Alpholica*, which along with al-Kindi's *Risalah* may have been influential upon Alphonsi's attitudes toward Islam. Finally, we could benefit from an edition of a vast anti-Judaic polemic written during the second half of the twelfth century in England by Peter of Cornwall, strongly influenced by Petrus Alphonsi's *Dialogi* and by Alphonsi's other writings, including some of his writings which seem to be no longer extant. However, even prior to the publication of these texts, with translation and commentary, we believe it to be not only possible, but contructive as well, to attempt a preliminary case in favor of the thesis that Petrus Alphonsi was the Annotator in the Toletano-Cluniac corpus. Hopefully this preliminary effort will encourage and stimulate other scholars to delve more deeply into this complex and controversial question and present further data which can help settle the matter definitively at some future date.

4. The Association of Jew with Muslim by Medieval Christians: A New Comparative Approach to the Origins of Modern Anti-Semitism *

PART ONE

TWENTIETH-CENTURY REVIVALS OF THE ASSOCIATION OF JEW WITH MUSLIM BY MEDIEVAL CHRISTIANS

"Is Christian theology responsible for anti-Semitism, for the Holocaust and its six million Jewish victims?" According to *The New York Times*, June 5, 1974, page 22, this was the main topic of debate at the second day's session of the Jewish-Christian symposium on Auschwitz, June 1974, Cathedral Church of St. John the Divine, New York City.[1]

One of the speakers, Rosemary Ruether, a Catholic scholar,[2] presented a harsh condemnation of Christianity:

> It was Christian theology which developed the thesis of the eternal reprobate status of the Jew in history and laid the foundation for the demonic view of the Jews which fanned the flames of popular hatred.

By contrast, Yosef Yerushalmi, a specialist on the Jewish encounter with the Inquisition,[3] offered a partial defense of the church. According to Yerushalmi Christian theology taught subjection but never extermination of the Jew. The crucial problem of Christian-Jewish relations is not why the medieval church persecuted the Jews but rather why it kept them alive. Crucial factors were the medieval church's "awareness of its Jewish matrix" and the decision by the church as early as the pre-Nicene period (even before Constantine made Christianity the majority religion of the Roman Empire during the early fourth century) to retain the Old Testament within its canon of scripture despite severe ideological attacks by Christian Gnostics on Judaism. According to Yerushalmi the relative silence of Popes Pius XI and XII

81

about the Nazi racial statutes and the mass slaughter of the Jews during World War II[4] was a radical break with the tradition of a *medieval* papacy that spoke out more forthrightly for Jews at times of severe persecution.

Thus, we have here the very interesting and progressive situation wherein a Christian scholar harshly condemns Christianity while a Jewish scholar partially defends the church. This is how far we have come in the movement for genuine Jewish-Christian dialogue and reconciliation, initiated by the late lamented Pope John XXIII at Vatican II in the early 1960s, a movement which deserves our strongest possible support.[5]

During the course of our own study of Christian-Jewish relations we have developed a position that has more affinity with that of Yerushalmi than Ruether. We do *not* believe that Christian theology has been primarily responsible for the tragic fate and destiny of the Jewish people in Europe during the past two thousand years. Rather, we emphasize the seventh-century rise of Islam and the great Islamic conquests, not only of the eastern, southern, and western Mediterranean littoral, but also of an empire that extended from the Atlantic to Central Asia and was greater in geographical size than any which had preceded it, including the Roman. Since the rise of Islam the *primary* (though by no means the only) factors in the history of anti-Semitism have been the following: the association of Jew with Muslim; the long-standing European Christian tendency to equate the Jew, of Middle Eastern origin, with the Muslim, also of Middle Eastern origin; the intensely held Christian feeling that the Jew was an ally of, and in league with, his ethnoreligious cousin the Muslim against the West; the deep-seated Christian apprehension that the Jew, the internal Semitic alien, was working hand in hand with the Muslim, the external Semitic enemy, to bring about the eventual destruction of Indo-European Christendom.

We commence this chapter by offering four examples from the twentieth century which testify to the continued power and contemporary relevance of the association of Jew with Muslim by medieval Christians. After a brief discussion of these initial examples, we proceed to attempt to explain why early medieval Christians associated Jew with Muslim circa 600–1100.

EXAMPLE ONE. The striking cover of *Newsweek* magazine, September 17, 1973, showed a red gasoline pump against a blue sky, with the headline "Arab Oil Squeeze" at a diagonal in the upper right-hand corner and a scowling, bearded Arab, with full-flowing Beduin headdress and robe, holding the gasoline hose. Irony of ironies! A week later (September 24, 1973, p. 64) *Time* magazine published a story which began by asking "What is a nice Jewish boy from Brooklyn doing posing as a hard-eyed Arab on the cover of *Newsweek?*" It seems that the Jew in question was 33-year-old Manhattan talent agent Steve Kaye. He explained what happened as follows. The firm he works for had been commissioned to find a model for the photo on the *Newsweek* cover. When they could not find any Arabs for the part, Kaye volunteered his own dark, bearded visage and even threw in the Beduin garb which he had bought in Israel, where his brother lives on a kibbutz. "How was *Newsweek* to know I'd been bar-mitzvahed 20 years ago?" said Kaye. "All they knew was that they needed an Arab fast and I looked like one." Kaye's identity was not revealed until one of his regular clients, in the radio business, saw the *Newsweek* cover and announced over the air waves to hundreds of astonished listeners: "That's no Arab; that's my Jewish agent."

Funny? Of course. Poignant too? Perhaps. Was what happened here pure coincidence or was it ultimately bound up with forces far greater than any which Mr. Kaye or most people in general would understand? We believe that in the *Newsweek* cover incident is an example of the centuries-old tendency to associate Jew with Muslim. Could it not have been the common Semitic ethnolinguistic heritage of both Jew and Arab that moved Kaye, perhaps unwittingly, to volunteer to pose as an Arab when no real Arab could be found? Could it not have been the long-standing Christian tendency to equate Jew with Muslim which moved the agency for which Kaye worked, again perhaps unwittingly, to allow Kaye to pose as an Arab and moved *Newsweek*, again perhaps unwittingly, to accept what Kaye's agency had done? But regardless of who was moved by what, when *Newsweek* put this picture of a Jew posing as an Arab on its September 17, 1973, cover, there can be no question but that it was providing a twentieth-century example of the association of Jew with Muslim by medieval Christians at the same time as it was reinforcing the continued power of this medieval Christian tendency in the contemporary world.

EXAMPLE TWO. Dan Kurzman's book *Genesis 1948: The First Arab-Israeli War*[6] tells the story of what happened to the Arab general, Fawzi el-Kaoukji (commander of the Arab Liberation Army, from whom the Israelis took the Christian holy city of Nazareth in July of 1948[7]) during his stay in Nazi Germany, where his hatred for British rule in the Middle East forced him to spend World War II. In 1941 the Nazis asked Kaoukji to lead a European Muslim army against the Allies. But because they would not guarantee the Arabs full independence if the Axis won the war, Kaoukji turned down the request. Thereupon a German officer snapped threateningly: *"Don't forget that you are a Semite like the Jews"* (and we can treat you accordingly by sending you to a concentration camp): Kaoukji, who together with his son was in a German hospital at this time recovering from wounds sustained in the unsuccessful German-backed Arab revolt against British rule in Iraq, replied as follows to the German officer's threat: *"True, I am a cousin of the Jews.* But I can prove that Arab blood has not been mixed with Jewish blood for hundreds of years. Could some Germans do the same?" This was an allusion to the rumor that Hitler was partly of Jewish descent himself, and it infuriated the Nazis to such an extent that they murdered Kaoukji's son (poisoning him in the hospital and making it seem like an accident). When the Germans invited Kaoukji to his own son's funeral, he replied: "Let those who murdered him go [but I won't]."

This story was told to Dan Kurzman by Kaoukji himself, and it represents eloquent testimony to the continued power of the association of Jew with Muslim by medieval Christians into modern times. Though the Nazis were profoundly anti-Christian, they maintained the long-standing Christian tendency to equate Jew with Muslim.

EXAMPLE THREE. Kurzman also tells the story of what happened during Golda Meir's important meeting with King Abdullah of Transjordan in May 1948.[8] During this meeting Abdullah proposed that the Jews should abandon the idea of an independent Jewish state and instead should join the Kingdom of Transjordan, in whose parliament and cabinet they could have 50 percent of the seats, thus creating a joint Arab-Jewish Palestinian country which would dominate the Middle East. This was unacceptable to Golda Meir. She told King Abdullah that he should be willing to permit an independent Jewish state in Palestine because "the Jews are the only friends you have." To which King Abdullah replied as follows:

I know that very well. I have no illusions. I know you and I believe in your good intentions. I believe with all my heart that divine provi-

dence has brought you back here [to Palestine and the Middle East],
restoring you, a Semitic people who were exiled to Europe and shared
in its progress, to the Semitic East which needs your knowledge and initiative. Only with your help and your guidance will the Semites be able
to revive their ancient glory. *We cannot expect genuine assistance from
the Christian world, which looks down on Semitic peoples* [italics ours]. We
will progress only as the result of joint efforts. I know all this and I
believe it sincerely, but conditions are difficult. One dare not take rash
steps. Therefore, I beg you once more to be patient.

King Abdullah, reflecting the views of many Arab intellectuals who
were moderates on the Zionist question, believed that the Arabs could
not "expect genuine assistance from the Christian world" because
that world "looks down on [all] Semitic peoples," both Arabs and
Jews, whom it equates with one another and believes to be in league
with one another against the West.

EXAMPLE FOUR. According to a story entitled "News Flashes: A
New 'Orleans Affair' Beginning," which appeared in one of the
leading Jewish newspapers in the United States, the Los Angeles *B'nai
B'rith Messenger*, Friday, November 29, 1974, p. 6:

A new 'Orleans affair' has broken out in the French city of Chalon-sur-
Saone [near Autun, Dijon, and Lyons, in east-central France] where
public rumors are being circulated that local Jews are 'kidnapping'
teenage girls and 'selling them abroad.' Jewish sources in Chalon-sur-
Saone said that the rumors started about two weeks ago in the local
high school for girls. From there they spread to the rest of the city's
population. Soon after the rumors first started, anti-Jewish slogans were
painted at night on Jewish-owned shops. Rumors, similar to those
which rocketed Orleans in the Spring of 1969, claim that Jewish shop
keepers drug and kidnap their non-Jewish customers, especially young
girls, to sell them abroad.

According to the rumors and printed reports thereof, to which
foreign lands were the Jews selling these young Christian girls into
white slavery?

An answer to this important question comes from the report on the
"Orleans Affair" itself (of which the Chalon affair was merely a repeti-
tion) which appeared in *Newsweek* magazine, June 30, 1969, page 52.

According to this report a story began to circulate through Orleans in late May 1969 to the effect that

> a worker accompanied his wife on an afternoon shopping trip to . . . a small boutique owned by Henri Licht, an Orleans Jewish businessman. The wife entered alone and when, half an hour later, her impatient husband went in looking for her, he was told by Licht that no woman answering his wife's description had ever been in the shop. At that, the irate husband called the police who made a thorough search of the shop and discovered not only the missing wife, but two other women, bound and drugged in the basement. Soon, the entire city was buzzing with the news: the quiet, bespectacled Monsieur Licht was actually the mastermind of a narcotics and white-slave ring that specialized in kidnapping comely Christian . . . [women of Orleans].

According to *Newsweek* the story was a complete fabrication. The Orleans police had received no complaints whatsoever about missing women and had discovered no one at all hidden in the basement of Licht's boutique. Investigators traced the inspiration for the white-slave story to a recent issue of a notorious scandal magazine.

But *Newsweek* continues:

> In Orleans the story spread like wildfire and was quickly embellished by such 'facts' as the existence of subterranean passages connecting Jewish shops and *submarines piloted by Israelis who peddled women to Arab harems* [italics ours].

Thus, the rumors and the printed reports thereof had it that it was specifically to Arab lands that the Jews were selling these young Christian girls into white slavery. What is more, the rumors, as reported in *Newsweek*, had the Israelis acting as intermediaries between the Jewish merchants of Orleans and the Arabs, this despite the fact that the Israelis and the Arabs have been bitter enemies not only since the Arab-Israeli War of 1948 but since the Balfour Declaration of 1917 as well.

What could have driven the Christians of Orleans to start a rumor which was at such variance with the known facts of Middle Eastern history since World War I? Was it not the long-standing Christian tendency to equate Jew with Muslim, which had led to an intensely held Christian feeling that the Jew was in league with the Muslim working to bring about the eventual destruction of Christendom? Does not the Orleans rumor, then, as reported in *Newsweek*, represent testimony more eloquent than even the stories of Steve Kaye, General Kaoukji, and Golda Meir to the continued power of the association of Jew with Muslim by medieval Christians into the twentieth century?

There clearly is something quite medieval about the "Orleans Affair" of 1969. *Newsweek* was aware of this, but the only medieval precedent it could think of was the burning of Joan of Arc as a witch in 1431 (mentioned in the very first sentence of its story). Edgar Morin, who wrote a book on the "Orleans Affair" entitled *Rumour In Orleans*,[9] was vaguely aware of the possibility of medieval precedents. One section of his book (pages 120–127) is called "The Middle Ages Today." Toward the end of this section Morin tells us:

> personally, I regard our contemporary society—the way it is developing—not so much as a society which still embodies traces of archaism, but rather as one which is actively promoting archaism of a new kind. . . . The Orleans affair should not be treated as a sequel (or throw-back) to the Middle Ages in the modern world; it is, rather, one symptom of our own modern Middle Ages.[10]

But why could not the 1969 "Orleans Affair" be a throwback to the Middle Ages? There was a very close medieval parallel to the "Orleans Affair" in Orleans itself, *the very same city*, circa 1010, at the time of a great persecution of the Jews of Western Europe that was a prelude to the persecutions at the time of the First Crusade. Both of the Christian chroniclers of the 1010 persecution, Adhemar of Chabannes (circa 1028) and the Cluniac Ralph Glaber (circa 1044), testify to the belief, widespread among the Christians of France, that the Jews were in league with the Muslims and that the destruction of the Holy Sepulchre in 1009 by the Fatimid Caliph of Egypt, al-Hakim, was a product of a joint Islamo/Judaic conspiracy. Glaber alone reports the rumor that the Jews of Orleans sent a message to the "Prince of Babylon" (= the Fatimid Caliph of Egypt) suggesting that the Muslims of the Middle East could protect themselves against the Christian danger only by destroying the Church of the Holy Sepulchre in Jerusalem, the most sacred Christian shrine in Palestine.[11]

Edgar Morin was not aware of the "Orleans Affair" of 1010. Had he known of it, would he not have seen the parallel? In 1010 the Jews of Orleans were accused of working with the Arabs to destroy Christian shrines. In 1969 the Jews of Orleans were accused of working with the Arabs to sell Christian girls into white slavery. Admittedly, the parallel is not 100 percent perfect. The Christians of the Middle Ages were more concerned about religion than sexuality. Hence they accused the Jews of conspiring with the Muslims to destroy Christian shrines. The Christians of the twentieth century are more concerned about sexuality than about religion. Hence they accuse the Jews of conspiring with the Muslims to sell Christian girls into white slavery. But in both cases, the "Orleans Affair" of 1010 and the "Orleans Affair" of 1969, the basic charge of Jews conspiring with Muslims against Christians was the same. Why, then, is not the "Orleans Affair" of 1969 a throwback to the Middle Ages? Why is not the "Orleans Affair" of 1969 the most eloquent of all possible testimony to the continued power of the association of Jew with Muslim by medieval Christians into modern times?

PART TWO

WHY DID EARLY MEDIEVAL CHRISTIANS ASSOCIATE JEW WITH MUSLIM (CIRCA 600–1100 A.D.)?[12]

Ever since our first introduction to the study of the Middle Ages,[13] we have been troubled by the question of why the High Middle Ages (1000–1300), the time when medieval Western European civilization reached such glorious heights of intellectual and cultural creativity, was also the period of the revival of anti-Semitism in Western Europe after it had been relatively dormant during the earlier, more primitive Carolingian-Ottonian period (700–1000). High medieval civilization produced such giants of the human spirit as St. Francis of Assisi and Jacopone da Todi, two genuine *alteri Christi*, in religion; St. Thomas Aquinas and Duns Scotus in philosophy; Robert Grosseteste and Roger Bacon in science; Dante, Juan Ruiz, and Chaucer in belles-lettres; Leonine and Perotine in music; Duccio and Giotto in painting; Niccolo and Giovanni Pisano in sculpture; as well as Villard de Honnecourt and Arnolfo di Cambio in architecture. How could this civilization also have been responsible for the terrible massacre of the Jews during the First Crusade, for the blood libel (the charge that Jews required Christian blood for the Passover ritual), for the desecration-of-the-host libel (the charge that the Jews stole and tortured the sacred

88

wafer used in the mass),[14] and for countless other unspeakable wrongs against a people who meant medieval Christians little harm and who desired primarily to live out their lives in peace, in accordance with the highest ideals of their ancient faith.

Since circa 1960, we have been diligently researching medieval Christian-*Islamic* relations, focussing on a study of Western Christian missions to the Muslims through the time of St. Francis of Assisi (1182–1226), for whom the problem of Islam was of central importance while the problem of Judaism, rather puzzlingly, was not. We have also published several articles on Palestinian Jewish history during the Greco-Roman period (circa 300 B.C. to 300 A.D.).[15] We feel that we have been able to develop a more cogent interpretation of the main dynamic in medieval anti-Semitism, and it is this interpretation that we would like to explain now.

Many factors contributed to the great outburst of anti-Semitism in Western Europe during the High Middle Ages, the aftereffects of which were felt in the later Middle Ages (1300–1500) and in modern times (after 1500). At least four main types of factors were at work helping to generate anti-Semitism in high medieval Western Europe: (1) religious factors, such as the deicide charge (the charge that the Jews killed Christ), Christian Messianic expectations (according to which the Jews had to be either converted or annihilated as agents of Antichrist before the Second Coming could take place), and Christian resentment of Jewish proselytising activities; (2) economic factors, such as economic competition between Christians and Jews and/or Christian resentment of Jewish money-lending activities; (3) political factors, such as the struggle for power between the monarchy, the nobility, and the urban middle class, and later the urban lower class, in which struggle the Jews were often caught; and (4) psychological factors, such as the deeply felt human need to find scapegoats for individual and/or societal shortcomings, the fear of what is different, and the Freudian-Oedipal interpretation of medieval anti-Semitism.[16]

However, a hitherto rather neglected factor which may well have made the most decisive contribution of all to the great outburst of anti-Semitism in the High Middle Ages was the following. Medieval Christians seem to have associated Jews with Muslims from the very beginning of the Arab conquests of Christian territory in the 630s; and, at times of special distress, to have considered the Jews allies of the Muslims and Islamic fifthcolumnists in Christian territory. Once the great anti-Muslim movement known as the Crusades began in the eleventh century, it was inevitable that the Jews, who had often in the past been looked upon as agents of a foreign Islamic conspiracy, would be considered more dangerous than ever and would be degraded, converted, exiled, or killed.[17]

*****

What examples are there of the association of Jew with Muslim by medieval Christians even before the rise of the crusading movement in the eleventh century?

Already in the 630s, the very decade of the Arab invasion of the Christian Middle East, the Byzantine Christians associated Jews with, and considered them agents of, the Muslims. This was a crucial factor in the severe persecution of the Jews throughout the Byzantine Empire instigated by Emperor Heraclius, which had echoes, even beyond the Byzantine frontiers in Merovingian France and Visigothic Spain during the same decade.[18]

In the 690s King Egica of Spain accused the Jews of his kingdom of being in league with their "Hebrew" (i.e., Muslim) brethren across the straits in North Africa. A severe persecution ensued throughout the Visigothic territories.[19]

The Carolingian King Pepin the Short established a semiautonomous Jewish state in southern France (centered at Narbonne) in the 760s. The head of this state was a Davidic prince named Natronai-Machir of Arab Iraq. He was sent to Western Europe by the caliph of Bagdad in part to play an important role in the new Abbasid-Carolingian alliance (which the semiautonomous Jewish state in southern France was to assist) against the Umayyads of Spain.[20] In ninth-century France, however, a century after the founding of the Jewish state, the Carolingians (patrons of the Jews) began to decline. The Christian clergy, strongly anti-Jewish (partly for fear of Judaizing tendencies within Christian ranks), tended to associate Jew with Muslim. They remembered that the founder of the semiautonomous Jewish state in southern France came originally from a *Muslim* land but forgot that this same Jewish princedom had been set up, from the very beginning, as a firm ally of the Christians against the Muslims of Spain (though not against the Muslims of Iraq).

The conversion to Judaism of the court chaplain Bodo-Elazar, which scandalized French Christians, both lay and clerical, during the 840s, undoubtedly served to strengthen the tendency to associate Jew with Muslim for the following four reasons. (1) Bodo fled for safety to *Muslim* Spain. (2) Those Christians who had accompanied Bodo on what they presumed was his journey to Rome, but who refused to convert to Judaism with him, were sold to *Muslim* slavers. (3) Bodo joined the army of *Muslim* Spain. (4) Bodo attempted to retaliate against his erstwhile French Christian coreligionists by endeavoring to persuade the ruler of *Muslim* Spain to force the Spanish Christians within his realm into either Judaism or Islam.[21]

In 848 Marseilles fell to the Arabs.[22] Although there is no record of a specific charge that the Jews betrayed Marseilles to the Arabs, there is, however, an eleventh-century tradition that the Jews betrayed Toulouse to the Arabs circa 756-788. However, Toulouse never fell to the Arabs; rather, it fell to the Normans in 848.[23] This tradition that the Jews betrayed Toulouse may reflect an earlier ninth- or tenth-century (and much more historically plausible) charge that the Jews betrayed Marseilles to the Arabs in 848.

Writing in the 850s, Prudence of Troyes accused the Jews of betraying Barcelona to the Muslims in 852, though the city would not seem to have been attacked by the Muslims that year.[24]

In the 930s a severe persecution of the Jews broke out in the Byzantine Empire (under Emperor Romanus Lecapenus). This persecution again had repercussions beyond the borders of the empire, *i.e.*, in Italy and Germany. The charge that the Jews were in league with the Muslims against the Christians—especially transmitted by the Venetians, perhaps partly because they resented Jewish economic competition—was a crucial factor in this persecution.[25]

Finally, circa 1010 a severe persecution of the Jews broke out in France, Germany, and Italy[26]—a crucial watershed in the history of Christian-Jewish relations during the Middle Ages for the following two reasons.

(1) It was the first major international persecution of the Jews in the Middle Ages since the Arab conquests of the 630s which clearly originated in Western Europe (France) rather than the Byzantine Empire.

(2) It was the first persecution of the Jews in the Middle Ages which involved *both* key countries of Western Europe, France and Germany.

This major international persecution of the Jews is clearly and un-equivocally attributed by the Christian primary sources to the charge that the Jews were in league with the Muslims (specifically, in league with al-Hakim, the Fatimid Caliph of Egypt, who destroyed the Holy Sepulchre in Jerusalem circa 1010).[27]

Like the persecution of 1010, the great persecution of the Jews dur-ing the First Crusade was also a major international persecution which originated in Western Europe rather than in Byzantium, involved both France and Germany, and seems to have been primarily the result of the association of Jew with Muslim by medieval Christians (though our primary sources are not as explicit about the operation of this factor in 1096 as they are about its operation circa 1010).[28] Hence the persecution of 1010 set the pattern for the great persecution of 1096.

*****

If, indeed, there is a significant number of examples of the associa-tion of Jew with Muslim by medieval European Christians even before the rise of the crusading movement in the eleventh century, *why* did the Christians tend to associate Jew with Muslim and, at times of special distress, persecute Jews for allegedly being agents of the Muslims?

We are nowhere near being able to present a definitive answer to this question. Nevertheless, it is possible to make certain tentative suggestions as to the direction in which we should look for answers.

One reason may have been because the Jews differed sharply from the Christians but possessed a close affinity with the Muslims in at least four major areas. Both Jews and Muslims (1) rejected the Trinity, (2) practiced circumcision of the flesh, (3) claimed physical descent from Abraham, and (4) considered Semitic languages their sacred tongues (Hebrew and Arabic). Christians, by contrast, affirmed the Trinity, valued only circumcision of the heart, claimed only spiritual descent from Abraham, and considered Indo-European languages their sacred tongues (Latin and Greek).[29]

Another reason why medieval European Christians would seem to have associated Jew with Muslim circa 600–1000 may have been because during the seventh century, the crucial century of the massive Arab conquests of Christian territory, the Jews usually rejoiced when

Christian territory fell into Islamic hands.[30] They did so for at least two major reasons. (1) The Jews knew that the Arabs extended toleration to all "peoples of the Book," including the Jews and the heretical Christian sects (the Monophysites in Armenia, Syria, and Egypt; the Nestorians in Iraq); whereas the seventh-century Byzantine and Western European Christian regimes severly persecuted these same religious minorities. (2) Certain Jewish apocalyptic visionaries saw the Muslim invasion as a necessary prerequisite to the coming of the (Jewish) Messiah.[31]

However, not only did the Jews rejoice when Christian territory fell into Islamic hands, but at times they may actually have collaborated with the Muslim invaders against the Christians. The Jews may well have assisted the Arab invaders of Spain in the 710s.[32] In the mid-ninth century it is quite possible that the deacon Bodo, who converted from Christianity to Judaism, did indeed do something similar to what he was accused of doing, namely, taking revenge upon his former co-religionists by encouraging the Muslims of Spain to oppress their Christian subjects.[33] In the tenth century Hasdai ibn Shaprut, the powerful Jewish vizier of two caliphs of Cordova, Abd ar-Rahman III (912–961) and his successor Hakam II (961–976), definitely assisted his Muslim masters against the Christians of Spain.[34] In the Middle East, Paltiel ben Sh'fatyah was the powerful Jewish vizier of Muizz (969–975), the Fatimid caliph of Egypt and Sicily. Manasseh ibn Ibrahim al-Q'zaz was the Jewish governor of Syria under al-Muizz's successor, al-Aziz (975–996).[35] The fact that the Fatimid caliphs of Egypt employed Jewish viziers in the second half of the tenth century may have contributed to the fact that the Jews of Western Europe were blamed when the Fatimid caliph destroyed the Holy Sepulchre in Jerusalem circa 1010.[36]

A final reason why medieval Western European Christians (in France and Germany) would seem to have associated Jew with Muslim even before the rise of the crusading movement in the eleventh century may have been because many of the Jewish inhabitants of Western Europe circa 700–1000 were immigrants from Islamic lands, maintaining considerable commercial and religious ties with the lands whence they had come.[37] Many Jewish settlers in Western Europe circa 700–1000 were immigrants either (1) directly from the Islamic lands of the Middle East (Palestine, Iraq),[38] (2) indirectly from these lands with a stopover in Italy,[39] or (3) from Muslim Spain.[40] As such, these Jews, at least in the first generation, must have been considerably Arabicized, so much so that it may have been quite easy for the average Christian to associate them with Muslim Arabs. In view of this immigration it is not difficult to see why Western European Christians tended to associate Jew and Muslim and even to consider the Jews agents of the Muslims. Indeed, it may have been precisely because the Carolingian rulers associated Jew with Muslim and considered the Jews close allies of the Muslims, making so significant a contribution as merchants to the development of Islamic society, that they encouraged Jewish immigration from Islamic lands into their own territories.[41] What better way could the Carolingians have found to strengthen themselves vis-à-vis their Arab opponents (especially the Umayyads of Spain; the Abbasids of the Muslim East were not considered enemies by Charlemagne) than to wean their Jewish merchant allies away from the Muslims over to the Christian side instead?[42]

*****

Thus, we argue that a hitherto neglected factor which contributed decisively to the great outburst of anti-Semitism in the High Middle Ages was the fact that medieval Christians seem to have associated Jews with Muslims from the very beginning of the Arab conquests of Christian territory and, at times of special distress, to have considered the Jews Islamic fifth columnists in Christian territory. Admittedly, even before the rise of Islam there already was a powerful anti-Semitic tendency within Christian society caused by both theological and sociological factors. However, the seventh-century rise of Islam completely altered the balance of religious power in the Western world and therefore the nature of Christian-Jewish relations as well. Thereafter Christian attitudes toward Muslims and Jews became inextricably bound up and have remained that way into the twentieth century. Thus, there were few anti-Semitic outbreaks in Western Europe during the Carolingian-Ottonian period. Neither was there any great special hatred of the Muslims at this time. The Muslims were dreaded invaders, like the Vikings,[43] Slavs, and Magyars. But they were not singled out for especial hatred, and no "holy war" was proclaimed against them. However, circa 1000 Western Christian attitudes toward Muslims changed dramatically from one of relative tolerance to one of fanatical antagonism, and Western Christian attitudes toward Jews underwent a similar change.

The reasons for these dramatic changes have not yet been fully explored by scholars, but we must explore them here at least tentatively because anti-Muslimism was a crucial factor in medieval anti-Semitism. Influenced by the compelling ideas of Lynn White,[44] we would suggest that the explanation can be found in the fact that circa 900–1100, contrary to the lay view, Western European civilization developed tremendous cultural dynamism, technologically, economically, politically, militarily, and demographically.[45] Indeed, Western Christian civilization became so dynamic at this time that it began to overflow its own geographical boundaries, becoming aggressively expansionistic and imperialistic. Of the three possible territories for expansion—the northeast European pagan, the Byzantine, and the Islamic—the Islamic was the territory that most powerfully attracted the Western European expansionist movement, though this movement also attacked Byzantium (the Fourth Crusade sacked Constantinople in 1204) and the Baltic pagans (cf. the founding of Memel in 1252 and Koenigsberg in 1255 by the Teutonic knights). First, the Islamic territory was the wealthiest of the three territories. Second, the Islamic was the only one of the three that was controlled by a non-Christian power expansionist in its own right, and therefore a very serious military threat to Western Christians. Third, the Islamic territory was once Christian territory and therefore had rich Christian associations. Seville, in Muslim Spain, was a holy city of Visigothic Catholicism. St. Augustine once lived and taught in what became Muslim North Africa. Jerusalem, in Muslim Palestine, was the city where Christ died to redeem mankind from the effects of original sin. Hence, the Islamic territory was subject to reconquest, always a more powerful motivation, and more morally justifiable excuse, for expansion than mere conquest. For these three reasons, then, the Islamic territory demanded the serious attention of Western Christians much more urgently than did the other two areas.

The result was that by circa 1000 Western European civilization began to expand against Islamic territory with tremendous force, sufficient in the eleventh century to reconquer New Castile and Sicily permanently, Syria-Palestine temporarily. This expansionist movement against Islamic territory (to which we usually give the name Crusades) naturally generated tremendous special hatred for the Muslims, the people who ruled this coveted territory. However, since even prior to the rise of the crusading movement in the eleventh century the Jews were, to a great extent, already associated with Muslims and, at times of special distress, considered Islamic fifth columnists in Christian territory, the crusading movement (born largely out of Christian expansionist desires against Islamic territory) soon involved attacks on the Jews as well.

Thus, the great outburst of anti-Semitism in Western Europe during the High Middle Ages was, to a great extent, the result of the dynamic expansion of Western European civilization between circa 900 and 1100. This expansion brought with it virulent anti-Muslimism (the Crusades), and, because of the preexisting association of Jew with Muslim in the mind of medieval Christians, virulent anti-Semitism as well.

*****

One major area in which we have attempted to develop this new approach of studying medieval Christian attitudes toward Jews in terms of medieval Christian attitudes toward Muslims is represented by Pope Innocent III's decision, embodied in a decree (Canon 68) of the Fourth Lateran Council (1215), to impose a "badge of shame" on the Jews. This decision is generally considered by Jewish historians to have been of crucial importance in the history of anti-Semitism and one of the most infamous things any pope has ever done to the Jewish people.[46] Yet, when we look at the decree of the Fourth Lateran Council imposing the Jewish badge, we find that it *also imposes a Muslim badge*. However, to our knowledge, this has been largely ignored. Despite the fact that almost certainly, to Pope Innocent III (1198–1216), Christian-*Islamic* relations (and the all-important question of the Crusade) were far more important than Christian-Jewish relations,[47] no one has ever attempted to study Pope Innocent III's Jewish policy in terms of his Muslim policy. It seemed to us that such a comparative approach was long overdue, and in attempting to develop it we came across evidence presented and developed infra in chapter six, "Why Did Pope Innocent III Want the Fourth Lateran Council (1215) to Impose a Distinction in Clothing on Muslims and Jews?" to support some rather challenging conclusions which the reader will want to consider later within context.[48]

*****

To sum up, medieval anti-Semitism (and thus, indirectly, modern anti-Semitism as well, which to a significant extent stems from medieval anti-Semitism) was primarily a function of medieval anti-Muslimism. Medieval anti-Muslimism, in turn, was called forth by powerful forces, both intellectual and socioeconomic, unleashed in the general development of Western European civilization taken as a whole. This type of approach sets Jewish history firmly within the context of general world history[49] when it calls upon us to reexamine the history of Christian attitudes toward Jews during the Middle Ages in the light of the closely related history of Christian attitudes toward Muslims. If it be found by other scholars to have some merit, we hope that it will have a salutary impact on the modern movement toward greater understanding and cooperation between the three major religious communities of the Western world (Christians, Muslims, and Jews).[50]

PART THREE

ADDITIONAL MEDIEVAL AND MODERN EXAMPLES OF THE CHRISTIAN EQUATION OF JEW WITH MUSLIM (CIRCA 1000–1975 A.D.)[51]

We would now like to present some additional medieval and modern examples, both vivid and concrete, of the Christian tendency to equate Jew with Muslim.

1. Ralph Glaber, the noted French Cluniac monastic historian (who wrote circa 1044), records an incident in the life of Abbot Majolus of Cluny which occurred in 972. When the abbot was captured by the Arab marauders based at La Garde-Fresnet in southeastern France, he dropped his Bible. One of the Arabs put his foot upon it, but was reproved by some of his milder comrades for insulting the Prophets. At this point in the story Glaber adds (1) that the Arabs believe the Old Testament prophecies were fulfilled in the Prophet Muhammad and (2) that the Arabs have genealogies tracing the descent of the Prophet Muhammad from Ishmael, similar to the genealogy of Christ found at the beginning of the Gospel of Matthew.[52]

97

What is the significance of Glaber's story for our purpose here? In actual fact Islam believes that both the Old and the New Testaments contain passages which predict the coming of the Prophet Muhammad. So why did Glaber single out the Old Testament for especial mention in this context?

Most likely, Glaber wanted to associate Jew with Muslim. He knew that the Jews and the Arabs were ethnolinguistic cousins with many religious affinities and believed that they were in league with each other against the Christians. After all, Glaber is also the Christian chronicler who tells us that the persecution of the Jews of Orleans circa 1010 was in retaliation for the fact that the Jews of France urged the Muslims of Egypt to destroy the Church of the Holy Sepulchre in Jerusalem.

2. In his *Social and Religious History* Salo Baron calls our attention to an amazing statement in the Latin translation of al-Kindi's *Risalah*, the Christian Arabic anti-Islamic polemic:

> Among Eastern Christians there was more resentment of the continued adherence to Jewish practices of converts than by professing Jews. They [Eastern Christians] sometimes actually pointed an accusing finger at the laxity of many Jews. A proverb cited in the Latin translation of Al-Kindi's renowned apology paradoxically claimed that 'A Jew is not [quite] a Jew until after he turns Saracen [Muslim]; hardly any of them [the Jews] cultivates his law, except when he accepts another.'[53]

In other words, when a Jew is a Jew he does not care about Judaism and its commandments. However, when a Jew converts to Islam, he suddenly becomes nostalgic for Judaism and begins to practice it. In its original Arabic version the *Risalah* reached Arabic-speaking Christians in Spain (the Mozarabs) between the ninth and the eleventh centuries. In its Latin translation of the 1140s by Peter of Toledo al-Kindi's *Risalah* was widely influential in the High Middle Ages (summarized in Vincent of Beauvais's massive midthirteenth-century Latin encyclopedia). Could we possibly have any testimony more eloquent than this totally explicit statement, "A Jew is not [quite] a Jew until after he turns Muslim," to the equation of Jew with Muslim by medieval Christians?

3. In a letter of April 6, 1233, to the archbishops and bishops of France, Pope Gregory IX, a relative of Pope Innocent III, asked Christians to show such kindliness to Jews as the Christians hope might be

shown to their brother Christians living in pagan (*i.e.*, Islamic) lands.[54]

Once we appreciate the long history of the Christian tendency to equate Jew with Muslim we can fully grasp the meaning of what Pope Gregory IX was saying here. The pope was not simply saying that if we Christians treat our minority group (the Jews) kindly, the Muslims will treat their minority group (the Christians, our brothers) kindly as well. He was saying much more! The pope was implying that Muslims and Jews were brothers. He was further intimating that if we want the Muslims to treat our brothers (the Christians) who live in their lands kindly, we must treat *their brothers* (the Jews) who live in our lands kindly. Here again we have a powerful example of the Christian tendency to associate Jew with Muslim.

4. The German pastor Ludolph von Suchem, in an account of his pilgrimage to the Holy Land written circa 1350, stated:

> the Muslims have as much respect for Christ's sepulchre [*i.e.*, no respect whatsoever] as Christians have for a Jewish synagogue [likewise, no respect whatsoever].[55]

Once we appreciate the long history of the Christian tendency to equate Jew with Muslim we can fully grasp the meaning of what Ludolph von Suchem was saying here, just as this same appreciation helps us to understand what Pope Gregory IX was saying in the passage cited immediately above. Ludolph was not simply saying that Muslims and Christians are alike in that both have no respect whatsoever for the houses of worship of religious minorities in their midst (Christians in the midst of Muslims; Jews in the midst of Christians). Von Suchem was saying much more! He was equating Muslims and Jews as cousins and collaborators. He was further intimating that Christian hatred of the houses of worship of the Jews (cousins and collaborators of the Muslims) who live in Christian lands was intimately bound up, as cause and effect, with Muslim hatred of the houses of worship of the Christians (cousins and collaborators of the Crusaders) who live in Islamic lands. Here again, as in the case of Pope Gregory IX's remarks, we have a powerful example of the Christian tendency to equate Jew with Muslim.

5. Again in his *Social and Religious History*, Baron calls our attention to another statement in a Christian work, this time the attribution of the cry "Mamet" (an obvious corruption from Mahomet-Muhammad) to Jews who are being executed by Christians.[56] The Jews

of Brussels (and Louvain) were burned at the stake for alleged desecration of the host in 1370. The Christian author of a poem entitled "Miracle de Sainte-Gudule" conjured up in his imagination a fantastic scene wherein the condemned Jews of Belgium danced around their own funeral pyre chanting "Mamet" (=Mahomet=Muhammad). Baron remarks that this scene was probably nothing more than a willful distortion of the *Shema* prayer, the final confession of God's strict unity as conceived of by the synagogue, which undoubtedly was recited by the Jewish martyrs as they were consumed by the flames. As Baron understands it, the Christian poem, when it depicted the dying Jews as calling upon Muhammad with their last breath, portrayed the Jews as calling upon Muhammad the *prophet* of Islam.

Even if we accept this interpretation of the poem, it would still be committing a flagrant factual error about the dying Jews (for Jews do not consider Muhammad their prophet) as part of its blatant attempt to equate Jew with Muslim. More likely, however, the author of this poem, following in the tradition of the authors of the great medieval French epics, the *chansons de geste*, held that Muhammad was not merely the prophet of Islam but rather the god of Islam (just as Jesus was the God of Christianity). Thus, when the Christian author of this poem depicted the dying Jews as calling upon Muhammad with their last breath, he was really portraying the Jews as calling upon the *god* of the Muslims for help, the god of the people who are the ethnolinguistic cousins of Jews and the god of the people with whom the Jews are in league against Christians. This was an even more flagrant factual error about the dying Jews (for Jews do not consider Muhammad their god, any more than Muslims do) as part of an even more blatant attempt to equate Jew with Muslim. Once again, could we possibly have any testimony more eloquent than this to the association of Jew with Muslim by medieval Christians and to the widespread medieval Christian belief that the Jews were in league with the Muslims planning the destruction of Christendom?

6. According to Ibn al-Athir, the great Arabic crusade chronicler who died in Iraq in 1233, when Saladin, the prototypical medieval Islamic warrior, paragon of both piety and chivalry, retook Jerusalem from the Crusaders in 1187, the Christians effectively regrouped at Acre:

> Here monks and priests and a crowd of Frankish knights and nobles
> dressed themselves in black and expressed great grief at the loss of

Jerusalem. The Patriarch of Jerusalem took them with him on a journey through the Frankish domains [Western Europe], calling on the people to help, invoking their aid and inciting them to avenge the loss of Jerusalem.

Among other things, they [the Christians] made a picture showing the Messiah [*i.e.*, Jesus], and an Arab striking Him, showing blood on the face of Christ—blessings on Him! [orthodox or Sunni Islam considers Jesus the Messiah, but neither God nor son of God]—and they said to the crowds: '*This is the Messiah, struck by Mahomet the prophet of the Muslims, who has wounded and killed him*' [italics ours].

This made a deep impression on the Franks . . . [as well it should have, so much so that] they flocked to the Patriarch, even the women. There were in fact in the army at Acre a certain number of women, who challenged their enemy's warriors to single combat.[57]

Thus, according to this Islamic chronicler the Christian charge that the Muslims crucified Christ spread far and wide throughout Western Europe at the time of the Third Crusade (circa 1190). It stirred up such a powerful hatred against the Muslims that not only Christian men, but Christian women as well, volunteered to fight the Muslims in the Holy Land.

This crucially important passage represents the earliest testimony we know of (dating from the first third of the thriteenth century)—and from a *Muslim* rather than a Christian source—to the Western Christian tendency (seen quite vividly in the art of the High Middle Ages and Renaissance) to blame the Muslims, as much as the Jews, for the crucifixion of Christ. Of course, it represents exceedingly eloquent testimony to the association of Jew with Muslim by medieval Christians. According to this passage the Christians accused the Prophet Muhammad, and, by implication, all Muslims, of participating in the scourging and crucifixion of Christ. Yet, not only was this a patent chronological absurdity (since the Prophet Muhammad and Islam did not arise until over five centuries after the death of Christ), but it was also an even greater theological absurdity. Islam seems to have accepted the Christian Docetist heresy that Jesus was never crucified at all, a theological position strongly at variance with both Judaism and Christianity, which concur in the view that Jesus was crucified in the flesh. According to Islam, God would never have allowed his Messiah Jesus to suffer such an excruciating death and ignominious fate. Rather, Jesus' phantom died on the cross. Jesus himself, like Enoch and Elijah, ascended directly to heaven when his allotted time on earth was completed.

How then could the Christians accuse the Muslims of crucifying Christ when such was both a chronological and theological absurdity? Was it not because of the Christian tendency to equate Jew with Muslim? Because of this equation, if the Christians believed that the Jews participated in the scourging and crucifixion of Jesus, eventually the Christians also had to believe that the Muslims, the ethnolinguistic cousins of the Jews for whom the Jews were acting as fifth columnists in Christian territory, must also have participated in the scourging and crucifixion of Jesus. Because of the association of Jew with Muslim by medieval Christians, *both* the Jews and the Muslims must be Christ-killers and deicides! Because of the equation of Jew with Muslim, *both* Jews and Muslims must have the Messiah's blood dripping from their equally Semitic hands!

7. According to our early thirteenth-century Islamic source (Ibn al-Athir) this devastating Christian tendency to associate Jew with Muslim was expressed most especially in Christian art. As Ibn al-Athir put it (quoted above): "they [the Christians] *made a picture* [italics ours] showing the Messiah [*i.e.*, Jesus], and an Arab striking Him, showing blood on the face of Christ." Are there any examples from Christian artistic sources of this Christian tendency to associate Jew with Muslim by making the Muslims equal participants with the Jews in Christ's final disgrace and death?

In the Historical Museum of Bergen, Norway, we had the startling experience of seeing a panel of a late medieval Norwegian altar frontal (dating from circa 1350), originally in a church in Roldal, Norway. The panel in question depicts a haloed and bearded Christ, bearing his cross and accompanied by two strange-looking figures. The bearded figure on the left who is scourging Christ over the naked portion of his body (arms, chest, calves, and feet), wears a weird type of hat from which it would seem that two horns are protruding. The beardless figure on the right, who holds the hammer and nails for the crucifixion proper, is hatless. His hair is quite short and curly; his face, dark and brownish.[58] The figure on the left, because of the beard and weird hat with horn-like protrusions, could well be a Jew; while the figure on the right, because of the curly hair and brownish face, could well be a North African Arab Muslim (with some black African Muslim racial admixture). Or, the figure on the left could be an Arab Muslim; the

Christ Bearing His Cross. Altar-Frontal from the Roldal Church, Sunnhordland, Norway, circa 1350; currently in the Historical Museum, Bergen, Norway.

Crucifixion Scene (detail). Fresco by Andrea di Buonaiuto, Front or Altar Wall, Spanish Chapel, Santa Maria Novella, Florence, Italy, circa 1350.

figure on the right a black Muslim. In the first possibility we would have a Christian depiction of a Jew and a Muslim jointly participating in the scourging and crucifixion of Christ. In the second possibility we would have two Muslims participating in the scourging and crucifixion of Christ. In either case we would have a rather striking artistic example of the medieval Christian tendency to associate Jew with Muslim.

8. For the third time in his *Social and Religious History* Baron calls our attention to a very important but far too little known book by Marcel Bulard, *Le Scorpion, Symbole du Peuple Juif dans l'Art Religieux des XIV, XV, XVI Siecles* (Paris: Boccard, 1935). According to Baron:

> Bulard also shows that the alleged Jewish collaboration with the Muslim enemies of Christianity caused some [Christian] artists to introduce Muslim flags and other paraphernalia into the very story of the Passion of Christ. Like the authors of many Passion plays, they [these Christian artists] evinced little concern about this palpable anachronism.[59]

When we turn to the Bulard book proper, we find at least eleven relevant artistic examples from the late fourteenth through sixteenth centuries. Ten are Italian. The eleventh comes from the Austrian Tyrol, just north of Italy. Seven examples (nos. 1, 4, 5, 7, 9, 10, and 11) explicitly depict both Jews and Muslims jointly participating in Christ's passion. Four examples (nos. 2, 3, 6, and 8) explicitly depict only Muslims participating in Christ's passion, though their painters assuredly believed that the Jews also participated therein. Let us now consider the eleven examples themselves in chronological order.

1. LATE FOURTEENTH-CENTURY ITALY (Bulard, 118-119, 225, and note 3).

CHRIST BEARING HIS CROSS, anonymous artist, wall painting, Benedictine monastery of the Sacro Speco at Subiaco, near Rome.

JEWS AND MUSLIMS: the fifth flag behind Jesus bears a Jewish scorpion; the sixth bears four Jewish badges; while the second flag behind Jesus probably bears the heads of four beardless black Muslims (Bulard, 232–234); the second (light-colored) flag in front of Jesus bears three separate (darker-colored) Muslim crescents, one on top and two below, separated by a darker horizontal band.

2. LATE FOURTEENTH-CENTURY ITALY (Bulard, 119–121).

CRUCIFIXION SCENE, anonymous artist, wall painting, Benedictine monastery of the Sacro Speco at Subiaco, near Rome.

MUSLIMS: the fourth of the five flags, to the right of Jesus' cross, bears four beardless black Muslim heads (Bulard, 232–234). In front of the Bad Thief's cross "four soldiers argue over Christ's tunic, placed on the knees of a fifth personage who is seated and surrounded by the other four; this figure sports long thin mustaches, like those of the Mongols, and wears a robe sown with ornaments in the shape of stylized leaves and a tall hat with raised brims culminating in a point." This fifth figure is undoubtedly a Muslim. But in another description of the same scene Bulard (page 184, note 5) suggests that the other four figures are also Muslims:

> Christ's tunic, coveted by four Orientals whose heads are covered by turbans or whose faces have veils pulled down over them, is placed within the lap of a seated personage, or sort of qadi [Muslim judge] with double beard, thin mustaches which hang down like those of a Mongol, and head covered by a pointed hat with raised brims. This judge seems to keep silent instead of rendering the decision awaited [by the other four].

3. CIRCA 1450 ITALY (Bulard, 135, no. 23; 232, note 4; and plate XXIV:1, rear of the volume).

CRUCIFIXION SCENE, anonymous painting attributed to Paolo di Stefano, disciple of Masolino, now in the Academy of Fine Arts, Florence.

MUSLIMS: the third flag near the Good Thief's cross bears the bearded head of a black Muslim (Bulard, 232–234) in profile turned toward the right, with a hooked nose; while "in the crowd, at the foot of Jesus's cross, there is a black Muslim [Bulard, 232–234] of a very pronounced racial type, wearing a white hat in the shape of a sugar-loaf."

4. CIRCA 1460 ITALY (Bulard, 229 and note 2; 250–251; and plate XLVII, rear of the volume).

CALVARY SCENE, painting by the famed Piero della Francesca, which in the 1930s was in the collection of Carl W. Hamilton, New York City.

JEWS AND MUSLIMS: in this painting a flag on the right bears a basilisk (a noxious Greek mythological dragon which, like the scorpion, was used to symbolize the Jews), while a flag in the center bears a Muslim crescent plus a star with four rays.[60]

5. CIRCA 1468 ITALY (Bulard, 140, no. 27, 193–195; 232 and note 4; and plate XXIX:1, rear of the volume; cf. also Frederick Hartt, *History of Italian Renaissance Art: Painting, Sculpture, Architecture*

[Englewood Cliffs, N.J., and New York City: Prentice-Hall and Abrams, 1969], 216 and figure 263).

STORY OF A JEW WHO DESECRATED THE HOST, painting of six panels by the famed Paolo Uccello, now in the Galleria Nazionale delle Marche Palazzo Ducale, Urbino (near San Marino and the Adriatic coast, between Ravenna and Ancona).

JEWS AND MUSLIMS: the first panel, which depicts the host being delivered to the home of the Jew by a Christian woman, features a back wall behind a floor fireplace; the wall is decorated with three cartouches; the center cartouche, the most prominent of the three, bears the head of a beardless black Muslim (Bulard, 232–234) in profile and turned toward the left, while the left cartouche bears a Jewish scorpion.

6. CIRCA 1482 ITALY (Bulard, 168, no. 71; 225 and note 4).

CHRIST BEARING HIS CROSS, wall painting by Giovanni Canavesi, Chapel of St. Bernard at Pigna, on the Riviera di Ponente (the Western Italian Riviera, in the Val di Nervia near Ventimiglia and Bordighera).

MUSLIMS: according to Bulard "the banner of one of the trumpets, which sound along the road to Calvary, is divided into four by white and green (green is the color of the flag of the Prophet [Muhammad]), with a yellow [Muslim] crescent standing out against the four squares thus formed."

7. LATE FIFTEENTH OR EARLY SIXTEENTH-CENTURY ITALY (Bulard, 167, no. 69; 231 and note 3; and plate XL:1, rear of the volume).

RESURRECTION, small bronze relief by an unknown artist who signed his name with the pseudonym "Moderno," now in the Museo Civico Cristiano at Brescia (central nothern Italy).

JEWS AND MUSLIMS: one of the guards at Christ's sepulchre holds a shield, whereon appears a large Jewish scorpion holding an Islamic crescent between his pincers.

8. CIRCA 1522 AUSTRIA (Bulard, 133–134, no. 20; 229–230 and note 1: and 231, note 1).

JESUS FALLING UNDER THE WEIGHT OF THE CROSS, anonymous wall painting (attributed by some to a Swabian Franciscan), east bay of the cloister, Franciscan Church of Schwaz (a town in the Inn River Valley, east of Innsbruck, Austrian Tyrol, i.e., western Austria, just north of the Italian frontier).

MUSLIMS: according to Bulard some of the spectators have "tall caps of felt [like the kind that] cover the heads of [Muslim] dervishes in ecstasy" or "wear . . . tall caps of white felt, like those of the [Muslim] dervishes, and have slit-like eyes, with long thin mustaches hanging down like those of the [Muslim] Mongols. Sometimes there are even some braids which, starting at their temples, come down all the way onto their chests."

9. CIRCA 1523 ITALY (Bulard 165–166, no. 67:1; 225 and note 2 plus plates XLI and XLII, rear of the volume).

CRUCIFIXION SCENE, painting by Gaudenzio Ferrari, a pupil of Leonardo da Vinci, Chapel of the Crucifix, Church of the Sacro Monte at Varallo-Sesia, province of Novara (in the Piedmont, northwestern Italy).

JEWS AND MUSLIMS: Bulard discerns a white flag with a black Jewish scorpion. He also discerns three (Muslim) dervish headdresses and a red flag with four white Muslim crescents.

Bulard (pages 229–230) further describes the Muslims in this painting as follows:

> If we examine closely this vast vivid tableau (plate XLI), wherein sculpture and painting combine their effects, adding thereto the effects of fabric and real accessories, if we enumerate those [Muslim] Mongolian visages with their prominent cheek-bones, their slit-like eyes, their long thin mustaches, those enormous [Muslim] turbans as round as pumpkins, those tall hats of felt covering the heads of [Muslim] dervishes in ecstasy, those vestments of white linen and those striped [Muslim] haiks, wouldn't we get the impression that all of this decor, whether alive or inanimate, has for its object to recall to the mind of the person who contemplates it, at least as much as the traditional tumult of Golgotha, the onslaught of the Asiatic [Muslim] hordes, in the terror of which all of Christendom had lived for so many centuries?

10. EARLY SIXTEENTH-CENTURY ITALY (Bulard, 127, no. 10; 225 and note 1).

CRUCIFIXION, anonymous wall painting, Church of San Mamante (or San Mamette), near Mezzovico, in the Ticino (southern or Italian Switzerland, between Lugano and Bellinzona).

JEWS AND MUSLIMS: Bulard discerns one yellow flag with black Jewish scorpion and another red flag with white Muslim crescent.

11. SECOND HALF OF SIXTEENTH-CENTURY ITALY (Bulard, 161, no. 60bis; 232 and note 2; and plate XXXIV:1, rear of the volume).

THE CROSSING OF THE RED SEA BY THE ISRAELITES, anonymous Italian woodcut of uncertain date but reproducing a design attributed to Paolo Farinati (second half of the sixteenth century; died circa 1606).

JEWS AND MUSLIIMS: in this woodcut the Egyptians, who give chase to the Israelites, carry a great flag which features a large Jewish scorpion and two Islamic crescents as well as two stars, (one with five points and the other with six).

In addition to these examples from Bulard, we would also like to offer an example from Frederick Hartt, the noted authority on Italian Renaissance art (cf. his *History of Italian Renaissance Art*, already cited above, 244-245; colorplate 31, facing 231).

CIRCA 1450-1460 ITALY.

FLAGELLATION OF CHRIST, painting by the famed Piero della Francesca, owned by the Galleria Nazionale delle Marche, Palazzo Ducale, Urbino.

In the left half of the painting, which is the the actual depiction of Christ's flagellation, the Jewish King Herod, according to Hartt, symbolizes Sultan Muhammad who conquered Constantinople in 1453. He looks on, while to his immediate right, with back turned toward us, stands a Turkish figure wearing a white turban and a long white rôbe. Thus, in a flagellation scene proper, we have a Jewish figure who represents a Muslim, and a Muslim figure representing himself, side by side watching Christ's disgrace and degradation.[61]

Thus, to summarize the eleven Bulard examples and the Hartt example, the four most powerful are no. 5, wherein the black Muslim in one cartouche looks leftward toward the Jewish scorpion in the neighboring cartouche; no. 7, the shield wherein the Jewish scorpion holds an Islamic crescent; no. 11, the Jewish scorpion and two Islamic crescents within one and the same flag; and the single Hartt example, wherein the Jew, who himself stands for a Muslim, and the Muslim are positioned side by side. Could there possibly be any testimony more eloquent than these Italian artistic examples from the late fourteenth through the sixteenth centuries, of the Christian tendency to equate Jew with Muslim and to believe that the two non-Christian Semitic groups were in league with one another planning the destruction of Christendom?

9. According to Ibn al-Athir, as we remember from paragraph 6 above, circa 1200 the Christians began to accuse the Muslims of complicity *with* the Jews in the crucifixion of Christ (the addition of the

Muslims to the picture did not mean the subtraction of the Jews therefrom). However, thus far the earliest example we have presented of the depiction of this accusation in Western European art is the Norwegian altar frontal circa 1350 (as discussed in paragraph 7 above), about a century and a half after the Ibn al-Athir reference. None of the eleven Bulard artistic examples, which come overwhelmingly from Italy, antedate the Norwegian altar frontal. Indeed, the earliest of the Bulard examples, no. 1 from the Sacro Speco at Subiaco, near Rome, dates from the late fourteenth century. The single Hartt example, Piero della Francesca's "Flagellation," dates from the mid-fifteenth century, about a century after the Norwegian example. Are there any Italian artistic examples of the Christian tendency to associate Jew with Muslim that antedate, or at least come from approximately the same time as, the Norwegian example and thus from a period of about a half century prior to Bulard's earliest example (no. 1 from Subiaco, late fourteenth century)?

A crucial Christian writer in this regard (as in so many others) is Dante (circa 1300). His *Inferno* (Canto XXVII, verses 85–90) contains an extremely intolerant outburst against Pope Boniface VIII, the Muslims, and the Jews, equating and damning all three. The passage in question is a bit difficult to interpret and reads as follows:

> Lo principe de' nuovi Farisei,
>> avendo guerra presso a Laterano,
>> e non con Saracin ne con Giudei,
> che ciascun suo nimico era cristiano
>> e nessuno era stato a vincer Acri,
>> ne mercatante in terra di Soldano

> The prince of the new Pharisees
>> wages war near the Lateran
>> but not against Muslims and Jews,
> for all of his enemies are Christians,
>> not the Muslims who conquered Acre
>> or the Jews who trade in the land of
>>> the Sultan.

Thus, according to Dante, Pope Boniface VIII, whom Dante intensely disliked, spent all his time waging war against his fellow Christians (especially the Colonna family of Rome who had a castle near the Lateran). He should have been fighting the true enemies of Christendom, the Muslims who took Acre in 1291, the last Christian bastion in the Holy Land, and the Jews who live in Christian lands but grow rich off trade and commerce with their Muslim cousins and allies. Here, then, we have a very powerful example of the association of Jew with Muslim by medieval Christians and of the Christian accusation that the Jews were in league with the Muslims in planning the destruction of Christendom.[62]

Following Dante's lead, Giotto (circa 1267–1337), the greatest Italian artist of Dante's generation and one of the greatest artists of all time, with the help of his disciples began to introduce the association of Jew with Muslim into contemporary art. Circa 1305 Giotto put a black Muslim into the flagellation scene, within the famous fresco cycle of Christ's passion, of the Arena (or Scrovegni) Chapel at Padua. Likewise, a disciple of Giotto put a black Muslim into the fresco of the "Raising of Lazarus," Chapel of St. Mary Magdalen, Lower Church of the great Double Basilica of St. Francis at Assisi, circa 1330. Around the same time Giotto and/or a disciple depicted black as well as Arab Muslims in the famous fresco of "St. Francis of Assisi and the Trial by Fire before the Sultan of Egypt," Bardi Chapel, Church of Santa Croce, Florence. As Hartt rightly remarks, the two black Muslims in this fresco "are among the earliest representations of colored persons known in Western art." Similarly, black Muslim heads appear on two of the shields worn by Moroccan Arab soldiers in a panel entitled "The Martyrdom of the Franciscan Friars at Ceuta," now in the Academy of Fine Arts, Florence, painted circa 1340 by Taddeo Gaddi, a disciple of Giotto.[63]

Shortly after this Gaddi work, Francesco Traini, the great Pisan artist (renowned for his midfourteenth-century fresco in the Campo Santo, Pisa, "The Triumph of Death," reflecting the havoc wrought by the Black Plague), painted an altarpiece (circa 1345) for the Church of St. Catherine at Pisa. It depicts the triumph of St. Thomas Aquinas, the Christian philosopher par excellence, over Averroes, considered by Traini and contemporaries to be the greatest Islamic philosopher. Averroes lies prostrate at St. Thomas' feet. However, characteristically enough, in the Traini conception Averroes, the great Muslim philosopher, wears the *Jewish* badge upon both of his shoulders. This very important particular is not only a poetic reference to the fact that it was the Jews, rather than the Muslims or the Christians, who played the primary role in preserving Averroes' Arabic commentaries on Aristotle (in Hebrew translation). It is also a rather striking example of the Christian tendency to equate Jew with Muslim and to believe that both non-Christian Semitic groups were conspiring together to over-throw Christendom. This Traini painting, unlike the work of Giotto and/or disciples at Padua and Assisi referred to immediately above, does not depict Muslim complicity (along with their Jewish cousins and allies) in Christ's passion. Nonetheless, it is still a major monu-ment in the history of the association of Jew with Muslim by medieval Christians.[64]

This leads us to what we believe is the most important fourteenth-century artistic monument of the association of Jew with Muslim by medieval Christians and of the anti-Islamic origins of modern anti-Semitism. We refer to the magnificent set of frescoes painted by An-drea di Buonaiuto (or da Firenze) which decorate the four walls and vaulting of the Spanish Chapel in the Dominican Church of Santa Maria Novella at Florence. These frescoes probably were inspired at least in part by two important Dominican priors and theologians at this church, Fra Zanobi de' Guasconi and Fra Giovanni di Giachinotto Corbinelli. The frescoes date from circa 1350 and therefore are more or less contemporaneous with the Norwegian altar frontal discussed in paragraph 7 above. Since the frescoes date from circa 1350, they there-fore postdate the Dante/Giotto/Gaddi/Traini works discussed immedi-ately above, just as they antedate the earliest Bulard example (from Subiaco, late fourteenth century) discussed previously. After studying the Spanish Chapel frescoes carefully, we came to the conclusion, even before studying the Bulard book in late 1974, that they contain-ed numerous instances of the Christian tendency to equate Jew with Muslim. Indeed, Bulard does not seem to analyze the Spanish Chapel frescoes in any special detail in his massive volume, primarily because they do not seem to depict the Jewish scorpion.

After studying Bulard, we realized that the conclusions we had come to independently were based on principles of analysis quite similar to those which Bulard had already employed, unbeknownst to us, about a generation earlier to develop the association of Jew with Muslim in Italian art in general from the late fourteenth through the sixteenth centuries.[65]

In the Spanish Chapel there are four great wall frescoes, and each has a corresponding fresco in the vaulting above:

I. The fresco of the front or altar wall, "Christ's Cross-Bearing, Crucifixion, and Descent into Hell," with its corresponding fresco in the vaulting above, "Christ's Resurrection from the Tomb."

II. The fresco of the right wall, "The Church Militant and Triumphant through the Dominican Order," with its corresponding fresco in the vaulting above, "The Ship of St. Peter on the Sea of Galilee."

III. The fresco of the left wall, "The Triumph of Catholic Doctrine through St. Thomas Aquinas As Well As the Religious and Liberal Arts," with its corresponding fresco in the vaulting above, "The Descent of the Holy Spirit at Pentecost."

IV. The fresco of the rear or entrance wall, "Preaching and Martyrdom Personified in the Dominican St. Peter Martyr," with its corresponding fresco in the vaulting above, "Christ's Ascension into Heaven in the Presence of Mary and the Apostles."

We can immediately dismiss number IV, the fresco of the rear or entrance wall (which is in a bad state of repair in any case), and the corresponding fresco in the vaulting above, as being of no relevance to our theme, the association of Jew with Muslim by medieval Christians.

However, the other three sets of wall and vaulting frescoes contain many powerful examples of this theme. The following discussion, to our knowledge, will be the first time the Spanish Chapel frescoes have been considered in this regard.

I. THE FRONT, OR ALTAR, WALL.

A. In the lower left-hand scene, "Christ Bearing His Cross," which includes many Jews, we can discern on the right, following Bulard's principles, two likely Muslims, with their backs turned toward us, in the crowd climbing the hill of Calvary:

1. one higher up on the hill, distinguishable by his white turban and long braid hanging down the middle of his back;

2. the other immediately below him and to his left, distinguishable by a tall pointed hat and two long braids hanging down the middle of his back;

3. while a third likely Muslim faces us directly above Christ's head (and also above the top of Christ's cross), wearing an unusual broad-brimmed, light-yellow hat and a forked beard.

B. In the main or central scene, "The Crucifixion," which again includes many Jews, we can discern a large number of likely Muslims who are distinguishable by either pointed hat or long braids:

1. the figure facing us on the extreme right of the total crucifixion scene (one of the soldiers fighting over the division of Christ's cloak), who wears a pointed red hat;

2. the figure standing with his back to us (below the Bad Thief's cross on the intermediate right side of the total crucifixion scene), with a single braid hanging down the middle of his back;

3. the figure with his back to us in the right center (mounted on a light-brown horse), wearing a light-green coat and a light-green pointed hat;

4. the figure directly above him but facing us (mounted on a light-grey horse), wearing a light conical hat that comes to a gradual point;

5. the figure standing on the immediate left of Christ's cross, partly hidden by it, wearing a light-green coat, a pointed brown beard, and a light-green hat (with a dark, round medallion in the center of the brim) that comes to a sharp point (in general, a figure quite similar to figure B:3 immediately above);

6. the figure (mounted on a light-grey horse), facing us on the right of the Good Thief's cross (which is itself on the left side of the total Crucifixion scene), who wears an unusual broad-brimmed, light-yellow hat and a forked beard (very similar to figure A:3 above); and

7. the figure (mounted on a dark-brown horse) with his back to us on the extreme left of the total crucifixion scene, wearing a light-green tunic, a single braid down the middle of his back, and a light-brown turban.

C. The lower right-hand scene, "Christ's Descent into Hell," does not seem to contain any Muslim figures.

D. The corresponding fresco in the vaulting, "Christ's Resurrection from the Tomb," would seem to depict two Muslims among the guards sleeping in front of the tomb:

1. the figure facing us in the center of the group of six guards, with light-grey beard and white turban; and

2. the figure with his back to us, second from the left in the group of guards, with yellow tunic, long braid hanging down the middle of his back, and strange white hat with what looks like a drooping antenna protruding from it.

II. THE RIGHT WALL.

A. In the lower right-hand corner of this fresco, entitled "The Church Militant and Triumphant through the Dominican Order," St.

Thomas Aquinas stands facing us. He is preaching successfully to a group of Jews and Muslims (intermingled with one another and crowded together in a tightly knit group) that the religion of Christ is superior to their combined faith. He holds open to them his great apology, the *Summa Contra Gentiles*, which sought to prove the truth of Christianity and the falsity of both Judaism and Islam by use of reason alone (without recourse to written revelation, because Judaism did not accept the New Testament, and Islam, neither the Old nor New Testament). The figure tearing up his own book, in the extreme lower right-hand corner of the total fresco, wearing a pink tunic and a red conical hat, may well be Averroes (cf. infra, III:A).

B. The corresponding fresco in the vaulting, "The Ship of St. Peter on the Sea of Galilee," does not seem to contain any Muslim figures.

III. LEFT WALL.

A. In the main fresco, entitled "The Triumph of Catholic Doctrine through St. Thomas Aquinas As Well As the Religious and the Liberal Arts," Averroes, the great Muslim philosopher, definitely appears. He is facing us and wearing a light-yellow tunic, light-grey forked beard, and a white turban. His head is leaning to the left, supported by his hand (a gesture of resignation). He is sitting, crushed and defeated at the feet of the enthroned St. Thomas. However, Averroes, in this context (as opposed to the Traini Averroes in the Church of St. Catherine, Pisa, discussed supra; or the possible Averroes discussed immediately supra, II:A), is not associated with the Jews. He wears no Jewish badge on his shoulders. His two companions who sit with him here in defeat at St. Thomas' feet are not Jews, but rather the two early Eastern Christian heretics Arius, of the fourth century, and Nestorius, of the fifth. Admittedly, five Jewish Old Testament prophets (Job, David with his harp, the horned Moses, Isaiah, and Solomon—the last the only one of the five to lack a halo, perhaps because he sinned through a multiplicity of wives) sit with five great New Testament figures (Matthew, Mark, Luke, John, and Paul), on the same level as St. Thomas Aquinas' throne. But these Jewish figures are supporters of St. Thomas, not of Averroes. They are an example of the association of Jew *with Christian* against Muslim rather than of the association of Jew with Muslim against Christian, which latter theme we are seeking examples of in this fresco cycle.

113

B. The corresponding fresco in the vaulting, "The Descent of the Holy Spirit at Pentecost," in addition to depicting Jews, would seem to depict five likely Muslims:

1. the figure facing us, six figures in from the lower right, wearing a light-green and gold tunic, as well as a strange hat whose brim is orange but whose cone is light green;

2. the figure facing us, eight figures in from the lower right and two figures to the left of the previous figure (B:1), wearing a red robe and a white turban;

3. the figure with his back to us in the direct center, one figure to the left of the previous (B:2), wearing a light-grey tunic, a long braid hanging down to the right, and a white hat with a drooping antenna (similar to figure I:D:2 above);

4. a black Muslim figure facing us, six figures in from the lower left and four figures to the left of the previously mentioned figure (B:3); and

5. the figure with his back to us, third from the lower left and three figures to the left of the previously mentioned figure (B:4), wearing a light-purple tunic and turban of the same color, sporting two braids which hang down onto his back.

To summarize, of the four wall and four vaulting frescoes in the Spanish Chapel, two wall frescoes (front/altar wall: "Crucifixion"; and right wall: "Church Militant") and two vaulting frescoes (front/altar vault: "Resurrection"; and left vault: "Pentecost"), or at least half of the total number of fresco scenes in the Spanish Chapel, clearly would seem to associate Jew with Muslim. The Spanish Chapel frescoes (circa 1350), great monuments of Italian Renaissance art in general, at the same time are among the most important (though hitherto not fully appreciated) artistic monuments of the Christian tendency to equate Jew with Muslim and to consider the two Semitic non-Christian groups coconspirators in a great international plot to destroy Christendom.

10. We now call into evidence an early sixteenth-century German woodcut from the workshop of Hans Burgkmair. Both the woodcut itself and the printed volume it serves to illustrate are eloquent testimony to the association of Jew with Muslim by medieval and early modern Christians. The woodcut serves as the frontispiece of a Latin religious disputation by a Dr. Oliverius entitled *Dialogus de Diversarum*

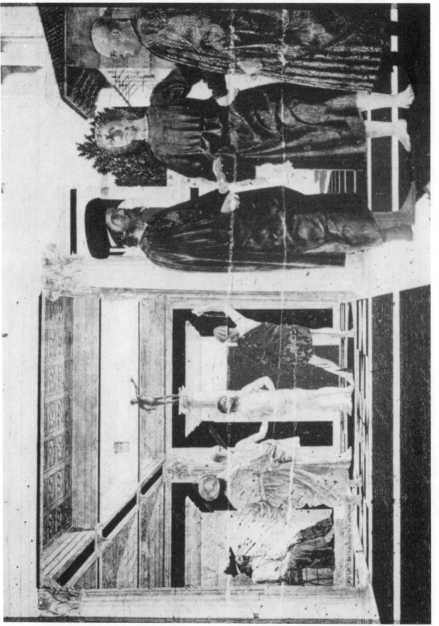

Flagellation of Christ. Painting by Piero della Francesca, Galleria Nazionale delle Marche, Palazzo Ducale, Urbino, Italy, circa 1450–1460.

Synagogue's Flag Bears the Name of the Prophet Muhammad. Detail of a woodcut entitled "Church, with Pope and Emperor," by Hans Burgkmair, German, circa 1508, frontispiece of Dr. Oliverius's *Dialogus de Diversarum Gentium Sectis et Mundi Religionibus*, printed at Augsburg, Bavaria, by Johannes Stamler in 1508.

Gentium Sectis et Mundi Religionibus, printed at Augsburg (Bavaria) by Johannes Stamler in 1508.

In the text proper the Christian theologian is confronted by both a Jewish and an Islamic clergyperson. While the Jew supports the Muslim by pointing to the yet unfulfilled promises of Christ and the failures of the church, it is to no avail. Both non-Christians (who share a common Semitic heritage and are considered allies) are won over in the end to the true faith and ask for baptism.

The woodcut proper, which serves to illustrate the text, shows Holy Mother Church sitting on a throne, under a cross, in the upper center of the composition, flanked by the pope on the left and the Holy Roman Emperor on the right. Four women, all with broken flagstaffs as signs of their captivity, sit humbly around the throne as subjects of the Holy Mother Church, pope, and emperor. The two women on the left represent Islam and Judaism; the two women on the right, the Greco-Roman pagans and the Mongols. By position in the composition the Jews are linked with the Muslims rather than the Greco-Roman pagans. But the Jews are also linked with the Muslims here by the flags that they carry. Judaism carries a flag on which is written the name *Machometus*, the Prophet Muhammad, the last and greatest of the Prophets according to Islam (or, as some Christians believed, the god of Islam; supra section 5, the Belgian "Miracle de Sainte-Gudule")! While Islam carries a flag on which is depicted a *Jew's* hat! Assuredly, the depiction here of this exchange of banners between Islam and Judaism was purposeful. If we look at the other two women, sitting on the right, we find that each of them carries the proper flag. The Greco-Roman pagans carry a flag on which the name "Jupiter" is written. The Mongols carry a flag on which the name *Chingista* (=Genghis Khan) is written. There is no exchange of flags here as there is between the two women sitting on the left, Islam and Judaism.

What was Burgkmair trying to say with his woodcut? According to Wolfgang Seiferth it was the following:

> One could regard this interchanging of the banners simply as an error on the part of the woodcarver who was unfamiliar with the previous history of his allegories. More likely, however, is the assumption that *the Jews were thereby being accused of collusion with the Turks* [italics ours], the enemies of the [German] nation; [for] both were enemies of

Christianity. Thus, to the many accusations heaped upon the Jews in the late Middle Ages, that of treason and conspiracy with the Turks was added.[66]

Of course, Seiferth should have been aware of the fact that the Christian belief in a Judaeo/Islamic conspiracy against the church can be traced back to the seventh century and was not simply something that "was added" in the early sixteenth century. Nevertheless, could there be any more eloquent testimony than the Burgkmair woodcut to the historic Christian tendency to equate Jew with Muslim and to consider the Jews allies of the Muslims in a great international conspiracy to destroy Christendom and the West?

11. In his compelling volume on *The Devil and the Jews*, Joshua Trachtenberg has collected some very powerful evidence of the association of Jew with Muslim (especially Turk) in early modern Europe which has not received sufficient attention. We believe it is important to present the Trachtenberg material at this point in order to supplement the material already developed above.

Trachtenberg states the following in the chapter of his book entitled "Infidel or Heretic?":

> It is not unusual to encounter [the Christian belief that] the Jew and the villainous Turk, the most powerful external foe and rival of Christendom in the later period, [were] conniving together against their common enemy [the Christians]. When the Turks moved north against the [Holy Roman] Empire in the sixteenth century, everywhere the cry arose spontaneously that the Jews were in league with them, serving as spies and in general as what we would call today "*fifth columnists*" [italics ours; Trachtenberg uses the same term here that was used by Cantera-Burgos and Baron to apply to the Spanish situation; cf. footnote 17 supra].[67]

What *historical* evidence does Trachtenberg cite for the Christian view that the Jews were a Turkish "fifth column"?

1. In 1538 the Jewish quarter of Candia, Crete, was attacked by the native Greek Christian population (though the Venetian occupation forces intervened in time to save the Jews from massacre) because of the Greek suspicion that the Jews were harboring Turkish spies.

2. In 1541 the Jews were expelled from Bohemia because, as a citizen of Prague wrote, "if the Turks should ever come into this coun-

try, which God forbid, it would be because of the Jews, *who showed them the way* [italics ours]."

3. The Jews were expelled from different parts of Austria three times, 1544, 1572, and 1602, for alleged collaboration with the Turks.

4. In 1566 the Spanish ambassador to England, referring to the Turkish invasion of Hungary, stated that "some Catholics think that the heretics [Protestants] are to blame for the enemy's attacks [*i.e.*, the attacks by the Turks], *and some even lay it to the Jews*" [italics ours].

5. When in 1684 the Christian armies attempting to retake Buda from the Turks were defeated, the Jews were held responsible. Mobs stormed the Jewish ghettos of a number of Italian cities to take vengeance on their inhabitants for alleged collusion with the Muslim enemies of Christendom.[68]

What *belletristic* evidence does Trachtenberg cite for the alleged Judaeo/Turkish alliance?

1. Martin Luther's frequent literary allusions to tales of Jewish collusion with the Turks.

2. A miracle play, whose earlier version presents a Turk piercing an image of Mary but whose later version assigns this same role to a Jew (the ally of the Turk).

3. Several dramas, like the French Besancon Antichrist play and the French *Mystere de la Sainte Hostie*, as well as the English *Three Ladies of London* (1584) by Robert Wilson, present a Jew who venerates the Prophet Muhammad (perhaps as the god of Islam; supra, section 5, the Belgian "Miracle de Sainte-Gudule") and swears by his name.

4. Christopher Marlowe's drama *The Jew of Malta* (circa 1592, published 1633), in which the Jewish archvillain Barabas is aided by his Turkish slave Ithamore in many nefarious activities (including the strangling of the Christian friar Father Bernardine), Barabas finally admitting the besieging Turks into the city. This Marlowe drama is one of the most overwhelming statements in the history of the association of Jew with Muslim by Christians, medieval or modern. Marlowe goes so far in his antipathy toward the Jewish people as to portray the Jew Barabas as eventually attempting to betray even his Turkish allies. The Jew, thus, becomes the ultimate traitor who betrays everyone, Christians and Muslims alike, in order to gain his own vicious ends. Primarily, however, the Jew attempts to betray the Christians to his Muslim cousins and allies.

117

5. Influenced by sixteenth-century English drama, Jakob Ayrer's (died Nuremberg, 1605) *Comoedie von Nikolaus* includes among its cast of characters the Jewish figure Moses, whose role it is to reveal the secrets of the Christians to the Turkish Sultan.[69]

12. From the midseventeenth-century we have a statement associating Jew with Muslim stemming from an English Royalist (High Anglican) writer serving as the exiled King Charles II's resident in Venice. We refer to the following statement made by Sir Peter Killigrew in February 1650:

> The danger to the Christian religion [*i.e.*, to High Anglicanism] is shown by the [Calvinist] sects which have sprung up in the new empire, to the number of fifty, all of which may be professed to-day in England with the utmost liberty. So also by the burning of the sacred liturgy [the Anglican *Book of Common Prayer*] by the [Calvinist] hangman and at the same time the publication of the Alcoran [the bible of Islam, which appeared at London in English translation, May 1649], translated from the Turkish, so that the people may be imbued with Turkish manners, which have much in common with the actions of the [Calvinist] rebels. The church of St. Paul [in London], comparable with St. Peter's at Rome, remains desolate and is said to have been sold to the Jews as a synagogue. The choir [of this church] will be profaned by the voices of the infidel [Jews] as soon as they receive possession from the troops of [Calvinist] soldiers, horse and foot, who have been lodged there.[70]

Thus, Killigrew equated all three non-Anglican groups, Calvinists, Muslims and Jews, and damned them all (as Dante had circa 1300 equated Pope Boniface VIII, the Muslims, and the Jews and had damned them all; supra, section 9). However, it is important to note that he equates Muslim with Calvinist by stating that the Calvinists published the Quran. He also equates Jew with Calvinist by stating that the Calvinists sold St. Paul's to the Jews. Hence, he also equates Muslim with Jew, according to the geometric principle that if B=A and C=A, B=C. Thus, Killigrew provides additional evidence of the persistence even into the middle of the seventeenth century (cf. likewise the violent equation of Jew with Turk in Italy as late as 1684 in the Trachtenberg material above) of the Christian tendency to equate Jew with Muslim and to consider the two non-Christian re-

118

ligious groups, who shared a common Semitic heritage, to be conspiring together to destroy Christendom and the West.

13. From England circa 1800 comes a startling statement associating Jew with Muslim written by William Blake, the great mystical and Romantic poet. Blake described John Henry Fuseli (born 1741 in Zurich; died 1825 as one of the most distinguished exiles in English art history, buried beside Sir Joshua Reynolds in St. Paul's Cathedral, London) as follows:

> The only man that e'er I knew
> Who did not make me almost spew
> Was Fuseli; and he was *both a Turk*
> *and a Jew*[Italics ours]—
> And so good Christian friends, how
> do you do?

William Blake thus asserts that Fuseli, who was his friend, was, figuratively speaking of course, both a Muslim and a Jew at one and the same time. This was a logical impossibility, but, then again, the history of Christian attitudes toward Jews is not noted for its logic! In reality, Fuseli was a Swiss Zwinglian minister whose liberal ideas had driven him out of Zurich and to England circa 1764 (at around age 23). Here he became an artist who, according to Sir Kenneth Clark, wanted "to render the most dramatic episodes of Shakespeare in the pictorial language of Michelangelo."[71] Thus, William Blake's poetic description of his artist friend John Henry Fuseli provides additional evidence of the persistence to around 1800, in highly civilized and advanced England, of the Christian tendency to equate Jew with Muslim.

14. Finally, we have a statement associating Jew with Muslim by Julian Armery, former British minister of state. He is quoted as describing Arab-Jewish affinity as follows in an address to the B'nai B'rith Lodge:

> Disraeli once said that Arabs were really Jews on horseback; today,
> it would perhaps be more apt to say that Arabs were Jews in Cadillacs.[72]

In Armery's remarks we have additional evidence of the persistence, in nineteenth- and twentieth-century England, of the Christian tendency to equate Jew with Muslim. After surveying the Middle Ages and early modern times, we have reached the twentieth century. Thereby we conclude this chapter as we began it, which was with four

119

examples of the twentieth-century tendency to equate Jew with Muslim and to consider both in league with each other conspiring against Christendom and the West.

5. The Association of Jew with Muslim by Medieval Jews: A Crucial Factor in the Association of Jew with Muslim by Medieval Christians*

We believe that by deepening our knowledge of medieval anti-Semitism our study can help in understanding twentieth-century anti-Semitism as well. The medieval origins of modern anti-Semitism have been the subject of two highly important and widely read books. We refer to (1) *The Devil and the Jews, the Medieval Conception of the Jew, and Its Relation to Modern Anti-Semitism*, by the late American Jewish scholar Joshua Trachtenberg, which first appeared through Yale University Press in the war year of 1943;[1] and (2) *The Pursuit of the Millennium: Revolutionary Messianism in Medieval and Reformation Europe and Its Bearing on Modern Totalitarian Movements*, by the Anglo-Jewish scholar Norman Cohn, which first appeared through Oxford University Press in 1957.[2] Both Trachtenberg and Cohn acknowledge the importance of the association of Jew with Muslim by medieval Christians as a factor in the history of anti-Semitism.[3]

The concept of the Jew as an internal ally of a foreign world conspiracy seems to us to be of primary importance to the medieval origins of modern anti-Semitism. This concept has certainly been an exceedingly damaging one in the twentieth century. During the Nasser era the governments and peoples of the various Arab states of the Middle East seemed to feel that the Israelis, who to them were an unwelcome Jewish island in the midst of the vast Islamic sea, were agents of the alleged American-British world conspiracy. Stalinist ruling circles in the Soviet Union even before World War II, and in Soviet-dominated Eastern Europe after World War II, entertained a similar belief about their own Jewish citizens. They saw (or pretended to see) the Jews living in their lands as dangerous internal allies of the alleged Western capitalist world conspiracy. The Nazis of Germany felt that the Ger-

121

man Jews and the rest of the Jews of Europe were simultaneously agents of two alleged world conspiracies, the Anglo-French capitalist and the Soviet Communist. The two other important European fascist leaders of the 1930s, Mussolini and Franco, did not generally hold these views with the same intensity as did Hitler (if they held them at all). In the seventeenth century many Catholic Poles felt that the Jews of their land were in league with the Protestant Swedes, who invaded Poland in the 1650s.[4] In sixteenth- and seventeenth-century Germanic Central Europe (and the Holy Roman Empire) a widespread popular feeling existed that the Jews were in league with the Muslims, i.e., the Ottoman Turks, who twice (unsuccessfully) beseiged Vienna, 1529 and 1683.[5] In the fifteenth century a widespread popular feeling among the Christians of Spain held that the Marranos (who, as Ben-Zion Netanyahu argues [infra, chapter 7], were far more willing converts from Judaism to Christianity than has previously been realized), as well as the unconverted Jews, were in league with the Muslims, especially with the Nasrid Kingdom of Granada and the Marinid dynasty in Morocco.[6] In the thirteenth century the Jews of Germany were accused of being in league with the dreaded Mongol invaders, who later converted from paganism to Islam after devastating Eastern Europe (circa 1240) and the Middle East (circa 1260), reaching the Adriatic at Spalato but never Jerusalem.[7]

Thus, it is easy to see that the twentieth-century anti-Semitic concept of the Jews as being in league with a foreign world conspiracy has definite medieval roots. The classical example of this concept, from which all subsequent varieties seem to stem, was the early medieval Christian belief circa 600–1000 that the Jews were in league with the Muslims against the West. There may have been some foreshadowing thereof in the pagan Roman and Byzantine Christian attitude toward the Jews as allies of the foreign pagan Parthian and later Zoroastrian Sassanian Persian conspiracy (from circa 63 B.C., when the Romans conquered Palestine, to circa 640 A.D., when the Arabs overwhelmed Persia.)[8] However, this earlier pre-600 charge was never as frequent chronologically or geographically nor its effect anywhere near as devastating as the later post-600 Christian charge that the Jews were in league with the Muslims. The Roman-Byzantine charge tended to equate unlike with unlike, i.e., the Jews (Semites and Abrahamitic in religion) with the Persians (Indo-Europeans and, as pagans or Zoroastrians, non-Abrahamitic in religion). The far more serious Christian charge tended to equate like with like, *i.e.*, the Jews (Semites and Abrahamitic in religion) with the Muslims (also Semites and Abrahamitic in religion). Indeed, the Arab relationship with the Jews could be traced back to around the thirteenth century B.C., *i.e.*, to the influence of the Midianite-Kenites (and Jethro) of northwestern Arabia upon Moses and upon the recently emancipated Israelite slaves (slowly making their difficult way across the Sinai desert to the east bank of the Jordan, thence into the Promised Land under Joshua).[9]

Once we realize that Jew-hatred in Western Europe during the period circa 600–1100 A.D. was largely an internal form of Muslim-hatred, the way is opened for us to understand the following. Minority groups quite frequently make a major contribution, unwittingly of course, to the hatred directed against them. When we examine several major historical works written by Jews in either the Hebrew or Arabic languages circa 600–1100, we discover the unsettling fact that the Jews themselves associated Jew with Muslim. Admittedly, most of these works were written by Jews in Islamic countries. For the Jews in Islamic countries to associate themselves with the Muslims in their major historical works would certainly pose no danger to the Jews in those lands. Indeed, if the Muslims became familiar with the contents of these works, the equation of Jew with Muslim expressed therein would enhance Jewish status within Islamic society.

However, if Jews migrated from Islamic countries to Western Europe in sizable numbers, and the contents of these works became generally known to Western Christians, the association of Jew with Muslim therein could prove potentially disastrous. Jewish literature itself would then serve to confirm Western Christian suspicion of the Jew as an ally of the Muslim, an agent of the foreign Islamic conspiracy. When Western European society was on the defensive vis-à-vis the Islamic world (circa 700-1000), this association of Jew with Muslim *by Jews* would do little harm. At that time Christians needed Jewish help against Islam. However, when Western European society began to take the offensive against the Muslims circa 1000, the association of Jew with Muslim *by Jews*, in their *own* historical literature circa 600-1100, could well have been a major factor in the tragic fate which the Jewish people suffered at the hands of the eleventh-century Crusaders who marched against the Muslims of Spain (circa 1010 and 1065) and the Middle East (circa 1096). During the crusading era Christians did not need Jewish help against Islam.

Let us examine, then, the association of Jew with Muslim in five major Jewish historical works circa 600-1100: (1) the story of Bustanai, circa 650-900; (2) the travel narrative of Eldad the Danite, ninth century; (3) the chronicle of Nathan the Babylonian, tenth century; (4) the exchange of letters between Hasdai the son of Shaprut, the high Jewish official of the caliphate of Cordova, and Joseph, the Jewish khan of the Khazars, tenth century; and (5) the chronicle of Ahima'atz, eleventh century. At the same time, however, let us also consider the several possible ways in which the contents of these works, written in Hebrew and/or Arabic, could have become known to the Christians of Western Europe (who, generally speaking, did not know Semitic languages).

Of the five major Jewish historical works circa 600–1100, only one comes from the Islamic East. We refer to the highly popular story of Bustanai. Bustanai (from the Persian, then Hebrew and Arabic, word for "garden") was a major Jewish historical personage who flourished at the time of Caliph Umar (634–644), though some versions of his story link him instead with Caliph Ali (656–661). He became the first exilarch, or political leader, of Davidic descent of the Iraqi Jewish millet or religious community under Arab rule (just as the Nestorian Catholicos was the political leader of the Christian millet). Bustanai's story is preserved in eight versions. Four would seem to stem from gaonic sources (*i.e.*, from Jewish ecclesiastical circles), which go back ultimately to circa 650–750 Arab Iraq. The other four would seem to stem from the official history (*Book of Memoirs*) of the exilarchate (*i.e.*, from Jewish political circles), which goes back ultimately to ninth-century Arab Iraq. Six of these versions (all four gaonic versions plus two of the exilarchic) are quite succinct and factual. Two versions (both exilarchic) are more prolix, and in them the legendary element seems at times almost to predominate.[10]

The second and third of these Jewish historical works come from nearer the geographical center of the Islamic Mediterranean. We refer to the city of Kairawan (located in present-day Tunisia), the great medieval emporium which stood at the commercial crossroads between Spain and Morocco in the west, Byzantium and Egypt in the east, and Italy to the north. The second historical work is the sensational travel narrative of Eldad the Danite (who claimed to have visited the Lost Ten Tribes in Ethiopia, Arabia, and Persia), a major landmark in the history of Western utopian literature.[11] The third is

124

the chronicle of Nathan the Babylonian, which treats the history of the Jews in Babylonia under the Arabs but was written in Kairawan.[12] Both of these works date from circa 850–950.

The fourth of these works basically originates in the Islamic West. We refer to the well-known exchange of letters between Hasdai the son of Shaprut, the Jewish foreign minister of the caliphs of Cordova during the middle tenth century, and Joseph the khan of the Khazars of the Volga River-Caucasus area, a Turkic people (closely related to the Magyars), whose ruling classes had largely been converted to Judaism. In this correspondence there is one letter from each of the two parties involved. Hasdai's letter is generally thought to have been written by his Hebrew-language secretary, the great lexicographer and poet M'nahem the son of Saruk. M'nahem died of the harsh treatment he later received at the hands of his erstwhile employer after the latter had turned violently against him for reasons that are not completely clear (they may have had something to do with Hasdai's fear of Karaism and heresy). The correspondence is usually considered to be genuine and is dated in the tenth century, the century in which both Hasdai and Joseph lived (though some hold that the correspondence is fictional, the creation of the fertile imagination of an eleventh-century Spanish Jewish writer).[13]

The fifth, and most pivotal, of these Jewish historical works comes from southern Italy, which, of course, was Christian rather than Islamic territory. However, southern Italy was a Christian territory exposed to constant attack from the Islamic outposts in the central Mediterranean. We refer to North Africa and especially to Sicily, whose Islamic history was initiated by the Aghlabid dynasty of Tunisia circa 825 and lasted until the Normans conquered the island, thereby shifting the balance of power in the central Mediterranean in favor of Christendom during the second half of the eleventh century. The work in question is the important and entertaining chronicle of Ahima'atz the son of Paltiel, written in the rhymed prose style that the great Islamic author Hariri brought to perfection circa 1100 in his *Maqamat*. In this chronicle, which interlaces a generally accurate narrative of events with interesting folklore, Ahima'atz (born 1017 in Capua, west coast of Italy; died 1060 in Oria, east coast of Italy), otherwise known as a synagogue poet, described the glorious history of his own courageous family, which provided religiopolitical leadership for south Italian Jewry during the 200-year period circa 850–1050.[14]

To sum up our introductory description of the Jewish historical works we propose to treat here with regard to their attitude toward the Arabs, the first work, the biography of Bustanai, is pro-Arab. The second, the travel narrative of Eldad the Danite, is anti-Arab. The third, the chronicle of Nathan the Babylonian, and the fourth, the epistolary exchange between Hasdai and Joseph, are both pro-Arab once again. The fifth work, the chronicle of Ahima'atz, after wavering between pro- and anti-Arab sentiments, finally embraces the Arab side.

These favorable Jewish attitudes toward Arabs, expressed in written form, are in marked contrast to the increasingly hostile Western Christian attitude toward the Arabs during the same period. Such a dichotomy may help explain in part why the crusading movement, which began primarily as an attempt to solve the problem of Islam, rapidly developed into an attack on the Jews as well.

*****

Let us turn now in greater detail to the five Jewish historical works that we wish to consider here.

The crucial essence of the earliest of these works, the story of Bustanai, is the statement that the caliph of the Arabs looked with great favor upon Bustanai, the political leader of the Iraqi Jews, and gave him a daughter of the late Sassanian Persian king to wed.

According to one Gaonic version of the Bustanai story (Tykocinski's second version), which goes back ultimately to circa 650–750, Biran, a wife of Sassanian King Chosroes II, and two of Chosroes' daughters, Izdadwar and her unnamed sister, were brought before Caliph Umar I. Umar took one of the sisters for his own harem and gave the other, Izdadwar, to Bustanai. However, Bustanai would not consummate the marriage until he had redeemed the Sassanian princess from slavery (at a cost of 52,000 zuzim). It was thereafter that she bore him three sons, Shahriyar, Goranshah, and Mardanshah, whom he treated as his own legitimate offspring. Nevertheless, when Bustanai died, Hasdai and Baradoi, his sons by another wife (Jewish by birth as well as religion), enslaved Bustanai's three sons by Izdadwar. Hasdai and Baradoi argued that since Izdadwar had been the daughter of a Sassanian king, she would never have consented to embrace Judaism and must therefore have been treated merely as a concubine by Bustanai. However, at a later date several prominent rabbis ordered that the three sons of Bustanai by Izdadwar be considered legitimate (and therefore be freed from bondage and treated as full-fledged members of the Jewish community). These rabbis reasoned that an exilarch would never have lived in sin with a woman and therefore Bustanai must have freed Izdadwar and converted her to Judaism in the presence of witnesses before marrying and cohabiting with her. Legitimized and emancipated by this liberal rabbinical ruling, Izdadwar's three sons soon married into powerful families that served the caliph. Their maternal uncle (Marzabana) had been governor of a border province under the Sassanians. Later, Bustanai's great grandson (unnamed in the source) married the daughter of Rabbi Haninai. This rabbi also ruled that the sons of Bustanai by Izdadwar were legitimate. Another of Bustanai's great grandsons, Zakkai the son of Ahunai the son of Shahriyar (the last being Bustanai's first born by Izdadwar), became exilarch circa 767 under the Abbasids. Bustanai's descendants by his purely Jewish wife ruled as exilarchs under the Umayyads, but the shift from Umayyads to Abbasids circa 750 probably played a role in bringing to power Bustanai's descendants by his Persian wife, led by Zakkai the son of Ahunai.[15]

According to one exilarchic version of the Bustanai story (Tykocinski's fifth; discovered in the Cairo Genizah), which seems to go back to a ninth-century source, a regent (called a *shaykh* in Arabic = *zaken* in Hebrew; possibly meaning an elderly man or a rabbi or both) served as exilarch during the minority of Bustanai. When Bustanai came of age at 16, the people demanded that the regent step down in favor of Bustanai. The regent refused and the case came before Caliph Umar I. The two parties to the dispute stood before the caliph. Each told his own side of the story in great detail. While they were arguing their respective cases, a wasp alighted on Bustanai's face and did not depart until it had bitten him. Bustanai, however, refused to brush the insect away from his face as long as he stood before the caliph, lest he seem to show disrespect thereby to the august majesty of the Islamic ruler. Bustanai's stoical ability to withstand pain and humble deference to duly constituted authority so impressed the caliph that he declared Bustanai the legitimate ruler of the Jews of Arab Iraq and gave him a seat in the inner council of the realm. From that day forth the Davidic dynasty of the exilarchs had the image of a wasp engraved upon their official signet rings.[16]

The eight versions of the Bustanai story attest to its immense popularity. It was well-known among the Jews of Arab Iraq through the thirteenth century at least, for the thirteenth is the century in which two of the exilarchic versions of the story (Tykocinski's fifth and seventh) were apparently reduced to writing in their present form, though they both go back to a ninth-century source.[17] What accounts for the popularity of the Bustanai story? First of all, the two feuding branches of the Bustanai family, those descended from his purely Jewish wife and those descended from his Persian wife, kept the story alive, each side in its own version. Those descended from Bustanai's purely Jewish wife claimed that the Persian wife had never been converted to Judaism. Those descended from the Persian wife claimed that she had indeed been converted. The story, then, played an important role in an intrafamily Jewish struggle for social standing and political power in Arab Iraq for many generations after the initial incident upon which it was based.[18] Second, the story was quite spicy, so that its considerable sexual interest also helped keep it alive. Third, and finally, the story (in both Tykocinski's fifth [from the Cairo Genizah] as well as his seventh versions)[19] also told about how a great hero could loyally overcome pain and suffering (the wasp bite) when the honor of his liege lord was at stake. This part of the story would have had great appeal to the medieval mind in general, which considered the concept of loyalty within a well-structured hierarchy a crucial value.

The Bustanai story, then, after originating in Arab Iraq, was transmitted westward all the way across the Mediterranean to Spain. There it was summarized (as Tykocinski's sixth version, an exilarchic version) in the great twelfth-century Hebrew chronicle *Sefer Ha-Kabbalah* (Book of Tradition). This work was written circa 1160 by Abraham ibn Daud, who was born around 1110 in Muslim Andalusia but lived and worked (Jewish Aristotelian philosophy, Jewish historiography, and the translation movement from Arabic into Latin) in Christian Toledo circa 1150–1175. In Toledo ibn Daud came into contact with such great Spanish Christian scholars as Dominicus Gundissalinus, and perhaps also with such great foreign Christian scholars (who came to Spain to study Arabic and/or to participate in the translation movement) as Gerard of Cremona from Italy and Alfred of Sareshal from England.[20] Even earlier than that, however, the Bustanai story was probably brought to Muslim Spain circa 1050 when two sons of the Exilarch Hezekiah, descendants of Bustanai (perhaps by his Persian wife), fled to Granada after their father was imprisoned and tortured by the caliph of Bagdad. Circa 1050–1150 the children of these two exiles moved from Granada to Christian Castile (perhaps to Toledo) and Muslim Saragossa (perhaps remaining there after the town was taken from the Muslims by Aragon in 1118 and/or moving from Muslim Saragossa to Christian Catalonia-Barcelona after Saragossa fell to Aragon). In Christian Castile and Aragon/Catalonia these descendants of Bustanai could easily have spread his story among their Spanish Jewish brethren and Christian neighbors. The latter, in turn, could have transmitted the story to some of the many French Christians (Crusaders, Cluniac monks, pilgrims to Santiago, etc.) who were such a powerful presence in Christian Spain at this time. They in turn, could have transmitted the story to the Christians back home, beyond the Pyrenees, in France (and Germany).[21]

However, it is highly probable that the Bustanai story was brought from Bagdad to southern France circa 768 by a descendant of Bustanai (via his purely Jewish wife rather than his Persian wife). We refer to Natronai-Machir, the first ruler of the semiautonomous "Jewish Princedom in Feudal France" which, according to Arthur Zuckerman, was set up to serve the interests of the Carolingian-Abbasid alliance directed against Umayyad Spain.[22] In view of the dealings of this semi-independent southern French Jewish dynasty with the Carolingian rulers of northern France circa 768–900, it is highly possible that the Bustanai story was proudly transmitted during this period by the Jewish dynasty to the political and ecclesiastical leaders of Christian Franco-Germany. It told in extremely vivid fashion of the Judaeo-Arabic alliance in Iraq that was a cornerstone of both the semiautonomous Jewish state in southern France as well as of the Carolingian-Abbasid alliance against Umayyad Spain. Another way in which the Bustanai story could have reached the Christians of Franco-Germany was via the Jew Isaac (who, Zuckerman argues, was none other than Count William of Toulouse, son of Natronai-Machir and, therefore, like his father, a descendant of Bustanai), Charlemagne's ambassador to the court of the Abbasid caliph in Bagdad circa 800.[23]

It is highly probable that Agobard of Lyons, the great French Christian churchman and writer of the first half of the ninth century, who was intensely anti-Jewish, knew the Bustanai story (though we have no *direct* evidence to this effect). Agobard knew about the food taboos of the Karaites (the Jewish sectarians of Arab Iraq whose movement was founded by Anan the son of David, a descendant of Bustanai, circa 760).[24] Further, Agobard also knew Jewish mystical ideas which were part of the Merkavah (or "Chariot") mysticism of the Jews of Arab Iraq (circa 600–1000).[25] If Agobard knew a subject as esoteric as the food taboos of a Jewish sectarian movement of Arab Iraq or as esoteric as the mystical ideas of the Jews of Arab Iraq, could not Agobard also have known the far less esoteric Bustanai story? As a general rule, Christian clerics and writers in ninth-century Franco-Germany (e.g., Paschasius Radbertus and Christian of Stavelot) were vitally interested in any data they could obtain about Jewish political rulers in the East. The existence or nonexistence of such rulers had a direct bearing on the question of whether or not God had forsaken the Jews and given their promise to the Christians, e.g., on whether or not the Christians were now the true Israel.[26] Agobard almost certainly shared this general ninth-century French Christian clerical interest in whether or not there were any Jewish political rulers in the East. The Bustanai story dealt with one of the great Jewish political rulers of the East, the refounder of the Jewish exilarchate in Iraq after the Arab conquest of the Middle East. This might be another reason why Agobard would have taken an especial interest in the story, particularly since Bustanai was also an ancestor of the ruler of the semi-independent Jewish princedom in southern France, of which Agobard was one of the principal Christian clerical enemies.

Further, in the 850s Natronai, the gaon (or head) of the Jewish talmudical seminary at Sura in Arab Iraq and a descendant of Bustanai by his Persian wife, could well have transmitted a version of the Bustanai story by letter to Rabbi Elazar of Spain (Rabbi Elazar Alluf of Ausona/Vich near Barcelona?).[27] Barcelona was a crucial border city. From the Jews of Barcelona information about Bustanai could have spread to the Jews and Christians of southern France, thence to the Jews and Christians of northern France and Germany after circa 850.[28]

Further, it is highly possible that the Radanites, the great Jewish international merchants of the ninth century (described by Ibn Khurradadhbih circa 870–892), transmitted the Bustanai story to Carolingian Franco-Germany. Acccording to Ibn Khurradadhbih these merchants visited Bagdad as well as the Carolingian court in France.[29] Morris Epstein has recently argued that the Radanites transmitted not only goods but culture as well (specifically, the Jewish Tales of Sendebar, which formed the basis for the later Latin Seven Sages of Rome).[30]

If so, perhaps the Radanites also transmitted the Bustanai story to the Christians of Franco-Germany at this same time.

The Bustanai story, after originating in Arab Iraq, was also transmitted westward to Italy, where it was summarized (Tykocinski's fourth, a Gaonic version) by Rabbi Isaiah ben Mali di Trani, who lived in southeastern Italy circa 1200–1260 but was in close contact with Jewish scholars in Germany as well as Greece and Palestine.[31] Did the Bustanai story reach the Jews of Italy before 1200 as well? There is no direct evidence that it did. However, it is highly possible that Aaron of Bagdad, who could have been the son of the exilarch (or the son of a relative of the exilarch), and thus a descendant of Bustanai, brought the Bustanai story with him when he came to Italy in the 850s.[32] According to thirteenth-century German Jewish tradition, this Aaron of Bagdad transmitted the mystical ideas of the Jews of Arab Iraq to the Jewish Kalonymid family of Lucca, which brought them to Franco-Germany when it moved to Mainz during the second half of the ninth century (in response to an invitation from the Carolingian rulers).[33] Even if this thirteenth-century tradition cannot be accepted at face value, perhaps it can be accepted as an indication of the fact that Jewish mystical ideas did travel from Arab Iraq through Italy to Franco-Germany circa 800–1100. If the mystical ideas of the Jews of Arab Iraq traveled to Franco-Germany circa 800–1100, how much the more so would the far less esoteric historical traditions of the Jews of Arab Iraq in general, and their Bustanai story in particular, have traveled that same route at the same time!

If Western Christians in northern France circa 800–1100 heard the Bustanai story from their Jewish neighbors (the Jews at this time, and even into the thirteenth century, were quite outspoken about their own religious traditions and past glories[34]), what would they have thought about it? How would it have struck them? Their Jewish neighbors undoubtedly would have told the story of Bustanai because they were proud of it. It showed how important the Jewish people were in the vast and powerful Islamic world from which many (if not most) of the Jews in northern France circa 800–1100 had come.[35] However, to the Christians this story would have been a scandal. It would have confirmed their belief in the Judaeo/Islamic conspiracy, that the Jews in their midst were allies of the Muslims, an Islamic fifth column in Christian territory. After all, do not the Jews themselves (so the

Franco-German Christians could easily have reasoned) say that the early Muslim Caliph Umar, the second successor of the Prophet Muhammad (the law-giver of the Islamic religion), gave Bustanai political power as well as a wife and brought him into the inner council of the realm? What more proof do we need (Franco-German Christians could easily have asked themselves) than this very story heard from the lips of the Jews themselves that they are in league with the Muslims?

What would have made this story even worse is that it not only suggests a two-way alliance, a Jewish-Islamic alliance, but it actually goes one step further to suggest a three-way alliance, a Jewish-Sassanian-Islamic alliance. This would have been especially important because the Christians of Western Europe at the time of the Crusades considered the Sassanians the forerunners of the Muslims, whose role as the great archenemy of Christianity for four centuries (third through seventh) Islam gladly took over.[36] The Bustanai story, then, speaks about the two great military archenemies of the Christian world, the Sassanians and the Muslims, and very dangerously links the Jews with both of these enemies *simultaneously*. What could possibly have been more explosive when heard by Western Christian ears? What kind of story could the Jews of northern France have possibly told their Christian neighbors which would have produced more suspicion of them as agents of a great foreign anti-Christian conspiracy?

$$*\ *\ *\ *\ *$$

The travel narrative of Eldad the Danite (written in Kairawan circa 850–900, or perhaps in the tenth century; Dunlop suggests that Eldad may have been a Khazar[37]) is itself unquestionably an anti-Arab document. But it is also anti-Christian, anti-Zoroastrian (the Zoroastrians are incestuous fire-worshippers[38]) and antiblack African (the black Africans are tall, naked, animal-like cannibals[39]). The best way to sum up Eldad's travel narrative is to say that it is an intensely pro-Jewish messianic document (Eldad was believed to have been sent by God as a herald of the messianic redemption) which considers all non-Jews either wicked or barbarian or both. Yet it is rather ironic that this anti-Arab document, as we shall soon see, could also have confirmed the suspicions of Western Christians that the Jews were in league with the Muslims.

132

There are at least four anti-Arab statements in the travel narrative of Eldad. The first is a reference to Mecca, the holiest city of the Islamic world, as the $ta^c\bar{u}t$ of the Ishmaelites, *i.e.*, the "going astray" or "error" of the Muslims. The Hebrew root here, ṭ-ᶜ-h, is the exact cognate of the Arabic root ṭ-ġ-w, to "overstep the bounds," with the noun derived therefrom *ṭaġūt*, meaning "idols" in the Quran. The Hebrew root, ṭ-ᶜ-h, is also the equivalent of the Arabic root ḍ-l-l, to "go astray, to err." In the Quran ḍ-l-l is used to refer to idolatry. It is highly possible that Eldad used the Hebrew root ṭ-ᶜ-h here in the same sense and that he was implying that he considered the pilgrimage rites connected with the shrine at Mecca to be a form of idolatry.[40]

Very shortly thereafter in the text Eldad mentions the fact that some Ishmaelites have to pay tribute to the Jewish tribes of Khazaria (he calls them the lost tribe of Simeon and the lost half tribe of Manasseh).[41] Undoubtedly Eldad rejoiced at this thought, for it meant that the Jews exercised power over the Arabs at least in this one place, whereas almost everywhere else it was the other way around. This local exercise of Jewish power was a foreshadowing of what the messianic redemption and the world-to-come would be like. At that time Jews would exercise power over all Arabs everywhere (as well as over all Christians and all other non-Jews, for that matter).

Immediately thereafter in the text Eldad links the pagan Romans, the Christian Romans/Byzantines, and the Arabs in one sweeping condemnation.[42] All are oppressors of the Jewish people, and all will soon get their just deserts. Eldad holds that the Jews who are scattered throughout the Christian and Islamic lands are living in lands where idolatry (ᶜavadoh zarah in Hebrew) and ritual impurity (ṭum' ah in Hebrew) prevail. The pagan Romans destroyed the Jewish Temple in Jerusalem in 70. Their successors, the Christian Romans/Byzantines and the Arabs, have been oppressing the Jewish people every since. Soon, however—and here Eldad quotes Psalm 37:15 (Dupont-Sommer tells us that the Qumranites also commented upon this verse[43])— "their swords [*i.e.*, those of the Christians] will come into their own hearts and their bows [*i.e.*, those of the Muslims] will be broken." Eldad, then, in this passage equates the Christians with the Muslims and declares both groups to be equally loathsome.

Finally, there may be be an invidious allusion to the Arabs in Eldad's description of the utopian commonwealth inhabited by the lost tribe of the B'ne Mosheh (sons of Moses), whose language is

Hebrew alone (they speak no Ethiopic nor Arabic) and whose Talmud, or post-biblical Jewish tradition literature, is written again solely in Hebrew (with no Aramaic admixture). Amongst the B'ne Mosheh, people are so honest that there is no need for the taking of an oath, no need to lock one's doors at night. All live to the ripe old age of 120, the mythical age which the Bible says Moses, the great emancipator, attained. Finally, all are equal and no person can be enslaved.[44] This last particular about the B'ne Mosheh may be a pejorative allusion by contrast to the Arab slave traders in East Africa and the vast numbers of black slaves employed in the ninth-century Arab Middle East. Eldad was probably aware of the great revolt of the black slaves in southern Iraq, at Basra, led by the Persian Kharijite anarchist-revolutionary Ali ibn Muhammad, which lasted circa 869–883.[45]

How, then, could a document which is as anti-Arab as the travel narrative of Eldad the Danite possibly confirm Western Christian suspicions that the Jews were in league with the Muslims? The key here is the geographical locations in which Eldad placed the Lost Ten Tribes, mighty warriors who venture at will into the territory of the non-Jewish tribes and peoples living in their vicinity, spreading havoc among the Gentiles and avenging past wrongs manyfold.

According to Eldad the Lost Ten Tribes were living in essentially three separate areas: (1) Persia and the Caucasus, (2) the Arabian Peninsula, and (3) Ethiopia. The tribes of Isaachar, Zebulun, Reuben, Simeon, and half of the tribe of Manasseh live in the Persian-Caucasus area. The tribe of Ephraim and the other half of the tribe of Manasseh live in the Arabian Peninsula, in the mountains *near Mecca!* Finally, the tribes of Dan, Naphtali, Gad, Asher, and the B'ne Mosheh live in the Ethiopian area.

All of these three areas in which Eldad placed the Lost Ten Tribes are either within Islamic territory or on its fringe. To Western European ears it would have sounded like the Lost Ten Tribes were living *among the Arabs!*

These Jewish tribes, as described by Eldad, were armed and courageous. They loved war and inflicted crushing defeats on the non-Jewish tribes and peoples who lived in their vicinity. The tribes living in the mountains near Mecca are described as being *z'ume nefesh* (angry, furious, stormy, of spirit) and *k'huye lev* (blunt, iron-hard, of heart). With their horses they cut their own paths (through their enemies). They have no mercy upon their foes. Booty is their only means of livelihood. Each one of these mighty warriors is worth a thousand of his enemies.[46]

This description of the Lost Ten Tribes living in the mountains near Mecca, among other places, sounds very much like the Arabs themselves who burst into the Middle East and conquered it in the 630s and 640s.[47] It seems probable that when the Christians of Western Europe heard the travel narrative of Eldad the Danite, they did not note his anti-Arab statements.[48] They noted, rather, what seemed to them to be far more striking, *i.e.*, Eldad's statements that the Lost Ten Tribes were living in Arab territories and behaved like the Arab invaders of the seventh century. The next step in the Western European thought process would have been to assume that the Lost Ten Tribes and the Arabs were in collusion with each other. Thus, it is highly possible that when the Christians of Western Europe heard Eldad's travel narrative, it confirmed their worst suspicions. The Jews in their midst, many of whom had come from Islamic lands to begin with, were nothing but Islamic fifth columnists in Christian territory, waiting for their opportunity to rise up in concert with a foreign Islamic and Jewish (Lost Ten Tribes) invasion to destroy Christendom forever.

*****

The chronicle of Nathan the Babylonian dates from the first half of the tenth century and was written in Kairawan (Tunisia) from material depicting the more or less contemporary situation in Iraq. It is clearly a pro-Arab document. This chronicle can be conveniently divided into three parts. Part one describes institutions, both religious (the two talmudical seminaries, Sura and Pumbedita) and political (the exilarchate). The second part of the chronicle describes personalities and their struggle with one another. This struggle was essentially a church-state struggle, between two heads of talmudical seminaries and two exilarchs, Rabbi Kohen Tzedek of Pumbedita against Exilarch Mar Uqba, then Rabbi Saadia Gaon of Sura against Exilarch David the son of Zakkai. The third part of the chronicle is also biographical, but instead of describing the church-state struggle, its subject is the third, or moderating, force within the community, the powerful banking family of the sons of Netira who had great influence at the court of the caliph. All three parts of Nathan's chronicle contain statements which would lead Western Christians to believe that the Jews were in

135

league with the Muslims, but the second and third parts would be most likely to have this kind of dangerous effect.

The second part of Nathan's chronicle, the biographical portion describing the church-state struggle within Babylonian Jewry during the two generation period circa 900–950, contains several statements which would do Jews living within Islamic countries much good but Jews living within Western Christian countries equal harm. According to Nathan the caliph of Bagdad can make and unmake exilarchs at will, under the influence of Jews who are powerful at court (especially the banking family of the sons of Netira). In the case of the Exilarch Mar Uqba, Caliph al-Muktadir (908–932) first deposed him (Mar Uqba leaving Bagdad and moving to Kirmanshah, relatively close in nearby western Iran); then reinstated him; finally deposed him again and exiled him to far-off Kairawan (Tunisia). But, Nathan tells us, the way the Exilarch Mar Uqba earned reinstatement after his first deposition was through his skill as an *Arab* poet. When Caliph al-Muktadir, who deposed him, summered at his palace in Safran, Mar Uqba devised a scheme to win the royal favor. He met the caliph's secretary daily in the gardens of the palace but did not reveal his true identity lest he be denied a hearing because of his past condemnation. Instead, Mar Uqba recited Arabic poetry that he had composed himself. These verses pleased al-Muktadir's secretary so much that he wrote them down in order to show them to his royal master. The caliph was so delighted with the verses that he sent for the otherwise unknown local poet, discovered in conversation with him that he was a worthy person, and asked him to express a wish. Mar Uqba, of course, now had his opportunity to come back from oblivion and asked to be reinstated as exilarch. The caliph was taken by complete surprise but had to grant the wish of this sly but talented Jewish suppliant of the house of David and restore him to his position as political leader of Iraqi Jewry.[49]

How would Nathan's story of Mar Uqba have sounded to Western Christians? First of all, it would have told them that the great Jewish bankers have influence at the court of the caliph. Second, it would have told Western Christians that the political leaders of Babylonian Jewry, the exilarchs, had to strive continually to win caliphal favor because the caliphs could make and unmake them at will. Third, and most importantly, it would have told them that the key way the exilarchs retain caliphal favor is by Arabicizing themselves and becoming great Arab poets. These views about the Jews living within the Islamic world would have led to attitudes among Western Christians which would have done the Jews living within their midst little good. This is especially the case since many of these Jews had come to Western Europe from Islamic lands to begin with and still continued to look actively to their brethren in those lands for religious guidance and inspiration.

In the third portion of his chronicle Nathan tells us, among other things, that during the reign of Caliph al-Muctadhid (891-902) the Jewish banker Netira (son-in-law of Joseph the son of Phineas who had served a former vizier, al-Khaquani, before 877) detected a high-ranking embezzler. Thereby, he saved the caliph's treasury from collapse and the caliph himself from a major scandal that could have led to his demise. This signal achievement, plus Netira's great personal magnanimity toward the caliph and his chief advisors (plus the Prophet Elijah, who, we are told, appeared to the caliph in a dream twice during the same night and warned him against persecuting the Jews, or else Elijah would punish him severely by amputating his hands and feet), persuaded the caliph to rescind a previously issued harshly anti-Jewish decree. Thus, the Jew Netira was able to achieve more than simply moving the caliph from a stance that was neutral toward the Jews to one that was mildly pro-Jewish. Rather, Netira was able to move the caliph from the extreme of a harshly anti-Jewish attitude to the opposite extreme of an exceedingly pro-Jewish attitude, a highly noteworthy achievement. Indeed, so far in the direction of the Jews did the caliphal pendulum swing that the Jews were freed from all distinctions in clothing required by Islamic law and allowed to wear the very same black garments worn by the royal Abbasid house.[50] What would Western Christians have thought about the Jews in their midst if they heard Nathan's story about Netira, the Jewish banker of Bagdad, and his relations with Caliph al-Muctadhid?

*****

The exchange of letters between Hasdai the son of Shaprut, the Jewish foreign minister of the caliphate of Cordova, and Joseph, the Jewish khan of the Khazars, tenth century, like the travel narrative of Eldad the Danite, ninth century, is heavily messianic in tone. Both Hasdai/Joseph and Eldad intensely hoped and prayed for the coming of the long-awaited Jewish Messiah, the true Messiah son of David as they believed, who would free all Jews everywhere from domination by non-Jews (Muslims, Christians, etc.). Indeed, in the Hasdai/Joseph exchange Hasdai's letter ends with warm praise for Eldad the Danite as one of the great personages of Jewish history. However, whereas Eldad's travel narrative is an openly anti-Islamic document, the Hasdai/Joseph exchange is, at least on the surface, strongly pro-Islamic. However, if we read carefully between the lines of Hasdai's letter to Joseph, we can detect, without too much difficulty, a latent Jewish antagonism to the Islamic world, not because it is Islamic but rather because it is not Jewish. The Jewish messianic ideal gave Hasdai the spiritual strength he needed to live and work as a Jew in an overwhelmingly non- (and at times even anti-) Jewish environment. Hasdai's ideal, by virtue of its emphasis on the apocalyptic victory of the Jewish people over all other peoples, was by implication anti-Islamic, as well as anti-Christian, anti-Zoroastrian, and anti every other non-Jewish group. However, Hasdai successfully masked the anti-Islamic implications of his strong Jewish religious nationalism in his exchange of letters with Joseph.

Why is the heavily messianic Hasdai/Joseph correspondence pro-Islamic, at least on the surface, whereas the equally heavily messianic Eldad travel narrative is so openly anti-Islamic? Was it because Hasdai held important political office (the equivalent of foreign minister) under a major Islamic ruler (the caliph of Cordova), whereas Eldad held no such office? Thus, Eldad had only his own life to lose if his criticisms of Islam were made known to the Islamic authorities, and to a perpetual exile like Eldad his own life probably would have seemed relatively cheap. Hasdai, by contrast, also had considerable power and wealth to lose if his criticisms of Islam were made known to those authorities. Or was it because Hasdai, by virtue of his high office, was leader of the Jewish community of the major Islamic land wherein he resided? Any open criticisms of Islam on his part might have endangered not only his own life, position, and wealth but also that of the entire Jewish community. Eldad, on the other hand, since he held no office in an Islamic state or even within the Jewish community but was completely his own person, endangered only his own life, not the lives of his people, by his criticisms of Islam. Or was it because Eldad came from the center of the Islamic world (the Middle East) where Islam was relatively strong and unthreatened? Thus, Eldad could afford to criticize the Muslims openly since he believed that the portion of the Islamic world wherein he lived was secure enough to tolerate his criticisms. Hasdai, by contrast, came from the western frontier of the Islamic world (Spain), where Islam was relatively weak and where it was engaged in a constant life-and-death struggle against Western Christendom. Thus, Hasdai could not afford to criticize the Muslims openly since he believed that the portion of the Islamic world wherein he lived was too insecure to tolerate any criticisms from subject peoples (Christians or Jews).

These factors were undoubtedly important in producing the divergent attitudes toward Islam expressed by Eldad and Hasdai. However, the most important reason why Hasdai masked his anti-Islamic feelings so well, whereas Eldad expressed them so openly, may be the following. Eldad actually visited militarily powerful Jewish tribes. This personal experience impelled him to conclude that Jews, by their own efforts, could bring about their own worldwide redemption. Hasdai could only *long* to visit the militarily powerful Jewish kingdom of Khazaria, but he never actually did see the Khazar state and territory with his own eyes. For him, therefore, Jewish military power was only a partial answer. The major military power which could help bring closer the day of the messianic deliverance of his people was Islamic. Thus, the existence of an independent Jewish kingdom for Hasdai meant two things: one openly expressed in his letter to Joseph and one hidden deep within his own heart. The openly expressed meaning was that the existence of an independent Jewish state in Khazaria would strengthen the Jewish position within Islamic Spain (no longer could Spanish Muslims say to their Jewish neighbors that the Jews were homeless vagabonds, a minority everywhere on earth). Hasdai's hidden dream was that the Jews of Spain could move the Muslims of Spain toward an alliance with the independent Jewish kingdom of Khazaria. With such an alliance the Ummayad caliphate of Cordova could overcome all its rivals, Islamic (*e.g.*, the Abbasid and Fatimid caliphates of Iraq and North Africa) as well as the Christian (the Byzantine and Holy Roman Empires). Once it had done that, the Jews within the caliphate of Cordova would rise up and, with the aid of the independent Jewish kingdom of Khazaria, overthrow the caliphate of Cordova. Jewish success in such an attempt would usher in the messianic redemption. However, the key to the international messianic redemption of the Jewish people was the caliphate of Cordova, which

Hasdai served so faithfully. Until it had achieved, with Jewish help, a worldwide victory over all its enemies, Muslim and Christian, thus paving the way for the ultimate Jewish victory to follow, no open criticisms of Islam could be tolerated. Why criticize the religion of a regime that is your primary means to eventual salvation? Why thereby jeopardize the crucial possibilities for an alliance between the caliphate of Cordova and the Khazars?

What are the statements in the Hasdai/Joseph correspondence that would have confirmed Western Christian suspicions that the Jews were in league with the Muslims?

In his letter to Joseph, Hasdai states that he is a servant of Abd-ar-Rahman, the king of Muslim Spain. Hasdai tells us that this land is called *al-Andalus* in the language of the Arabs, the dominant group therein, who have their capital at Cordova. This Abd-ar-Rahman is greater than any king who ever lived. He is the *amir al-mu'minina*, "the commander of the faithful," and Hasdai specifically asks God to be propitious to him.[51] Would not these highly positive statements about Abd-ar-Rahman on the part of Hasdai have made Western Christians think that the Jews were in league with the Muslims?

But, more specifically, Hasdai tells us that when God saw the misery, agony, and helplessness of his people Israel throughout the world, he inspired Hasdai to be so bold as to present himself before the caliph and inclined the caliph's heart toward Hasdai. God did this, we are told, because he is merciful toward his people Israel, the Jewish people, and because he remembers his covenant with the patriarchs (Abraham, Isaac, and Jacob), the fathers of the Jewish people. After Abd-ar-Rahman accepted Hasdai into his loyal service, Hasdai continues, the poor of the Jewish flock were exalted to safety. All the oppressors of the Jews stayed their hands and refrained from any further persecution of God's people. Thus, God, in his mercy, lightened the yoke which Israel was bearing in the Diaspora by inspiring Abd-ar-Rahman to accept Hasdai into his employ.[52] Would not these statements by Hasdai have sounded to Franco-German Christians like a description of the Judaeo-Islamic alliance?

Another example of the same is mentioned a bit further into Hasdai's letter when he tells us that Abd-ar-Rahman has collected a very large treasure of silver and gold, such as no king has ever collected. Indeed, the caliph's yearly revenue amounts to the immense sum of about 100,000 gold pieces! Most of this is derived from tariffs on imports from the various countries of the Mediterranean, especially Islamic Egypt (the very country where the persecution of Christians circa 1010 simultaneously triggered a great international persecution of the Jews of Western Europe). Who supervises the collection of the tariffs from these foreign merchants? Hasdai of course![53] Thus, a Jewish minister of state, by his own admission, is responsible for the financial support of the Islamic war-machine in Spain, which is surely a scandalous thorn in the side of Western Christendom, if it is not much more, *i.e.*, a direct threat to the very existence of Western Christendom itself.

Additional examples of what would sound to Western Christians like a description of the Jewish-Islamic alliance are mentioned a bit further into Hasdai's letter when he tells us who first informed him of the existence of an independent Jewish kingdom called Khazaria. Hasdai always asked the ambassadors sent to the court of the caliph of Cordova by the Holy Roman and Byzantine emperors if they had ever heard about an independent Jewish kingdom anywhere in the world (*e.g.*, the Lost Ten Tribes mentioned by Eldad). The ambassadors of these Christian powers, who said that they knew of no such kingdom, could have been sincere, or could merely have been pretending ignorance. It was *Islamic* (or possibly Islamicized Jewish) merchants (rather than the Christian ambassadors) who *first* informed Hasdai about the independent Jewish kingdom. These merchants came from the land of Khurasan (northeastern Iran, which at the time of the First Crusade was considered a heartland of the Islamic anti-Christian world conspiracy).[54] A little later in the letter Hasdai tells us that Islamic caravans proceed from Khurasan, from Bardha'ah (a city between Baku and Tiflis, just south of the Kura River), and from Bab al-Abwab (*i.e.*, Darband, a city just north of Baku, on the Caspian Sea) into the neighboring land of this independent Jewish kingdom of Khazaria. All of these three place names near Khazaria—Khurasan, Bardha'ah, and Bab al-Abwab—whence the caravans come, are Islamic in sound. Thus, from Hasdai's letter it becomes clear that this independent Jewish kingdom is adjacent to the lands of the Islamic East and is in close commercial contact with them.[55] Finally, when Hasdai attempted to send Mar Isaac the son of Nathan as a messenger to the Khazars via Byzantium, the Byzantine emperor detained him, though treating him honorably and including him among the regular ambassadors of the caliph of Cordova to Byzantium.[56] Thus, in the letter of Hasdai to Joseph, *Muslims*, not Christians, are the first to tell

141

Hasdai about the independent Jewish kingdom of Khazaria. This kingdom is geographically and commercially linked not with Christian but rather with *Islamic* countries in the Middle East. Hasdai's messenger to this kingdom is treated by a great Christian ruler (the Byzantine emperor) as an ambassador not of a Jewish but rather of an *Islamic* potentate, *i.e.*, the caliph of Cordova. What more would Western Christians have needed to confirm their worst suspicions about a Jewish-Islamic alliance directed against them?

In the reply to Hasdai by Joseph, the Khazar khan, there are two passages which would confirm Western Christian suspicions of a Jewish-Islamic alliance.

Joseph's reply to Hasdai contains the famous story of how Khan Bulan was approached by both the Christians and the Muslims, each religious group attempting to convert the Khazars to its own respective faith. The way this story develops is as follows. On the third day, in the presence of the entire Khazar nation, the Christian priest is asked which religion, Judaism or Islam, he ranks second to Christianity. He chooses Judaism. Immediately thereafter the Muslim qadi is asked which religion, Judaism or Christianity, he ranks second to Islam. He too chooses Judaism.[57] However, immediately above in this same letter there is a description of a private audience between the khan and the Christian priest on the first day, and a similar private audience between the khan and the Muslim qadi on the second day.[58] In the account of the way each non-Jewish missionary spoke when he stood before the khan *alone* (rather than in the presence of the entire Khazar nation) there are important hints of a Jewish-Islamic alliance.

To begin with, on the first day, when Bulan asked the Christian priest which religion is "better," Judaism or Islam, the priest does not state explicitly that Judaism is "better" than Islam. He merely says that no religion in the whole world can be compared to Judaism.[59] But the Islamic qadi, on the second day, when asked by the khan which religion is "better," Judaism or Christianity, does state explicitly and in so many words that Judaism is "better" than Christianity.[60] The Christian avoids a direct answer to the khan's question. The Muslim makes a clear choice between the two pre-Islamic monotheistic faiths and chooses Judaism over Christianity without hesitation as the religion to be ranked second in God's sight after Islam. Thus, to Western Christians, this aspect of the private audiences of the first and second days would have sounded as follows. In a Jewish document a Christian will not clearly state that Judaism is superior to Islam, but a Muslim will clearly state that Judaism is superior to Christianity. The Muslim is more willing to accept Jewish religious superiority than is the Christian. Therefore, the Jews (as can be seen from their own document) must be on the side of the Muslims against the Christians.

Second, in private audience with the Khan the priest merely praises Judaism; he does not attack Islam.[61] But when asked to compare Judaism and Christianity in his private audience, the Muslim qadi not only praises Judaism; he also attacks Christians as eaters of unclean animals (and/or of animals slaughtered without the *bismillah*, *i.e.*, without solemnly pronouncing the name of God over the animals as they are being slaughtered; pronouncing the name of God over the animal to be slaughtered is something Jews and Muslims do, but not Christians) and as idol worshippers (because, unlike Jews and Muslims, the Christians allow the use of paintings and even sculpture in worship, *e.g.*, icons and crucifixes).[62] Thus, again, to Western Christians this aspect of the private audiences would have sounded more or less as follows. In a Jewish document Muslims are allowed to attack Christians theologically, but Christians are not allowed to attack Muslims theologically. Therefore, the Jews (as it emerges from their own literature) must be on the side of the Muslims against the Christians.

Finally, after the priest and qadi conclude their respective private audiences, Khan Bulan responds to the priest by saying merely "thus you have spoken your words."[63] However, the Khan responds to the Muslim qadi "you have already told me the truth."[64] Thus, a third time, to Western Christians, this aspect of the private audiences would have sounded more or less as follows. When both the Christian and the Muslim acknowledge Jewish superiority, the Jew considers the Christian's acknowledgment mere "words" but the Muslim's acknowledgment "truth." Does this not show, Western Christians could well have thought, that the Jew really favors the Muslim and is in league with him against the West?

The second passage in Joseph's reply to Hasdai which would have confirmed Western Christian suspicions of a Jewish-Islamic alliance occurs at the end of a description by Joseph of the strategic geographical location of his independent Jewish country. Joseph tells us that his country controls the mouth of the Volga River and that he regularly wages grievous wars against the Russians. Why does Joseph fight the Russians? According to Joseph's reply to Hasdai the reason is to prevent them from laying waste the entire land *of the Muslims* as far south as *Bagdad*[65] Thus, the Khazar attitude toward the Russians is based on a desire to protect *the Muslims* with their great city of Bagdad, the seat of the Eastern Islamic caliphate! Does not this fact, then, Western Christians might well have reasoned, prove once again the existence of the international Jewish-Islamic world conspiracy? At present the eastern branch of this world conspiracy is attacking the pagan Russians. But suppose that the eastern Jewish(Khazar)-Islamic conspiracy is able to break through the pagan Russian buffer and invade Ottonian Germany, the Holy Roman Empire. Suppose also that such an invasion can be coordinated with a similar invasion of Carolingian France by the troops of the western Jewish-Islamic conspiracy, represented by the caliph of Cordova, Abd-ar-Rahman, and his Jewish foreign minister, Hasdai ibn Shaprut. Would not such a two-pronged Islamic invasion mean the end of Western Christendom? Would not this soon be followed by the end of Eastern Christendom (for the Muslims would then be able to attack Byzantium from the rear, from Franco-Germany and the Balkans, as well as from the front, from Syria) and the complete victory of the heresy of Muhammad over the truth of Christ everywhere on the face of the globe?

*****

How could information about the compromising contents of these three Jewish historical works—Eldad the Danite, Nathan the Babylonian, and the epistolary exchange between Hasdai and Joseph—have reached French and German Christians in the late tenth or early eleventh century? Geographically, the line of transmission probably went from Kairawan to Muslim Spain to Christian Spain to southern France to northern France, and thence to Germany. But an alternate route may also have existed that went from Muslin Spain to Germany via Byzantium.

We know that Hasdai himself was familiar with the work of Eldad the Danite, for he mentions Eldad quite prominently at the end of his letter to Joseph.[66] Hasdai calls Eldad a man of understanding (*n'von davar*) who spoke pure Hebrew and was able to call everything by its proper name in that language. When Eldad discussed halachic (*i.e.,* Jewish religiolegal) questions, he always claimed that he was relying upon the tradition which he received from Othniel the son of Kenaz, who received it from Joshua, who received it from Moses, who received it from God himself. Hasdai's description of Eldad is loaded with messianic symbols. These include the reference to "pure" Hebrew, as well as to the three greats of the Jewish past, Othniel, Joshua, and Moses, who are associated in the Bible with military might and prophecy, characteristics of the final redemption of the Jewish people. Hence, Hasdai's mention of Eldad in this context probably means that Hasdai was really asking the Khazars if they could be that portion of the Lost Ten Tribes who Eldad said lived near Persia. It is also likely from the context of Hasdai's letter (the nineteen lines which follow the mention of Eldad, which are also the final nineteen lines of the letter as a whole[67]) that Hasdai believed the final redemption would be ushered in partly through the help of the Lost Ten Tribes. Armed to the teeth, they would invade the Islamic and Christian lands, overthrow their governments, free the Jewish people from the bondage of exile, and lead them back home again in triumph to Palestine.

If Hasdai knew the work of Eldad, it is also highly likely that he knew the work of Nathan the Babylonian, which also was originally written in Kairawan, about 50 to 75 years after the time of Eldad. In part one of his chronicle[68] Nathan, like Eldad, describes Jewish power here on earth. He glorifies the Babylonian exilarch, the head of the Jewish community of Arab Iraq, as a veritable king within his own community, considered by tradition a descendant of King David, like the Messiah himself.[69]

From Muslim Spain, then, information about the contents of the three works together, Eldad, Nathan the Babylonian, and the Hasdai/ Joseph correspondence, could easily have traveled north to Christian Spain, thence over the Pyrenees to France and Germany (via Alsace-Lorraine). One way this could have happened is as follows. Hasdai, as foreign minister of the caliph of Cordova, had frequent diplomatic dealings with the minor Christian potentates of northern Spain in the 950s (especially of Leon and Navarre).[70] He was quite successful at pitting them against each other and subjecting them to caliphal influence. It seems likely that while carrying out caliphal diplomatic policy vis-à-vis the various Christian potentates of northern Spain during the mid-tenth century, Hasdai could well have leaked information to them about the Jewish-Islamic alliance as described in Eldad, Nathan, and his own correspondence with Joseph (circa 955). He would have done this to enhance the importance of the Jewish people in the eyes of the Christians of northern Spain so that they would deal more readily and respectfully with him, a Jewish agent of the caliph. These northern Spanish Christian potentates could easily have transmitted any information given them by Hasdai about the Jewish-Islamic alliance over the Pyrenees to the Christian political leadership of France, who, in turn, could have transmitted it to their counterparts in Germany.[71]

Or material about the Judaeo/Islamic alliance could have reached Germany more directly via John of Gorz. John was the ambassador of the Holy Roman emperor (Otto I) to the caliph of Cordova in the 950s, and John praised Hasdai's diplomatic skills to the skies.[72] Apparently the two, Hasdai and John (a monk), had significant diplomatic (and perhaps even theological) discussions. It seems likely, again, that in the course of such discussions Hasdai told John about the Jewish-Islamic alliance as described in Eldad, Nathan, and the Hasdai/Joseph correspondence for the same reason that he would have leaked information about the Jewish-Islamic alliance to the various Christian potentates of northern Spain. John of Gorz, then, could easily have related this material to the Holy Roman emperor (Otto I). From the emperor it could have spread to the various German nobles and high ecclesiastics, thence to their counterparts in northern France.

A third way the material about the Jewish-Islamic alliance could have reached the Christian ruling classes in Franco-Germany was via the Jewish messengers (Saul, Joseph, and Isaac the son of Eliezer) who carried Hasdai's letter to Khazaria circa 955 (via Germany, Hungary, Russia, and the Volga Bulgars).[73] These messengers may well have leaked some of the contents of the Hasdai/Joseph correspondence accidentally or purposefully at this time or a later date and have reiterated the material about the Jewish-Islamic alliance from Eldad and Nathan. They may have done so to magnify and exalt the power and prestige of Hasdai (as the caliph of Cordova's foreign minister) in the eyes of the Germans and other non-Jewish peoples through whose lands they passed. In so doing they may have felt that the Germans would assuredly have to negotiate with Hasdai now. Soon, after Hasdai entered into communication with the Khazars, the Jewish-Islamic alliance would be able to attack the Germans, if that should prove necessary or desirable, on two fronts, from the west (Spain) and the east (Khazaria). Of course, it is also possible that the success of Hasdai's plans required secrecy. However, this is doubtful because Hasdai's letter itself tells how he would always ask emissaries to the caliph of Cordova from Christian Germany and Byzantium if they knew anything about the Lost Ten Tribes.[74] Apparently Hasdai did not mind if the Christians knew what his intentions were in this regard. On the contrary, he probably used the fear of a Jewish-Islamic alliance, which seemed like a genuine possibility at that time, as a means of exerting pressure on the Christians to refrain from mistreating the Jews living in their midst.

A fourth way the material about the Jewish-Islamic alliance could have reached the Christian ruling classes of Franco-Germany was indirectly, via the Byzantine emperor. Hasdai is generally believed to have been the person who intervened circa 948 to stop the persecution of the Jews in the Byzantine Empire, including southern Italy, instigated by Emperor Romanus Lecapenus (coruler with Constantine VII Porphyrogenetos) in the 930s.[75] On the occasion of this intervention it is highly likely that Hasdai used the material about the Jewish-Islamic alliance (based on Eldad and Nathan) to persuade the Byzantine emperor to relax the pressure upon the Jews. What other leverage would Hasdai have had to save his coreligionists in the Byzantine Empire from persecution? Hasdai could have threatened to launch a major persecution of the Christians in Muslim Spain in retaliation if the Byzantine emperor did not relax the pressure on the Jews. However, such a threat would not have been very effective since the Christians of Muslim Spain were Latin Christians by historical tradition, owing spiritual allegiance to Rome. The Byzantines would not have been as concerned about their welfare as about the welfare of Greek Orthodox Christians owing spiritual allegiance to Constantinople. In view of the fact that the Byzantines were seeking an alliance with the caliph of Cordova (against the Fatimids and/or Ottonian Germany), leaking information about the Jewish-Islamic alliance (from Eldad and Nathan) would have been the best means available whereby Hasdai could persuade the Byzantines to relax their pressure on the Jews.

Further, Hasdai's letter (circa 955) to Joseph tells us that the first ambassador Hasdai sent to the Khazars, Mar Isaac the son of Nathan, set out for Khazaria via Byzantium. Upon arriving in Byzantium (circa 948), he was detained by the emperor himself (Constantine VII Porphyrogenetos, who reigned until 959) for six months and then sent home to Muslim Spain.[76] During the six months that Mar Isaac was detained in Byzantium, he could well have related information about the Jewish-Islamic alliance (from Eldad and Nathan) to the Byzantine emperor himself and/or Christian political and ecclesiastical leaders in Byzantium, hoping that this material would be efficacious in persuading them to allow him to continue on his way to Khazaria. Mar Isaac could have reasoned that this material about the Jewish-Islamic alliance could help persuade the Byzantines that to continue to detain him would be an insult not only to the Jews but to their far more powerful Muslim allies as well. However, such information may have had the opposite effect. Fear of a combined Western Jewish-Islamic alliance joining forces with the Khazars of the Caucasus against Byzantium may have reinforced the determination of the Byzantine emperor to prevent Mar Isaac from reaching Khazaria and to send him back to Muslim Spain instead.

Further, Emperor Constantine VII Porphyrogenetos sent several diplomatic missions to the caliph of Cordova circa 947–952 (as well as a Greek copy of the medical work of Dioscorides, along with the monk Nicholas to help translate it into Arabic, via Latin, with the aid of Hasdai the son of Shaprut and several Muslim scholars).[77] It is highly possible that Hasdai used these opportunities to reiterate material about the Jewish-Islamic alliance (from Eldad and Nathan) to the Byzantine ambassadors in order to strenghthen his own hand in dealing with them on behalf of the caliph of Cordova. From the Byzantine emperor news about the Jewish-Islamic alliance could easily have reached the German area, because the Byzantines were in diplomatic contact with the Holy Roman Emperor Otto I.[78] From Otto I information about the Jewish-Islamic alliance could have spread to the German nobles and high ecclesiastics, thence to their counterparts in nothern France.

*****

The chronicle of Ahima'atz revolves around the life and work of five prominent Jews in southeastern Italy, the beautiful and romantic land of Apulia. All of these five Jewish leaders, whose dates extend from circa 850 to 1000, are described as entering into relationships with the Arabs, some of which might sound quite suspicious to any Franco-German Christians who heard about them. The five prominent Jews in question are the following:

148

1. Aaron of Bagdad, circa 850;
2. Sh'fatyah the son of Amittai, also circa 850;
3. Hananel II (son of Paltiel I), circa 925;
4. Paltiel II (son of Kassia II, grandson of Paltiel I), circa 950; and
5. Samuel II (son of Paltiel II), circa 1000.

All of these notables except Aaron of Bagdad were members of the same family, the family to which the author of the chronicle of Ahima'atz also belonged circa 1050.

(1) Aaron of Bagdad would have seemed to Franco-German Christians to be pro-Arab. He left Bagdad around the time of the persecution of the Jews by Caliph al-Mutawakkil, circa 850, and remained in southern Italy until circa 870, the beginning of the reign of Byzantine Emperor Basil I, who severely persecuted the Jews in the 880s. (2) Sh'fatyah the son of Amittai would have seemed anti-Arab, a position which he adopted at least partly in order to save the Jews of Oria from Byzantine persecution under Emperor Basil I. (3) Hananel II would not have seemed pro-Arab, for he was seized by Arab raiders at Oria and taken to Tunisia, where he sought and received permission from the Arab ruler to return home to southern Italy *via Byzantium*. (4) Paltiel II would have seemed pro-Arab, for he loyally served the Fatimid rulers in Sicily, North Africa, and Egypt in very high position. Finally, (5) Samuel II, the son of Paltiel II, would also have seemed pro-Arab, because he followed in his father's footsteps by serving the Fatimids in high position.

Thus, of the five, three would have seemed pro-Arab—Aaron, Paltiel, and Samuel—while two would not: Sh'fatyah and Hananel. What is more, those whose careers would have seemed pro-Arab come at the beginning and end of the chronicle (*i.e.*, Aaron and then Paltiel and Samuel), all the more effectively obscuring the lives and work of the two middle Jewish personalities, Sh'fatyah and Hananel, who were not pro-Arab. On the whole, therefore, the impression which Franco-German Christians would have received from the data presented in the chronicle of Ahima'atz about the five was that the Jews were allies of the Arabs, in league with them against the Christian world, both East and West.

1. There is considerable material in the story of Aaron of Bagdad, circa 850-870, which would have confirmed the suspicions of Franco-German Christians that the Jew was an ally of the Muslim. This material can easily be grouped under four main headings: (a) Aaron's

origin in Arab Iraq, *i.e.*, in Bagdad, the seat of the Abbasid caliphate; (b) his white or good magic in Italy; (c) his "Arab-like" harshness in the application of the Jewish penal code; and (d) Aaron and the "Saudan," *i.e.*, the Arab governor of Bari, circa 870.

A. Aaron's origin in Arab Iraq, *i.e.*, Bagdad, the seat of the Abbasid caliphate.[79] Aaron came from Bagdad, whose Jews are called "beloved." He was an esteemed man, of distinguished family (perhaps the son of the Exilarch Samuel, 773-816[80]), an illustrious scholar. Before Aaron left Iraq, he is said to have harnessed a lion to his mill to turn the grinding stones (this lion had previously killed the mule which had formerly done such work for Aaron). Aaron's father accused him of humiliating the lion, "king of the beasts," and of breaking the lion's strength. We suspect that the "lion" here stands either for the Jewish "king," *i.e.*, the exilarch (believed to be descended from King David), head of the semiautonomous Jewish millet in the Abbasid caliphate, or for the Arab "king," the Abbasid caliph himself (al-Mutawakkil, who persecuted the Jews circa 850[81]). Aaron could have incurred the severe displeasure of either ruler because of some insulting remarks against them or by becoming involved in conspiracies (real or imagined) against them. Aaron's father sent him into exile for three years because Aaron had broken the lion to the mill. The exile went to southern Italy via Jaffa in *Arab* Palestine, not via Byzantium (even though southern Italy, Aaron's destination, had long been Byzantine dominated). This particular of the story probably would have served as a reconfirmation to Western Christians of Aaron's Arab connections and associations.

B. Aaron's white or good magic in Italy.[82] From Jaffa, Aaron sailed to Gaeta, a southwestern Italian port just north of Naples, where there was considerable sentiment for collaboration with the Arabs during the ninth century.[83] At Gaeta, Aaron restored to human form the son of a Spanish Jewish merchant. This young man had been transformed into a mule by a local sorceress. However, Aaron did not put to death the witch who had transformed the young man. This particular of the story might have indicated to Western Christians that the Jews were too lenient toward the practitioners of black magic. Aaron did put Jews to death for serious crimes against Jewish law. However, the sorceress may have been a non-Jew, and this may have been the reason why Aaron could not punish her.

From Gaeta, Aaron traveled inland to Benevento, where he discovered that the highly esteemed young cantor of the local synagogue,
who had such a beautiful voice but who stopped short of pronouncing
the name of God in the liturgy, was actually a living dead person.[84]
Upon hearing the young cantor tell his story (which story some scholars
consider a very early version of the legend of the Wandering Jew[85])
and accepting his confession of sin, Aaron drew out of the youth's
lifeless body whatever shadow of the human soul was unnaturally left
therein and gave him a decent burial. Again we have the image of the
Jew as magician; albeit this time his magic is on the side of good and
right. Yet this Jewish practitioner of the magic arts did come from the
land of the Arabs and travel to Italy by way of Muslim Palestine and
semicollaborationist Gaeta rather than by way of solidly Christian and
anti-Arab Byzantium. Could not the Christians of Franco-Germany
who heard this story have concluded that the Jews, the Arabs, and the
magical arts were all intimately bound together?[86]

C. Aaron's "Arab-like" harshness in the application of the Jewish
penal code.[87] When Aaron finally reached Oria (between Brindisi and
Taranto), he set up a school for higher Jewish learning. As a leading
authority on Jewish law, criminal cases were referred to him for decision. Aaron was a veritable "hanging judge," merciless in the application of the death penalty. Indeed, he is said to have applied all four
of the traditional types of death penalty provided by Jewish law, *i.e.*,
death by strangulation, the sword, stoning, and burning. An adulterer
(a Jew with the Greek name of Theophilus) was condemned to death
by the sword (*i.e.*, beheading); a man who had fallen into idolatry was
condemned to death by stoning; and a man who had committed incest
(with his mother-in-law) was condemned to death by burning. If Aaron
was able to carry out these death penalties (for it is always possible that
our chronicle was exaggerating), this would seem to indicate his awe-
inspiring (almost prophetic and messianic) charismatic power and
authority over non-Jews as well as his own people for the following
reasons.

By the ninth century, Aaron's lifetime, there generally was considerable opposition from the non-Jewish governments (Muslim and
Christian), and from many members of the Jewish community itself,
to the imposition of the death penalty by Jewish religious courts. The
non-Jewish governments were opposed to the imposition of the death

penalty by Jewish religious courts because the right to impose that penalty gave these courts too much power. The theory was that the more power the Jewish religious courts and the Jewish people exercised in the Diaspora, the less likely were the Jews to convert to either Islam or Christianity. Many Jews were also opposed to the imposition of the death penalty by Jewish religious courts because the Jews were a persecuted minority in non-Jewish lands. Every member of the group was badly needed in order to insure its survival. The community as a whole could not really afford the luxury of executing its own members, no matter how great their sin or crime.[88] Aaron of Bagdad was apparently able to overcome such opposition from both non-Jews and Jews if he was able to apply the death penalty. However, Aaron's striking imposition of all four types of death penalty might have reconfirmed the suspicion in the mind of Western Christians that he was indeed a close associate of the Arabs, whom Christians generally considered models of cruelty and savagery.[89] What other kind of behavior could have been expected (these Christians might well have reasoned) from a Jew hailing from an Arab land, a land ruled by the same cruel and savage people now ruling much of formerly all-Christian Spain and formerly all-Christian Sicily?

D. Aaron and the "Saudan," the Arab governor of Bari, circa 870.[90] After an interval of several pages, the chronicle of Ahima'atz resumes the story and concludes it in a way which clearly seems to associate Jew with Muslim. In the midninth century, our chronicler tells us, the Arabs invaded the lands of the Christians (here called "uncircumcised idolaters"), advancing up through Calabria (the foot of the Italian boot) into Apulia (the heel of the Italian boot). Bari, the great seaport on the Adriatic, fell to the Arabs in 849. Thereafter Aaron of Bagdad moved to the city. When the Arab commander, whom our chronicler very vaguely calls "Saudan," heard about this, he came to visit Aaron and bestowed a great honor upon him. Indeed, Aaron stayed with the "Saudan" for six months. During this time the "Saudan's" love for Aaron was more wonderful, so we are told, than the love of men for women. The "Saudan" sought Aaron's counsel on numerous occasions and never swerved therefrom. Aaron's advice to the "Saudan" was clear. Indeed, it seemed almost as if it had resulted from a consultation with the priestly Urim and Thumim of the Old Testament (i.e., seemed almost inspired by God).

However, Aaron began to be moved by severe feelings of nostalgia for his home in Iraq. Without telling the "Saudan," he went down to the dock. There he found a ship ready to set sail for Arab Egypt and immediately booked passage thereon. As the ship moved out into the harbor, the "Saudan," having discovered that Aaron had left him, sent his own vessels after the ship. The Arab could not bear to part with his trusted Jewish advisor and may also have feared that Aaron's departure would make it more difficult to keep the Jews of southeastern Italy on his side in the struggle against the Christians. Since Aaron wanted to go back home to Arab Iraq, he stopped the pursuing ships from gliding over the waves by pronouncing the ineffable name of the Lord against them. Then the sailors on board Aaron's ship, upon realizing that they were carrying a fugitive, decided to turn back toward the dock. However, the power of the ineffable name also prevented them from returning. When the "Saudan" saw what had happened, his anger at Aaron's betrayal of their friendship subsided. He realized that something greater than the merely mortal was at work here.

Finally, the "Saudan" called out to Aaron: "My master, my master, my father, my father, my cavalry and my chariots, why hast thou left and forsaken me?" The "Saudan" is quoted here by the chronicle of Ahima'atz as applying the same terminology to Aaron of Bagdad that Elisha had applied to his own teacher, Elijah, when Elijah was taken bodily up into Heaven (2 Kings 2:12). So great was the "Saudan's" esteem for Aaron! Of course, we have here a clear case of the association of Jew with Muslim by medieval Jews in that an Arab quotes the Jewish scriptures to a Jew and considers a medieval Jew to be the equivalent of the Prophet Elijah, the forerunner of the Messiah. The "Saudan" continued by promising to give Aaron all of his wealth if he would only return to him. Aaron responded that the good Lord had already made an irrevocable decision that he should return home. However, Aaron said he would answer any questions which the "Saudan" would care to ask him. The "Saudan" then proceeded to ask Aaron many questions, the last of which was whether the "Saudan" would succeed in entering the powerful inland Christian fortress-city of Benevento (half way to Naples). To this question Aaron replied: "Yes [you will enter it], but not willingly [not b'ratzon]; rather, you will enter it only under compulsion [b'ones; i.e., as a prisoner]." Indeed, so our chronicler tells us, what happened to the "Saudan" was precisely what Aaron had predicted. Meanwhile, Aaron sailed away to Egypt, thence returning home to Arab Iraq, where, apparently, he lived happily ever after.

How would this final fourth story about Aaron of Bagdad in the chronicle of Ahima'atz have sounded to Franco-German Christians? The first part, about Aaron's six-month stay with the "Saudan" in Bari as the "Saudan's" chief advisor, would clearly have been taken as a definite association of Jew with Muslim, a clear indication that the Jews were in league with the Muslims and that the two Semitic groups were close allies in the struggle against the West.

The second part of the story, wherein Aaron fled the "Saudan," might not seem to associate Jew with Muslim quite as much. However, Aaron did return to Arab Iraq via Arab Egypt. Further, the "Saudan" made every effort to bring Aaron back after Aaron had sailed out to sea, and he even quoted the Jewish scriptures to Aaron in considering him the equivalent of the Prophet Elijah, the forerunner of the Messiah. These facts would seem to associate Jew with Muslim and to indicate that the Muslims prefer to be in permanent league with the Jews, even if the Jews occasionally, on the surface at least, appear reluctant to accommodate them. Of course, the fact that Aaron predicted the "Saudan's" defeat in the siege of Benevento, rather than his victory, would seem to indicate a dissociation of Jew and Muslim. Indeed, this may be why Aaron decided to return home. He foresaw that Arab power in southeastern Italy would soon be broken by a joint Franco-Byzantine Reconquista in 871. However, the language Aaron uses in the chronicle to predict the Arab defeat is so equivocal that it might not necessarily have led northern European Christians to any clear and distinct conclusion that the two groups, the Jews as led by Aaron of Bagdad and the Arabs as led by the "Saudan" of Bari, had definitely come to a parting of the ways. Christians in France and Germany would probably have remembered the first part of the story, Aaron's six-month stay with the "Saudan" as his chief counselor, rather than the second part of the story, Aaron's departure. Aaron's departure was under rather miraculous circumstances. Christians might not have wanted to believe that a Jew could work such miracles with ships, preferring to think that only Christian saints could do so.

2. There is even some material in the story of Rabbi Sh'fatyah the

son of Amittai of Oria circa 850–870, as told in the chronicle of Ahima'atz, which would make it seem to Franco-German Christians as if the Jew was an ally of the Muslim, in league with him against the West. On the whole, however, the rabbi was anti-Arab and pro-Byzantine, a position which he was forced to adopt partly in order to save the Jews of Oria from Byzantine persecution during the reign of Emperor Basil I.

When the Byzantine Emperor Basil I (circa 867–886) ascended the throne by overthrowing the previous emperor, Michael III, he launched a severe persecution against the Jews of his realm. He was using anti-Semitism to consolidate his position after usurping the throne of the previous ruler and/or feared a Jewish fifth column as he began a great new offensive against the Arabs. Emperor Basil ordered the Jews to embrace Christianity, then summoned Rabbi Sh'fatyah, the leader of the Jewish community of Byzantine-dominated southeastern Italy, to Constantinople under a safe-conduct pass.[91] However, nothing the rabbi is described in the chronicle of Ahima'atz as doing in Constantinople could possibly give anyone the impression that the Jew was an ally of the Muslim or in league with him against the Christian world.

In Byzantium Rabbi Sh'fatyah entered into a theological discussion with the emperor on the relative merits of Christianity and Judaism. The rabbi defeated the emperor therein by demonstrating from the scriptures that the amount of money spent by kings David and Solomon on the construction of the First Temple in Jerusalem (circa 950 B.C.) exceeded the amount spent by Emperor Justinian on the Christian Hagia Sophia in Byzantium (circa 535 A.D.). The emperor then invited Rabbi Sh'fatyah to partake of refreshments at his own royal table, taking special pains to see to it that the food served the rabbi and the utensils in which it was served were both kosher. After refreshments, Rabbi Sh'fatyah exorcised an evil spirit from the emperor's daughter and put it into a leaden chest, sealing it up tight with the aid of the ineffable name of God and casting it into the sea. The emperor's response to the rabbi's exorcism was to attempt in a serious way to convert him to Christianity. He offered Rabbi Sh'fatyah a large bribe, ordering his aids to accompany the rabbi and put pressure upon him until he consented to convert. However, the rabbi refused to be intimidated and demanded the right to depart in peace. The emperor reluctantly granted Rabbi Sh'fatyah's request, and the queen, in gratitude for all that he had done for her daughter, gave him her two heavy gold earrings and her heavy golden girdle as gifts for his own two daughters.

The emperor offered the rabbi a parting gift for having come all the way from southeastern Italy to Byzantium. Whatever Rabbi Sh'fatyah wanted, whether money or towns, it did not matter to the emperor. However, the rabbi shocked the emperor by asking that as his gift the emperor stop persecuting the Jews throughout his realm and forcing them to embrace Christianity against their will. The emperor wanted to punish Rabbi Sh'fatyah for his insolence. However, he reminded himself that he had brought the rabbi to Byzantium under a safe-conduct pass, and the emperor felt morally obligated, despite everything, to honor that pass. So he consented to Rabbi Sh'fatyah's request in part, by exempting his home town, Oria, from the general persecution of the Jews then raging throughout the Byzantine Empire, and which continued to rage, we are told by the chronicler, for the full "twenty-five years" Basil I was in power (actually he only reigned 19 years, 867–886). Basil's son, Leo VI, came to power in 886 and halted the persecution, allowing the Jews of the empire to return unhindered to their ancestral faith.

Nothing specific in this story of the exploits of Rabbi Sh'fatyah the son of Amittai in Byzantium at the time of Emperor Basil I would have suggested to Franco-German Christians that the Jew was an ally of the Muslim or in league with him. However, northern European Christians who were especially well-informed about world affairs during the ninth and tenth centuries might well have imagined that one of the reasons why the Byzantine Emperor Basil I decided upon a severe persecution of the Jews was because he associated them with the Muslims and suspected them of being in league with the Muslims. However, they would essentially have had to come to such a conclusion upon the basis of evidence derived from other sources and then have had to read it into the story as told in the chronicle of Ahima'atz. Nothing specific in the story proper would necessarily have led them to this conclusion.

We suspect that one of the reasons Emperor Basil I did indeed launch a persecution against the Jews of his realm was because of real (or imagined) instances of Jewish collaboration with the Arabs on the Byzantine eastern Anatolian frontier during the reign of his predecessor, Michael III (842–868).[92] By the same token, Basil may have decided to exempt the Jews of Byzantine southeastern Italy (or some of them) from the persecution because they held the crucial balance of power between the Byzantines and the Arabs in that very strategic portion of the Mediterranean. The power that controlled the heel of the Italian boot could cut off communication by water between Byzantium and its western outposts, Venice and southern Italy/Sicily. If the Jews of southeastern Italy tipped the balance of power in strategic Apulia and the Straits of Otranto permanently in favor of the Arabs, the entire Byzantine western front against the Arabs would collapse. The Arabs could then cross the Straits with relative ease, seize Corfu and the Ionian islands (Levkas, Cephalonia, and Zante), and use them as bases for major attacks through the Gulf of Corinth on Athens and the Aegean itself, the very heartland of the Byzantine Empire.[93] Nothing was more important than retaining control of southeastern Italy at all costs. If that meant relaxing some or all of the pressure on the Jews of that area, such was indeed a small enough price to pay for the very safety of the empire itself. Indeed, this may have been precisely the argument that Rabbi Sh'fatyah used to persuade Emperor Basil I to exempt the Jews of Oria from the general persecution then raging throughout the Byzantine Empire. This geopolitical argument based on the balance of power which the Jews held in strategic southeastern Italy, rather than the exorcism of an evil spirit from the daughter of the emperor, may have been the main reason why Rabbi Sh'fatyah was successful in Byzantium when the emperor summoned him to answer for the Jews who dwelt in the crucially important heel of the Italian boot.

The next time Rabbi Sh'fatyah is mentioned in the chronicle of Ahima'atz we find him serving as an emissary from the Byzantine governor of Bari to the Arabs who had invaded southeastern Italy. We already have met the same Arabs supra, under their "Saudan," when they took Bari circa 849 and held it until circa 871. Aaron of Bagdad served them as advisor for six months before abandoning them to return home to Iraq.[94] The fact that Rabbi Sh'fatyah was sent as an emissary to the Arabs (by a Byzantine governor who regrouped his forces in Oria, the rabbi's city, after the fall of Bari to the Arabs) probably would have indicated to most Franco-German Christians that the Jews had a special affinity with the Arabs and that the reason the Jew was sent as emissary to the Arabs was because he knew their language and customs. Alternatively, some northern European Christians could have concluded that the Byzantine governor sent the rabbi as an emissary to the Arabs because he trusted him, and if the Byzantine governor trusted Rabbi Sh'fatyah, the latter could not have been in league with the Arabs. This alternative, however, might have been countered by the argument that perhaps the Byzantine governor made an error in judgment (after all, he was only a local governor, not the emperor himself) and put his trust in a person who was really loyal, not to him at all, but rather to his Arab enemies.

Indeed, when Rabbi Sh'fatyah reached the Arab camp, after setting out north from Oria toward Bari, the "Saudan" went out of his way to receive him with honor, speaking to him cordially and lavishing attention upon him in the presence of the "Saudan's" chief lieutenants. Apparently the "Saudan" insisted on detaining the rabbi indefinitely. According to the chronicle this was because the "Saudan" feared that if Rabbi Sh'fatyah returned to the Christian camp, he would reveal the Arab plan. The plan was to beguile Oria into submitting by offering to spare lives in exchange for tribute, them massacring all later and destroying the town. But how could the rabbi reveal their plan unless the Arabs had already shared it with him? Unless they had asked for his cooperation and that of the Jews of Oria, promising in return to spare them at the same time that they slew the Christians? If the chronicle can so easily be interpreted as indicating that the Arabs had shared their plan with the rabbi, would not it thereby have served to reconfirm the preexisting Franco-German equation of Jew with Muslim?

However, Rabbi Sh'fatyah, according to the chronicler, pondered the treachery the Arab commander was planning against the Christians and, after refusing to transfer to the Arab side, insisted upon the right to return to the Christian lines, even though it was very late Friday afternoon and the Jewish Sabbath was about to begin at sundown. The "Saudan" attempted to prevent the rabbi's departure by arguing that he would never reach home at Oria before dark. Since Jewish law prohibited travel on the Sabbath and punished the violation of that prohibition by death, if darkness should fall upon Rabbi Sh'fatyah while en route back home, he would forfeit his life. This particular of the story would have seemed very suspicious to northern European Christians. Why should an Arab commander have been so concerned lest a Jew violate the Jewish Sabbath unless Judaism and Islam were one and the same religion and in league with one another against the Christians?

However, Rabbi Sh'fatyah demanded the right to depart and told the Arab not to worry about the Jewish Sabbath. The "Saudan" finally relented. With the aid of the ineffable name of God, the rabbi's horse was able to gallop at unheard of speeds (while the very ground under its hooves contracted), so that the rabbi did indeed make it back home safe and sound before dark. When Rabbi Sh'fatyah reached Oria he cried out, as it were, "the Arabs are coming, the Arabs are coming" and urged the people to take refuge within the powerful walls of the citadel, perched atop the hill along whose slopes Oria was built. The rabbi went to the Byzantine governor of the city and reported faithfully everything that had transpired between himself and the "Saudan" in Bari. Thereupon Rabbi Sh'fatyah and the Byzantine governor took counsel together on how to defeat the Arabs if indeed they should attack Oria. Finally, the rabbi went home to his wife and children. He washed, bathed, and put on his finest festive garments, all in honor of the Sabbath that was about to commence and which the rabbi welcomed as was proper.

The next morning the Arabs approached the city. It was the Jewish Sabbath, and the besiegers probably hoped that the Jews would not fight on that holy day,[95] thus allowing the Arabs an easy victory over the Byzantines in the city. However, the enemy found the the Byzantines and Jews united and fully prepared for them inside the fortress. The Arabs decided that they were too few in number to launch a frontal attack against such a powerful position. Thereupon, according to the chronicle of Ahima'atz, the "Saudan" of the Arabs demanded that the Byzantines turn over Rabbi Sh'fatyah to him. The rabbi was alleged to have violated the Jewish Sabbath by traveling on that sacred day, when Jewish religious law forbade it. The "Saudan" wanted to make absolutely certain that the full letter of the Jewish law would be applied against Rabbi Sh'fatyah, who was supposed to set an example unto his community of faithfulness to the Mosaic law and the later Jewish tradition. Was this not a crystal clear example of the association of Jew with Muslim by medieval Jews, *i.e.*, by the author of the chronicle of Ahima'atz, reflecting prevailing Jewish attitudes in southeastern Italy at that time? Would not northern European (Franco-German) Christians who heard this story have been duly impressed? Would they not have concluded therefrom that Judaism and Islam were one and the same religion? In actual fact, of course, such was far from the case, especially since Islam's Friday Sabbath has far less of a rest element than Judaism's Saturday (or Christianity's Sunday) Sabbath. Would not Franco-German Christians have concluded from the story of how the "Saudan" wanted to impose the death penalty for a violation of the Jewish Sabbath that the Jews and Arabs were in league with each other, even though Rabbi Sh'fatyah served as a faithful emissary for the Byzantine governor?

In reality, the extraordinary concern shown in the story by the Arab commander for the sanctity of the Jewish Sabbath is probably only a fictional veil for what most likely really did happen. The "Saudan" probably demanded the head of the rabbi, the leader of the Jews, as the price for his departure from the city, in the hope that he would thus be able to drive a wedge between the two groups of defenders, turn Christian against Jew. He probably imagined either one of two possible scenarios. The Christians would turn Rabbi Sh'fatyah over to him, as the small price they would be all too willing to pay to be rid of the Arabs on this particular occasion. This act of betrayal would so incense the Jews that they would then secretly decide to attempt to surpass the Christians in the art of betrayal, as it were, by opening the gates of the citadel to the Arabs in revenge. Or the "Saudan" may have reasoned the other way around. The Jews would indignantly refuse to hear anything further about the outrageous idea of buying off the Arabs at the cost of the life of their great spiritual leader. The Christians, in revenge for the stubborn refusal of the Jews to sacrifice one single person for the good of the entire city, would turn against their Jewish allies and either massacre them or else drive them out of the city. The result would be that the Jews of southeastern Italy as a whole, now wavering between the Arabs and Byzantium, would go over en masse to the Arab side, once and for all, and the Byzantine position in the heel of the Italian boot would totally collapse, never to be rebuilt again.

The "Saudan's" plan was shrewd but it did not work. Rabbi Sh'fatyah explained to the "Saudan" that he had not violated the Jewish Sabbath, so says our chronicler, because with divine assistance the rabbi arrived home on time. The Arab commander had no other choice but to depart with his men. Again we would have a manifestation of the Judaeo/Islamic alliance—or so it would have seemed to northern European (Franco-German) Christians. Why else would a Jew explain his religious behavior to an Arab—over such a fundamental principle of Judaism as the observance of the Saturday Sabbath—unless the two non-Christian Semitic groups were truly one and the same, in league with each other against the Christians? What really happened in southern Italy at this time, in all probability, was that Rabbi Sh'fatyah was able to persuade both Christians and Jews inside the Oria citadel that the Arab commander was only trying to divide and conquer. If both groups, Christians and Jews, held firm and allowed nothing to disrupt their unity of purpose against the common enemy, the "Saudan's" forces were too weak to be able to do anything but retreat. Indeed, it may have been at this time of the "Saudan's" failure to win the Jews of Oria to his side by driving a wedge between them and the Christians that Aaron of Bagdad, then in the camp of the "Saudan" and serving as his advisor, decided to abandon the Arab side in southeastern Italy to return home to Iraq via Egypt.

Rabbi Sh'fatyah's persistent loyalty to the Byzantine side almost certainly was the price he paid for the exemption of the Jewish community (or a portion thereof) of southeastern Italy from Basil I's edict of forced conversion for the Jews of the empire. What the rabbi promised the emperor in person in Byzantium, i.e., Jewish loyalty to the Greek cause in the highly strategic area of the Straits of Otranto, he was able to deliver on the field of battle, as it were, in southeastern Italy. However, despite the clear loyalty of Rabbi Sh'fatyah to the Christian side, there were still certain particulars within his story as told by the chronicle of Ahima'atz that might have conveyed a contrary impression. The rabbi was sent as an emissary to the Arabs, presumably because he knew their language and customs. The Arab commander was exceedingly solicitous about the proper observance of the Jewish Sabbath. These particulars might have sounded quite suspicious to northern European (Franco-German) Christians. Despite all indications to the contrary in the story of Rabbi Sh'fatyah, they might have concluded that the Jews were really allies of the Muslims according to the testimony of the very literature of the Jews themselves.

3. There is little if any material in the story of Hananel II, son of Paltiel I, circa 925, as told in the chronicle of Ahima'atz, which would sound to northern European (Franco-German) Christians as if the Jew was an ally of the Muslim. There is hardly anything in the story of Hananel II to create the suspicion that the Jews were in league with the Muslims.[96]

Hananel II was seized by Arab raiders at Oria in southeastern Italy and taken captive to Tunisia, where he asked permission of the caliph of Ifrikiya (Tunisia) to return home to Italy via Byzantium. Hananel felt that he had to stop in Byzantium first in order to obtain the support of the Byzantine emperor for his desire to reenter southern Italy (a Byzantine sphere of influence) and to reclaim his property. It had been taken by other Jews who escaped the Arab attack on Oria by fleeing to other Byzantine held cities, north to Bari or south to Otranto.

Hananel II succeeded in obtaining permission from the caliph to travel to Byzantium. There he was able to persuade the Byzantine emperor to give him a sealed edict that would assist him in reentering Byzantine territory in southern Italy and in reclaiming his lost property.

This situation was finally resolved when Hananel II divided the property which he considered rightfully his own with the Jews of Bari who had fled with it from Oria. Hananel took the old (valuable) manuscripts of the scriptures and the women's robes (*m'ilim*). The other Jews kept the (gold?) ornaments from the women's robes.

How would this story of Hananel II have sounded to northern European Christians? On the whole we feel that it would have tended to exonerate the Jews by indicating that they were not in league with the Muslims.

Admittedly, the particular about Hananel beginning his journey back to Italy from *Arab* territory could have been held against him by northern European Christians if they forgot that he had been taken prisoner by the Arabs in the first place.

Further, the particulars that Hananel desired to leave Arab territory, and that the caliph of Ifrikiya was willing to allow him to leave, could have been interpreted by northern European Christians favorably to the Jews if they so chose to interpret. Under such an interpretation the particulars would have indicated that the Jew did not desire to serve the Arabs and the caliph did not desire the services of the Jew. However, these particulars could also have been interpreted unfavorably to the Jews if northern Europeans were so inclined. Under such an interpretation Christians would have assumed that the only reason the caliph allowed the Jew to leave Arab territory and return to southern Italy (via Byzantium) was because the Jew had secretly promised to serve as a spy for the Arabs.

However, the particular that the Byzantine emperor gave Hananel II a sealed edict allowing him to reenter Byzantine territory in southern Italy and to reclaim his lost property could not easily have been interpreted unfavorably to the Jews, even by the most suspicious of northern European (Franco-German) Christians. If northern European Christians would have been willing to accept this particular of the story of Hananel as fact, its interpretation would have been rather clear. It could hardly have been interpreted otherwise than as indicating that the Byzantine emperor himself did not consider Hananel II to be in league with the Arabs. If the Byzantine emperor did not suspect the presence here of any Jewish-Islamic alliance against the Christians, northern European Christians could have reasoned, there really could not have been such an alliance, at least in the specific case of Hananel II, the leader of the Jewish community of southern Italy circa 925.

4. The story of Paltiel II (son of Kassia II, grandson of Paltiel I), circa 950, as told in the chronicle of Ahima'atz, abounds with material which would have made it seem to northern European (Franco-German) Christians as if the Jew were an ally of the Muslim, in league with him against the West. This material can be grouped under eight main headings. (A) The Arab commander (here called al-Muizz) who took Oria circa 952 put the Christian inhabitants of the city to the sword. But he spared the descendants of the Jew Rabbi Sh'fatyah, especially Paltiel II, whom he took into his own service. (B) Paltiel, an accomplished astrologer, predicted from the stars that the Arab commander would become the ruler of a great (Fatimid) empire (including Sicily, North Africa, and Egypt). When these predictions came true for Sicily and North Africa, al-Muizz made the Jew Paltiel his vizier. (C) Paltiel won a victory over the Byzantine ambassador to the court of al-Muizz in North Africa. This ambassador would not deal at first with the Arab ruler's Jewish vizier. (D) Paltiel arranged all the details of his master al-Muizz's triumphal march across Libya to Egypt and entrance into Cairo as the new ruler of the land of the Pharaohs. (E) Paltiel became the vizier of al-Muizz's expanded empire and ruled the Middle East, including Syria-Palestine, for his master. (F) Upon the death of al-Muizz, circa 975, his son al-Aziz, who succeeded to the throne, retained the Jew Paltiel as his vizier. Together the two, Arab ruler and Jewish vizier, confounded the jealous Arab critics of Paltiel's administration. (G) Paltiel predicted from the stars the simultaneous death of three great rulers in the Mediterranean basin, one Christian (John of Byzantium) and two Muslim (Hakam, the Umayyad Caliph of Spain, and al-Muti, the Abbasid Caliph of Iraq.) But al-Aziz said that Paltiel would die at the same time as these other three rulers, because the Jew was

also a true king. (H) This heading describes the vast extent of the power wielded by the Jew Paltiel within the Islamic world.[97]

A. Circa 952, so the story in the chronicle of Ahima'atz goes, the Arabs attacked southern Italy in force, landing in Calabria and moving up from the foot of the Italian boot toward the heel.[98] When they reached Oria, they laid siege to this strategic inland city. When the siege had weakened the defenders in the powerful citadel, the Arabs successfully stormed the fortress and overcame the garrison. Most of the inhabitants of the city were massacred and the rest sold into slavery. However, the Arab commander (here called al-Muizz) spared the lives of the family of *Rabbi Sh'fatyah* (the same great Jewish personality who circa 867 had negotiated with the Byzantine Emperor Basil I and the Arab commander, the "Saudan" of Bari). This particular of the story would certainly have confirmed the suspicions of northern European Christians that the rabbi (circa 850–870), even though he sided with the Byzantines, was secretly sympathetic to the Arabs (and that is why the "Saudan" was so solicitous about his possible violation of the Jewish Sabbath). The most prominent member of the family of Rabbi Sh'fatyah then alive in Oria was Paltiel II. According to the chronicle, Paltiel II found favor in the eyes of the Arab commander, who bestowed kindness upon the Jew, "brought him into his tent, kept him at his side, and retained him in his service." Apparently the Arab commander was working for an alliance with the Jews of southeastern Italy circa 950, for the Jews continued to hold the balance of power between the Arabs and the Byzantines in that area. Paltiel II, the leader of the Jewish community of Oria, apparently was willing to work on behalf of such an alliance by entering the service of al-Muizz. If this part of the story reached northern European Christians, would it not have confirmed their worst suspicions about the Jewish-Islamic alliance?

B. As the chronicle of Ahima'atz continues with the story of Paltiel II, one night Paltiel, a skilled astrologer, went outside to observe the stars with al-Muizz.[99] As they were gazing at the heavens, they saw al-Muizz's star consume three others. Al-Muizz asked Paltiel how he interpreted this astrological phenomenon. Paltiel wisely turned the question around so that he could have the last word and asked al-Muizz instead how he interpreted it. Al-Muizz, very accommodatingly, allowed the Jew to protect himself in this way and went on to explain that he interpreted the astrological phenomenon to mean that he would conquer three additional southeastern Italian cities from the Byzantines: Taranto, Otranto, and Bari. Paltiel, very sagaciously, then gave his own interpretation of the stars, which was much more favorable and flattering to the Arab commander and his ego. According to Paltiel the three stars consumed by al-Muizz's were Sicily, North Africa, and finally Egypt—entire countries, not mere cities! Al-Muizz believed so completely in his Jewish astrologer that he began to rejoice then and there, as if he had already conquered the three countries in question. He embraced Paltiel, we are told, kissed him, and gave him his own ring, in the firm and unshakable belief that the words of his Jewish servant would come true.

And so they did! A mere seven days later word came from Sicily that upon the death of the local amir the Arab notables of the island had invited al-Muizz to rule over them. Sicily was his, without the use of force, offered to him, as it were, on a silver platter. The first part of Paltiel's prediction came true, as al-Muizz was certain it would, and the Arab ruler appointed Paltiel the master of his household. In actual fact the Fatimids began as the rulers of North Africa, then advanced north into Sicily (and southern Italy) and east to Egypt. However, the chronicle of Ahima'atz, true to its south Italian provenance, orientation, and patriotism, had the Fatimids begin in southern Italy, then move to Sicily and from there to North Africa and Egypt.[100] Nevertheless, this discrepancy between historical fact and the chronicle of Ahima'atz on this point would not have affected the way this portion of Ahima'atz's story would have sounded to northern European Christian ears. A Jew predicted that an Arab commander would become ruler of a vast empire, and this prediction began to come true almost immediately. The Arab believed implicitly in the Jew's predictions even before they came true, and when they began to come true, he quickly rewarded the Jew by making him master of his household. Would not these particulars of the continuing story of Paltiel II have provided further confirmation of the worst suspicions and fears of northern European Christians about the Jewish-Islamic alliance?

C. As the chronicle of Ahima'atz continues with the story of Paltiel II, al-Muizz, in fulfillment of the prediction which his Jewish advisor had made several years before, became the ruler of North Africa.[101] He left his brother behind to rule in Sicily but took his Jewish advisor, Paltiel, with him to North Africa and made him his vizier, second in power after himself. In this capacity Paltiel received all ambassadors to al-Muizz from foreign countries, including those sent from Christian lands. One day an ambassador came from Byzantium with gifts for al-Muizz and sought an audience with the Arab ruler. According to the chronicle of Ahima'atz the ambassador went into a state of shock when he learned that the vizier of al-Muizz was a Jew, whose advice the Arab ruler always followed. This Jew was in complete control of who did and did not see al-Muizz. The Greek ambassador threatened to go home forthwith, without delivering his gifts and conveying his message, if he was not allowed to see the Arab ruler immediately, without having to suffer the humiliation of first presenting his credentials to a Jew. Paltiel knew that he could not afford to antagonize the Byzantine ambassador too much, lest he depart and take with him any possibilities there might have been for a Byzantine-Fatimid alliance against their mutual enemies (the Umayyads of Spain and the Ottonians of Germany/Italy). On the other hand, he could not allow the religious prejudice of this Christian foreigner to undermine his own power and authority with the Arab ruler. Hence, Paltiel decided to proceed as follows in the matter.

He commanded that nobody at the Arab court have anything to do with the Byzantine ambassador until the Greek should modify his opinions. Thus, the Christian was not specifically told that if he was unwilling to see the Jewish vizier, he could not see the Arab ruler. Nor was he told the contrary. He was simply ignored. After putting up with this treatment for ten days, the Byzantine ambassador finally admitted his arrogance and religious intolerance and expressed a willingness to see the Jewish vizier. Even then Paltiel kept him waiting for two additional days before he would see him. Finally, on the thirteenth day the Byzantine ambassador was admitted into the presence of the Jewish vizier, who proceeded to dazzle him with the splendor of the Arab court, real and feigned. At the gate of his palace Paltiel greeted the Byzantine ambassador with lavish gifts, making whatever gifts the Greek wanted to present to the Arab ruler seem insignificant by comparison. Music, dancing girls, perfumes, and precious stones overwhelmed the Byzantine ambassador as he walked from the gate of Paltiel's palace to the dining hall. The walls and floors of the palace were covered with tapestries of silk, wool, scarlet, and linen, as well as with rugs of silk. The ambassador was asked to sit on a chair of gold. Then Paltiel deceived the ambassador by saying that everyday Paltiel washed his hands in a bowl of precious stones (onyx and jasper) which he broke immediately thereafter and discarded, while his master, al-Muizz, did the same. The Greek ambassador was forced to admit that the Byzantine court used less expensive golden bowls which, of course, it did not discard after each and every individual use.

The Jewish vizier had clearly won a great moral victory over the Byzantine ambassador for himself, and presumably for his Arab master as well. Thereafter the Greek left the court of al-Muizz, and we are not told whether he ever did see the Arab ruler. Apparently the Byzantine ambassador had been so deeply impressed by the Arab ruler's Jewish vizier that he considered a meeting with the Arab ruler himself to be superfluous and was happy to transact all his business with the Jew. Whatever chance there was for a Byzantine-Fatimid alliance was not lost. At the same time the power and authority of al-Muizz's Jewish vizier was not undermined. The Jew and the Arab here combined to put the Christian to shame by their joint wealth and splendor. The Arab had the real power and wealth, which the Jew used to dazzle and overwhelm the Christian. If this story about Paltiel and the Byzantine ambassador to the North African court of al-Muizz reached northern European Christians in France or Germany, how could it have helped but provide further confirmation of the Jewish-Islamic alliance against the Christians?

D. As the chronicle of Ahima'atz continues with the story of Paltiel II, thus far two of Paltiel's three predictions have come true about al-Muizz. The Arab commander already ruled both Sicily and North Africa. The only area which still remained beyond his control was Egypt. This land now fell into his power in a way that was very similar to the way he came into control of Sicily.[102] The last Ikshidid ruler of Egypt died, and the nobles decided to ask al-Muizz to take over the country for two main reasons: his military prowess and his wisdom. Again a land was al-Muizz's without the use of violence. Couriers were sent from Egypt to al-Muizz's headquarters in North Africa inviting him to rule over the land of the pharaohs. However, the problem which he faced was how to march his army across the harsh and barren terrain of Libya on his way from Tunisia to Egypt. Libya was believed to be completely lacking in water, food, and inns for the traveler. Who else could solve this problem but al-Muizz's brilliant Jewish vizier Paltiel? Paltiel did much more than merely build inns for travelers, which would only have been a temporary solution of the Libyan problem. He decided to take drastic action, *i.e.*, to civilize the entire Libyan area and turn it into a flourishing part of the new and expanded Fatimid empire. He set up merchant cities along the route from Tunisia to Egypt. These were the cities that harbored the army of al-Muizz as it moved eastward toward the land of the Nile.

When the new ruler's armies reached Cairo, they encamped three miles outside the city to await the homage of the people, both nobles and masses. Meanwhile, the task of securing the city of Cairo for the entry of the new ruler was assumed by Paltiel. He entered the city with a division of troops and stationed them at every strategic spot: on the walls, in the towers, in the private palaces and public buildings, at the gates, and in the suburbs. This massive show of force, maintained around the clock, day and night, made the safe entry of the new Egyptian ruler a total certainty. Once within the city, thanks to the two-fold effort of his Jewish vizier (who made possible both the march across the Libyan desert and the safe entry into the capital), al-Muizz received the homage of the Egyptian people. Here, then, we have the Jew Paltiel making possible the establishment of the Fatimid regime in what became its true heartland, Egypt. If this portion of the story of Paltiel II reached northern European Christians in France and Germany, how could it have helped but provide overwhelming confirmation of the Jewish-Islamic alliance?

E. As the chronicle of Ahima'atz continues with the story of Paltiel II, we are told that after the arrival of al-Muizz in Egypt, the Fatimid Empire now included Egypt, Palestine (the Holy Land), and Syria, all the way to the border of Iraq (the territory of the rival Abbasid caliphate).[103] Paltiel II, as al-Muizz's vizier, ruled over these territories for the caliph, including all of their inhabitants, whether Muslim, Christian, or Jew. But he also was head of the organized Jewish community or millet of the Fatimid realm. Such an exalted position, of course, brought Paltiel much eminence, power, and wealth, by which the Arab ruler chose to honor and distinguish him. Finally we are told that all of Paltiel's exploits were written down in the annals of the kingdom of Nof and Anamim, i.e., Egypt. Again, if these particulars of the story of Paltiel reached northern European Christians, they would have further confirmed their suspicions about the Jewish-Islamic alliance.

F. As the chronicle of Ahima'atz continues with the story of Paltiel II, we are told that when death claimed al-Muizz, the Fatimid ruler of Egypt (Sicily/North Africa and Syria/Palestine), his wishes that his son al-Aziz should succeed him were honored by the Egyptian nobility.

His wishes that his son retain the Jewish vizier Paltiel II were also honored.[104] Thus, the Jewish-Islamic alliance continued into the next generation. However, most of the Arab advisors of the caliph saw the transfer of rule from father to son as their opportunity to attempt to have the Jewish vizier replaced by an Arab Muslim. They slandered Paltiel to the new caliph. However, al-Aziz rejected their insinuations and rebuked them personally. Thus, the new ruler came to the verbal defence of his Jewish vizier against Arab detractors. What is more, al-Aziz told Paltiel about the slanders. The two of them took counsel together on how best to deal with the resentful Arab courtiers. They decided to silence their criticisms of Paltiel without depriving them of life, *i.e.*, in a nonviolent and relatively compassionate way. This was the plan which the two of them devised together.

Paltiel and his family and friends retreated to the lavish estate which the former caliph had given him and which the new caliph had been happy to allow him to retain. A few days later the caliph, feigning ignorance of Paltiel's whereabouts, asked where Paltiel had gone. Upon being told that his Jewish vizier had gone to his private estate, the caliph commanded his entire court, including Paltiel's enemies, to join him in a special trip to see the Jewish vizier, so highly did the caliph say he thought of Paltiel. The caliph, accompanied by his entourage, arrived at the estate and pretended that his visit was a complete surprise. He approached Paltiel, embraced him, kissed him (all in the presence of his enemies, the jealous Arab courtiers), took him by the hand and led him away from the others. Then everyone sat down for the entertainment, with the caliph and Paltiel occupying the seats of honor, everyone else, including Paltiel's enemies, off to the side. The entertainment was lavish and lasted the whole day: jesters; musicians playing viols, harps, pipes, timbrels, and cymbals; and singers. Then the caliph arose and rode back home to Cairo. The whole charade was perfectly calculated to exalt Paltiel and discredit his accusers. It worked brilliantly. From that time forth no Arab member of al-Aziz's court ever uttered a word against Paltiel so long as the Jewish vizier lived. In this spectacular way the caliph showed his great trust in, and affection for, his Jewish right hand. Thus, the Jewish-Islamic alliance continued in Egypt into the second generation. And for northern European Christians there would be further confirmation of their worst suspicions and fears that the Jew was in league with the Muslim.

G. As the chronicle of Ahima'atz continues with the story of Paltiel

II, we are told that one night Paltiel received a final opportunity to demonstrate his astrological skill.[105] He and the new caliph, al-Aziz, were walking in the open and saw three bright stars (the same number as Paltiel had seen with al-Aziz's father, al-Muizz, back in southern Italy many years ago). But this time, instead of a fourth star (that of the caliph) consuming the other three, the three stars suddenly disappeared completely. Paltiel did not ask the caliph for his interpretation of the astrological phenomenon first. Rather, the Jewish vizier did not hesitate a moment before giving his own interpretation thereof. The three stars represented three kings, all of whom would die within the year. According to Paltiel these rulers were John I Tzimisces of Byzantium (died 976); the Abbasid caliph of Bagdad (al-Muti, died 974); and the Umayyad caliph of Cordova (Hakam II, died 976).[106] Caliph al-Aziz, however, had a slightly different interpretation of whom the three disappearing stars represented. He agreed that two of the three stars represented respectively John of Byzantium and the Abbasid caliph of Bagdad. But he very sorrowfully had to state that in his view the third star was not the Umayyad caliph of Cordova but rather Paltiel himself.

In actual fact, seven important political leaders of the Mediterranean basin died around the very same time, *i.e.*, circa 975: the Holy Roman Emperor Otto I (who also dominated Italy); John I Tzimisces of Byzantium; Al-Muti of Bagdad; al-Muizz of Egypt; and Hakam II of Cordova; plus two important Jewish political leaders: Paltiel himself, the Jewish vizier of Fatimid Egypt, and propably also Hasdai ibn Shaprut, the Jewish foreign minister of the caliphs of Cordova. Thus, both Paltiel and al-Aziz were partly correct and partly incorrect in their interpretation of the astrological phenomenon of the three stars which suddenly disappeared. Paltiel was correct in saying that the ruler of Cordova would die but was wrong in thinking that he himself would continue in life. Al-Aziz was correct in thinking that Paltiel would die but wrong in believing that the ruler of Cordova would continue in life. Both the ruler of Cordova and Paltiel died more or less at the same time as the rulers of Byzantium, Bagdad, and Egypt (al-Muizz, the father of al-Aziz).

However, the important particular in this story is not that Caliph al-Aziz was correct in predicting Paltiel's death (which was due to old age). Rather, it was that al-Aziz actually called Paltiel a "king," the king of *Teman*, a Hebrew term meaning Yemen and/or "the South," but here used for Egypt. Paltiel answered that he could not be the king of Egypt because he was only a Jew, and Jews can not be kings in Arab lands—only viziers. The caliph responded that Paltiel was a king because the caliph said he was; that Paltiel was the caliph's equal; and therefore that he would die during the same year as the other kings. Subsequent events, we are told in the chronicle, proved that the caliph was correct about Paltiel's imminent death. But if the caliph's feeling that Paltiel would soon die proved to be correct, what about the caliph's feeling that Paltiel was his royal equal? Does not the chronicle of Ahima'atz imply that this caliphal feeling was also correct? If so, and if the particulars of this further story about Paltiel (Paltiel, al-Aziz, and the death of the three kings) reached northern European Christians in France and Germany, would they not have been very seriously disturbed at the Arab ruler saying that his Jewish vizier was his equal and also a king? Would not this have been the final and ultimate confirmation of their worst suspicions and fears about the Jewish-Islamic alliance?

H. As the chronicle of Ahima'atz finally concludes the story of Paltiel II, we are told, by way of summation, that when Paltiel died, he was vizier of a vast (Fatimid) Arab empire which included Arabia, Syria, Palestine, and Egypt.[107] At the same time Paltiel was head of the Jewish communities not only of these lands but of North Africa and Sicily as well. He was a generous person, giving 5,000 gold dinars to charity for: Jewish religious scholars in Palestine; the Jewish semi-monastic brotherhood of Jerusalem called "the Mourners of Zion"; Jewish religious scholars in Iraq; the poor of the Holy Land; and oil with which to light the lamps of the synagogues in the Holy Land. What is more, he organized a special caravan (of horses and mules) which he sent, under heavy guard, to the Holy Land. It bore the gold he had donated for the various charitable purposes outlined above. Paltiel was a model leader of his own Jewish religious community and also a model vizier of the Fatimid caliphs, helping them administer their vast empire with skill and dedication. Paltiel was great both among his own people and among the Muslims. He represented the perfect embodiment of the *Jewish-Islamic alliance*. Here was a person, then, whose life and work, if it became known to the northern European (Franco-German) Christians, would have served as the perfect confirmation of their suspicion that the Jew was in league with the Muslim against the Christian.

5. Samuel II, circa 1000, as we are told in the chronicle of Ahima'atz, continued in his father Paltiel II's footsteps by serving the Fatimid caliphs of Egypt. This would, of course, have sounded to northern European (Franco-German) Christians as if the Jew was a continuing ally of the Muslim. However, there are few specific details about the Jewish-Islamic alliance *per se* in the rather brief account of Samuel II in this chronicle.[108]

We are told that Samuel II brought the remains of his father (Paltiel II) and mother to Jerusalem, the Holy City, for burial. He also brought the embalmed bones of Rabbi Hananel II, his own great-uncle, to Jerusalem for burial alongside his parents. We are told further that Samuel personally was wealthy and generous enough to donate during his lifetime a total of 20,000 silver drachmae to charity for, among other purposes, money to buy oil for the lamps of the synagogue at the Wailing Wall in Jerusalem and of other synagogues both near and far; the "Mourners of Zion," who lived in Jerusalem; and institutions of higher Jewish learning in Palestine and Babylonia.[109]

However, there are no details in the chronicle of Ahima'atz about Samuel II's politics or his dealings with Muslims and Christians. Did he inherit his wealth from his father Paltiel II and then remain only a private business person and philanthropist? Or did he also assume his father's high office of vizier (or another high office like treasurer or master of the household) in the service of the Fatimid caliph? The answer revolves around the meaning of the statement in the chronicle of Ahima'atz that Samuel "arose . . . to fill the place of his father." Does this mean Paltiel II's place within the Jewish community alone, or his place in both the Jewish community and the caliph's government? We think that the second possibility is more likely. Just as Joseph Ha-Nagid succeeded his father Samuel Ha-Nagid as vizier of the Berber ruler of Granada and head of the Granadan Jewish community in the 1060s,[110] so Samuel II succeeded his father Paltiel II as vizier of the Fatimid caliph of Egypt and head of the Jewish community of the Fatimid Empire circe 975 (approximately three-quarters of a century earlier). If this is the proper interpretation of the statement in the chronicle of Ahima'atz, two Jewish viziers (father and son, Paltiel and Samuel) rendered yeoman services unto two Fatimid caliphs (also father and son, al-Muizz and al-Aziz) over a period of approximately three-quarters of a century, *i.e.*, from circa 925 to 1000. When the Franco-German Christians learnt of such important Jewish services to the Arabs, is it any wonder that they blamed the Jews for the great persecution of the Christians of Egypt and Palestine engineered by the mad Fatimid caliph, Hakim, circa 1010?

*****

How could material associating Jew with Muslim, from either the chronicle of Ahima'atz or from the actual history of his family, have reached northern European Christians in France and Germany?

1. The Kalonymid family. One Jewish tradition of the High Middle Ages maintains that the founder of the distinguished Kalonymid family of Mainz came to Germany from Lucca, Italy, circa 875, and was a disciple of Aaron of Bagdad.[111]

Another tradition holds that the founder of this family came to Germany from southern Italy circa 982, after rescuing the Holy Roman Emperor Otto II from death.[112]

If we work under the assumption that the second tradition is more likely to be true and that the Kalonymid family came to Germany from Italy in the second half of the tenth rather than in the ninth century, perhaps this Kalonymid ancestor from southern Italy gave information about Aaron of Bagdad, Rabbi Sh'fatyah, Hananel II, and Paltiel II (who died only circa 975), as well as information about Bustanai, Eldad the Danite, Nathan the Babylonian, and the Hasdai/Joseph correspondence, to the German emperor and nobility.

Even if the second of the two traditions discussed above is more likely to be true, there could still be a kernel of truth in the first tradition. There may indeed have been a disciple of Aaron of Bagdad who either went from southern Italy to Germany circa 875 or else settled in Lucca. If he crossed the Alps to Germany, he could have given information about Aaron of Bagdad and Rabbi Sh'fatyah (as well as Bustanai) to the German emperor and nobility as early as the late ninth century. If he settled in Lucca, he and/or his descendants in tenth-century Tuscany could have given information about Aaron, Sh'fatyah, Hananel, and Paltiel (as well as about Bustanai, Eldad, Nathan, and Hasdai/Joseph) to Geman and French Christian (and/or Jewish) merchants who came down over the Alps to Lucca. They, in turn, could have relayed this information to the German and French rulers and nobility. This late ninth-century Luccan disciple of Aaron of Bagdad, if he existed, could also have given the information in ques-

173

tion to the Christians of northern Italy, who could have relayed it to the Christians of Germany and France.

2. Rabbi Sh'fatyah the son of Amittai, circa 870, who was summoned to Byzantium by Emperor Basil to discuss the question of forced baptism, may have given information about Aaron of Bagdad (and Bustanai) to the Byzantine emperor, who in turn, may have relayed it to the Christians of Italy, Germany, and France.[113]

3. Rabbi Sh'fatyah, who worked with the Byzantine governor of Oria to save this city from the Arabs of Bari and their "Saudan," may have given information about Aaron (and Bustanai) to the governor. Hence the information could have been relayed by the governor to the Christian rulers of Italy, Germany, and France through the Byzantine emperor; or directly by the governor to the Christian rulers of Italy, who, in turn, could have relayed it to the Christian rulers of Germany and France.[114]

4. Rabbi Hananel I, the brother of Rabbi Sh'fatyah, circa 875, entered into serious discussion with the (Greek Orthodox) archbishop of Oria about *historical questions* (archival matters) and about astronomy. In their discussion of astronomy the archbishop attempted to entrap Hananel and thereby compel him to embrace Christianity. However, as we are told, God worked a miracle to save Hananel, and the archbishop ended up having to pay Hananel 300 gold pieces instead.[115] It is certainly possible that Hananel gave the archbishop information about Aaron of Bagdad and about Hananel's own brother, Rabbi Sh'fatyah (as well as about Bustanai). The archbishop could have relayed this information to the patriarch of Constantinople (in turn, transmitting it to other church figures in Italy, Germany, and France) or to the Byzantine emperor (in turn, transmitting it to the Christian political leaders of Italy, Germany, and France). It is also possible that the archbishop of Oria relayed the information directly to other Italian church figures who, in turn, transmitted it to their German and French counterparts. Some of these church figures in Italy, Germany, and France could then have shared this information with the political leaders of their respective countries.

5. Moses of Pavia, circa 900, was driven out of Oria by Amittai the son of Sh'fatyah on suspicion of bearing false witness in an adultery case. The two had quarreled earlier over Amittai's conduct at the funeral of Moses's brother, conduct which Moses considered an insult to his family. Moses went to Pavia (Lombardy) via Capua (near Na-

ples).[116] Possibly Moses gave information about Aaron of Bagdad and Rabbi Sh'fatyah, perhaps in part out of enmity toward the family of Ahima'atz, as well as information about Bustanai and Eldad, to German and French Christian (and/or Jewish) merchants who came down over the Alps to trade in Pavia. They, in turn, could have relayed this information to the Christian political and religious leaders of Germany and France. Moses of Pavia could also have given such information directly to the aforementioned Christian leaders of Germany and France if he himself ever crossed the Alps.

6. Hananel II (uncle of the great Jewish vizier Paltiel II), circa 925, was taken captive by Arabs and brought to Tunisia. There he was able to persuade the Arab ruler to allow him to return home to southern Italy via Byzantium. Hananel II may have given information about Aaron of Bagdad and Rabbi Sh'fatyah (as well as about Bustanai and Eldad) to the Byzantine emperor (who allowed him to return home to reclaim lost property). The emperor, in turn, could have relayed this information to the Christians of Italy, Germany, and France.[117]

7. Paltiel II, the great Jewish vizier, circa 950, was visited, when serving al-Muizz in North Africa, by the Byzantine ambassador (over whom he won such a brilliant victory). Paltiel II could have given this ambassador information about Aaron of Bagdad, Rabbi Sh'fatyah, Hananel II, and even about himself (as well as about Bustanai and Eldad). The Byzantine ambassador, in turn, could have transmitted this information dutifully to the emperor upon his return to Constantinople. The emperor, in turn, could have relayed it to the Christians of Italy, Germany, and France.[118]

8. The doge of Amalfi, circa 950, entered into a special relationship with Paltiel II, then al-Muizz's vizier in North Africa, through Paltiel's cousins Shabbethai and Papoleon, and perhaps through other Jewish and Christian intermediaries as well.[119] It is possible that Shabbethai and Papoleon (and/or Paltiel II himself) gave information about Aaron of Bagdad, Rabbi Sh'fatyah, Hananel II, and even about Paltiel II (as well as about Bustanai and Eldad) to the doge. The latter could have relayed this information to the Christian political leaders of Italy, Germany, and France, either directly, or indirectly via the Byzantine emperor (and/or his representatives in southeastern Italy), or via the doges of the other southwestern Italian maritime republics.

9. Shabbethai Donnolo (born Oria, circa 913; died southern Italy, after 982), a great Italian Jewish intellectual, was a member of the

family of Ahima'atz and a contemporary of Hananel II, Paltiel II, and Samuel II, his relatives. Circa 950 Donnolo entered into relationships with a very important south Italian Byzantine church figure, St. Nilus, archbishop of Rossano (in Calabria), and an important Byzantine political figure, Eupraxius, the governor of Calabria.[120] It is highly possible that Donnolo gave them information about such persons as Aaron of Bagdad, Rabbi Sh'fatyah, Hananel II, and Paltiel II (as well as about Bustanai and Eldad). These two Byzantine notables, in turn, could have relayed such information to the patriarch of Constantinople and the Byzantine emperor. They, in turn, could have transmitted it to the Christian ecclesiastical and political leaders of Italy, Germany, and France. Alternatively, Nilus and Eupraxius could have relayed any information which they received from Donnolo directly to the Christian ecclesiastical and political leaders of Italy, who, in turn, could have transmitted it to their counterparts in Germany and France.[121]

What is more, not only is it highly possible that Shabbethai Donnolo gave information from Jewish sources which associated Jew with Muslim, but he himself was also a living example of this association. Hence, his own career could not help but lend added confirmation to the tendency on the part of Western Christians to think in terms of the Jewish-Islamic alliance. Donnolo, like his relative Hananel II in the chronicle of Ahima'atz, was taken captive by Arab raiders who swooped down on Oria circa 925. Fortunately he was ransomed by relatives in Taranto. His parents, however, who were also taken captive, apparently had to remain in bondage (either in Sicily or North Africa) for some time thereafter. Normally Jews strove to ransome their coreligionists at the earliest opportunity. However, certain exceptional circumstances, of which we are not told, could have intervened in the case of the parents of Donnolo, which prevented their being ransomed until a considerable time after the ransom of their brilliant son. Perhaps there was only enough money to ransom one member of the family, and the parents purposefully declined ransom in favor of the son, on the theory that his life was still ahead of him while theirs was nearly over. Thus, it is possible that Donnolo had to remain in touch with the Arabs for several years after his own ransom with regard to the fate and destiny of his parents. This factor may already have tended to associate him with the Muslims. Second, Donnolo was known as a student of the (scientific) wisdom of the *Arabs, Babylonians, and Indians* (in addition to that of the Jews, Greeks, and

Latins). This factor may also have tended to equate him with the Muslims. Finally, Donnolo studied this Eastern wisdom under an Arab teacher named Bagoas, who came from Bagdad itself, the capital of the Abbasid caliphate. This final factor would clearly have tended to stereotype him as a Jewish ally of the Muslims.

These three factors, then—Donollo's lengthy negotiations with the Arabs for the release of his parents from their captivity, his studies of Arabic wisdom, and his Arab teacher from Bagdad—made Donnolo a living example of the association of Jew with Muslim. His own illustrious career, along with the information which he may have given to his Christian acquaintances about the equation of Jew with Muslim in the activities of Aaron of Bagdad, Sh'fatyah, Hananel II, and Paltiel II (as well as Bustanai and Eldad), may well have added even further confirmation to what by now assuredly needed little additional confirmation. In the eyes of northern European (Franco-German) Christians, the Jews and Muslims were allies, in league with each other against the Christian world, East and West.[122]

*****

We would like to suggest that the chronicle of Ahima'atz may have been written in reaction to the persecution of the Jews in Tunisia during the reign of the Zirid ruler al-Muizz (1016-1062).[123] The chronicle's purpose would have been to supply the Jews of Tunisia with information about how the Jews of southern Italy directly across the Mediterranean had sided with the Muslims (and had been persecuted by the Christian Byzantines) circa 850 to 1000. Thus, the stories about Jewish-Arab cooperation might hopefully help the Jews of Tunisia regain the favor of the Arab rulers of their land.

Alternatively, the chronicle of Ahima'atz may have been written in response to a need arising solely from within the Mediterranean Jewish community rather than from persecution from without by non-Jews. The chronicle may have been written in part out of jealousy of the two great Spanish Jewish politicians and statesmen Hasdai the son of Shaprut and Samuel Ha-Nagid (the Prince; also called Samuel ibn Nagdela or ibn Nagrela). Hasdai served as foreign minister of the Arab caliphs of Cordova in the midtenth century; Samuel, as vizier of the Berber rulers of Granada in the first half of the following century. Hasdai was an almost exact contemporary of Paltiel II; Samuel, an

177

almost exact contemporary of Ahima'atz.[124] Did Ahima'atz intend his
family chronicle to demonstrate to his fellow Jews throughout the
Arab world that the Spanish Jewish leaders Hasdai the son of Shaprut
and Samuel Ha-Nagid were really not as great as the Jewish leaders of
southern Italy? The family of Ahima'atz had served the Arabs equally
well, but in the central Mediterranean and the Middle East, areas of
even greater strategic and religious importance than Spain. Two of its
most illustrious members, Paltiel II and his son Samuel II, had served
the Fatimid caliph of Egypt. This empire extended much further, and
was much closer to the Islamic and Jewish heartlands (Arabia and
Palestine), than the territory of the Umayyad caliph of Cordova whom
Hasdai had served or of the Berber king of Granada whom Samuel had
served. Indeed, the caliphate of Cordova had ceased to exist by the
time Ahima'atz wrote, i.e., by circa 1054, because it fell to the Berbers
circa 1013. By contrast, the Fatimid Empire continued into the midtwelfth century until finally overthrown by Saladin. Likewise, the
Muslims of Granada would rise up and slay Joseph Ha-Nagid, Samuel
Ha-Nagid's son and successor in the vizierate, and massacre the Jews
of Granada in 1066, only twelve years after Ahima'atz wrote his
chronicle. No such tragedy occurred to Samuel II, Paltiel II's son and
successor in the vizierate, nor were the Jews of Egypt massacred during
Samuel II's lifetime. Clearly, the Jewish leaders of south Italian provenance in the tenth century were better able to protect themselves and
their people from Islamic vengeance than were the Jewish leaders of
Spain in the tenth and eleventh centuries.[125]

Thus, the chronicle of Ahima'atz, we would suggest, was probably
written to magnify and exalt the Jewish-Islamic alliance in general and
the south Italian Jewish contribution thereto in particular. Its purpose
was to help the Jews of North Africa overcome Arab persecution
and/or to demonstrate the superiority of south Italian Jewry (and its
heroic personalities, especially Paltiel II and his son Samuel II) over
Spanish Jewry (and its heroic personalities, Hasdai ibn Shaprut and
Samuel Ha-Nagid). To magnify and exalt the Judaeo-Islamic alliance
in general could not harm Jews living in Islamic lands. Quite the contrary! It could only help them. However, the material about the Judaeo-
Islamic alliance in the chronicle of Ahima'atz probably became known
to Franco-German Christians. This was brought about either through
Jews and/or converts from Judaism to Christianity who opposed the
family of Ahima'atz and wanted to denounce its pro-Arab exploits to

the Christians, or through Jews who supported the family of Ahima'atz and were not afraid to boast of its pro-Arab exploits to the Christians. Such material about the Judaeo-Islamic alliance would have been very dangerous to Jews living in Franco-Germany. It would have served to fan the flames of already-existing Franco-German Christian suspicions against Jews as agents of the Islamic world conspiracy and to confirm these suspicions via the very best kind of proof. The historical literature of the Jews themselves associated Jew with Muslim and clearly indicated that the two groups were in league with each other. What further proof beyond the data furnished by the chronicle of Ahima'atz would the Franco-German Christians have required to conclude that the Jews and Muslims (both of Middle Eastern origin, rejecting the Trinity, claiming physical descent from Abraham, utilizing Semitic languages in their scriptures and liturgies, and practicing circumcision of the flesh) were in league with each other against the Christians, with the Muslims attacking from without and the Jews, their cousins and allies, attacking from within?[126]

The favorable Italian Jewish attitude toward the Arabs reflected in the mideleventh-century chronicle of Ahima'atz sharply contrasts with the increasingly hostile Western Christian attitude toward the Arabs during this very same period. Such a dichotomy may help explain in part why the crusading movement, which began primarily as an attempt to solve the problem of Islam, rapidly developed into an attack on the Jews as well.

*****

Thus, we have attempted to demonstrate the following in the text and footnotes of this chapter of our book.

1. The Bustanai story was possibly known to the Christians of France in the second half of the eighth century (brought by Natronai/Machir from Bagdad) or the first half of the ninth century (Agobard). Aaron of Bagdad could have brought it to the Jews of southern Italy circa 850. They, in turn, could have transmitted it (perhaps via the Kalonymids of Lucca and Mainz) to the Christians of Franco-Germany circa 850–1000. Therefore, the description of the Judaeo/Islamic alliance in the Bustanai story could well have reinforced the Christian equation of Jew with Muslim at work in ninth-century France, in tenth-century Western Europe (the persecution of the 930s), and in eleventh-century Western Europe (the persecutions of 1010, the 1060s, and 1096).

2. The Eldad material was definitely known to the Jews of Spain in the 880s and again in the 950s (the Hasdai/Joseph correspondence). Via Hasdai the son of Shaprut and other sources it probably became known to the Christians of France (Fulbert of Chartres) circa 1010. This would have been in time for Eldad's description of the Judaeo/Islamic alliance to reinforce the Christian equation of Jew with Muslim during the persecutions of the Jews in eleventh-century Western Europe. The Eldad material was definitely known to Rashi and his grandson Jacob Tam (France circa 1075–1175) and probably influenced the development of the Prester John legend among the Christians of Western Europe in the twelfth century. Eldad's description of the Judaeo/Islamic alliance would have reinforced the Christian equation of Jew with Muslim during the Second and Third Crusades.

3. Nathan the Babylonian's chronicle was probably known to Hasdai the son of Shaprut. Information from it (along with information from Bustanai, Eldad, and Hasdai/Joseph) could have been transmitted by Hasdai to the Christians of Franco-Germany either directly or indirectly via Byzantium. This would have been in time for the description of the Judaeo/Islamic alliance in Nathan (as well as in Bustanai, Eldad, and Hasdai/Joseph) to reinforce the Christian equation of Jew with Muslim at work in the persecutions of the Jews of Western Europe during the eleventh century. Information from Nathan's chronicle could also have been transmitted by the Jews of Kairawan to the Jews of nearby southern Italy in the second half of the tenth century. They, in turn, could have transmitted it (along with information from the chronicle of Ahima'atz) over the Alps to the Jews and Christians of Franco-Germany in the second half of the tenth or during the eleventh centuries. This would have been in time for Nathan's description of the Judaeo/Islamic alliance to reinforce the Christian equation of Jew with Muslim at work in the eleventh-century persecutions of the Jews of Western Europe.

4. Information, including the description of the Judaeo/Islamic alliance, from the Hasdai/Joseph correspondence was probably transmitted by Hasdai himself (along with similar data from Bustanai, Eldad, and Nathan) to the Christians of Franco-Germany in the tenth century, either directly or indirectly via Byzantium. This would have been in time to reinforce the Christian equation of Jew with Muslim at work in the eleventh-century persecutions of the Jews of Western Europe. Such information from the Hasdai/Joseph correspondence was probably also known to Rashi and his grandson Jacob Tam (France circa

1075-1175). Both knew the work of Menahem ben Saruk, a very close associate of Haśdai the son of Shaprut in midtenth-century Cordova. From the broad Jewish circles linked with Rashi and Jacob Tam, the description of the Judaeo/Islamic alliance in the Hasdai/Joseph correspondence could have been transmitted to the Christians of Franco-Germany in the twelfth-century, in time to reinforce the Christian equation of Jew with Muslim at work in the Second and Third Crusades.

5. Information from the chronicle of Ahima'atz could have reached the Christians of Franco-Germany in the tenth century, directly via the Kalonymids of Lucca and Mainz and/or via Christian religious (St. Nilus of Rossano) and political (Eupraxius) leaders in Italy, or indirectly via Byzantium. This would have been in time for Ahima'atz's description of the Judaeo/Islamic alliance to reinforce the Christian equation of Jew with Muslim at work in the persecutions of the Jews of Western Europe during the eleventh century. Such information could also have reached the Christians of Franco-Germany in the eleventh century via converts from Judaism and/or Jews who taught Christians Hebrew. The chronicle of Ahima'atz was possibly known to Rashi and his grandson Jacob Tam (who knew the work of Shabbetai Donnolo and the rabbinical scholars of tenth-century southern Italy). From the broad Jewish circles linked with Rashi and Jacob Tam, details from the chronicle of Ahima'atz could have been transmitted to the Christians of Franco-Germany in the twelfth century. This would have been in time for Ahima'atz's description of the Judaeo/Islamic alliance to reinforce the Christian equation of Jew with Muslim at work in the Second and Third Crusades. Information from the chronicle of Ahima'atz was probably known as well to Rabbi Judah the Pious and Rabbi Elazar Rokeach (Germany circa 1172-1225). It could have been transmitted by Jewish circles linked with these great mystics (who were quite open to Christian religious influence) to the Christians of Germany in the thirteenth century. This would have been in time to reinforce the Christian equation of Jew with Muslim at work in Central Europe during the thirteenth century (the century of five Crusades: 1204, 1219, 1229, 1250, and 1270).

To summarize the burden of the argument in chapter five, the association of Jew with Muslim in the mind of medieval Christians was the crucial factor which led to the great revival of anti-Semitism in Western Europe during the High Middle Ages (circa 1000–1300, the classic period of the medieval Crusades against the Muslims), after anti-Semitism had been relatively dormant in Western Europe during the earlier Carolingian-Ottonian period (circa 700–1000). The first and in many ways most fundamental chapter in the great revival of anti-Semitism in Western Europe during the High Middle Ages, under the crucial influence of the association of Jew with Muslim in the minds of medieval Christians, was the major persecution of the Jews of Western Europe during the early eleventh century, circa 1010, in France, Germany, and Italy. Further persecutions during the eleventh century, in which the association of Jew with Muslim in the minds of medieval Christians played a primary role, were those of the midcentury, circa 1065, and of the end of the century, circa 1096, the First Crusade. Modern scholarship has generally considered the persecution at the end of the eleventh century, during the First Crusade, to be the most important indication of the radical shift toward the negative which characterized Western Christian attitudes toward Jews during the High Middle Ages (and thereafter into the Later Middle Ages and early modern times). However, we have suggested that the great persecution at the beginning of the century, circa 1010, about which we admittedly have much less information, was really a more important watershed in the history of Christian-Jewish relations than was the First Crusade.

Be that as it may, the association of Jew with Muslim *by medieval Jews* was a pivotal factor in five major Jewish historical works written circa 600–1100: (1) the story of Bustanai, circa 650–900; (2) the travel narrative of Eldad the Danite, ninth century; (3) the chronicle of Nathan the Babylonian, tenth century; (4) the exchange of letters between Hasdai the son of Shaprut, the Jewish foreign minister of the caliphs of Cordova, and Joseph, the Jewish khan of the Khazars, tenth century; and (5) the chronicle of Ahima'atz, eleventh century (but with most of its material describing great personalities and events of the ninth and tenth centuries). We have little doubt that the association of Jew with Muslim *by medieval Jews* played a crucial role in the association of Jew with Muslim by medieval Christians. The former association nurtured the latter and made it seem much more plausible. Of course, as we argue, it was the latter association, of Jew with Muslim *by medieval Christians*, that led, in turn, to the great revival of anti-Semitism in Western Europe during the High Middle Ages (circa 1000–1300, the classic period of medieval imperialist expansion), beginning with the major persecution of the Jews of Western Europe circa 1010.

6. Why Did Pope Innocent III Want the Fourth Lateran Council (1215) to Impose a Distinction in Clothing on Muslims and Jews?*

We have attempted, thus far, to demonstrate that the association of Jew with Muslim by medieval Jews was a crucial factor in the association of Jew with Muslim by medieval Christians (chapter five) and that the latter association was a crucial factor in the great ōutburst of anti-Semitism in Western Europe during the High Middle Ages (chapter four). The climax of high medieval anti-Semitism was the Jewish badge imposed by Pope Innocent III at the Fourth Lateran Council in 1215. That badge was a key element in the ghettoization process of Central Europe (from Italy to Germany). This process began in earnest in the fourteenth century (after the Black Plague, during which frightful massacres of the Jews were perpetrated) and lasted to the time of the French Revolution/Napoleon. The badge was revived along with the ghettoization process by Hitler's Nazi movement, leading ultimately to the gas ovens and the extermination of six million Jews. It is to the hitherto largely unrecognized *anti-Islamic* origins of the high medieval Jewish badge that we now turn.

This sixth chapter of the book, then, argues that during the latter part of his pontificate (certainly from April 1213 onward) Pope Innocent III (1198–1216) came to hold the following beliefs:

1. The Second Coming of Christ would take place in 1284.

2. In order to pave the way for this eschatological event, the Muslims of the Middle East would have to be converted to Christianity.

3. To achieve the conversion of the Muslims of the Middle East, missionaries would have to be sent among them.

In order to facilitate the work of these missionaries,

4. a great (Fifth) Crusade would have to be launched that would conquer and occupy the Islamic lands in the Middle East; and

5. the conquered Muslims in these lands would have to be de-

graded socially by means of a distinction in clothing imposed upon them by their Christian conquerors.

Concomitant with this, the pope believed, the Jews living in Western Europe, who were equated with the Muslims and considered an Islamic "fifth column" in Christian territory, would also have to be degraded socially by means of a distinction in clothing, in order to facilitate their conversion en masse as part of the same preparation for the Second Coming of Christ in 1284.

*****

What evidence is there to support the view that during the latter part of his pontificate Pope Innocent III came to believe that the Second Coming of Christ would take place in 1284?

In a key passage in his Crusade appeal of April 19, 1213, addressed to every part of Western Europe except Spain, Pope Innocent III expressly identified Muhammad (i.e., Islam) with the Beast of the Apocalypse (i.e., Antichrist), "whose number is concluded in 666." The pope argued that since almost 600 years of this number (i.e., of the number 666) have already passed, the end of the Beast (i.e., Islam) is at hand.[1]

From what date did Pope Innocent III begin to count these 666 years? Richard William Southern suggests that he started counting either from 622, the year of the hijrah (the "emigration," Muhammad's flight from Mecca to Medina), or from 632, the year of Muhammad's death.[2] However, our suggestion is that Innocent started counting from 618, the same year from which the ninth-century Spanish martyrs' movement started counting.[3] If so, then adding to 618 the 600 years which, in 1213, Innocent said were almost completed, we obtain 1218, only five years after the date of Innocent's Crusade appeal. 1218 was the year in which the Fifth Crusade in the East gathered genuine momentum with the siege of Damietta, and it was precisely this (Fifth) Crusade that Innocent was attempting to launch in his Crusade appeal of April 19, 1213.[4] Again, if we add to 618 the 666 years which Innocent said were the total number of years allotted to the Beast (i.e., Islam), 1284 would be the year of the end of Islam. Thus the 66-year, or two generation, period between 1218 and 1284 was the period during which, Pope Innocent III believed, Islam would disap-

184

pear from the face of the earth. We should note that the disappearance of Islam foreseen here would assuredly not have been a simple, natural phenomenon. On the contrary, it would have been a supernatural phenomenon of monumental proportions. The identification of Muhammad (*i.e.*, Islam) with the Beast of the Apocalypse (*i.e.*, Antichrist) would seem to mean that, in the mind of Pope Innocent III, the end of Islam was closely associated with the Second Coming of Christ.[5] If so, then, according to Innocent's letter, 1284 was both the year of the end of Islam and also the year of the Second Coming.[6]

To sum up so far. In our view, this crucial passage in Pope Innocent III's Crusade appeal of April 19, 1213, would seem to mean that the pope believed that

1. 618 was the year when Islam began;

2. 1218 was the 600th year after the beginning of Islam and the beginning of a 66-year period during which Islam would disappear from the face of the earth; and

3. 1284 was the 666th year after the beginning of Islam, the year of the final disappearance of Islam and the year of the Second Coming of Christ. Southern states that "it would be interesting to know the inspiration of this letter" of Pope Innocent III.[7] What Southern does not realize is that he himself may have provided an answer to this question in an earlier section of his book. From Southern's discussion of the ninth-century Spanish martyrs' movement, led by Eulogius and Alvarus, it is clear that this movement also expressly identified Muhammad (*i.e.*, Islam) with the Beast of the Apocalypse (*i.e.* Antichrist), whose number was 666.[8] Relying on its own messianic computations, the martyrs' movement came to believe that the end of Islam and the Second Coming of Christ would take place in 863.[9] When this eschatological event failed to materialize in 863, it may be that the author of the so-called *Cronica Prophetica* revised the computations of the ninth-century Spanish martyrs' movement slightly in order to postpone the end approximately twenty-one years, from 863 to 884.[10] We have already marshalled some evidence elsewhere in support of the view that both the memory of the ninth century Spanish martyrs' movement and the actual writings of its two leaders, Eulogius and Alvarus, lived on into the High Middle Ages and were known in Spain circa 1050 to 1250.[11] The *Cronica Prophetica* also would seem to have lived on and may have been read as a supplement to the writtings of Eulogius/Alvarus.[12]

185

In the early 1180's certain Spanish apocalypticists of Toledo circulated, in the name of Johannes Davidis Hispalensis (Johannes Avendauth), the so-called "Letter of Toledo," addressed to Pope Lucius III (1181–1185). This letter foretold that by 1186 the world would be devastated; a faithful Christian remnant would survive; Jews and Muslims would forsake their houses of worship, and their "sect" (apparently Jews were equated with Muslims) would be utterly destroyed; after which an age of great well-being would begin.[13] Perhaps this "Letter of Toledo" drew inspiration, at least in part, from the *Cronica Prophetica*, but revised the *Cronica*'s computations in order to postpone the end approximately 300 years, from 884 to 1186.[14] However, when the eschatological event again failed to material in 1186, it may be that these same Spanish apocalypticists of Toledo revised their own computations in order to postpone the end approximately 100 more years, from 1186 to 1284.[15] Was it from these circles that Pope Innocent III derived the belief, expressed in his Crusade appeal of April 1213, that the end would occur in 1284? If so, was Rodrigo Jimenez de Rada, archbishop of Toledo, with whom Pope Innocent III was in frequent communication with regard to the Crusade in Spain, 1212–1213, the link connecting the pope with the Spanish apocalypticists of Toledo?[16]

*****

James Brundage, in a letter to us of December 9, 1965, expressed the following caveats regarding the above-outlined thesis about Pope Innocent III's millenarianism:

> How far is it really possible to extrapolate from one sentence in one letter a general theory of Innocent III's millenarian ideas? Indeed, how certain is it that this particular letter represents in all details the pope's mind, bearing in mind the elaborate chancery organization of Innocent's pontificate? And, for that matter, what is the textual history of this particular letter? It is easy to raise the questions; it is much less easy, I know, to answer them. Still, I should think that they would need to be investigated and answered so far as possible before you can safely rest an interpretative structure upon this passage.

We agree with Brundage that until a thorough study of the textual history of Pope Innocent III's Crusade appeal of April 19, 1213, is made by experts on the papal chancery in the High Middle Ages,[17] there can be no *certainty* in regard to the thesis outlined here about Pope Innocent III's millenarianism. We hope that this chapter will serve to stimulate such a study by those qualified to make it.

However, if this particular millenarian passage in the pope's letter of April 1213 is not a post-Innocentian interpolation,[18] then even at such an early stage in the investigation of this question we would argue the likelihood that this particular letter does indeed represent the pope's mind *in all details*. The letter was simply too monumentally important for Innocent to have allowed it to go out containing *anything* that did not represent his mind. To the great importance of this letter the following two facts attest: (1) the letter launched a new (the Fifth) Crusade (one of the most important matters, if not *the* most important matter, that Innocent dealt with during the last two to three years of his pontificate), and (2) it was addressed to every part of Western Europe except Spain.[19]

If indeed this eschatological passage in Pope Innocent III's Crusade appeal of April 19, 1213, does represent the pope's mind, how do we know that Innocent sincerely believed in this kind of thinking? Perhaps he did not credit millenarianism at all but merely used it to rally support for the Fifth Crusade because he thought that other, more gullible, Christians, the potential crusaders, would credit it. After all, some may argue, Innocent's forte was canon law and administration, and lawyer-administrators allegedly are not the kind of people who believe in eschatological predictions.

In reply, we would point out a parallel in the thought of the greatest "canon lawyer" of medieval Judaism, Moses Maimonides (1135-1204). Author of the *Mishneh Torah*, a monumental fourteen-volume code of Jewish religious law which was of considerable importance in the history of Judaism, Maimonides was also one of the greatest medieval Jewish Aristotelian *rationalists*. This same person believed that the return of prophecy, the sign heralding the coming of the Messiah, would take place in 1216.[20] Maimonides, almost an exact contemporary of Pope Innocent III, traced his messianic prediction back through his father, grandfather, and their ancestors. All lived in Spain, the very same land whence, we have suggested, Pope Innocent III's not too dissimilar messianic views may have come.[21] Another parallel can be seen in the early Franciscan movement during Pope Innocent III's own lifetime (*i.e.*, circa 1209–1216). This was a utopian religious

187

movement with a significant millenarian ingredient.[22] Yet, among the very earliest disciples of St. Francis were Elias of Assisi and Peter Catanii, both of whom had studied law at Bologna. There were at least four other Bolognese lawyers upon whom the early Franciscan ideal, in its most utopian form, made a powerful impression, *i.e.*, John Parenti and John of Parma (two generals of the order), plus Nicholas of Pepoli and Accursius.[23] Thus, the fact that Pope Innocent III's forte may have been law and administration does not *ipso facto* preclude the possibility that he also believed in eschatological predictions.

Granted that Pope Innocent III was a great lawyer-administrator, was this all that he was? Did his devotion to law and administration mean that he was not also a deeply religious Christian? For such Christians eschatology has always been an important matter.[24]

If indeed Pope Innocent III was really only a lawyer-administrator, how do we account for the significant amount of private religious writing that he produced, which had little if anything to do with law and administration?

Prior to his pontificate Innocent wrote at least three religious treatises:

1. *De Miseria Humanae Conditionis* (an ascetic treatise in the tradition of extreme Christian pessimism about human nature and the world)

2. *De Sacro Altaris Mysterio* (a long allegorical and mystical commentary on the Mass)

3. *De Quadripartita Specie Nuptiarum Liber* (an allegorioal and mystical commentary on Psalm 44 [45]).[25]

Even during his pontificate, which was an extremely busy one, Innocent struggled mightily to find time, despite his many official tasks,[26] to write

4. *Sermones*
   a. *De Tempore*
   b. *De Sanctis*
   c. *Communes*
   d. *De Diversis*
5. *Dialogus inter Deum et Peccatorem*
6. *Libellus de Eleemosyna*
7. *Encomium Charitatis*
8. *De Beatissima Virgine Maria et Filio Ejus Jesu Christo Encomium*
9. *De Vita et Passione Domini Nostri Jesu Christi Orationes Tres*
10. *Orationes Tres de Omnibus Sanctis, pro Defensione et Tranquilitate Catholicae et Orthodoxae Ecclesiae*

11. *Hymnus (et Oratio) de Christo et Beatissima Virgine Maria Dignissima Matre Ejus*

12. *Commentarium in Septem Psalmos Poenitentiales* (Psalms 6, 31, 37, 50, 101, 129, 142).[27]

Notice the concern here with asceticism, the *mystery* of the Mass, the saints, sin, charity, the Virgin Mary, the *passion* of Christ, and the *penitential* Psalms. Surely these writings were not the work of only a lawyer-administrator.

Even Pope Innocent III's official papal letters, like his private religious writings, are filled with theology, scriptural citations, and allegorical interpretations, far more than would be normal, it seems to us, for only a lawyer-administrator.

Furthermore, Fulk of Neuilly, a popular northern French preacher circa 1200, had a reputation as a worker of miracles, including even raising the dead. He called for a new Crusade exclusively of the poor (like Peter the Hermit and his followers in 1096). Yet, Pope Innocent III commissioned Fulk to preach the Fourth Crusade (November 5, 1198).[28] Would a pope who was really only a lawyer-adminstrator have commissioned a utopian religious enthusiast, potentially dangerous to the establishment because he stirred up the lower classes, to preach a new Crusade? Did Pope Urban II bless the work of Peter the Hermit and his followers, who called forth the so-called "Peasants' Crusade" in Central Europe in 1096?

Furthermore, it is well known that of the two great early thirteenth-century founders of new mendicant orders, St. Francis of Assisi and St. Dominic de Guzman, St. Dominic was a far better administrator. St. Dominic, unlike St. Francis, did not lose control of the movement which he had founded and did not see his movement tear itself apart in internecine strife during his very own lifetime! Yet, of these two equally devoted sons of the church, Pope Innocent III clearly preferred St. Francis to St. Dominic. If Pope Innocent III had really been only a lawyer-administrator, he either would asuredly have favored St. Dominic over St. Francis or would at least have treated both St. Dominic and St. Francis with equal respect. He would never have favored St. Francis *over* St. Dominic!

Indeed, in 1209 St. Francis of Assisi came to Pope Innocent III seeking papal approval for a new type of monastic order, whose way of life was almost totally unprecedented in the history of Western Christianity. The life of the new order, whose members would be called friars rather than monks, was to be based on several exceedingly radical principles:

1. Friars should not flee the world, by going to live in places remote from civilizaton, but rather should work within the world, especially within the slums of the big cities of medieval Western Europe where the presence of the church was far from adequately felt at that time.

2. Friars should adhere to total apostolic poverty. Neither the individual monk nor the monastic group as a whole should own any property. Rather, the monks should earn their daily bread by taking odd jobs or, if that be impossible, by begging from door to door (with begging considered a holy task, almost a form of worship).

3. Friars should not stay in one place all of their lives but rather should go wherever their fellow Christians need help.

4. Friars should obey all of the injunctions of the Gospel literally and should endeavor with all of their body and soul to imitate Christ, the crucified and suffering Savior, at all times and places.[29]

The early Franciscan movement was not too different from the new utopian order of monks envisioned by Joachim of Flora, and it had a significant millenarian ingredient.[30] Yet, Pope Innocent III, who was allegedly only a lawyer-administrator, gave St. Francis his verbal approval for the new order and promised that even more support would follow at a later date if the order would prove itself, which it most certainly did.[31]

In 1215 St. Clare of Assisi sought Pope Innocent III's approval for an order of Franciscan nuns. What St. Francis wanted men to attempt, total individual *and group* poverty, was radical enough. But for *women* to attempt to live in total poverty, without monastic endowments, relying instead upon the daily kindness of the local Christian populace, failing which they would starve to death, was the ultimate in religious utopianism. Yet, according to Thomas of Celano's *Vita Sanctae Clarae Virginis* (circa 1255–1256), the pope said that St. Clare's rule was totally unprecedented and then proceeded with great joy to write out, at least partly in his own hand, an official approval for the new order of nuns.[32]

At the Fourth Lateran Council (1215) the older monastic orders (*e.g.*, Cistercians) forced the adoption of a prohibition against all new monastic rules. In order to save the early Franciscan rule, Pope Innocent III declared to the council that he had already approved the early Franciscan rule verbally in 1209. As far as he was concerned, verbal approval was the equivalent of written approval. Thus the early Franciscan rule was not a new rule and therefore was not included within the prohibition just enacted.[33] The significance of what Pope Innocent III did for St. Francis of Assisi at the Fourth Lateran Council cannot be fully comprehended until we realize that the prohibition of new monastic rules by the Fourth Lateran Council also put the early Dominican rule in jeopardy. However, Pope Innocent III did nothing to help *St. Dominic* circumvent this prohibition.[34] Could it have been that the more utopian early Franciscan rule, with its greater emphasis on poverty and imitation of the crucified Christ, struck a far more responsive chord in the heart of this very deeply religious pope than did the more "practical" early Dominican rule?[35]

Granted that Pope Innocent III was not only a great lawyer-administrator but also a deeply religious Christian,[36] is there anything more specific which might lead us to believe that Innocent credited millenarian ideas? The following considerations militate in favor of the likelihood that Pope Innocent III indeed did.

1. In his *De Miseria Humanae Conditionis* Innocent cites the New Testament Book of Revelation (Apocalypse of John) eighteen times.[37] Furthermore, in book III, chapter 3 of this work Innocent speaks of the four different comings of Christ, including Christ's "Second [Coming] for Judgment."[38] Book III, chapters 15–20, contains a detailed description of what happens at the end, including "On the Day of Judgment" (title of chapter 15); "On the Tribulation That Precedes [It]" (title of chapter 16); "How the Lord [*i.e.,* Jesus Christ] Will Come [a second time] for [the Last] Judgment" (title of chapter 17); "On the Power and the Wisdom and the Justice of [Christ] the Judge" (title of chapter 18); "On the Divine Judgment" (title of chapter 19); and "That Nothing Will Benefit Those Worthy of Damnation" (title of chapter 20).[39]

2. Innocent probably knew the apocalyptic writings of Joachim of Flora (died 1202) for the following reasons. (1) According to Canon 2 of the Fourth Lateran Council Joachim commanded that all of his writings "be assigned . . . [to the pope] to be approved by the Apostolic See or else corrected."[40] (2) Innocent clearly knew Joachim's treatise on the Trinity, for he condemned it at the Fourth Lateran Council.[41] Yet, Joachim's trinitarian ideas (bordering on tritheism) and his apocalyptic ideas (three successive ages, that of the Father, Son, and Holy Spirit) are closely related.

Innocent condemned Joachim's trinitarian ideas at the Fourth Lateran Council, but not Joachim's apocalyptic writings. If both Joachim's trinitarian treatise and his apocalyptic writings were available to Innocent, as we think likely, Innocent's failure to condemn the apocalyptic writings may well mean that he saw nothing objectionable in—nay, perhaps even approved—Joachim's apocalyptic theology of history. Joachim's theology of history called for a new, more spiritual order of monks to pave the way for the utopian age of the Holy Spirit. We have already discussed Innocent's very favorable attitude toward St. Francis of Assisi's new order of monks and toward the early Franciscan movement, in which there was a significant millenarian ingredient.[42]

It cannot be argued that Pope Innocent III would never have approved Joachim's apocalyptic ideas because they made the organized church seem superfluous.[43] In some of Joachim's apocalyptic works the partial survival of a purified church bureaucracy is envisioned.[44] Furthermore, we know that Innocent, a major reformer of the organized church in his own right, was willing to listen to attacks on the church bureaucracy.[45] This may have been because he well knew that it was inefficient and corrupt in many places and wanted to change the situation for the better as soon as possible, to prevent the heretical movements, which had threatened to destroy the organized church completely, from using the situation to their own great advantage.

3. Both Pope Innocent III's nephew, Pope Gregory IX (1227–1241), and his protege, Emperor Frederick II (1212–1250), accepted millenarian ideas. Pope Gregory IX introduced the eschatological formulae *diebus novissimis* and *cum hora undecima* into his great mission bulls of the 1230s dealing with the conversion of the Muslims.[46] Could he have derived this millenarianism from his uncle, Pope Innocent III, with whom he worked so closely for so many years? Innocents's millenarianism, like that of Gregory IX, expressed itself in connection with the problem of Islam. Emperor Frederick II "claimed a messianic role for himself."[47] Could he also have received this millenarianism from his guardian, Pope Innocent III? The two met and seemed to be on good terms circa 1212–1215, when Innocent's millenarianism reached its peak.[48] The young Frederick II was certainly influenced by Innocent's attempt (1215) to launch a Fifth Crusade.[49] Why could he not also have been influenced by Innocent's millenarian ideas which, as we have seen, the pope linked to this Crusade in his Crusade appeal of April 19, 1213? If indeed, as we argue, Pope Innocent III did accept

millenarian ideas, this would certainly help explain the origins of the unexpected and rather startling millenarianism of both Pope Gregory IX and Emperor Frederick II.[50]

*****

If indeed we are correct that in 1213 Pope Innocent III sincerely believed that Islam would disappear from the face of the earth circa 1284 as part of the Second Coming of Christ, the following question remains. In the mind of Pope Innocent III did Christinas have a role to play in bringing about the end of Islam? The answer is certainly Yes, for if Innocent imagined that the end of Islam would be solely the result of God's doing, would Innocent have envisioned a 66-year period leading up to the final disappearance of Islam? Would a pope depict God as requiring 66 years to achieve His ends unless he thought that God had assigned to Christian people a crucial role in their realization?[51]

Did Pope Innocent III foresee the role of Christians as an indirect, passive one, e.g., doing complete penance for their sins during this 66-year period (1218–1284) so as to merit God's bringing Islam to an end for them in 1284? Given Innocent's tremendous dynamism and vast Crusade plans, it would seem much more likely that he foresaw Christians playing a significantly more direct and active role in the ending of Islam.

How did Pope Innocent III conceive this role? We can only think of two possibilities: (1) killing most of the Muslims in the world or (2) converting most of them to Christianity.

We can rule out possibility one immediately. Pope Innocent III's attitude toward the Muslims, comparatively speaking, was one of the most tolerant during the entire High Middle Ages (1000–1300). In his letter of April 26, 1213 (only seven days after his crucial millenarian letter of April 19, 1213), to Malik al-Adil, the Ayyubid sultan of Egypt, Innocent genuinely deplored the shedding of Muslim blood.[52] According to Norman Daniel, whose Islam and the West embodies the results of an extremely intensive study of Western Christian attitudes toward Islam during the High Middle Ages, Innocent's tolerant attitude toward the Muslims as expressed in this letter has only one parallel during the entire 300-year period 1000–1300, that of the Liber Nicholay (midthirteen century? Italy?).[53]

This leaves us with possibility two, converting the Muslims to Christianity, as the only possibility.[54] Indeed, we have a significant amount of evidence indicating that Pope Innocent III was seriously interested in the conversion of the Muslims to Christianity and encouraged St. Francis of Assisi's efforts along these lines.[55]

How did Pope Innocent III believe the Christians would accomplish the mass conversion of the Muslims in the 66-year period, 1218–1284? The first step, Innocent must have reasoned, would have to be conquest of the Muslim lands in the Middle East by the greatest crusading force Western Christians had ever mustered. The conquest of these Muslim lands, Innocent probably thought, was an absolutely fundamental precondition for the mass conversion of the Muslims for the following two reasons. (1) The conquest of the Muslim lands in the Middle East would deal Islam a crippling psychological blow, by proving once and for all to the people of the mosque that Christ was more powerful than Muhammad.[56] (2) It would insure that the Muslims would be unable to inflict the death penalty prescribed by Islamic law upon the numerous Christian missionaries Innocent hoped to send them.[57] Thus, we are arguing here that the purpose of the great Fifth Crusade, called for by Innocent at the Fourth Lateran Council (November 1215), was the conquest of the Muslim lands in the Middle East as the first, but absolutely crucial, step in the mass conversion of the Muslims to Christianity. As we believe the pope envisioned it, this great Crusade would begin operations in the summer of 1217. Counting from November 1215, the time of the Fourth Lateran Council, the Crusade would take no more than three to four years, e.g., until late 1218 or late 1219, to conquer the Muslim lands in the Middle East.[58] Hopefully the Crusade would finish its operations by the end of 1218, the crucial 600th year after the birth of Islam (in 618). Christian missionaries could then proceed to work in earnest among the conquered Muslims.

It is in the light of these plans of Pope Innocent III that we believe we must see the imposition of a distinction in clothing[59] upon Muslims at the Fourth Lateran Council, primarily *the Muslims he hoped to conquer in the Middle East*. The imposition of a distinction in clothing upon the conquered Muslims of that strategic region of the world was closely related to the attempt to convert them to Christianity.[60] Distinction in clothing imposed by a conqueror upon the conquered implies social degradation.[61] The social degradation of the conquered

Muslims was closely related in the following two ways to the attempt to convert them to Christianity.

(1) It was absolutely indispensable for the success of the missionaries. Without the social degradation of the conquered Muslims, the highly attractive Islamic civilization would probably assimilate most of the Christian occupation force culturally, and perhaps much of it even religiously (*i.e.*, convert some of it to Islam!).[62] Thus, if the Christian missionaries were to have a fair chance of success in converting the conquered Muslims, something would have to be done to prevent this. Christians were less likely to be attracted by the culture and religion of a people that was both conquered and made to wear a "badge of shame." (2) The social degradation of the conquered Muslims would also act as a powerful sociological pressure, supporting the preaching and example of the missionaries Innocent hoped to send among them.[63] The only way available to the conquered Muslims to escape this social degradation would be to heed the Christian missionaries and accept baptism at their hands.

As the pope probably envisioned it, these missionaries would work for the conversion of the conquered Muslims by both deed and word. (1) They would live an exemplary Christian life ethically, by loving one another and by dissuading the Christian occupation force from abusing the conquered Muslims in their persons or their property; and ritually, by encouraging the devotion to the sacraments of each other and of the Christian occupation force. (2) They would also preach the Gospel to the conquered Muslims in all its beauty and simplicity, demonstrating how the Gospel was the fulfillment of the highest ideals of the Islamic faith.[64] We would suggest that Innocent intended to use the newly founded Franciscan order as the backbone of the corps of missionaries he proposed to send to work among the conquered Muslims.[65]

Innocent probably believed that with God's help, plus the crippling psychological blow an overwhelmingly victorious Crusade would give Islam, plus the social degradation of the conquered Muslims enforced by a visible distinction in clothing, the missionaries would succeed if devoted enough (St. Francis and his closest disciples were all highly dedicated). By the twofold method of deed and word they would convert the majority of the conquered Muslims to Christianity during the 66-year period, 1218–1284, thus paving the way for the Second Coming of Christ.

*****

What relevance did all this have to the Jews?

Ever since circa 1000, as we have argued, Western Christians seem to have equated Jews and Muslims and to have considered Jews to be Islamic fifth columnists in Christian society. In fact, this equation of Jew with Muslim (rather than the belief that the Jews killed Christ) was the crucial factor in the great outburst of anti-Semitism in Western Europe during the High Middle Ages (1000–1300) and subsequent thereto.[66] Suffice it to say that Canon 68, the distinction in clothing canon of the Fourth Lateran Council, offers a good example of this equation when it implies that Moses imposed a distinction in clothing (i.e., fringes; cf. Numbers 15:38) upon both Jews *and Muslims!*[67] Apparently the author of this canon considered Moses the lawgiver of Islam as well as Judaism. Canon 69 of the Fourth Lateran Council links Jews and Muslims in forbidding members of either group to hold office among Christians.[68] Numerous other examples have been given supra in chapter four.

In the light of this equation of Jew with Muslim we think it safe to assume that when Pope Innocent III foresaw the end of Islam circa 1284 he foresaw the end of Judaism along with it. The "Letter of Toledo," which may have been one of the sources of Innocent's eschatology, also equated Jew with Muslim and foresaw the end of their common religion in 1186.[69] Similarly, Joachim of Flora, who died during the early part of the pontificate of Pope Innocent III, linked Jew and Muslim. He foresaw the conversion of both groups in 1260, immediately prior to the transition from the second age, the age of the Son, to the third age, the utopian age of the Holy Spirit.[70] Similarly, we would argue, Pope Innocent III equated Jew with Muslim and expected the end of both faiths preparatory to the Second Coming of Christ in 1284.

We would further argue that just as Innocent believed Christians had an active role to play in the ending of Islam through the conversion of Muslims, so he believed they had an active role to play in the ending of Judaism through the conversion of most of the Jews in the world to Christianity. However, unlike the Mulims who lived in their own lands, most of the Jews lived within Christian society. Therefore, unlike the Muslims, the Jews would not have to be conquered by a Crusade as an indispensable precondition for the Christian attempt to convert them en masse. But, like the Muslims whom Innocent hoped to conquer, the Jews (and the relatively few Muslims[71]) living in Christian society would also be forced to adopt an externally imposed distinction in clothing as a means of degrading them socially,[72] as an aid in the attempt to convert them en masse. Also the social degradation of the Jews would make it much more difficult for the Jews living within Christian society to convert Christians to Judaism and through such conversions prolong the existence of their faith beyond 1284.[73] Such social degradation would also make it much more difficult for any Jews living within Christian society to marry their Christian neighbors and either convert their Christian spouses to Judaism or raise the children of these mixed marriages as Jews, thereby again prolonging the existence of their faith beyond 1284.[74] Finally, the social degradation of the Jews living within Christian society would act as a powerful sociological pressure to support the preaching and example of the missionaries Innocent probably also hoped to send to work among the Jews.[75]

*****

We agree with Israel Abrahams, Henry Charles Lea, Johann E. Scherer, Joseph Jacobs, Simon Dubnow, Solomon Grayzel, and Azriel Shochat that the prevention of intermarriage between Christian and Jew could not have been the primary reason (though it certainly could have been and probably was a subsidiary reason) behind the distinction in clothing requirement introduced by the Fourth Lateran Council in 1215.[76] Some of the arguments *against* the view that the prevention of intermarriage was the primary factor behind the distinction in clothing requirement are as follows.

1. Those who hold that the prevention of intermarriage was the primary factor behind the distinction in clothing requirement tend to assume that Christians who married Jews at the time of the Fourth Lateran Council did so innocently, *i.e.*, mistakenly thinking that their prospective spouses were Christians. Had they known they were Jews, they would not have married them. However, if Jews were required to wear distinctive clothing, no Christian could innocently mistake them for Christians. Hence the distinction in clothing requirement would eliminate intermarriages between Christians and Jews.

The problem with this line of thinking is that by 1215 almost all

Christians of Western Europe would have known who the Jews residing in their particular community were. The towns were relatively small. Most Jews voluntarily lived in their own neighborhoods, apart from Christians.[77] In some regions Jews may already have been distinguished, on their own initiative, by beard and headgear.[78] Many Jews were beginning to take up, partly against their will, a notorious occupation, *i.e.* moneylending, which clearly set them apart.[79] Jews were conspicuous by their absence from church-related celebrations which played such a key role in medieval life. Jews frequently challenged Christians to debate and ridiculed what Christians held dear.[80] It was obvious, to all Christians, who the local Jews were.[81] A special distinction in clothing, imposed by Christians, was not needed for this purpose.

One might argue that Jews traveled around frequently (as merchants), and the identity of these travelers might not have been so obvious in a strange community. This argument has no validity, however, because from the time of the First Crusade Jewish travel on the roads had become increasingly dangerous, thus less and less frequent. Furthermore, travelers, as strangers, would have been even more obvious in the communities which they entered. Finally, Jews traveling on the roads were early exempted from the distinction in clothing requirement, and this exemption may have originated with Pope Innocent III himself, 1215–1216.[82]

2. Canon 68 begins with the admission that Jews in some Christian provinces, on their own initiative, had already distinguished themselves in appearance from the Christians. Grayzel, Kisch, and Blumenkranz hold that the reference here is, not to being distinguished in clothing, but rather to being distinguished by beard and headgear.[83] However, the concluding portion of Canon 68 which actually mentions the imposition of a distinction in clothing does not seem to take this preexisting distinction in appearance into consideration. This portion of Canon 68 speaks as if it were imposing the distinction in clothing upon *all* Jews in *all* Christian provinces.[84] It does not clearly specify that those Jews in some Christians provinces who, on their own initiative, had already distinguished themselves in appearance from the Christians were exempt from the new decree. The implication is that even those Jews who had already distinguished themselves in appearance would nevertheless have to assume a special, additional distinction imposed by non-Jews. If Canon 68's primary motive had been the prevention of intermarriage, why should a special, additional

distinction have been decreed even for these Jews? If, however, the primary motive was social degradation in order to encourage conversion, the special, additional distinction in clothing (which Innocent probably thought should be a blue badge in the form of the Greek letter Tau[85]) is easily understandable.

3. There is little if any evidence that intermarriage between Christians and Jews was widespread at this time. Canon 68 itself admits that such intermarriages occurred only *interdum*, "occasionally." If so, why such a harsh and totally unprecedented measure to prevent such comparatively rare occurrences? Kisch attempts to refute this last argument by maintaining that such intermarriages, though perhaps only occasional, were still extremely serious breaches. Intermarriage was considered heresy, and heresy was an especially critical problem for the church at this time (*e.g.*, the Albigensian situation in southern France which called forth a Crusade circa 1209).[86] Kisch does not document this intriguing suggestion sufficiently. In its support one could cite the fact that Emperor Frederick II, Pope Innocent III's protege, did give the Inquisition jurisdiction over intermarriages between Christians and Jews.[87]

However, even if Kisch is correct and the church did indeed consider intermarriage between Christian and Jew as serious a threat as heresy, would not the church merely have decreed more severe punishment (or more ruthless enforcement of existing punishments) for Jews who broke the laws of both their own faith and Christianity by marrying Christians? Did the church have to punish all Jews everywhere in Western Europe, the overwhelming majority of whom married within their faith, by making them all wear a special badge of shame? If the church did have to punish all Jews for the sins of the few who married Christians, would not the church merely have imposed a badge of shame upon the Jews of regions (*e.g.*, southern France) where the problem of heresy was more flagrant rather than on the Jews throughout all of Western Europe, including regions (*e.g.*, England) where the problem of heresy was less flagrant? Moreover, even if Kisch's refutation of our third argument is valid, this would still leave us with our first and second arguments above, either one of which is sufficient in itself to refute the view that the prevention of intermarriage was the *primary* factor behind the distinction in clothing requirement. Even if Kisch is correct that the church equated intermarriage with heresy, the church did not have to attempt to prevent such inter-

THE JEW AS ALLY OF THE MUSLIM

marriage by making the Jews wear a badge. The Christians already knew who the local Jews were from the way the Jews *behaved* and from the fact that the Jews in many Christian lands were already distinguished from the Christians by beard and headgear.

The history of intermarriage between Christian and Jew has not yet been written.[88] Until the data on intermarriage between Christian and Jew in the Middle Ages is collected, a *final* judgment about the primary motive for the distinction in clothing requirement imposed by Canon 68 is impossible. However, at this stage we are arguing that the prevention of intermarriage could not have been the primary reason for the distinction in clothing requirement, though it most certainly could have been and probably was a subsidiary reason. If it was a subsidiary reason, however, it was considered, not an end in itself, but rather merely a means of achieving a more important end, *i.e.*, preventing Jews from using intermarriage (involving the possible conversion of the non-Jewish spouse to Judaism and/or the raising of the children as Jews) as a means of preserving their faith beyond 1284. The main reason for the distinction in clothing requirement was to degrade the Jews (not to prevent intermarriage between them and the Christians). But, again, degradation was considered, not an end in itself, but rather merely a means of achieving a more important end, *i.e.*, a sociological pressure to support the work of the missionaries Innocent hoped to send to the Jews to bring about their conversion en masse, along with the similar mass conversion of the Muslims, preparatory to the Second Coming of Christ in 1284.

*****

In this chapter we have argued that the imposition of a distinction in clothing on non-Christian Abrahamitic monotheists, decreed by Pope Innocent III and the Fourth Lateran Council in 1215, was primarily directed against *the Muslims* that the pope hoped to conquer in the Middle East, not the Jews (and the few Muslims) living in Christian society. This view, of course, is not the generally prevailing opinion. The generally prevailing opinion is well represented by Blumenkranz:

> Both the allusion [in Canon 68 of the Fourth Lateran Council] to Biblical law (Leviticus 19), and the inclusion of the canon among a series of others regulating the Jewish position, indicate that the decree was directed especially against the Jews.[89]

The problem with Blumenkranz's argument is that it fails to take into consideration the long history of the Christian tendency to equate Jew with Muslim.

Thus, the mere fact that Canon 68 quotes the Old Testament (actually Numbers 15:38 rather than Leviticus 19:19[90]) does not mean that Canon 68's imposition of the distinction in clothing was directed primarily against the Jews. As we have already demonstrated,[91] their historic tendency to equate Jew with Muslim impelled the Christians of Western Europe to consider both Moses and the Old Testament to be as much *Islamic* as Jewish. Second, though it may be true that Canon 68 fits into the immediate context of four canons of the Fourth Lateran Council (Canons 67–70) treating Christian-Jewish relations, it is also true that two of these same four canons (Canons 68 and 69) treat Christian-Islamic relations and mention the Muslims as well (called "Saracens" in Canon 68 and "Pagans" in Canon 69[92]).

More importantly, though the immediate context of Canon 68 seems to reflect greater Christian concern about Jews than about Muslims, the *larger* context of both Pope Innocent III's life and work in general, and of the primary purposes for which the Fourth Lateran Council was called into session in particular, must also be taken into consideration. This context and these purposes were the Crusade against the Muslims and the reform of the church. Both were seen by the pope and the council as being intimately related.[93] Of course, if we consider only the immediate context of Canon 68 of the Fourth Lateran Council, we could easily come to the mistaken conclusion that the distinction in clothing requirement of 1215 was directed primarily against the Jews rather than the Muslims. However, if we consider the larger context of the main purposes of Pope Innocent III and the Lateran Council in general, we cannot avoid coming to precisely the opposite conclusion. The distinction in clothing requirement was directed *primarily against the Muslims*, not the Jews.

However, in opposition to our thesis one might want to argue that if Canon 68's distinction in clothing requirement of 1215 was directed primarily against the Muslims, why were the Jews mentioned *first*, the Muslims only second, in that portion of the canon which imposes the badge? One would think, at least at first glance, that if the primary thrust of the new decree was directed against the Muslims they would be mentioned first therein.

In reply to this argument, several logical and plausible reasons can be suggested why Pope Innocent III and the Fourth Lateran Council mentioned the Jews first in Canon 68, even thought the main thrust of Canon 68's distinction in clothing requirements was directed against the Muslims. These same reasons can also explain why chapter twenty-two of book two of St. Anselm's *Cur Deus Homo*, written in the 1090s (the very decade of the First Crusade), one of the greatest monuments in the history of Christians missions to the Muslims, mentions the Jews first, even though, according to Rene Roques and Julia Gauss,[94] the main thrust of the *Cur Deus Homo* was directed against the Muslims.

1. Pope Innocent III and the Fourth Lateran Council followed the chronological principle. Since Moses' life and work antedated that of (Christ and) Muhammad, while Muhammad's life and work postdated that of Moses (and Christ), Canon 68 mentioned the Jews first and the Muslims only second.

2. Pope Innocent III and the Fourth Lateran Council mentioned the Jews first because Jesus himself, in his human aspect, had been born to a Jewish couple (Joseph and Mary) rather than to a Muslim couple. Jesus also entered into discussion at age twelve with the Jewish rabbis at the Jerusalem Temple rather than with the Muslim ulama at the Meccan Ka'aba.

3. Pope Innocent III and the Fourth Lateran Council mentioned the Jews first because Christianity emerged more out of Judaism than out of Islam. This can be seen from the facts that the early Apostles came out of a Jewish rather than an Islamic background and that the Jewish scripture, the Old Testament, was incorporated into the Christian scripture, whereas the Muslim scripture, the Quran, was not.

4. Pope Innocent III and the Fourth Lateran Council mentioned the Jews first because a greater proportion of the world Jewish population than of the world Muslim population lived in Western Christian countries. Moreover, Jews were present in all five of the major countries of Western Europe in the early thirteenth century—Italy, Spain, France, Germany, and England—whereas Muslims were at most present within only three of the major countries: Italy, Spain, and France.

5. Pope Innocent III and the Fourth Lateran Council were thinking in terms of the relative ease with which the threat posed by each of the two infidel groups could be dealt with. The Jews were mentioned first because the threat which they posed was considered easier to deal with in that the Jews represented only a spiritual but not a military

threat. By contrast, the threat which the Muslims posed was considered more difficult to deal with in that the Muslims represented not only a spiritual but a military threat as well.

We must remember that the distinction in clothing requirement was not an end in itself, but a part of the social degradation connected with the missionary program that would bring about the Second Coming of Christ. But, first and foremost, the Christians had to have political control over the non-Christian group in question. The Christians already had political control over Jews, for in the early thirteenth century most of the Jews in the world lived in Western Christian lands. Thus, it would have been easy to start the eschatological chain reaction in motion by imposing a distinction in clothing upon them, leading to social degradation and missionary persuasion. In the early thirteenth century most of the Muslims in the world lived in their own independent kingdoms. They had to be conquered first by a massive new (Fifth) Crusade which had not yet achieved success. Thus, the reason Canon 68 mentioned the Jews first when it imposed the distinction in clothing requirements was because it was beginning with those already under Christian control, with those upon whom the imposition of the distinction in clothing would have already been possible. The Muslims were mentioned second because most of them were not yet under Christian control. Imposition upon them of the distinction in clothing awaited the successful outcome of a gigantic struggle, the Fifth Crusade. Though the Muslims were the primary target, the Jews were mentioned first because the pope and the council preferred to think of the easier target first, the relatively powerless Jews, and the much more difficult target second, the fierce Muslims who could not be conquered without the shedding of an immense amount of Christian blood.

6. Finally, the recent Second Vatican Council's practice in this regard is quite instructive. It is well known that the main thrust of *Nostra Aetate*, Vatican II's "Declaration on the Relationship of the Church to Non-Christian Religions," as can be seen from the history of the evolution of this document as well as the amount of lines it gives to a particular question, was reconciliation between Christians and Jews rather than reconciliation between Christians and Muslims (which the document, of course, also considered an important goal). Nevertheless, Christian reconciliation with the Muslims is mentioned first therein (paragraph no. 3), while Christian reconciliation with the

Jews is mentioned only second (paragraph no. 4). Thus, first in order of mention is not necessarily first in order of importance. Indeed, it could well be argued that St. Anselm's *Cur Deus Homo*, the Fourth Lateran Council's Canon 68, and Vatican II's *Nostra Aetate* all followed the principle of building to a crescendo by mentioning what was of lesser importance first and of greater importance last. Thus, St. Anselm and the Fourth Lateran Council mentioned the Jews first even though the main thrust of their concern was the Muslims, while Vatican II mentioned the Muslims first even though the main thrust of its concern was the Jews.

*****

To summarize this chapter. Canon 68, the distinction in clothing canon, of the Fourth Lateran Council (1215) was directed at both Muslims and Jews, but primarily at the Muslims whom Pope Innocent III expected his Fifth Crusade to conquer in the Middle East, and only secondarily at the Jews (and the relatively few Muslims) living in Western European Christian society. The purpose of the distinction in clothing in the case of both the Muslims and the Jews was to degrade these non-Christians socially. Degrading them socially was conceived of, not as an end in itself, however, but rather merely as a means of facilitating their conversion to Christianity, which the missionaries (especially the Franciscans) whom Innocent hoped to send to both groups would strive to achieve by both word and example. The conversion of these peoples en masse was seen as mankind's crucially indispensable role in preparing the way for the Second Coming of Christ, which Pope Innocent III expected in 1284.

Thus, Pope Innocent III's primary concern was the imposition of a "badge of shame" on the Muslims he hoped to conquer in the Middle East, not the Jews of Western Europe. It was the Muslims of the Middle East whom he wanted to convert much more so than the Jews. The Jews were brought into the picture primarily because the Christians equated them with the Muslims and considered them Islamic fifth columnists in Christian territory. Hence, Christian-Islamic relations determined Christian-Jewish relations in one of the most crucial episodes in the history of the Jewish people in the Diaspora, the imposition of the Jewish badge at the Fourth Lateran Council (1215).

7. The Netanyahu Thesis on the Marranos: A New Ethnic Approach to the Origins of the Spanish Inquisition*

Benzion Netanyahu has challenged us of late to come to serious grips with the highly controversial problem of Christian-Jewish relations in Renaissance Spain in his compelling book *The Marranos of Spain, From the Late XIVth to the Early XVIth Century, According to Contemporary Hebrew Sources* (New York: American Academy for Jewish Research, 1st edition, 1966; 2nd edition, 1972; reprinted by the Kraus Reprint Co.).[1] This book represents a sequel to Netanyahu's thorough earlier work *Don Isaac Abravanel, Statesman and Philosopher* (Philadelphia: Jewish Publication Society of America, 1st edition, 1953; 2nd edition, 1968; 3rd edition, 1972). Netanyahu's *Marranos* develops at length a new thesis about the fifteenth-century Marranos, *i.e.*, the thousands of Jews who converted to Christianity in Spain largely in two great waves, which is as follows.

(1) The wave of 1391 seemed on the surface to be one of completely forced conversions, but beneath it flowed a strong eddy of voluntarism. These conversions were occasioned by a series of frightful riots against and massacres of the Jews of Spain (Castile and Aragon; the Jews of Portugal, Granada, and Navarre more or less escaped attack) which first broke out in the city of Seville in response to the fiery preaching of Archdeacon Ferrand Martinez. (2) The wave of circa 1410–1415, more voluntary than the previous wave, arose in response to the powerful missionary preaching of the great Dominican chiliast San Vicente Ferrer and the harsh anti-Jewish social legislation enacted at this time by the crown of Castile and imitated by the crown of Aragon. The element of force involved in the first wave of 1391 was fear of cruel torture and/or violent death at the hands of the mob. This same coercive element was not present in quite the same way in the wave of circa 1410–1415. In this later wave the main factors which

drove the Jews to convert en masse were persuasive preaching (that Jesus was the true Jewish Messiah whose coming was predicted by not only the Bible *but the Talmud as well* and that the Messiah the Jews had so long awaited in the Diaspora would never come) as well as fear of a new harsh program of ghettoization which Castile and Aragon decided to introduce for the Jews at this time.[2]

As Netanyahu points out (*Marranos*, 124), Joseph Albo, the Aragonese Jewish popular philosopher of the first half of the fifteenth-century, held the following view. If Jews were forced to convert to Christianity but later experienced no regret at their conversion (presumably, according to Albo, this regret had to be accompanied by emigration from Spain and open return to Judaism in a land where such would be permitted), these Jews were *voluntary* converts to Christianity, even if at the time they converted they did so only out of fear of death. Thus, according to the Albo criterion even the first wave of Jewish conversions to Christianity, the wave of the 1390s in which the fear of death was an overwhelming factor, was basically a voluntary one. The converts of the 1390s never experienced regret. Indeed, though a priori they might have continued to remain Jews had they not been threatened with massacre in the 1390s for failure to convert, a posteriori they were happy that they had indeed been forced to convert.

How much the more so would the Albo criterion apply to the second wave of Jewish conversions to Christianity, the wave of the 1410s in which the fear of death was not as important a factor. These converts also never experienced regret. But neither had they been forced to convert primarily out of fear of death. Thus, the wave of the 1410s was a doubly voluntary wave, voluntary because, unlike the wave of the 1390s, it was not primarily motivated by the fear of death, and voluntary, according to the Albo criterion, because, like the wave of the 1390s, it never experienced regret.

As Netanyahu also points out (*Marranos*, 157–158), Isaac Caro of Toledo, in the second half of the fifteenth-century, like Albo in the first half of the same century, held as follows. Even though the converts of the 1390s converted out of compulsion (fear of death), while the converts of the 1410s did not convert out of a similar compulsion, the converts of the 1390s were just as much voluntary converts as were those of the 1410s. According to Caro it was a capital offense under *Jewish* law for a Jew to become a Christian, whether he did so willingly (*b'ratzon*) or only under compulsion (*b'hehreah*). In this one instance alone, where a Jew converts to Christianity, *compulsion is also will*, i.e., forced conversion is the same as voluntary conversion. Why so? Because in essence, according to Caro, there is no such thing as forced conversion. No one who was truly loyal to Judaism would ever be converted to Christianity even under compulsion. He would die first (either at the hand of the Christians or at his own hand in ritual suicide), or flee, or die trying to flee. Here Caro was adopting a northern European Jewish point of view. The Jews of Franco-Germany rarely converted to Christianity under compulsion, generally choosing death or flight instead. These northern European Jews, Caro probably held, were true Jews, while the Spanish Jews, even those who converted primarily out of fear of death, were traitors. Thus, according to Caro the converts of the 1410s were certainly voluntary converts, because they did not convert primarily out of fear of death. However, even the converts of the 1390s were voluntary converts as well, because even though they did convert primarily out of fear of death, they still had had a choice. They could have chosen death or flight. The fact that they chose conversion means that they *preferred* conversion. If they preferred conversion, that means that they were *voluntary* converts.

Thus, for both Albo and Caro even the converts of the 1390s, though admittedly motivated primarily by fear of death, were as much voluntary converts as the converts of the 1410s who were not motivated primarily by fear of death. However, Albo and Caro differed on why they considered even the converts of the 1390s to be voluntary converts. For Albo the converts of the 1390s were voluntary converts because they did not later regret what they had earlier done (and express such regret by emigrating to a foreign land where they could openly return to Judaism). For Caro, on the other hand, who represented a much more conservative point of view, the converts of the 1390s were voluntary converts, because all conversion is voluntary in that it prefers conversion to death or flight. Thus, Albo held that while failure to repent at a later date equals willingness, failure to chose death or flight instead of conversion does not equal willingness. Caro, on the other hand, held that both failures, failure to repent at a later date and failure to chose death or flight instead of conversion, equal willingness. To put it another way, Albo held that someone could still be considered loyal to Judaism even if he converted to Christianity out of fear of death. Forced conversion did not ipso facto

equal voluntary treason, provided there was later repentance and return to Judaism. Caro, on the other hand, held that the only loyal Jew
was one who never converted to another religion at all. To Caro any
conversion at all equals voluntary treason, even if it arose out of fear
of death and was followed by genuine repentance. Albo, therefore, put
the emphasis on a decision which could be made after the time of the
crisis had passed, whereas Caro put the emphasis upon the decision
which was in fact made at the very time of the crisis itself. However,
both Albo and Caro agreed that the conversions of the 1390s and the
conversions of the 1410s were basically waves of voluntary conversions.

We would agree with Albo, Caro, and Netanyahu that the application of Christian pressure on the Jews, whether by the mob (who offered the choice of conversion or death) in the 1390s or by the kings
(who offered the choice of conversion or ghettoization) in the 1410s,
was only a secondary factor. The primary factor was the attitude of the
Jews themselves and their conscious, or unconscious, decision to opt
out of what they considered the second-class citizenship and alienated
minority status of Judaism and into what they considered the first-class
citizenship and integrated majority status of Christianity. Christian
pressure in itself, even the threat of death, could not have produced
mass permanent Jewish conversion to Christianity in Spain circa 1400
if the Spanish Jews themselves had not previously come to believe that
mass permanent assimilation was both possible and desirable. This is
precisely what both waves of Jewish converts to Christianity, the
basically voluntary wave of the 1390s and the even more voluntary
wave of the 1410s, had come to believe.

*****

According to regnant modern Jewish scholarly opinion (best represented by Cecil Roth and Yitzhak Baer), the Spanish Inquisition was
established circa 1480 for exclusively religious reasons. The Marranos,
who had been forcibly converted to Christianity in 1391 and circa
1410–1415 (the assumption of this school of thought being that there
was no voluntary element whatsoever in either wave of conversion),
remained Jews at heart. Though externally they pretended to be Christians, in secret they kept alive their Jewish faith. Eventually, so this
theory holds, Christian patience with their crypto-Judaism became ex-
hausted, and the Spanish Inquisition was established to transform
them into good Christians, private as well as public.

Modern Spanish authorities on the Marranos (*e.g.*, Bernardino Llorca and Nicolas Lopez Martinez) agree with the traditional Jewish scholarly view that the Marranos were secret Jews. However, according to these Spanish scholars the crypto-Judaism of the Marranos, though the main factor behind the Spanish Inquisition, was not the only factor. There were also socioeconomic factors. Because these secret Jews had at least formally been converted to Christianity, they were no longer subjected to most of the economic, social, and political limitations that unconverted Jews were subjected to. By their own native genius and hard work they quickly achieved positions of great power and prominence in the fields of business, governmental service, and the church. Along with this great success went an equally great arrogance that led them to express open contempt for the Old Christians (not of Jewish descent). By circa 1480—or so this theory holds—the great success and equally great arrogance of the neophytes, compounded by the fact that they were only pretending to be Christians while in secret remaining loyal to their old Jewish faith, finally provoked the violent reaction against them known as the Spanish Inquisition.

To summarize, then, according to regnant *Jewish* scholarly opinion the fifteenth-century Marranos were secret Jews. Thus, the Spanish Inquisition was established because of religion. The modern Spanish historians believe that important socioeconomic factors were also at work. However, even for the Spanish historians, religion, *i.e.*, the crypto-Judaism of the Marranos, was still the *main* factor behind the Spanish Inquisition.[3]

Relying upon the hitherto largely neglected fifteenth-century Spanish Jewish (Hebrew language) sources—*i.e.*, on rabbinic responsa (answers to questions about Jewish law), philosophical treatises, literary polemics against Christianity, sermon collections, and Bible commentaries—Netanyahu demonstrates that the overwhelming majority of the Marranos in the late fifteenth century, even before the establishment of the Inquisition (circa 1480), were not secret Jews at all. Their forefathers of 1391, once driven into Christianity by fear of torture and/or death (though even for these Jews a strong subconscious element of voluntarism was operating beneath the surface of their conversion), were gradually seduced by the tremendous facilities offered by the majority of Spanish Christian civilization. In due course they attempted to assimilate completely and become Christians in private as well as public. Of course, the relatively less-forced converts of circa

209

1410–1415, who did not convert to Christianity out of fear of torture and/or death but rather in response to missionary preaching and restrictive legislation, put up even less resistance to assimilationist pressures than did the relatively more-forced converts of 1391.

Though Netanyahu himself does not discuss this particular point in his book, it may be suggested that prior to their conversion to Christianity the faith in Judaism of the converts of both 1391 and 1410–1415 (especially of the relatively more voluntary converts of 1410–1415) had been undermined to a significant extent by the cosmopolitan intellectual and cultural atmosphere of Spain. This atmosphere prevailed for five centuries, from the tenth through the fourteenth centuries, under both the Muslims (especially during the caliphate of Cordova, tenth century, the golden age of Spanish Islam) and the Christians (especially during the rule of King Alphonso X of Castile, circa 1252 to 1284, the golden age of medieval Christian Spain). Moreover, the Muslims developed the first great civilization in medieval Spain. Their physical presence and cultural influence, both of which continued into the Later Middle Ages when Christianity effectively dominated the Iberian peninsula, may have been the decisive factor in the collapse of the Spanish Jewish community circa 1400 and its mass conversion to Christianity.[4]

Considerable fifteenth-century Spanish Jewish opinion (followed by some modern Jewish writers of traditional religious leanings) blamed philosophical speculation for the mass conversion. Such speculation flourished among the Jews of medieval Spain, where the Islamic presence was very strong, more than among the Jews of any other medieval Western European country. Conversely, philosophy was practically nonexistent among the Jews of medieval northern France and Germany, where the Islamic presence was negligible, and these Jews never converted to Christianity *en masse*. Philosophy, argued these late medieval Jewish writers, was especially responsible for undermining the kind of blind faith in God needed to withstand persecution. Others in fifteenth-century Spain blamed not philosophical speculation in general, which could be made to serve as the handmaiden of faith, but rather a certain extremist type of philosophy, *i.e.*, Averroism. This radical secularizing type of Aristotelianism arose in Spain and Western Europe in general circa 1200 and was difficult if not impossible to reconcile with the prevailing theism of the Bible and the Talmud. Averroism, argued these late medieval Jewish writers, was especially responsible for undermining Jewish religious zeal and paving the way for the mass conversion of the Spanish Jews at the end of the fourteenth and the beginning of the fifteenth centuries.[5]

In any case, for the third-generation Marranos of the late fifteenth century Judaism was a thing of the past. In fact, they hated Judaism as much as did the Old Christians and wanted no relationship whatsoever with the unconverted Jews still residing in Spain. All that the late fifteenth-century Marranos wanted was to participate fully and completely, on an equal basis with the Old Christians, in the exciting and dynamic Spanish Christian civilization which would soon (in the sixteenth century) spill over its borders, colonize the New World, and become the chief power in the Old World.

As Netanyahu himself puts it (*Marranos*, 75, 207):

what we gather about the Marranos from the responsa literature can be broadly outlined as follows: the camp of the forced converts of 1391 began to turn away from Judaism already in the first generation. By the end of the second generation, the majority of them had stopped observing Jewish law, while in the middle of the century that majority became so overwhelming that at times it appeared . . . that no more crypto-Jews remained in the Marrano camp. Sizeable migration of Marranos from Spain stopped already in the first generation, and from then on it gradually diminished until it reached the vanishing point. In Spain, itself, however, pockets of secret Jews, or at least of practitioners of some Jewish rites, remained in certain *localities*. But these, too, were constantly narrowing in scope and weakening in the intensity of their Jewish devotion, as their practice of Judaism was limited to the performance of *certain* Jewish rites only. While crypto-Judaism was thus dwindling, the process of assimilation, both social and religious, was advancing without letup, so much so that when the Inquisition was established, it [*i.e.*, the process of assimilation] was so deep and thorough-going that the Marrano camp as a whole appeared to Spain's Jews as a predominantly gentile camp. . . .

Having thus arrived at the conclusion that the Marranos, in general, were *semi-gentilized*, there is hardly any need to consider further the strength of the Judaic element among them. Surely a segment of secret Jews survived, in semi-dormant fashion, up to the days of the Inquisition; and, shortly before the establishment of the latter, it may have even been "revived" or strengthened by some sort of "awakening."

211

But . . . the pro-Jewish element among the Marranos, consisting as it did of "platonic" Jews as well as of performers of "some precepts," belonged to the very fringes of the camp, while the broad current of the Marrano force moved incessantly forward toward its desired goals without sharing in any Judaizing effort. In fact, if there was a religious process still astir among the Marranos, it was not of *Judaization* but of *dejudaization*—and this to the very limit.

Thus, according to the Netanyahu thesis, the Marranos were permitted to assimilate fully into Spanish Christian society during the first two-thirds of the fifteenth century. However, the establishment of the Inquisition circa 1480 halted and began to partially reverse that movement. Given the sincere Christianity of the Marranos, the Spanish Inquisition could not have been established for religious reasons, *i.e.*, to suppress the alleged secret Judaism of the Marranos. If the Spanish Inquisition was not motivated by religion, what then was it motivated by? According to Netanyahu (*Marranos*, 3 and note 6; citing his *Abravanel*, 275, note 25), the Inquisition was a product of "racial [ethnic] hatred and political considerations." The Spanish Inquisition persecuted the Marranos of the late fifteenth century essentially because of their race, *i.e.*, their Jewish ethnic background. The contemporary Spanish documents actually use the term *raza* ("race"). They also speak about *limpieza de sangre* ("purity of blood"). The "political considerations" included the desire of the monarchy to use the Inquisition to forge a unified modern nation state in Spain by suppressing regionalism and the nobility (with whom the Marranos were generally allied). The alleged secret Judaism of the Marranos was not the motivating factor behind the Inquisition but did provide this institution with a convenient pretext to mask its true motives. The establishment of the Inquisition represented a decision by Spanish Christian society to reject the Marranos as converts to Christianity even though their conversion was sincere, because such rejection satisfied ethnic emotions and served political considerations which seemed overwhelmingly more important than the true teaching of the church at the time.

In shocked and bewildered response to the sudden turn of events in the 1480s—their persecution by the Inquisition and rejection by Spanish Christian society for ethnic and political reasons—*some* (but not most) of the Marranos did as follows. They attempted to defy inquisitorial tyranny by rediscovering their origins, the Jewish heritage of their grandfathers of circa 1400. To accomplish this they either fled Spain in order to return to Judaism in a more tolerant foreign land (especially an Islamic land like Ottoman Turkey) or, more frequently, remained in Spain but began to practice Judaism in secret. As this minority group among the Marranos probably reasoned circa and after 1480, if we are going to be persecuted for crypto-Judaism, something we are not practicing, perhaps we ought to begin practicing it, in order to make our suffering meaningful and to force our persecutors to become honest, instead of allowing them the luxury of hypocrisy.

Thus, according to the Netanyahu thesis, and this is where it so radically revises previous views, the Spanish Inquisition was not a *response* to the secret Judaism of the Marranos. Rather, the Inquisition may have caused some of the Marranos to become secret Jews. As Netanyahu puts it (*Marranos*, 3):

> The minority [of the Marranos] that still adhered to Judaism in the three decades preceding the establishment of the Inquisition was, save for temporary and inconsequential reactions, constantly diminishing in size and influence. . . . It would have, in all likelihood, soon faded into nothingness, had not the process of assimilation been violently interfered with by the Inquisition. . . . Thus it was due to the Inquisition itself that the dying Marranism in Spain was given a new lease on life. . . . What actually happened was the reverse of what is generally assumed: *It was not a powerful Marrano movement that provoked the establishment of the Inquisition, but it was the establishment of the Inquisition that caused the temporary resurgence of the Spanish Marrano movement.*

The Spanish Inquisition, then, was inspired by ethnic and political considerations, not religious prejudice. However, the Inquisition did attempt to use a religious justification. It sought to legitimatize its terror by means of a fictitious religious charge, the alleged crypto-Judaism of the Marranos. According to Netanyahu (*Marranos*, 3-4):

> This fiction was in no way a product of misinformation or self-delusion, but of deliberate and careful calculation. . . . Those who used these tactics knew precisely what they were doing. The fact that there was a striking difference between the official campaign slogans of the Inquisition and the real, unpublished aims of its advocates should surprise no one at all familiar with the history of persecution. Campaign

slogans of mass persecution movements rarely agree with their actual aims. . . .

Now religious motivation, however distorted, has always some nobility to it, and in the Middle Ages in particular it had, besides an appeal, also an explosive force. That it was brought to the fore in the campaign against the Marranos was, therefore, merely part of a *modus operandi*, a means for attaining a certain end; but it was not really the religion of the Marranos with which the Inquisition was concerned. Its concern were the *bearers* of that religion. Its purpose was to degrade, impoverish and ruin the influence of the Marranos in all spheres of life, to terrorize and demoralize them individually and collectively—in brief, to destroy them psychologically and physically so as to make it impossible for them to rise again as a factor of any consequence in Spain. The aim of the Inquisition, therefore, as I see it, was *not to eradicate a Jewish heresy from the midst* of the Marrano group, but to eradicate the Marrano group from the midst of the Spanish people.

Finally Netanyahu, in explanation of the ethnic reason (one of what he considers the two real reasons for the establishment of the Inquisition, the other being "political considerations"), presents an extremely significant quotation from the writings of Isaac Arama, one of the leading Jewish religious thinkers in fifteenth-century Spain. In his commentary on the biblical book of Lamentations, Arama has the Jewish people as a whole address God as follows (*Marranos*, 208):

> You, God, know, and You are my witness, that in all the evils they have perpetrated against me, and in all the acts of vengeance they have wrought upon me, their sole intent was to annihilate and destroy me not because of my sins, but because of *what I am*.

According to Netanyahu, what Arama said about the unconverted Jews of Spain could also apply, with equal appropriateness, to the Marranos as well.

Thus, the Netanyahu thesis demonstrates that in the establishment of the Spanish Inquisition much stronger than the forces of religion were the concerns and demands of everyday life and the internal divisions within the body politic of the Spanish people emanating from powerful socioethnic and historical causes. The blame for the Spanish Inquisition, therefore, cannot fall primarily upon Christian theology or on the Roman Catholic Church, both of which served here only as a medium and an excuse. Though it is true that the Spanish church to a great extent allowed itself to be used as a vehicle of oppression, the primary responsibility for the Inquisition must fall rather on certain segments of the Spanish people and their leaders, who finally allowed themselves to succumb to the easy temptation to use ethnic hatred against the Marranos as a means of advancing their own class interest and/or of achieving national unity, despite the teachings of their own Christian faith, according to which "there cannot be [in Christ] Greek and Jew, circumcised and uncircumcised, barbarian, Scythian, slave, freeman, but Christ is all and in all" (Colossians 3:11).

From the foreword and first chapter of the book (as well as from the preface to the second edition of the book, written October 20, 1971, page vii) it would seem that Netanyahu is working on a sequel volume which will deal with the Christian (Spanish and Latin) sources for the history of the Marranos in the fifteenth-century. Therein he will attempt to show that these Christian sources have hitherto been misread because of the romantic notions which have prevailed among scholars working in this field. A proper understanding of the Christian sources will reveal the same startling conclusion that emerges from a study of the Jewish sources. The fifteenth-century Marranos were out and out Christians, not secret Jews. The Spanish Inquisition was established because of ethnic and political considerations, not religious prejudice.

Netanyahu is also at work on two other related books, a history of the Marranos in recent Spanish and Jewish scholarship and a history of the Inquisition from the fifteenth to the early nineteenth centuries.[6] At the same time he has gathered material for a comprehensive history of medieval Christian-Jewish polemics and a history of the medieval Christian practice of treating the Jews as *servi camerae*, serfs of the royal treasury, semifree agents of the various medieval monarchies, an ambivalent practice which both degraded the Jews and yet helped insure their survival within medieval Western Christian society. Both of these areas of study, medieval Christian-Jewish polemics and the Jews as *servi camerae*, despite their tremendous importance, are very far from having been definitively studied.[7] Netanyahu has also been attempting to rally support for the publication of a *Monumenta Judaeorum Hispaniae Historica* (similar to the *Monumenta Germaniae Historica*), a multivolume collection of all the texts (whether in Hebrew,

Arabic, Latin, Spanish, etc.) relevant to the history of the Jews in Spain. Finally, Netanyahu hopes to be able to summarize all of his research in a work of creative synthesis that would survey the long and significant history of the Jewish people in the Iberian peninsula. This history has previously been studied by such distinguished scholars as Jose Amador de los Rios, Solomon Katz, Eliyahu Ashtor, Meyer Kayserling, Abraham Neuman, Yitzhak Baer, Jose Maria Millas-Valli-crosa, Francisco Cantera Burgos, Julio Caro Baroja, and Americo Castro.[8]

It is impossible within the limitations imposed upon us in this chapter to discuss in detail all of the various proofs which Netanyahu adduces throughout his book in support of the thesis that the fifteenth-century Marranos were not secret Jews.[9] However, suffice it to say that chief among these proofs are the following facts which emerge clearly and unequivocally from a study of the Jewish sources.

(1) Contrary to long-standing Jewish tradition, which taught that kindness should be shown to Jews who had been forcibly converted to Christianity but who remained Jews at heart, the unconverted Jews of Spain despised the Marranos. Why should this have been the case? It was because the Marranos were not Jews at heart! The unconverted Jews of Spain saw the Marranos as betrayers of Judaism, because the Marranos lived like Christians and acted like Christians in *private* as well as in public.[10] (2) The Marranos hated the unconverted Jews and campaigned actively for their destruction as well as for the suppression of the Jewish religion within Spain.[11] (3) When the Spanish Inquisition was established in the 1480s, the unconverted Jews did not lament the fact that the Marranos were being singled out for such cruel and unusual persecution. Quite the contrary, the unconverted Jews rejoiced that the Marranos were finally being punished by God, via the Inquisition, for their betrayal of Judaism and their idolatrous worship of foreign gods.[12] (4) When the establishment of the Inquisition did produce a reaction in the direction of Judaism among some of the Marranos, the overwhelming majority of the Spanish rabbinical authorities of the day refused to treat these Judaizing Marranos as penitent Jews (*shavim bi-t'shuvah*) but rather defined them instead as proselytes (*gerim*), as regular converts to Judaism from some other religion. This was because the rabbis knew that the Marranos by this time, *as a group*, were out and out Gentiles and not secret Jews.[13] (5) Most Marranos who fled Spain after the establishment of the Inquisition went to Christian

216

lands, where it was relatively more difficult to return to the open practice of Judaism, rather than to Islamic lands, where it was relatively
easier to return to the open practice of Judaism. This was because most
of the Marranos were no longer secret Jews by the end of the fifteenth
century but instead were Christians, through and through, who continued to want, in vain, to be accepted as such within or without
Spain. They preferred to risk persecution in Christian lands for trying
to be Christians rather than to be relatively well treated in Islamic
lands for being content to be Jews.[14]

✳✳✳✳✳

The published reviews of Netanyahu's *Marranos* have suggested no
serious criticisms of his thesis. If the Netanyahu thesis proves to be
correct, which seems highly likely especially because of the way it
radically rejects romantic illusion, its implications for the study of
medieval anti-Semitism and for the continuing modern Christian-
Jewish dialogue are vast.

What are these implications?

(1) *Jews living in the Christian world would theoretically prefer to*
assimilate completely and to disappear as Jews.

Alexis Khomiakov, the great nineteenth-century Russian Orthodox
lay theologian and Slavophile philosopher, held that "all Protestants
were crypto-Papists" (*i.e.*, would-be Roman Catholics).[15] The reverse
is probably also true, as we see in the post-Vatican II Roman Catholic
Church's attempt to reach out for Christian unity in part by diluting
its traditional distinctiveness. "Roman Catholics are would-be Protestants." What is true about relations between the two great divisions
of the Western Christian church, the Germanic Protestants and the
Latin Roman Catholics, may also be true about relations between
Christians and Jews. One could argue that "Christians are would-be
Jews," citing the numerous Judaizing movements which have arisen during the long history of the Christian church.[16] One could also argue
the reverse, that "Jews are would-be Christians," citing the Spanish
situation of the fifteenth century. This argument could also cite such
more recent phenomena as the Frankist movement in eighteenth-
century Eastern and Central Europe, as well as the waves of Jewish
conversion to Christianity in both Germany and England circa 1800.[17]
Analogous thereto would be the German Jewish assimilationist drive

between 1870 and 1930, dramatically and violently reversed when Hitler came to power,[18] as well as the heavy assimilationist pressures which have been successfully at work on the Jewish communities in the Soviet Union, the United States, and Palestine/Israel since World War I.

The Netanyahu thesis is the first approach to the study of Jewish history in Renaissance Spain which is aware of this important principle of interreligious relations in the Western World. The two sides of any given coin have more in common with each other than they do with any single side of any other coin. Protestantism and Catholicism are two side of the same coin called Western Christendom. Christianity and Judaism are two sides of the same coin called Judaeo-Christianity, or biblicism. The subconscious attraction of each for the other can occasionally burst into the open and powerfully affect the course of history, as it did, with such tragic consequences, in Renaissance Spain before and after the establishment of the Inquisition.

Thus, the Netanyahu thesis demonstrates that the Roman Catholic religion and Spanish Christian society were both attractive enough spiritually and materially to inspire, after a relatively short period of time, the enthusiastic devotion of thousands of Jews. This was despite the fact that most of these same Jews had been harshly treated by the Christian majority culture a short while before when they apparently had been driven by brute force into abandoning their ancestral faith in the persecution of 1391.

2. *Jewish attempts at complete assimilation may be tolerated for a time, e.g., two generations, by a given Christian country.*

Thus, the Netanyahu thesis demonstrates that Spanish Christian society for two generations (circa 1420–1480) was willing to give these seemingly forced converts from Judaism the benefit of the doubt, to accept the genuine nature of their sincere endeavor to behave as Christians, to allow them to assimilate and rapidly ascend the ladder of success and power in the fields of business, governmental service, and even the church. However, it turned against them in the end and attempted to destroy them via the Inquisition of the 1480s. Likewise, German Christian society for two generations (circa 1870–1930) was equally willing to allow the newly emancipated Jews, emerging from the ghetto, to assimilate and rapidly ascend the ladder of success and power in the fields of business and governmental service, only to turn against them in the end as well and attempt to destroy them via the Nazi movement of the 1930s.

3. *Ultimately, Jewish assimilation and disappearance is impossible, because the Christian world will not allow this to happen for very good reasons of its own.*

This implication of the Netanyahu thesis will be more fully developed infra.

Our understanding of the three implications of the Netanyahu thesis as developed above can be facilitated by a comparison of its more realistic approach with the more romantic view of Cecil Roth currently dominating the study of the Marrano problem. According to Roth, Jews and Christians are primarily religious communities. Jews do not seek complete assimilation (conversion) within the Christian world. This is the case because the Jews consider their religion to be superior (older, purer, and such) to Christianity. Christians, on the other hand, do seek complete Jewish assimilation (conversion). This relieves the Christians of the religious inferiority complex with which they are burdened because their religion is younger than Judaism, as well as more easily tempted by the seductions of paganism and the worship of nature and/or power. Finally, according to Roth, the Jews of Spain and of Franco-Germany were exactly the same in that neither group wanted to assimilate into the Christian world.

The great weakness in the Roth approach is that it downplays the significance of the Marrano phenomenon among the Jews *of Spain*. If both the Jews of Spain and of Franco-Germany were exactly the same in that neither group wanted complete assimilation, why did thousands of Jews convert to Christianity in Spain when no similar development ever took place in Franco-Germany? If we answer that the Jews of Spain were only attempting to avoid massacre by their mass conversion, why did the Jews of Franco-Germany not seek to avoid massacre by mass conversion around the same time (*i.e.*, circa 1400)?

According to the Netanyahu approach, Jews and Christians are primarily ethnic communities, the Jews being Semites and the Christians Indo-Europeans, that are fundamentally and totally irreconcilable. Jews do, however, seek complete assimilation within Christian majority society, because they cannot bear the psychological and physical deprivations of being a small and at times heavily persecuted minority. Christians, on the other hand, do not want the Jews to seek

219

complete assimilation. This is because it is precisely the exclusion of the Jews from the main sources of economic, social, and political power within a given country that allows Christians to relieve their feelings of inferiority at being a younger religious group, more easily swayed by those forces at work in the world which oppose ethical monotheism. Both the Jews of Spain and Franco-Germany would have wanted to assimilate completely within the Christian world. However, the Jews of Franco-Germany were wise enough to realize correctly that complete assimilation was impossible, whereas the Jews of Spain made the tragic mistake of thinking that complete assimilation was possible.

We suggest that it was the Islamic factor that made the difference. The presence of Muslims in Spain complicated the Spanish situation and made it possible for the Jews to deceive themselves into thinking that complete assimilation was a genuine possibility, on the false assumption that Spanish Christendom would accept the Jews without reservation as permanent allies against the Islamic danger. By contrast, there were no Muslims in Franco-Germany to give the Jews the false hope that they could be completely accepted by the Christians. The Franco-German Jews realized that the only things the Jews could do at times of persecution were either die as martyrs (often by self-immolation in ritual suicide), which they believed would guarantee them heavenly bliss, or else flee to another land and there attempt to rebuild their lives. Because of the complicating presence of the Muslims, the Spanish Jews mistakenly thought that there was a way out of the Jewish dilemma other than by dying or through flight, i.e., that complete assimilation to avoid persecution was a viable alternative.

Another way of outlining the major differences between the more romantic Roth approach and the more realistic Netanyahu approach would be as follows. According to Roth:

GROUP OF JEWS	IN PUBLIC	IN PRIVATE
Franco-German Jews	Jews	Jews
Spanish Jews (Marranos)	Christians	Jews

The situation of the Jews of Franco-Germany was the same as that of the Jews of Spain (Marranos) in the fifteenth century with regard to the weightier question of what each group was doing in private, i.e., in the home. Here both groups were Jews. But the two groups of Jews, the Franco-German and the Spanish (Marranos), differed with regard to the less important question of whether they had to live a lie. In this respect the Spanish Jews (Marranos), unlike those of Franco-Germany, had to develop a split personality and be one thing in public (*i.e.*, Christians), another in private (*i.e.*, Jews).

According to Netanyahu:

GROUP OF JEWS	IN PUBLIC	IN PRIVATE
Franco-German Jews	Jews	Jews
Spanish Jews (Marranos)	Christians	Christians

The situation of the Jews of Franco-Germany was different from that of the Jews of Spain (Marranos) in the fifteenth century with regard to the weightier question of what each group did in private, *i.e.*, in the home. In this area the Franco-German Jews remained Jews; the Spanish Jews (Marranos) became Christians. But the situation of the two groups of Jews, Franco-German and Spanish (Marranos), was the same with regard to the less important question, the question of the extent to which each group had to live a lie. Neither group had to develop a split personality and be one thing in public, another in private. Neither group was hypocritical. Both were honest according to their own lights. The Franco-German Jews were consistently Jews, in public as well as in private. The Spanish Jews (Marranos) were equally consistent, but, by contrast with the Jews of northern Europe, *consistent as Christians*, again in public as well as in private.

Thus the Roth approach makes the Franco-German and Spanish (Marranos) Jews essentially the same because both groups of Jews agreed in the weightier area of what they were in private, *i.e.*, Jews. The Netanyahu approach distinguishes clearly between the two groups, the northern European Ashkenazim and the Iberian Sefardim, and holds that all they agreed on was their consistency, in whatever path they chose. If the Jews of Franco-Gemany chose Judaism they were faithful to it both at home as well as on the street. If the Marranos of Spain chose to abandon Judaism and adopt Christianity instead, they were totally faithful to their new religion both at home as well as on the street. But, and this is especially important, the two groups of Jews differed radically in the fundamental and basic question of *which religion they ultimately preferred* to give their loyalty to. The Franco-German Jews realized that there was no way to escape the Jewish predicament and that the only way to avoid being persecuted for being different was either martyrdom or flight. The Spanish Jews (Marranos) did not realize that there was no way to escape the Jewish predicament and mistakenly thought that they could avoid being persecuted for being different by becoming like their persecutors via conversion to Christianity.

The Jewish people of today know what great losses they have suffered in the modern world (since circa 1789 when the French Revolution freed the Jews of Central Europe from the ghetto) and are continuing to suffer due to the powerful forces to assimilation, aided by the breakdown of the traditional Jewish faith. But even in the Middle Ages, when religion undoubtedly played a far greater role in the lives of the Jewish people (and all people) than it does today, as is clear from the Netanyahu thesis, the Jews also suffered tremendous losses due to a theoretical desire for complete assimilation carried out in practice by the Marranos of fifteenth-century Spain. In fact, as the fifteenth-century Spanish Jewish writers themselves (like Abravanel) pointed out, the Jews lost more people throughout the entire Middle Ages due to the desire for complete assimilation (i.e., in the case of the thousands of fifteenth-century Spanish Marranos) than to actual physical annihilation (e.g., in the First Crusade, 1095–1096; or the Black Plague, circa 1348, both of which led to frightful massacres of the Jews of Western Europe).

In the Middle Ages, the "Age of Faith," the Jewish people suffered greater losses from the desire for complete assimilation than they did from physical annihilation. But in our own secular "post-Christian" twentieth century the Jews have suffered greater losses due to physical annihilation (i.e., the tragic loss of 6 million Jews in the great struggle against Nazism) than to the desire for complete assimilation. This startling knowledge gained from the Netanyahu thesis can throw considerable new light not only on the Christian-Jewish relations of the past but also on those which people of good will on both sides of the dialogue would hope to see established in the future. Today, in the nuclear and space ages, perhaps the greatest enemy of the Jewish people is not Christianity or any other religion but rather the dehumanizing and secularizing forces of uninhibited technology and rampant materialism which are also enemies of Christianity, of Islam, and of all religious traditions and spiritually inclined people everywhere, East and West.

*****

Let us pause now to reflect at greater length and in greater depth on the third of the three implications of the Netanyahu thesis developed above, *i.e.*, that ultimately complete Jewish assimilation and disappearance is impossible because the Christian world will not allow this to happen for good reasons of its own. In this regard, Isaac Abravanel, the great Spanish Jewish statesman, author, and thinker of the second half of the fifteenth century, already pointed out that there is no way the Jewish people as a whole can opt out of Judaism permanently, since complete assimilation is ultimately impossible. As Abravanel put it:

> Even though they [*i.e.*, the Marranos] and their children after them strive to be completely like the Gentiles, behold such will never be, for the families of the earth [*i.e.*, the Gentiles] will always call them Jews and designate them as Israelites even against their will, will consider them Jews and slander them by saying that they are practicing Judaism in secret and for this trumped up reason will burn them with fire and flames.[19]

Thus, as Abravanel realized almost five centuries ago, the more Jews try to be like Christians, the more Christians will persecute them for being Jews. The converse of this, however, may also be true. The more Jews try to segregate themselves from the surrounding Christian society and cultivate instead their own unique traditions, the less Christians will persecute them for being Jews. For example, the Spanish Inquisition was set up circa 1480 to annihilate those Jews who wanted to be like Christians (*i.e.*, the Marranos). However, those Jews who wanted to remain loyal to Judaism and who therefore had segregated themselves from the surrounding Christian society were only punished with exile by the expulsion order of 1492. Those Jews who wanted to be Christians (the Marranos) gained in the short run, during the first two generations of the fifteenth century, and were temporarily allowed to climb rapidly the economic, social, and political ladder in Spain. But in the long run, *i.e.*, from circa 1480 onward, all they gained was psychological and physical torture by the Inquisition. Those Jews who did not want to be Christians but were content to remain loyal to their ancestral faith lost out in the short run, because they continued to suffer discrimination as Jews throughout the fifteenth century. But in the long run, after 1492, they were the real winners, because they were expelled from the country and could start life over again in friendlier lands (like Ottoman Turkey) and prosper.

The twentieth-century situation of the Jews, however, has not been quite like that in fifteenth-century Spain. In the great Hitlerite persecution of the Jews in the 1930s and 1940s both the assimilated and the nonassimilated suffered equally. Both groups ended up in the same gas chambers. Neither assimilation nor self-segregation could completely save a community. Yet, even in those hellish times the nonassimilated were still better off psychologically, because they could at least blame their deaths on their religiocultural uniqueness. But on what could the assimilated Jews blame their deaths? One can comprehend being killed for being different, but can anyone comprehend being killed for being like the persecutor? Perhaps the best course—if a choice is ever really given by history—is the middle path, between total assimilation (as the left wing of Reform Judaism) and total self-segregation (as the right wing of Orthodox Judaism). We refer to the path of moderate assimilation combined with moderate loyalty to the uniqueness of the Jewish tradition. Such a position (plus their relative paucity of numbers and the highly idealistic character of their Christian fellow countrymen) may be what saved the Jews of Denmark from destruction at the hands of the Nazis during World War II.[20]

The middle path, moderate assimilation and moderate distinctiveness, may not necessarily ward off all persecution. But neither may the two other extremes, total assimilation and total self-segregation. Yet the middle path has a double advantage over each of the two extremes. It does not raise any false hopes which lead to bitter disillusionment later (as in the case of those who seek total assimilation). Nor does it cut the Jews off from as many potential allies among the Christians by overemphasizing Jewish uniqueness (the main weakness in the position of the total self-segregators). However, if the middle path becomes untenable because the pressure from the extremes is too great, the extreme of total self-segregation will either lead to less persecution or make whatever persecution is destined to come more meaningful than the extreme of the attempt to achieve complete assimilation, the path of the Marranos. Jewish movements toward radical assimilation, as in the case of the fifteenth-century Marranos and the Jews of Germany circa 1870–1930, are often followed by movements of totalitarianism, as in the Inquisition and Nazism. Indeed, the two types of movements, the Jewish attempt at complete assimilation and totalitarianism, may in part be cause and effect.

Reflecting further on the third implication of the Netanyahu thesis, the impossibility of Jewish assimilation, it would seem that when Jewish usefulness in a given Christian country is over (as was the case in Spain circa 1400 and in Germany circa 1930), only two real options remain viable for Jews. They are death within the country which they have hitherto considered their home, or flight to another more hospitable country where the cycle of Jewish usefulness has only just begun or has not yet reached its culmination. Complete assimilation and/or conversion to Christianity cannot be used as a means of escaping death or the necessity of flight. The attempt to achieve complete assimilation only hastens the inevitable and/or is a clear sign that the inevitable is approaching. Why should this be the case? Why should complete assimilation be impossible? The answer to this question may lie in the historical necessity of perpetual Jewish emigration. If this is indeed the case, since complete assimilation, in which the Jews become totally absorbed into the culture of a given locality, is the very negation of perpetual emigration, complete assimilation can be no more than a temporary interlude.

Why would history require perpetual Jewish emigration? Perpetual Jewish emigration is a crucial means of bringing about change in the inner spiritual culture of the Jews themselves and of enriching the general Christian culture in the largest possible number of countries. It is true that the Jewish people have a permanent center of their own in Palestine, but even here the necessity of emigration has prevailed on numerous occasions in the past. History itself began, according to the Book of Genesis, with Adam and Eve's emigration from the garden. Abraham began the Palestinian center by emigrating from Babylonia. This was followed by Joseph and the Hebrew emigration to Egypt. Moses laid the groundwork for the revival of the Palestinian center by leading the Israelites in their emigration out of Egypt through the Sinai to the east bank of the Jordan. This was followed by the Israelite emigration to Assyria and the Judean emigration to Babylonia in the eighth and sixth centuries B.C. respectively. The Jewish emigration into the Greco-Roman Diaspora was speeded considerably by the destruction of the Second Temple in Jerusalem during the great Jewish revolt against Rome circa 66–73 A.D. (chronicled by Josephus).

225

What is true about the Jewish center in Palestine certainly is true about the Jewish periphery in the Diaspora. Here emigration has been even more the rule: (1) emigration of the Sefardim (Iberian Jews) from Palestine to Babylonia, Spain, Turkey, and the Low Countries, the British Isles and the Americas; and (2) emigration of the Ashkenazim (Franco-German Jews) from Palestine to Italy, Franco-Germany, Poland, the United States, Palestine, Argentina, South Africa, Australia, and so on. Jewish history during the past 4,000 years has in large part been shaped by the tension between the relative stability provided by the Jewish home in Palestine and the relative flexibility provided by the Jewish settlement in the Diaspora. The relative stability provided by the Palestinian center helps the Jewish Diaspora to survive and find meaning in its life of service to the nations. The Diaspora, on the other hand, because it is continually on the move, assists the Palestinian center by preventing its petrification and ossification. Palestine represents the centripetal force in Jewish history, but the Diaspora represents the equally neccessary centrifugal force in this history. Each force requires the other's counterforce if the wheel of Jewish history is to function properly. But the essence of the Diaspora is perpetual emigration. Hence complete assimilation is an impossible dream, or, even worse than that, a terrifying nightmare. The historical necessity of perpetual Jewish emigration in the Diaspora makes the attempt at complete assimilation no more than a temporary remedy at best to buy time for flight, at worst a prelude to totalitarianism, Inquisition, and the death camp.

But perhaps the real reason why Jews have not been allowed the luxury of successful total assimilation is not so much because history does not want this to come about, but rather because *the Christian world* does not want this to come about. Individual Jews, of course, may be able to achieve complete assimilation into Christian society. However, what may hold good for the individual Jew does not hold good for the Jewish people as a whole. Why should the Christian world (except perhaps for the millenarians like Pope Innocent III and others), contrary to the impression which its attempt to evangelize the Jews over the centuries may have given, really *not* want the Jews to convert to Christianity en masse? Why did Spanish Christian society, through the Inquisition established circa 1480, decide to reject the Marranos, despite their sincere conversion, when it had accepted them during the first two-thirds of that century? In short, why did

226

Spanish Christian society refuse to permit total Jewish assimilation and disappearance? Netanyahu's response, as explained above, is "race" and "politics." In the following pages we briefly develop eight possible additional reasons why the Christian world in general does not, and Spanish Christian society circa and after 1480 in particular did not, desire final and complete Jewish assimilation. Admittedly, these factors contradict each other. However, that is not difficult to comprehend inasmuch as they operate within the collective Christian unconscious mind, which, of course, is no more rational than the collective Jewish or Islamic mind. All of these factors are important. However, the eighth may be the most basic and fundamental. It is that Christianity is a delicate, even precarious, balance between three forces—(1) Indo-Europeanism, (2) Christianism, and (3) Semiticism—and that the continued existence of the Jews as Jews is crucial to the maintenance of this balance, without which Christianity could not survive as a world religion.

(1)*The Indo-European Christian world does not want to lose the services of the Semitic Jews as a crucially indispensable link with the Semitic Islamic world against which it has felt the need to wage virtually perpetual war.*

Due to the efforts of St. Paul and his disciples Christianity, which began as a Semitic religion, became ever increasingly Indo-European. During the Middle Ages it is true that not all Christians were Indo-Europeans. Some Christians, like the Monophysites of Syria and Ethiopia, were Semites, as were the Nestorian Christians who fled Byzantine persecution in the fifth century to sanctuary in Zoroastrian and later Islamic Iraq. It is also true that not all Indo-Europeans were Christians. Some Indo-Europeans, like the Iranians (along with the Kurds and Afghans), were Muslims (though prior to their adoption of Islam the Iranians had long been influenced by the ideals of the Prophet Zoroaster and the rituals of the magi). Others, like the Aryans of northern India, were Hindus. However, by and large the overwhelming majority of Christians were Indo-Europeans, and the overwhelming majority of Indo-Europeans were Christians. On the other hand, the overwhelming majority of Semites were Muslims, though there were many non-Semites in medieval Islam as well, *e.g.*, the Ural-Altaic Turks, such Southeast Asian peoples as the Malays and Indonesians, the Hamitic Berbers, and black Africans. The Semitic Middle East was the birthplace of Islam and its heartland thereafter.

With the rise of Islam in the seventh century, the Prophet Muham-

227

mad and his successors (the four orthodox caliphs: Abu Bakr, Umar, Uthman, and Ali) restored Semitic supremacy in the Middle East, after the Indo-Europeans (Persians, Greeks, Romans, and Byzantines) had ruled there for almost twelve centuries (*i.e.*, ever since the time of King Nebuchadnezzar and the Chaldean Empire of the sixth century B.C., the last great Semitic empire to rule the Middle East before the rise of Islam). Since that crucial seventh century the Indo-European Christians, deeply resentful over the loss of the Holy Land to the Muslims, and the Semitic Muslims, just as deeply resentful over the Christian effort to reconquer the Holy Land, have been at war. This great war, exacerbated by the crusading movement which arose in the eleventh century, has been a war in which each side hoped for total victory. Hence, each side was exceedingly reluctant to consider a resolution of the conflict via compromise and synthesis.

The Semitic Jews were allowed by the Indo-European Christians to settle in their midst in order to serve as a link between the Indo-European Christian and the Semitic Islamic worlds. The function of this link was twofold. On the one hand, it was to help the Indo-Europeans negotiate truces between themselves and the enemy when it suited their purposes to be temporarily at peace with Islam, *i.e.* when the Christians needed to rest and recuperate before the next armed encounter. On the other hand, the Semitic Jews were allowed to settle in the Indo-European Christian world in order to help that world learn about, and from, its Semitic Islamic enemy so that it could utilize this knowledge to win the eventual victory. If the Semitic Jews would not have been able and willing to perform these two vital functions for the Indo-European Christians, they would not have been allowed to settle and/or to remain within the Indo-European Christian world. Hence, to allow the Semitic Jews to assimilate completely into the Indo-European world via mass conversion would have meant that the Jews would no longer be able to function as a crucially indispensable link with the Semitic Islamic world. The absence of such a Jewish link would have critically weakened and debilitated the Indo-European Christian world, rendering it unable to defend itself against the onslaughts of the Semitic Islamic world, totally incapable of ever conquering that world and thereby of completely eliminating the powerful threat which it represented.

(2) *The Christian world wants to become Jewish instead of allowing the Jews to become Christians because in reality the Christians believe that the*

Jewish religion is superior to their own, i.e., that the mother is superior to the daughter.

Why do Christians believe that the Jewish religion is superior to their own? Jesus, the early Apostles, and even the Apostle Paul himself, responsible for transforming Christianity from a Semitic into an Indo-European ethnolinguistic movement, were all Jews. The New Testament depends upon the Old for its validity rather than vice versa, which means that the Jewish scriptures have greater independence than do the Christian. The monotheistic unitarian theology of Judaism, which believes only in the Father, in one person who is only one God, is simpler and more readily comprehensible than the equally monotheistic but trinitarian theology of Christianity, which believes in the Father, the Son, and the Holy Spirit, three persons who are really only one God. Judaism is thisworldly, whereas Christianity is otherworldly. Judaism believes that wealth is a greater religious virtue than poverty, whereas Christianity believes that poverty is a greater religious virtue than wealth. Judaism believes that sexual fulfillment is a higher religious virtue than celibacy, and yet Jews are better able to preserve the nuclear family and keep down the number of illegitimate births; whereas Christianity believes that celibacy is a higher religious virtue than sexual fulfillment, and yet Christians are less able to preserve the nuclear family and keep down the number of illegitimate births. Jews are so much more cosmopolitan than Christians and are apparently able to live in (and adjust successfully to) so many different societies, speak so many different languages, and know so many different literatures; whereas Christians are more deeply rooted in the soil of a given country, more closely bound to place and space, and much less capable of leading the kind of seemingly exciting life (of being able to cross national and cultural boundaries freely) that Jews are forced to live (by necessity of their Diaspora predicament). Jews, as Semites who came originally from the Middle East, represent to the Christian mind the attractions of the warm sand and relaxing surf of the Mediterranean; whereas Christians, as Indo-Europeans whose home is the more northerly climes, think of themselves in terms of such highly unattractive images as cold snow and dark forests, in which great exertion and effort are required simply to stay alive, let alone to create a system of meaningful values.

For all of the above outlined reasons, and many others, the Christians consider the Jewish religion to be superior to their own and look

229

upon the Jews with secret admiration and envy. When they see the Jews as a whole actively seeking complete assimilation and disappearance into the Christian world, which the Christians themselves consider inferior to the Jewish, the reaction of the Christians is at first one of shocked surprise, then one of angry outrage, and finally one of uncontrollable desire to visit death and destruction upon the betrayers of the very ideal which the Christians themselves hold dearest, *i.e.*, Judaism. Since the Christians secretly admire Judaism more than their own religion, they punish Jews who seek complete assimilation far more harshly and cruelly than they punish Jews who remain loyal to their ancestral faith and traditions.

(3) The Christian world wants to keep the Jews apart, segregated, so that it can punish them for having foisted one of their own, i.e., Jesus of Nazareth, off upon the Christians as God, a God who demands the impossible of people and at the same time dies powerless upon the cross and requires His followers to imitate His example.

How does Jesus demand the impossible? A literal interpretation of the Sermon on the Mount (and other Gospel material) provides a very bountiful answer to this question. If we ever become angry against our neighbor, insult him, or even call him a fool, we will suffer the severest of punishments in this life and the next (Matt. 5:22). Men cannot be girl-watchers because mere girl-watching is already equivalent to fornication or adultery (Matt. 5:28). Men cannot divorce their wives on grounds of infertility, debility, incompatibility, insanity or criminality; only on grounds of adultery. Nor can they marry a divorcee no matter how attractive (Matt. 5:32). We cannot take any oath, neither to the church nor to the state (whether to the legislative, executive, or judicial brances thereof) (Matt. 5:34). We cannot resist an evil person who mistreats us; neither can we fight back against him. If he hits us on one cheek, we must turn the other to him. If he takes us to court to sue us undeservedly for part of our wealth, we must give him the rest of it without a contest.

When we give charity, we must give it in secret. We cannot donate a building to a hospital or university and have it named after ourselves (Matt. 6:2). When we pray, we must pray alone, behind closed doors. We cannot go to church to pray together with our neighbors (Matt. 6:6). We cannot save up our money and have a bank account (Matt. 6:19). We cannot judge anyone else or condemn him, whether privately or in court, for we have made as many mistakes in life as he has

(Matt. 7:1). If we are rich, we should sell what we have and give the money raised thereby to the poor, for "it is easier for a camel to go through the eye of a needle than for a rich person to enter the kingdom of God" (Matt. 19:21, 24). When we know one of our own followers or disciples is going to betray us, we should not do anything to try to stop the betrayal (Matt. 26:20–25). When we are falsely accused and are brought to trial, we should not lift a finger in our own defence (Matt. 26:64, 27:11–12). When we are being put to death for a crime which we did not commit, we should not hate or curse those who put us to death but rather love and forgive them (Luke 23:34). What is more, we should tell all our followers that they should do the same (Matt. 16:24), behave not like human beings, made out of flesh and blood, but rather like angels made out of pure spirit.

We would suggest that the Christian world reasons as follows. The God whom the Jews have foisted off onto us is the kind of God who demands the impossible, who lived and died to teach us that defeat is really victory. We have no choice but to consider Jesus as our God because we are Indo-Europeans, and in him our ancestors have believed for generations past. But we do not have to love the people who gave Jesus to the world. Quite the contrary, the wrath which we do not dare to vent upon Jesus, our insufferable God, we vent upon the defenseless people who produced him. We make them pay for everything that Jesus does to us. If we allow the Jews to join us through complete assimilation, how can we make them pay for foisting Jesus onto us?

(4) *The mass conversion of the Jews means that the Second Coming of Christ is at hand; Christians, like all peoples who rule over others more than others rule over them, are terribly afraid of realized eschatology, because they prefer the life and values of this world to the bloodless and gutless world of the angels and saints in heaven.*

In medieval Christian thought the mass conversion of the Jews was viewed as intimately bound up with the Second Coming of Christ, as both cause and effect. However, if medieval Christians did not desire the Second Coming or wanted to postpone it, then they would not have been enthusiastic about the mass conversion of the Jews but rather would have opposed it.

The *locus classicus* for the antieschatological preference in Western European medieval literature is that passage early in the great French romance *Aucassin and Nicolette* (circa 1200), wherein Aucassin asks

231

the viscount of the town of Beaucaire what he has done with Aucassin's beloved, Nicolette, the viscount's goddaughter. The viscount says that Aucassin could never hope to marry the girl, because Aucassin is a nobleman and Nicolette (at least as far as anyone knew at that time) was a former Muslim slave girl who had been converted to Christianity. According to the viscount the most Nicolette could ever be to Aucassin would be a mistress. But if Aucassin took her for a mistress, he would burn in hell forever.

To which Aucassin replies that hell is precisely where he wants to go. Why should he want heaven? The only people he would have for companions there would be old crippled priests who do nothing but crouch before altars and pray in church crypts all day, who go around barefoot in worn garments and cloaks, dying of hunger and thirst, of cold and misery, their bodies covered with sores. What young, vital person would want to go to a bloodless and gutless place like that when he could go to an exciting place like hell? The people who go to hell are handsome priests, good-looking knights who gain glory and fame by dying in tourneys or battle, stout archers and their loyal aids. Hell is also the place whither go all the beautiful and graceful women who are interested in the opposite sex and have two or three lovers in addition to their own husbands. Hell also boasts material things like gold, silver, ermine and squirrel furs. The riches of the world are found *in hell*, not in heaven. What is more, hell is where all the minstrels and musicians go, all the popular entertainers. Hell is where real happiness lies. Who would want to go to heaven?[21]

Of course, Aucassin was speaking here about the first judgment, i.e., the judgment of the soul alone immediately after death rather than the final judgment, that of the soul together with its resurrected body after the Second Coming. But he probably would have felt the same way about what would happen when the Messiah comes. When the Messiah comes and the world is finally perfected, much of what characterizes normal human existence will no longer take place. Human sexuality will disappear completely (Matt. 22:30). No one will marry and no one will get divorced. By the same token, no one will have mistresses, whether before or after marriage. No one will bear children, nor will anyone raise them. No one will go through the rites of puberty. No one will court members of the opposite sex. Further, working for a living will disappear. No one will have to farm, handicraft, manufacture, buy and sell, or bank ever again. Economic inequality will disappear. There will no longer be any rich and any poor. No one will become a soldier because there will not be any wars. No one will become a policeperson, lawyer, or judge because there will not be any more crime. The legislative and executive branches of government will disappear because all people will get along with each other in perfect harmony without the need for any type of governmental supervision or interference.

Missionary activity will disappear because all people will believe the same thing, i.e., the truth. Almsgiving will disappear because all will be provided with whatever they need. Because no one will ever sin again, fasting and pilgrimages to great shrines will disappear as ways of attempting to atone for sin. Just as pilgrimages will disappear, so will all domestic and foreign travel. Prayer will not disappear. However, it will now be nothing more than a recitation of God's glory. Prayers of petition will no longer be necessary because people will have everything they need. Since prayers of petition will no longer be necessary, prayers of thanksgiving for receipt of that for which we have petitioned will also disappear. Clergymen will disappear because all will worship God properly and of their own accord. Physicians will disappear because no one will ever be sick. Professors will disappear because God will teach people directly.

What then will remain? Eating and drinking sumptuously at the messianic banquet; singing hymns of praise to God; the study of sacred texts. But all these things—eating and drinking, singing, study—will no longer provide an escape from the workaday world. Instead, they will become the workaday world. Once they become work rather than respite, they will lose most of the beauty and meaning which they provided before the Messiah came. People will become automatons and robots, always doing God's will automatically, not their own. All values will be destroyed because there will no longer be any free choice. All will be forced to be free, forced to be good.

No wonder people do not want the Messiah to come! No wonder medieval Christians did not want the Jews to convert. If the Jews converted en masse, it would mean the end of everything that was truly human in the world, and society would become, to use the words of Aucassin, nothing but an aggregate of old crippled priests praying before altars and in church crypts all day long, wearing worn garments, going about barefoot, their bodies covered with sores. Everyone would become a saint, and any normal human being would be *damned* first before wanting to live in that kind of world!

(5) *The Christian world needs to keep the Jews apart, segregated, so that the Jews can perform the unpopular role of being society's entrepreneurs, especially in occupations and regions of the country where few Christians prefer to be.*

In the Early Middle Ages (circa 600–1000) the Carolingian-Ottonian period, when the overwhelming majority of Western Christians were engaged in agricultural pursuits, the Jews were forced to become the merchants, a very important yet at the same time very unpopular occupation. The merchant was viewed as almost a practitioner of black magic because he became rich, not by producing goods from the soil (believed to be the only honest occupation), but rather by moving goods around and often engaging in what seemed like shady dealings to the simpler and more naive members of society from whom he bought and to whom he sold.

In the High Middle Ages (circa 1000–1300), the Romanesque-Gothic period of medieval urbanization, commerce was no longer considered an odious occupation for Christians, and they became the merchants. Jews were forced to become the moneylenders, again a very important occupation but one which was even less popular during the High Middle Ages than the occupation of merchant had been during the Early Middle Ages. The moneylender was viewed as being an even worse practitioner of black magic than the merchant because, while the merchant made his money by moving rather than producing goods, at least the merchant dealt in goods, with something *substantial and tangible*. The moneylender made his money not by moving *goods* but rather by moving money, something artificial and symbolic that was even further removed from the soil than goods. Moreover, the moneylender had to charge "interest," forbidden by the Scriptures; and more often than the merchant, he often had to punish people for their inability to pay debts, a punishment that was deeply resented, because the more one was punished for the inability to pay, the less able he became to pay, and a vicious circle ensued.

In the Later Middle Ages (circa 1300–1500), the period of the Black Plague and the Hundred Years War which marked the decline and fall of the Middle Ages, moneylending was no longer considered an odious occupation for Christians, and they became the moneylenders. The

Jews, in order to survive, had to become both merchants and money-lenders, but now on a minor rather than a major scale. The Jews had to become petty merchants, *i.e.*, dealers in used goods, and petty money-lenders, i.e., pawnbrokers primarily to knights and students. Thus, in the Later Middle Ages the Jews were doubly suspect both as tricky movers of goods and as Shylockian movers of money (rather than honest and noble producers of goods from the soil). But this time the Jews operated on a small rather than a grandiose scale. In earlier periods at least the magnitude of Jewish enterprises in these necessary but odious occupations earned them significant governmental protection from public enmity. But in the Later Middle Ages this factor was considerably diminished because the Jews were now forced into economic activities on a relatively small and insignificant scale. Thus, their situation became doubly precarious. (1) They now were considered both types of sorcerer simultaneously, merchant sorcerer and money-lender sorcerer, and (2) their enterprises were now only on a petty and prosaic scale rather than on a powerful and glorious one.

In early modern times (circa 1500–1800), when the center of the world Jewish population had shifted from Western Europe to Poland, German Christians and German Jews were the two main components of the Polish middle class. However, the Jews were the primary one of the two Polish middle-class groups forced to go to the Polish south-eastern frontier, *i.e.*, the Ukraine, and take up the two odious occupations of steward for the absentee Polish landlords and tavernkeepers. As steward the Jew at least came close to the soil. Yet, his job was not to grow anything but rather to force others, *i.e.*, the peasants, to grow things to enrich the absentee landlord. As tavernkeeper the Jew helped the peasant escape temporarily, via alcoholic beverages, from the misery of his daily existence, to which misery the Jew contributed in part as steward. Thus, the Jew was caught in a vicious economic circle. Oppress the peasant and then help him escape his oppression temporarily through drink. Both occupations were as necessary as they were odious. Without temporary escape the peasant could not have kept working. Without working the peasant would have been thrown off the land by the absentee landlord and would have starved.

If the Christian world had allowed the Jews to assimilate completely and/or to convert to Christianity en masse in the Early Middle Ages, who would have performed the highly necessary but unpopular function of merchant? Christians did not want to do this kind of work at that time. The only people who could have been forced to do it were the ethnoreligiously different. The Jews were the only ethnoreligiously different group in Western Europe at that time. They were also talented and creative, so that the Christians could be sure that they would do their job well. If the Christians would have allowed the Jews to do what the Jews really wanted to do, *i.e.*, become an equal part of the Christian world through assimilation or conversion, society in general would have been severely crippled because no one would have been left to do the necessary but odious work of moving rather than producing goods.

What is true for the Early Middle Ages is true as well for all subsequent periods. If the Christian world would have allowed the Jews to assimilate completely and/or convert en masse to Christianity, who in the High Middle Ages would have performed the highly necessary but unpopular function of moneylender; in the Later Middle Ages, of dealer in used goods and pawnbroker; in early modern times, of stewards (for absentee landlords) and tavernkeepers? If the Jews had not existed to perform these occupations in Christian society, certain groups from among the Christian populace would have had to suffer the discrimination of being forced to perform them. The Jews saved Christians from the bitter necessity of having had to discriminate against their own kind and allowed them the luxury of discriminating against an out-group instead, that was both religiously and ethnolinguistically different. Discriminating against aliens is always easier to justify to one's conscience than discriminating against one's own kind. Could the Christian world give up the luxury of having a pool of talented people to do highly important but unpopular jobs upon which the continued existence and welfare of the entire society depended? Allowing the Jews to assimilate completely and/or convert en masse to Christianity would have meant giving up that luxury.[22]

(6) *The Christian world requires the continued physical existence of the Jews as Jews in order to combat the ever-present and extremely subversive Monophysite heresy, i.e., the doctrine that Jesus was not both God and man but rather God alone.*

The Jews must be kept alive as Jews in order to witness against the Monophysite doctrine and in favor of the historical fact that there did indeed once live a human person named Jesus. The continued existence of the Jews as Jews provides crucial support for the fact that the

Savior was human as well as divine, perhaps the most fundamental tenet of orthodox Christianity theology.

During the period of the seven classical ecumenical councils (the first at Nicea, 325; the seventh, also at Nicea, 787), the church faced danger from two opposite extremes, the Nestorians and the Monophysites. The Nestorians had to flee Byzantium to refuge in Iraq, living as a minority first among the Zoroastrian Persians, then among the Muslim Arabs. The Monophysites were the more dangerous heretics because the more widespread and politically powerful. They created national churches in four different lands: Armenia, Syria, Egypt, and Ethiopia, forming the majority in these four lands from the fifth until the ninth centuries, as well as in Armenia and Ethiopia ever thereafter. The Monophysites emphasized Christ's divinity to the neglect of his humanity; the Nestorians, his humanity to the neglect of his divinity. Orthodox Christology, to the contrary of both, held that unless Christ were simultaneously divine and human there was no hope for mankind's salvation. If Christ were totally human (the way the orthodox understood the Nestorian position), admittedly he would have felt compassion for humanity and have desired to save it but, because he was not divine, would have had no power to do so. On the other hand, if Christ were totally divine (the way the orthodox understood the Monophysite position), admittedly he would have had the power to save humanity but, because he was not human, would not have felt any compassion for it and would not have desired to save it. Hence, orthodox Christology insisted that Christ must have been both fully human as well as fully divine for the mystery of redemption to have taken place and to continue to take place in every successive generation.

This is where the Jews come into the picture. They are badly needed to help the orthodox fend off the challenge of the more powerful and dangerous of the two heresies outlined above, *i.e.*, the Monophysites, who deny Christ's humanity. The continued existence of the Jews, the actual physical people into which the Savior was born, makes it easier to argue convincingly that the Savior is both *human* and divine, very *man* and very God, thereby undercutting the Monophysite position. If the Christian world would allow Jews to assimilate completely and/or convert en masse to Christianity, thereby disappearing as an easily identifiable entity, orthodox theology would lose much of its credibil-

237

ity, and the leadership of the Christian world might well pass from the overwhelmingly Indo-European orthodox to the primarily Semitic Monophysites of the Middle East.[23]

(7) The Christian world requires the continued existence of the Jews as Jews in order to help Christianity overcome the constant temptation to worship the God of space rather than the God of time, i.e., the constant temptation of paganism and the adoration of nature and/or power.

If Judaism and the Jews stand for law, justice, and discipline, while Christianity and Christians stand for love, mercy, and freedom (this contrast is not completely valid because there is considerable emphasis on love, mercy, and freedom in Judaism, especially Hasidism; and upon law, justice, and discipline in Christianity, especially Calvinism), Christianity needs Judaism because love, mercy, and freedom without law, justice, and discipline become anarchy, barbarism, and the war of all against all. But if the Jews were allowed to assimilate completely and/or convert en masse to Christianity and thus to disappear as a separate entity, who would have continued to perform the crucially indispensable role of helping love, mercy, and freedom continue to prevail by standing for their required opposites?[24]

Another way to understand this same contradiction is through the ideas and terminology of Franz Rosenzweig (1886-1929), one of the most influential Jewish theologians of the twentieth century. According to Rosenzweig Christianity desperately needs Judaism as a corrective because the mission of Christianity is to convert pagans, in the course of which it runs the risk of being partly converted by them. The task of the Jews who live among Christians is to help Christians remain faithful to Christianity, as the Christians persuade pagans to accept true religion. Thus, Christians convert pagans to ethical monotheism, while Jews keep Christians faithful to the same. To put it another way, the task of Christians is to convert pagans to Christianity, whilst the task of the Jews is to convert Christians to Christiantity. But if Jews were allowed to assimilate completely and/or to convert en masse to Christianity and thus to disappear as a separate entity, who would remain to perform the vitally necessary role of keeping the Christians faithful to ethical monotheism or to Christianity?

Judaism, according to Rosenzweig, is the fire, while Christianity is the rays of light which emanate from the fire. Without the fire there can be no rays of light. The Jews cannot be allowed to assimilate completely because if they do, the fire (Judaism) will go out, the rays (Christianity) will cease to emanate, and the people who walk in darkness (the pagans) will never see a great light. If the Jews are allowed to assimilate completely, Judaism will disappear. But so will Christianity, because it will no longer be able to perform its role as world missionary, and thus paganism will never be transformed into higher religion. As much as the Jews may want to assimilate completely, this luxury cannot be allowed them because the consequence for the rest of the world would be disastrous.[25]

Paul Tillich, pondering this same problem in an insufficiently appreciated series of four lectures entitled *Die Judenfrage, ein Christliches und ein Deutsches Problem*, Schriftenreihe der Deutschen Hochschule fuer Politik (Berlin: Weiss, 1953), 48 pp., especially lecture three, understood the situation in a slightly different but fundamentally similar way.[26] According to Tillich there are two basic conceptions of the holy, or two basic types of religion: the priestly and the prophetic. Both tendencies are present within Judaism and both within Christianity. However, when the Jews lost their land to the Romans (to Pompey, 63 B.C.), as well as their temple to the same people (to Titus, 70 A.D.), and were forced into the Diaspora, the prophetic tendency was able to win a clear and distinct victory over the priestly within their religion. Whereas when Christianity became the state religion of the Roman Empire from the time of Constantine circa 313, by contrast with the Jewish situation at that same time, the priestly tendency was able to win a clear and distinct victory over the prophetic within the Christian world. It continues to maintain this superiority, especially within Roman Catholicism, the most hierarchical and the largest of the four main branches of Christendom (the other three being Protestantism, Eastern Orthodoxy, and Monophysitism).

The chief characteristics of each respective conception of the holy, as Tillich understood them, can be outlined as follows:

PRIESTLY	PROPHETIC
sacrament	kerygma
magic	law
ritual	ethics
the community	the individual
hierarchy	democracy
infallibility of the religious leaders	fallibility of the religious leaders

SPACE	TIME
STATIC	DYNAMIC
PAST AND PRESENT	FUTURE
POLYTHEISM	MONOTHEISM
NATIONALISM	INTERNATIONALISM
WAR	PEACE

According to Tillich both conceptions of the holy are equally necessary. Each corrects and makes possible the continued existence of the other.

The priestly conception of the holy assumes that people are animals; the prophetic, that they are angels. The priestly conception of the holy assumes that people are basically bad; the prophetic, that they are basically good. The priestly conception demands too little of people; the prophetic, too much. The priestly conception is too concrete; the prophetic, too abstract. The priestly conception is too realistic; the prophetic, too idealistic. Both conceptions, the priestly and the prophetic, are equally necessary. Either without the other would become distorted and unrecognizable. The priestly conception of the holy, without the prophetic corrective, leads to barbarism because it allows people to surrender to their own worst instincts. The prophetic conception of the holy, without the priestly corrective, leads to disillusionment because people can only maintain the prophetic for a short period of time before it totally exhausts and depletes them both spiritually and physically. Civilization would be impossible if either conception would be allowed to run wild with no contrary conception to keep it in check.

This is where the Jews come into the picture. Ever since the destruction of the Second Temple in 70 and the beginning of the Diaspora, the Jews have been a people forced by history to overemphasize the prophetic at the expense of the priestly. By contrast, ever since the time of Constantine circa 313 and the victory of Christianity over Mithraism within the Roman Empire, the Christians have been a people forced by history to overemphasize the priestly at the expense of the prophetic. But if the Jews were allowed to assimilate completely and/or convert en masse to Christianity, thus to disappear as a separate entity, who would remain within the Indo-European Christian civilizational area to perform the crucially indispensable role of keeping the priestly in check by standing for its required opposite, the prophetic?

240

Who would continue to keep sacrament in check by kerygma, magic by law, ritual by ethics, the community by the individual, hierarchy by democracy, infallibility of religious leaders by their fallibility, SPACE by TIME, the STATIC by the DYNAMIC, the PAST AND PRESENT by the FUTURE, POLYTHEISM by MONOTHEISM, NATIONALISM by INTERNATIONALISM, and WAR by PEACE? Thus, the Jews cannot be allowed to assimilate completely because their disappearance would mean the eventual disappearance of the prophetic within the Indo-European Christian civilizational area. The disappearance of the prophetic would allow the priestly to run wild. If the priestly runs wild, the Western world will return to utter barbarism and degradation as the priestly allows and encourages this world to surrender to its own worst instincts.

(8) *The Christian world requires the continued existence of the Jews as Jews in order to help it maintain the delicate balance within its own psyche between its Indo-European, its purely Christian, and its Semitic elements. Should this delicate balance be upset, Christianity would be seriously endangered as an ideology and would no longer be able to serve its primary historical function, as the means by which the Indo-European peoples express their will to survive and dominate.*

Christianity, as a cultural system, is made up of three component and coequal parts: its Semitic-Judaic heritage represented by the Old Testament; its Indo-European/Greco-Roman heritage, especially its philosophical (Plato, Aristotle, and the Stoics) and literary (Homer, Vergil, and others) traditions; and finally the purely Christian component, represented by the New Testament, patristic literature, the medieval Scholastics, and so on. The third transforms the other two component parts into a highly effective synthesis capable of satisfying millions of people both intellectually and emotionally, as well as helping them find salvation. Thus, Christianity can be compared to a balance and two scales. One scale is the Semitic-Judaic heritage (the Old Testament). The other scale is the Indo-European/Greco-Roman heritage (Plato, Aristotle, Homer, Vergil and, so on). The balance proper, which holds the two scales together and puts them to work in the service of civilization, is the purely Christian component (New Testament, patristic literature, Scholasticism, and such). Such is Christianity as a cultural system.[27]

However, if the soul of Christianity, its culture, is only one-third Indo-European, its body, the world Christian population, is 90 percent

Indo-European ethnolinguistically. This disparity puts tremendous pressure upon Christian culture. It attempts to make the Indo-European component thereof weigh far more than the one-third allotted to it within the Christian cultural synthesis and as close as possible to the 90 percent which the Indo-European component represents within the world Christian population. Hence, the disparity in question tends to upset the delicate balance between the coequal Semitic, Christian, and Indo-European components of Christian culture, thereby threatening to destroy the entire Christian cultural system.

This is where the Jews come into the picture. When the Semitic Jews are allowed to live and work as Jews amongst the Indo-European Christians, they moderate by their mere presence and example the tremendous pressure which the overwhelming Indo-European component of the world Christian population exerts upon Christian culture, thus helping that culture retain the crucially indispensable tripartite balance between its Semitic-Judaic, purely Christian, and Indo-European/Greco-Roman component parts. If the Jews were allowed to assimilate completely and/or convert en masse to Christianity and thus to disappear as a separate entity within the Christian world, there would no longer be any such countervailing force to preserve the delicate balance and scales of Christian culture capable of uniting the Indo-European peoples and giving them the will to survive and dominate.

Thus, to sum up this section of the chapter, perhaps the real reason why the Jews have never been allowed the luxury of successful total assimilation and mass conversion is because the Christian world does not want this to happen, for the eight possible reasons outlined above, especially the last. The Christian world requires the continued existence of the Jews as Jews in order to help it maintain the delicate balance within its own psyche between its Indo-European, purely Christian, and Semitic elements. Should this delicate balance be upset, Christianity would be seriously endangered as an ideology and would no longer be able to serve its primary historical function, *i.e.*, as the means by which the Indo-European peoples express their will to survive and dominate. This, then, may be the ultimate reason why Spanish Christendom could not allow the Jews (the Marranos) to achieve complete assimilation as mightily as, the Netanyahu thesis demonstrates, the Jews of Spain strove to accomplish that purpose. After two generations (by circa 1480) Spanish Christians had to create the Inquistion, one of the most powerful engines of torture and repression ever invented, to attempt to drive the Jews back to Judaism by crucifying those who had sought to become Christians.

*****

Netanyahu's conclusions about the fifteenth-century Spanish Marranos are among the first to come to serious grips with the fundamental truth of Christian-Jewish relations for the past 2000 years, *i.e.*, that the Jews desperately seek complete assimilation into the Christian world, but the Christian world, just as desperately, cannot afford to allow them to assimilate completely. These conclusions have cleared the ground for a thorough and complete reevaluation of the social and religious history of the Jewish people in the Iberian peninsula, from Roman to modern times. In this reevaluation we suggest that the comparative approach may well offer the best opportunity for a genuine understanding of what really happened in Spain.[28]

Can we really understand the Jewish fate in Visigothic Spain if we do not simultaneously analyze in equivalent depth the fate of the Arian (and other) heretics during this same period, comparing and contrasting their situation in detail with that of the Jews? Can we really understand the Jewish fate in Muslim Spain if we do not simultaneously analyze in equivalent depth the fate of the Mozarabs (Arabic-speaking Christians) during this same period, comparing and contrasting their situation in detail with that of the Jews?[29] Can we really understand the Jewish fate in Christian Spain from the *Reconquista* (circa 1000) to the Expulsion (1492) if we do not simultaneously analyze in equivalent depth the fate of the *Mudejars* (Muslims living under Christian rule), comparing and contrasting in detail their situation with that of the Jews?[30] Can we really understand the fate of the Jews and Marranos in Spain before and after the Inquisition (circa 1480) and Expulsion (1492), or the Jewish and Marrano Diaspora after 1480/ 1492 in Europe, the Middle East (especially Ottoman Turkey), and the Americas, if we do not simultaneously analyze in equivalent depth the fate of the Moriscos (forced Muslim converts to Christianity) and their Diaspora, especially in North Africa, during this same period, comparing and contrasting their situation in detail with that of the Jews and Marranos?[31]

Similarly, can we really understand how the *Christians* of Spain treated their two creative minority groups, the Muslims (the *largest* of the two) and the Jews, in the Later Middle Ages and early modern times, if we do not compare and contrast it with how the *Muslims* of Spain treated their two creative minority groups, the Mozarabs (the largest of the two) and the Jews; and how the Catholic Visigoths (of the seventh century) treated their two minority groups, the Arian heretics (the largest of the two) and the Jews? Similarly, can we really understand how the Christians of *Spain* treated, first Mudejars *and* Jews, then Moriscos *and* Marranos, if we do not compare and contrast in depth their treatment of these two creative minority groups with how their Portuguese cousins treated them?[32]

When the Fourth Lateran Council in 1215 decreed a distinction in clothing for Jews, it also decreed a distinction in clothing for Muslims. During the following three centuries the story of Christian attempts to impose a badge upon the Jews of Spain and of Jewish resistance to these attempts also has an equivalent story as far as the Mudejars are concerned. However, on which minority group, Jews or Muslims, did the Christians of Spain make the greater effort to impose a badge and why? Which minority group, Jews or Muslims, was better able to resist these efforts and why? Likewise, from the early to midfourteenth century there were attacks against the Jews of (northeast) Spain (Navarre, Aragon, etc.) during the 1320s and again during the Black Plague (1348–1349), though these attacks were nowhere near as serious as those upon the Jews of France and Germany at those times. However, were there also attacks against the Mudejars during the 1320s and the Black Plague? If not, why not? Further, it is generally held that the Jewish position in Castile deteriorated considerably during the great civil war between King Pedro the Cruel and his half-brother Count Henry of Trastamara (circa 1350–1370) and during the victor Henry's reign (circa 1369–1379) because the Jews had backed the wrong side, the loser Pedro. However, did the position of the Mudejars also deteriorate during and because of this civil war (they too supported Pedro)? If not, why not? The Jewish community of Spain was shaken to its very foundations by the terrible massacres of 1391 which originated in Seville. However, was there an equivalent of the massacres of 1391 for the Mudejars? If not, why not?[33]

The subconscious desire of the Jewish people in Spain to assimilate completely and disappear as Jews was strongly encouraged by the efforts of learned apostates from Judaism to Christianity who, upon con-version, launched a ceaseless and powerful polemic against their former religion and coreligionists the likes of which had rarely been seen before in Jewish history and were rarely equaled thereafter. We refer to the work of Abner of Burgos and John (called Alphonso) of Valladolid during the fourteenth century; Paul of Burgos (originally Solomon Ha-Levi) with his disciple Geronimo de Sante Fe (originally Joshua Ha-Lorki) as well as Franciscus de Sant Jordi/Dios Carne (Astruc Rimoch), Pedro Ferrus, Diego de Valencia, and Maestro Juan de Espanya El Viejo of Toledo, all of the early fifteenth century. Were there similar apostates from Islam to Christianity in late medieval and early modern Spain whose attacks upon their former religion and coreli-gionists helped stimulate the Morisco movement?[34]

San Vicente Ferrer played a major role in the second and even more voluntary wave of conversion of Jews to Christianity in Spain circa 1410–1415. However, this saint, as a revolutionary messianist and leader of a wandering band of flagellants, was not solely concerned with the conversion of the Jews. He was equally if not even more con-cerned with the conversion of the far more numerous Mudejars. The harsh anti-Jewish legislation which he helped persuade the govern-ment of Castile to enact in 1412 was also directed against the Mude-jars. If so, then San Vicente Ferrer's messianism and his attitudes toward the Mudejars must be taken into consideration in evaluating his crucial role in the tragic demise of the Jewish community of Spain.[35]

Paul of Burgos, San Vicente Ferrer, and others were behind the nightmarish Tortosa disputation, which lasted a year and nine months (from February 1413 to November 1414), the most horrible of all of the theological tournaments into which the Jews were forced during the Middle Ages. However, was there also a Tortosa disputation for the Mudejars? If not, why not?[36]

At this point it is proper to note that three great Christian apolo-gists in fifteenth-century Spain, all three of whom may well have been of Jewish descent, wrote not only against the Jews but against the Muslims as well. Pedro Bonafus de la Cavalleria, baptized as a child at the time of the Tortosa disputation, a famous lawyer and high ju-dicial counselor of the king of Aragon, wrote the *Zelus Christi contra Judaeos, Saracenos et Infideles* (1450), in which the author demonstrated a remarkable knowledge of Jewish (especially mystical) literature. As can be seen by the title, the *Zelus Christi* also attacked the Muslims, though its attack was primarily directed against the Jews.[37] Alphonso de Spina, the Franciscan rector of the University of Salamanca (historically one of the key centers of liberal thought in Spain!), wrote *Fortalitium Fidei* (1460). This work is considered one of the greatest landmarks in the history of anti-Semitic literature. However, it was also directed against the Muslims as can be seen from its full title, *Fortalitium Fidei contra Judaeos, Saracenos, Aliosque Christianae Fidei Inimicos*. The *Aliosque . . . Inimicos* are heretics and sorcerers. The fifteenth century also saw the great expansion of the witch-hunting frenzy and of a volume as notorious in the history of intolerance and persecution as the *Fortalitium Fidei*. We refer to the *Malleus Maleficarum* by Heinrich Institoris and Jakob Sprenger, 1487.[38]

Similarly, Cardinal Juan de Torquemada (1388–1468) wrote the *Defensorium Fidei contra Judaeos* which was directed, not solely against Jews, but also against Muslims as can be seen from its full title, *Defensorium Fidei contra Judaeos, Hereticos et Saracenos*. This same author also published a special treatise directed against the Muslims alone, the *Tractatus contra Principales Errores Perfidi Machometi et Turchorum sive Saracenorum Festinanter Copulatus*, while, to our knowledge, he wrote no such special treatise directed against the Jews alone.[39] Should not what Pedro Bonafus de la Cavalleria, Alphonso de Spina, and Juan de Torquemada wrote against the Jews be carefully compared and contrasted with what they wrote against the Muslims, the larger and more powerful minority group in fifteenth-century Christian Spain? Is not their combined literary-polemical attack on both Judaism and Islam further support for the thesis of the final section of this chapter, that the fate and destiny of the Jews (Marranos) in Renaissance Spain should be studied against the background of the highly similar fate and destiny of the Muslims (Moriscos) in Renaissance Spain.

Was it mere coincidence that the Expulsion of the Jews from Spain took place in 1492, the very same year in which Granada fell and Columbus set sail for the Far East only to discover the Americas? The precise relationship between these three events still awaits final elucidation. However, it is unlikely that we will ever be able to understand any one without also attempting to understand the other two.[40] Further, there were several revolts against the crown by the Moriscos in sixteenth-century Spain. Were there simultaneous and/or similar revolts against the crown among the Marranos? If not, why not?[41] Finally, the Marranos and Jews who departed Spain after circa 1480

/1492 and into the sixteenth and seventeenth centuries went to Christian lands (Italy, the Low Countries, Hamburg, Vienna, England, and, most importantly for the future of the Jewish people in the nineteenth and twentieth centuries, the New World), as well as to Islamic lands (North Africa and Ottoman Turkey). Did a similar proportion of the Moriscos who departed Spain circa 1600 go to Christian lands or Ottoman Turkey? Both the Marranos and the Moriscos were equally forced converts to Christianity, or were they? If they were, why did only the Marrano Diaspora reach as far as Holland, England, and the New World but not the Morisco Diaspora? Why were there so few (if any) Moriscos in Lima and Mexico City, Brazil, Curacao, and New Amsterdam? These questions must be asked and answered if we hope to achieve a genuine understanding of the history of the Jewish people in Spain and Portugal.[42]

Thus, the work of Netanyahu is laying the foundation for a thorough and complete reevaluation of the social and religious history of the Jewish people in the Iberian peninsula from Roman to modern times. Very few contemporary scholars are as much at home in the noble cultural traditions of both the Jewish and Spanish peoples. Yet, despite the fact that both peoples are naively idealistic in their attitudes toward life and the world, Netanyahu is a realist. As such, he is not content with the outmoded romantic notions about the Marranos which have so long impeded scholarly progress in the highly important field of the origins of the Spanish Inquisition. At the same time Netanyahu's work is laying the foundation for a more balanced evaluation of the long and significant history of the Jewish people in Spain and Portugal.

When his work is finished (and even to some extent while it is still in process), we will be able to take the second step in the complete rewriting of the history of the Jewish people in the Iberian peninsula in accordance with more modern scholarly ideas. This second step would be the systematic introduction of the comparative approach, the simultaneous in-depth study of the fate and destiny of Jews and Arian heretics under the Visigothic Catholics, of Jews and Mozarabs under the Muslims, of Jews and Mudejars as well as Marranos and Moriscos under the Christians, in both Spain and Portugal. This kind of comparative approach is the primary approach upon which future, ecumenically oriented scholarship on the Marranos should concentrate. It may also offer the best hope for a thorough modern under-

247

standing of the genuine dynamic of interreligious relations in Iberia throughout the centuries, especially during the Renaissance period (circa 1400 to 1600). It may take another century before a comparative approach of this kind will be able to lead us to a fuller understanding of what happened in Spain, but let us hope that its time will be shorter.

In conclusion, we note that the main thrust of Netanyahu's work is to demonstrate that medieval anti-Semitism (and, therefore, modern anti-Semitism as well, which stems from medieval anti-Semitism) was not the result of Christian theology or the Christian religion per se but rather of powerful forces, both intellectual and socioeconomic, which were unleashed in the general development of Western European civilization taken as a whole. Netanyahu's approach, thus, is similar to that of Bernhard Blumenkranz. Each one's work supports the other's. Blumenkranz's *Le Juif Medieval au Miroir de l'Art Chretien* concludes, as we recall, with the following statement:

> The struggle of Christianity against Judaism . . . is a product of general conditions emerging out of internal and external politics and of sociological facts.[43]

Our own thinking regarding the medieval origins of modern anti-Semitism follows the trail so ably blazed by Netanyahu in the United States and Blumenkranz in Europe. Without their efforts in this field we would all be wandering aimlessly in the wilderness. Our debt to them is great, for their work has laid the crucial foundations for the revival of research on the history of Christian-Jewish relations in ancient, medieval, and modern times, and for a genuine Christian-Jewish dialogue leading toward the true reconciliation between church and synagogue that all people of good will everywhere hope to see develop in the coming generations.[44]

8. The Crucial Influence of Islam upon the Collapse of the Jewish Community of Spain (Circa 1400) and the Jewish Community of Southern Italy (Circa 1300) *

Once we accept the Netanyahu thesis, that the overwhelming majority of the Spanish Marranos of the fifteenth century were sincere Christians, we are faced with the serious historiographical problem which Netanyahu has not yet addressed. That problem is what factors caused the unprecedented sincere mass conversion to Christianity of the Jews of Spain and southern Italy during the Later Middle Ages. Such is the topic of this eighth chapter of our book. The word "collapse" in the title of this chapter means "sincere Jewish mass conversion to Christianity." During the Middle Ages and the Renaissance, to our knowledge, this phenomenon of sincere Jewish mass conversion to another religion ocurred uniquely in the Mediterranean area, *i.e.*, in Spain and southern Italy. That apparent singularity of the south Italian and Spanish situations (circa 1300 and 1400 respectively) is set into even deeper relief by the fact that simultaneously therewith, north of the Pyrenees and the Alps, Jews seemed to be much more willing to suffer voluntary mass martydom (often self-inflicted, *i.e.*,, by ritual suicide) or exile rather than yield to Christian pressure for conversion. This is what happened in and around Prague, circa 1390, as well as Vienna, circa 1420, more or less contemporaneously with the mass conversion of the Jews of Spain circa 1400.[1]

The following are the factors which we feel should be considered as *possible* explanations (they are only hypotheses) as to why the Jewish community of Spain collapsed so totally circa 1400 that it sincerely converted en masse to Christianity at that time:

1. Spanish Jewry's especially strong power drive;

2. the Spanish civil war circa 1350–1370, between King Pedro the Cruel and his rebel half-brother Count Henry of Trastamara, in which the Jews chose to support the loser, Pedro;

3. Spanish Jewry's excessive social sophistication (really social pseudosophistication) which misled it into thinking that it could escape the law of "superfluous people" as well as the Jewish fate and destiny in general (*i.e.*, perpetual migration);

4. Spanish Jewish desire for revenge upon the Muslims, the other and even larger non-Christian ethnoreligious minority in the Iberian peninsula, and the equally intense Spanish Jewish desire to refute, once and for all, the devastating Christian charge that the Jews were in league with the Muslims;

5. Spain's geography and climate;

6. ethnic tensions within the Spanish Jewish community itself;

7. the geriatric factor and Spanish Jewry's desire for cultural rejuvenation;

8. the role of philosophy;

9. the role of mysticism;

10. the economic interpretation, *i.e.*, Spanish Jewry's excessive wealth;

11. the constant shifting of the majority culture within the Iberian peninsula; and, perhaps most importantly,

12. the especial attraction of Spanish Christian culture as *a heavily Semiticized Christian culture.*[2]

The primary effects of the sincere mass conversion of the Spanish Jews were as follows: to help generate (1) a major Spanish exploration and colonization effort in the New World, as well as (2) powerful currents of theological and philosophical liberalism and skepticism that would make intellectual and cultural freedom and individualism far more possible in eighteenth- than in fifteenth-century Europe.

The Jews of southern Italy also converted to Christianity en masse and with relative sincerity circa 1290, about a century earlier than their Spanish Jewish brethren. The same factors which may well have been operative in Spain circa 1400 would also seem to have been operative in southern Italy circa 1300.

However, the crucial overarching factor which made the Spanish and south Italian Jewish communities so uniquely susceptible to the desire for mass conversion and complete assimilation was undoubtedly the same factor which made both Spain and southern Italy in general so unique in Western Europe. This factor cuts across most of the tentative explanations suggested above which will be developed below. We refer to *the overpowering presence of the Muslims* and the centuries-long threat, implicit as well as explicit, which Islam posed to Christian religious and social values within both the Iberian and the Italian peninsulas.

Thus, once again it was Christian-Islamic relations which crucially determined Christian-Jewish relations in one of the most tragic episodes of Jewish history and Western civilization. The Iberian Inquisition and its demonic attack upon thousands of innocent people in Europe and the New World circa 1480-1825 must ultimately be traced to the Islamic conquest of Spain in 711!

1. Spanish Jewry's Especially Strong Power-Drive[3]

Was it the tremendous desire for power rather uniquely developed by Spanish Jewry which encouraged its willingness to do anything, including conversion to Christianity in relative sincerity if necessary, to defend and enhance that power?

What factors produced the excessive power drive of Spanish Jewry? Was it the general harshness and inhospitality of the Spanish landscape (i.e., the relative paucity of water, arable land, trees, and birds)? Did this kind of landscape require of Spaniards in general and Spanish Jews in particular, who wanted to survive, an especially gargantuan effort to achieve power over nature, which when successful stimulated an equally gargantuan effort to achieve power over people? Was it the inordinate wealth which Spanish Jewry was able to accumulate, partly because at one time Andalusia was part of an exceedingly prosperous Islamic empire that extended from the Atlantic to the Indian ocean; and partly because the Jews of Iberia could serve as economic intermediaries between the warring Christians and Muslims? Or, and perhaps most importantly, was it that the Jews represented the strategic balance of social force between the warring Christian and Islamic camps?

Was it that the equally dynamic Christian and Islamic ethnoreligious communities (both more heavily represented than the Jews in the rural, agricultural areas, the less influential portion of the country), each wielded about 40 percent of the total social force in medieval Iberia? Did the Jews (because they were so overwhelmingly concentrated in the Spanish urban centers, the more influential portion of the country) represent the remaining 20 percent of the total social force in the peninsula? Did this 20 percent then give them the balance of power between the Christian 40 percent and the Muslim 40 per-

251

cent? Or was it a combination of all three factors, ecological necessity (the general harshness and inhospitality of the Spanish landscape) which applied to all Spaniards alike regardless of ethnoreligious background, plus surplus Jewish capital (accumulated in large part because of the Islamic presence within Spain) and the strategic balance of total social force (between the warring Christian and Islamic camps) represented by the Jewish community, with the last named perhaps the weightiest of the three factors, all conspiring together, which generated the excessive power drive of medieval Spanish Jewry?

Fairly convincing proof of the excessive power drive of the Spanish Jewish establishment and the role of this drive in the collapse of the Spanish Jewish community circa 1390–1415 is offered by the following. Jewish religious tribunals north of the Pyrenees enjoyed only the right to try civil cases and punish by the imposition of fines; but Jewish religious tribunals in Spain enjoyed the right to try both civil *and criminal* cases and to punish by the imposition of both fines *and death*.[4] The reason the Jewish religious tribunals of Spain enjoyed this unusual privilege may well have been because the Jewish magnates of Spain insisted upon it with Herculean determination and made it the sine qua non for their collaboration with the Christian establishment. The Spanish Christian establishment, in turn, desperately needed the help of the Jewish grandees during the long struggle against the Muslims, one gigantic destruction and rebuilding project circa 711–1350, by which latter date the ultimate Christian victory in the Iberian peninsula seemed assured. Thus, though the Spanish Christian establishment would have preferred to withhold from the Jewish religious tribunals in Spain the right to try criminal cases and to impose the death penalty, it had no alternative for many generations but to pay the price required by the Jewish establishment for its collaboration.

At least two important Jewish literary sources circa 1375–1425, the anonymous and radically mystical treatise *Sefer Ha-Kanah* and Solomon Alami's incisive moral treatise *Iggeret Musar*, claim that the power drive of the Spanish Jewish establishment played a major role in the collapse of Spanish Jewry circa 1390–1415.

Netanyahu cites the *Sefer Ha-Kanah* as stating that Spanish Jews "apostasized in order to acquire for themselves kingship and rule [Hebrew: *malchut* and *memshalah*, which, of course, equals power drive] and they would take for themselves foreign [*i.e.*, Old Christian] wives."[5] Thus, with what seems to be a considerable degree of social insight, the *Sefer Ha-Kanah* links the power drive of the Jewish converts with their desire to marry Old Christians (of non-Jewish descent) instead of New Christians (other Jewish converts to Christianity like themselves). Of course, had the Jewish converts to Christianity really been secret Jews, they would not have preferred Old Christian wives. Rather, they would either have married only among themselves or else married un-converted Jews.

The *Sefer Ha-Kanah* would seem to imply that the Jewish converts' power drive came first and eventually led them to desire genuine conversion to Christianity and intermarriage with Old Christians. The situation was not the reverse. It was *not* that the desire for genuine conversion to Christianity came first; when this desire was achieved during the "time of troubles" (circa 1390–1415) it led to an equally intense desire for intermarriage with Old Christians; when this desire was achieved (circa 1415–1440) it opened up genuine access to power for the Jewish converts, who then developed their power drive. Rather, the power drive of the Jewish converts to Christianity existed long be-fore their mass conversion circa 1390–1415. Indeed, it helped cause that mass conversion. It did not suddenly arise after the conversion; nor was it a later effect of the conversion.

Netanyahu also cites Solomon Alami's *Iggeret Musar* as suggesting that it was the casuistic, truth-evading, and self-seeking rabbinic scholars and the power-hungry, wily, and unprincipled Jewish courtiers who were the secondary cause of the mass conversion (Alami considered the philosophical movement among Spanish Jews to have been the primary cause).[6] Assuredly, however, the power-hungry Jewish cour-tiers were far more responsible than the self-seeking rabbis, for "who pays the piper calls the tune." By the second half of the fourteenth century, in Castile at least, the rabbis were totally dependent upon the Jewish courtiers for their socioeconomic survival and were mere agents of the secular leaders of the Spanish Jewish establishment.[7] This can be quite clearly seen through the contrast between the way Rabbi Asher the son of Y'hiel dominated the Jewish grandees in Toledo dur-ing the first quarter of the fourteenth century and the way Rabbi M'nahem the son of Zerah capitulated to them completely during the final quarter of the fourteenth century.

Admittedly, Rabbi Asher's back was stiffened by the fact that he had been born and bred in Germany, where the Jewish religiolegal tradition was stricter than it was in Spain and where the Christian presence was undiluted by any Islamic civilizational admixture. It was also stiffened by the fact that he was one of the greatest authorities on Jewish religious law during the entire Middle Ages. By contrast, Rabbi M'nahem was a native of Spain, where the Jewish religiolegal tradition was more lax and the Islamic presence was very strong. He was only a minor authority on Jewish religious law. Hence, it was M'nahem, not Asher, who stood helplessly by while his patron, Samuel Abravanel (grandfather of the great Isaac Abravanel, of late fifteenth-century Spanish and Italian fame), treasurer of King John I of Castile, converted to Christianity in 1385 (only six years before the terrible massacres of 1391; Samuel Abravanel may well have seen the hand-writing on the wall). Taking the baptismal name of Juan Sanchez de Sevilla, he converted under considerable sociolegal but certainly under no physical compulsion in order to retain his exalted position in the royal bureacracy.[8]

Thus, two important Jewish texts from the crisis period circa 1375-1425, the *Sefer Ha-Kanah* and Solomon Alami's *Iggeret Musar*, both written in relative independence of one another, consider the power drive of the Spanish Jewish establishment (the courtiers) to have been a major factor in the collapse of the Spanish Jewish community circa 1390-1415.

2. The Spanish Civil War Circa 1350-1370

The Jews of Spain were uniquely powerful enough, economically, socially, and politically, to take sides in the terrible civil war circa 1350-1370, which was a struggle between King Pedro the Cruel, the legitimate ruler, and his half-brother, Count Henry of Trastamara, the rebel. Like the tragic Spanish Civil War of the 1930s, the Spanish civil war of the fourteenth century soon escalated into a great international conflagration, with France backing Henry, and England, Pedro. The Jews of Spain chose to support the legitimate ruler, Pedro, but they chose unwisely, because it was the rebel Henry who eventually proved to be victorious with French assistance. Active Jewish involvement in the civil war represented a catastrophic blunder. Both sides to the conflict (even King Pedro's) perpetrated frightful massacres of Jews. The victorious Henry imposed huge fines upon the Jews for having backed the wrong side. For the same reason the Cortes (parliament) which met at Toro in 1371 finally imposed the "badge of shame" upon the Jews who had been able to stave off its official introduction into Castile for about a century and a half (after it was required by the Fourth Lateran Council in 1215).[9]

Did the blunder of active Jewish involvement in the civil war and choice of the wrong side totally undermine Jewish self-confidence and lead the majority of the Spanish Jewish community to opt out of Judaism and into Christianity with relative sincerity a generation later, circa 1390–1415? Because the Jewish establishment of Castile was wrong so catastrophically during the civil war, did it then decide never to be wrong again? Because the Jewish establishment of Burgos and Toledo (traditionally considered the leading Jewish communities of Castile) supported the losing side during the civil war and paid dearly for this mistake, spiritually (having now to wear the "badge of shame") even more than physically (and the physical price was high indeed: massacre, huge fines, etc.), did these proud establishments decide never to support the losing side again? When intense Christian pressure was applied to the Jews of Spain circa 1390-1415, did the Jews decide to be right? Did the Jews who had been so clearly on the losing side between circa 1350-1370 now decide to be on the winning side? Was this the kind of thinking that led to mass and relatively voluntary Jewish conversion to Christianity in Spain circa 1400, an event almost totally unprecedented in Jewish history?

Were the Jewish establishments of Burgos and Toledo totally depleted psychologically and physically by their ill-fated role in the terrible Spanish civil war of the midfourteenth century? They had suffered many cruel psychological and physical blows during the twenty-year period of the civil war, circa 1350-1370. During the subsequent twenty-year period did they have too little time to rebuild their psychological and physical defenses and/or reserves? Was this why, when intense Christian pressure was applied to the Jews of Spain circa 1400, they had no will whatsoever left to resist and surrendered completely with mass Jewish conversion to Christianity in relative sincerity?

Something drastic assuredly had happened to Jewish morale in Burgos between 1368 and 1391. Thus, the Jews of Burgos took up arms for Pedro the Cruel and against Henry of Trastamara in 1368.[10] However, in 1391 the Jews of Burgos offered no armed resistance at all to the Christian mobs who attacked them.[11] In 1368 the Jews were willing to fight with weapons to save the *Christians* (Pedro the Cruel). Yet, in 1391 the Jews were unwilling to fight with weapons to save *them-*

selves. Instead, they voluntarily gave up one eminently defensible group position, their virtually "impregnable" fortress, and moved into a large number of indefensible individual positions (*i.e.*, the homes of friendly Christians). This was the case even though the mob that attacked them did so *without royal approval* and was nowhere near as well armed as had been the soldiers of Henry of Trastamara, against whom the Jews had been willing to fight with weapons in 1368. Clearly, the Jewish defeat in the civil war of the 1360s had devastated them psychologically to the point where they decided that they would never fight again. Hence, they opted to save their lives by converting to Christianity in 1391.

3. Spanish Jewry's Excessive Social Sophistication

Tremendous social sophistication was rather uniquely developed by Spanish Jewry, again perhaps because in order to survive, the Spanish Jews had to play off one side against the other, Muslim against Christian and vice versa. This sophistication enabled them to understand better than any other medieval European Jewish community the law of "superfluous people," that circa 1400 their help was no longer needed by the Christians of Spain against the Muslims. The Castilian *Reconquista* reached the mouth of the Guadalquivir and the Atlantic Ocean at Cadiz circa 1252 under King Alfonso X of Castile. The last great Islamic threat to Christian Andalusia was defeated by King Alfonso XI of Castile circa 1340.[12] Did Spanish Jewry's unique grasp of social realities lead it to attempt to obviate the application of the law of "superfluous people" to itself circa 1390–1415 via conversion en masse to Christianity with relative sincerity?

This Spanish Jewish attempt worked for a time (two generations). But what the Jews of Spain did not realize, despite their social sophistication (which thus proved to be only pseudosophistication), was that once a Jew, always a Jew. The ethnic factor is the determining factor. It can never be erased. Conversion to Christianity might defeat the law of "superfluous people" for two generations. But it could never defeat that law forever.

The Jews north of the Pyrenees, in Franco-Germany, were not socially "sophisticated." Nor were they pseudosophisticated. They were simple and uncomplicated Jews, overwhelmingly loyal to Jewish piety and religious law, without complaint or protestation. They imitated their enemies. They mistakenly thought their enemies selfless. They would be equally selfless as well! They mistakenly thought that they were being attacked by the Christians for idealistic reasons of religion, for having killed Christ. They responded by offering the attackers an idealistic response, martyrdom or flight.

The Jews south of the Pyrenees in Spain, however, knew that they were not being attacked for idealistic reasons of religion, for having killed Christ. They knew the real reasons why they were being attacked were economic, social, and political, i.e., because they were "superfluous people," no longer needed by Christian society. They knew that they were being attacked out of motives of pure self-interest. Thus, they offered the attackers no idealistic response, such as martyrdom or flight. They offered them an economic, social, and political response, a response based upon what they thought was pure self-interest, i.e., the response of mass conversion to Christianity in relative sincerity. They too imitated their enemies. They correctly thought their enemies were acting out of motives of self-interest. They would act out of precisely the same motives as well! If the Christians could act out of motives of self-interest in massacring the Jews, motives far different from those the Christians publicly expressed, the Jews could similarly act out of motives of self-interest by converting en masse to Christianity in relative sincerity (with no thought of practicing Judaism in secret) in order to attempt to obviate the disaster which the application to them of the law of "superfluous people" would have meant.

History proved the Spanish Jews to have been tragically wrong. Their attempt to defeat the law of "superfluous people" by conversion to Christianity eventually brought on the Spanish Inquisition. Its horrors (psychological as well as merely physical) were far greater than the mere physical extinction of death (which also offered the psychological victory of dying as martyrs for a cause without ever having betrayed that cause by conversion to its opposite) which the Jews of northern Europe were willing, and at times even eager, to suffer courageously and unflinchingly. The fate and destiny of Spanish Jewry, in the long run, would have been less tragic if it had not been socially sophisticated (pseudosophisticated) enough to understand the law of "superfluous people" circa 1390–1415. Or, if it had chosen not to attempt to thwart the operation of this law by conversion en masse to Christianity but rather had chosen to die as martyrs (as did their less socially sophisticated brothers north of the Pyrenees). Could the Inquisition have tortured the minds and bodies of the Marranos after circa 1480 if their grandfathers, the Jews of Spain, had chosen to die as martyrs, in imitation of the behavior of their Franco-German brethren, during the crisis period circa 1390–1415?

4. Spanish Jewish Hatred of the Muslims

The Jews of Spain may well have converted circa 1390–1415 in part out of an intense (perhaps even obsessed) desire to participate actively and energetically, on a more direct and equal basis, in the Christian effort to destroy the last vestiges of independent Islamic power in the Iberian peninsula, the Nasrid kingdom of Granada (supported morally, and at times militarily, by the Merinid sultanate of Morocco and the rest of the Muslims of the Mediterranean).

Of course, the crucial question would then remain as to why the Jews of Spain would so intensely have desired the destruction of the Nasrid kingdom of Granada? To this question there are at least two answers.

First, the Jews of Spain may well have intensely desired the destruction of the Nasrid kingdom of Granada because of their feeling of having been betrayed, especially during the twelfth century, in the cruelest and most vicious way by the Muslims of Spain, whom they had once considered their brothers, (i.e., during the period of the emirate and caliphate of Cordova, circa 750–1000). This feeling of betrayal was strongly reinforced by the way the Nasrid rulers of Granada and/or their Merinid Moroccan allies behaved toward the Jews during the crucial fourteenth century.

There were at least thirteen possible reasons why the Jews could have felt betrayed by the Muslims of Spain/Morocco:

1. The Muslim massacre of the Jews of Fez, Morocco, circa 1035.[13]

2. The Muslim massacre of the Jews of Granada, Andalusia, circa 1066 (considered by some the first pogrom of Jews on European soil).[14]

3. The Muslim suppression of the Jewish revolt in Lucena, Andalusia, circa 1090.[15]

4. The fearsome Muslim threat to impose forced conversion upon the Jews of Lucena, circa 1105 (avoided by the payment of an especially heavy fine).[16]

5. The Muslim suppression of the Jewish messianic revolt in Cordova, Andalusia, circa 1117.[17]

6. The Muslim suppression of the Jewish messianic revolt in Fez, circa 1127.[18]

7. The Muslim threat of death leveled against the Jews of Aghmat-Ailan, Morocco, if they dared to move to the capital at Marrakesh, circa 1106–1143.[19]

8. The forced conversion of the Jews of Muslim Spain circa 1146–1163.[20]

9. The forced conversion of the Jews of Muslim Morocco circa 1164–1185.[21]

10. The prohibition upon Jewish forced converts to Islam from marrying into "Old" Muslim families or engaging in any kind of economic activity above petty trade, and compelling the forced converts to wear hats and tunics of degrading shapes and distinctive colors (blue) as well as "badges of shame," circa 1184–1199.[22]

11. The continuation of the prohibition upon Jewish forced converts to marry into "Old" Muslim families and the retention of the requirement that the forced converts wear garments of distinctive colors (though the distinctive color was now changed from blue to yellow), circa 1199–1213.[23]

12. The Muslim massacre of the Jews of Marrakesh, Morocco, 1232.[24]

13. The Muslim massacre of the Jews of Fez, 1275.[25]

All of these serious Islamic attacks upon the Jews, but especially numbers 2, 4, and 8 to 10, could not help but create a deep sense of Jewish betrayal by, along with an equally intense Jewish desire for revenge upon, the Muslims of Spain/Morocco. They had treated the Jews harshly and cruelly after the fall of the caliphate of Cordova, when the Christians slowly and gradually retook most of Muslim Spain (circa 1000–1300).

But what happened circa 1000–1300 does not end the story of Islamic attacks upon the Jews of Spain/Morocco. The story continued into the fourteenth century. The main Islamic actor now was not the Almoravides or the Almohades, the dynasties which dominated Muslim Spain and Morocco from the late eleventh to the midthirteenth centuries. Rather it was the Nasrids, the dynasty that ruled the last remaining independent Islamic bastion in the Iberian peninsula, and brilliantly managed to stave off the fall of Granada to the far superior Christian forces of the north for over two and one-half centuries (circa 1235–1492).

The story of Nasrid betrayal of the Jews in the fourteenth century is relatively obscure, but two main events stand out in rather clear relief. First, circa 1320 the Nasrid ruler of Granada, Ismail I (also called Abu-l-Walid ibn Abi-Zaid Faraj), imposed the "badge of shame" upon the Jews of his kingdom. The great act of betrayal represented herein can only be understood when we realize that the "badge of shame" in general would not be seriously required by the Christians of Castile for another fifty years. Thereby Granada revived a particularly igno-minious portion of the anti-Jewish policy of the great Almohade ruler Yaqub al-Mansur (1184–1199) (number 10 as discussed immediately above) and also emulated those Christian lands (outside of the Iberian peninsula) which enforced the decree of the Fourth Lateran Council (1215) imposing the "badges of shame" upon all Jews (and Muslims, for that matter) living within Christian territory.[26]

Second, in 1368, as the Spanish Civil War of the fourteenth cen-tury was reaching its final and decisive hour, King Pedro called upon the Nasrid ruler of Granada, Muhammad V, for help. Muhammad's forces were too ineffective to take the great southern Trastamaran bas-tion at Cordova (though they did take the smaller Trastamaran towns of Jaen and Ubeda) and were forced to withdraw. But this was not before they had enslaved and held for ransom the entire Jewish popu-lation (about 300 families; perhaps 1200–1800 people) of the town of Jaen, thus reviving the bitter memories of the two earlier Muslim ac-tions against the Jewish community of Lucena, not too far to the south of Jaen, circa 1090 and 1105 (numbers 3 and 4 discussed immediately above).[27]

These two anti-Jewish Muslim actions of the fourteenth century, the enslavement for ransom of the Jews of Jaen in 1368 and the im-position of the "badge of shame" upon the Jews of Granada circa 1320, together with the thirteen anti-Jewish Islamic actions circa 1000–1300 as outlined above, could have served to produce an ex-ceedingly deep and abiding hatred of the Muslims within the soul and consciousness of the Jews of Christian Spain. This powerful hatred may well have driven the Jews to the decision to convert to Christian-ity en masse and with relative sincerity in order to participate actively and energetically, on a more direct and equal basis, in the Christian effort to destroy the last vestiges of Islamic power in the Iberian peninsula, the Nasrid kingdom of Granada.

Second, in addition to desiring intensely the destruction of the Nasrid kingdom of Granada because of their feeling of having been betrayed by the Muslims of Spain, whom they once had considered their brothers, the Jews of Spain also may well have highly desired the destruction of the Nasrid kingdom of Granada for another reason. This would have been as part of a vain attempt to refute, once and for all, the devastating Christian charge that the Jews were in league with the Muslims against the Christians and were veritable Islamic fifth columnists in Christian territory.

This charge played a major role in medieval Christian anti-Semitism. It surfaced with tremendous force circa 1321 in France, almost affecting the Papal States in Italy as well and definitely spreading to northeastern Spain (Navarre and Aragon).[28] The charge appeared in the late 1330s in Castile and almost led to the expulsion of the Jews from this most important of the Spanish kingdoms.[29] Finally, it is highly likely that the charge also surfaced toward the end of the century, with perhaps an intensity as great as that by which its appearances circa 1321 and in the late 1330s were characterized, as the Ottoman Turkish invasion of the southern Balkans (Greece, Bulgaria, and Serbia) terrified Christian Europe during the 1380s.[30] This third major fourteenth-century appearance of the charge that the Jews were in league with the Muslims may have been the proverbial straw that broke the camel's back. Perhaps it drove the Jews of Spain to the ineluctable conclusion that the only way they could defend themselves against massacre in Spain as Islamic fifth columnists, while all of Christian Europe was in a state of panic over the Ottoman advance into the Balkans circa 1390, was to convert to Christianity en masse and with relative sincerity circa 1390–1415. As new Christians they could then actively assist the Old Christians of Spain in destroying the Islamic kingdom of Granada, the last vestige of independent Islamic power in the Iberian peninsula, thus proving that the Jews were not in league with the Muslims after all!

5. Spain's Geography and Climate

Was it the relative vastness of the distances between major Jewish centers of population within Spain itself that prevented the development of Spanish Jewish unity against Christian pressure? These distances were vast not only in actual miles but also because of the Spanish terrain, which was either unbroken, seemingly infinite, treeless plain, or broken by the highest internal mountain chains in all of Atlantic Europe west of the Alps. They are also vast because of the relative impossiblity of using the Spanish rivers as arteries of transportation. Since there is so little rain and whatever rain there is often comes down in torrents, the result is that the river channels are either totally dry or else too flooded for successful navigation.[31]

Or was it the geographical isolation of Spain itself from the rest of the world which made Jewish flight to avoid persecution extremely difficult if not impossible? Spain is cut off to the north, from France, by the lofty Pyrenees traversed by fewer passes than the Alps, and from the British Isles, by the Bay of Biscay; to the east, from Italy, by the Mediterranean; to the south, from Morocco, by the Straits of Gibraltar; and to the west, from the New World, by the Atlantic.

Or was it Spain's balmy Mediterranean climate which enervated the Jews and sapped their will to resist Christian pressure? Or did the climate deceive the Jews into thinking that they were back home in equally Mediterranean Palestine, and, thus, into thinking that in Spain they were no longer in *galut*, in exile? If so, the result would have been that they could not bear the thought of leaving Spain and were willing to pay any price, including mass conversion to Christianity in relative sincerity if need be, for the privilege of remaining.

Or was it the greater power of regionalism in Spain (itself perhaps caused by the combination of the three previously discussed factors: vastness, isolation, and climate) which prevented the development of Jewish unity against Christian pressure?

After all, pursuing this factor a bit further, it is generally acknowledged that the power and problem of regionalism and secessionist movements are far greater in Spain than in most other Western European countries. Of the three great Atlantic powers in the sixteenth century—England, France, and Spain—Spain was undoubtedly the last to develop a sense of national unity. What is more, the Spanish story in the seventeenth, nineteenth, and twentieth centuries at least has been primarily one of fission, successful or merely attempted, rather than fusion. We refer to the successful breakaway of the Portuguese from Spain circa 1640, and the unsuccessful but nonetheless intense secessionist efforts by the Catalans circa 1650 and in the 1930s and by the Basques in the 1830s (the Carlist Revolt) and the 1930s. By contrast, the story during these same centuries in England, France, Germany, and Italy has been primarily one of fusion, rather than fission, with England and Scotland uniting; Richelieu-Mazarin-Louis XIV centralizing in France; Bismarck uniting Germany, and Cavour, Italy. Of course the most violent secessionist movements in contemporary Western Europe are those of the Basques of northeastern Spain and the Catholics of Northern Ireland. The German-speaking South Tyrolean secessionist movement in northern Italy, the Breton secessionist movement in Western France, as well as the Welsh and Scottish secessionist movements in Britain may all set off dynamite charges from time to time. But only the Basque nationalists assassinate hated government officials in the capital city of the enemy (Madrid) and kidnap foreign consuls. All of this demonstrates once again that the power and problem of regionalism are far greater in Spain than in most other Western European countries.

The way this regionalism affected Spanish Jewish history may well have been that in the late fourteenth century the Jewish communities of the various sovereign and independent regions of Iberia, *i.e.*, Portugal, Castile, Granada, Aragon, and Navarre, had relatively little communication among themselves.[32] The Jewish communities of each of these five kingdoms, like the kingdoms themselves, were more or less hermetically sealed off from each other. When the great time of troubles and intense pressure for Christianization came circa 1390–1415, the Jewish community of each sovereign and independent region was totally alone and isolated. No community may have had a fervent feeling of belonging to a greater Jewish whole within the Iberian peninsula or within the world at large. Therefore, each isolated and alienated Jewish community could put up little or no resistance to Christianization and would have to succumb relatively quickly if intense pressure was applied. Each isolated and alienated Jewish community would have to opt to end its isolation and alienation by acquiring a new sense of belonging to a greater whole, *i.e.*, the greater whole of world *Christendom*. This world was more united than Judaism because it was still in control of its own religious center, Rome, and because it at least had one primate for all of the Iberian peninsula in the archbishop of Toledo, and one great pilgrimage shrine which drew Christians from all over Western Europe, Santiago de Compostela in far northwestern Galicia. The Jews had lost control of their religious

263

center, Jerusalem, centuries earlier; the concept of ecclesiastical primacy in the hierarchical sense was unknown to the Jewish rabbinate; and the Jews had no pilgrimage shrine in Spain of world-historical importance. The only way the Jews of Spain could finally unite with each other was to join the Christian church!

6. Ethnic Tensions within the Spanish Jewish Community Itself

Did ethnic tensions within the Spanish Jewish community itself, tensions apparently not as readily felt within other major medieval European Jewish communities, help undermine Spanish Jewish unity as well as its strength to resist the intense pressures to conform exerted by the Spanish Christian majority circa 1390–1415? We would suggest that ethnically the Spanish Jewish community was divided into two warring camps:

1. the "natives," whose ancestors had come to Spain before the Islamic conquest in 711; and

2. the "foreigners," whose ancestors came to Spain only after the Islamic conquest in 711.

The "natives" and "foreigners" differed in the following ways.

The ancestors of the "natives" had been in Spain since the crystallization of the first historically significant Spanish Jewish community in the first century A.D.[33] The ancestors of the "foreigners" came to Spain at least 700 years later.

The ancestors of the "natives" had been in Spain at a time when it was dominated by only one ethnoreligious tradition, either Roman pagan, or Roman Christian, or Visigothic Christian. Admittedly, however, circa 400–600 Spain was divided ideologically between heretical Arian Christian Visigoths and orthodox Catholic Christian Romans. However, both groups were Indo-European and Christian. The ancestors of the "foreigners" never knew a time when Spain was dominated by a single ethnoreligious tradition. They came to Spain only after it was divided between the Christians and the Muslims, who fought each other for centuries before the Christians emerged victorious (from the midthirteenth century on).

The ancestors of the "natives" came originally from Palestine and had been heavily influenced culturally by the following non-Jewish ethnolinguistic groups *resident in Spain:* the Semitic Phoenician-Carthaginians, the Indo-European Celts, the Indo-European Romans, and the Indo-European Visigoths, three out of four of which groups were Indo-European. By contrast, the ancestors of the "foreigners" came originally from Iraq (the dominant subgroup numerically and politically within the camp of the "foreigners") or North Africa. Those who came from Iraq had been heavily influenced culturally by two non-Jewish ethnolinguistic groups, the Indo-European Iranians and the Semitic Arabs, and thus only half of the non-Jewish cultural influence upon them before they came to Spain was Indo-European. Those who came from North Africa had been heavily influenced culturally by the following non-Jewish ethnolinguistic groups: the Hamitic Berbers, the Semitic Carthaginians, the Indo-European Romans, the Indo-European Vandals, and the Semitic Arabs, only two out of five of which groups were Indo-European.

Thus, all the non-Jewish cultural influence upon the "native" Jews of Spain was Spanish, and three-quarters of that non-Jewish cultural influence was Indo-European, whereas all of the non-Jewish cultural influence upon the "foreign" Jews of Spain was non-Spanish, and only about half of it was Indo-European. It is clear, then, that the "native" Jews of Spain were far more heavily Indo-Europeanized than the "foreigners"; the "foreign" Jews of Spain were far more heavily Semiticized than the "natives."

Finally, after the Islamic conquest in 711 the "native" Jews tended to prefer the northern part of Spain and thus to live in an ecological environment that was cooler and rainier climatologically and thus grassier and more heavily forested, an area which looked geographically and commercially toward France. By contrast, after the Islamic conquest in 711 the "foreign" Jews tended to prefer the southern part of Spain and thus to live in an ecological environment that was warmer and drier, with the hills and valleys much more barren, an area which looked geographically and commercially toward Morocco.

Hence, we would interpret some of the quarrels and struggles famous in Spanish Jewish history as follows. Two southern "foreigners" (*i.e.*, Jews whose ancestors were not present in Spain before the Islamic conquest in 711), the statesperson Hasdai ibn Shaprut and the poet Dunash ben Labrat, joined together to destroy the northern "native" poet M'nahem ibn Saruk in the tenth century.[34] The "foreign" Talmudic scholar Enoch ben Moses defeated the "native" Talmudic scholar Joseph the son of Isaac ibn Abitur, who then went into exile, also in the tenth century.[35]

The "north" versus the "south" was also an important factor in the following struggles (in which it may have been that the "northerners" were the "natives," whereas the "southerners" were the "foreigners"): the eleventh-century struggle between the great statesperson and scholar Samuel Ha-Nagid (ibn Nagdela or Nagrela), Jewish vizier of the southerly Berber kingdom of Granada circa 1025–1050, and Jonah ibn Janah, the greatest Hebrew grammarian of medieval Spain, who lived in northerly Saragossa;[36] and the thirteenth- through early fifteenth-century struggle between the northerly Abulafia family (which dominated the Jewish communities of Burgos and Toledo, in Old and New Castile respectively, in northern and central Castile) and the southerly Abravanel family (which dominated the Jewish Community of Seville, in Andalusia, southern Castile). In this latter struggle the Abulafias prevailed in the thirteenth century (Meir b. Todros Abulafia, Todros ben Joseph Halevi II, etc.). Southerners from Seville (Judah Abravanel, Joseph of Ecija) prevailed circa 1300-1340. The Abulafias (Joseph ben Meir Abulafia, Samuel Halevi Abulafia) prevailed again circa 1340-1360. Seville (Joseph Pichon and Samuel Abravanel) prevailed again circa 1360-1390. The Abulafias prevailed at the end (though only after most of the Jews of Spain had converted to Christianity) through the Marrano Paul of Burgos circa 1390-1420.[37]

Finally, we would interpret the heretical Karaite movement (which arose in Iraq-Iran in the eighth century and spread westward to Italy, Algeria, and Spain[38]), finally crushed in Spain circa 1200, as a protest by old "native" Jews of Roman-Visigothic background against domination by the newcomers, the "foreign" Jews of Arabic-Berber background from Iraq and North Africa.[39]

Was it that Spanish Jewish history from the time of the Islamic conquest tended to be dominated by the "foreigners" rather than the "natives" even though the "natives" probably represented a majority of the Spanish Jewish community? After suffering under this "foreign" domination for seven centuries (eighth through the fourteenth), were the majority "native" Jews of Spain inspired by the successful revolt of Count Henry of Trastamara against the rule of his half-brother King Pedro the Cruel, which revolt in part relied upon *nativist* Spanish Christian hatred of the Muslims and Jews who were the allies of Pedro? Did this inspiration lead the "native" Jews to attempt to throw off the yoke of their "foreign" brethren by converting to Christianity en masse and with relative sincerity circa 1390–1415 as the only available means by which they could end the tyranny of the minority over their lives? When the revolt of the "native" Jews (the suppressed majority of Jews of Roman-Visigothic background) via mass conversion to Christianity began, were the dominant "foreigners," the minority elite who came from Iraq and North Africa, compelled to follow suit by likewise converting to Christianity en masse and with relative sincerity? Was it that otherwise they would no longer have had anybody left within the synagogue to dominate and the only place they could have found new groups to dominate was within the Church? Thus, was the relatively sincere mass conversion of the Jews of Spain circa 1390–1415 one way of resolving long-standing ethnic tensions within the Spanish Jewish community itself, between the larger but submerged group of "native" Jews of Roman-Visigothic background and the smaller but dominant groups of "foreign" Jews of Iraqi and North African background?

7. The Geriatric Factor and Spanish Jewry's Desire for Cultural Rejuvenation.

If Judaism is the oldest or first generation, the grandmother, Christianity is the middle or second generation, the mother, and Islam is the youngest or third generation, the granddaughter. Could it have been that the Jews of Spain circa 1390–1415 decided to attempt rejuvenation, perhaps under the influence of the sunny Mediterranean climate of Spain and/or the contemporary Italian Renaissance effort to achieve cultural rejuvenation by returning to classical pagan antiquity as well as the pre-Reformation (Wycliffe in England; Huss in Bohemia) longing to achieve religious rejuvenation by returning to the ideals of the early (pre-Constantinian and pre-Nicene) church? Weary of playing the role of the aged grandmother, did the Jews of Spain attempt, en masse and with relative sincerity, to join those who were only middle-aged by converting to Christianity, the religious civilization that was the equivalent of the second generation, as the maximum possible rejuvenation they could have hoped to achieve?

Admittedly, the Jews of Spain, once they had decided to attempt to turn back the generational clock, would probably have preferred to skip over Christianity completely, the middle or second generation, in order to retreat all the way back to childhood, to the youngest generation, to Islam. However, we suggest that such was psychologically and culturally impossible. The most a people could hope for was to re-

267

juvenate itself by one step, to move down from old to middle age, from Judaism to Christianity. The shock involved in such a moderate move of a single step would have been severe but still bearable. However, a radical move of two steps from old age down to youth, from Judaism down to Islam, would have been too psychologically and culturally unsettling. The shock involved in such a radical jump of two steps would have been unbearable. It would have destroyed rather than rejuvenated.

At least five different situations involving relations between Christians, Muslims, and Jews, and cutting directly across the question of Jewish attempts at ethnoreligious rejuvenation by mass conversion, can be distinguished as follows.

1. SITUATION NUMBER ONE. The Jews are the majority, the Muslims and Christians both present as minorities. Historically this is a very rare situation and prevails now only in the State of Israel. In this situation the Jews will certainly not attempt to seek rejuvenation by conversion to Christianity or Islam because the Jews are already the majority. The only time a people seeks ethnoreligious rejuvenation by mass conversion is when it is in the minority, since ethnoreligious rejuvenation by mass conversion is a means by which a minority attempts to discover the additional spiritual and physical energy required for a meaningful future existence (albeit in an altered state of cultural consciousness).

2. SITUATION NUMBER TWO. The Christians are in the majority, the Jews in the minority, but no Muslims at all are present. This was the situation north of the Pyrenees in medieval Franco-Germany. In this situation the Jews will again not attempt to seek rejuvenation by mass conversion (in this case the mass conversion could only be to Christianity since no Muslims at all are present) because the Jews will not feel their age. In order to feel their age, the Jews must be living in a country where *both* younger ethnoreligious traditions are present, both Christianity *and* Islam. Since only one younger ethnoreligious tradition was present north of the Pyrenees, *i.e.*, Christianity, while the Muslims were totally absent, the Jews of Franco-Germany felt no real pressure for rejuvenation and thus never seriously entertained the thought of mass conversion to Christianity.

3. SITUATION NUMBER THREE. The Muslims are in the majority, the Jews are in the minority, but no Christians at all are present. This was the situation in Yemen. In this situation the Jews will

again not attempt to seek rejuvenation by mass conversion (in this case the mass conversion could only be to Islam since no Christians at all are present) for two reasons. (1) As in the situation no. 2 immediately above, only one younger ethnoreligious tradition is present, *i.e.*, Islam, and thus the Jews feel no real pressure for ethnoreligious rejuvenation. (2) Even if the Jews did feel real pressure for ethnoreligious rejuvenation, the only way they could have achieved it would have been by converting to Islam, involving a jump of two generational steps, from grandmother down to granddaughter; and the Jews would have considered this a psychological and cultural impossibility as suggested above.

4. SITUATION NUMBER FOUR. The Muslims are the majority; Christians and Jews are both present as minorities. This was the situation in Spain during the period of the caliphate of Cordova (circa 750–1000). In this situation the Jews will again not attempt to seek rejuvenation by mass conversion. Though both younger ethnoreligious traditions are present in this situation and thus the Jews really feel their age, the only option that means anything is conversion to Islam, the majority culture. But that is impossible because it involves jumping *two* generational steps, from grandmother to granddaughter, a psychological and cultural impossibility as suggested above. Conversion to Christianity, though possible psychologically and culturally because it would only involve jumping one generational step, from grandmother to mother, would be pointless. It would simply mean that the Jews were moving from one type of minority status into another, a move also illegal, because Islamic society only permits non-Muslims to convert to Islam, not to any other religious tradition.

5. SITUATION NUMBER FIVE. The Christians are the majority, Muslims and Jews are both present as minorities. This was the situation in Spain circa 1390–1415. In this situation the Jews *would* attempt to seek rejuvenation by mass conversion (in this case conversion to Christianity) for the three crucial reasons: (1) since both younger ethnoreligious traditions (Christianity and Islam) are present, the Jews definitely feel their age; (2) since the majority group in this case is Christianity, conversion would be possible psychologically and culturally because it would only involve jumping one generational step, from grandmother to mother; and (3) because by conversion the Jews gain admission to the majority group.

Thus, the last situation, which was found in Christian Spain circa

1400, was unique because it was the only one of the five situations outlined above in which all three crucial reasons why Jews would attempt to seek rejuvenation by mass conversion were present. All three reasons were present in none of the four other situations. Situation 1, the modern State of Israel, lacks condition 3, the possibility of moving by mass conversion from a minority to a majority group status, since the Jews in the State of Israel are already in the majority. Situations 2 and 3, medieval Franco-Germany and medieval/modern Yemen, lacked condition 1, the presence of *both* younger ethnoreligious traditions to make the Jews really feel their age, for Franco-Germany lacked Muslims and Yemen lacked Christians. Situation 4, the caliphate of Cordova, lacked condition 2. Here mass conversion to the majority religious culture would have involved jumping two generational steps, from grandmother to granddaughter, a psychological and cultural impossibility. Only in situation 5, Christian Spain circa 1400, were all three crucial reasons present. Only Christian Spain circa 1400, rather than the modern State of Israel, medieval Franco-Germany, medieval and modern Yemen, or the caliphate of Cordova, represented a situation where the Jews could and would attempt to achieve ethnoreligious rejuvenation by mass conversion with relative sincerity.

8. The Role of Philosophy

Philosophy (especially Aristotelian), which was more fully developed by Spanish than by any other medieval European Jewry (assuredly under Islamic influence), may well have undermined Jewish belief in the fundamental dogmas of their own revealed religion.[40] Given an enthusiastic belief in those dogmas, the Jewish masses would respond to persecution idealistically and choose to die as martyrs for their faith. Lacking an enthusiastic belief in those dogmas, the Jewish masses would respond to persecution in a way that would advance their own self-interest and would convert to Christianity en masse and with relative sincerity.

The more idealistic Neo-Platonist Avicennan interpretation of Aristotle prevailed among the Jewish philosphers of Spain circa 1150–1300 and was fostered by Abraham ibn Daud and Maimonides (who spent most of his life as an exile from Spain in Egypt). The more scientific-naturalistic Averroist interpretation of Aristotle prevailed among the Jewish philosophers of Spain circa 1300–1400 and was fostered by the lesser known but almost equally influential Moses of Narbonne, who lived and worked in Castile in the mid-fourteenth century.[41] What in the Aristotelian system undermined the traditional Jewish system of belief and practice in Spain and thus paved the way for the mass conversion of the Jews to Christianity in relative sincerity circa 1390–1415?

In the Aristotelian system God is an impersonal force, not a personal being. This primary and general postulate of Aristotelianism engendered a whole series of secondary but more specific philsophical challenges to the traditional Jewish system of belief and practice.

1. If God is an impersonal force rather than a personal being, he did not *create* the universe. The universe must have been eternally existent. If so, God is not the sole power in the universe. The universe represents a power independent and perhaps even older than God. If so, God is not omnipotent.

2. If God is an impersonal force rather than a personal being, he does not work miracles like those which the Bible says God worked on Moses's behalf, *e.g.*, the miracle of the burning bush or the miracle of the parting of the Red Sea. If there are no miracles, how can the truth of the divine revelation be confirmed unto the skeptical and how can God save his people when they are in distress?

3. If God is an impersonal force rather than a personal being, he does not hear prayers. If he does not hear prayers, he cannot answer requests for help, whether individual or communal. If God cannot answer requests for help, he cannot save Jews from persecution and help them survive, individually or collectively, as a minority group within a non-Jewish society.

4. If God is an impersonal force rather than a personal being, he does not reveal his will through the Prophets (*e.g.*, Moses). There is no such thing as revelation. The Torah and its 613 commandments are not God's work but rather a product of the human imagination. If so, why should the Jews die as martyrs to defend them? If all religion is human rather than divine, should not the Jews become Christians instead of suffering as Jews?

5. If God is an impersonal force rather than a personal being, he does not care what people do. Hence, there is no divine reward or punishment either in this life or the next. If so, there will be no divine reward for resisting majority group pressure to convert and conform. Nor will any divine punishment be visited upon the Jews for abandon-

ing the religion of their ancestors and transferring en masse and with relative sincerity to Christianity.

6. If God is an impersonal force rather than a personal being, there is no immortality of the individual soul. At most there is only immortality of the collective soul, of the human species as a whole. If so, why should the Jews hold out as a small and weak minority within an overwhelmingly large and powerful Christian majority? Since only the collective soul survives, why should the Jews not become part of the collective body as well, join the majority, become Christian en masse and with relative sincerity?

7. If God is an impersonal force rather than a personal being, he would not "choose" any single people or group as his own special treasure or representative of true religion unto a pagan world. Hence, the Jewish people could not be God's "elect," because God does not have an "elect." If so, there cannot possibly be any meaning or purpose in the suffering of the Jewish people during its long and harsh exile in the Diaspora? Then why should the Jews continue to suffer in exile? Why should they not attempt to end their misery by relatively sincere mass conversion to Christianity?

8. If God is an impersonal force rather than a personal being, he does not care if mankind as a whole is redeemed from oppression; nor does he care if history comes to an eschatolgical end with the ultimate triumph of good. If so, God will not send the Messiah (son of David) to redeem the Jewish people from the darkness of their exile. Nor will he bring them back to the Holy Land whence they came; nor preside over the last judgment, where the synagogue will finally triumph over the church and mosque, as the Jews are assigned to heaven but their tormentors and oppressors to hell. If the Jewish Messiah is not going to come, should not the Jews join the Christians who are the majority? Should not they convert to Christianity en masse and with relative sincerity, making their mass conversion and their new religion their Messiah?

The majority of the Jewish Aristotelians in fourteenth-century Spain did not carry their philosophical beliefs out to their ultimate conclusions. But a small minority did, and this minority apparently exerted an increasing influence upon the Jewish upper class in both Castile and Aragon as the fourteenth century moved inexorably to its tragic conclusion.[42] Did the Jewish middle and lower classes follow the example set by their natural leaders, the Jewish upper classes, in accepting some or all of this extreme type of Aristotelianism? If they did, they would thereby have been undermining the kind of blind faith in the traditional Jewish system of belief and practice required if the Jewish community of Spain was to avoid mass conversion to Christianity in relative sincerity when intense pressure toward this end was applied by the Christian majority circa 1390–1415. Does not this Aristotelian danger explain why the great Jewish scholar of late fourteenth- and early fifteenth-century Catalonia, Hasdai Crescas, had to devote the major portion of his life after 1390 to a highly creative attempt to destroy the Aristotelian stranglehold over the Jewish philosophical movement in Spain? This attempt was only partly successful, but it later influenced an equally if not even more brilliant Jewish philosopher of Spanish-Portuguese background, Baruch Spinoza, in seventeenth-century Holland, to create a non-Aristotelian philosophical system of his own.[43]

Netanyahu cites at least four fifteenth-century Spanish Jewish writers who would seem to have argued that the philosophical movement was the primary cause of the total Spanish Jewish collapse and relatively sincere mass conversion to Christianity circa 1390–1415. Two are from the early fifteenth century, Solomon Alami and Shem Tov the son of Shem Tov; and two from the mid- to late-fifteenth century, the great Isaac Arama and Joel ibn Shuaib.

Solomon Alami held that the philosophical movement was the main cause of the Jewish collapse because the philosophical movement taught that knowledge (philosophy, intellect, rational search, and inquiry into the nature of the universe) was the key to salvation, while Judaism taught that action (the performance of mitzvot, God's commandments) was the key to salvation. The danger in the philosophical approach was that under the stress of persecution, something which Jews had to endure periodically if not constantly, it is impossible to seek salvation by knowledge but not impossible to seek it by action. Knowledge requires peace of mind and thus cannot be pursued during times of persecution, whereas action requires no such peace of mind and can be performed during times of the greatest stress. What is more, action can help people suffering persecution to overcome their psychological anxiety, but knowledge cannot. If Judaism is to be understood as salvation through knowledge, as the philosophers taught, such a Judaism was bound to collapse during the great persecution of circa 1390–1415. During this long twenty-five year period Jews had little if any peace of mind, and those Jews who preferred this philosophical conception, or were strongly influenced by it, were bound to transfer to Christianity where they could certainly find more peace of mind to pursue their concept of salvation by knowledge. Only those Jews who understood Judaism to be salvation through action would have been able to avoid conversion during the time of troubles. However, the philosophers were persuasive enough during the fourteenth century to turn too many of the Jews, especially their leaders, away from the traditional and safe action-centered approach to Judaism, which would have enabled the Jews to survive the great persecution as Jews, toward the new and dangerous knowledge-centered approach to Judaism, which was totally incapable of helping the Jews survive the great persecution as Jews. The result was mass and relatively sincere conversion to Christianity circa 1390–1415. So argued Solomon Alami.[44]

Alami's contemporary, Shem Tov the son of Shem Tov, also blamed the philosophers for the collapse. But this was not because they taught salvation through knowledge. That doctrine in itself would not have been harmful. The real threat posed by the philosophical movement was that it taught the wrong *type* of knowledge. Its extreme Aristotelianism (with an impersonal God concept) undermined the traditional Jewish belief that God judges people, rewarding the righteous and punishing the wicked either in this life or the next. The philosophical movement, in opposing these traditional Jewish beliefs, taught the people not to believe in the last judgment, heaven, and hell. Without belief in reward and punishment there was no reason to do what was right, no reason to stay faithful to Judaism, and no reason to avoid what was wrong, no reason to avoid mass conversion to Christianity. Thus, Shem Tov the son of Shem Tov understood the threat of the philosophical movement.[45]

Isaac Arama also blamed not the more moderate Jewish Avicennans but rather the more radical Jewish Averroists. These intellectuals, who interpreted Aristotle too literally, believed that God was an impersonal force but not a personal being. Therefore they were compelled to deny that God was omnipotent or omniscient. They then went on to reason as follows. Since God is not omniscient, he may not know that we plan to sin by relatively sincere mass conversion to Christianity. But even if he does know that we plan to sin by mass conversion, since he is not omnipotent, perhaps he does not have

274

enough power to punish us for it. Therefore, why not surrender to majority group pressure and save our lives via relatively sincere mass conversion? Thus did Isaac Arama understand the baneful effect of the philosophical movement upon the Jewish will to resist Christian conversion pressures in Spain circa 1400.[46]

Finally, Joel ibn Shuaib, about the time of the expulsion of the Jews from Spain in 1492, argued that the main cause of the total Jewish collapse a century earlier was the fact that the Jews had ceased to believe in the imminent coming of the Jewish Messiah son of David.[47] Ibn Shuaib did not offer any explanations as to why the Spanish Jews should suddenly have abandoned their expectation of the messianic redemption at the end of the fourteenth century. However, should we not place a major portion of the blame upon the philosophical movement, especially the Jewish Averroists, who taught that God was an impersonal force, not a personal being? The logical conclusion from the doctrine of God's impersonality was that God had no intention of redeeming the world and, therefore, that history was cyclical rather than goal-oriented. But if history is cyclical, there would be no hope for the Jews to end their sufferings in exile through divine intervention. That suffering would continue forever. The Messiah would never come. Hence, why should the Jews of Spain not end their suffering in exile through relatively sincere mass conversion to Christianity circa 1390–1415?

9. The Role of Mysticism

If philosophy contributed in a major way to the mass and relatively sincere conversion of Spanish Jews to Christianity circa 1390–1415, mysticism may also have played a part. The law (halachah) as action (mitzvot) was traditionally the essence of Judaism and the main principle behind its resistance to Christian pressure for conversion. The philosophical movement offered a distinct alternative to the law by arguing that knowledge not action was the key to salvation. By so doing it undermined the chief principle whereby Judaism resisted Christian pressure for conversion. Likewise, the mystical movement offered an alternative to the law by arguing that emotion, not action, was the key to salvation.[48] By so doing, it too undermined the chief principle whereby Judaism resisted Christian pressure for conversion.

We would suggest that the law was the main principle around which rallied the Spanish Jewish middle class, the largest of the three Jewish socioeconomic classes. The Spanish Jewish upper class embraced the philosophical movement as salvation by knowledge rather than action, and the Spanish Jewish lower class embraced the mystical movement as salvation by emotion rather than action, both to spite the Spanish Jewish middle class that adhered to the law. Thereby, both the upper and lower classes undermined Judaism, which could only exist as an independent religious force if it adhered fanatically to the law as the only key to salvation. When the great pressure for conversion began in Spain circa 1390, mass apostasy to Christianity was the Spanish Jewish upper class's means of demonstrating its superiority, and that of its principle of salvation by knowledge, over the Jewish middle class with its principle of salvation by law, and over the Jewish lower class with its principle of salvation by emotion. At the same time, mass apostasy to Christianity was the Spanish Jewish lower class's means of demonstrating its superiority, and that of its principle of salvation by emotion, over the Jewish middle class with its principle of salvation by law, and over the Jewish upper class with its principle of salvation by knowledge. The Spanish Jewish middle class saw both its rival classes, the upper and lower, converting to Christianity simultaneously, each to spite it and to spite the other. Thereupon, the Spanish Jewish middle class decided that there was no point in dying or suffering for its conception of Judaism (salavation through law) when neither of the two other Jewish social classes were willing to die or suffer for their conceptions of Judaism (salvation through knowledge and salvation through emotion). The result was that the Spanish Jewish middle class joined the other two Jewish socioeconomic classes by converting to Christianity en masse and with relative sincerity.

But were there any specific ideas, peculiar to the Jewish mystical tradition, which helped undermine the Jewish will to resist Christian pressure? Indeed, there may well have been two: (1) the doctrine of the holiness of evil and (2) the belief in reincarnation.

THE DOCTRINE OF THE HOLINESS OF EVIL. According to this doctrine, since God created the universe and was radically present throughout his creation, God must have created evil (as well as good) and must be present within evil (as well as good). If so, evil could not be totally bad. There must be something good within it. Traditionally the Jewish people had believed that the worst possible evil a Jew could commit was conversion to another religion, which was considered treason to the ancestral faith. But, if we are to say that there is some good even in the worst evil, if we are to say that evil is in part holy, conversion to Christianity could not be totally bad. Indeed, there must be some good even within such a decision. If so, why should the Jews not convert to Christianity en masse and with relative sincerity to save their lives?

Further, this doctrine of the holiness of evil became closely bound up with messianism. According to the traditional orthodox Jewish messianic doctrine things must get worse before they can get better. Indeed, the worse they get the greater the chances for their getting better. In messianic terms this was the doctrine of the "birth pangs of the Messiah" (*hevle Mashiah*). Just as a woman must endure the harshest suffering, birth pangs, before she can have her child, so the world as a whole must endure the harshest suffering, the temporary victory of evil over good, before it can have its child, the Messiah, who will usher in the permanent and eternal victory of good over evil. But mankind has a role to play in the coming of the Messiah. If so, perhaps this role is to help bring on the "birth pangs of the Messiah," *i.e.*, to help insure the temporary victory of evil over good in order to hasten the permanent and eternal victory of good over evil. Now the worst possible evil a Jew can commit is to betray his ancestral faith and convert to another religion. Thus, mass and relatively sincere Jewish conversion to Christianity, the worst possible evil, would bring on the "birth pangs of the Messiah," the temporary victory of evil over good in the world. However, because of the holiness of evil, because evil leads to good, these "birth pangs of the Messiah," this temporary victory of evil over good, will soon bring about the messianic redemption, the permanent and eternal victory of good over evil. If so, why should the Jews not convert en masse and with relative sincerity to Christianity? This relatively sincere mass committing of evil will hasten the final redemption of the world!

Is there any evidence that the doctrine of the "holiness of evil" was known to Spanish Jewish mystical circles at this time? There are at least two pieces of such evidence. One comes from the famous *Sefer Bahir*, written circa 1180 in southern France (whence its views easily could have reached Castile via Catalonia), the first great Jewish mystical classic written on Western European soil. Probably influenced by the Manichean ideas then dominating southern France, this book in-

277

troduced the concept of the holiness of evil into the Jewish mystical tradition. For this reason, among others, the *Sefer Bahir* was considered blasphemous by thirteenth-century southern French Talmudic scholars. According to this book there is an evil principle in God himself, and it lies within God's north side. Furthermore, even the "gates of Zion," where the creative energy of the Jewish people is concentrated and through which it is communicated to the world, are "on the side" of evil.[49]

Further evidence that the doctrine of the holiness of evil was known to Jewish mystics in thirteenth- and fourteenth-century Spain comes from the *Zohar*, the bible of the Jewish mystical tradition, written in late thirteenth-century Castile by Moses de Leon. According to the *Zohar*, evil is rooted in the essence of the theosophic process itself. Its main source is not human sin. Evil did not come into the world because of Adam's fall, although his fall did indeed enhance the power of evil. Evil is woven into the texture of the universe itself, indeed into God's very own existence. God can be compared to a tree, a nut, and a woman. Evil can be compared to tree bark, a nut shell, and a woman's menstrual blood. Just as a tree cannot exist without its bark, a nut without its shell, and a woman (in her premenopause years) without her period, so God cannot exist without evil. Everything that is demonic has its root somewhere in the mystery of God. What is more, though evil is dead, it comes to life when a ray of light, however faint, emanating from the essence of God's *own* holy being, falls upon it. A spark of God's own holiness burns even in the devil himself.[50]

If the Spanish Jewish masses, especially the lower class, began to listen to the mystics who taught the doctrine of the holiness of evil as developed in the *Sefer Bahir* and the *Zohar*, they almost certainly would have begun to wonder why they should not convert to Christianity. For if evil is a part of God and is rooted in the essence of the theosophic process itself, then, as some radical fourteenth-century Spanish Jewish mystics may well have argued, why should not the Jews attempt to commune with that side of the divine nature which is evil via the worst possible evil a Jew could commit, betrayal of his ancestors by converting to another religion? For centuries the Jews had attempted to redeem themselves from exile by doing good. But this only linked them with part of God, God's goodness. Perhaps the time has now come for the Jews to link themselves with the other part of God, God's evil. Perhaps this is what is now required before the Messiah can come. But the primary way a Jew can commune with God's evil is by committing the cardinal sin, conversion to Christianity. Hence, the Jewish mystics, by their doctrine of the holiness of evil and their teaching that evil is part of God himself, may very well have contributed, and in a major way, to the collapse of the Jewish community in Spain circa 1390–1415.

Certainly this doctrine of the holiness of evil played a major role in the Jewish mystical and messianic movements of the seventeenth and eighteenth centuries. It played a crucial role in the Shabbetai Tzvi movement in the seventeenth-century Ottoman Empire.[51] It played an equally crucial role in the Jacob Frank movement in eighteenth-century Poland.[52] In both movements the doctrine of the holiness of evil led to the equally radical doctrine of the "apostasy of the Messiah."[53] Before the Jewish Messiah could save his own people from exile and redeem the world, he first had to convert to another religion. In Shabbetai Tzvi's case this other religion was Turkish Islam. In Jacob Frank's case it was Polish Catholicism. But in both cases the doctrine of the holiness of evil led, as a natural result, to the doctrine of the holiness of *apostasy* or conversion to another religion. The Shabbetaian movement was *by no means* a mere transitory phenomenon without influence upon subsequent Jewish religious history. It played an important role in the development of modern Hasidism and Zionism,[54] as well as Reform Judaism.[55] Such major Jewish mystical-messianic movements as the Shabbetaian in the seventeenth and the Frankist in the eighteenth centuries demonstrate how masses of Jews could be led by the mystical doctrine of the holiness of evil into the more radical doctrine of the holiness of apostasy. Could not this same doctrine, the holiness of evil, which was known to Jewish mystical circles in Spain during the thirteenth and fourteenth centuries, likewise have led many Spanish Jews to the more radical doctrine of the holiness of apostasy, and thus have played a crucial role in the Jewish collapse of circa 1390–1415 and the mass conversion of Jews to Christianity in relative sincerity?

THE BELIEF IN REINCARNATION. The classical geographical area where the doctrine of reincarnation developed seems to be India, and the classical religious tradition wherein it developed seems to be Hinduism. We refer especially to the Hinduism of the Upanishads, circa 600–300 B.C., perhaps under the influence of the native Dravidian inhabitants of India (because the Vedic religion of the Aryan invaders of India would not seem to have known the doctrine of reincarnation).[56] From Hinduism this doctrine moved into Buddhism and Jainism (in each case perhaps as early as the founders, the Buddha and the Mahavira, both sixth century B.C.).[57] From India the doctrine also spread westward, and its first important appearance in the Mediterranean area seems to have been in Greek Pythagoreanism (also sixth century B.C.).[58] After the decline of Pythagoreanism the doctrine of reincarnation was revived by Manicheanism (third century A.D. Iran; Mani, the founder, had spent time in the borderland between Iran and India, where Buddhist influence was strong) and carried into the Mediterranean basin by Manichean missionaries during the fourth and fifth centuries. After the decline of Manicheanism in the western Mediterranean area circa 500, the doctrine of reincarnation was revived by the new Manicheans, the Paulicians, who arose in Syria after the Islamic conquest in the seventh century. From the Paulicians the doctrine of reincarnation eventually spread into Shiism, the great Islamic sectarian tradition, and was embraced by the Druzes, who arose in Syria during the eleventh century.[59] From the Paulicians the doctrine also eventually spread westward (in part via the Bogomils of Bosnia) to the Manicheans of southern France in the twelfth century, thence to the early Franciscans[60] and to the Jewish mystics of southern France and Spain. It was kept alive by the Jewish mystical tradition (especially in Palestine and Poland) at least into the eighteenth century. Indeed, it may well be that the Jewish mystical tradition was the main defender of the doctrine of reincarnation in the Western civilizational area after the disappearance of southern French Manicheanism circa 1300.[61]

But what was there in the doctrine of reincarnation, as taught by the Jewish mystics of southern France and Spain in the thirteenth and fourteenth centuries, that would have encouraged Jewish conversion to Christianity in Spain circa 1390–1415? According to the doctrine of reincarnation the soul of the average (sinful) individual must endure an endless series of rebirths. If so, this means that the soul of the average Jew will keep being reborn into a world that persecutes Jews. In the traditional Jewish theology, which taught the immortality of the soul and the resurrection of the body, the average Jewish soul only has to live in the world once. It has to suffer persecution for being Jewish only once. Then it returns to heaven to await the messianic redemption and the last judgment. But the Jewish mystics, by teaching the doctrine of reincarnation, were teaching that the average Jewish soul has to live in the world many times. It therefore has to suffer endless persecution for being a Jew. Suffering as a Jew was bearable when the Jewish people believed that their souls would only have to suffer in the world once. But if the Jewish people believed that their souls would have to suffer for being a Jew over and over again, through many lifetimes, they might well have preferred to convert to Christianity en masse and enjoy this lifetime before being reincarnated as a persecuted Jew once more.

Further, according to the traditional Jewish theology, if a Jew committed the cardinal sin, betrayal of the ancestral belief by conversion to another religion, he was punished for it by eternal damnation. But the new doctrine of reincarnation taught that there was no such punishment. Rather, the way God punished the sinner was by temporarily bringing his soul back again in a lower form of life. But if in this subsequent earthly life the sinner behaved, he could rise up the ladder of rebirth and come back as a person again in his next reincarnation. Thus, punishment for sin was not eternal, and punishment for the ultimate sin of apostasy was also not eternal. Such being the case, why should the Jews not convert en masse and with relative sincerity to Christianity and end their minority group suffering in exile? The punishment for such mass sin would not be eternal damnation in the fires of Hell. At most it would be temporary rebirth in lower forms of life (animals, plants, or stones). That was certainly a small price to pay for the bliss of liberation from minority group suffering in this life. The Jews would not have to worry about being reborn until the approach of death by old age. Meanwhile, they could convert to Christianity and enjoy their status as members of the majority.[62]

Is there any evidence that the doctrine of reincarnation was known in Spanish Jewish mystical circles at this time? Apparently this doctrine (like that of the holiness of evil) first entered the Jewish religious tradition in Spain and southern France during the late twelfth century under Manichean influence.[63] The doctrine of reincarnation can be found in the *Sefer Bahir*, circa 1180,[64] and is also associated with Isaac the Blind, circa 1160–1235, one of the great southern French Jewish mystics of the time.[65] The *Zohar*, thirteenth-century Spain, accepted this doctrine but limited it to exceptional cases. A man who did not marry and have children would be reincarnated as a punishment, as would a man who married but died childless (leaving his widow to perform the levirate marriage, *i.e.*, to marry the brother of her dead husband). The *Zohar* specifically rejected the view, held by other Spanish Jewish mystics of the thirteenth, that people could be reincarnated into lower forms of life. The *Zohar* also specifically rejected the view that reincarnation (rather than the last judgment) was the primary form of divine retribution.[66] Another great thirteenth-century Spanish Jewish mystic, Isaac ibn Latif of Toledo, also specifically rejected the same view.[67]

The fact that two thirteenth-century Spanish Jewish mystics, Moses de Leon (author of the *Zohar*) and Isaac ibn Latif, rejected the view that reincarnation was the primary form of divine retribution undoubtedly means that other thirteenth-century Spanish Jewish mystics (perhaps many others) held to the contrary. Indeed, the Spanish Jewish mystic of the early fourteenth century, Joseph ben Shalom of Barcelona, based his entire mystical system upon reincarnation as the primary form of divine retribution, thereby creating a Hinduizing form of Jewish mysticism.[68] Finally, according to Netanyahu, the Spanish Jewish mystic Shem Tov the son of Shem Tov, late fourteenth century to early fifteenth century, in his *Sefer Ha-Emunot* attempted to use the doctrine of reincarnation to prove the truth of the traditional Jewish theological doctrines of reward and punishment.[69] Circa 1400, then, at the very time of the mass conversion of the Jews of Spain to Christianity Shem Tov the son of Shem Tov was attempting to use the doctrine of reincarnation to defend orthodox Jewish theology, perhaps in part trying thereby to undercut the use which certain radical Jewish mystics had made of this doctrine to support the precise opposite of Jewish orthodoxy, *i.e.*, mass conversion to Christianity.

If we look north of the Pyrenees, at the Jews of Franco-Germany, who never converted en masse to Christianity, we find that they had practically no philosophical movement whatsoever, but they did have a mystical movement of considerable importance from circa 1175 (German Hasidism, the chief lights of which were Rabbi Judah He-Hasid, late twelfth century, and Rabbi Elazar Rokeah, early thirteenth century).[70] Thus, in the case of Franco-German Jewry we have the presence of a mystical tradition but no real philosophical tradition and also no collapse. But in the case of Spanish Jewry we have the presence of both a mystical tradition and a philosophical tradition and a definite collapse. Therefore, would not philosophy rather than mysticism have been the crucial factor which weakened the will of the Spanish Jews to resist Christian conversion pressure circa 1400?

Not necessarily! It may have been neither philosophy nor mysticism in or of themselves which led to the collapse of Spanish Jewry circa 1400. Rather, it may have been the *combination* of both philosophy and mysticism in Spain which led to the collapse. Franco-German Jewry knew only one challenge to the Jewish legal system, the mystical challenge, which the Jewish legal system was able to cope with and neutralize, thereby saving the traditional basis of the Jewish religion and community from collapse. But Spanish Jewry knew a double challenge to the Jewish legal system, both the philosophical *and* the mystical challenge, and this two-pronged assault proved too much for the Jewish legal system to cope with and neutralize. The result was that the Jewish legal system eventually collapsed entirely in Spain circa 1400 and along with it collapsed the traditional basis of the Jewish religion and community. The result was mass and relatively sincere conversion to Christianity.

10. The Economic Interpretation.[71]

The Jews of Spain prospered economically more than any other medieval Jewry. Their excessive economic prosperity made them greedy for gain, explained by the principle that the more one has, the more one wants. Faced with the choice of conversion or death circa 1390, they had to choose conversion because they had too much wealth to lose if they chose death, and they stood to gain too much additional wealth if they chose conversion. What is more, their excessive wealth made the Spanish Jews lovers of luxury. As such, all they could cope with was pleasure. They were completely incapable of dealing with pain. When the choice of death or conversion was presented to them circa 1390, they had to chose conversion because their excessive wealth had corrupted them to the point where they could no longer stand the thought of the physical pain involved in dying as martyrs for their faith.

Why did the Jews of Spain grow so excessively wealthy? The Jews were the economic intermediaries between Christians and Muslims. They could live in Christian Spain as well as in Muslim Spain, in Christian Franco-Germany as well as in Muslim North Africa. On the other hand, no Spanish Christian could live as easily in Muslim Spain or Muslim North Africa. Nor could any Spanish Muslim live as easily in Christian Spain or in Christian Franco-Germany. The Jews, therefore, as the economic intermediaries between the Christians and Muslims, grew rich through the unique and special economic service they rendered the peoples of the Iberian peninsula, helping them overcome economically the deep ethnoreligious and political chasm which separated the Christian north and the Muslim south.

Furthermore, few Spanish Jews were engaged in agriculture. Generally speaking, farmers are the economic group within society which work the hardest but reap the smallest financial rewards for their labor. At least 50 percent of both the Christians and the Muslims of Spain were engaged in agriculture. No more than 25 percent of the Jews of Spain (if that many) were engaged in agriculture (though the avoidance of agriculture did not represent an exclusively voluntary choice on the part of most Jews). By avoiding the occupation within society that required the most work for the least reward, the Jews of Spain gained great economic advantage.[72]

Further, the Jews of Spain were overwhelmingly concentrated in the cities, especially in the large cities, and generally speaking, it is in the cities that most of the wealth of a given society is generated. By living more or less where the money was, the Jews of Spain had a great advantage in the struggle to acquire a portion of the wealth of the country far greater than their percentage of the population.

Further, the Jews of Spain, highly educated in such economically significant fields as philosophy, science, medicine, and engineering, controlled and dominated three highly lucrative economic endeavors: (1) tax farming, (2) military contracting, and (3) moneylending in general (to the nobility, church, and middle class).[73] Of course, these same economic endeavors were also highly risky. If the monarch changed his attitude toward the tax-farmer, or if there was a revolution and/or change of dynasty, the tax farmer could lose everything. If the war ended in defeat, the military contractor could lose everything. If the debtors rioted and destroyed his records, the moneylender could lose everything. In addition, all of these economic endeavors were very heavily taxed. Despite these two drawbacks, riskiness and heavy taxation, tax-farming, military contracting, and moneylending were immensely lucrative and made the Jews of Spain, who controlled and dominated these endeavors, fabulously wealthy by the midfourteenth century.

Is there any evidence from fourteenth- and fifteenth-century Spanish Jewish writers that the economic factor did indeed play a major role in the collapse of Spanish Jewry circa 1400? First we have a power-ful attack on the luxury-loving Jewish upper class by the anonymous Jewish mystic who wrote the *Sefer Ha-Kanah* and the *Sefer Ha-Peliah* circa 1375–1425. The author of these twin treatises tells about one Jewish courtier who disgusted him so much that he prayed to God to bring the man's house crashing down upon him and God heeded his prayer. This courtier had an angry and nasty disposition; was vain (he pulled his beard for affect) and a lover of food, wine, and Gentile con-cubines. He believed that God had created people so that they could indulge in the sensual pleasures of this world. Undoubtedly there were many other Jewish courtiers like him, for this same anonymous mystic goes on to call down the direst woes upon the entire Jewish upper class in general for building palatial homes, neglecting the study of the Torah, robbing and lying in order to accumulate wealth, flaunting their brightly colored garments (instead of wearing black), allowing their children to indulge in food and wine as well as to engage in levity and to dance with members of the opposite sex. All of this is obscene and blasphe-mous because the Jewish people are in exile from the Holy Land. They should be in mourning, not rejoicing. These Jewish courtiers accumu-late wealth in vain, because the Gentiles can and will take it away from them any moment they so desire.

This same author goes on to condemn Jews for lending money at interest to Gentiles. Traditional Jewish law only condemned Jews for lending money at interest to their fellow Jews, but it permitted lending money at interest to non-Jews. Canon law imitated Jewish law, permit-ting Christians to lend money at interest to non-Christians but not to their fellow coreligionists, hence the need for Jewish moneylenders to lend money to Christian borrowers. He also condemns the levirate marriage (which, in the strict sense, is incest since it permits marriage between brother-in-law and sister-in-law). Finally, he rebukes those rabbis who accept a salary for teaching people how to study the sacred texts. This is something the rabbis should really be doing *gratis* for the love of God.[74]

Another writer, Solomon Alami, who lived in the late fourteenth and early fifteenth centuries (and, like the author of the *Sefer Ha-Kanah*, has also been mentioned previously in this chapter), condemned the luxury-loving Jewish courtiers in terms as harsh as those of the author of the *Sefer Ha-Kanah*. According to Alami, they pride them-selves on their dignities and wealth but are totally oblivious to the sufferings of the Jewish poor. The courtiers build themselves palatial residences, travel around in splendid carriages, ride on richly caparisoned mules, wear magnificent garments, deck their wives and daughters in gold and pearls. They hate manual labor and live in luxury and idleness. The courtiers are arrogant and totally indifferent to the religion of their fathers. They love to dance, gamble, and vainly stroke their beards. The courtiers love gourmet meals, while the scholars of the sacred texts starve to death on the meager donations which the courtiers give them. In the synagogues the courtiers sleep or talk to one another while the rabbis deliver the sermons. The Jewish courtiers love to fight with each other on the most trivial of questions. They are violently jealous of one another and are ready to slander each other to the king at the drop of a hat, even to the point of engineering the cruel death of their rivals at court.[75]

Netanyahu cites two Spanish Jewish writers of the second half of the fifteenth century, about a century after the author of the *Sefer Ha-Kanah/Sefer Ha-Peliah* and Solomon Alami, who also held that the economic factor played a major role in the Jewish collapse of circa 1400. According to Isaac Arama the Marranos converted en masse and with relative sincerity to Christianity out of a desire for material success and in the hope of accumulating additional property.[76] Isaac Caro, a noted homiletician and exegete, held that materialism and the desire for wealth were more important factors in the Jewish collapse than the influence of Aristotelian/Averroist philosophical ideas. The philosophical movement was restricted only to small circles of Jewish intellectuals and their supporters among the upper-class Jewish courtiers, so argued Caro; whereas materialism and the desire for wealth penetrated every stratum of Jewish society, the upper, middle, and especially lower class. Inasmuch as the conversion to Christianity was a mass conversion, affecting every class within the Jewish community, the factor which likewise affected all three classes—materialism and the desire for wealth—must have played a far greater role in the collapse of the Jewish community of Spain circa 1400 than philosophy, which affected only the Jewish upper class. So Isaac Caro.[77]

11. The Constant Shifting of the Majority Culture within the Iberian Peninsula

There were continual shifts and changes in the majority, or ruling, culture within the Iberian peninsula during the 1100-year period circa

300–1400. Did these shifts so thoroughly bewilder and confuse the Jewish minority in Spain that by circa 1400 whatever psychological defense mechanisms they had been able to set up against the majority culture broke down totally and completely in the face of intense Christian pressure ? Was the result mass voluntary conversion of the Jews of Spain to Christianity? Had the majority culture in Spain remained more stable, which was the case north of the Pyrenees in Franco-Germany, would not Jewish ability to set up successful psychological defense mechanisms against the majority culture in Spain have equalled that of the Jews of Central Europe? Would not the Jews of Spain circa 1400 have come much closer to imitating their Franco-German brothers by choosing death as martyrs instead of mass conversion to Christianity?

How many shifts and changes were there in the majority, or ruling, culture within the Iberian peninsula during the 1100-year period circa 300–1400? We count nine such changes, and most were radical. Below we have attempted to rate each change, both in its religious and in its ethnic or dynastic aspect, on a scale of 1 to 3 with regard to the degree of its radicality. What were these changes?

In 300 the majority culture in Spain was pagan Roman (with two important substrata, the Phoenician-Carthaginian and the Celt-Iberian). The following 1100 years would see nine major shifts in the majority culture.

1. A major shift to Catholic Christian Roman in the fourth century, a religious shift (from pagan to Christian) worth 2 points on the 1 to 3 scale (because a shift to a completely new religion) but no ethnic shift at all.

2. To Arian Christian Visigothic in the fifth century, a religious shift (from Catholicism to Arianism) worth 1 point (because still within the same religion) and an ethnic shift (from Romans to Germanic Visigoths) worth only 1 point (because still within the general Indo-European ethnolinguistic family).

3. To Catholic Christian Visigothic by the seventh century, a religious shift (from Arianism to Catholicism) worth 1 point but no ethnic shift at all.

4. To Islamic Arab in the eighth century, a religious shift (from Christianity to Islam) worth 2 points and an ethnic shift (from Germanic Visigoths to Arabs) also worth 2 points (because from Indo-Europeans to Semites).

5. To the Islamic period of the "Party Kings" (*Reyes de Taifas* in Spanish; *Muluk at-Tawa'if* in Arabic) in the eleventh century, divided ethnically into three warring factions: the Arabs (in Seville), the Berbers (in Granada, Toledo, and Saragossa), and the Slavs (in Almeria, Murcia, Denia, Valencia, Tortosa, and the Balearic Islands); no religious shift at all because still Islamic but an ethnic shift worth about 2 points (because two-thirds of the power now was openly controlled by non-Semitic Arabs, by Hamitic Berbers and Indo-European Slavs).

6. To the moderately intolerant Islamic Berbers, the Almoravides, circa 1090–1150; no religious shift at all because still Islamic but an ethnic shift worth about 1 point (instead of power being divided between the Semitic Arabs, the Hamitic Berbers, and Indo-European Slavs, it was all concentrated into the hands of the Hamitic Berbers, though Berber invaders from North Africa, not Berbers with a longer residence in Spain, as had been the case in the previous period of the "Party Kings").

7. To the radically intolerant Islamic Berbers, the Almohades, circa 1150–1200, a religious shift worth 1 point because Islam now became sectarian and radically intolerant of non-Muslims, and a tribal dynastic shift worth 1 point (from the Lamtuna tribe, Senegal River region, for the Almoravides; to the Masmuda tribe, Atlas mountains of Morocco, for the Almohades[78]).

8. To the tolerant Christian rulers of Castile and Aragon in the thirteenth century (still strongly influenced by Islamic religious and cultural ideals), a religious shift worth 2 points (because from Islam to Christianity) and an ethnic shift worth 2 points (because from Hamitic Berbers to Indo-European Spaniards).

9. To the less tolerant Christian rulers of Castile and Aragon circa 1370 (heavily Frenchified, with much less Islamic influence especially in Castile where the French put the rebel Henry of Trastamara on the throne after years of a devastating civil war), a religious shift worth 1 point, because Christianity now became radically intolerant of non-Christians, and a dynastic shift worth 1 point.

Thus, in the 1100 years circa 300–1400 there were nine major shifts within the majority culture of Spain. Considered with regard to their magnitude (on the scale of 1 to 3), the religious changes amounted to a total of 10 points and the ethnic/dynastic changes also to 10 points. Both sets of changes, the religious and the ethnic/dynastic, together equal 20 points.

Were the shifts and changes within the majority, or ruling, culture in Spain really that serious circa 300–1400? The only way to answer this question is by the comparative method. Only if we compare the number and magnitude of the shifts within the majority culture in France or Germany with what was happening in Spain can we come to a genuine appreciation of this factor as a cause of the Jewish collapse in Spain circa 1400.

If we look at what was happening in France, we note only five shifts in the majority culture in the 1100 years circa 300-1400. Beginning circa 300 with the majority culture being pagan Roman, we move to (1) Catholic Christian Roman in the fourth century, a religious shift of 2 points but no ethnic shift; (2) Catholic Christian Germanic-Frankish Merovingian in the fifth century, no religious shift but an ethnic shift worth 1 point; (3) Catholic Christian Germanic-Frankish Carolingian in the eighth century, no religious shift but a major dynastic shift of 1 point; (4) Catholic Christian Capetian in the eleventh century, no religious shift but a minor dynastic shift worth 1/2 point; (5) Catholic Christian House of Valois in the fourteenth century, no religious shift but a minor dynastic shift of 1/2 point. These represent a total of only five shifts in 1100 years, adding up to only 5 points in their magnitude, as compared with nine shifts in Spain adding up to 20 points in their magnitude. Obviously, the number and intensity of the shifts and changes in the majority, or ruling, culture in Spain were about 300 percent greater than in France.

The same thing is true when we compare Spain with Germany. If we look at what was happening here, we note only four shifts in the majority culture in the 1100 years circa 300-1400. Beginnning circa 300 with the majority culture being pagan Germanic, we move to (1) Catholic Christian Germanic-Frankish Carolingian in the ninth century, a religious shift of 2 points and an ethnic-dynastic shift of 1 point; (2) Catholic Christian Germanic Saxon and Salian dynasties, tenth and eleventh centuries, a minor dynastic shift of 1/2 point; (3) Catholic Christian Germanic Welf and Hohenstaufen dynasties, circa 1100–1250, a major dynastic shift of 1 point (because the Welfs and the Hohenstaufens were bitter rivals); (4) Catholic Christian Germanic Hapsburg dynasty, from circa 1270, a major dynastic shift of 1 point (because the center of gravity of the Holy Roman Empire shifted radically toward Austria and the Danube River basin). These represent a total of only four shifts in 1100 years adding up to only 5 1/2 points in their magnitude, as compared with nine shifts in Spain adding up to 20 points in their magnitude. Obviously the number and intensity of the shifts and changes in the majority, or ruling, culture in Spain were about 300 percent greater than in Germany.

Obviously there were a much greater number and intensity of shifts and changes within the majority, or ruling, culture in Spain circa 300–1400 than within the majority, or ruling, culture in France or Germany during this same period.

	NUMBER OF SHIFTS	MAGNITUDE OF SHIFTS
Spain	9	20 points
France	5	5 points
Germany	4	5 1/2 points

This factor would help explain why it was the Jews of Spain, rather than the Jews of France or Germany, who collapsed under pressure and converted en masse with relative sincerity to Christianity circa 1400.

Jews live in two cultures at once, the majority culture, which is independent and primary, and their own minority culture, which is dependent and secondary. If the majority culture suddenly changes, this causes profound psychological dislocation within the Jewish minority culture as it realigns its defenses and makes the Jews much less resistant to the pressures of assimilation. The majority culture surrounding the Jews can change in two ways: (1) by an invasion of the country, a revolution, or a dynastic change, or (2) by mass Jewish emigration into a new majority culture area. If the majority culture changes because of either (1) invasion/revolution or (2) Jewish emigration, it takes the Jews about three generations, or a century, to adjust to the new majority culture and thus rebuild their defenses against assimilation.[79] But the majority culture in Spain shifted nine times (and usually very intensely) in 1100 years, or about one shift every 120 years. That meant that just as the Jews were finished adjusting to the first shift, the next shift took place. Eventually, after the ninth shift in 1100 years, something had to give way. After the successful Trastamaran revolt of circa 1370, the Jews simply could not adjust any longer. They could not rebuild their defenses against assimilation one more time. They simply gave up trying. When the intense pressure for conversion came circa 1400, the Jews went more or less voluntarily and en masse to the baptismal fonts, thanking God they did not have to attempt to adjust to the majority culture ever again. Now they could be part of it!

12. The Especial Attraction of Spanish Christian Culture as a Semiticized Christian Culture

The Jews of Spain converted to Christianity en masse and with relative sincerity circa 1400 because the Christianity that was offered to them was a unique form of Christianity, heavily influenced by Islamic culture. Spanish Christianity was certainly heavily influenced by Islam during the time when Islam dominated the Iberian peninsula (circa 700-1200). However, it was also influenced by Islam (though to a lesser extent) after the Christians clearly emerged triumphant in the thirteenth century. The large number of Muslim Mudejars who lived under Christian rule proved to be more stubbornly resistant than the Jews to assimilation because they led more rural lives and could rely psychologically upon the independence of the Islamic kingdom of Granada and the vast Islamic world in general. These Mudejars helped to keep alive during the thirteenth and fourteenth centuries the many Islamic elements incorporated into Spanish Christianity circa 700-1200.

We would suggest that Jews resist conversion unto the death if the conversion required of them is to pure Indo-European Christianity or to pure Semitic Islam. However, the unique combination of Indo-European Latin with Semitic (Arabic, plus earlier Phoenician/Carthaginian) elements in *Spanish* Christianity, as opposed to the Christianity of Franco-Germany which was purely Indo-European (Latin and Germanic), totally undermined the Jewish will to resist. In opting for Christianity over Judaism in Spain circa 1400, the Jews, the grandmother, were opting, really, for both Christianity, the mother, and Islam, the granddaughter, *simultaneously*. Christianity, the mother, predominated in the mixture over Islam, the granddaughter, but Islam was still present in an important way therein. This type of combined Indo-European Christian *and* Semitic Islamic majority culture was something which prevailed in few if any other countries and in few if any other periods in the history of the Jewish people in the Diaspora after the destruction of the Second Jerusalem Temple in 70 A.D.

What evidence is there that the Christianity to which the Jews of Spain converted en masse and with relative sincerity circa 1400 was really a heavily Semiticized Christianity?

Semitic influence upon Spanish culture in general, of course, went back to long before Islam conquered the Iberian peninsula in the eighth century, and even before Christianity became the majority religion in the peninsula (from the fourth century). The Phoenician (Tyrian) presence in southeastern Spain goes back to circa 1000 B.C., and the Carthaginians took over from the Phoenicians circa 600 B.C. to influence Spain until they were overwhelmed by the Romans circa 200 B.C.[80] Thus, Semitic culture influenced Spain for 800 years, circa 1000-200 B.C. During half this period it was Middle Eastern Semites (Phoenician/Tyrians) who influenced Spain; during the other half it was North African Semites (Carthaginians). This Middle Eastern influence in the Iberian peninsula was temporarily revived circa 550—625 A.D. by the Byzantine Greeks who conquered southeastern Spain, the very same territory which had been so strongly influenced by the Semitic Phoenicians/Carthaginians circa 1000-200 B.C.[81]

The Semitic Muslims conquered Spain in the eighth century. They, too, like their earlier Semitic Phoenician/Carthaginian cousins, were present in the Iberian peninsula for about 800 years, circa 700 (the conquest under Musa ibn Nusayr) -1500 (the fall of Granada). Circa 700-1100 it was Middle Eastern Semites (the Arabs) who influenced Spain; circa 1100-1500 it was North Africans. We refer to the Hamitic Berbers, i.e., the Almoravide Berbers of Morocco who controlled Muslim Spain circa 1090–1150, followed by the Almohade Berbers of Morocco who controlled Muslim Spain circa 1150–1250, followed by the Merinid Berbers of Morocco who influenced the Arab Nasrid dynasty that ruled Granada circa 1250–1500. The Berbers were heavily indebted both religiously and culturally to the Semitic Arabs.

Thus, we have an interesting parallel between the two major periods of Middle Eastern/North African influence upon the Iberian peninsula, with the Islamic influence of the Middle Ages reinforcing earlier Phoenician influence during the pre-Roman period:

	PHOENICIAN INFLUENCE	ISLAMIC INFLUENCE
800 years	1000–200 B.C.	700–1500 A.D.
Middle Eastern phase	Phoenician-Tyrian Semites 400 years 1000–600 B.C.	Arab Semites 400 years 700–1100 A.D.

North African phase	Carthaginian Semites	Berber Hamites (heavily indebted religiously and culturally to the Arabs)
	400 years	400 years
	600–200 B.C.	1100–1500 A.D.
Concentrated in what part of Spain?	Southeast	South

Thus, how could the Christian culture of Spain, to which the Jews converted en masse and with relative sincerity circa 1400, have been anything but a heavily Semiticized Christian culture when the Middle Eastern/North African presence had been felt in the Iberian peninsula in a major way for 1,600 years of the 2,400-year period circa 1000 B.C. —1400 A.D.; and when the Muslims had dominated the peninsula during the previous 500 years of the 700-year period circa 700–1400 A.D.? Indeed, if we examine certain of the key cities of the Christian Iberian peninsula circa 1400, we find that Lisbon was Islamic for about 450 years (circa 700–1150) of the 700 years circa 700–1400, or over half of the time. Toledo was Islamic for over 350 years (circa 711-1085). Seville was Islamic for about 550 years (circa 700-1250). Granada was still Islamic in 1400 (i.e., Granada had been Islamic for the entire 700-year period). Valencia was Islamic for over 500 years (circa 711-1238). Saragossa was Islamic for over 400 years (circa 711-1118). Thus, for half or more of the period circa 700-1400 about half of the great cities of Spain (including one city in the northeast, Saragossa) were dominated by Islamic culture.

Americo Castro has powerfully argued that Islam heavily influenced three key institutions or ideas in medieval Spain: the military orders, the concept of the holy war (i.e., the Reconquista), and the concept of toleration (which coexisted with the concept of holy war until circa 1375, after which date toleration was increasingly supplanted by intolerance and eventually by the Inquisition).[82] The great hero of medieval Spain, the Cid, and his epic (which was completed by the middle of the twelfth century) were heavily influenced by Islamic chivalric ideals and attitudes toward conquered and subjected peoples.[83] Intellectually, Christian nonfictional literature in Spain was dominated through the twelfth century by the Mozarabs. They included Domingo Gundisalvo (Dominicus Gundissalinus), the greatest Spanish Christian intellectual of the twelfth century, among the greatest of the entire Middle Ages. The Mozarabs, as Arabic-speaking Christians, were heavily Islamicized in culture, though not in religion.[84] Spanish Christian scientific and technological knowledge was heavily influenced by Islam during the High and Later Middle Ages.

The four greatest literary figures of Christian Spain circa 1250-1350 were all heavily influenced by Islamic culture: King Alfonso X el Sabio (1252-1284), Ramon Lull, Don Juan Manuel, and Juan Ruiz.[85] Spanish Christian music was heavily Islamicized, and Mudejar architecture was a powerful influence in the Iberian peninsula during the thirteenth to fifteenth centuries.[86] Indeed, architecturally (and perhaps in other ways as well, for King Pedro the Cruel, circa 1350–1370, even offered his vizierate to the great Arabic philosopher and historian Ibn Khaldun), Kings Alfonso X (1252–1284), Alfonso XI (1312–1350), Pedro the Cruel (1350–1369), and Enrique IV (1454–1474), all of Castile, built no buildings at all that were not Mudejar.[87] Thus, all royal building was strongly influenced by Islamic architectural ideas for about 90 of the 150 years circa 1250–1400.

When the Jews of Spain converted to Christianity circa 1400, what they were really converting to was a heavily Islamicized form of Spanish Christian culture. This, surely, must have been the primary reason why they did convert, when their brothers north of the Pyrenees died as martyrs for their faith during the very same period. Had their brothers in Franco-Germany also been given the opportunity of converting to a heavily Islamicized instead of a heavily Germanicized Christianity, they too might have preferred baptism to martyrdom.

Thus, we would argue, the main reason why the Jews of Spain converted to Christianity en masse and with relative sincerity circa 1400 was because what they were really converting to was a heavily Islamicized (and therefore a heavily Semiticized) Christianity, wherein the Christian Indo-European (Latin-Germanic) elements amounted to about 60 percent of the mixture while the Islamic Semitic (Phoenician/Carthaginian, Arabic, and Arabicized Berber) elements amounted to about 40 percent of the mixture. The Jews would never have converted en masse and with relative sincerity to pure Semitic Islam, because that would have been too close to the Semitic culture which the Jews already possessed. Nor would the Jews have converted en masse and with relative sincerity to pure Indo-European (especially Germanic) Christianity, because that would have been too far away from the culture the Jews already possessed. The Jews would only have converted to a heavily Islamicized (and therefore a heavily Semiticized) Christianity. Such was close enough, because of its strong (40 percent) Semitic component, to the Semitic culture of the Jews to permit them to make a smooth transition into a new cultural allegiance. But it was also far enough away (because of its dominant 60 percent Indo-European component) from the Semitic culture of the Jews to tempt them into adopting something new and different. There were few if any other countries in the world at that time other than Spain where the majority religion to which the Jews were impelled to convert was Christianity, the second generation or mother, with a strong admixture of Islam, the third generation or granddaughter. It was this unique combination of Indo-European Christianity and Semitic Islam which attracted the Jews of Spain so powerfully circa 1400. It was this peculiar combination which broke down all Jewish defenses against majority-group pressure and persuaded the Jews of Spain to prefer the easier choice of the baptismal font to the more difficult choice of death as martyrs (and/or by ritual suicide or flight), which is what their brethren north of the Pyrenees in Franco-Germany were opting for at this very same time.

*****

Two of the most important effects which the mass conversion of the Jews of Spain circa 1400 helped bring about were (1) a major Spanish exploration and colonization effort in the New World from circa 1492 and (2) a powerful current of theological and philosophical liberalism and skepticism, making intellectual and cultural freedom and individualism far more possible in eighteenth- than in fifteenth-century Europe.

Had the Jews of Spain circa 1390-1415 not attempted with relative sincerity to enter directly into Spanish Christian society through mass conversion, there might have been no major attempt by Spain to explore and colonize the New World from circa 1492. The sudden mass influx of internal aliens, the Jews, into the mainstream of Spanish society circa 1390-1415 may have blocked opportunities for Old Christians, who, then, may have attempted to compensate therefore by raising their birth rate, eventually bringing on a severe overpopulation problem. This overpopulation problem produced deep tensions within

Spanish society that could only be resolved by the expansion of Spanish civilization into new frontiers across the sea. Thus, the collapse of the Jewish community of Spain circa 1400 helped create the conditions within Spain that led Cortes and Pizarro to overwhelm the Aztecs and Incas in conquering Mexico and Peru for Old Spain in the sixteenth century.

Not only did the Spanish Jews, by the tensions which their mass conversion produced within Christian society, contribute indirectly to the Spanish exploration and colonization effort in the New World. They also contributed directly to the Spanish expansionist movement by emigrating abroad themselves, bearing Spanish civilization with them. Actually there were two distinct but related waves of Jewish emigration from Spain after circa 1480. The first wave consisted of Marranos, Jewish converts to Christianity, motivated to leave Spain by the introduction of the Inquisition. They carried Spanish civilization with them into two main parts of the globe, the New World and northwestern Europe.[88] The second wave consisted of regular Jews, those who had never been converted to Christianity, motivated to leave Spain by the expulsion order of 1492. They carried Spanish civilization with them into two other parts of the globe, North Africa and (eventually, via Italy) the Ottoman Empire (which straddled the Balkans and the Middle East, linking Europe, Asia, and Africa).[89] These two waves of emigration, the Marrano beginning circa 1480 and continuing into the seventeenth century, and the regular Jewish wave beginning in 1492 and ending the same year (because the assumption is that few if any unconverted Jews survived in Spain after the expulsion), were closely related. The Inquisition helped produce both the Marrano wave directly and the regular Jewish wave indirectly via the fall of Granada.

The fall of Granada in 1492 led to the expulsion of the regular Jews from Spain that same year (again Christian-Islamic relations determined Christian-Jewish relations) because Jewish help was no longer needed against the Muslims. But the Marranos in the 1480s were among the primary advocates of the great religious crusade which overwhelmed Granada in 1492.[90] They would have pressed hard for this crusade for two main reasons. Their strong advocacy of the Holy War against the Muslim infidel, by making the Marranos seem like exceedingly patriotic Christians, would help the Marranos score important psychological points against the Inquisition. The Marranos also

296

badly needed the immense financial rewards (booty, captives held for ransom, confiscated lands, etc.) which awaited those who financed a successful conquest of Granada, to use in attempting to obtain political help from the nobility, as well as the civil and ecclesiastical bureaucracy, against the Inquisition. The introduction of the Inquisition circa 1480 forced the Marranos to push for the conquest of Granada. The fall of Granada circa 1492 allowed the Spanish Christians to expel the no-longer needed unconverted Jews that same year. Thus, not only did the Inquisition directly cause the immigration of the Marranos beginning circa 1480 into the New World and northwestern Europe, but it also indirectly caused the immigration of the unconverted Jews in 1492 to North Africa and (eventually, via Italy) to the Ottoman Empire.

In short, the mass conversion of the Jews of Spain circa 1390–1415 led to the expansion of Spanish culture into the New World and northwestern Europe in the sixteenth century. This is because the conversion movement led to the Inquisition circa 1480, which in turn impelled the Marranos to carry Spanish culture to the New World and northwestern Europe in the sixteenth century. By the same token, the mass conversion of the Jews of Spain circa 1390-1415 also led to the expansion of Spanish culture into North Africa and (eventually, via Italy) into the Ottoman Empire in the sixteenth century. This is because the conversion movement again led to the Inquisition circa 1480, which in turn forced the Marranos to press for the conquest of Granada. This, when successful in 1492, allowed Spain to expel the unconverted Jews, who carried Spanish culture with them into North Africa and (eventually, via Italy) into the Ottoman Empire in the sixteenth century. Thus, the mass conversion of the Jews of Spain circa 1390-1415 caused Spanish culture to expand not only into the New World and northwestern Europe but also into North Africa and the Ottoman Empire. Ferrand Martinez and Vicente Ferrer may well have wrought far more than they imagined, unless by prophetic vision they foresaw the great Spanish expansionist movement of the sixteenth-century Golden Age.

We move now to a consideration of the second effect. The Jews of Spain circa 1390-1415 also had to attempt with relative sincerity to enter directly into the mainstream of Spanish Christian society through mass conversion, else there might well have been no powerful current of theological and philosophical liberalism and skepticism to make intellectual and cultural freedom and individualism far more possible in eighteenth century than it had been in fifteenth-century Europe.[91]

History may well have required the existence of a group like the Marranos, who were at home neither in Judaism nor in Christianity, but who lived in a spiritual and psychological wilderness of their own midway between these two ethnoreligious traditions, in order to stimulate the development of liberalism and skepticism in Western Europe in the sixteenth and seventeenth centuries. The cornerstone of this new flowering of liberal and progressive thought in early modern Western Europe was the dogma of the dignity of the individual, whose worth was not dependent upon membership in any ethnoreligious group but was determined rather by having been created in the image of God as a unique being with certain natural and inalienable rights. This dogma, in turn, when applied to the religious sphere, led to the development of the concept of religious toleration and the separation of church and state. When applied to the political sphere, it led to the development of the concepts of republicanism and democracy. When applied to the economic sphere, it led to the concept of the free market, where people interact with each other solely according to the law of supply and demand (rather than according to any ideological criteria). When applied to the scientific and technological sphere, it led to new inventions which greatly enhanced the socioeconomic (and especially the medical) well-being of the populace. When applied to the cultural sphere, it led to creative new breakthroughs in art (the Dutch bourgeois-Baroque painters like Rembrandt).

Why did the Marranos play such an important role in encouraging the development of European free thought? The answer to this question is that after the rise of the Inquisition circa 1480 the Marranos hated both Judaism and Christianity with equal passion. They hated Judaism for giving them the ethnic impediment which made it impossible for them ever to be accepted fully by Spanish Christian society after the rise of the Inquisition, no matter how much they out-Christianed the Christians. They hated Christianity for first accepting them (in the first two-thirds of the fifteenth century), then rejecting them (during the final third of the fifteenth century), treatment that was even more enraging than never accepting them at all. Because the Marranos hated both Judaism and Christianity alike, they attempted to develop a new third force, a new religion of their own, where they could be spiritually at home, to supplant both older faiths. What they developed was a new gospel of reason and science whose chief dogma was the dignity of the individual and his total liberation from all ethno-religious prejudices or stigmas.

In order to develop this new religion of their own, the religion of reason and science, the Marrano intellectuals first had to destroy the two older religions, Judaism and Christianity. In going about this task they attacked the scriptural underpinnings of both Judaism and Christianity, especially attacking the Old Testament, for by destroying its credibility they destroyed both Judaism and Christianity, since the New Testament rests upon the Old. The Marrano intellectuals also stood less chance of being persecuted by the Christian establishment if they attacked the Old Testament because they could always claim that their attacks were against Judaism, not Christianity. The Marrano intellectuals developed a scientific biblical criticism to prove that Moses was not the author of the full Pentateuch, which rather had developed over a period of many centuries and thus could not have been the product of a single revelational experience at Mt. Sinai. They blamed Jewish and Christian ritual ceremonies for obscuring the enduring moral and ethical values which the founders of these religions preached but which their followers never practiced. They criticized the undemocratic ecclesiastical regimes which stifled creative new ideas and ignored the views of the majority of the laity in both religions. They opposed both Judaism and Christianity for their views about the afterlife, either by attacking the doctrine of the resurrection of the body as a primitive notion or by going even further to attack this doctrine along with that of the immortality of the soul as unscientific.

Who were some of the Marrano intellectuals of the sixteenth and seventeenth centuries who played such an important role in the development of Western European free thought? In the sixteenth century we have such figures of Marrano background as the Spanish scholastic Francisco de Vitoria (died 1592), who stressed the importance of universal law and natural rights;[92] Juan Luis Vives (1492–1540), author of De Veritate Fidei (1543), a major exponent of Erasmian humanism who argued that the state, not the church, should control education and social welfare;[93] Michel de Montaigne (1533–1592), author of the famous Essays (1540), a father of modern skepticism and common sense naturalism;[94] Montaigne's friend the French humanist Etienne de la Boetie (1530-1563), the author of Discours de la Servitude Volontaire (1576), a plea for human dignity and freedom against tyrannical rulers and for the use of nonviolent means of social protest;[95] and Jean Bodin (1530–1596), author of *Methodus ad Facilem Historiarum Cognitionem* (1566), a founder of modern scientific-critical historiography (though twentieth-century scholarship has questioned Bodin's Marrano origin).[96] In the seventeenth century this movement reached its culmination in the towering figure of Baruch Spinoza (1632–1677), who powerfully advocated such radical ideas as pantheism and naturalism, scientific biblical criticism, and a social contract idea which held that sovereignty resides in the people, whose freedom of thought and expression should never be abridged.[97] Three contemporaries of Spinoza in the Low Countries entertained very similar ideas, especially in the realm of theology and philosophy, which in some cases directly influenced Spinoza's views: Uriel da Costa (1585–1640), author of *Exemplar Humanae Vitae* (1687);[98] Isaac La Peyrere (1594–1676), author of *Rappel des Juifs* (1643) and *Praeadamitae* (1655);[99] and Juan de Prado (1615–1670).[100]

Our right to indulge in the kind of historical speculation about the effects of the mass conversion developed above is based upon the precedent provided within the writings of the fifteenth-century Spanish Jewish thinkers themselves. Why did God allow the Old Christians to accept the Marranos in the first half of the fifteenth century but then allow them to attempt to destroy the Marranos through the Inquisition in the second half of the very same century? According to Netanyahu, an answer to this question was given by the anonymous fifteenth-century Spanish Jewish personality who authored the *Sefer Alilot D'varim* circa 1468.[101] According to this author, the Marranos, by first leaving the Jewish camp for Christianity and then returning to Judaism after the establishment of the Inquisition (which this author foresaw), would make the following very important contributions to Judaism:

1. increased numbers (because for a period of two generations the Marranos were no longer subject to discrimination, forced conversion, or massacre as Jews, and thus could multiply unhindered);[102]

2. biological rejuvenation (through the new genes, acquired by intermarriage with Old Christians, which the Marranos brought back to the Jewish community);

3. enhanced wealth (acquired when they were freed from the traditional economic restrictions Christians placed upon Jews, *e.g.*, exorbitant taxes);

4. important new connections in the highest echelons of the Christian civil bureaucracy;

5. new ideas (acquired by being part of the majority culture for two generations and hence looking at the world from Christianity's majority point of view instead of from Judaism's minority point of view, but also acquired by studying in Christian universities, an activity not ordinarily open to unconverted Jews); and

6. the intense zeal, enthusiasm, energy, and devotion which characterize the behavior of repentant sinners, people who, after having been brought up in an alien tradition by their parents, return to the tradition in which their grandparents had been raised.

History impelled the Jews of Spain to convert to Christianity en masse and with relative sincerity circa 1390 to 1415 because history wanted their grandchildren to return to Judaism after the establishment of the Inquisition circa 1480, bringing with them increased numbers, biological rejuvenation, enhanced wealth, important new political connections, new ideas, and new enthusiasm.

＊＊＊＊＊

A key to understanding the Spanish situation lies in what happened in southern Italy (but not Sicily) circa 1300, about a century earlier than the collapse of the Jewish community of Spain. The fate of the Jewish community of southern Italy circa 1300 offers us an instructive parallel to the fate of the Jewish community of Spain a century later.

This is assuredly no mere historical coincidence, because circa 1300–1700 the fate and destiny of Spain and Italy in general converged (as they did for an even longer period from the Roman conquest of Spain circa 200 B.C. to the Visigothic invasion circa 400 A.D.[103]). In the fourteenth century Aragon controlled Sardinia; in the fifteenth century Aragon added Sicily to Sardinia and then had two Italian possessions. In the sixteenth century the combined Kingdom of Castile and Aragon added Naples and Milan to Sardinia and Sicily. Thus, Spain had four Italian possessions, two islands and two crucial territories on the mainland, one in the south and the other in the north. These mainland territories put central Italy (Tuscany and the Papal States) in a Spanish vice. Was it mere historical coincidence that at the very time Spanish and Italian history began increasingly to converge circa 1300–1400, Spanish and south Italian Jewish history would also converge? Was it mere historical coincidence that the Jewish communities of both Spain and southern Italy would suffer the similar fate of mass conversion to Christianity in relative sincerity, in each case at the end of a century: southern Italy circa 1300 and Spain circa 1400?

Admittedly, the number of Jews who converted to Christianity in Spain circa 1400, about 250,000, was greater in absolute terms than the number of Jews who converted to Christianity in southern Italy circa 1300, around 10,000. Even more importantly, a far greater proportion of the Jews of Spain (50 percent) than of the Jews of southern Italy (25 percent) opted to remain within Christianity when the initial pressure let up. Finally, in Spain the intense pressure upon the Jews during the first decade, the 1390s, resumed in the third decade, 1410-1415, under a new ruler (Juan II of Castile). By contrast, in southern Italy the intense pressure upon the Jews during the first decade, the 1290s, let up in the second decade, 1300-1310, under the same ruler (Charles II of Naples).

What exactly did happen to the Jews of southern Italy circa 1300?[104] It all began in France in 1288. King Charles II of Naples, perhaps in response to pressure from the French lower and lower-middle classes (who may have been especially hard pressed economically around this time by poor harvests due to drought, cold, or flood) demanding that something be done about the moneylenders, expelled all Jews, Lombards, and Cahorsins from his home provinces of Anjou and Maine in west-central France. The Cahorsins withdrew to southern France; the Lombards, to northern Italy. Most of the Jews probably moved north to the Isle de France. But some may have moved to Charles's possessions in southern Italy, where they found a situation that was even more explosive. The same kinds of pressures that were operating against the Jews (and others) as moneylenders in west-central France circa 1288 were probably also operating against them, with as much or perhaps even greater force, in southern Italy at this same time.

An influential Dominican friar, Bartolomeo da Aquila, under the pretext (almost certainly a fiction) that the Jews of Apulia had crucified a Christian child in ceremonies designed to mock Jesus's passion, apparently persuaded King Charles to issue an edict circa 1290 which offered the Jews the choice of conversion, expulsion, or death. At the same time two *Spanish* monks, Juan and Sancho, perhaps coming by way of the Balearic Islands and/or Sicily, began to move from city to city in southern Italy (very much like San Vicente Ferrer's procedure in Spain during the 1410s), preaching to Jews, probably with the help of converts from Judaism to Christianity who knew Hebrew well, and attempting to persuade the Jews to convert to Christianity (instead of leaving the country or dying as martyrs). The result of this combined pressure, royal edict and missionary sermons, was that about half the Jewish community of southern Italy converted to Christianity. The other half either quit the country (a significant number going north to Mantua; others probably going to nearby Sicily) or else survived as Jews either by paying large bribes to local officials, who then looked the other way when these Jews continued to practice their religion, and/or by going into hiding with sympathetic Christian friends and acquaintances.

By 1294, the height of the persecution, no less than 1,300 newly converted Jewish families were granted immunity from the taxes which they had previously paid as Jews. We should assume about eight people per family, two parents and six children. Jews were compelled to have large families if they were to survive as a people through all the persecutions which they continually had to endure; moreover, such large families would have been consistent with the general practice of the Christian and Islamic peoples of the Mediterranean area.[105] We then arrive at a total of about 10,000 Jewish converts to Christianity in southern Italy circa 1294. Most likely another 10,000 either left the country or managed somehow to survive as Jews, even though they remained in southern Italy.

In Apulia, on the eastern coast of southern Italy, the great Jewish community of Trani, famous for its scholars and royal advisors, counted about 350 Jewish families (or about 2,800 Jews) who converted to Christianity. The Jewish community of Taranto, further south, counted about 170 Jewish families (or about 1,360 Jews) who converted. In Campania, on the western coast of southern Italy, Salerno counted about 150 Jewish families (or about 1,200 Jews) who converted to Christianity; while Naples, further north, counted about 140 Jewish families (or about 1,120 Jews) who converted. Many other important south Italian Jewish communities, like Bari in Apulia, were also affected. A royal decree of May 1, 1294, provided for the assumption of Christian family names by the Jewish converts. These were usually the names of those Christians (often members of the highest echelons of the nobility) who stood godfather for the Jews at their baptisms.

303

However, even at the very height of the persecution the pendulum was beginning to swing back toward toleration of Judaism and toward the restoration of the flourishing Jewish community in southern Italy. Already in 1294 a group of Jews, who had fled the country rather than convert to Christianity or die as martyrs, successfully negotiated an agreement with King Charles whereby they could return to their homes and live openly as Jews "under the king's trust." Certainly the royal decree requiring conversion, expulsion, or death was now revoked. Those Jews who had remained in southern Italy and yet had escaped conversion either by bribery or by going into hiding could now live openly as Jews. The missionary sermons of Juan and Sancho probably ceased. The only thing remaining before the pendulum could swing full arc was an official decree allowing those Jews who had converted to Christianity to return to their ancestral religion. This King Charles II could not do without antagonizing the church. However, the king could look the other way when Jews who had indeed converted to Christianity did return to Judaism, quietly and without fanfare. A few Jewish converts to Christianity probably did take advantage of this implied royal permission to resume their Judaism.

When King Charles was succeeded by his son, Robert the Wise (who reigned circa 1309–1343), known to be much more friendly to the Jews than his father, the number of erstwhile Jewish converts to Christianity who now began quietly returning to Judaism increased manyfold. The result was that the Jewish quarter of Gerace (in the toe of the Italian boot) was attacked during Easter week of 1311, and the church demanded a royal decree specifically forbidding returns to Judaism. Such a decree was issued but was surely honored by the monarchy far more in the breach than in the keeping. This is evidenced by the fact that in the very same year King Robert allowed the Jews of Gerace significant tax relief to help restore their damaged homes and synagogues and permitted them to bear arms to ward off any future resumption of the attack upon them by the local Christian populace. During the years 1315–1316 twenty-three Jews of Salerno, on the west coast, and twenty-one Jews of Trani, on the east coast, were allowed to bear arms, at least during their commercial journeys. In 1321–1322, when Pope John XXII in Avignon reputedly ordered the expulsion of the Jews from all the papal possessions, King Robert is reported to have intervened to obtain the repeal of the decree. In 1324 the king granted the Jewish communities of Rossano and Crotone in Calabria permission to remodel their old synagogues. In 1328

King Robert claimed that the Jews of southern Italy, under his protection, were better off than the Jews of any other country in Christendom, even despite a special tax then being imposed upon them in his kingdom.

In 1329 the king even went so far as to invite Jews from the Balearic Islands to settle in his kingdom. Certainly King Robert would not have been inviting foreign Jews to settle in southern Italy if at the same time he was not also ignoring the royal decree of 1311 issued only to placate the church when Jewish converts to Christianity from the early 1290s quietly resumed the practice of Judaism. In 1342, a year before his death, King Robert repealed an old law which required Jews to live in separate quarters within the cities. In 1343 the church took advantage of the temporary weakness of the state occasioned by the death of the king that very year to obtain a renewal of the royal decree of 1311 prohibiting Jewish converts to Christianity from returning to Judaism. This renewal of 1343, like the original decree of 1311, undoubtedly was more honored in the breach than in the keeping. Robert's granddaughter and successor, Queen Joanna I, continued the same friendly policy toward the Jews which had characterized the reign of her grandfather King Robert.

Thus, to summarize what happened to south Italian Jewry circa 1280–1340, we estimate that circa 1280 there were 20,000 Jews in southern Italy (perhaps 7,000 Jews on the west coast, the Naples-Salerno area; another 7,000 on the east coast, in Apulia, the Trani-Bari-Brindisi-Taranto area; another 4,000 in the far south, Calabria; and another 2,000 in the interior between Naples and Bari).[106]

Circa 1290 we estimate that 50 percent of the south Italian Jews, or 10,000, converted to Christianity, while the other 50 percent, or 10,000, remained faithful to Judaism and survived as Jews, either fleeing the country temporarily or remaining in southern Italy.

Circa 1294–1340 we estimate that half the Jewish converts of circa 1290, 5,000, opted to remain within the church. The other half opted to return to the synagogue, joining the 10,000 who had remained faithful to Judaism during the period of persecution.

Thus, to sum up graphically the south Italian situation:

1280	20,000 Jews in south Italy.
1290-1294	50 percent of the Jews, 10,000, convert to Christianity. 50 percent of the Jews, 10,000, survive as Jews.

1294-1340   25 percent of the Jews, 5,000, remain Christian. 25 percent of the Jews, 5,000, return to Judaism, to join the 50 percent of the Jews, 10,000, who had survived as Jews and had never converted to Christianity.

Therefore circa 1280–1340 approximately 25 percent of south Italian Jewry converted to Christianity in relative sincerity. Their sincerity is evidenced by their refusal to return to Judaism when such opportunity was presented to them after the great persecution of the 1290s had ended and the pendulum had swung back in the direction of Christian toleration of Judaism as well as encouragement of Jewish economic enterprise.

Let us now present similar data about what happened to Spanish Jewry circa 1380–1440, or about a century after what happened to south Italian Jewry. We must approach the demographic figures for Spanish Jewry circa 1380 through the better-known demographic figures for Spanish Jewry circa 1480, when the Spanish Inquisition was established.

Around 1480 there were approximately 10 million Spaniards. About 70 percent (or 7 million) were Christians; 20 percent (or 2 million), Muslims (living primarily in Andalusia, Granada, Murcia, and Valencia); around 10 percent (or 1 million), Jews. Looking more closely at this 1 million Jews, about seven-tenths of them, or 700,000 souls, were Marranos (Jews who had converted to Christianity in relative sincerity circa 1390–1415 but were having increasing difficulty being accepted as full-fledged Christians toward the end of the fifteenth century). About three-tenths of them, or 300,000 souls, were Jews who had never been converted to Christianity. Thus, there were over twice as many Marranos as unconverted Jews in Spain circa 1480.[107]

Now that we have established the Spanish demographic figures and percentages circa 1480, we can more easily move back in time about a century. Circa 1380, about ten years before the great persecution of the Jews which began in Seville, we estimate that there were about 5 million Spaniards (half the number of Spaniards living a century later). Around 70 percent (or 3.5 million) were Christians; another 20 percent (or 1 million), Muslims; around 10 percent (or 500,000), Jews. The same percentages of the total population for the Christians, Muslims, and Jews—70, 20, and 10 percent respectively— prevailed in 1380 as in 1480.[108]

During the long period of persecution which lasted about twenty-five years circa 1390–1415, about 50 percent of the Spanish Jews, or around 250,000 souls, converted to Christianity. Another 25 percent of the Spanish Jews, or around 125,000 souls, were massacred. The remaining 25 percent, or around 125,000 souls, somehow managed to survive as Jews. In Castile or Aragon this was accomplished by bribery or hiding out with friends (far fewer escaped by temporary migration than in southern Italy circa 1290). In Portugal, Granada, and Navarre all of the Jews survived as Jews because there were no serious persecutions at this time.[109]

During the subsequent period of circa 1415–1440 in Spain, when the severe pressure upon the Jews let up, hardly any of the 250,000 Spanish Jews who had converted to Christianity returned to Judaism. Instead, they went on to achieve great success within the economic, social, political, cultural, and even the (Christian) religious life of the Spanish people in general. Their numbers increased from around 250,000 circa 1415 to around 700,000 circa 1480, a jump of about 180 percent. By contrast, the 125,000 Jews who had remained loyal to the synagogue and somehow avoided conversion or massacre during the same "time of troubles" circa 1390–1415 also prospered during the economic and demographic expansion which characterized fifteenth-century Spain. Their numbers increased from around 125,000 circa 1415 to around 300,000 circa 1480, a jump of about 140 percent.

Why did the number of Marranos, Jews within the Christian camp, increase by 180 percent circa 1415–1480, whereas the number of the unconverted Jews, Jews outside the Christian camp, increased by only 140 percent during the same period? Actually, the unconverted Jews probably had a higher birthrate than did the Marranos because the unconverted Jews were poorer. Yet at the same time, though the unconverted Jews had a higher birthrate, their relative poverty resulted in many defections from their ranks into the ranks of the Marranos during the course of the fifteenth century. The unconverted Jews, because they were poorer, bore the children. However, once the children of the unconverted Jews grew up and saw how much better off materially the Marranos were than their own parents who had remained loyal to Judaism, large numbers of these children sought baptism and moved into the Marrano camp.

Thus, to sum up graphically the Spanish situation:

1380   500,000 Jews in Spain.

1390-1415	50 percent of the Jews, 250,000, convert to Christianity.
	25 percent of the Jews, 125,000, massacred.
	25 percent of the Jews, 125,000, survive as Jews.
1415-1440	50 percent of the Jews, 250,000, remain Christian.
	25 percent of the Jews, 125,000, continue as Jews.
1415-1480	Marranos increase 180 percent form 250,000 to 700,000. Unconverted Jews increase 140 percent from 125,000 to 300,000.

Therefore, circa 1380–1440 approximately 50 percent of Spanish Jewry converted to Christianity in relative sincerity. Their sincerity is evidenced by their refusal to return to Judaism when such opportunity was presented to them after the great persecution of 1390–1415 had ended and the pendulum had swung back in the direction of Christian toleration of Judaism.

We are now ready for a close comparison and summary of the fate and destiny of the Jewish communities in southern Italy circa 1300 and Spain circa 1400. Thus, in southern Italy, circa 1300, 50 percent of the Jews converted to Christianity; and in Spain, circa 1400, 50 percent of the Jews likewise converted to Christianity. However, in southern Italy, by circa 1340, a generation after the great time of troubles, only 25 percent of the Jews remained permanent converts to Christianity; whereas in Spain, circa 1440, likewise a generation after the great time of troubles, 50 percent of the Jews remained permanent converts to Christianity.

Comparing southern Italy circa 1340 and Spain circa 1440, in each case one generation after the time of troubles, we find that a far greater percentage of the Jewish converts to Christianity were sincere and remained within the church in Spain than in southern Italy. In Spain all of the converts from Judaism to Christianity (50 percent of the entire Jewish community) opted to remain within the church, whereas in southern Italy only half of the converts from Judaism to Christianity (only about 25 percent of the entire Jewish community) opted to remain within the church. Thus, the Spanish situation circa 1380–1440 was twice as severe a disaster for the Jewish community as was the south Italian a century earlier circa 1280–1340.

Moreover, in absolute numbers the Spanish situation was infinitely more serious. A total of no more than 5,000 Jews opted for *permanent* conversion to Christianity in southern Italy between 1280 and 1340, whereas a total of about 250,000 Jews, or over fifty times as many Jews in absolute numbers, opted for permanent conversion to Christianity in Spain between 1380 and 1440. No wonder, then, that though the two situations have more in common with each other than either has with what was happening to the Jews north of the Pyrenees/Alps in the Franco-German area at this same time, the Spanish situation has captured the attention and the imagination of the world, whereas the south Italian situation, which was almost equally important qualitatively but far less significant quantitatively, has been almost totally forgotten. It was the Spanish situation, rather than the south Italian, which led to the creation of the more powerful inquisitorial engine of repression, to punish the Jewish converts (Marranos) for their attempt to violate the iron law of Christian-Jewish relations, that the continued existence of the church is dependent on the continued existence of the synagogue. It was the Spanish situation, rather than the south Italian, which more strongly encouraged such important historical developments as the exploration of the New World and the rise of liberalism and skepticism in Western Europe during the sixteenth and seventeenth centuries.

Thus, the Spanish situation circa 1400 was more truly monumental than the south Italian. However, the south Italian situation around a century earlier was also unprecedented for its time. Never before had as many as 25 percent of the Jewish community of a given country opted for permanent conversion to Christianity. It can shed crucial light on the later Spanish situation and help determine which of the twelve factors discussed above as possible explanations for the total collapse of the Jewish community of Spain circa 1390-1415 were more influential. In both situations, the Spanish circa 1400 and the south Italian circa 1300, we find a willingness on the part of a highly significant percentage of the Jewish population (at least 25 percent in both southern Italy circa 1300 and Spain circa 1400) to opt out of Judaism and to join Christianity. North of the Pyrenees and the Alps, among the Jews of Franco-Germany, the maximum percentage of relatively sincere converts from Judaism to Christianity during any single period would not have been more than 10 percent. Which of the factors discussed above fit both the Spanish situation circa 1400 and the south Italian situation circa 1300? When we carefully compare both situations, we discover that all factors discussed above as possible contrib-

309

utors to the collapse of Spanish Jewry were also operative in southern Italy as well, some to a greater and others to only a lesser extent.

1. The Power Drive

It is highly likely that south Italian Jewry had a strong power drive because some of the same factors which helped induce this drive in Spanish Jews were also present in southern Italy. We refer to the general harshness and inhospitability of the landscape (relative paucity of water, arable land, trees, and birds) and inordinate Jewish wealth. This wealth was accumulated because Sicily, like Spain, was once part of the far-flung Islamic empire, and southern Italy was very closely associated with Sicily. Another reason was that the Jews of southern Italy/Sicily, like those of Spain, could serve as economic intermediaries between the Christians of Italy and the Muslims of Sicily/North Africa. However, the Jews of southern Italy did not hold the same balance of power between the Christians and Muslims of Italy as the Jews of Spain held between the Christians and Muslims of the Iberian peninsula. Islamic power in Italy was far weaker than it was in the Iberian peninsula. Hence, the south Italian Jewish power drive was nowhere near as strong as that of Spanish Jewry. This is evidenced by the fact that south Italian Jewish religious courts were not as noted as the Jewish religious courts of Spain for trying criminal as well as civil cases and for imposing the death penalty as well as fines.[110] Thus, the power drive was certainly operative among the Jews of southern Italy circa 1300 but perhaps with only half the force which this same factor commanded among the Jews of Spain circa 1400.

2. The Impact of Civil War

Just as Spain was torn by civil war (between Pedro and Henry) during the fourteenth century, the century at the end of which the Jewish community totally collapsed, so southern Italy was torn by civil war during the thirteenth century, the century at the end of which its Jewish community totally collapsed. However, the Italian civil war of the thirteenth century was twice as serious as the Spanish civil war of the fourteenth century. The Italian civil war raged about fifty years in two different time periods (circa 1227-1268 and 1282-1291), whereas the Spanish civil war lasted only twenty years. The Italian civil war of the thirteenth century was fought between the Guelphs and the Ghibellines. The generally victorious Guelphs were the party of the church and the rising middle class, supported by the French and the Angevin dynasty. The losing Ghibellines were the party of the nobility, supported by the Germans, led by the Hohenstaufen dynasty of Sicily/southern Italy (Frederick II, Conrad IV, Manfred, Conradino) and the Aragonese in the 1280s. The Spanish civil war of the fourteenth century was fought between Pedroists and Trastamarans. The victorious Trastamarans were supported by the church, the nobility, and the French. The losing Pedroists were supported by the middle class, the Jews, Muslims, and English. The church and the French were on the winning side in both these civil wars. However, while the middle class won in southern Italy, it lost in Spain.

Thus, thirteenth-century southern Italy, like fourteenth-century Spain, was devastated by a terrible civil war that undoubtedly had something to do with the total Jewish collapse and mass conversion in *both* countries. However, the civil war in southern Italy played less of a role because the Jews there were not really powerful enough to take sides in the struggle in a major way (though they probably supported the losing Ghibellines as did the Muslims of southern Italy). The civil war played more of a role in Spain because the Spanish Jews were powerful enough to take sides in the struggle in a major way (the Jews of Spain and the Muslims of Granada supported the losing Pedroists). The Jews of southern Italy, to our knowledge, suffered no major massacres, fines, or enslavements during the civil war there (1227–1268, 1282–1291). The Jews of Spain did suffer such agonies during the Spanish civil war (1350–1370). Thus, we would estimate that at most this factor, civil war, was operative in the south Italian Jewish collapse circa 1300 with only half the force it commanded in the Jewish collapse in Spain circa 1400.

3. Excessive Jewish Social Sophistication

The Jews of southern Italy were probably as socially sophisticated as the Jews of Spain (and thus, they too, like their Spanish Jewish cousins, probably thought they understood the "law of superfluous people"). Like the Jews of Spain, the Jews of southern Italy had to learn how to play off one side against the other, the Muslims of Sicily circa 800–1050 (who controlled Bari, Apulia, circa 841–871; invaded

Apulia again in the late ninth and early tenth centuries; and threat-ened it thereafter) against the Christians (both the Latins backed by the Holy Roman Empire and the papacy, as well as the Greeks backed by the Byzantine Empire) and vice versa, the Christians against the Muslims. Yet southern Italy proper was never really held by the Mus-lims for very long. Moreover, the Christians of southern Italy them-selves were divided into two increasingly antagonistic camps, the Latin (and German) Catholic and the Greek Orthodox. The split be-gan in earnest in the ninth century and reached its culmination in the sack of Eastern Orthodox Constantinople by Latin (French and Vene-tian) crusaders in 1204. Hence the necessity for the Jews of southern Italy to learn to play each non-Jewish force off against the other was never as great as it was in Spain, where the Muslims were far more powerful and where the Christians were unified in a single camp (all Latin Catholics). Thus, as in the cases of factors 1 and 2, this third factor, excessive social sophistication, was only operative among the Jews of southern Italy in the thirteenth century with about half the force it commanded among the Jews of Spain in the fourteenth century.

4. Jewish Hatred of the Muslims

The Jews of Spain may have converted to Christianity en masse and with relative sincerity circa 1400 in part out of an intense desire to participate actively and energetically, on a more direct and equal basis, in the Christian effort to destroy the last vestige of indepen-dent Islamic power in the Iberian peninsula, the Nasrid kingdom of Granada. The Jews of southern Italy, likewise, may well have con-verted to Christianity en masse and with relative sincerity circa 1300 in part out of a similar desire to participate actively and equally in the Christian effort to destroy the last vestige of Islamic independence in the Italian peninsula, the semiautonomous Muslim city of Lucera.[111] However, Granada did not fall by conquest until circa 1500, about a century after the mass Jewish conversion. Lucera fell by mass conver-sion circa 1300, the very same time that the Jews of southern Italy were also converting en masse to Christianity. Muslim Granada, as an independent kingdom on the sea, reinforced from North Africa, could hold out for about a century after the mass Jewish conversion. But Muslim Lucera, being only a semiautonomous city, far from the sea, and thus impossible to reinforce from North Africa, could not hold out any longer than the mass Jewish conversion.

Did the Jews of southern Italy desire to exact revenge upon the Muslims of Lucera circa 1300 in the same way that the Jews of Spain desired to exact revenge upon the Muslims of Granada circa 1400? Did the Muslims of Sicily/southern Italy wrong the Jews as did the Muslims of Spain circa 1000–1300 (especially under the Almohades), then in the fourteenth century? The Almohades of twelfth-century Spain were notorious for forcing the Jews into Islam, then making the forced converts wear degrading forms of clothing. Likewise, the Muslims of Sicily made the Jews wear degrading forms of clothing in the second half of the ninth century. Further, the Muslims did enslave and thereby decimate entire Jewish communities in Sicily/southern Italy on at least three occasions: when the Arabs took Syracuse in Sicily in 878, as well as when they took Oria in southeastern Italy in 925 and 952 (the 925 raid on Oria affecting both Hananel II and Shabbetai Donnolo, the latter the greatest Italian Jewish scholar of the tenth century; the 952 raid on Oria affecting Paltiel II, the famous Fatimid official).[112] What the Arabs did to the Jews of Syracuse in 878 and of Oria in 925 and 952 is not too dissimilar to what the Nasrids of Granada did to the Jews of Jaen in 1368 during the Spanish civil war of the fourteenth century. However, the wrongs inflicted by Muslims upon Jews in Spain lasted the entire four-century period leading up to the mass Jewish conversion circa 1400. By contrast, the wrongs inflicted by Muslims upon the Jews in Sicily/southern Italy took place only about 400 years before the mass Jewish conversion circa 1300. However, Jews, like Arabs, are noted for their long memories (indeed, the Jews remembered Zion for about 2,100 years before they had their opportunity in 1948 to revive the last independent, Maccabean, Jewish state in Palestine, overwhelmed by the Romans in 63 B.C.). Thus, the Jewish desire for revenge upon the Muslims as a factor in mass Jewish conversion to Christianity may have been operative both in Spain circa 1400 and southern Italy circa 1300. But the power of this factor in southern Italy would only have been about one-fourth of what it was in Spain.

Did the Jews of southern Italy circa 1300 feel the same desperate need to defend themselves against the charge that the Jews were in league with the Muslims which the Jews of Spain felt circa 1400? The Arab threat to Spain, which made the Spanish Jews especially sensitive to this charge, was much greater than the Arab threat to Italy. The Arabs once dominated all of Spain, whereas at most the Arabs dominated all of Sicily but never all of Italy. Moreover, the Arab domination of Spain lasted about 500 years (circa 700–1200), whereas the Arab domination of Sicily only lasted about 300 years (circa 800–1100). Nevertheless, the Arab threat to Italy was still quite a serious one, especially in view of the fact that Rome, the religious center of Western Christendom, was in Italy, and it almost fell to the Arabs in 846. The Christians of Sicily/southern Italy had good reason to fear an Islamic attempt at reconquest from North Africa after 1100. Thus, there was a major Islamic attempt at such a reconquest in the Spanish Almoravide and Tunisian Zirid attack on Norman Sicily in 1122, avenged by the Norman attack on North Africa 1148–1149. Because the Christians of Sicily/southern Italy had good reason to fear an Islamic attempt at reconquest, they may well have been seriously tempted to suspect the Jews of Sicily/southern Italy of being in league with the foreign Muslim enemy.[113] Of course, the Christians of central and northern Italy continued to associate Jew with Muslim as is evidenced both by the decrees of the Fourth Lateran Council (1215), which reflected in large part the outlook of Pope Innocent III, and by the views of Dante (circa 1300).[114]

Indeed, the Christians of Spain (though at the other end of the Mediterranean) were deeply disturbed by the Ottoman Turkish advance into the Balkans in the 1380s. The Christian attack on the Jews of Spain circa 1390 may have been in part due to the belief that the Jews were in league with the advancing Ottoman Muslims. So the Christians of southern Italy (who were much closer than the Christians of Spain to the advancing Muslims of the eastern Mediterranean) would have been equally disturbed by the Mamluk Egyptian offensive which destroyed Acre circa 1291, the last Christian stronghold in Palestine. The Christian attack on the Jews of southern Italy circa 1300 may have been in part due to the belief that the Jews were in league with the advancing Mamluk Muslims. Thus, an intense Jewish desire to defend themselves against the charge that the Jews were Islamic fifth columnists in Christian territory may well have been a factor in both the mass conversion of the Jews of Spain circa 1400 and the mass conversion of the Jews of southern Italy circa 1300. If so, the force of this factor was probably as great in southern Italy circa 1300 as it was in Spain circa 1400.

5. Geography and Climate

The geography and climate of Spain and Italy are quite similar in so many ways. If geography and climate were important factors in the collapse of Spanish Jewry circa 1400, they would have been equally important factors in the collapse of south Italian Jewry circa 1300.

The distances between major Jewish centers of population within southern Italy were not quite as great as they were in Spain. Neither is southern Italy as strongly characterized by unbroken treeless plains (though Apulia is a plain). However, the south Italian terrain, like the Spanish, is very mountainous. In southern Italy, as in Spain, rivers do not serve as major arteries of communication (though southern Italy, which has far fewer square miles of inland territory than does Spain, made up for its fluvial deficiency by a much heavier use of seaborne routes of communication than did Spain).

As to their geographical isolation, Spain and Italy are close parallels. Both are peninsulas. Both are cut off on the north from the rest of Europe by towering mountains (Pyrenees and Alps). Spain is even more cut off by bodies of water than is Italy, for Spain has the Bay of Biscay on the north in addition to the Pyrenees, while Italy has no body of water to its north in addition to the Alps. Spain has the vast and stormy Atlantic to its west, while Italy has only the smaller and calmer Mediterranean Sea (and two islands, Corsica and Sardinia) to its west. Spain has the broad Mediterranean to its east (with the Balearic Islands), while Italy has only the relatively narrow Adriatic to its east. To the south both Spain and Italy are separated from important land masses by narrow straits (Spain, the Straits of Gibraltar; Italy, the Straits of Messina). In the case of Spain an entire continent (Africa) lies immediately across the straits, whereas in the case of Italy an important island (Sicily) lies immediately across the straits, and south of that island is the Mediterranean once again. On the whole, however, though the geographical isolation of the Iberian peninsula is greater than that of the Italian peninsula, Italy is certainly more isolated geographically from the rest of continental Western Europe than any country other than Spain.

The Mediterranean climates of Spain and Italy are also very similar, as is the power of regionalism in both countries. Though Spain lagged behind England and France in developing a sense of national unity, Italy lagged behind Spain. Spain became united circa 1500. It took Italy until 1870. Spain can be divided into south (Andalusia), central (Portugal, New Castile with the national religious center at Toledo, and Valencia), north (Galicia, Asturias, Leon, Navarre, Aragon, and Catalonia), and the islands (Balearics). Italy, likewise, can be divided into south (Sicily, Calabria, Campania, Apulia, etc.), central (the Papal States, with the national religious center at Rome; and Tuscany), north (Liguria, Piedmont, Lombardy, Romagna, Venice, and Trieste), and the islands (Corsica and Sardinia). The Spanish north was primarily Latin; the south, Arab; and the center, more or less equally divided between the two circa 711–1212. The Italian north was primarily Germanic; the center, Etruscan-Latin; and the south, Greek and Arab. Pushing the parallel even further, the northern Spanish provinces are similar to the northern Italian provinces, Galicia to Liguria, Asturias to Piedmont, Catalonia to Venice. Old Castile and Burgos compare with Tuscany and Florence. New Castile and Madrid/Toledo compare with Latium and Rome. Naples and Campania compare with Cordova and Andalusia. Apulia compares with Valencia. Calabria compares with Granada. The Basque separatist mountaineers in northern Spain are similar to the Tyrolean separatist mountaineers in northern Italy.

The power of regionalism in Spain may have kept its Jewish communities from uniting against the Christian danger and thus have contributed in an important way to the total collapse of Spanish Jewry circa 1400. However, the power of regionalism was also felt throughout Italy in general and in southern Italy in particular. After all, Sicily was uniquely influenced by Arabic civilization; Apulia, by Greek; Benevento, by Germanic-Lombard; and Campania, by Latin. Would not the almost equal power of regionalism in Italy in general and southern Italy in particular also have kept the Jewish communities therein from uniting against the Christian danger and thus have contributed in an important way to the total collapse of south Italian Jewry circa 1300?

Thus, the geographical and climatological factors were operative among the Jews of southern Italy circa 1300 with a force nearly equal to that which these factors exerted upon the Jews of Spain circa 1400.

6. *Ethnic Tensions within the Jewish Community Itself*

If ethnic tensions within the Spanish Jewish community helped undermine Spanish Jewish unity as well as its will to resist intense pressure to convert circa 1400, ethnic tensions within the Italian Jewish community also helped undermine Italian Jewish unity as well as its will to resist intense pressure to convert circa 1300.

The Spanish Jewish community was probably divided into two warring groups, the "natives" whose roots in Spain antedated the Islamic conquest of the early eighth century and the "foreigners" who came to Spain only after the Islamic conquest. Likewise, the Italian Jewish community may also have been divided into two similar warring groups, the "natives" whose roots in Italy antedated the Islamic conquest of Sicily in the ninth century and the "foreigners" who came to Italy only after the Islamic conquest.

As in Spain, the roots of the Italian Jewish "native" group in Italy went back centuries earlier than those of the "foreigners." Moreover, the ancestors of the "natives" had lived in both Spain and Italy when both countries were still part of the Roman Empire and thus when both countries were still united. The ancestors of the "foreign" group in Spain never knew a time when Spain was not divided between Muslim and Christian; the ancestors of the "foreign" group in Italy never knew a time when Italy was not divided between the Germans in the north, the Latins in the center, and the Greeks and Arabs in the south. As in Spain, the ancestors of the "native" Jews of Italy came from Palestine. Moreover, the ancestors of the "native" Jews of Spain were influenced ethnically by such non-Jewish peoples as the Phoenician-Carthaginians, Celts, Romans, and Visigoths, the last three being Indo-European. The ancestors of the "native" Jews of Italy were influenced ethnically by such non-Jewish peoples as the Carthaginians (in western Sicily), Etruscans, Romans, and Ostrogoths, the last two being Indo-European. Whereas the "native" Jews of Spain preferred the northern part of that country, and the "foreigners" the south, in Italy the "native" Jews and the "foreigners" were more or less evenly distributed throughout the land.

A further difference between the Jews of Spain and those of Italy was that whereas in Spain the "native" Jews dominated numerically but the "foreign" Jews dominated politically, in Italy it was the other way around, the "foreign" Jews probably dominated numerically but the "native" Jews dominated politically. Thus, in Spanish Jewry it would have been the "native" majority rebelling against domination by the "foreign" minority that began the mass movement into Christianity circa 1400, whereas in south Italian Jewry it would have been the other way around, the "foreign" majority rebelling against domi-

317

nation by the "native" minority that began the mass movement into Christianity circa 1300.

The reason why the "foreign" Jews in Italy would have dominated numerically but not politically, while the "foreign" Jews in Spain would have dominated politically but not numerically, was as follows. Because Italy was located in the central Mediterranean while Spain was located in the far western corner thereof, the "foreign" group of Jews in Italy was made up of people from many more countries than the "foreign" group of Jews in Spain. The "foreign" group of Jews in Spain was made up of two main subgroups: (1) Jews from Arab Iraq and (2) Jews from Arab North Africa (who generally followed the lead of the Iraqi Jews). On the other hand, the "foreign" group of Jews in Italy was made up of about six subgroups: (1) Greek Jews from the Byzantine Empire, (2) Jews from Arab Palestine, (3) Jews from Arab Iraq, (4) Jews from Arab North Africa, (5) Jews from Christian Franco-Germany, and (6) Jews from Islamic, then Christian, Spain. Thus, the reason the "native" Jews of Spain, though a numerical majority, were dominated by the "foreign" Jews was because the "foreign" Jews in Spain were more or less united among themselves. They also were culturally more advanced than the "native" Jews, inasmuch as the "foreign" Jews in Spain came primarily from Iraq, the greatest center of Jewish religious learning in the world at that time. Spain was a Jewish religious frontier circa 700-1000, whereas Iraq's tradition of Jewish religious learning went back at least to the third century A.D. On the other hand, the "foreign" Jews of Italy, though a numerical majority, were dominated by the "native" Jews, precisely the reverse of what occurred in Spain, because the "foreign" Jewish group in Italy was composed of so many divergent groups and the "native" Jews could rule by "dividing and conquering" them.

Likewise, more Karaite heretics were present in Spain than in Italy. This was the case not only because the Karaites, who arose in eighth-century Arab Iraq, tended to prefer lands where Islam dominated at one time or another (Islam dominated Spain at one time but never was able to dominate Italy) but also because the Karaites generally tended to appear in a country where "native" Jews wanted to protest against domination by "foreign" Jews. In Spain, where the Karaites posed a threat serious enough that it had to be dealt with by force and violence, the "native" Jewish majority was dominated by the "foreign" Jewish minority. However, in Italy the "native" Jews, though a minority, dominated the "foreign" Jews. Hence, there was less need for the development of a Karaite heretical protest movement among the Jews of Italy, while there was definitely such a need among the Jews of Spain circa 900-1200.[115]

Thus, we would suggest that this factor, ethnic tensions within the Jewish community itself, operated with as much force in southern Italy circa 1300 as in Spain circa 1400 and played an equal role in the collapse of both communities.

7. The Geriatric Factor and the Desire for Cultural Rejuvenation

Some of the same factors which may have influenced the Jews of Spain to seek cultural and religious rejuvenation by conversion to Christianity would also have been operative in southern Italy. The Italian Renaissance attempt to return to the culture of classical antiquity (which began at least with the great Tuscan sculptor Nicola Pisano, circa 1250-1275[116]) certainly would have been even more influential upon southern Italy than upon Spain. The pre-Reformation (Wycliffe and Huss) attempt to achieve religious rejuvenation within Western Christianity by returning to the ideals of the early church could not have been an influence upon the south Italian Jews circa 1300 (because the Wycliffe-Huss movement did not begin until circa 1375), though it could have been an influence upon Spanish Jewry's attempt to seek cultural and religious rejuvenation circa 1400. However, Dante, under Spiritual Franciscan influence, made a conscious attempt to revive the Roman imperial tradition in his antipapal De Monarchia circa 1300. This, in turn, influenced the antipapal activities and writings of English Spiritual Franciscans like William of Ockham in the first half of the fourteenth century, who, in turn, influenced the equally antipapal pre-Reformation activities and writings of Wycliffe and Huss.[117]

Of course, the same three factors which made Spain (situation no. 5) so different from the State of Israel (situation no. 1), medieval Franco-Germany (situation no. 2), Yemen (situation no. 3), and the medieval caliphate of Cordova (situation no. 4), were also operative in southern Italy.[118] We refer to (1) the presence in a major way of both younger ethnoreligious traditions, Christianity and Islam, in addition to Judaism, making the Jews really feel their age; (2) the possibility of moving via mass conversion from a minority- into a majority-group status; and

319

(3) the mass conversion only involving a jump of one generational step, from grandmother to mother, from Judaism to Christianity, rather than two generational steps, from grandmother to granddaughter, from Judaism to Islam.

In southern Italy circa 1300, as in Spain circa 1400, both Christians and Muslims were present in addition to Jews. Indeed, just as in Christian Spain, the Muslims of southern Italy (concentrated in and around Lucera and numbering at least around 40,000[119]) were the larger minority, and the Jews of southern Italy (numbering around 20,000) were the smaller minority. Indeed, the Islamic presence in southern Italy circa 1300 was felt to be even more dangerous than the Jewish, because the Muslims were more numerous than the Jews and were armed. Indeed, they had revolted unsuccessfully against the Angevins in 1269 and 1284, though without suffering any immediate reprisals.[120] More intense pressure for conversion was applied to the Muslims of Lucera circa 1300 than to the Jews circa 1290. The result was that almost all the Muslims of Lucera converted to Christianity and were more or less permanently absorbed into the Christian population of southern Italy, whereas only about 25 percent of the Jews of southern Italy were sincere converts to Christianity in the early 1290s who refused to return to Judaism when they had opportunity to do so during the more tolerant first half of the fourteenth century.

Likewise, in southern Italy circa 1300, as in Spain circa 1400, by converting to Christianity the Jews could abandon minority and attain majority status. Moreover, such a conversion movement would only have meant jumping a possible one generational step, from Judaism to Christianity, not an impossible two-generational step, from Judaism to Islam. Thus, the geriatric factor and the desire for cultural rejuvenation were operative amongst the Jews of southern Italy circa 1300 with almost as much force as amongst the Jews of Spain circa 1400.

8. The Role of Philosophy

If the philosophical movement played an important role in the collapse of Spanish Jewry circa 1400, it may also have played an important role in the collapse of south Italian Jewry circa 1300. Indeed, the only three Western European areas where the Jewish philosophical movement had deep roots were Spain, southern France, and Italy (it was not well represented in northern France or Germany). All three areas were in close proximity to the Islamic world, where the medieval Jewish philosophical tradition began (Saadia Gaon, tenth century, Iraq) and reached its climax (Maimonides, twelfth century, Egypt).

If the Jews of Spain were distinguished from those of Franco-Germany by their love of philosophy in general and of Aristotelian philosophy in particular (from circa 1150), so were the Jews of Italy. Indeed, the greatest Jewish Aristotelian (and partly Averroist) philosopher of the thirteenth century was probably the Italian follower of Maimonides, Hillel of Verona (circa 1220–1295). Though his family was from Verona, he himself had studied in *Spain*, then lived in Rome and *southern Italy*.[121] Hillel's rival, who worked in central Italy (Rome) was Zerahiah ben Isaac ben Sh'altiel Gracian (Hen) (second half of the thirteenth century), another Jewish Aristotelian (and partly Averroist) follower of Maimonides.[122] Zerahiah was born in Spain, which in part explains his rivalry with Hillel, a native Italian who had merely studied in Spain. Thus, both Hillel and Zerahiah link the Jewish philosophical traditions of Spain and Italy. Further, Immanuel of Rome (and later of northern Italy; late thirteenth and early fourteenth centuries), the Jewish Dante, though primarily a poet, was also a Jewish Aristotelian (and partly Averroist) philosopher in close touch with Hillel of Verona.[123]

In southern Italy proper was Jacob Anatoli (first half of the thirteenth century), the important Jewish Aristotelian philosophical follower of Maimonides and friend of Emperor Frederick II as well as of Michael Scot (the well-known Christian translator from the Arabic).[124] Jacob's son, Samson ben Jacob Anatoli, and his grandson, Jacob ben Samson Anatoli, were both also Jewish Aristotelian philosophical followers of Maimonides in southern Italy (second half of the thirteenth century).[125] The Jewish Aristotelian philosophical follower of Maimonides, Moses ben Solomon of Salerno (circa 1250), was a disciple of Jacob Anatoli.[126] Other late thirteenth-century south Italian/ Sicilian Jewish Aristotelian philosophers, scientists, and translators (from the Arabic) who followed in the footsteps of Jacob Anatoli were Faraj (Ferragut) ben Solomon of Agrigento (who commented on the philosophical works of Maimonides and translated medical treatises from the Arabic); Ahitub of Palermo (who wrote a literary work very similar to that of Immanuel of Rome and Dante); and Moses of Palermo (who translated an Arabic work on the diseases of horses).[127] There were many other Jewish Aristotelian-Averroist scientists and translators in Italy during the thirteenth and early fourteenth centuries.[128]

Indeed, those rabbinic scholars who feared the corrosive effects of the philosophical movement upon Jewish piety were as apprehensive about the work of the Italian, as of the Spanish, Jewish Aristotelians. Solomon ibn Adret, the great Talmudic authority of late thirteenth-century Barcelona, considered the philosophical work of the south Italian Jacob Anatoli to be extremely dangerous.[129] Ibn Adret may have influenced the south Italian Talmudic scholar Isaiah ben Elijah di Trani the Younger (died circa 1280) to adopt a far less tolerant attitude toward philosophy and science than did his more famous grandfather, the south Italian Isaiah ben Mali di Trani the Elder (circa 1200-1260).[130] Apparently the Jewish philosophical movements of both Spain and southern Italy were heading in a direction that seemed to some important rabbinic scholars in both countries to be dangerous to the kind of blind faith that was needed if Jews were to resist Christian conversionist pressures. These rabbinic scholars were probably right! The philosophical movement, by its support of Aristotelian ideas, which it interpreted in increasingly Averroist terms as the thirteenth century wore on, probably did help to bring about a situation in the Jewish communities of both Spain and southern Italy which led both communities to collapse totally under Christian pressure. Nevertheless, the power of the philosophical factor in the Jewish community of southern Italy circa 1300 probably was half what it was in the Jewish community of Spain about a century later.

9. The Role of Mysticism

If the mystical movement played an important role in the collapse of Spanish Jewry circa 1400, it may also have played an important role in the collapse of south Italian Jewry circa 1300. Indeed, there were important representatives of the Jewish mystical movement in thirteenth-century southern Italy. The leading native Italian Jewish mystic circa 1300 was M'nahem Recanati.[131] The surname, of course, would seem to indicate an east-central Italian origin (Recanati, a town near Ancona). However, we would suggest that Recanati probably worked in *central and southern Italy* (just as Hillel of Verona's name indicates a northern Italian origin, though he worked in *central and southern Italy*). The philosophical and mystical movements within Judaism were still closely connected in the thirteenth century, as is evidenced by the fact that the great Spanish Jewish mystic Abraham

Abulafia was a colleague of Hillel of Verona and of Ahitub of Palermo, two of the leading Jewish philosophers of late thirteenth-century Italy.[132] All of the Jewish philosophers and scientists of thirteenth-century Italy—Hillel of Verona, Zerahiah Gracian, Jacob Anatoli (as well as his son and grandson), Moses of Salerno, Ahitub of Palermo, and Moses of Palermo—worked in *central and southern Italy*. Though Immanuel of Rome died in northern Italy, he at least began his career in *central* Italy. Immanuel is in part the exception that proves the rule that most Italian Jewish intellectuals, whether philosophical or mystical, worked in *central and southern Italy*.

Likewise, when Abraham Abulafia, one of the two greatest Jewish mystics of the thirteenth century (the other being Moses de Leon, the author of the *Zohar*, the bible of Jewish Mysticism), came from Barcelona to Italy, he spent most of his time in *central* (Rome) *and southern Italy* (Capua; probably also Apulia since Abulafia traveled extensively in Greece, which lies directly across the Adriatic from Apulia) as well as Sicily. Indeed, though Abulafia was of Spanish origin, he spent most of his life in Italy. Born in Aragon, circa 1240, he spent the 1260s and circa 1275-1290 in Italy and Greece. Abulafia's disappearance from view in the 1290s, implying death or loss of creativity for some other reason (such as disillusionment with the world), may have been connected in some way with the mass conversion of the Jews of southern Italy circa 1290. About twenty-five years of Abulafia's fifty-year life-span (circa 1240-1290) were spent in Italy, and he wrote all of his extant works in Italy circa 1280-1290.[133] Thus, the mystic Abulafia (like the philosopher Zerahiah), though of Spanish birth, did most of his work in Italy and can therefore be considered a *central to south Italian* Jewish mystic.

Further, the Jewish mystic, Isaac ben Samuel of Acre, who fled the Holy Land when Acre fell to the Muslims in 1291, spent about fifteen years in Italy (circa 1291-1305), probably in Rome or Sicily, again in *central and southern Italy*, though probably not in Naples or Apulia where the Jewish communities were in turmoil due to the mass conversion of circa 1290. He then moved on to Spain, where he spent the rest of his life, meeting Moses de Leon in Castile and working with Solomon ibn Adret in Barcelona, the enemy of philosophy. Hence, Isaac of Acre can also in part be considered a *central to south Italian* Jewish mystic.[134]

It is likely that Recanati, like Abulafia and Isaac of Acre, lived and worked in *central to southern Italy*. The Jewish mystical movement in central and southern Italy in the thirteenth century definitely endorsed the doctrine of reincarnation (documented from the writings of Recanati[135]). It probably endorsed the doctrine of the holiness of evil as well, although we have no specific documentation thereof in thirteenth-century Italian Jewish mysticism. The facts that both Spanish and southern French Jewish mysticism in the thirteenth century taught both doctrines, reincarnation and the holiness of evil, closely relating one to the other, and that there were considerable cultural interrelationships between Spanish and Italian Jewry during the thirteenth century, make it seem highly likely that the Jewish mystics of southern Italy also taught both doctrines prior to the collapse of the Jewish community therein circa 1300. If so, the Jewish mystical movement may well have contributed as much to the collapse of south Italian Jewry circa 1300 as it did to the collapse of Spanish Jewry a century later. However, we would estimate that the force of the mystical factor in southern Italy in the thirteenth century was probably only half that of its force in Spain in the fourteenth century.

10. The Economic Interpretation

If its excessive economic prosperity played an important role in the collapse of Spanish Jewry circa 1400, this same factor may also have played an important role in the collapse of south Italian Jewry circa 1300, for the Jews of southern Italy were almost as wealthy as those of Spain and for many of the same reasons. Like the Jews of Spain, who were economic intermediaries between the Christians of the north and the Muslims of Andalusia, the Jews of southern Italy were economic intermediaries between the Christians (both Latin and Greek) and the Muslims (of Sicily and North Africa) circa 800–1300. The Amalfitans, by their policy of appeasing the Arabs circa 800–1100, offered the Jews considerable competition as intermediaries between Christians and Arabs, though Amalfi caught the crusading fever and became anti-Arab after 1100, to decline rapidly in any case after it was sacked by the Pisans in the 1130s.[136] The Jews of Spain could live with relative ease in the Christian north and in Arab Andalusia and thus help link these two parts of Spain together economically. Likewise, the Jews of southern Italy could live with relative ease in Byzantine Apulia and in Arab Sicily and thus help link these two parts of southern Italy together economically. Further, like the Spanish Jews, the Jews of southern Italy were not engaged in agriculture in any important way but were rather concentrated primarily in the (coastal port) cities. Further, like the Spanish Jews, the Jews of southern Italy (especially Apulia) were highly educated in such economically significant fields as philosophy, science, medicine, and engineering.[137] But, unlike the Jews of Spain whose economic elite earned its money primarily by tax-farming, military-contracting, and moneylending, the economic elite of the Jews of southern Italy, because of the strong Italian maritime tradition, was primarily engaged in trade and commerce (especially waterborne). Thus, we would argue, the economic factor (excessive wealth) was operative in both the Spanish Jewish collapse circa 1400 and the south Italian Jewish collapse circa 1300 with equal power.

11. The Constant Shifting of the Majority Culture

If the continual shifts and changes in the majority, or ruling, culture within the Iberian peninsula during the 1,100-year period circa 300-1400 contributed to the collapse of the Jewish community of Spain, the continual shifts and changes in the majority, or ruling, culture in southern Italy during the rather similar 1,000-year period circa 300-1300 may have contributed to the collapse of the Jewish community of southern Italy.

How many shifts and changes were there in the majority, or ruling, culture within southern Italy during the 1,000-year period circa 300-1300? We count twelve such changes in southern Italy as against only nine in Spain.

Beginning with the pagan Roman majority culture in southern Italy circa 300 A.D., we move to

1. Catholic Christian Roman in the fourth century, a religious shift worth 2 points but no ethnic shift at all.

2. To Arian Christian Ostrogothic in the early sixth century, a religious shift worth 1 point and an ethnic shift worth 1 point.

3. To Eastern Orthodox Christian Byzantine Greek in the mid-sixth century, a religious shift worth 1 point and an ethnic shift worth 1 point.

4. To an Arian Christian Lombard challenge to Byzantine rule in the late sixth century, a religious shift worth 1 point and an ethnic shift also worth 1 point.

5. To a Catholic Christian Lombard challenge to Byzantine rule by the early eighth century, a religious shift worth 1 point but no ethnic shift at all.

6. To the Sunni orthodox Islamic Arab Aghlabid dynasty's challenge to Byzantine rule circa 827-909, a religious shift worth 2 points and an ethnic shift worth 2 points.

7. To the Shii sectarian Islamic Arab (and Berber) Fatimid dynasty's challenge to Byzantine rule circa 909-948, a religious shift worth 1 point but not much of an ethnic shift.

8. To the Sunni orthodox Islamic Arab Kalbite (Yemeni) dynasty's challenge to Byzantine rule circa 948-1091, a religious shift worth 1 point and an ethnic shift worth 1 point.

9. To Catholic Christian Norman rule (under significant Islamic influence) in the twelfth century, a religious shift worth 2 points and an ethnic shift likewise worth 2 points.

10. To Catholic Christian German (Hohenstaufen-Swabian) rule (still under Islamic influence) circa 1200–1260, no religious shift at all but an ethnic shift worth 1 point.

11. To Catholic Christian French (Angevin) rule (Islamic influence virtually disappearing) circa 1260–1280, after a religious crusade, a religious shift worth 1 point and an ethnic shift worth 1 point.

12. To a major Catholic Christian Spanish (Aragonese) challenge to French (Angevin) rule, especially in Sicily, from the 1280s, no religious shift at all but an ethnic shift worth 1 point.

To sum up the cultural changes in southern Italy during the 1,000-year period circa 300–1300 and compare them with the cultural changes in Spain during the 1,100-year period circa 300–1400, we find that the number of major cultural shifts in southern Italy was twelve as compared to only nine in Spain. The religious shifts amounted to a total of 13 points in Italy as compared to only 10 in Spain; the ethnic/dynastic shifts, to a total of 11 points in Italy as compared to only 10 in Spain; and both religious and ethnic/dynastic shifts, to a total of 24 points in Italy as compared to only 20 in Spain. Clearly, then, if the continual shifts and changes in the majority, or ruling, culture in the Iberian peninsula helped bring about the collapse of the Spanish Jewish community circa 1400, how much the more so did the continual shifts and changes in the majority or ruling culture in southern Italy help bring about the collapse of the south Italian Jewish community circa 1300.

12. *The Especial Attraction of a* Semiticized *Christian Culture*

The Jews of Spain may have converted to Christianity en masse and with relative sincerity circa 1400 because the Christianity that was offered to them was a unique form of Christianity, heavily influenced by Islamic culture. Islamic influence on Spanish culture was pronounced when Islam dominated the Iberian peninsula (circa 700–1200). It continued, though to a lesser extent, even after the Christians emerged triumphant in the thirteenth century, inasmuch as large numbers of Muslims continued to live in central and southern Spain under Christian rule. Likewise, the Jews of southern Italy may have converted to Christianity en masse and with relative sincerity circa 1300 because the Christianity that was offered to them was also a unique form of Christianity, heavily influenced by Islamic culture. Islamic influence on Italian culture was pronounced when Islam dominated Sicily (circa 800–1100). It continued, though to a lesser extent, even after the Norman Christians emerged triumphant in the late eleventh century, inasmuch as large numbers of Muslims continued to live in Sicily under Christian rule.

What evidence is there that the Christianity to which the Jews of southern Italy converted en masse and with relative sincerity circa 1300 was a heavily Semiticized Christianity? Just as there was a Semitic (Tyrian, then Carthaginian) presence in Spain during the first millenium B.C., so there was a Semitic (also Tyrian, then Carthaginian) presence in Italy during the first millenium B.C. However, the Semitic presence was much greater during the first millenium B.C. in Spain than in Italy. In Spain the Semitic presence lasted about 800 years (Tyre, circa 1000–600 B.C.; Carthage, circa 600–200 B.C.) and was felt directly on the Iberian peninsula (in the southeast). In Italy the Semitic presence only lasted about 550 years (Tyre, circa 800–500 B.C.; Carthage, circa 500–250 B.C.) and was not felt as directly on the Italian peninsula (rather, it was centered in northwestern Sicily,[138] though recently traces of Phoenician influence in the food customs of some of the people in mainland southern Italy have been noticed by Waverly Root[139]). Yet, precisely as in Spain, first millenium B.C. Semitic influence in Sicily was equally divided chronologically between the Semites of the Middle East (Tyre) and the Semites of North Africa (Carthage). The Tyrians were in Spain for about 400 years (1000–600 B.C.) and the Carthaginians for about 400 years (600–200

B.C.). The Tyrians were in Sicily for about 300 years (800–500 B.C.). and the Carthaginians for about 250 years (500–250 B.C.).

Likewise, just as the Byzantine Greeks reinforced the Middle Eastern influence in Spain by their conquest of the Phoenician-Carthaginian south-east for 75 years (circa 550–625), so the Byzantine Greeks reinforced the Middle Eastern influence in Italy by their conquests which lasted about 500 years (circa 550–1050) on the south Italian mainland and about 350 years (circa 550–900) in Sicily. However, when the Byzantines held southern Italy and Sicily, they were more heavily Middle Eastern in their culture than they were when they held southeastern Spain. This was because the Byzantine occupation of Italian territory coincides with the imperially sponsored iconoclastic movement (circa 700–850), which attacked the use of art in Christian worship. In so doing, iconoclasm was influenced by the Middle Eastern desert ideal, which favors the use of poetry and music to communicate with the divine but does not favor the use of art for this purpose. Even after 850, when the iconoclastic movement ended, though religious painting was allowed, religious sculpture was more or less forbidden. This was in large part a concession to those Middle Eastern non-Christian religious faiths (Judaism, Zoroastrianism, Manicheanism, and Islam) which strongly opposed the use of sculpture.[140] Thus, the Byzantine presence in southern Italy and Sicily exerted much more of a Middle Easternizing and even Semiticizing influence than did the Byzantine presence in southeastern Spain.

What about Islamic influence per se (rather than Phoenician or Byzantine) upon Italy in general and southern Italy in particular? Of course, Islamic influence in Sicily was overwhelming during the more or less 300-year period when the Arabs dominated the island (circa 800–1100). But even afterwards, during the period of the Norman and Hohenstaufen/Swabian rule, the Muslims remained a major military force.[141] The Arabs were a crucial component in the Norman and Hohenstaufen armies and as such even attacked Assisi in the 1240s, whence according to tradition they were driven off by St. Clare, who held up to them a monstrance containing the sacred host.[142] They also were an intellectual and cultural force. There was a major movement to translate Arabic scientific and medical treatises in both Sicily and southern Italy in the twelfth and thirteenth centuries, which continued even under the far less tolerant Angevins toward the end of the thirteenth century.[143] Islamic architectural/artistic influence (e.g., in

328

the Martorana and San Cataldo churches in Palermo as well as the monastery of Monreale near Palermo) continued to be felt in an important way.[144] To this day the Sicilian puppet shows and painted wagons continue to be overwhelmingly concerned with the problem of Islam.[145]

The Normans and Hohenstaufen/Swabians also carried Islamic influence and culture across the Straits of Messina into their domains in southern Italy (all the way to Apulia). However, Islamic influence in these areas had already preceded the Normans by several centuries, radiating out from Arab-held Sicily during the ninth through eleventh centuries, especially into the Campanian area, where such cities as Naples and Amalfi were distinguished by their penchant for collaboration with the Arabs.[146] Islamic influence can still be seen in the Cathedral of St. Andrew in Amalfi, which dates from the eleventh century (especially in the thirteenth-century bell tower and the Cloisters of Paradise). There is also the famed legend of the four physicians (Latin Christian, Greek Christian, Arab Muslim, and Jew) who founded the medical school at Salerno circa 1000, to which Constantine the African made such an important contribution by translations from Arabic into Latin in the late eleventh century.[147] However, would-be Italian collaborators with the Arabs were not found only in Campania. Bertha of Tuscany was a would-be collaborator with the Arabs in the early tenth century.[148] Indeed, Islamic architectural influence is quite strong in the twelfth- and thirteenth-century cathedrals of Tuscany and Latium (at least in those which use the rather unique striped-marble effect); just as there were Arab merchant colonies in such important Italian commercial cities as Genoa, Pisa (where the Arabs resided south of the Arno while the Jewish merchants resided north of it), Ferrara (where cases involving intermarriage between Arab merchants and local Christian women came to the attention of Pope Innocent III around 1199), and Venice (whence, later, Otello, the Moor, black Muslim, of Venice).[149]

St. Francis of Assisi himself used an Arab physician (from Rome or Lucera?) in Rieti in the 1220s (who, however, did not help him very much).[150] One of the Franciscan Moroccan martyrs of 1220, Berardo, is said to have known Arabic, and he may well have taught some of the language to St. Francis for use in the saint's attempt to convert the Sultan of Egypt, Malik al-Kamil, Saladin's nephew, during a temporary lull in the fierce fighting of the Fifth Crusade before Damietta, in September of 1219.[151] Indeed, the problem of Islam was the crucial concern of the main portion of St. Francis' life and work (circa 1212-1226), and the saint went on three missions to the Muslims: of the Middle East, 1212; of Spain, 1213-1215; and of Egypt, 1219.[152] St. Francis' stigmata have recently been convincingly interpreted by Father Giulio Basetti-Sani, Louis Massignon's leading Italian Franciscan disciple, against the backdrop of the Christian-Islamic dialogue. They represented an attempt to prove the truth of Christ's crucifixion to Islam, which believes that only a phantom died on the cross since Christ himself ascended to heaven alive (at the same time as Islam considers Jesus the Messiah but does not consider him the Son of God).[153] Certainly there was considerable, though indirect, Islamic influence upon thirteenth-century Italian poetry, for this poetry owes much to twelfth-century southern French troubadour lyrics, and these in turn owe much to eleventh-century Hispano-Arabic love songs.[154]

The Islamic influence upon Dante's *Divine Comedy* (via thirteenth-century Latin translations prepared in Spain of important Arabic documents such as the so-called *Libro della Scala*) has convincingly been demonstrated by Miguel Asin-Palacios, Jose Munyoz-Sendino, and Enrico Cerulli.[155] Petrarch's interest in Arabic culture has recently been discussed by Francesco Gabrieli.[156] Boccaccio's famed retelling (in the *Decameron*, First Day, Third Tale) of the story of the three rings (involving the legendary and chivalrous Arabic ruler Saladin and the wise Jew Melchisedek) is a powerful example of an Islamic and Jewishly influenced Italian concept of religious toleration.[157] The same thing is true of the equally famed legend of the three imposters (Moses, Jesus, and Muhammed), so closely associated with the name of Emperor Frederick II of Sicily/southern Italy during the first half of the thirteenth century but itself of Islamic origin.[158] Petrarch's Latin epic poem *Africa* (1337-1347), which ostensibly chronicles the story of the Roman struggle against Carthage, probably refers to the Christian-Islamic encounter and may be a call for the revival of the crusading movement which had lost Acre to the Mamluks of Egypt in 1291. The great Italian epic poems of the fourteenth through the sixteenth centuries—Pulci's *Morgante Maggiore* (1460-1483), Boiardo's *Orlando Innamorato* (1484-1494), Ariosto's *Orlando Furioso* (1516-1532), and Tasso's *Gerusalemme Liberata* (1575)—deal overwhelmingly with the problem of Islam.[159] At the same time the Italians were the leading Western Christian exponents of Arabic Averroist thought (Marsilio of Padua, fourteenth century; Pietro Pomponazzi, fifteenth century; Agostino Nifo and Jacopo Zabarella in the sixteenth century).[160] Quite recently Waverly Root has written about the extensive Arabic influence upon modern Italian cuisine.[161]

Thus, the Christian culture of Italy in general, and of southern Italy in particular, was a heavily Semiticized Christian culture (because of its Tyrian-Carthaginian, Byzantine-Greek-iconoclast, and Arabic legacies), as was that of Spain. Hence, when the Jews of southern Italy converted en masse to Christianity circa 1300, they, like the Jews of Spain who did the same thing circa 1400, were really converting to a combination of Christianity (the second generation, the mother) and Islam (the third generation, the granddaughter), with Christianity predominating. However, the Arabs themselves only controlled Sicily for about 300 years (circa 800-1100), whereas they controlled Spain for about 500 years (circa 700-1200). Moreover, Arabic culture in Italy was found primarily upon the island of Sicily, while Arabic culture in Spain was represented on the Spanish mainland itself. Hence, we would suggest that the force with which the factor of a Semitic Christian culture was operative in southern Italy was only about half that with which this same factor was operative in Spain. Therefore, its influence upon mass Jewish conversion to Christianity in southern Italy circa 1300 was only about half what its influence was upon mass Jewish conversion to Christianity in Spain a century later.

*****

If the mass conversion of the Jews of Spain to Christianity circa 1400 helped generate (1) the Spanish exploration and colonization effort in the New World and (2) a powerful current of theological and philosophical liberalism and skepticism in Western Europe, could the mass conversion of the Jews of southern Italy to Christianity circa 1300 have had· the same two effects?

Did the mass conversion of the Jews of southern Italy circa 1300 help generate an Italian exploration and colonization effort in the New World? The movement to explore and colonize the New World was primarily developed and controlled by the Atlantic nations of Western Europe: Portugal, Spain, France, The Netherlands, and England. Indeed, this very movement passed central and eastern Europe by and probably helped retard the growth of the modern national state in both Germany and Italy until comparatively late (the midnineteenth century). Yet the Italians did make a contribution to the exploration and colonization of the New World. The achievements of medieval Italian seafarers (primarily Genoese and Venetian in the Mediterranean) and of Italian explorers (especially the Polos, who ventured as far as China) certainly helped pave the way for Columbus, who had Genoa in his background. A Florentine explorer of the South American coast in the late 1490s and early 1500s gave his name to the New World (Amerigo Vespucci). Another Florentine seafarer made an important contribution to the exploration of the North American coast circa 1524 (Giovanni da Verrazano). Indeed, Spain itself administered Sicily and southern Italy in the sixteenth and seventeenth centuries, and undoubtedly some Sicilians and south Italians participated in the movement to colonize and develop the Spanish territories in the New World. The many Italian immigrants into Latin America (especially Brazil and Argentina)[162] in the nineteenth and twentieth centuries (almost as many as to the United States) may well have been continuing the Italian participation in the Spanish exploration and colonization efforts of the sixteenth and seventeenth centuries.

But, to our knowledge, the mass conversion of the Jews of southern Italy circa 1300 did not play anywhere near the same kind of role in the exploration and colonization of the New World as did the mass conversion of the Jews of Spain circa 1400. This may have been, in part, because in absolute terms the number of Jews who became permanent converts to Christianity in southern Italy circa 1300 was no more than several thousand, whereas the number of Jews who became permanent converts to Christianity in Spain circa 1400 was several *hundred* thousand. Obviously, the several hundred thousand Spanish Marranos could have played a major role in the development of the New World. The several thousand south Italian Marranos could have played nowhere near the same kind of role.

Did the mass conversion of the Jews of southern Italy circa 1300 help generate a powerful current of intellectual liberalism in Western Europe? Certainly the Italian contribution to the development of intellectual liberalism in Western Europe from the fourteenth to the eighteenth centuries was much more significant than it was to the exploration of the New World. The list of major Italian pioneers of intellectual liberalism circa 1300-1800 is a long one. It begins with Marsilio of Padua (circa 1270-1342), the Averroist who liberalized political theory, and ends with Cesare Becaria (1735-1793), the liberalizer of penological thought.[163] However, to our knowledge, the mass conversion of the Jews of southern Italy circa 1300 did not play anywhere near the kind of role in the development of a powerful current of intellectual liberalism in Western Europe as did the mass conversion of the Jews of Spain circa 1400. Again this may well be due to the fact that, in absolute terms, the number of permanent Jewish converts to Christianity in southern Italy circa 1300 was only several thousand, whereas the number of permanent Jewish converts to Christianity in Spain circa 1400 was several *hundreds* of thousands. Again, the several hundred thousand Spanish Marranos could have played a major role in the development of Western European liberalism. The several thousand south Italian Marranos could have played nowhere near the same kind of role.

*****

As we have attempted to demonstrate above, seven of the twelve factors—numbers 1 through 4, 8 through 9, and 12—operated in southern Italy circa 1300 with only about half the force which they commanded in Spain circa 1400. However, four of the thirteen factors—numbers 5 through 7 and 10—operated in southern Italy circa 1300 with about the same force which they commanded in Spain circa 1400. One exceptional factor, number 11, cultural shifting, operated with about 30 percent greater force in southern Italy than in Spain. Thus, a clear majority of the factors, seven out of twelve, operated in southern Italy circa 1300 with only about half of the force which they commanded in Spain circa 1400. This may help explain why only 25 percent of the Jews of southern Italy became permanent converts to Christianity circa 1300, whereas about 50 percent of the Jews of Spain became permanent converts to Christianity circa 1400.

But the factor that we believe was the most important of all was number 12. When the Jews of Spain and of southern Italy were converting to Christianity en masse and with relative sincerity, they were doing so because the Christian culture they were offered was heavily Semiticized. Had the Jews of Spain and southern Italy been pressured to join a purely Indo-European Christian culture, something they never had an opportunity to do because of the overwhelming Islamic influence in Spain and southern Italy, they would have chosen the

333

same path their brethren north of the Pyrenees/Alps chose when pressured to join a purely Indo-European Christian culture: mass martyrdom (often by ritual suicide) or flight. Or, vice versa, had the Jews of Franco-Germany been pressured to join a heavily Semiticized Christianity, something they never had an opportunity to do because Islam had never been a lasting presence north of the Pyrenees/Alps, they would have chosen the same path their Spanish and south Italian brethren chose when pressured to join a heavily Semiticized Christian culture: mass conversion with relative sincerity. But the Jews of Franco-Germany were never pressured to join a heavily Semiticized Christianity, and the Jews of Spain and southern Italy were never pressured to join a purely Indo-European Christian culture. Rather, the Jews of Spain and southern Italy were pressured to join a heavily Semiticized Christian culture, and the Jews of Franco-Germany were pressured to join a heavily Indo-European Christian culture. This, then, is the crucial distinction and here, we believe, is our basic explanation!

Thus, why did the Jewish communities of Spain and southern Italy (but not those of France or Germany) collapse so totally circa 1400 and 1300 respectively? Primarily because the Jewish communities of Spain and southern Italy (but not those of France or Germany) were given the opportunity of joining heavily Semiticized forms of Christian culture. They were the only Jewish communities in the history of the Jewish people in Europe that were given such an opportunity. Is it any wonder, then, that the Jewish communities of Spain and southern Italy were the only Jewish communities in the history of the Jewish people in Europe that converted to Christianity en masse and with relative sincerity?[164]

9. Louis Massignon (1883-1962) and the Contemporary Ramifications of the Thesis about the Anti-Islamic Origins of Modern Anti-Semitism*

What are the contemporary implications of the thesis developed in this book that Christian anti-Muslimism was the primary (though not the only) factor in medieval Christian anti-Semitism? We maintain that medieval anti-Muslimism was a crucial factor in medieval anti-Semitism. According to such scholars as Joshua Trachtenberg and Norman Cohn medieval anti-Semitism is a crucial factor in modern anti-Semitism. Therefore, medieval anti-Muslimism may also be a crucial factor in modern anti-Semitism.[1]

If this is true, then by solving the problem of anti-Muslimism we would go a long way toward solving the problem of anti-Semitism. The best way to solve the problem of anti-Muslimism is to accept the Massignonian teaching, which will be discussed in greater detail infra, that Judaism, Christianity, and Islam are not three separate religions but rather *three branches of the same religion, the religion of Abraham.* Until Christians and Muslims embrace the Massignonian vision and end the states of war and belligerency which have prevailed between them for the past fourteen centuries, we may not see the end of the long nightmare of Christian anti-Semitism in the West.

*****

Let us look a little deeper into the contemporary ramifications of the unique triangular relationship between Judaism, Christianity, and Islam.

Israeli antagonism toward Arabs may in part be affected by a Jewish desire (perhaps more subconscious than conscious) to disprove the historic Christian belief that the Jews are in league with the Muslims against the West.

335

On the other hand, a deeper awareness throughout the Arab world of this historic Christian belief that the Jews are in league with the Muslims against the West could well soften Arab antagonism toward Israel and help pave the way for peace in the Middle East.

The most important and crucial problem in interreligious relations in the Western civilizational area (which includes the Middle East/North Africa, Europe, and the Americas) is the problem of Christian-Islamic relations, not the problem of Christian-Jewish or of Islamic-Jewish relations. The problem of Christian-Islamic relations involves the two largest and most powerful of the three great Western monotheistic faiths, Christianity and Islam, with approximately 1 billion and 500 million believers respectively. The Christian-Jewish problem involves only the largest and the smallest of the three great Western monotheistic faiths, with 1 billion and 13.5 million believers respectively, and the Islamic-Jewish problem likewise involves only the second largest and the smallest of the three great Western monotheistic faiths, with 500 million and 13.5 million believers respectively. Far and away the Christian-Islamic controversy is much weightier and more serious than the Christian-Jewish or the Islamic-Jewish controversies.

If we solve the problem of Christian-Islamic antagonism, there would be no need for Israel to treat the Arabs with hostility as a means of allaying Christian fears of a Judaeo/Islamic alliance, just as there would be no need for the Arabs to fear the Israelis as agents of Western colonialism and imperialism.

We are, thus, living at a crucial watershed of human history. The decade of the 1970s witnessed the rise of the Islamic peoples via the massive transfer of wealth from the Atlantic powers to the oil-rich countries of the Third World. In the 1980s the peoples of the Mosque are on the verge of attaining a position of power and influence which they have not had since the golden age of Ottoman Turkey under Sultan Sulayman the Magnificent in the sixteenth century, or Saladin's reconquest of Jerusalem from the Crusaders in the late twelfth century, or the creation by the Arabs in the century after the Prophet Muhammad (died 632) of a vast empire stretching from the Atlantic to Central Asia that was greater than any the world had ever seen prior to that time (including the Roman). The twentieth century has seen the power equation between Christianity and Islam shift from an overwhelming imbalance in Christianity's favor, when Allenby conquered Jerusalem from the Turks in 1917, to a balance of much closer to par at the present time, surely one of the most radical shifts in the balance of power that the world has seen.

This new balance in the power equation between Christianity and Islam which we see emerging in our own lifetimes may well lead to genuine Christian-Islamic dialogue and reconciliation in the spirit of Vatican II's epoch-making "Declaration on the Muslims," (inspired by Louis Massignon, more about whom infra), which attempted to discredit the crusading ideology forever. This declaration formed the third section of the very same document of world-historical import whose fourth section, the "Declaration on the Jews" (inspired by Christian remorse at the church's failure to prevent Hitler's murder of 6 million Jews during World War II and by Christian sympathy for the creation of the State of Israel after the Jews had been homeless for 2,000 years), called likewise for a new era of Christian-Jewish dialogue and reconciliation after attempting to discredit the deicide charge forever.[2]

Once we solve the larger problem of Christian-Islamic relations, it will be far easier for us to solve the smaller problems of Christian-Jewish relations and Islamic-Jewish relations. A breakthrough in the area of Christian-Islamic reconciliation will create an atmosphere of interreligious amity and cooperation overwhelmingly conducive to the solution of all other problems of interreligious relations in the world in general and in the West in particular.

If we can solve the greater problem of Christian-Islamic relations, we would be very optimistic about our ability to, or our likelihood of, solving the lesser problems of Christian-Jewish and Islamic-Jewish relations. On the other hand, if we ignore, fail to solve, or even exacerbate, the greater problem of Christian-Islamic relations, we would be very pessimistic about our ability to, or our likelihood of, solving the lesser problems of Christian-Jewish and Islamic-Jewish relations.

Our analysis of the crucial impact of Christian-Islamic upon Christian-Jewish relations may not be correct. But if it is, it would seem that American and world Jewry should be ready and willing to put much more of its community-relations time, money, energy, and imagination into urging Christians and Muslims to enter into genuine dialogue and reconciliation.

Surely the Jewish people should fight Christian anti-Semitism. But it should also fight Christian anti-Muslimism, for the good of the Jewish people, the West, and the world at large!

337

Likewise, the Jewish people should fight Arab anti-Semitism. But it should also fight Arab anti-Christianism, again for the good of the Jewish people, the West, and the world at large!

Our goal should be to create a new spiritual *and institutional* unity between Jews, Christians, and Muslims. This unity would be centered around the holy city of Jerusalem and a central titular spiritual figure who would take up residence in this holy city. Perhaps this figure should be the pope, who would first have to transform his office and mission from a more narrowly Christian into a more broadly Abrahamitic one, encompassing all three great Western monotheistic faiths seen as coequals in the sight of God and man.

This dream is inspired by the ideals of Louis Massignon (1883–1962), about whom we have had the privilege of publishing a book.[3] Massignon, the greatest French Islamologist of the twentieth century, father of Vatican II's epoch-making "Declaration on the Muslims," was the person who, in this century of all-out war, issued a prophetic call for genuine dialogue and reconciliation between Judaism, Christianity, and Islam. He argued that they were not three separate religions but rather three branches *of the same religion.* This was not the religion of Muhammad, or of Jesus, or of Moses, but rather the religion of the world historical figure who preceded all three of these equally great prophets. It was the religion of *Abraham*, from whom both Jews and Muslims claim physical descent (the Jews through Isaac; the Muslims through Ishmael) and Christians claim spiritual descent (through Jesus, though Jesus himself is said by the Gospel of Matthew, chapter 1, to have been a *physical* descendant of Abraham through Isaac, like the Jewish people in general).

Massignon was perhaps the twentieth-century European religious figure with the most unique ability to fathom the souls of all three great Western monotheistic faiths. His mentors in Islamology (Hartwig Derenbourg of France and Ignaz Goldziher of Hungary) and Indology (Sylvain Levi of France) were *Jews.* But Arab *Muslims* in Bagdad (during the spring of 1908) saved him from execution by the Turks (on a false charge of spying), helping him rediscover the intense, mystical *Catholicism* of his Breton ancestors.

Massignon himself represented a uniquely powerful combination of *Catholic* mysticism (centering in the stigmata of St. Francis of Assisi and of Melanie Calvet of La Salette); the *Jewish* spiritual Zionism of Ahad Ha-Am and Judah Magnes (though Massignon strongly, perhaps overzealously, opposed Herzlian political Zionism); the *Islamic* mystical tradition called Sufism (interpreting the great tenth-century *crucified* Islamic mystic of Bagdad, al-Hallaj, was Massignon's lifework and probably his greatest Islamological contribution); and *Gandhian* nonviolent resistance to colonialism and tyranny.

According to Massignon, then, Judaism, Christianity, and Islam are not three separate religions but rather three denominations of the same religion, the religion of Abraham. They are not three separate trees, but rather three branches of the same tree, the tree of Abraham.

Massignon was unique in his emphasis upon the common Semitic character, even into the twentieth century, *of all three* great Western monotheistic faiths. He considered Judaism the monotheistic expression of the *Hebrew*-speaking Semites, Christianity the monotheistic expression of the *Aramaic*-speaking Semites, and Islam the monotheistic expression of the *Arabic*-speaking Semites. He believed that all three Semitic language and religious groups were equal sons of their common father Abraham and equal branches of Abraham's tree of life.

In the Massignonian conception Judaism, the earliest of the branches to sprout, is the branch of the tree of Abraham that puts the greatest emphasis upon hope, the intensest kind of hope in the coming of the Messiah. The Jews were the only one of the three great Western monotheistic faith-communities to wander in exile for 2,000 years, during which time they never ceased to expect the messianic redemption, never gave up hope that someday their Messiah would come to lead them back home.

Christianity, the second in time of the branches to sprout, is the branch of the tree of Abraham that puts the greatest emphasis upon love, the intensest kind of love for the suffering and oppressed of mankind. The Christians are the only one of the three great Western monotheistic faith-communities to consider the crucifixion of Jesus a positive symbol, a symbol of victory, not defeat, a symbol of victory through total selflessness, total selflessness in the service and love of one's fellow human beings.

Islam, the third in time of the branches to sprout, is the branch of the tree of Abraham that puts the greatest emphasis upon faith. The Muslims have the intensest faith in the wisdom of God's governance of the universe and submit the most wholeheartedly to his inscrutable decrees. How can Muslims doubt God when it was he who ordained that Islam would be the Western monotheistic faith which would have to suffer the least amount of persecution? The Muslims were in the Meccan catacombs, as it were, for only twelve years, circa 610–622, during the Prophet Muhammad's totally nonviolent period; while the Christians were in the Roman catacombs for three centuries, circa 30–313, during their totally nonviolent period; and the Jews were in the catacombs of the world at large for about 2,000 years, from 135, the failure of the Bar Kochba revolt, the last great Jewish revolt against pagan Roman rule in Palestine, to 1948, when the State of Israel was born, during which period of nearly two millenia the Jews were almost always nonviolent.

In the Middle Ages the greatest Jewish thinker to deal with the problem of the metahistorical relationship between Judaism, Christianity, and Islam was Maimonides, the medieval Jewish Massignon, as it were.[4] In the Maimonidean conception all three great Western monotheistic faith-communities had important missions to fulfill in the world. It was not that one of the three had an important mission to fulfill whilst the other two were purposeless or, even worse, did the Devil's work. All three had a constructive role to play—but not an equal role. Judaism's role was superior to the role of the other two, for the Jewish mission was to bring monotheism into the world, to give it to the Christians and Muslims, and to make certain that the Christians and Muslims remained faithful to it. The Christian mission was no more than to bring Jewish monotheism to the Indo-European peoples, and the Islamic mission was no more than to bring Jewish monotheism to the peoples of Afro-Asia.

Massignon agreed with Maimonides that all three great Western monotheistic faiths had an important mission to fulfill. None of the three was without a purpose in the world. None of the three did the Devil's work. But Massignon differed from Maimonides by holding that all three had *an equal role* to play. Judaism's role was not superior to the role of the other two. Neither was Christianity's nor Islam's. They each had different missions, but none had a mission that was more important than the mission of the others. In the Massignonian as opposed to the Maimonidean conception, all have equally important roles. All are equally beloved children of their father Abraham. All are branches of Abraham's tree which perform an equally vital role in keeping the tree alive. This is Massignon's distinct advance on Maimonides' understanding of the unity within diversity represented by the three great Western monotheistic faiths. This is where the most progressive twentieth-century thinker on the question of the metahistorical relationships between the peoples of the synagogue, the church, and the mosque moves ahead of the most progressive medieval Jewish thinker on this same question.

Louis Massignon was a great twentieth-century prophetic figure who was ahead of his time. We believe that the world will eventually be forced to join him in recognizing the essential unity of the three great Western monotheistic faiths. It will be forced to do so through the inexorable progress of human events. These events include such powerful world unifying factors as (1) the common threat to all three Abrahamitic religions—Judaism, Christianity, and Islam—posed by an all-triumphant modern materialism (scientism, secularism, automation, computerization, pollution, and the danger of nuclear holocaust); (2) the common bond created by the revolution in telecommunications and the development of mass international tourism; and (3) the common challenge of space exploration (John F. Kennedy's true New Frontier), which is an extension of the common bond represented by factor two and offers an eventual avenue of escape from part of the common threat represented by factor one. We sincerely hope that through the ideas and facts of our book as developed above we can help bring about a climate of opinion which will make possible the realization of the Massignonian ideal and dream of Jewish-Christian-Islamic dialogue and reconciliation within our own lifetimes rather than a century hence!

In August and September, 1983, Pope John Paul II made two historic pronouncements which indicate that he has been influenced by the ideals of Louis Massignon. Thus, on or about August 15, 1983, the pope concluded an historic pilgrimage to the great southern French shrine of Lourdes, the holy place where in 1858 the fourteen-year-old Marie Bernadette Soubirous saw the Virgin Mary appear on eighteen occasions. At this sacred spot just north of the Pyrenees, amid the crippled and the maimed, Pope John Paul II called for "harmony and collaboration among Christians, Jews and Moslems, in order to fight prejudice."[5]

Less than a month later, on or about September 10, 1983, the pope traveled to Vienna to help celebrate the third centennial of the Christian defeat of the Turks besieging Vienna. On this historic occasion Pope John Paul II warned against making the celebration of the victory over the Muslim Turks an opportunity to engage in "one-sided blame or praise," because Christians committed atrocities before the gates of Vienna as did the Turks. The pope also gave thanks for the fact that the Muslims, the former enemies, now live at peace among the Christians of Austria, as do the Jews, whose presence in Austria serves as a reminder. "The fate of the Jewish community, once so fruitfully involved with the people of Europe and now so tragically decimated, admonishes us by its very presence to use every opportunity to promote human and spiritual understanding."[6]

Let us pray that in the coming generations the papacy will view as its primary mission the struggle to achieve the Massignonian ideal. In so doing, the papacy will take the lead in working for reconciliation between the three branches of the religion of Abraham: Judaism, Christianity, and Islam.

Notes

Acknowledgments

1. For the life and the work of Queller, infra, note 13 to chapter four; Dales, idem; White, infra, note 45 to chapter four; Burns, infra, note 1 to chapter two; Synan, infra, notes 1 and 5 to chapter one; Kritzeck, infra, note 2 to chapter two; Netanyahu, infra, note 1 to chapter seven.

Introduction

1. On Massignon cf. Giulio Basetti-Sani, *Louis Massignon (1883-1962): Christian Prophet of Inter-Religious Reconciliation*, ed. and trans. A. H. Cutler (Chicago: Franciscan Herald Press, 1974); infra, chapter nine and note 3 thereto.

2. Henry Kamm, "Pope, at Lourdes, Seeks to Console the Suffering," *New York Times*, August 16, 1983, part 1, 3.

3. "Pope, in Vienna, Stresses Christian Heritage," *New York Times*, September 11, 1983, part 1, 9.

4. Bernhard Blumenkranz, *Le Juif Medieval au Miroir de l'Art Chretien* (Paris: Etudes Augustiniennes, 1966), 136 = Blumenkranz's *Juden und Judentum in der Mittelalterliche Kunst* (Stuttgart: Kohlhammer, 1965), 80. For Blumenkranz's life, Colette Sirat, "Blumenkranz, Bernhard," *Ency. Judaica* 4 (1971): 1141; ibid. 1 (1971): 28; *Who's Who in World Jewry* (1978), 112. For Blumenkranz's bibliography, *Repertoire des Medievistes Europeens* (1960), 28, no. 136; *Repertoire International des Medievistes* (1965), 64, no. 303; ibid. (1971), 73, no. 377; ibid. (1979), 73, no. 513.

Infra, note 17 to chapter 4, for Blumenkranz's view that anti-Muslimism rather than the deicide charge was the primary factor in high medieval anti-Semitism. Infra, note 43 to chapter 7, for the similarity between Blumenkranz and Netanyahu, who both deemphasize the deicide charge.

5. Infra, note 53 to chapter 4.

6. As did leprosy, "Leprosy," *Ency. Brit.* 16 (1926): 480; Omer Englebert, *St. Francis of Assisi: A Biography*, trans. E.M. Cooper, ed. Ignatius Brady and Raphael Brown (2nd ed.; Chicago: Franciscan Herald Press, 1965), 462–463, note 25.

1. Toward a New Comparative Approach to the History of Papal-Jewish Relations

* Chapter one goes back ultimately to ideas which came to us in the mid-1950s. An earlier version appeared in *Journal of Ecumenical Studies* 5 (1968): 153–155. With

the permission of its editors, Leonard and Arlene Swidler, it is reproduced here after further revisions. We thank Edward Synan and Solomon Grayzel for reading the earlier version before it appeared in that journal.

1. Edward A. Synan, *The Popes and the Jews in the Middle Ages*, preface by John M. Oesterreicher (New York and London: Macmillan, 1965); reviews by Solomon Grayzel, *Central Conference of American Rabbis Journal* 13 (April 1966): 82-86; Cecil Roth, *Jewish Social Studies* 18 (1966): 192; James Parkes, *Judaism* 16 (1967): 242-246.

2. Christian-Islamic relations may have played an important role in Pope John XXIII's philo-Semitism. He traveled an ecumenical road which led him from sympathetic interest in Eastern Orthodoxy (Bulgaria, 1925-1934), to sympathetic interest in Islam (Istanbul, 1934-1944), to sympathetic interest in Judaism (during World War II). If so, Christian-Islamic relations preceded, and perhaps influenced, Christian-Jewish relations in the case of the pope responsible for Vatican II's "Declaration on the Jews."

On Vatican II and the Jewish people, Oesterreicher, "Declaration on the Relationship of the Church to Non-Christian Religions, Introduction and Commentary," in Herbert Vorgrimler, ed., *Commentary on the Documents of Vatican II* (New York: Herder and Herder, 1969), III: 1-136; Tommaso Federici, "Ebrei," in Salvatore Garofalo and Federici, eds., *Dizionario del Concilio Ecumenico Vaticano Secondo* (Rome: Unione Editoriale, 1969), 1043-1063.

3. Judah Goldin, *The Fathers according to Rabbi Nathan* (New Haven: Yale University Press, 1955), 117, 233; and his *The Living Talmud: The Wisdom of the Fathers* (New York: New American Library/Mentor, 1957), 86, 88-89; Isaac Unterman, *Pirke Aboth: Sayings of the Fathers* (New York: Twayne, 1964), 111; Irving M. Bunim, *Ethics from Sinai* (2nd ed.; New York: Feldheim, 1964), I: 145, 149-150.

4. Edward H. Flannery, *The Anguish of the Jews: Twenty-Three Centuries of Anti-Semitism*, preface by Oesterreicher (New York and London: Macmillan, 1965); review by A. Roy Eckardt, *Jewish Social Studies* 18 (1966): 172-174.

5. For Synan's biography and bibliography, *Directory of American Scholars* 4 (1963): 194; 4 (1969): 361; 4 (1974): 416; 4 (1978): 463; 4 (1982): 528; *Repertoire International des Medievistes* (1965), 604, no. 3125; ibid. (1971), 745, no. 4183; (1979), 714, no. 4864.

In the field of medieval philosophy Synan is editor of *The Works of Richard of Campsall*, 2 vols. (Toronto: Pontifical Institute of Mediaeval Studies, 1968 and 1982.) Synan is also editor/translator of Godfrey of St. Victor's *Fons Philosophiae* (Toronto: Pontifical Institute of Mediaeval Studies, 1972), containing interesting references to the Jews. Synan is also the author of a series of articles on such medieval philosophers as St. Thomas Aquinas, St. Bonaventure, Peter Bradley, Adam Burley, Richard of Campsall, Walter of Chatton, Peter Lombard, and Roger of Nottingham. See in general Synan's "Latin Philosophies of the Middle Ages," in James M. Powell, ed., *Medieval Studies: An Introduction* (New York: Syracuse University Press, 1976), 277-311; and his "Aquinas and His Age," in Anthony Parel, ed., *Calgary Aquinas Studies* (Toronto: Pontifical Institute of Mediaeval Studies, 1978), 1-25.

Synan has also taken an especial interest in Christian-Jewish relations and Jewish studies. He served as associate editor for vols. 3 (1958) and 4 (1962) of *The Bridge: A*

Yearbook of Judaeo-Christian Studies, published by the Institute of Judaeo-Christian Studies, Seton Hall University, directed by Oesterreicher. This journal pioneered in the Catholic-Jewish dialogue in the United States after World War II. For the fifth volume, Oesterreicher, ed., *Brothers in Hope* (New York: Herder and Herder, 1970).

Synan contributed four articles to *The Bridge:* "Abraham Heschel and Prayer," 1 (1955): 256–265; "Jacob B. Agus's *Guideposts in Modern Judaism:* A Review Article," 2 (1956): 322–331; "Covenant of Husband and Wife," 4 (1962): 149–170; with M. R. de Sion, "Bahya b. Pakuda, Tutor of Hearts," ibid, 252–273.

Synan has also helped encourage publication of English translations of two important texts in the area of medieval interreligious relations: Joseph Ramon Jones and John Esten Keller, *The Scholar's Guide: A Translation of the Twelfth-Century Disciplina Clericalis of Pedro Alfonso* (Toronto: Pontifical Institute of Mediaeval Studies, 1969), and Frank Talmage, *Joseph Kimhi's Book of the Covenant* (Toronto: Pontifical Institute of Mediaeval Studies, 1973).

Synan informed us that he had completed a manuscript translation of Peter Abelard's *Dialogue between a Christian, Jew and Philosopher (Muslim?)* which he hoped to publish. This important text, written circa 1140, may have served as a crucial link between the writings of Petrus Alphonsi and Peter the Venerable on Jews and Muslims. Meanwhile, cf. Synan's "The *Exortacio* against Peter Abelard's Dialogues inter Philosophum, Iudaeum et Christianum," in J. Reginald O'Donnel, ed., *Essays in Honour of Anton Charles Pegis* (Toronto: Pontifical Institute of Mediaeval Studies, 1974), 176–192. Infra, note 25 to chapter 2.

6. Infra, notes 11, 26–27 to chapter 4.

Three other popes whose potentially important dealings with Jews are not discussed by Synan are Sylvester I (314–335), Boniface IV (608–615), and Benedict VIII (1012–1024). Blumenkranz, *Juifs et Chretiens dans le Monde Occidental 430–1096* (Paris and The Hague: Mouton, 1960), index, *s.v.*

7. These Christian historians of the papacy include Rudolf Baxmann, Ottorino Bertolini, Erich Caspar, Mandell Creighton, Louis Duchesne, Ferdinand Gregorovius, Hartmann Grisar, Johannes Haller, Joseph Langen, Horace Kinder Mann, Carlo Marcora, Henry Hart Milman, Guillaume Mollat, Vicenzo Monachino, Pio Paschini, Ludwig von Pastor, Leopold von Ranke, Agostino Saba, Joseph Schmidlin, Franz Xaver Seppelt, Walter Ullmann, and Noel Valois. The main Christian historian of papal-Jewish relations is Peter Browe. The leading Jewish historians of the Jewish people include Yitzhak Baer, Salo Baron, Ben-Zion Dinur, Simon Dubnow, Heinrich Graetz, Isaac Markus Jost, Joseph Klausner, and Gershom Scholem. The Jewish historians of papal-Jewish relations include Abraham Berliner, Bernhard Blumenkranz, Solomon Grayzel, Leon Poliakov, Paul Rieger, Moritz Stern, and Hermann Vogelstein.

8. On Vatican II and Islam, Georges Anawati, "Excursus on Islam," in Vorgrimler, ed., *Commentary on the Documents of Vatican II,* III: 151–154; and Federici, "Musulmani," in Garofalo and Federici, eds., *Dizionario del Concilio Ecumenico Vaticano Secondo,* 1514–1526.

In a speech delivered in Ankara, Turkey, on Thursday, November 29, 1979, before he flew to Istanbul to visit Patriarch Demetrios I of Constantinpole, Pope John Paul II "called for urgent steps to establish closer ties between Christians and Moslems" in the spirit of Vatican II on Islam. L. Fleming, "Pope Urges Closer Ties with Moslems," *Los Angeles Times*, November 30, 1979, part 1, 5. Supra, notes 2 and 3 to the introduction; infra, notes 5 and 6 to chapter 9.

Cf. also the important work of Giulio Basetti-Sani, the leading Italian Franciscan disciple of Louis Massignon (the greatest twentieth-century French Islamologist and father of Vatican II's "Declaration on Islam"): *Muhammed et Saint Francois* (Ottawa: Commissariat de Terre Sainte, 1959); *Introduzione allo Studio del Corano* (Brescia: Edizioni Civilta, 1967); *Per un Dialogo Christano-Musulmano: Mohammed, Damietta e La Verna* (Milan: Vita e Pensiero, 1969), currently being translated into English; *Louis Massignon: Orientalista Cristiano* (Milan: Vita e Pensiero, 1971), edited and translated by us and published as *Louis Massignon (1883–1962): Christian Prophet of Inter-Religious Reconciliation* (Chicago: Franciscan Herald Press, 1974), as reviewed by S.A. Quitslund, *Journal of Ecumenical Studies* 14 (1977): 503–504, and by R.M. Speight, *The Muslim World* 68 (1978): 292–293; *The Koran in the Light of Christ: A Christian Interpretation of the Sacred Book of Islam*, trans. W. Carroll and B. Dauphinee (Chicago: Franciscan Herald Press, 1977), as reviewed by J.A. Saliba, *Theological Studies* 40 (1979): 221; and *L'Islam e Francesco d'Assisi: La Missione Profetica per il Dialogo* (Florence: La Nuova Italia Editrice, 1975), currently being translated into English and as reviewed by James Kritzeck, *Catholic Historical Review* 64 (1978): 293–295. Cf. also Basetti-Sani, *Muhammad, St. Francis of Assisi and Alvernia* (Fiesole: Convento di San Francesco, 1975) (an adaptation of two articles published in *The Cord*, March 1956 and November 1967); and his "For a Dialogue between Christians and Muslims," *Muslim World* 57 (1967): 126–137, 186–196. On Basetti-Sani, also Marshall G.S. Hodgson, *The Venture of Islam: Conscience and History in a World Civilization* (Chicago and London: University of Chicago Press, 1974), I: 29.

9. Kenneth R. Stow, *Catholic Thought and Papal Jewry Policy 1555–1593* (New York: Jewish Theological Seminary of America, 1977), and as reviewed by Grayzel, *Jewish Quarterly Review* 68 (1978): 177–178, represents the kind of approach to a new history of papal-Jewish relations called for in this chapter of our book. The Stow volume offers an excellent synthesis by a Jewish intellectual of the best in both the modern Catholic (Stow knows the work of Synan; Stow, xviii, note 7) and Jewish traditions of religiolegal and historical scholarship. At the same time he is aware of the role played by the Christian equation of Jew with Muslim (Turk) in sixteenth century Christian-Jewish relations (Stow, 227, and notes 6–7; 243, note 76; 264, note 179). Hopefully Stow will continue to enlighten us with further studies of papal-Jewish relations informed by the comparative approach in general and by an even fuller appreciation of the crucial impact of Christian-Islamic relations upon Christian-Jewish relations in particular. For a reaction to Stow, David Berger, "*Cum Nimis Absurdum* and the Conversion of the Jews," *Jewish Quarterly Review* 70 (1979): 41–49.

2. Peter the Venerable (1094–1156) and Islam

* An earlier version of chapter two appeared in the *Journal of the American Oriental Society* 86 (1966): 184–198. With the permission of its editor, Ernest Bender, it is reproduced here after further revisions. We thank George F. Hourani and James Kritzeck for their criticisms of the earlier version prior to its publication in that journal.

1. In the footnotes to this chapter the following abbreviations are used: *PV=* James Kritzeck's book *Peter the Venerable and Islam; TC* = the Toletano-Cluniac corpus. The following are among the major literary monuments in the field of the history of *Western* Christian attitudes toward Muslims published since 1945:

Marie-Therese d'Alverny's many articles on this subject, infra, note 5;

Giulio Basetti-Sani, supra, note 8 to chapter 1;

Robert Ignatius Burns, *The Crusader Kingdom of Valencia: Reconstruction on a Thirteenth Century Frontier*, 2 vols. (Cambridge: Harvard University Press, 1967); *Islam under the Crusaders: Colonial Survival in the Thirteenth Century Kingdom of Valencia* (Princeton: Princeton University Press, 1973); *Medieval Colonialism: Postcrusade Exploitation of Islamic Valencia* (Princeton: Princeton University Press, 1976); *Moors and Crusaders in Mediterranean Spain: Collected Studies* (London: Variorum, 1978); *Jaume I i els Valencians del Segle XIII* (Valencia: Tres i Quatre, 1981), including chapters on the Jews and Muslims, *i.e.*, chapter 4, "Jaume I i els Jueus," and chapter 5, "La Historia dels Mudejars Avui en Dia"; *The Crusader-Muslim Predicament: Colonial Confrontation in the Conquered Kingdom of Valencia* (Princeton: Princeton University Press, forthcoming); his three-volume transcription, with book-length introduction, of King James I of Aragon's *Diplomatarium*, a collection of about 10,000 documents dealing with Valencia and written on paper instead of parchment (Princeton: Princeton University Press, forthcoming); *Muslims, Christians and Jews in the Crusader Kingdom of Valencia* (Cambridge University Press, forthcoming); a volume of collected articles forthcoming in Barcelona (via El-Albir Press); plus several recent articles, "Mudejar History Today: New Directions," *Viator* 8 (1977): 127-143; "The Language Barrier: The Problem of Bilingualism and Muslim-Christian Interchange in the Medieval Kingdom of Valencia," *Journal of the Faculty of Arts, University of Malta* 6 (1977): 116-136; "Muslim-Christian Conflict and Contact in Medieval Spain: Context and Methodology," *Thought* 54 (1979): 238-252; "Societies in Symbiosis: The Mudejar-Crusader Experiment in Thirteenth-Century Mediterranean Spain," *International History Review* 2 (1980): 349-385; "The Paper Revolution in Europe: Crusader Valencia's Paper Industry—A Technological and Behavioral Breakthrough," *Pacific Historical Review* 50 (1981): 1-30; "Relic Vendors, Barefoot Friars, and Spanish Muslims: Reflections on Medieval Economic and Religious History, a Review Article," *Comparative Studies in Society and History* 24 (1982): 153-163; infra, note 28 to chapter 7.

On Burns' life and work cf. *Directory of American Scholars* 1 (1982): 101; *Repertoire International des Medievistes* (1979), 104, no. 731.

Enrico Cerulli, *Il 'Libro della Scala' e la Questione delle Fonte Arabo Spagnole della Divina Commedia* (Vatican City: Biblioteca Apostolica Vaticana, 1949); *Nuove Richerche sul 'Libro della Scala' e la Conoscenza dell'Islam in Occidente* (Vatican City: Biblioteca Apostolica Vaticana, 1972);

Edward P. Colbert, infra, note 30;

Norman Daniel, *Islam and the West: The Making of an Image* (Edinburgh: Edinburgh University Press, 1960); *Islam, Europe and Empire* (Edinburgh: Edinburgh University Press, 1966); *The Arabs and Mediaeval Europe* (1st ed.; London and Beirut: Longman and Librairie du Liban, 1975; 2nd ed., 1979); *Cultural Barrier: Problems in the Exchange of Ideas* (Edinburgh: Edinburgh University Press, 1975); *Heroes and Saracens: A Reinterpretation of the Chansons of Geste* (Edinburgh: Edinburgh University Press, 1983).

Dario Cabanelas Rodriguez, *Juan de Segovia y el Problema Islamica* (Madrid: Universidad de Madrid, Facultad de Filosofia y Letras, 1952);

Johann Fueck, *Die Arabischen Studien in Europa bis in den Anfang des 20, Jahrhunderts* (2nd ed.; Leipzig: Harrassowitz, 1955);

James Kritzeck, infra, note 2;

Aldobrandino Malvezzi, *L'Islamismo e la Cultura Europea: Critica e Storia* (Florence: Sansoni, 1956);

Ugo Monneret de Villard, *Lo Studio dell'Islam in Europa nel XII e nel XIII Secolo* (Vatican City: Biblioteca Apostolica Vaticana, 1944); *Il Libro della Peregrinazione nell Parti d'Oriente di Frate Ricoldo da Montecroce* (Rome: Instituto Storico Santa Sabina, 1948);

James T. Monroe, *Islam and the Arabs in Spanish Scholarship (Sixteenth Century to the Present)* (Leiden: Brill, 1970);

Jose Munyoz Sendino, *La Escala de Mahoma* (Madrid: Ministerio de Asuntos Exteriores: Direccion General de Relaciones Culturales, 1949);

Robert Schwoebel, infra, note 3;

Richard William Southern, *Western Views of Islam in the Middle Ages* (Cambridge: Harvard University Press, 1962);

J. Windrow Sweetman, *Islam and Christian Theology: A Study of the Interpretation of Theological Ideas in the Two Religions*, 3 vols. (London: Lutterworth, 1945–1955);

Jean Jacques Waardenburg, *L'Islam dans le Miroir de l'Occident: Comment Quelques Orientalistes Occidentaux Se Sont Penches sur l'Islam et Se Sont Formes Une Image de Cette Religion* (3rd ed.; Paris and The Hague: Mouton, 1969).

2. Since the completion of his dissertation Kritzeck has been responsible for at least the following books: with Giles Constable, *Petrus Venerabilis (1156–1956): Studies and Texts Commemorating the Eighth Centenary of His Death* (Rome: Herder, 1956); with R. Bayly Winder, *The World of Islam: Studies in Honor of Philip K. Hitti* (London: Macmillan, 1959); *Peter the Venerable and Islam* (Princeton: Princeton University Press, 1964); *Anthology of Islamic Literature* (New York: Holt, Rinehart and Winston, 1964); *Sons of Abraham, Jews, Christians and Moslems* (Baltimore: Helicon, 1965); with William H. Lewis, *Islam in Africa* (New York: Van Nostrand-Reinhold, 1969); *Modern Islamic Literature* (New York: Holt, Rinehart and Winston, 1970).

At present Kritzeck is completing a study of the life and work of Ali ibn Hazm (eleventh century Muslim Spain), the greatest Islamic theologian of medieval Spain, a major Islamic writer against Judaism and Christianity and a father of the modern study of world religions; Kritzeck is also writing a book on Islam in Southeast Asia.

For more information on Kritzeck's life and work, *Directory of American Scholars* 1 (1963): 170–171; 4 (1969): 203; 1 (1974): 353; 1 (1978): 385; *Repertoire International des Medievistes* (1971), 423–424, no. 2358.

3. We may be able to learn a great deal about contemporary relations between the capitalist (and social democratic) West and the communist East by studying medieval relations between the Christian West and the Islamic East. G. Whitmarsh, *New Perspectives in the Teaching of History, A British Commentary on American Developments* (Wilmington, Delaware: Wemyss Foundation, 1965), 11 and note 4, citing a similar view of A.J.P. Taylor. Robert Schwoebel, *The Shadow of the Crescent: The Renaissance*

Image of the Turk (1453–1517) (New York: St. Martin's, 1967), ix; and our review of this book, *The Muslim World* 60 (1970): 180–181.

4. M.C. Diaz y Diaz, *Index Scriptorum Latinorum Medii Aevi Hispanorum* (Salamanca: Consejo Superior de Investigaciones Cientificas y Universidad de Salamanca, 1958), I: 202. The curators of the Latin manuscript collections of Western Europe have called our attention to two twelfth-century manuscripts of the *Dialogi* unlisted by Diaz y Diaz: Bern lll (from Metz) and Dijon 230 (from Citeaux). Infra, chapter 3.

For the manuscripts of *TC*, two articles by Marie-Therese d'Alverny, "Deux Traductions du Coran au Moyen Age," *Archives d'Histoire Doctrinale et Litteraire du Moyen Age* [hereinafter = *AHDLMA*] 16 (1947–1948): 69–131; "Quelques Manuscrits de la 'Collectio Toletana'," in Constable and Kritzeck, eds., *Petrus Venerabilis*, 202–218. A detailed study of the various manuscript traditions of *TC*, though a great *desideratum* because it will help us understand the influence of *TC* upon later generations, has not yet been done, probably because our possession of the autograph manuscript of *TC*, Arsenal 1162, makes a study of the later manuscripts of *TC* unnecessary for a critical edition of its texts.

5. Marcel Devic, "Une Traduction Inedite du Coran," *Journal Asiatique*, 8 serie, 1 (April–June 1883): 343–406 (cf. Kritzeck, *PV*, ix, note 5, and 68, note 70); d'Alverny, *AHDLMA*, XVI: 69–131.

For d'Alverny's bibliography, Etienne Gilson, *History of Christian Philosophy in the Middle Ages* (New York: Random, 1955), index, *s.v.*; *Repertoire des Medievistes d'Europe=Melanges de Science Religieuse* 11 (1954), *Cahier Supplementaire*, 7; *Repertoire des Medievistes Europeens* (1960), 10, no. 23; *Repertoire International des Medievistes* (1965), 16–17, no. 50; ibid. (1971), 17, no. 52; ibid. (1979), 12, no. 100; *International Who's Who* (1982–1983), 27.

6. In the third impression (1966) of *Islam and the West* Daniel updated his bibliography slightly. Cf. the forward, vi–vii, and bibliography no. 3, 432. Cf. also the separate bibliography appended to Daniel's sequel volume, *Islam, Europe and Empire* (1966), 566–594. Daniel's *Arabs and Mediaeval Europe* (1975) has a brief "Bibliographical Note," 356–357; helpful bibliographical footnotes, 328–355; and an index to the scholars cited in those footnotes, 358–361. Kritzeck reviewed Daniel's *Islam and the West*, "Moslem-Christian Understanding in Mediaeval Times," *Comparative Studies in Society and History* 4 (1962): 388–401; we reviewed Daniel's sequel, *Islam, Europe and Empire, The Muslim World* 60 (1970): 182–184.

7. Cf. our "Who Was the 'Monk of France' and When Did He Write? A Note on D.M. Dunlop's 'A Christian Mission to Muslim Spain in the Eleventh Century'," *Al-Andalus* 28 (1963): 249–269. The Dunlop article appeared ibid. 17 (1952): 259–310. Our views on the "Monk of France" were partly anticipated by Jacinto Bosch Vila, "A Proposito de Una Mision Cristiana a la Corte de al-Muqtadir ibn Hud," *Tamuda* 2 (1954): 97–105. Abdel-Magid Turki, "La Lettre du 'Moine de France' a al-Muqtadir Billah, Roi de Saragosse, et le Repose d'al-Bayi Le Faqih Andalou," *Al-Andalus* 31 (1966): 73–153, argues unconvincingly against Brockelmann, Dunlop, Bosch Vila, and the Cutlers that the "Monk of France's" letter is not genuine but was rather written by the Muslim legist who replied to it, al-Baji, who flourished at Saragossa in the 1070s.

8. For the Byzantine and/or Eastern Christian polemic against Islam, "Bibliographie de Armand Abel," in Pierre Salmon, ed., *Melanges d'Islamologie: Volume dedie a la Memoire de Armand Abel par ses Collegues, ses Eleves et ses Amis* (Leiden: Brill, 1974), 270–278; Karl E. Gueterbock, *Der Islam im Lichte der Byzantinischen Polemik* (Berlin: Guttentag, 1912); W. Eichner, "Die Nachrichten ueber den Islam bei den Byzantinern," *Der Islam* 23 (1936): 133–162, 197–244; Hildebrand Beck, *Vorsehung und Vorherbestimmung in der Theologischen Literatur der Byzantiner*, Orientalia Christiana Analecta 114 (Rome: Pontificium Institutum Orientalium Studiorum, 1937), 32–65; Hans-Georg Beck, *Kirche und Theologische Literatur im Byzantinischen Reich* (Munich: Beck, 1959), 337–339 and index *s.v.* "Islam"; Julia Gauss, "Glaubensdiskussion zwischen Ostkirche und Islam im 8–11. Jahrhundert," *Theologische Zeitschrift* 19 (1963): 14–28; Hagop A. Chakmakjian, *Armenian Christology and the Evangelization of Islam* (Leiden: Brill, 1965); John Meyendorff, "Byzantine Views of Islam," *Dumbarton Oaks Papers* 18 (1965): 115–132; Walter Emil Kaegi, Jr., "Initial Byzantine Reactions to the Arab Conquest," *Church History* 38 (1969): 139–149; Speros J. Vryonis, Jr., "Byzantine Attitudes toward Islam during the Late Middle Ages," *Greek, Roman and Byzantine Studies* 12 (1971): 263–286 = pp. 421–436 of his *The Decline of Medieval Hellenism in Asia Minor and the Process of Islamization* [Eleventh through Fifteenth Centuries] (Berkeley: University of California Press, 1971); Daniel Sahas, *John of Damascus on Islam* (Leiden: Brill, 1972); Demetrios Constantelos, "The Moslem Conquests of the Near East as Revealed in the Greek Sources of the Seventh and Eighth Centuries," *Byzantion* 42 (1972): 325–357; four books by Adel Theodore Khoury: *Manuel II Paleologue: Entretiens avec un Musulman* (Paris: Cerf, 1966), *Der Theologische Streit der Byzantiner mit dem Islam* (Paderborn: Schoeningh, 1969), *Les Theologiens Byzantins et l'Islam, Textes et Auteurs* (VIIIe–XIIIe Siecles) (Louvain and Paris: Nauwelaerts, 1969), *Polemique Byzantine contre l'Islam* (VIIIe–XIIIe Siecles) (Leiden: Brill, 1972); "Apologetique Byzantine contre l'Islam (VIIIe—XIIIe Siecle)," *Proche Orient Chretien* 29 (1979): 242–300; J. Moorhead, "The Monophysite Response to the Arab Invasions," *Byzantion* 51 (1981); 579–591.

9. Infra, notes 43–45 and accompanying text to chapter 4.

10. The fact that Islamic law imposed the death penalty upon Christian missionaries is relevant. However, the letter of the law was not always enforced (especially for the first offense). Furthermore, northeast European pagans also killed Christian missionaries at times, and the threat of death would not always have been sufficient to quench missionary zeal.

A more important factor helping explain why the medieval Christian mission to the Muslims was so late in developing may well be ethnolinguistic. Northern European pagans were ethnolinguistically Indo-European, as were the Christian missionaries (whether Byzantine or Latin). By contrast, the Muslims were ethnolinguistically Semitic. Thus, the northern European pagans were ethnolinguistic cousins of the Christian missionaries; the Muslims were not. The Christian missionaries preferred to work among their own ethnolinguistic kind first. Only after converting the northern European pagans (circa 1000) could the Christian missionaries think seriously about the Muslims.

11. Neither does Norman Daniel's *Islam and the West*. Daniel's sequel volume *Islam, Europe and Empire*, dealing primarily with the period after 1800, does not pro-

vide the necessary corrective. Both books are organized topically rather than chronologically. Daniel's most recent book, *The Arabs and Mediaeval Europe*, follows the chronological principle.

12. Cf. the data collected in our article "The First Crusade and the Idea of 'Conversion'," *The Muslim World* 58 (1968): 57-71, 155-164; with the reply thereto by James Calvin Waltz, "Historical Perspectives on Early 'Missions' to Muslims: A Response to Allan Cutler," ibid. 61 (1971): 170-186. Our article of 1968 served as the "springboard" for John France, "The First Crusade and Islam," ibid. 67 (1977): 247-257 (cf. especially the remarks of the journal's editor, p. 246, and the article itself, p. 247 and notes 1, 3 and 4). By contrast, H. Dajani-Shaked, "Displacement of the Palestinians during the Crusades," *The Muslim World* 68 (1978): 157-175, emphasizes the flight rather than the conversion of the Muslims of the Middle East during the Crusader Period.

13. We hope to demonstrate this in a forthcoming book tentatively entitled *St. Francis of Assisi and Islam: Revisionary Studies in the Early Franciscan Mission to the Muslims*. Basetti-Sani (supra, note 8 to chapter 1) holds that St. Francis was opposed to the Crusades *per se* and attempted unsuccessfully to persuade the papacy to end them. We disagree. St. Francis opposed only the view that the successful Crusade should be followed by the massacre, expulsion, or exploitation of the conquered Muslims. He favored the view that the successful Crusade should be followed by the conversion of the Muslims.

14. (Philadephia: Jewish Publication Society of America, 1956) IV: 122, 301-302, note 44; V: 116, 341, note 41. Kritzeck, *PV*, 26, note 81, disapprovingly cites the *Geschichte der Juden* by the great nineteenth century Jewish historian, Heinrich Graetz, with whom Baron agrees on this question. Cf. also now Yvonne Friedman, "An Anatomy of Anti-Semitism: Peter the Venerable's Letter to Louis VII, King of France (1146)," *Bar-Ilan Studies in History* 1978: 87-102.

15. John Robert Sommerfeldt, "The Epistemological Value of Mysticism in the Thought of Bernard of Clairvaux," in Sommerfeldt, ed., *Studies in Medieval Culture* (Kalamazoo: Western Michigan University Press for The Medieval Institute, 1964) I: 48-58.

16. Thomas W. Arnold, *The Preaching of Islam: A History of the Propagation of the Muslim Faith* (1st ed.; Westminster: Constable, 1896; 2nd ed.; New York: Scribner's, 1913; 3rd ed. by R.A. Nicholson; London: Luzac, 1935; 4th ed. by J.A. Saiyid; Lahore: Shirkat-i-Qualam, 1956), still seems to be the best work available on this question.

Cf. also Richard W. Bulliet, *Conversion to Islam in the Medieval Period: An Essay in Quantitative History* (Cambridge, Massachusetts, and London: Harvard University Press, 1979); and, more generally, N. Levtzion, ed., *Conversion to Islam* (New York and London: Holmes and Meier, 1979).

17. For Archbishop John of Seville circa 1140, Joseph F. O'Callaghan, *History of Medieval Spain* (Ithaca and London: Cornell University Press, 1975), 308. For the persecution of the Christians in Muslim Spain by the Almoravides and Almohades circa 1100-1150, Carl Brockelmann, *History of the Islamic Peoples*, trans. Joel Carmichael and Moshe Perlmann (New York: Capricorn, 1960), 206; Philip K. Hitti, *History of the Arabs* (8th ed.; London and New York: Macmillan and St. Martin's

1963), 544; R. Hitchcock, "Muslim Spain (711–1492)," in P.E. Russell, *Spain: A Companion to Spanish Studies* (London: Methuen, 1973), 56; O'Callaghan, 220–221, 285–286; S.M. Imamuddin, *Political History of Muslim Spain* (2nd. ed.; Dacca: Najmah, 1969), 264.

18. Cf. C. Nedelcou, "Sur la Date de la Naissance de Pierre Alphonsi," *Romania* 35 (1906): 462–463; infra, note 17 to chapter 3. On Petrus Alphonsi's work and travels after his conversion in 1106, Baron, *Social and Religious History*, V: 115–116, 120, 342, note 43, 344–346, notes 49–50; VIII: 173–174, 363–364, note 40; infra, chapter 3 in general.

19. In addition to the bibliography cited in Kritzeck, *PV*, 99, notes 117–118; M.M. Moreno, "E Lecito ai Musulmani Tradurre il Corano?" *Oriente Moderno* 5 (1925): 532–543; Muhammad Shakir, "On the Translation of the Koran into Foreign Languages," *The Muslim World* 16 (1926): 161–165; W.G. Shellabear, "Can a Moslem Translate the Koran?" ibid. 21 (1931): 287–303; J.K. Birge, "Turkish Translations of the Koran," ibid. 28 (1938): 394–399; J. Fueck, "Zur Frage der Koranuebersetzung," *Orientalistische Literaturzeitung* 47 (1944): 165–168; G.M. Meredith-Owens, "Notes on an Old Ottoman Translation of the Kuran," *Oriens* 10 (1957): 258–276; A.L. Tibawi, "Is the Quran Translatable?" *The Muslim World* 52 (1962): 4–16; J.D. Pearson, "Al-Kuran: Translations of the Kur'an," *Ency. of Islam* 5 (1981): 429–432; M.H. Kahn, "A History of Bengali Translations of the Holy Qur'an," *The Muslim World* 72 (1982): 129–136.

20. The style of Ketton's twelfth-century Latin Quran translation should be compared with that of Mark of Toledo's early thirteenth-century Latin Quran translation (as Kritzeck has done, though all too briefly), as well as with the Latin Quran translation of Ludovico Maracci (circa 1698), the great seventeenth-century Italian Islamologist. However, Mark of Toledo's translation still remains in manuscript, primarily Paris Bibliotheque Nationale Latin 14503 (fourteenth century). d'Alverny, *AHDLMA*, XVI: 120. At pp. 116–117 of this same article d'Alverny presents side by side seven Christian versions of the first Sura (chapter) of the Quran, the *Fatiha* (Opening), considered "the Lord's Prayer of Islam." These versions are Ketton's free Latin translation; plus the more literal Latin translations of the Annotator (= Peter of Toledo = Petrus Alphonsi?), Mark of Toledo, and Guillaume Postel (sixteenth century); plus the early seventeenth-century literal French translation by Andre du Ryer; plus two late-seventeenth-century literal Latin translations by Maracci.

21. Cf. J. Munyoz-Sendino, "La Apologia del Cristianismo de al-Kindi," *Miscelanea Comillas* 11–12 (1949): 375. In our article "The Ninth Century Spanish Martyrs' Movement and the Origins of Western Christian Missions to the Muslims," *The Muslim World* 55 (1965): 326–328 and notes 21–37, we have placed al-Kindi's *Risalah*, as traditionally dated, in the context of whatever preliminary evidence we had been able to collect on the relatively unexplored topic of Middle Eastern and Byzantine Christian interest in the conversion of the Muslims circa 750 to 900.

22. On the still unpublished *Contrarietas*, an anti-Islamic polemic originally written in Arabic (but apparently preserved only in Mark of Toledo's early thirteenth-century Latin translation, of which only one postmedieval manuscript would seem to be extant) purportedly by a convert from Islam, d'Alverny, "La Connaissance de l'Islam en Occident du IXe au Milieu XIIe Siecle," in *L'Occidente e l'Islam nell'Alto*

Medioevo (Spoleto: Centro Italiano di Studi sull'Alto Medioevo, 1965), II: 591–592 and notes 27–28; her earlier articles, AHDLMA, XVI: 125–127, and (with G. Vajda) "Marc de Tolede, Traducteur d'Ibn Tumart," Al-Andalus 16 (1951): 124–131; Cerulli, Il 'Libro della Scala', 354, note 1, and 406; Daniel, Islam and the West, index, s.v.; our article, Al-Andalus, XXVIII: 265 and note 75. For the influence of al-Kindi's Risalah upon the ninth-century Spanish martyrs' movement, the article by Franke cited infra, note 30.

23. Southern, Western Views, 24–25; our article, The Muslim World, LV: 334–338 and notes 61–94.

24. On Pope Gregory VII and Islam, our article, Al-Andalus, XXVIII: 261–269; also Horace Kinder Mann, Lives of the Popes in the Middle Ages (2nd ed.; London and St. Louis: Kegan Paul, Trench, Trubner and Herder, 1925), VII: 193–195; Daniel, Islam and the West, 27, 43, 114, 333, note 103, 347, note 43, 349, note 16; Basetti-Sani, Per Un Dialogo Christiano-Musulmano, 83–84; Andre d'Algerny and Guglielmo Narducci, "St. Gregorei VII et l'Islam," En Terre d'Islam 14(1939): 147–154; Christian Courtois, "Gregoire VII et l'Afrique du Nord," Revue Historique 195 (1945): 97–226; Robert S. Lopez, "Le Facteur Economique dans la Politique Africaine des Papes," ibid. 197 (1947): 178–188.

In our forthcoming book St. Francis of Assisi and Islam we argue that St. Francis studied the Latin translation of the Quran (by Ketton and/or Marc of Toledo), and perhaps even the Arabic original thereof, in preparation for his mission to the Muslims of Egypt during the Fifth Crusade in 1219. Meanwhile, Odulphus van der Vat, Die Anfaenge der Franziskanermissionen und Ihre Weiterentwicklung im Nahen Orient und in den Mohammedanischen Laendern Waehrend des 13. Jahrhunderts (Werl in Westfallen: Franziskus Druckerei, 1934), 58, note 78. On St. Francis and Islam, also the work of Basetti-Sani, supra, note 8 to chapter 1.

25. The relevent Abelardian text is Dialogus inter Philosophum [Musulmanum?], Judaeum et Christianum, ed. Rudolf Thomas (Stuttgart and Bad Cannstatt: Frommann, 1970); Synan had prepared an English translation (supra, note 5 to chapter 1); cf. now Peter Abelard, Dialogue of a Philosopher with a Jew and a Christian, trans. P.J. Payer (Toronto: Pontifical Institute of Mediaeval Studies, 1979).

For Abelard and the Jews, articles on Abelard by A.H. Newman, Jewish Ency. 1 (1901): 51, N. S. Arnoff, Universal Jewish Ency. 1 (1939): 18; Hans Liebeschutz, Ency. Judaica 2 (1971): 59–60, and his "The Significance of Judaism in Peter Abelard's Dialogus," Journal of Jewish Studies 12:1–2 (1961): 1–18; Baron, Social and Religious History, VI: 272–273, 462–463, note 51; VIII: 67, 310–311, note 21; Robert Chazan, Medieval Jewry in Northern France: A Political and Social History (Baltimore: Johns Hopkins, 1973), 33, 39, 52, 87; M. Kurdzialek, "Beurteilung der Philosophie im Dialogus inter Philosophum, Iudaeum et Christianum," in E.M. Buytaert, ed., Peter Abelard: Proceedings of the International Conference, Louvain, May 10–12, 1971 (Louvain and The Hague: Nijhoff, 1974), 85–98.

For Abelard and Islam, d'Alverny, in L'Occidente e l'Islam, II: 599 and note 48, plus the discussion thereof (comments of Jean Leclercq), ibid., 791–793; Rene Roques, "La Methode du Cur Deus Homo de St. Anselme de Cantorbery," in his Structures Theologiques de la "Gnose" a Richard de Saint-Victor: Essais et Analyses Critiques (Paris: Presses Universitaires de France, 1962), 260–264; Edouard Jeauneau, La Philosophie

Medievale (1st ed.; Paris: Presses Universitaires de France, 1963), 62–63; Jean Jolivet, "Abelard et la Philosophie (Occident et Islam au XIIe Siecle)," *Revue de l'Histoire des Religions* 164:2 (October–December 1963), 181–189; Kritzeck, "De l'Influence de Pierre Abelard sur Pierre le Venerable dans ses Oeuvres sur l'Islam," a manuscript copy of which Kritzeck was kind enough to furnish us with, the published version appearing in *Pierre Abelard-Pierre le Venerable: Les Courants Philosophiques, Litteraires et Artistiques en Occident au Milieu de XIIe Siecle: Abbaye de Cluny 2 au 9 Juillet 1972* (Paris: Editions du Centre National de la Recherche Scientifique, 1975), 205–214; George Makdisi, "The Scholastic Method in Medieval Education: An Inquiry into Its Origins in Law and Theology, *Speculum* 49 (1974): 640–661.

26. Daniel, *Islam and the West*, 54 (followed by Kritzeck, *PV*, 177): "The plain fact is that the text of Ketton's Quran which Peter claimed to have searched in vain, made clear sense of verses which assert or imply *tahrif*, the corruption of Scripture." Daniel, 54, 335–336, note 24; *PV*, Kritzeck, 177 and notes 87–89.

27. Miguel Asin Palacios, *Abenhazam de Cordoba y su Historia Critica de las Ideas Religiosas* (Madrid: Revista de Archivos, 1927–1932), 5 vols.; I. di Matteo, "Il *Tahrif* od Alterazione della Bibbia secondo i Musulmani," *Bessarione* 38 (1922): 64–111, 223–260, and his "Le Pretese Contraddizioni della Sacra Scrittura secondo Ibn Hazm," ibid. 39 (1923): 77–127; Sweetman, *Islam and Christian Theology*, pt. 2, vol. 1, 178–262; Moshe Perlmann, "Eleventh-Century Andalusian Authors on the Jews of Granada," *Proceedings of the American Academy for Jewish Research* 18 (1948–1949): 269–284; Baron, *Social and Religious History*, V: 85, 88, 327, note 4, 330, note 8; Shlomo Pines, "Judaeo-Christian Materials in an Arabic Jewish Treatise," *Proceedings of the American Academy for Jewish Research* 35 (1967): 213–217. Also in general two articles on Ibn Hazm, C. Van Arendonk, *Ency. of Islam* 2 (1927): 384–386, and R. Arnaldez, ibid. 3 (1971): 790–799. Kritzeck's forthcoming book on Ibn Hazm is eagerly awaited.

28. Migne, *Patrologia Latina* [hereinafter=MPL], CLVII: 601, lines 13–16.

29. Infra, chapters 4 and 6 of this book.

30. On Felix, Speraindeo, Eulogius, Alvarus, and Petrus Alphonsi, d'Alverny, in *L'Occidente e l'Islam*, II, 586–595. On the ninth-century Spanish martyrs' movement, our article, *The Muslim World*, LV: 321–339; F.R. Franke, "Die Freiwilligen Maertyrer von Cordova und das Verhaeltnis der Mozaraber zum Islam," *Gesammelte Aufsaetze zur Kulturgeschichte Spaniens (Spanische Forschungen der Goerresgesellschaft)* 13 (1958): 1–170; Edward P. Colbert, *The Martyrs of Cordoba (850–859): A Study of the Sources* (Washington, D.C.: Catholic University of America Press, 1962); James Calvin Waltz, "The Significance of the Voluntary Martyrs of Ninth-Century Cordoba," *The Muslim World* 60 (1970): 143–159, 226–236, arguing against our interpretation of this movement published in the same journal, 1965; Daniel, *Arabs and Mediaeval Europe*, 23–48; Miguel Jose Hagerty, *Los Cuervos de San Vicente: Escatologia Mozarabe* (Madrid: Editora Nacional, 1978); infra, notes 29 to chapter 7 and 84 to chapter 8.

31. Daniel, *Islam and the West*, 231. Also of general relevance here is Gregory G. Guzman, "The Encyclopedist Vincent of Beauvais and His Mongol Extracts from John of Piano Carpini and Simon of St. Quentin," *Speculum* 49 (1974): 287–307.

32. Daniel, *Islam and the West*, 233.

33. Gilson, *History of Christian Philosophy in the Middle Ages*, 172–178, 635–636, notes 124–134; Daniel, *Islam and the West*, 167, 189, 204; d'Alverny, *Alain de Lille: Textes Inedits, avec une Introduction sur sa Vie et ses Oeuvres* (Paris: Vrin, 1965), 68–69, 156–162; Guy Raynaud de Lage, *Alain de Lille: Poete du XII Siecle* (Montreal: Universite de Montreal Institut d'Etudes Medievales, 1951), 28–31. Cf. also two recent articles, P.G. Walsh, "Alan of Lille as a Renaissance Figure," and Michael Wilks, "Alan of Lille and the New Man," in Derek Baker, ed., *Renaissance and Renewal in Christian History* (Oxford: Blackwell, 1977), 117–135 and 137–157 respectively.

Amos Funkenstein, "Ha-T'murot B'Vikuah Ha-Dat She-Ben Y'hudim L'Notzrim B'Meah Ha-Yud Bet" [The Changes in the Religious Disputations between Jews and Christians during the Twelfth Century], *Zion* 33:3–4 (1968): iii and 126–144, suggests that Alan of Lille attempted to demonstrate that the Talmud contains explicit hints at the truth of Christian dogma and in so doing influenced Raymond Martin in thirteenth-century Spain and the Christian Kabbalists of the Renaissance. Likewise, Christian polemicists attemped to demonstrate that the Quran contains explicit hints at the truth of Christian dogma, Daniel, *Islam and the West*, 166–184, and Baron, *Social and Religious History*, V: 329, note 4.

David Berger, "Gilbert Crispin, Alan of Lille and Jacob Ben Reuben: A Study in the Transmission of Medieval Polemic," *Speculum* 49 (1974): 34–47, marshals the evidence in favor of the conclusion that Alan of Lille's anti-Jewish polemic relies, verbatim in many places, on Gilbert Crispin's anti-Jewish polemic written under the influence of St. Anselm in England during the 1090s.

34. John Beckwith, *Early Medieval Art* (New York: Praeger, 1964), 202, 204.

35. Kritzeck, *PV*, 12.

36. Beckwith, *Early Medieval Art*, 215; infra, note 42.

37. Kritzeck, *PV*, 4, note 4.

38. A.J. Denomy, "Concerning the Accessibility of Arabic Influences to the Earliest Provencal Troubadours," *Mediaeval Studies* 15 (1953): 148–149 and notes 10, 13–14; relying upon Emile Male, *Art et Artistes du Moyen Age* (2nd ed.; Paris: Colin, 1928), 41–44, 46, and upon Joan Evans, *Romanesque Architecture of the Order of Cluny* (Cambridge: Cambridge University Press, 1938), 125.

39. Beckwith, *Early Medieval Art*, 165.

40. Ibid., 206–207.

41. Ibid., 207. Beckwith's footnote at this point, 250, note 80, is to his own article, "The Influence of Islamic Art on Western Medieval Art," *Middle East Forum* 36 (1960): 25–26. Beckwith, *Early Medieval Art*, 251, note 84, also cites Meyer Schapiro, "The Romanesque Sculpture of Moissac," *Art Bulletin* 13 (1931): 249ff, 464ff, discussing cultural syncretism in southern France at this time and its influence on sculpture.

On the artistic monuments at Moissac, in addition to Beckwith and Schapiro, H.W. and D.J. Janson, *History of Art* (Englewood Cliffs, New Jersey, and New York City: Prentice-Hall and Abrams, 1968), 221–223; Vera and Hellmut Hell, *The Great Pilgrimage of the Middle Ages: The Road to St. James of Compostella*, introduction by Sir Thomas Kendrick, trans. Alisa Jaffa (New York: Potter, 1966), 103–104, 116–119; Henry Kraus, *The Living Theatre of Medieval Art*, foreword by Harry Bober (Bloomington: Indiana University Press, 1967), 183–184.

42. Beckwith, *Early Medieval Art*, 214–215, 218. In his footnote, 252, note 88, Beckwith cites A. Katzenellenbogen, "The Central Tympanum at Vezelay, Its Encyclopaedic Meaning and Its Relation to the First Crusade," *Art Bulletin* 26 (1944): 141ff, and refers the reader as well to an abbreviated version of the Vezelay scene, illustrating the mass of the Pentecost, in the Sacramentary of Saint-Etienne de Limoges = Paris, Bibliotheque Nationale, Latin manuscript no. 9438, fol. 87, published by J. Porcher, *Le Sacramentaire de Saint-Etienne de Limoges* (Paris: Nomis, 1953), plate XII, the sacramentary dating from circa 1100. In his previous footnote, 252, note 87, Beckwith had told us that the famous sculptor Gislebertus, who served his apprenticeship at Cluny, probably worked at Vezelay between 1120 and 1125, and had referred us to D. Grivot and G. Zarnecki, *Gislebertus: Sculptor of Autun* (London: Trianon, 1961).

Cf. also John Block Friedman, *The Monstrous Races in Medieval Art and Thought* (Cambridge, Massachusetts, and London: Harvard University Press, 1981). According to Friedman it is "likely" that Peter the Venerable "contributed to the imagery of the [Vezelay] tympanum." Friedman, 78, 230, note 54. Peter the Venerable was interested in the conversion of the Muslims. Friedman, 65–66, 227, notes 22–23. The cynocephali, or dog-headed people, in the Vezelay tympanum (Friedman, 78–79 and figure 29e, p. 81) are probably Muslims. Cf. Friedman, 67–69.

43. The Jansons, *History of Art*, 222–223. On Vezelay, also V. and H. Hell, *The Great Pilgrimage of the Middle Ages*, 59, 70–71; Kraus, *Living Theatre of Medieval Art*, index, *s.v.*

44. See our "Who Was the 'Monk of France' and When Did He Write?" supra, note 7.

45. Ibid.

46. Kraus, *Living Theatre of Medieval Art*, 35–36.

47. For Peter the Venerable's awareness of the problem of Muslims held in captivity by Christians, see the text between notes 25 and 26 of this chapter. The great importance of the *TC* and Peter the Venerable's interest in the conversion of the Muslims continues to be discussed in the scholarly literature. Thus, Hans E. Keller, "La Conversion de Bramimonde," *Olifant* 1 (1973): 3–22, argues that the concluding episode of the *Chanson de Roland* was strongly influenced by the *TC* and Peter the Venerable's interest in the conversion of the Muslims. In this episode Charlemagne succeeds in converting Bramimonde by persuasion. She is the widow of Marsile, the Muslim king of Saragossa, all of whose Muslim inhabitants Charlemagne is earlier described as conquering and then as forcing into baptism. Likewise, James Calvin Waltz, "Muhammad and the Muslims in St. Thomas Aquinas," *The Muslim World* 66 (1976): 81–95, argues that the *TC* and Peter the Venerable were major influences upon St. Thomas Aquinas' knowledge of Islam.

3. *Petrus Alphonsi (1076–1146) and Peter the Venerable*

* Chapter three goes back ultimately to three papers: the two closely related papers (1) "The Anti-Islamic (the 5th) Chapter of Petrus Alphonsi's *Dialogi* against the Jews (circa 1110 A.D., Spain)," delivered at the fourteenth annual meeting,

Western Branch, American Oriental Society, Los Angeles, April 10, 1965, and (2) "The Legend of Muhammad Contained in the 5th or anti-Islamic Chapter of Petrus Alphonsi's *Dialogi* against the Jews," delivered at the 175th annual meeting, American Oriental Society, Chicago, April 15, 1965, plus (3) "Petrus Alphonsi and the Toletano-Cluniac Corpus," delivered at the 180th annual meeting, American Oriental Society, Baltimore, Maryland, April 15, 1970. We thank the late Walter Fischel for his comments on the Los Angeles paper, both Nabia Abbot and the late Marshall Hodgson for their reactions to the Chicago paper, George F. Hourani for his suggestions after the Baltimore paper. An earlier version of the first quarter of this chapter appeared in *Year Book 1968 of the American Philosophical Society*, 1969, 552-555. With the permission of its editor, George W. Corner, it is reproduced here after further revisions. The research for this chapter was assisted by a grant from the American Philosophical Society, Philadelphia, December 1964. We express our gratitude to the society for its support of our work.

1. Petrus Alphonsi's other work, the *Disciplina Clericalis* (Migne, *Patrologia Latina*, CLVII: 671-706), has long since been available in an excellent twentieth-century edition befitting its importance in the history of medieval belles-lettres. We refer to the critical edition of A. Hilka and W. Soederhjelm (Helsinki: Druckerei der Finnischen Litteraturgesellschaft, 1911), 2 vols. The Hilka-Soederhjelm text, minus its magnificent *apparatus criticus*, was reproduced, along with an Old Castilian translation and a good introduction by A. Gonzalez-Palencia (Madrid-Granada: Consejo Superior de Investigaciones Cientificas, Patronato Menendez y Pelayo-Instituto Miguel Asin, 1948), a testimony to the exacting standards and continuing scholarly validity of the Hilka-Soederhjelm edition.

Cf. also Haim Schwarzbaum, "International Folklore Motifs in Petrus Alphonsi's *Disciplina Clericalis*," *Sefarad* 21 (1961): 267-299; 22 (1962): 17-59, 321-344; and 23 (1963): 54-73; Joseph Ramon Jones and John Esten Keller, *The Scholar's Guide: A Translation of the Twelfth Century Disciplina Clericalis of Pedro Alfonso* (Toronto: Pontifical Institute of Mediaeval Studies, 1969), with helpful introduction by the translators (9-29); Edward D. Montgomery, Jr., *Le Chastoiement d'Un Pere a Son Fils: A Critical Edition* [of the Old French verse version] (Chapel Hill: University of North Carolina Press, 1971); Eberhard Hermes, ed., *The Disciplina Clericalis of Petrus Alphonsi*, trans. P. R. Quarrie (Berkeley and Los Angeles: University of California Press, 1977), with helpful introduction by Hermes (3-99); and the *Disciplina Clericalis* in the most recent Spanish edition and translation, ed. Maria Jesus Lacarra, trans. E. Ducay (Saragossa: Guara, 1980).

2. British Museum, *General Catalogue of Printed Books* 3 (1968): 564; 128 (1962): 93; Bibliotheque Nationale, *Catalogue General des Livres Imprimes: Auteurs* 80 (1925): 462-464.

Cf. now Barbara P. Hurwitz, *Fidei Causa et Tui Amore: The Role of Petrus Alphonsi's Dialogues in the History of Jewish-Christian Debate* (Dissertation; New Haven, Connecticut: Yale University, 1983), 260 pp. The author sent us a copy of her important dissertation in October 1983. Ms. Hurwitz hopes to revise the dissertation and complete an English translation of the *Dialogi* for publication. We wish her every success.

3. For the influence of Petrus Alphonsi's *Dialogi* upon anti-Judaic polemic in twelfth-century England (Bartholomew of Exeter and Peter of Cornwall), Richard

William Hunt, "The Disputation of Peter of Cornwall against Symon the Jew," in Hunt et al., eds., *Studies in Medieval History Presented to Frederick Maurice Powicke* (Oxford: Clarendon, 1948), 143–156, especially 147, note 1. For the influence of the *Dialogi* in twelfth-century France (Peter the Venerable), Baron, *Social and Religious History*, V: 115–116; Kritzeck, *Peter the Venerable and Islam*, 25–27, especially 27, note 83; Joel Rembaum, "The Influence of *Sefer Nestor Hakomer* on Medieval Jewish Polemics," *Proceedings of the American Academy for Jewish Research* 45 (1978): 157, note 5. For the influence of the *Dialogi* in twelfth-century Italy (Joachim of Flora), Morton W. Bloomfield, "Joachim of Flora: A Critical Survey of His Canon, Teachings, Sources, Biography and Influence," *Traditio* 13 (1957): 278, note 121; Yitzhak Baer, *History of the Jews in Christian Spain*, trans. Louis Schoffman (Philadelphia: Jewish Publication Society of America, 1961), I: 438, note 25; Beatrice Hirsch-Reich, "Joachim von Fiore und das Judentum," in Paul Wilpert and Willehad Eckert, eds., *Judentum im Mittelalter: Beitraege zum Christlich-Juedischen Gespraech*, Miscellanea Mediaevalia 4 (Berlin: de Gruyter, 1966), 228–263, especially 228–236.

Cf. Peter Browe, *Die Judenmission im Mittelalter und die Paepste* (Rome: Herder, 1942), pp. 101–103, for a list of the most important Christian anti-Judaic polemics circa 1000–1250. We have already discussed the influence of Petrus Alphonsi's *Dialogi* upon two of the writers in this list, Peter the Venerable and Joachim of Flora. Browe himself states that the *Dialogi* influenced Vincent of Beauvais, the last mentioned in the list. In view of the *Dialogi*'s proven influence in England (Bartholomew of Exeter and Peter of Cornwall), France (Peter the Venerable and Vincent of Beauvais), and Italy (Joachim of Flora), it is highly possible that they also influenced the other Christian anti-Jewish writers in this list, especially the French: Guibert of Nogent, Hildebert of Lavardin, pseudo William of Champeaux, Abelard, Walter of Chatillon, Richard of St. Victor, Alan of Lille, Adam the Cistercian, Peter of Blois, and William of Bourges, though these writers undoubtedly were also influenced by the anti-Judaic polemic of St. Anselm's English disciple Gilbert Crispin written in the 1090s.

Did Petrus Alphonsi's *Dialogi* exert any influence on the Christian Hebraists of the twelfth-century Victorine school, Hugh of St. Victor circa 1125–1140, Hugh's disciple Andrew of St. Victor circa 1150, and Andrew's English disciple Herbert of Bosham circa 1175? On these Christian Hebraists, Raphael Loewe, "Hebraists, Christian," *Ency. Judaica* 8 (1971): 11–13; Baron, *Social and Religious History*, VI: 272–273. Charles Homer Haskins, *Studies in Mediaeval Culture* (Oxford: Clarendon, 1929), 78, links Petrus Alphonsi's *Disciplina Clericalis* with Hugh of St. Victor. Perhaps Hugh also knew Petrus Alphonsi's *Dialogi*.

Did Petrus Alphonsi influence Abelard's interest in Jews and Muslims (perhaps also the interest in the Hebrew language of the Abelard student who wrote *Ysagoge in Theologiam* circa 1150; Baron, VI: 272–273)? Kritzeck considers this a possibility worth further study, in his article that appeared in *Pierre Abelard-Pierre le Venerable*, 208 and n.18; supra, note 25 to chapter 2.

Did Petrus Alphonsi influence those twelfth-century Cistercians especially interested in the Jewish question and/or Hebraic Studies, *e.g.*, Stephen Harding (died 1134), Nicholas Manjacoria (Rome circa 1150), and St. Bernard of Clairvaux? For their interest in Jews and/or Hebrew, Monneret de Villard, *Lo Studio dell'Islam in Europa nel XII e nel XIII Secolo*, 17; Baron, VI: 273; Loewe, *Ency. Judaica*, VIII: 37,

45; David Berger, "The Attitude of St. Bernard of Clairvaux Toward the Jews," *Proceedings of the American Academy for Jewish Research* 40 (1972): 89–108. Did Petrus Alphonsi visit both Stephen Harding and St. Bernard at Citeaux in the 1110s?

4. Infra, chapter 7.

For the influence of Petrus Alphonsi's *Dialogi* upon the Christian-Jewish dialogue in the Iberian peninsula into the Later Middle Ages, Diaz y Diaz, *Index Scriptorum Latinorum Medii Aevi Hispanorum*, I: 202, no. 893; M. Martins, "A Polemica Religiosa nalguns Codices de Alcobaca," *Broteria* 42 (1946): 241–250; Francisco Cantera Burgos, *El Tratado "Contra Caecitatem Iudaeorum" de Fray Bernardo Oliver* (Madrid and Barcelona: Consejo Superior de Investigaciones Cientificas, Instituto "Arias Montano," 1965), 49–50; J.J. Ainaud de Lesarte, "Una Version Catalana Desconocida de los *Dialogi* de Pedro Alfonso," *Sefarad* 3 (1943): 356–376; Antonio Pacios Lopez, *La Disputa de Tortosa* (Madrid and Barcelona: Consejo Superior de Investigaciones Cientificas, Instituto "Arias Montano," 1957), I: 25–30, 41, 88, 195–196, 242–243, 248–252, 262, 265, 293, 297, 299, 305–309; Netanyahu, *Marranos*, 132; Federico Perez Castro, *El Manuscrito Apologetico de Alfonso de Zamora* (Madrid and Barcelona: Consejo Superior de Investigaciones Cientificas, Instituto "Arias Montano," 1950), xcvii; Nicholas Antonio and J. Labouderie, cited in *MPL*, CLVII: 529–531; Soederhjelm, "Bemerkungen zur *Disciplina Clericalis* und ihren Franzoesischen Bearbeitungen," *Neuphilologische Mitteilungen* 12 (1910): 52 and note 3; infra, note 38 to chapter 7.

5. Supra, note 4 to chapter 2.

6. For Petrus Alphonsi's contribution to twelfth-century science, Baron, *Social and Religious History*, VIII: 173–174, 363–364, note 40; Jones and Keller, *Scholar's Guide*, 13–16; Gonzalez Palencia, *Pedro Alfonso: Disciplina Clericalis*, ix–xiv; all three relying upon Jose-Maria Millas Vallicrosa, "Avodato Shel Mosheh S'fardi (Petrus Alfonsus) Al Hohmat Ha-T'hunah" [Moses the Spaniard's (Petrus Alphonsi's) Work in the Field of Astronomy], *Tarbitz* 9 (October 1937): 55–64; his "La Aportacion Astronomica de Pedro Alfonso," *Sefarad* 3 (1943): 65–105, partly reprinted in Millas-Vallicrosa's *Estudios sobre Historia de la Ciencia Espanyola* (Barcelona: Consejo Superior de Investigaciones Cientificas, 1949), 197–218; his "La Corriente de las Traducciones Cientificas de Origen Oriental hasta Fines del Siglo XIII," *Journal of World History* 2 (1954): 411–413. Cf. also Francisco Vera, *Los Judios Espanyoles y su Contribucion a las Ciencias Exactas* (Buenos Aires: Fundacion para el Fomento de la Cultura Hebrea, 1948), 60–65; George Sarton, *Introduction to the History of Science* (Baltimore: Williams and Wilkins for the Carnegie Institution, 1931), II: 15, 40, 118, 121, 124, 130, 199–200, 210, 595, 960; Charles Homer Haskins, *Studies in the History of Mediaeval Science* (Cambridge: Harvard University Press, 1924), 10, 18, 22–24, 35, 113, 115–119; Lynn Thorndike, *History of Magic and Experimental Science during the First Thirteen Centuries of our Era* (New York: Macmillan, 1929), II: 66–73, 650, 777–778; Lynn Thorndike and Pearl Kibre, *Catalogue of Incipits of Mediaeval Scientific Writings in Latin* (2nd ed.; Cambridge: Mediaeval Academy of America, 1963), 590, 769, 963, 1159, 1604; A.C. Crombie, *Robert Grosseteste and the Origins of Experimental Science 1100-1700* (Oxford: Clarendon, 1953), 19, note 8; G. Beaujouan, "La Science dans l'Occident Medieval Chretien," in Rene Taton, ed., *Histoire Generale des Sciences* (Paris: Presses Universitaires de France, 1957), I: 528; Hermes, *Disciplina Clericalis*, 40, 67-80.

7. The published catalogues are utilized by Diaz y Diaz, *Index Scriptorum Latinorum*

Medii Aevi Hispanorum, 2 vols., and listed in Paul O. Kristeller, *Latin Manuscript Books before 1600: A List of the Printed Catalogues and Unpublished Inventories of Extant Collections* (3rd ed.; New York: Fordham University Press, 1965).

8. The most detailed scholarly communication we received from the curators of the European Latin manuscript collections was from Mariano Santamaria, Canonigo Archivero of Santo Domingo de la Calzada, and we offer him sincerest thanks. In his letter of May 9, 1968, Santamaria made at least four points worthy of consideration, though not necessarily of acceptance. (1) We cannot be certain that Petrus Alphonsi was *born* in Huesca. All the introduction to the Dialogi (*MPL*, CLVII: 537:B) says is that he was baptized in Huesca. His place of baptism need not have been his place of birth. (2) The reason Petrus Alphonsi began his life of wandering was that, after he converted to Christianity in 1106 and wrote his *Dialogi* shortly thereafter, the Jews of Aragon were so incensed against him that they tried to kill him. (3) Though Petrus Alphonsi wrote his anti-Judaic polemic in dialogue form, he never actually called it *Dialogi*. (4) Though many claim that the twelfth-century Santo Domingo de la Calzada manuscript is the actual autograph of the *Dialogi*, this is not really true. It is close to the autograph but not the autograph itself.

9. Blumenkranz advised us about his procedure in a letter of May 6, 1966. Before publishing the text of Crispin's *Disputatio* in 1956, he earlier published an analysis of the manuscript traditions in "La *Disputatio Judei cum Christiano* de Gilbert Crispin, Abbe de Westminster," *Revue du Moyen Age Latin* 4 (1948): 237–252.

10. The Christians reconquered Huesca in 1096. If Petrus Alphonsi was born in Huesca circa 1076, as we suggest, he would have spent the crucially formative first twenty years of his life in an Arabic-speaking Islamic environment. The Islamicization pressures upon Jews in northeastern Muslim Spain were great because the main Jewish population concentrations were far to the southwest, in Andalusia. Moreover, Huesca, while it had an important Jewish colony at this time, was not the main Jewish center in northeastern Muslim Spain. That was Saragossa. "Saragossa," *Ency. Judaica* 14 (1971): 858–859. Evidence for the extent of Islamicization pressures on the Jews of late eleventh-century Huesca is provided by the correspondence of Basaam ibn Simeon, for which, Haim Zev Hirschberg, "Huesca," *Ency. Judaica* 8 (1971): 1058; as well as by the preference for Islam over Christianity expressed by Moyses, Petrus Alphonsi's Huescan Jewish alter ego, in the fifth, or anti-Islamic, chapter of the *Dialogi*, for which *MPL*, CLVII: 597:B–C; 602:A.

According to Soederhjelm, *Neuphilologische Mitteilungen*, XII: 51–52, Petrus Alphonsi's *Disciplina Clericalis* could have been written as late as 1114. But Alphonsi tells us in the *Prologus* to the *Disciplina* (Hilka-Soederhjelm edition of the Latin text, I: 1, lines 10–11 = Jones and Keller's English translation, 33, lines 16–18) that he wrote the *Disciplina* in Arabic, then translated it into Latin. Likewise, in his astronomical treatise of circa 1115 (preserved in MS 283, Corpus Christi College, Oxford; Haskins, *Studies in Mediaeval Science*, 117), Petrus Alphonsi calls himself *translatorque huius libri*, which would seem to mean that he wrote the book first in Arabic, then translated it into Latin. Finally, Petrus Alphonsi's important astronomical/astrological treatise, *De Dracone*, circa 1120, bears the following Latin title: *Sententia Petri Ebrei cognomento Anphus de Dracone quam Dominus Walcerus Prior Malvernensis Ecclesie in Latinam Transtulit Linguam* (Haskins, *Studies in Mediaeval Science*, 116). This would seem to indicate that Petrus Alphonsi wrote the *De Dracone* in Arabic and Walcher of Malvern translated it into Latin. Thus, from three of Petrus Alphonsi's treatises, written in the 1110s, we have evidence that Alphonsi felt more at home in Arabic than Latin as late as 1120, almost twenty-five years after Huesca was reconquered by the Christians in 1096.

For Petrus Alphonsi's Jewish knowledge, Josef Oesterreicher, "Die Gespraeche des Petrus Alfonsi und ihre Haggadischen Bestandteile," *Jahres-Bericht der Deutschen Landes-Oberrealschule in Goeding* 5 (1903): 3–40; Arthur Lukyn Williams, *Adversus Judaeos: A Bird's Eye View of Christian Apologiae until the Renaissance* (Cambridge: Cambridge University Press, 1935), 233–240; Saul Lieberman, *Shkiin: D'varim Ahadim al Aggadot* etc. [A Few Comments on Forgotten Jewish Legends etc.] (Jerusalem: Bamberger and Wahrmann, 1939), 19—20, 27-42; Gerson Cohen, "The Story of the Four Captives," *Proceedings of the American Academy for Jewish Research* 29 (1960-1961): 79-80; Funkenstein, *Zion*, XXXIII: 3-4, 133-137; Funkenstein, "Basic Types of Christian Anti-Jewish Polemics in the Later Middle Ages," *Viator* 2 (1971): 378-379; H.M. Merhavya, *Ha-Talmud BiR'i Ha-Natzrut: Ha-Yahas L'Safrut Yisrael She'l'ahar Ha-Mikra Ba-Olam Ha-Notzri Bime-Ha-Benayyim (500-1248)* [The Talmud as Reflected in Christianity: The Medieval Christian World's Attitude toward Post-Biblical Jewish Literature (500-1248)] (Jerusalem: Bialik Institute, 1970), 93-127; M. Kniewasser, "Die Anti-juedische Polemik des Petrus Alphonsi (getauft 1106) und des Abtes Petrus Venerabilis von Cluny (+ 1156)," *Kairos*, n.s. 22 (1980): 34-76; B. Septimus, "Petrus Alphonsi on the Cult at Mecca," *Speculum* 56 (1981): 517-533; Jeremy Cohen, *The Friars and the Jews: The Evolution of Medieval Anti-Judaism* (Ithaca: Cornell University Press, 1982), 27-32; Hurwitz, *Fidei Causa*, passim.

11. Supra, note 27 to chapter 2.

12. Gerson Cohen, *Book of Tradition (Sefer Ha-Qabbalah) By Abraham Ibn Daud* (Philadelphia: Jewish Publication Society of America, 1967), xliv-xlv and xlv, notes 5–6. Cf. Cohen, *Book of Tradition*, xlvi-xlix, for a discussion of the Karaite challenge to Rabbanite Judaism in Spain circa 850–1300. Circa 1050 the Karaite movement entered a period of revival in Castile under Ibn al-Taras and his wife. However, circa 1090 Cidellus, the Jewish physician to King Alfonso VI of Castile, drove most of the Karaites out of the kingdom. Some may have fled to northeastern Spain, for the Rabbanite scholar, Judah ibn Barzilai of Barcelona, knew their ideas in the early twelfth-century. Cohen, *Book of Tradition*, xlviii and note 18. There was a Karaite community in Muslim Saragossa, only forty miles south of Huesca, in the eleventh century. "Saragossa," *Ency. Judaica*, XIV, 859. Cf. also E. Ashtor, *Jews of Moslem Spain*, trans A. and J.M. Klein (Philadelphia: Jewish Publication Society of America, 1979), II: 273; Septimus, *Speculum*, LVI: 529-530 and notes 54-56.

13. D'Alverny, *Occidente e l'Islam*, II: 594, revising Daniel, *Islam and the West*, 12. On the Risalah, d'Alverny, II: 592–593; Kritzeck, *Peter the Venerable and Islam*, 31–35, 101–107; supra, notes 21–22 to chapter 2.

14. Supra, note 22 to chapter 2.

15. "Samuel Ha-Nagid," *Ency. Judaica* 14 (1971): 817; Baron, *Social and Religious History*, V: 95, 333–334, note 19; Perlmann, *Proceedings of the American Academy for Jewish Research*, XVIII, 280–284; E. Garcia-Gomez, "Polemica Religiosa entre Ibn Hazm e Ibn al-Nagrila," *Al-Andalus* 4 (1936): 1–28.

16. George Alexander Kohut, "Alfonsi, Petrus," *Jewish Ency.* 1 (1901): 377, with the mistaken birth dates, cites the view of Moritz Steinschneider, the great nine-teenth-century authority on medieval intellectual relations between Christians, Muslims, and Jews (for Steinschneider's prodigious accomplishments, Alexander Marx, *Essays in Jewish Biography* [Philadelphia: Jewish Publication Society of America, 1947], 112-184), that Petrus Alphonsi's *Dialogi* "fully merits the oblivion into which it has fallen." Cf. Kohut's references to six of Steinschneider's many valuable works that discuss Petrus Alphonsi. Though Steinschneider was among the first to suggest that Petrus Alphonsi contributed to medieval science as well as theology and belles lettres, his bias against Alphonsi's *Dialogi* may have discouraged scholarly research on Alphonsi's life and work.

17. Nedelcou, *Romania*, XXV: 462-463; Soederhjelm, *Neuphilologische Mit-teilungen*, XII: 50-51. Both Nedelcou in 1906 and Soederhjelm in 1910 corrected the mistaken notion that Petrus Alphonsi was born in 1062. Nevertheless, this same mistaken date was repeated by P. Fournier, "Alphonse, Pierre," *Dictionnaire d'Histoire et de Geographie Ecclesiastiques* 2 (1914): 743; Haskins, *Studies in the History of Mediaeval Science*, 118; Thorndike, *Magic and Experimental Science*, II: 69; Sarton, *Introduction to the History of Science*, II: 199; Williams, *Adversus Judaeos*, 233; Gonzalez Palencia, *Pedro Alphonso: Disciplina Clericalis*, vii; Baron, *Social and Religious History*, V: 115; J. Vincke, "Petrus Alphonsi," *Lexikon fuer Theologie und Kirche* 8 (1963): 332; A. O'Malley, "Petrus Alphonsi," *New Cath. Ency.* 11 (1967): 209; Daniel, *Islam and the West*, 7; Jones and Keller, *Scholar's Guide*, 13; Kenneth R. Scholberg, "Petrus Alphonsi," *Ency. Judaica* 13 (1971): 347; supra, note 18 to chapter 2.

18. Baron, *Social and Religious History*, VIII: 173-174, 363-364, note 40. For Petrus Alphonsi's possible visit to France in the 1110s, Baron, VIII: 363, note 40; Thorndike, *Magic and Experimental Science*, II: 70-72; Hermes, *Disciplina Clericalis*, 40, 67-72. In France Alphonsi could have met Abelard and other leading French religious and intellectual figures of the early twelfth-century. Supra, notes 25 to chapter 2 and 3 to this chapter.

19. Millas-Vallicrosa, "Un Nuevo Dato Sobre Pedro Alfonso," *Sefarad* 7 (1947): 136-137; Hermes, *Disciplina Clericalis*, 64.

20. The following medieval personalities, Christian, Muslim, and Jew, lived circa 70 years or more.

CHRISTIAN. (1) Adalbert of Bremen (1000-1072)=72 years; (2) St. Anselm of Canterbury (1033-1109)=76 years; (3) Gilbert La Porree (1075-1154)=79 years; (4) William of Conches (1080-1154)=74 years; (5) Hildegard of Bingen (1098-1179)=81 years; (6) Gerard of Cremona (1114-1187)=73 years; (7) Alan of Lille (1116-1202) = 86 years (confirmed from skeletal evidence; Walsh, in Baker, *Renaissance and Renewal in Christian History*, 119).

MUSLIM (Aguado-Bleye, *Manual de Historia de Espanya*, I: 541, 952-954). (1) Yusuf ibn Abd al Barr (978-1070) = 92 years; (2) Abu Umar Uthman ibn Said of Denia (981-1053) = 72 years; (3) al-Udhri (1003-1085) = 82 years; (4) Abu Bakr ibn al-Arabi (1076-1149) = 73 years; (5) Ibn Sahl al Darir (1096-1175) = 79 years; (6) Ibn Hubaykh (1110-1188) = 78 years; (7) Ibn Rushd (1126-1198) = 72 years; (8) Abul Abas Abas ibn Arrumia (1161-1239) + 78 years.

JEW (Max L. Margolis and Alexander Marx, *History of the Jewish People* [Philadelphia: Jewish Publication Society of America, 1953], 449, 761-766.) (1) Paul de Santa Maria of Burgos (originally Solomon Ha-Levi), the famous convert to Christianity, the Petrus Alphonsi of the early fifteenth century (1352-1435) = 83 years; (2) Isaac Alfasi (1013-1103) = 90 years; (3) Abraham bar Hiyya (1065-1136) = 71 years; (4) Abraham ibn Ezra (1092-1167) = 75 years; (5) Abraham ibn Daud (1110-1180) = 70 years; (6) Maimonides (1135-1204) = 69 years; (7) Azriel the Kabbalist (1160-1238) = 78 years; (8) Nahmanides (1194-1270) = 76 years; (9) Solomon ibn Adret (1235-1310) = 75 years; (10) Isaac Barfat (1326-1408) = 84 years; (11) Hasdai Crescas 1340-1410) = 70 years; (12) Isaac Abravanel (1437-1509) = 72 years.

21. We would suggest that Petrus Alphonsi lived from circa 1076 to 1146. He was probably born at Huesca (where he was baptized at circa age 30 in 1106) or Saragossa (to which city he returned from England and perhaps France at circa age forty-five circa 1121), and he probably died at Toledo (where he played a major role in the Toletano-Cluniac corpus of Peter the Venerable during the early 1140s).

According to Septimus, *Speculum*, LVI: 517 and note 1, relying on F. Rosenthal, "Literature," in Joseph Schacht and Clifford E. Bosworth, eds., *The Legacy of Islam* (Oxford: Clarendon, 1974), 343, note 2, Mr. Cutler has estimated "Alfonsi's lifetime . . . as 1076-1140." That is not quite correct for two reasons. First, it omits the word "circa" from that estimate. Second, 1140 is too early as a death date—circa 1146 is better—because it does not permit Petrus Alphonsi to play any role in the Toletano-Clunaic corpus of the early 1140s.

Petrus Alphonsi certainly did not die in 1110 (against Kohut, *Jewish Ency.*, I: 377; Sarton, *Introduction to the History of Science*, II: 199; Williams, *Adversus Judaeos*, 233). This supposed death date of 1110 was already discussed and rejected by Soederhjelm, *Neuphilologische Mitteilungen*, XII: 51 and notes 2-3; Haskins, *Studies in the History of Mediaeval Science*, 118–119 and note 16; and Millas Vallicrosa, *Sefarad*, III: 66 and note 2. Cf. also Baron, *Social and Religious History*, VIII: 174. Vincke, *Lex. Theol. Kirche*, VIII: 332, and O'Malley, *New Cath. Ency.*, XI: 209, give "circa 1140" as Alphonsi's death date, close to our own suggestion that he died circa 1146. Cohen, *Proceedings of the American Academy for Jewish Research*, XXIX: 79–80, by associating Petrus Alphonsi with Toledo ("Thus Petrus Alphonsi *of Toledo* [italics ours] in his diatribe against the Jews etc.") and with Abraham ibn Daud, the great Jewish philosopher and historian who only came to Toledo in the 1150s, would seem to reflect a view close to Vincke, O' Malley, and ourselves regarding Alphonsi's death date (*i.e.*, circa 1146).

Jose Amador de los Rios, the nineteenth-century historian of Spanish literature and of Spanish Jewry, perhaps in part due to Castilian patriotism, held that Petrus Alphonsi was named after Alphonso VI of Castile, not Alphonso I of Aragon, therefore that Petrus Alphonsi must have been baptized (and probably born as well) in Burgo de Osma, Castile (= *Osmensis* in Latin), rather than in Huesca, Aragon (= *Oscensis* in Latin). To our knowledge, this view has not won general acceptance. Soederhjelm, *Neuphilologische Mitteilungen*, XII: 51 and note 4; Millas Vallicrosa, *Sefarad*, III: 65 and note 1.

Yitzhak Baer suggested that the Cluniac movement and its anti-Jewish propaganda played a major role in Petrus Alphonsi's conversion. Baer, "Ha-Matzav Ha-Politi Shel Y'hude S'farad B'Doro Shel Rabbi Y'hudah Ha-Levi" [The Political Situation of the Jews of Spain during the Generation of Rabbi Judah Ha-Levi], *Zion* 1 (1935): 8; Baer, *History of the Jews in Christian Spain*, I: 59. Millas Vallicrosa, *Sefarad*, III: 65–66 and 66, note 1, calls Baer's suggestion "bien probable;" and it is strengthened by our article on the "Monk of France," *Al-Andalus*, XXVIII: 249–269, demonstrating that there was a major Cluniac attempt to convert the Muslim ruler of Saragossa in the 1070s. Abbot Hugh of Cluny, deeply involved in this attempt, equated Jew with Muslim. Cf. the Letter of the "Monk of France," in Dunlop, *Al-Andalus*, XVII: 265. Hence, if the Cluniacs attempted to convert the Muslims of Spain in the 1070s, they may well have also attempted to convert the Jews of Spain (including Petrus Alphonsi) in the late eleventh century.

In addition to the Cluniac factor, the failure of the Jewish messianic movement in Andalusia circa 1105 (on which, Abba Hillel Silver, *History of Messianic Speculation in Israel: From the First through the Seventeenth Centuries* [Boston: Beacon, 1959], 68–69; Baron, *Social and Religious History*, III: 124) may have induced Petrus Alphonsi to convert to Christianity the following year in 1106. Just as the failure of the Jewish messianic movement in Avila circa 1295 induced some of the Jews of that city to convert to Christianity shortly thereafter. Baer, *History of the Jews in Christian Spain*, I: 278–281, 288, 439; "Avila, Prophet of," *Ency. Judaica* 3 (1971): 970.

In addition to the Cluniac and messianic factors, the heroic example of the Cid won the hearts of members of all three faith-communities, Christians, Muslims, and Jews. Many of the Cid's Muslim followers converted to Christianity. Pascual de Gayangos, *History of the Mohammedan Dynasties in Spain by Ahmed ibn Mohammed al-Makkari* (London: Oriental Translation Fund of Great Britain and Ireland, 1840), II, appendix, xxxix–xl (cf. also II, appendix, xxii and note 1; I, appendix, xliii–xliv); Robert Ignatius Burns, "Christian-Islamic Confrontation in the West: The Thirteenth-Century Dream of Conversion," *American Historical Review* 76 (1971): 1389, note 12. We know of at least one Jew of Arabic-speaking background (like Petrus Alphonsi) who converted to Christianity in 1094 under the influence of the Cid. Isaac Broyde, "Ibn Alfange," *Jewish Ency.* 6 (1904): 519. Could the Cid also have influenced the conversion of Petrus Alphonsi, especially in view of the fact that the Cid strongly influenced Petrus Alphonsi's godfather, King Alfonso I of Aragon? Pedro Aguado Bleye, *Manual de Historia de Espanya* (6th ed.; Madrid: Espasa-Calpe, 1947), I: 629 and note 1.

In addition to the Clunaic and messianic factors, as well as the example of the Cid and Ibn Alfange, Petrus Alphonsi may also have been influenced by Rabbi Samuel of Morocco, another Jew of Arabic-speaking background who purportedly converted to Christianity in the early 1070s and wrote two Arabic treatises (today preserved only in the midfourteenth-century Latin translations of Alfonso Buenhombre, the Spanish Dominican): the *Tractatus*, primarily directed against the Jews, and the *Disputatio*, primarily directed against the Muslims. Williams, *Adversus Judaeos*, 228–232; Daniel, *Islam and the West*, 7, 54, 189, 335, note 23; Hermes, *Disciplina Clericalis*, 50-51.

It would be interesting to compare Petrus Alphonsi with another late eleventh-century convert from Judaism of Arabic-speaking background (like Petrus Alphonsi), who hailed from northeastern Muslim Spain (like Alphonsi) and specialized in belles lettres, medicine, mathematics, and astronomy (like Alphonsi), who converted not from Judaism to Christianity (as did Alphonsi) but rather from Judaism to Islam. Isaac Broyde, "Hasdai (Hisdai), Abu al-Fadl ben Joseph ibn," *Jewish Ency.* 6 (1904): 248; Baron, *Social and Religious History*, III: 158.

Petrus Alphonsi could also have converted to Christianity in 1106 in order to protect his position as court physician to King Alfonso I of Aragon (*infra*, note 26, para. 5) from attack by Cidellus, the powerful Jewish physician of King Alfonso VI of Castile. Castile and Aragon were then growing closer (they would unite temporarily in 1109, upon Alfonso VI of Castile's death, when his daughter Urraca married Alfonso I of Aragon). Petrus Alphonsi may have feared that Cidellus would soon be powerful enough to put one of his own relatives or friends into Petrus Alphonsi's position as physician to King Alfonso I of Aragon. Indeed, Cidellus' nephew, Solomon, was sent on a diplomatic mission to Aragon in 1108. Baer, *History of the Jews in Christian Spain*, I: 50–51.

For the possible influence of the Karaite factor on Petrus Alphonsi's conversion, supra, note 12.

22. Supra, text at and following note 18 to chapter 2.

23. These two arguments are Baron's, *Social and Religious History*, V: 342, note 43. Kritzeck, *Peter the Venerable and Islam*, 56 and note 23 (cf. 27 and note 83), also rejects the view that Petrus Alphonsi = Peter of Toledo. However, Kritzeck does associate Petrus Alphonsi with Toledo ("Peter Alphonsi, *a learned Toledan* [italics ours] with whose work the abbot [Peter the Venerable] became acquainted while in Spain"); as did Gerson Cohen (supra, note 21, para. 1). Kritzeck also knew that Petrus Alphonsi's *Dialogi* strongly influenced Peter the Venerable's anti-Judaic polemic of the 1140s and allowed that when Peter the Venerable called Peter of Toledo "Master Peter," the title "master" might have been a reference not only to erudition but to age as well. The age implication would also apply to Petrus Alphonsi, for if he was born in 1076, as we suggest, he would have been around 66 years of age in 1142, when Peter the Venerable came to Spain. Kritzeck is now more willing than he had been when he wrote *Peter the Venerable and Islam* in 1964 to entertain seriously the possibility that Petrus Alphonsi = Peter of Toledo. Cf. his article in *Pierre Abelard-Pierre le Venerable*, 208 and note 18; supra, note 3 to this chapter.

Both Baron and Kritzeck, in *Peter the Venerable and Islam*, base their rejection of the view that Petrus Alphonsi = Peter of Toledo upon Monneret de Villard, *Lo Studio dell'Islam in Europa*, 9ff, and especially 14. However, Monneret de Villard's reasons for dismissing the possibility that the two Peters were one are extremely flimsy.

Thus, Monneret's first argument assumes the mistaken birth date of 1062 for Petrus Alphonsi and holds that though Alphonsi could have lived until the time of the Toletano-Cluniac corpus circa 1142, at this time (80 years old) he would have been too feeble to translate a work as long as al-Kindi's *Risalah*. In reply, if we assume a more likely birth date for Petrus Alphonsi of circa 1076, he would only have been around 66 years old at the time of the Toletano-Cluniac corpus circa 1142 and a 66-year-old could well have had enough energy to translate the *Risalah*, especially with the help of another. We know that Peter of Toledo had the help of Peter of Poitiers in the translation of this work. After all, Abraham ibn Ezra, the great Spanish-Jewish intellectual of the midtwelfth-century, poet, grammarian, Bible commentator, theologian, scientist, and translator, lived circa 75 years (1092–1167). During the last 27 years of his life (from circa 1140) he wandered from Andalusia to the Middle East, Italy, southern France, northern France, England, northern France, southern France, Italy, and perhaps back home to Spain, and was busy writing original works until the day he died. Margolis and Marx, *History of the Jewish People*, 333; Tovia Preschel, "Ibn Ezra, Abraham: As Commentator on the Bible," *Ency. Judaica* 8 (1971): 1166. If Abraham ibn Ezra could write original works, unaided, while wandering, during the last 27 of his 75 years, could not Petrus Alphonsi have translated (the *Risalah*), with help (Peter of Poitiers), while residing in the same place (Toledo) at around age 66?

Monneret's second argument is that Petrus Alphonsi could not be Peter of Toledo because what Petrus Alphonsi wrote about Islam in the fifth, or anti-Islamic, chapter of his *Dialogi* does not coincide with the excerpts from the Latin translation of al-Kindi's *Risalah* (translated by Peter of Toledo) as quoted by Vincent of Beauvais. This entire argument collapses because if Monneret would have had the full text of the Latin *Risalah* before him (instead of merely the excerpts therefrom in Vincent of Beauvais), he would have realized that there is considerable similarity between the fifth, or anti-Islamic, chapter of Petrus Alphonsi's *Dialogi* and al-Kindi's *Risalah*, so much similarity that it is highly likely that al-Kindi's *Risalah* was the major source of the fifth chapter of the *Dialogi*. D'Alverny, in *Occidente e l'Islam*, II: 594.

Finally, Monneret's third argument is that though Peter the Venerable definitely relied heavily upon Petrus Alphonsi's *Dialogi* in his own anti-Judaic polemic of the 1140s, this still does not prove that Petrus Alphonsi is Peter of Toledo. The influence of Petrus Alphonsi's *Dialogi* upon Peter the Venerable is, according to Monneret, "easily explainable," though Monneret does not offer any explanation thereof. We agree with Monneret but contend that the "easiest explanation" for this influence is that Petrus Alphonsi is Peter of Toledo.

Thus, none of Monneret's three arguments against the view that Petrus Alphonsi is Peter of Toledo stand up under close analysis.

24. The question of the relative incidence of the name Pedro in Spanish life and history in general and during the lifetime of Petrus Alphonsi in particular deserves further study. *E.g.*, cf. Aguado-Bleye, *Manual de Historia de Espanya*, I: 628, for the facts that King Pedro I of Aragon (died 1104) named his only son (who predeceased him in 1103) Pedro and that when Pedro I of Aragon took Huesca from the Muslims in 1096, Pedro, a Mozarab from Almeria, received a considerable portion of the spoils, from which he made a donation to the Mozarab church of Huesca called "San Pedro the Old." Of the two arguments against the view that Petrus Alphonsi is Peter of Toledo, the argument from the alleged frequency of the name Peter is considerably stronger than the argument from Petrus Alphonsi's advanced age circa 1142.

25. For Huesca, Petrus Alphonsi, *Dialogi*, MPL, CLVII: 537:B–C to 538: A. For Saragossa, supra, note 19.

26. Cf. in general Baron, *Social and Religious History*, V: 114-115, 341-342, note 43; VIII: 173-174, 363-364, note 40; Dorothee Metlitzki, *The Matter of Araby in Medieval England* (New Haven: Yale University Press, 1977), 18-29, 95-106, 199ff, 202ff, 210ff.

For the relations of St. Anselm of Canterbury and his disciple Gilbert Crispin with the Jews, Baron, V: 114–115, 341–342. note 42; Blumenkranz, *Juifs et Chretiens*, index *s.v.* "Anselme de Cantorbery" and "Gilbert Crispin"; Blumenkranz, *Les Auteurs Chretiens Latins du Moyen Age sur Les Juifs et le Judaisme* (Paris and The Hague: Mouton, 1963), 279–287; Blumenkranz, "The Roman Church and the Jews," in Cecil Roth, ed., *The Dark Ages 711–1966,* World History of the Jewish People 11 (New Brunswick, New Jersey: Rutgers University Press, 1966), 89–94, 97; Blumenkranz, "Anselm of Canterbury" and Crispin, Gilbert," *Ency. Judaica.* 3 (1971): 33, and 5 (1971): 1113–1114 respectively; R.W. Southern, "St. Anselm and Gilbert Crispin, Abbot of Westminster," *Medieval and Renaissance Studies* 3 (1954): 78-115; Gillian R. Evans, *Anselm and a New Generation* (Oxford: Clarendon, 1980), 35-41; P.G. van der Plaas, "Des Hl. Anselm *Cur Deus Homo* auf dem Boden der Juedisch-Christlichen Polemik des Mittelalters," *Divus Thomas* 7 (1929): 446-467; 8(1930): 18-32.

For the relations of St. Anselm and Crispin with the Muslims, Roques, *Structures Theologiques de la "Gnose" a Richard de Saint-Victor,* "La Methode du 'Cur Deus Homo' de Saint Anselme de Cantorbery," 243–293; Julia Gauss, "Anselm von Canterbury und die Islamfrage," *Theologische Zeitschrift* 19 (1963): 250–272; Gauss, *Ost und West in der Kirchen- und Papstgeschichte des 11. Jahrhunderts* (Zurich: E.V.Z. Verlag, 1967), "Anselm von Canterburys Weg zur Begegnung mit Judentum und Islam," 103–126, 138–139; Gauss, "Anselm von Canterbury: Zur Begegnung und Auseinandersetzung der Religionen," *Saeculum* 17 (1966): 277–363; Gauss, "Toleranz und Intoleranz zwischen Christen und Muslimen in der Zeit vor den Kreuzzuegen," ibid. 19 (1969): 362–389; Gauss, "Die Auseinandersetzung mit Judentum und Islam bei Anselm," *Analecta Anselmiana* 4 (1975): 101-109; J. Slomp, "An Early Medieval Dialogue with Islam Written by Anselm of Canterbury [the *Cur Deus Homo*]," *Bulletin of the Christian Institutes of Islamic Studies* [Henry Martyn Institute, Lucknow, India] 5 (1971): 23-34.

Thus, if both St. Anselm of Canterbury and his disciple Gilbert Crispin were interested in the dialogue with Jews as well as Muslims, this could help explain why Petrus Alphonsi came to England in the 1110s and why Anselm, Crispin, and/or their circle might have taken an especial interest in Petrus Alphonsi, for he combined the zealous loyalty to Christianity of the neophyte with an extensive knowledge of both Judaism and Islam, as well as their sacred languages (Hebrew and Arabic) along with their sacred and secular literatures. St. Anselm was especially sympathetic to converts from Judaism to Christianity. Blumenkranz, *Ency. Judaica,* III: 33.

Petrus Alphonsi may also have come to England to serve as physician to the English king. Alfonso de Spina, writing in fifteenth-century Spain, reported that Petrus Alphonsi was the physician of King Alfonso I of Aragon (reigned from 1104). Soederhjelm, *Neuphilologische Mitteilungen,* XII: 52 and note 3. A thirteenth-century Cambridge University MS of the *Disciplina Clericalis* states that Petrus Alphonsi was the physician of King Henry I of England (reigned from 1100). Cf. the Hilka-Soederhjelm edition, Latin text of the *Disciplina,* I: xi, xix; Soederhjelm, *Neuphilologische Mitteilungen,* XII: 52 and note 4; Haskins, *Studies in the History of Mediaeval Science,* 119 and note 17; Hermes, *Disciplina Clericalis,* 66. Hilka-Soederhjelm and Soederhjelm alone hold that Petrus Alphonsi was physician only to the king of Aragon but not to the English king. Haskins holds that he was physician to both kings, and he is followed in this view by Sarton, *Introduction,* II:1, 199; O'Malley, *New Cath. Ency.,* XI: 209; Jones and Keller, *Scholar's Guide,* 27. Southern, *Western Views of Islam*, 35, and Scholberg, *Ency. Judaica*, XIII: 347, hold that he was at least physician to the English king. Infra, note 40. Petrus Alphonsi may have become physician of King Henry I of England in part on the recommendation of St. Anselm, Crispin, and/or their circle.

It may also have been that King Alfonso I of Aragon sent Petrus Alphonsi to England as an ambassador to work for an alliance between Aragon (united with Castile in 1109 through the marriage of King Alfonso I of Aragon and Queen Urraca of Castile, and dominating Castile through this union) and the Anglo-Normans of the English Channel area. Hermes, *Disciplina Clericalis*, 66. Through such an alliance the Aragonese may have hoped to obtain Anglo-Norman military help for two purposes: (1) to put down the Galician revolt against Aragonese domination of Castile and/or (2) to reconquer Saragossa, the last great bastion of Islamic rule in northeastern Spain. For the Galician revolt and the Aragonese reconquest of the 1110s, Aguado-Bleye, *Manual*, I: 618–622, 628–629; O'Callaghan, *History of Medieval Spain*, 216–220. For Anglo-Norman interest in Castile, Galicia, and Santiago de Compostela circa 1066–1125, David C. Douglas, *William the Conqueror: The Norman Impact upon England* (Berkeley and Los Angeles: University of California Press, 1964), 393–394; Pedro de Palol and Max Hirmer, *Early Medieval Art in Spain* (New York: Abrams, 1967), 113; Bernard Reilly, "Santiago and St. Denis: The French Presence in Eleventh-Century Spain," *Catholic Historical Review* 54 (1968): 474–475; Kendrick, in the Hells, *Great Pilgrimage of the Middle Ages*, 17–18; Gauss, *Theologische Zeitschrift*, XIX: 254 and note 10; F.S. Schmitt, *S. Anselmi Cantuariensis Archiepiscopi Opera Omnia* (1st ed.; Edinburgh: Nelson, 1946), IV: 178; VI: 113; index, *s.v.* "Diacus, Episcopus Sancti Iacobi Compostellani." For important Norman participation in the Aragonese Crusade that reconquered Tudela and Saragossa in 1110s, Prosper Boissonnade, *Du Nouveau sur la Chanson de Roland* (Paris: Champion, 1923), 44–49.

It may also have been that Petrus Alphonsi came to England in order to enter into close personal relationship with the important school of Arabic scientific studies which flourished there in the eleventh century; for which Lynn White, "Eilmer of Malmesbury, An Eleventh Century Aviator," *Technology and Culture* 2 (1961): 97–111; Haskins, *Studies in the History of Mediaeval Science*, 113–119, 334; J.W. Thompson, "The Introduction of Arabic Science into Lorraine in the Tenth Century," *Isis* 12 (1929): 191; M.C. Welborn, "Lotharingia as a Center of Arabic and Scientific Influence in the Eleventh Century," ibid. 16 (1931): 196–198; Monneret de Villard, *Lo Studio dell'Islam in Europa*, 2 and note 2.

Or perhaps Petrus Alphonsi came to England specifically in order to enter into close personal relationship with the greatest English Arabic and scientific scholar of the first half of the twelfth century, Adelard of Bath. For Petrus Alphonsi and Adelard in England, Haskins, *Studies in the History of Mediaeval Science*, 22–23, 117–119; Hermes, *Disciplina Clericalis*, 75. Perhaps they had earlier met in Aragon. Between circa 1109 and 1126 Adelard had traveled widely in the Mediterranean (southern Italy, possibly Sicily, Cilicia, Syria, possibly Palestine). He could also have visited Spain following the example of Thomas of York circa 1050 (Welborn, *Isis*, XVI: 197–198) and Gerbert of Aurillac (Pope Sylvester II) circa 975 (Haskins, 8–9). Haskins (34 and note 75) holds that "it seems probable that Adelard visited Spain." Indeed, Adelard may have visited Spain (including Aragon), on his way back to England from Italy, in order to pray at the shrine of Santiago de Compostela. Cf. Kendrick, in Hells, *Great Pilgrimage of the Middle Ages*, 17–18, 20, for visits to Santiago by the first known English pilgrim to the shrine, Ansgot of Burwell in Lincolnshire, late eleventh century; Matilda, daughter of King Henry I of England, after 1125; and Bishop Henry of Winchester, brother of King Stephen, on his way back to England from Rome in 1151.

27. The great early twelfth-century French intellectual centers included (1) Bec, with which both St. Anselm and Gilbert Crispin were very closely linked; (2) Paris and vicinity, where Alphonsi could well have met William of Champeaux (circa 1070–1122), to whom an anti-Judaic polemic has long been ascribed; Hugh of St. Victor (died 1141), who was influenced by William of Champeaux; and Peter Abelard (1079–1142), who toward the end of his life wrote on the problem of Islam and Judaism and came into close association with Peter the Venerable at Cluny; (3) Chartres, where Alphonsi could well have met Ivo of Chartres (1040–1116), the great canonist who had to ponder the kinds of restrictions which were to be placed upon the Jews in Western Christian society; Bernard of Chartres (died circa 1127); and Gilbert of La Porree (circa 1075–1154); and (4) the related abbeys of Citeaux and Clairvaux, where Alphonsi could have met St. Stephen Harding (died 1134), who was an important Christian Hebraist, and St. Bernard of Clairvaux (1090-1153), who would later appear as the great defender of the Jewish people against Christian persecution during the Second Crusade. Supra, notes 3 and 18.

We also think it highly possible that if Petrus Alphonsi did travel to France in the 1110s, he would have met Anselm of Laon (died 1117), the great Bible commentator who had been influenced by St. Anselm of Canterbury, plus the following three who wrote polemics against the Jews: Odo, Bishop of Cambrai, who wrote against the Jews circa 1106–1113; Guibert of Nogent, who was also influenced by St. Anselm of Canterbury and who wrote against the Jews circa 1104–1121; and Hildebert of Lavardin, associated with both Le Mans and Tours, who wrote against the Jews sometime before his death in 1133. Browe, *Judenmission*, 101; supra, note 3.

28. For the French contribution to the *Reconquista*, Marcelin Defourneaux, *Les Francais en Espagne aux XIe et XIIe Siecles* (Paris: Presses Universitaires de France, 1949); Jose Maria Lacarra y de Miguel, "Los Franceses en la Reconquista y Repoblacion del Valle del Ebro en Tiempos de Alfonso [I] el Batallador," *Cuadernos de Historia de Espanya* 2 (1968): 65–80.

29. P.G. Thery, *Tolede: Grande Ville de la Renaissance Medievale: Point de Jonction entre les Cultures Musulmane et Chretienne* (Oran: Heintz Freres, 1944); Cohen, *Book of Tradition*, xxvii; Kritzeck *Peter the Venerable and Islam*, 52–53; Haskins, *Studies in the History of Mediaeval Science*, 12–16, and his *Renaissance of the Twelfth Century* (Cleveland and New York: World/Meridian, 1961), 52–53, 285–287.

30. Hilka-Soederhjelm edition, Latin text of the *Disciplina Clericalis*, I: 4–6; 17, variant to line 4; 47, col. b; Hermes, *Disciplina Clericalis*, 107. For the role of Bagdad and the Islamic East in Spain during Petrus Alphonsi's lifetime, Emilio Garcia-Gomez, "Bagdad y los Reinos de Taifas," *Revista de Occidente* 43 (1934): 1–22; Brockelmann, *History of the Islamic Peoples*, 205; Hitti, *History of the Arabs*, 542; Imamuddin, *Political*

History of Muslim Spain, 238, 265–266; Cohen, *Book of Tradition*, index, *s.v.* "Babylonia" and "Bagdad"; J.H. Schirmann, "Ibn Ezra, Isaac," *Ency. Judaica* 8 (1971): 1170.

31. Cf. Baer, *History of the Jews in Christian Spain*, II: 99, for Samuel Bienveniste, a Jewish notable of *Soria*, who settled in *Saragossa* in the 1380s but continued to visit his native town of Soria from time to time and found refuge from the anti-Jewish excesses of 1391 in a castle belonging to the bishop of *Osma*. Donya Maria, queen of Aragon, wrote the bishop of Osma and the archbishop of *Toledo* asking them to arrange the return of her subject to Saragossa.

Likewise, Moses of Narbonne (on whom, infra, note 41 to chapter 8), the great fourteenth-century Jewish Averroist, linked Barcelona, Soria, and Toledo by his travels between circa 1340 and 1370. Alfred L. Ivry, "Moses Ben Joshua Of Narbonne," *Ency. Judaica* 12 (1971): 422-423.

32. Kritzeck, *Peter the Venerable and Islam*, 54; Haskins, *Studies in the History of Mediaeval Science*, 9–12, 33, 67–81; Thorndike, *Magic and Experimental Science*, II: 85–87, 119, 230, 257; Sarton, *Introduction to the History of Science*, II:1, 174–175; Millas-Vallicrosa, *Journal of World History*, II: 417; Francis J. Carmody, *Arabic Astronomical and Astrological Sciences in Latin Translation: A Critical Bibliography* (Berkeley and Los Angeles: University of California Press, 1956), index, *s.v.* "Hugh of Santalla."

33. Kritzeck, *Peter the Venerable and Islam*, 52–54; Pierre Duhem, *Systeme du Monde: Histoire des Doctrines Cosmologiques de Platon a Copernic* (Paris: Hermann, 1915), III: 177–183; Haskins, *Studies in the History of Mediaeval Science*, 9–10, 13, 67, 70, 279, 283; Thorndike, *Magic and Experimental Science*, II: 73, 78–82, 177, 180, 346, 449; Sarton, *Introduction to the History of Science*, II:1, 172–173; Angel Gonzalez Palencia, *El Arzobispo Don Raimundo de Toledo* (Barcelona: Editorial Labor, 1942); Aguado-Bleye, *Manual*, I: 933–934; Millas-Vallicrosa, *Journal of World History*, II: 417–421; Gilson, *History of Christian Philosophy in the Middle Ages*, 237–239; Baron, *Social and Religious History*, VIII: 61–62, 174–175; Richard Lemay, *Abu Ma'shar and Latin Aristotelianism in the Twelfth Century: The Recovery of Aristotle's Natural Philosophy through Arabic Astrology* (Beirut: American University, 1962), xxii, 10–12, 18, 27, 38, 57, 143, 198, 236, 242, 247; d'Alverny, "Dominic Gundisalvi," *New Cath. Ency.* 4 (1967): 966–967.

34. For Raimundo's Cluniac background, Gonzalez Palencia, *El Arzobispo Don Raimundo de Toledo*, 48. For Michael's Cluniac background, Haskins, *Studies in the History of Mediaeval Science*, 72. For the link between Cluny and Arabic studies before Peter the Venerable, cf. supra notes 7, 34-43, to chapter 2.

35. Kritzeck, *Peter the Venerable and Islam*, 54; Duhem, *Systeme du Monde*, III: 198–201; IV: 577; Haskins, *Studies in the History of Mediaeval Science*, 9–11, 14, 17–18, 51, 67–68, 98, 110, 121; Thorndike, *Magic and Experimental Science*, II: 75, 82–83, 85, 119, 449; Sarton, *Introduction to the History of Science*, II:1, 177–179, 206-208; Carmody, *Arabic Astronomical and Astrological Science in Latin Translation*, index, *s.v.* "Abraham bar Hiyya" and "Plato of Tivoli"; Lemay, *Abu Ma'shar and Latin Aristotelianism in the Twelfth Century*, 46, 390; Marshall Clagett, *Archimedes in the Middles Ages* (Madison: University of Wisconsin Press, 1964), I: 4, 16–29, 40, 358–359, 636: Millas-Vallicrosa, *Estudios Sobre Historia de la Ciencia Espanyola*, 219–262, and

his article, *Journal of World History*, II: 413–414; Vera, *Los Judios Espanyoles y su Contribucion a las Ciencias Exactas*, 36–59; F. Cantera Burgos, "Christian Spain," in Roth, *Dark Ages*, 380; Baron, *Social and Religious History*, index to volumes I-VIII *s.v.* "Bar Hiyya, Abraham (Savasorda)"; M. Levey, "The Encyclopedia of Abraham Savasorda: A Departure in Mathematical Methodology," *Isis* 43 (1952): 257–264, and his "Abraham Savasorda and His Allegorism: A Study in Early European Logistic," *Osiris* 11 (1954): 50–64; Baer, *History of the Jews in Christian Spain*, I: 54, 59, 66, 334, 389, 391; Leon D. Stitskin, *Judaism as a Philosophy: The Philosophy of Abraham Bar Hiyya (1065–1143)* (New York: Bloch, 1960); Geoffrey Wigoder, "Abraham Bar Hiyya," *Ency. Judaica* 2 (1971): 130–133; Hermes, *Disciplina Clericalis*, 66, 174, note 47.

More so than being associated with Toledo, both Robert of Ketton as well as his close friend and fellow translator, Herman of Dalmatia, were associated with Plato of Tivoli at Barcelona as well as with the Basque country of northeastern Spain (Robert at Pamplona and Herman at Tolosa de Guipuzcoa). Kritzeck, *Peter the Venerable and Islam*, 62–63, 66–67. On Herman, cf. also now H.L.L. Busard, *The Translation of the Elements of Euclid from the Arabic into Latin by Hermann of Carinthia (?)* (Leiden: Brill, 1968), I (books 1–6), and (Amsterdam: Mathematisch Centrum, 1977), II (books 7–12), and as reviewed by G. Tee, *Journal for the History of Arabic Science* 2 (1978): 403-404; C.F. Burnett, "Arabic into Latin in Twelfth Century Spain: The Works of Hermann of Carinthia," *Mittellateinisches Jahrbuch* 13 (1978): 100-134.

The roots of the early twelfth-century Barcelona school of translators from the Arabic (Plato of Tivoli and Abraham bar Hiyya/Savasorda) go back to the tenth-century school of translators from the Arabic at the Monastery of Ripoll in Catalonia (about 50 miles north of Barcelona); on which, Millas-Vallicrosa, *Estudios Sobre Historia de la Ciencia Espanyola*, 43–64, and his article, *Journal of World History*, II: 404–409; D.M. Dunlop, "Arabic Science in the West, I: The Beginnings of Transmission," *Journal of the Pakistan Historical Society* 5 (1957): 1–22. There may also have been an influence from southern Italy. Thus, Petrus Alphonsi seems to have known the works of Constantine the African, the great eleventh-century south Italian translator from the Arabic. Thorndike, *Magic and Experimental Science*, II: 72 and note 1; Hermes, *Disciplina Clericalis*, 69.

36. Kritzeck, *Peter the Venerable and Islam*, 62–67, especially 62 and note 46, 66 and note 61. Robert of Ketton returned to London circa 1150, and this is the last we hear of him. Kritzeck, 63. Was London the scene of his early education? Was he moved to devote his life to translating from the Arabic by Petrus Alphonsi, who visited England in the 1110s, and/or by any of the English scholars interested in Arabic and Islamic studies with whom Petrus Alphonsi may well have associated at that time: Crispin, Walcher, and/or Adelard? Baron, *Social and Religious History*, VIII: 174. There was also an important group of English translators from the Arabic in the late twelfth century, especially Roger of Hereford, Daniel of Morley, and Alfred of Sareshal. Haskins, *Studies in the History of Mediaeval Science*, 123–129; Monneret de Villard, *Lo Studio dell'Islam in Europa*, 5–6; Josiah Cox Russell, "Hereford and Arabic Science in England," *Isis* 18 (1932): 14–25; Charles Singer, "Daniel of Morley: an English Philosopher of the XIIth Century," *Isis* 3 (1920): 263–269; James Otte, "The Life and Writings of Alfredus Anglicus," *Viator* 3 (1972): 275–291.

For the scholars of Chartres, *supra*, note 27.

37. Baron, *Social and Religious History*, VIII: 174; Haskins, *Studies in the History of Mediaeval Science*, 22, 24, 114–119.

38. Petrus Alphonsi, *Dialogi*, MPL, CLVII: 538:A: *Petrus Alfunsi*. Cf. also Petrus Alphonsi, *Disciplina Clericalis*, Hilka-Soederhjelm edition of the Latin text, I: 1, line 1: *Dixit Petrus Alfunsus*, with the following variant readings in the *apparatus criticus*: *Aldefulsi, Aldefunsus, Adelfonsus, Adelphusus, Adevultus, Alfusus, Alphunsus, Alfonsus, Alphonsus, Anfusus, Anfonsus, Anfulsus, Amphulsus, Amfulsus, Amphusus*, and *Ambfonsus*. Cf. the title of Petrus Alphonsi's *De Dracone: Sententia Petris Ebrei Cognomento Anphus*, in Haskins, *Studies in the History of Mediaeval Science*, 116. Cf. the beginning of Petrus Alphonsi's explanation of the use of the chronological tables (Oxford, Corpus Christi College, MS 283, f. 142v): *Dixit Petrus Anfulsus*, in Haskins, 117. Cf. also the reading *Anidefunfus* in the *Epistola de Studio Artium Liberalium Praecipue Astronomiae ad Peripateticos Aliosque Philosophicos* (British Museum Arundel MS 270, ff., 40–44v) in Thorndike and Kibre, *Catalogue of Incipits of Mediaeval Scientific Writing in Latin*, 1604, and Thorndike, *Magic and Experimental Science*, II: 70. Cf. also Millas-Vallicrosa, *Sefarad*, VII: 136, for Petrus Alphonsi witnessing a document in Saragossa (April 14, 1121) as *Petrus Alphons*.

39. Petrus Alphonsi says that Moses, the Jewish debater in the *Dialogi*, was his boyhood friend: MPL, CLVII: 537:D. However, most scholars assume that Moses was really Petrus Alphonsi's Jewish name before his conversion, that his Jewish name was Moses or *Rabbi Mosheh Ha-S'fardi* [Rabbi Moses the Spaniard], therefore that in the *Dialogi* he is arguing with himself. For the view that Petrus Alphonsi's Jewish name was Moses, Baron, *Social and Religious History*, V. 115; VIII: 173–174; Sarton, *Introduction to the History of Science*, II:1, 199; Millas-Vallicrosa, *Sefarad*, III: 65, and *Journal of World History*, II: 411; Baer, *History of the Jews in Christian Spain*, I: 59; Gonzalez Palencia, *Pedro Alfonso: Disiplina Clericalis*, vii; Jones and Keller, *Scholar's Guide*, 13; O'Malley, *New Cath. Ency.*, XI: 209; Scholberg, *Ency. Judaica*, XIII: 347.

40. Supra, note 26, para. 5.

41. Supra, note 35.

42. Ibid.

43. Supra, note 19. Petrus Alphonsi could have returned from England to Saragossa circa 1121 in the hope of obtaining property there after the city fell to the Christians in 1118, either property that had once belonged to his parents and/or relatives, or property confiscated from the conquered Muslims and waiting to be parceled out by the king to his favorites. It is possible that Petrus Alphonsi was thwarted in his hope by Eleazar of Saragossa, the powerful leader of the Jewish community of this city after its reconquest (on whom, Baer, *History of the Jews in Christian Spain*, I: 53), perhaps working in concert with some of Petrus Alphonsi's Christian enemies at the court of King Alphonso I of Aragon, for Eleazar of Saragossa had many dealings with the king.

If Petrus Alphonsi hoped to recover property in Saragossa that had once belonged to his parents and/or relatives, his enemies (Jewish and/or Christian) could well have argued successfully against him as follows. Admittedly, in Spain Jewish converts to Christianity could inherit the property of their parents. Baron, *Social and Religious History*, III: 10: Baer, *History of the Jews in Christian Spain*, I: 20. But, Jewish converts to Christianity north of the Pyrenees (in France, England, and Germany) could not do so. Grayzel, *Church and the Jews in the XIIIth Century*, 18–19, especially 19, note 36. Since Petrus Alphonsi had spent so much time north of the Pyrenees (the decade of the 1110s in England and perhaps France as well), he should be treated like the Jewish converts to Christianity in France, England, and Germany and should not be allowed to inherit the property of his parents and/or relatives in Saragossa.

If Petrus Alphonsi hoped to be awarded property confiscated from the Muslims, his enemies (Jewish and/or Christian) could well have argued successfully against him as follows. Admittedly, when Saragossa fell to the Christians in 1118, all Muslim houses and mosques inside the city walls were confiscated (just as they were when Tudela fell to the Christians in 1115, and Valencia to the Cid in 1095). However, to spare the feelings of the conquered Muslims, Christians were the only ones allowed to obtain this confiscated Muslim property. Jews could not. Baer, I: 52–53. To allow Petrus Alphonsi, a Jewish convert to Christianity, to obtain some of this confiscated Muslim property would be as much of an insult to the Muslims as to allow an un-converted Jew to obtain some of this same property because Islamic tradition held that Jews should not be allowed to convert to Christianity (for if they were to convert at all, they should only be allowed to convert to Islam). Baron, III: 131.

44. Cf. supra, note 26, for positive reasons why King Alfonso I of Aragon might have sent Petrus Alphonsi to England. However, it is also possible that Petrus Alphonsi left Aragon for negative reasons.

Santamaria, the *canonigo archivero* of Santo Domingo de la Calzada, suggested that Petrus Alphonsi left Aragon for England because the Jews of Aragon tried to kill him after his conversion to Christianity circa 1106. Supra, note 8. This seems doubtful because it is unlikely that the Jews of Aragon would have felt powerful enough to at-tempt to *kill* Petrus Alphonsi at this time. The Jewish situation in Christian Spain circa 1110 was deteriorating. Alfonso VI of Castile acted to curtail the rights of the Jews in his kingdom circa 1091. Baer, *History of the Jews in Christian Spain*, I: 44. In early twelfth-century Aragon the Jews could not even dominate the Muslims. Baer, I: 52–56. If the Aragonese Jews could not even dominate the Muslims, how could they dominate the Christians (or converts from Judaism to Christianity like Petrus Al-phonsi) by trying to kill them? In Aragon before Alphonsi's conversion in 1106 the Jews might have had enough power (working in concert with highly placed Christian courtiers) to drive Alphonsi from office as physician to the crown. Supra, note 21, para. 8. However, once he converted to Christianity in 1106, Alphonsi's prestige would probably have been too great among the Christians for him to be driven from office as royal physician. If so, how could the Jews of Aragon have attempted some-thing as drastic as killing Alphonsi. Admittedly, Petrus Alphonsi's Jewish and Chris-tian enemies might have been able to thwart his hope of obtaining property in Sara-gossa circa 1121. Supra, note 43. However, that would have been after Petrus Al-phonsi had spent about a decade abroad and his personal contacts at court had lapsed. However, even circa 1121 his Jewish and Christian enemies probably would still never have attempted something as drastic as killing him.

Perhaps Petrus Alphonsi went abroad because he opposed the marriage of King Alphonso I of Aragon to Queen Urraca of Castile (September 1109), as did Bernard of Cluny, archbishop of Toledo, because the marriage was within the forbidden degrees of consanguinity. The marriage finally broke up around 1114, but it is possible that King Alfonso I of Aragon never forgave his physician for having opposed it and blamed the break up of the marriage in part on this opposition. If this could have been a factor in Petrus Alphonsi's decision to go abroad circa 1110, King Alfonso need not necessarily have forgiven Petrus Alphonsi for his opposition to the marriage when Alphonsi returned to Saragossa circa 1121. On the ill-fated marriage of Alfonso and Urraca, Aguado-Bleye, Manual, I: 618–622; O'Callaghan, History of Medieval Spain 216–218.

45. For the Almoravide pressure on the Jews of Muslim Spain circa 1106, Baron, Social and Religious History, III: 124; V: 200–201. For the massacre of the Jews of Central Europe during the First Crusade, Baron, IV: 89–106. For the riots which broke out against the Jews of Castile upon the death of King Alfonso VI in 1109, Baer, History of the Jews in Christian Spain, I: 51.

46. Cf. Baer, History of the Jews in Christian Spain, I: 51, for the harsh anti-Jewish legislation of King Alfonso VII of Castile (1126–1157): (1) The king cancelled all fines and wergild due him from the murder of Jews during the massacres of 1109. (2) The king established that in the future the wergild due for the murder of a Jew would be no more than the wergild due for the murder of a peasant (a return to the Castilian policy of 974, laying aside the Castilian policy of the early eleventh century which held that the wergild due for the murder of a Jew was at least the same as that due for the murder of a knight or priest; Baer, I: 43). (3) In Toledo all suits between a Jew and a Christian were henceforth to be tried before a Christian court.

Worst of all and most significant because of its possible application to Petrus Alphonsi, King Alfonso VII of Castile decreed that in Toledo and vicinity no Jew, nor recent convert from Judaism (Petrus Alphonsi could have been included in this part of the prohibition), could hold any office which gave them power over Christians.

Baer, I: 60, attributes the departure from Toledo of Isaac ibn Ezra after 1119 to "disturbed conditions prevailing at the time throughout Castile." It could also have been due partly to the anti-Jewish attitude of the Christian populace of Toledo at this time. Baer, I: 50–51.

The attitude toward the Jews in the Song of the Cid (completed circa 1140) may also reflect the anti-Jewish attitudes of the crown and the people of Castile during the reign of King Alfonso VII. The Cid himself, a generation earlier, was quite sympathetic to the Jews, many of whom were found in his entourage. Cantera Burgos, in Roth, Dark Ages, 374–375; Baer, I: 58. Thus, the anti-Jewish attitude of the story of how the Cid tricked the Jewish couple of Burgos, Vidas = Hayyim and his wife Raquel, must reflect the following generation (the generation of circa 1140). So Baer, I: 58, 388–389, note 32; against Cantera Burgos, in Roth, Dark Ages, 374–375, who holds that this episode reflects the period of the Cid himself. Cf. also N. Salvador Miguel, "Reflexiones sobre el Episodio de Rachel y Vidas en el Cantar de Mio Cid," Revista de Filologia Espanyola 59 (1977): 183-224; C.I. Nepaulsingh, "Review Essay," The American Sephardi 9 (1978): 149-153; J. England, "The Second Appearance of Rachel and Vidas in the Poema de Mio Cid," in J. England, ed., Hispanic Studies in Honour of Frank Pierce (Sheffield: Department of Hispanic Studies and Sheffield University Press, 1980), 51-58.

Cf. also Baer, I: 43, 51, for the riots against and massacre of the Jews of Castrojeriz, near Burgos, 1035, and of Burgos itself, 1109; supra, note 21, para. 5, for another discussion of the Cid and Petrus Alphonsi.

47. Baer, *History of the Jews in Christian Spain*, I: 52, 387, note 22; Baron, *Social and Religious History*, IV: 32–33.

48. Baron, *Social and Religious History*, VIII: 173–174, 363–364, note 40; also V: 342, note 43; supra, note 6 of this chapter.

49. Hermes, *Disciplina Clericalis*, 42; infra, note 55. Cf. Petrus Alphonsi, *Disciplina Clericalis*, Hilka-Soederhjelm edition of the Latin text, I: 37, line 18, for one reference to the Jews in general, *Iudaeorum auctoritas*; and I: 24, line 14, for one reference to the Jewish lawgiver Moses, *Moysis praeceptum*. These references do not seem to be pejorative. Nor would there seem to be any attacks in the *Disciplina* on the Pharisees (e.g., their alleged hypocrisy) or the synagogues (*e.g.*, their alleged link with Satan). Thus, Petrus Alphonsi's *Disciplina Clericalis*, in contrast to the *Dialogi*, seems to be free of anti-Jewish bias. However, there is one example of the tendency to equate Jew with Muslim by medieval Christians in the *apparatus criticus* to the *Disciplina*, ibid., I: 2, line 16, where the *lingua Arabica* of the text becomes *lingua Hebraica* in one fourteenth-century Breslau manuscript (on which, I: viii, MS no. 33).

50. After hearing the earlier version of this chapter which was delivered as a paper entitled "Petrus Alphonsi and the Toletano-Cluniac Corpus," 180th Annual Meeting, American Oriental Society, Baltimore, April 15, 1970, George F. Hourani suggested that the reason Petrus Alphonsi may have changed his name to Peter of Toledo by the 1140s was to please his patron, archbishop Raimundo *of Toledo*. This suggestion is eminently plausible.

51. Kritzeck, *Peter the Venerable and Islam*, 56.

52. Cf. ibid. 57, for both Blachere's view that Peter of Toledo was a convert from Islam and Kritzeck's suggestion that he just as easily could have been a Mozarab (of course, our suggestion as developed in this chapter was that he was a convert from Judaism). Daniel, *Islam and the West*, 399–400, held that the Annotator was a Mozarab (though Daniel did not suggest that Peter of Toledo himself was a Mozarab or that Peter of Toledo = the Annotator). Kritzeck has suggested that Peter of Toledo = the Annotator. If we combine Daniel's view that the Annotator was a Mozarab with Kritzeck's view that Peter of Toledo = the Annotator, we arrive at the view that Peter of Toledo was a Mozarab, the suggestion Kritzeck presents on p. 57, as an alternative to that of Blachere. The possibility that Peter of Toledo was an unconverted Muslim (Kritzeck, 57 and note 28, 68 and note 70) is extremely remote. It is almost impossible to imagine that Peter the Venerable would have put an unconverted Muslim in charge of the Toletano-Cluniac corpus, a project directed at refuting Islam (just as it is very difficult to imagine that any loyal Muslim would have wanted to be put in charge of such a project, though a loyal Muslim might have been willing to play a small role therein, as did the unconverted Muslim Muhammad, for whom, Kritzeck, 68–69). Would not Peter the Venerable have feared that an unconverted Muslim, if put in charge of the project, would attempt to sabotage it? Furthermore, even if Peter the Venerable had been willing to put an unconverted Muslim in charge of the project (which is highly doubtful), would this unconverted Muslim have felt secure enough in his position to call in a second unconverted Muslim, Muhammad, as an assistant,

even for a relatively small role? In the context of the times one loyal Muslim working on the project in any capacity was already stretching the bonds of Christian toleration for non-Christian religions to the limit. But since we know that Peter of Toledo did indeed call in an unconverted Muslim, Muhammad, to assist in the project, it would seem to follow that Peter of Toledo almost certainly was not an unconverted Muslim himself. Cf. also supra, text of chapter 2 between notes 17 and 18.

53. Kritzeck, *Peter the Venerable and Islam*, 56 and note 25, as well as 31 and note 100. Peter of Toledo is described in the Christian sources as *perito utriusque linguae . . . sed . . . lingua Latina non adeo ei familiaris vel nota erat ut Arabica.* This would fit Petrus Alphonsi perfectly. Supra, note 10 to this chapter.

54. Kritzeck, *Peter the Venerable and Islam*, 33 and note 105, 34–35, 68–69. For Peter of Toledo and Muhammad, Kritzeck, 57–58 and note 31.

55. Alphonsi's contemporaries who wrote against Islam were: Hugh of Fleury (circa 1110), Guibert of Nogent (circa 1112), Sigebert of Gembloux (circa 1112), Embrico of Mainz (or Hildebert of Mans; died circa 1112), Ekkehard of Aura (circa 1115), William of Malmesbury (circa 1120), Pseudo-Ildefonsus of Toledo (circa 1130?), Walter of Compiegne (circa 1140, relating information allegedly derived from Islamic converts to Christianity), or Euthemius Zigabenus (flourished under Emperor Alexius Comnenus, 1081-1118, in Byzantium).

For the relative tolerance of Petrus Alphonsi's attitude toward Islam even in the fifth chapter of the *Dialogi* (which is far less tolerant than the *Disciplina Clericalis*), Daniel, *Islam and the West*, 7; Southern, *Western Views of Islam*, 35 and note 2; d'Alverny, *Occidente e l'Islam*, II: 593–595; Septimus, *Speculum*, LVI: 533 and note 64.

In general, on the Christian "biographies" of the Prophet Muhammad available at the time of the First Crusade (circa 1100), Alessandro d'Ancona, "La Leggenda di Maometto in Occidente," *Giornale Storico della Letteratura Italiana* 13 (1889): 216–229; Daniel, *Islam and the West*, 29–35; Southern, *Western Views of Islam*, 27–36; d'Alverny, *Occidente e l'Islam*, II: 595–600.

Southern, *Western Views*, 34–35, speaks of William of Malmesbury's relatively tolerant view of Islam circa 1120; d'Alverny, *Occidente e l'Islam*, II: 599, by contrast, does not consider William of Malmesbury very tolerant of Islam; cf. also Daniel, *Islam and the West*, 348; S.C. Chew, *The Crescent and the Rose* (New York: Oxford University Press, 1937), 387–388. William of Malmesbury could have been influenced by the fifth, or anti-Islamic, chapter of Petrus Alphonsi's *Dialogi* and/or have received information about Islam from Alphonsi (in England during the 1110s) by letter or in conversation. Petrus Alphonsi was associated with Walcher of Malvern in England (supra, note 36), and Malvern is no more than forty miles north of Malmesbury. On Malmesbury and Arabic science, White, *Technology and Culture*, II: 97–111. Cf. also Monneret, *Lo Studio dell 'Islam*, 2, who links Walcher of Malvern with William of Malmesbury.

Likewise, Geoffrey of Monmouth, in his famed *History of the Kings of England*, written circa 1136, relates some material about Islam. John S.P. Tatlock, "Certain Contemporaneous Matters in Geoffrey of Monmouth," *Speculum* 6 (1931): 206–211. Geoffrey of Monmouth could have received his information about Islam from Petrus Alphonsi either directly or indirectly (via William of Malmesbury). Monmouth was only forty miles from Malmesbury and about an equal distance from Malvern. Robert of Gloucester was patron of both William of Malmesbury and Geoffrey of Monmouth. Haskins, *Renaissance of the Twelfth Century*, 57.

56. Kritzeck, *Peter the Venerable and Islam*, 56; Daniel, *Islam and the West*, 320–322; Petrus Alphonsi, *Dialogi*, MPL, CLVII: 601:C-D, 604:D to 605:A; Petrus Alphonsi, *Disciplina Clericalis*, Hilka-Soederhjelm edition of the Latin text, I: 14–16 = Jones and Keller, *Scholar's Guide*, 56–60.

57. Kritzeck, *Peter the Venerable and Islam*, 56. Cf. also d'Alverny, *Occidente e l'Islam*, II; 594. According to Daniel, *Islam and the West*, 12, the written sources for Petrus Alphonsi's statements about Islam in the fifth chapter of the *Dialogi* were not known. However, Daniel was corrected by d'Alverny on this point. Indeed, when we consult Daniel's own book, especially the footnotes, we can easily see the close connection between the fifth, or anti-Islamic, chapter of Petrus Alphonsi's *Dialogi* and al-Kindi's *Risalah*. Cf. e.g. Daniel, 31, 328, note 55; 106; etc.

58. Petrus Alphonsi, *Dialogi*, MPL, CLVII: 597:B-C.

59. Petrus Alphonsi, *Dialogi*, MPL, CLVII: 600:B. For Kab al-Ahbar, Kritzeck, *Peter the Venerable and Islam*, 84–88, 105; Haim Zev Hirschberg, "Ka'b Al-Ahbar," *Ency. Judaica* 10 (1971): 488. For Abdallah ibn Salam, Kritzeck, 33, 89–96, 105, 162; Josef Horovitz, "Abdallah Ibn Salam," *Ency. Judaica* 2 (1971): 54. For the medieval Christian view that Muhammad had important Jewish helpers, cf. in general, Daniel, *Islam and the West*, index, *s.v.* "Jews," especially the reference to pp. 343–344. Cf. also Moshe Perlmann, *Samau'al Al-Maghribi: Ifham Al-Yahud: Silencing the Jews*, published as *Proceedings of the American Academy for Jewish Research* 32 (1964): 58–62, 98, note B52; Jacob Mann, "A Polemical Work against Karaite and Other Sectaries," *Jewish Quarterly Review* 12 (1921): 123–150, and Addenda, ibid. 16 (1925–1926): 89–91; J. Leveen, "Mohammad and His Jewish Companions," ibid. 16 (1925–1926): 399–406; S. Gandz, "Notes on Mr. Leveen's Article," ibid. 17 (1926–1927): 235–236; Leveen, "Addenda to Mohammed and His Jewish Companions," ibid. 17 (1926–1927): 237; Boaz Cohen, "Une Legende Juive de Mahomet," *Revue des Etudes Juives* 88 (1929): 1–17; M. Schwabe, "Aseret Haverav Ha-Y'hudim Shel Muhammad" [Muhammad's Ten Jewish Companions], *Tarbitz* 2 (1930–1931): 74–89; David Tzvi Baneth, "Al Aseret Haverav Ha-Y'hudim Shel Muhammad" [On Muhammad's Ten Jewish Companions], ibid. 3 (1931–1932): 112–116; Mann, "An Early Theologico-Polemical Work," *Hebrew Union College Annual* 12–13 (1937–1938): 411–459; Myron Weinstein, "A Hebrew Quran Manuscript [Post-Medieval]," *Studies in Bibliography and Booklore* 10 (1971–1972): 19–52; Septimus, *Speculum*, LVI: 517-533 passim.

60. Kritzeck, *Peter the Venerable and Islam*, 105, note 146. Cf. also supra, note 59; infra, note 68.

61. Kritzeck, *Peter the Venerable and Islam*, 21–22, 25–27, 192; Baron, *Social and Religious History*, IV: 122, 155, 301ff; V: 116, 341; VI: 169. Cf. also d'Ancona, *Giornale Storico della Letteratura Italiana*, XIII: 230; Daniel, *Islam and the West*, 84–85, 343–344, 350, note 18; infra, note 29 to chapter 4.

Peter the Venerable also wrote against the Petrobrusian heretics circa 1137–1138, then again 1140–1141 and 1143. Marcia Colish, "Peter of Bruys, Henry of Lausanne and the Facade of St. Gilles," *Traditio*, 28 (1972): 456 and note 32. Abelard also opposed the Petrobrusian heretics. Colish, 454 and note 14. Again we may have an

Abelardian influence on Peter the Venerable in that both attempted to deal with the challenge posed by the heretics (Petrobrusians), in addition to that posed by the Muslims and Jews, to Western Christian Orthodoxy.

62. Kritzeck, *Peter the Venerable and Islam*, 156; also 45, 158–159. Cf. also supra, text and note 16, as well as text between notes 24 and 25, to chapter 2.

63. Kritzek, *Peter the Venerable and Islam*, 58, note 31: "Daniel . . . [*Islam and the West*] passim, emphasizes the influence of this annotator." Southern does not seem to cite the Annotator in his *Western Views of Islam*. However, in his other volume, *The Making of the Middle Ages* (New Haven and London: Yale University Press, 1964), 40, Southern does cite the Annotator, relying on d'Alverny, *AHDLMA*, XVI: 101 and note 2, though Southern may be exaggerating the "profoundly hostile spirit" of the Annotator. If the Annotator was Petrus Alphonsi, his epithet of "madman" [*insanus*] for Muhammad would have been consistent with the traditional Jewish attitude toward Muhammad (as *m'shugga* = "mad," based on Hosea 9:7, "the man of the spirit [the prophet] is mad"). Perlmann, *Samau'al Al-Maghribi*, 62, 99, note B66. Cf. also Daniel, *Islam and the West*, 27–32, for the medieval Christian view that Muhammad was a "madman" and an "epileptic." However, Southern may well be correct when he suggests that the statement of the Annotator which he cites represents "the words of a man in the Schools," for Petrus Alphonsi's life and work could easily qualify him as one of the leading "Schoolmen" of the first half of the twelfth century.

64. For the Angel Gabriel in the Annotator, Daniel, *Islam and the West*, 32, 328, note 58; 37, 332, note 81. For the Angel Gabriel in Petrus Alphonsi's *Dialogi*, MPL, CLVII: 601:C. For the Angel Gabriel in Peter of Toledo's Latin *Risalah*, Munyoz-Sendino, *Miscellanea Comillas*, XI–XII: 402, lines 22–36. For the Angel Gabriel in the *Contrarietas*, cf. the only MS of this unpublished work, Paris, Bibliotheque Nationale, Latin 3394, f. 242v, line 18 (which we have examined on microfilm).

65. For Islamic bellicosity in the Annotator, Daniel, *Islam and the West*, 38; also 123, 353, note 32. For Islamic bellicosity in Petrus Alphonsi's *Dialogi*, MPL, CLVII: 598:B. For Islamic bellicosity in Peter of Toledo's Latin *Risalah*, Kritzeck, *Peter the Venerable and Islam*, 103–105 and note 139, as well as p. 145; Daniel, 123, 353, note 32. For Islamic bellicosity in the *Contrarietas*, Daniel, 123, 353, note 32; and the entire fourth chapter of the *Contrarietas* entitled *Quod per gladium et falsas visiones populum congregavit*, for which, d'Alverny, *AHDLMA*, XVI: 127.

66. For Muhammad's lust and adultery in the Annotator, Daniel, *Islam and the West*, 99, 346, note 54; and p. 102. In Petrus Alphonsi, supra, note 56. In Peter of Toledo's Latin *Risalah*, Kritzeck, *Peter the Venerable and Islam*, 104 and note 141; Daniel, 101, 347, note 60. Muhammad's lusting after Zaynab, the wife of his adopted son Zayd, is reported by Petrus Alphonsi, Peter of Toledo's *Risalah*, and the *Contrarietas*, so Daniel, 31, 328, note 55; 97–98, 346, notes 50–51.

67. For contradictions in the Quran as reported by the Annotator, Daniel, *Islam and the West*, 64, 338, note 46. By Petrus Alphonsi, *Dialogi*, MPL, CLVII: 603:D, 604:A–C. By Peter of Toledo's Latin *Risalah*, Daniel, 64; and Kritzeck, *Peter the Venerable and Islam*, 105. By the *Contrarietas*, Daniel, 64, as well as 35, 333, note 69; and the entire ninth chapter of the *Contrarietas* entitled *De multis in quibus contradicit sibi ipsi*, for which, d'Alverny, *AHDLMA*, XVI: 127.

68. Cf. Daniel, *Islam and the West*, 62, 337, notes 37-38; 84, 343-344, note 21; 86, 344, note 27, for all three writings—the Annotator, Petrus Alphonsi, and the *Contrarietas*—sharing similar views about Jewish influence on Muhammad. Cf. Kritzeck, *Peter the Venerable and Islam*, 105, for Peter of Toledo's Latin *Risalah*'s agreement on this point.

69. Daniel, *Islam and the West*, 62.

70. Petrus Alphonsi, *Dialogi*, MPL, CLVII: 597:A; 600:B, line 11; and 605:D, line 8.

71. Petrus Alphonsi, *Dialogi*, MPL, CLVII: 601:A, line 11: *Frivola sunt* [*ista miracula*] *quae prosequeris.* . . .

72. Petrus Alphonsi, *Dialogi*, MPL, CLVII: 605:C, line 4; 606:A, line 8-14, especially lines 9, 11, and 12; also 601:B, line 2. Cf. also Petrus Alphonsi, *Disciplina Clericalis*, Hilka-Soederhjelm edition of the Latin text, I: 11, *De Mendacio*, lines 3-4: *Correxit quidam philosophus filium suum: Cave mendacium, quia dulcius est carne volucrum.* For Islam as *error*, Alphonsi's *Dialogi*, MPL, CLVII: 606:A, line 14; also earlier in the text, col. 605:D, line 2. For Judaism as *error*, ibid., col. 597:B.

73. Daniel, *Islam and the West*, 62.

74. For *nequitia*, Petrus Alphonsi, *Dialogi*, MPL, CLVII: 605:D, line 11. For the *nequitia* of women in Alphonsi's *Disciplina Clericalis*, the Hilka-Soederhjelm edition of the Latin text, I: 14, line 8.

75. For *inconstans* and *irrationabile*, Petrus Alphonsi, *Dialogi*, MPL, CLVII: 597:B, lines 2-3. For the close relationship between Judaism and Islam, ibid., 597:B, 600:A-B.

76. For *inanis*, Petrus Alphonsi, *Dialogi*, MPL, CLVII: 599:C, line 12.

77. Daniel, *Islam and the West*, 63, 338, note 43; Southern, *Making of the Middle Ages*, 40; d'Alverny, *AHDLMA*, XVI: 101 and note 2; supra, note 63.

78. Daniel, *Islam and the West*, 83, 343, note 17, cites a discrepancy between Petrus Alphonsi's *Dialogi* and Peter of Toledo (= the Annotator) in translating the Quran, Sura 93: 6-8. However, Petrus Alphonsi = Peter of Toledo = the Annotator of circa 1142 could easily have decided, for polemical reasons or otherwise, to translate this Quranic passage differently from the way he had translated it for the *Dialogi* circa 1110, over thirty years before.

4. *The Association of Jew with Muslim by Medieval Christians*

*Chapter four is based on a paper delivered, with continuous revisions, on five separate occasions during 1967-1968 and one occasion during 1969-1970: (1) annual meeting, American Academy of Religion, Chicago, October 21, 1967; (2) 82nd annual meeting, American Historical Association, Toronto, December 20, 1967; (3) symposium entitled "Aspects of Medieval Anti-Judaism," sponsored by the UCLA Center for Medieval and Renaissance Studies, April 21, 1968; (4) quarterly meeting, Los Angeles Society for Jewish Research, April 28, 1968; (5) special lecture sponsored by the departments of philosophy and history, University of California at La Jolla, June 3, 1968; and (6) quarterly meeting, Committee on Middle Eastern Studies, Indiana University, Bloomington, March 17, 1970.

The Toronto paper was presented as part of the session "Anti-Semitism in Western Europe 1000–1500." The two other papers therein, "Causes and Symptoms of Anti-Semitism in the West" and "From Xenophobia to Prejudice: The Emergence of Anti-Semitism in the Thirteenth-Century," were delivered by B. Netanyahu and Gavin Langmuir. Robert Lopez served as critic of the three papers. We thank Professors Lopez, Netanyahu, and Langmuir for their suggestions regarding the Toronto paper.

The paper delivered at UCLA was part of a symposium in which the following members of the UCLA faculty participated: (1) Lynn White, (2) the late Gustave von Grunebaum, (3) Gerhart Ladner, (4) Moshe Perlmann, and (5) Amos Funkenstein. The following scholars from other universities also participated: Gavin Langmuir, B. Netanyahu, Adolf Leschnitzer, and Isadore Twersky. Ladner, von Grunebaum, Funkenstein, Langmuir, and Leschnitzer, "Reflections on Medieval Anti-Judaism," *Viator* 2 (1971): 355–396. For their comments on our paper we thank the participants in the symposium; as well as Richard Popkin, Edward Peters, and James Monroe, then all of the University of California at La Jolla, for their reactions to our lecture at their university.

We also express appreciation to colleagues in the Department of Near Eastern Languages and Literature, Indiana University, Bloomington, 1969–1970—Senior Judaica Scholar Henry Fischel and five Islamologists: Wadi Jwaideh, Salih Altoma, Salman Alani, Mohammed Alwan, and Victor Danner—for their encouragement of our work. An earlier version of this chapter appeared in *Judaism: A Quarterly Journal of Jewish Life and Thought* 17 (1968): 469–474. We thank Robert Gordis, its editor, for his permission to reproduce the chapter here after further revisions. The research for this chapter was assisted by a fellowship for "Younger Teacher-Scholars" from the National Endowment for the Humanities, Washington, D.C., and a grant from the UCLA Center for Medieval and Renaissance Studies, both during 1967–1968. We express gratitude to Barnaby Keeney, first director of the National Endowment for the Humanities, himself a medieval historian by training, and to Lynn White, then director, UCLA Center for Medieval and Renaissance Studies, for their support of our research.

Barbara Tuchman, the double Pulitzer Prize-winning historian, published a brilliant essay, "They Poisoned the Wells," *Newsweek*, February 3, 1975, 11, dealing with the scapegoat concept in Jewish history as well as its contemporary application to the Middle East crisis and those who blame the Jews for the Arab oil squeeze on the West. There is very little to criticize in this essay except to point out that she apparently failed to refer therein to the important role played by "the association of Jew with Muslim by medieval Christians" in the origins of modern anti-Semitism. This factor would have been extremely relevant in an article dealing in large part with the Arab-Israeli struggle and its effect upon the contemporary Christian West. Indeed, Tuchman begins her essay by discussing the persecution of the Jews of Western Europe at the time of the Black Plague (circa 1350), a result of the accusation that the Jews had caused the plague by poisoning the wells. However, she fails to note that a generation earlier, circa 1320, the Jews of France were accused of having instigated the lepers to poison the wells, with the crucial particular added to the story as it then circulated that the Jews and lepers had acted in concert *with the Muslims of Spain*. Thus, in the dress rehearsal, as it were, for the persecution of the Jews of Western Europe during the Black Plague the association of Jew with Muslim by medieval Christians played a crucial role. In her well-written and best-selling book, *A Distant Mirror: The Calamitous Fourteenth Century* (New York: Knopf, 1978), 109, Tuchman corrects the omission in her *Newsweek* essay. She points out that the Christians who accused the Jews and lepers of poisoning the wells circa 1320 accused them of doing so in concert with the Muslims of Granada and that the charge of well-poisoning circa 1320 was revived by, and influenced, the persecution during the Black Plague circa 1350. She is also aware of the fact that the Fouth Lateran Council imposed a badge of shame upon the Muslims as well as the Jews. Tuchman, 112; infra, chapter 6.

For the persecution of the Jews of France circa 1320 in which the Islamic factor played a major role, James Parkes, *The Jew in the Medieval Community: A Study of His Political and Economic Situation* (London: Soncino, 1938), 125–126, 174; Joshua Trachtenberg, *The Devil and the Jews: The Medieval Conception of the Jew and Its Relation to Modern Antisemitism* (Cleveland, New York, and Philadelphia: World/Meridian and Jewish Publication Society of America, 1961), 101–102; Baron, *Social and Religious History*, X: 68–70; XI: 159–161, 219–222, 250–252; Baer, *History of the Jews in Christian Spain*, II: 15–17; Ephraim Kupfer, "Sikili, Jacob ben Hananel," *Ency. Judaica* 14 (1971): 1530; Synan, *Popes and the Jews*, 129–130, 209, note 36; infra, note 114 to chapter 8.

On the persecution in general at this time, John E. Weakland, "Pastorelli, Pope, and Persecution: A Tragic Episode in 1320," *Jewish Social Studies*, 38 (1976): 73–76.

1. For the first day's session, Israel Shenker, "An Awesome Reliving of Auschwitz Unfolds at St. John's," *New York Times*, June 4, 1974, part 1, 33. On the symposium in general, Gregory Baum, "Theology after Auschwitz: A Conference Report," *Ecumenist* 12:5 (August 1974) (entire issue devoted to Baum's report). The symposium's proceedings were published as *Auschwitz, Beginning of a New Era?: Reflections on the Holocaust: Papers Given at the International Symposium on the Holocaust, Held at the Cathedral of St. John the Divine, New York City, June 3–6, 1974*, ed. Eva Fleischner (New York: K'tav for Cathedral Church of St. John the Divine and Anti-Defamation League of B'nai B'rith, 1977).

2. Rosemary Ruether, "Anti-Semitism in Christian Theology," in *Auschwitz, Beginning of a New Era?* 79–92, 447–449 (the quoted passage is at page 79).

Cf. Ruether's *Faith and Fratricide: The Image of the Jews in Early Christianity* (New York: Seabury, 1974), based on her patristic studies as reflected, *e.g.*, in her *Gregory Nazianzus: Rhetor and Philosopher* (Oxford: Clarendon, 1969).

Cf. also Ruether's "The 'Adversus Judaeos' Tradition in the Church Fathers: The Exegesis of Christian Anti-Judaism," in Paul E. Szarmach, ed., *Aspects of Jewish Culture in the Middle Ages* (Albany: State University of New York Press, 1979), 27–50.

Cf. also Thomas A. Idinopulos and Roy Bowen Ward, "Is Christology Inherently Anti-Semitic? A Critical Review of Rosemary Ruether's *Faith and Fratricide*," *Journal of the American Academy of Religion* 45 (1977): 193–214; Alan T. Davies, ed., *Anti-Semitism and the Foundations of Christianity* (New York: Paulist Press, 1979) (discussion of the Ruether book *Faith and Fratricide*).

For other recent studies of patristic attitudes toward the Jews, Robert Wilken, *Judaism and the Early Christian Mind: A Study of Cyril of Alexandria's Exegesis and*

Theology (New Haven: Yale University Press, 1971); and his *John Chrysostom and the Jews* (University of California Press, forthcoming); Nicholas R.M. de Lange, *Origen and the Jews: Studies in Jewish-Christian Relations in Second Century Palestine* (New York: Cambridge University Press, 1976); Claude Aziza, *Tertullien et le Judaisme* (Paris: Belles Lettres, 1977).

The following works remain of classical importance in the study of patristic attitudes toward the Jews: S. Krauss, "The Jews in the Works of the Church Fathers," *Jewish Quarterly Review* 5 (1892): 122–157; 6 (1894): 82–99, 225–261; James Parkes, *The Conflict of the Church and the Synagogue* (Cleveland, New York, and Philadelphia: World/Meridian/Jewish Publication Society of America, 1961 [originally published in 1934]), passim; Williams, *Adversus Judaeos*, 3–104, 117–140; Marcel Simon, *Verus Israel: Etude sur les Relations entre Chretiens et Juifs dans l'Empire Romain, 135–425* (1st ed.; Paris: Boccard, 1948; 2nd ed.; Paris: Boccard, 1964); and his *Recherches d'Histoire Judeo-Chretienne* (Paris and The Hague: Mouton, 1962); Bernhard Blumenkranz, *Die Judenpredigt Augustins: Ein Beitrag zur Geschichte der Juedisch-Christlichen Beziehungen in den Ersten Jahrhunderten* (1st ed.; Basel: Halbing and Lichtenhahn, 1946; 2nd ed.; Paris: Etudes Augustiniennes, 1973); his "Augustin et les Juifs: Augustin et le Judaisme," *Recherches Augustiniennes* 1 (1958): 225–241; and his "Church Fathers," *Ency. Judaica* 5 (1971): 550–553.

In a lettter to us of April 7, 1975, Ruether stated that our thesis with regard to the anti-Islamic origins of modern anti-Semitism "seems nonsense to me, confusing secondary and late symptoms with cause." Ruether holds that the theological anti-Semitism of the church fathers is the primary cause of Western Christian anti-Semitism. No one would want to deny that patristic anti-Semitism was important. However, patrisitic anti-Semitism cannot explain why anti-Semitism almost died out completely in Western Europe during the Carolingian-Ottonian period (circa 700–1000) or why anti-Semitism was revived with explosive force during the High Middle Ages (circa 1000–1300), the Romanesque-Gothic period of medieval urbanization. The temporary near demise and the permanent rebirth of anti-Semitism in Western Europe circa 700–1300 were both intimately bound up with the birth of Islam in the seventh century. Islam created an empire stretching from the Atlantic to central Asia larger than that of the Romans, an empire which threatened the destruction of Christendom. The birth of Islam completely altered the religious equation in the Western civilizational area from what it had been during the patristic period (two monotheistic faiths, Judaism and Christianity, competing for the role of successor to the dying Greco-Roman pagan civilization) to what it has been from the seventh century until the present (two great monotheistic faiths, Christianity and Islam, competing for dominance over the Mediterranean, with the third monotheistic faith, Judaism, caught in the middle). The thesis about the anti-Islamic origins of modern anti-Semitism offers us the primary explanation of the history of anti-Semitism in Western Christendom since the birth of Islam in the seventh century.

3. Yosef Yerushalmi, "Response to Rosemary Ruether," in *Auschwitz, Beginning of a New Era?* 97–107.

Yerushalmi has published *From Spanish Court to Italian Ghetto: Isaac Cardoso: A Study in Seventeenth-Century Marranism and Jewish Apologetics* (New York and London: Columbia University Press, 1971); *Haggadah and History: A Panorama in Facsimile of*

Five Centuries of the Printed Haggadah (Philadelphia: Jewish Publication Society of America, 1975); *The Lisbon Massacre of 1506 and the Royal Image in the Shebet Yehudah*, Hebrew Union College Annual Supplements, no. 1 (Cincinnati: Hebrew Union College Press and K'tav, 1976); *Zakhor: Jewish History and Jewish Memory* (Seattle: University of Washington Press, 1982). Cf. *Directory of American Scholars* 1 (1982): 850.

4. Startling new information about modern Vatican-Jewish relations came to light in anticipation of Golda Meir's historic visit and conversation with Pope Paul VI. Paul Hofmann, "Mrs. Meir Confers with Pope in Vatican," *New York Times*, January 16, 1973, part 1, 1 and 16; "Mrs. Meir Says Tension Marked Talk with Pope," ibid., January 20, 1973, part 1, 1 and 12; *Time*, January 29, 1973, 27; *Newsweek*, same date, 36. In June 1938 Pope Pius XI ordered an American Jesuit, John LaFarge, to write an encyclical condemning Nazi anti-Semitism which might have saved thousands of Jewish lives during World War II had not the pope died in 1939 before the document could be officially promulgated. *Time*, December 25, 1972, 48; *B'nai B'rith Messenger* (Los Angeles), December 22, 1972, 4.

5. Eliezer Whartman, "Our Letter From Israel: Israel and the Catholic Church," *Bnai B'rith Messenger* (Los Angeles), October 18, 1974, 33 and 39, cites another Christian spokesperson, Gerald Noel, a leading English Catholic intellectual (writing in the *London Catholic Herald*) whose views on anti-Semitism parallel those of Ruether, and another Jewish spokesperson, David Flusser, the Hebrew University's authority on comparative religion and Christian-Jewish relations, whose views on anti-Semitism parallel those of Yerushalmi. Thus, Noel and Ruether, the two Christians (both Catholic), believe that the primary responsibility for anti-Semitism over the centuries belongs to the church, whereas Flusser and Yerushalmi, the two Jews, believe that the primary responsibility for anti-Semitism over the centuries lies elsewhere. We basically agree with Flusser and Yerushalmi, except that we argue that the primary factor in anti-Semitism since the seventh century has been *anti-Muslimism*.

6. (New York: Signet Books, New American Library, 1972), 93.

7. Kurzman, *Genesis 1948*, 378–380, 594–596, and the strong reaction of Louis Massignon, Catholic mystic and greatest French Islamologist of the twentieth century, against the Israeli capture of Nazareth, as reported in Basetti-Sani, *Louis Massignon (1883–1962): Christian Ecumenist, Prophet of Inter-Religious Reconciliation*, 29, 76–77, 137, 178. But certainly the Christian holy places in Nazareth have flourished since the Israeli conquest of the city in 1948. Shlomo Hasson, "Nazareth," *Ency. Judaica* 12 (1971): 901–904.

8. Kurzman, *Genesis 1948*, 209.

9. Translated by Peter Green (New York: Pantheon Books/Random House, 1971). On the "Orleans Affair" of May-June 1969, also Renee Winegarten, "Jews in the Mind of France," *Commentary* 50:5 (November 1970): 67–68: Arnold Mandel, "France," *American Jewish Year Book* 71 (1970): 419–420; Bernhard Blumenkranz, "Orleans," *Ency. Judaica* 12 (1971): 1470.

10. Morin, *Rumour in Orleans*, 126.

11. Parkes, *Jew in the Medieval Community*, 37–39; Trachtenberg, *Devil and the Jews*, 184: Baron, *Social and Religious History*, IV; 17, 55–58, 66–67, 77; Blumenkranz, *Juifs et Chretiens*, 380–381, his *Auteurs*, 236–259, and his "The Roman Church and the Jews," in Roth, *Dark Ages*, 74, 76, 79, 81, 84, 87–89; Roth, "Italy," ibid.,

119–120; S. Schwarzfuchs, "France under the Early Capets," ibid., 145–150; Blumenkranz, "Germany 843–1096," ibid., 172–174. On Caliph Hakim of Egypt, whose persecution of the Christians (and Jews) of Egypt and Palestine circa 1010 triggered the persecutions of the Jews of Western Europe at the same time, the articles in the *Ency. of Islam* by E. Graefe, 2 (1927): 224–225, and M. Canard, 3 (1971): 76–82.

Cf. also Robert Chazan, "1007–1012: Initial Crisis for Northern European Jewry," *Proceedings of the American Academy for Jewish Research* 38–39 (1972): 101–117, especially 109–110, and 110, note 27. Despite the views of Parkes, Trachtenberg, Baron, and Blumenkranz (who rely upon two French Christian chroniclers of the first half of the eleventh century, Ralph Glaber and Adhemar de Chabannes, on whom infra, note 27), all four recognizing the crucial importance of the association of Jew with Muslim by medieval Christians in the great persecution of the Jews of Western Europe during the early eleventh century, Chazan holds that the association of Jew with Muslim by medieval Christians played *no real role* in this persecution. The persecution, according to Chazan, was solely the result of the association of Jew with *Christian heretic*.

According to Blumenkranz, *Juifs et Chretiens*, 71, note 14, followed by Roth, "Italy," in Roth, *Dark Ages*, 120, 406, note 68, and David Berger, "St. Peter Damian: His Attitude toward the Jews and the Old Testament," *Yavneh Review: A Religious Jewish Collegiate Magazine* 4 (Spring 1965): 82, 106, note 9, St. Simeon the Anchorite was responsible for the conversion of some of the Jews of Lucca in 1016. However, 1016 was not the date St. Simeon came to Lucca but rather the date he died. S. Baring-Gould, *Lives of the Saints* (Edinburgh: Grant, 1914), VIII: 574; Felice da Mareto, "Simeone di Polirone," *Encic. Catt.* 11 (1963): 625; F.D. Lazenby, "Simeon of Polirone," *New Cath.Ency.* 13 (1967): 218; Filippo Caraffa, "Simeone, Eremita di Polirone," *Bib. Sanct.* 11 (1968): 1114. It would seem that this St. Simeon, probably born in Armenia, went via Jerusalem to Rome in 983, thence via Pisa to Lucca circa 985, and it was at this time that he converted some of the local Jews. Baring-Gould, VIII: 571–573; A. Zimmerman, "Simeon von Polirone," *Lexikon fuer Theologie und Kirche* 9 (1937): 566; Mareto, 625; Herbert Thurston and Donald Attwater, eds., *Butler's Lives of the Saints* (London: Burns and Oates, 1956), III: 190; Lazenby, 218.

If, indeed, the conversion of some of the Jews of Lucca by St. Simeon the Anchorite took place circa 985 (and not in 1016, which was rather the year of his death), then, because of St. Simeon's Eastern Christian origins and connections, his missionary activity at Lucca could well have been influenced by the expulsion of the Jews from Sparta, Greece, circa 985, ordered by St. Nikon Metanoeite. Joshua Starr, *The Jews in the Byzantine Empire 641–1204* (New York: Burt Franklin, 1970), 9, 167–168; Andrew Sharf, *Byzantine Jewry from Justinian to the Fourth Crusade* (New York: Shocken, 1971), 126, 130, note 70. St. Nikon himself may well have associated Jew with Muslim and have considered the Jews Islamic fifth columnists in Christian territory, for St. Nikon was the Apostle of Crete who reconverted the Islamic upper class of the island to Christianity after Emperor Nicephorus Phocas reconquered it from the Muslims in 961. F.H. Marshall, "Byzantine Literature," in Norman H. Baynes and H. St. L.B. Moss, eds., *Byzantium: An Introduction to East Roman Civilization* (Oxford: Clarendon, 1961), 236–237, 236, note 1; E. Voulgarakis, "Nikon Metanoeite und die Rechristianisierung der Kreter vom Islam," *Zeitschrift fuer Missionswissenschaft und*

Religionswissenschaft 47 (1963): 192–204, 258–269; Marilyn Dunn, "Evangelism or Repentance? The Re-Christianization of the Pelopponese in the Ninth and Tenth Centuries," in Baker, *Renaissance and Renewal in Christian History*, 82–83. St. Simeon the Anchorite may well have agreed with St. Nikon Metanoeite that the Jews were an Islamic fifth column in Christian society but disagreed with St. Nikon in favoring conversion rather than expulsion as the most authentically Christian way of dealing with this fifth column.

It is also possible that St. Simeon the Anchorite's effort to convert the Jews of Lucca circa 985 should be viewed against the backdrop of Emperor Otto II's campaign against the Arabs in southern Italy, for which, Alexander A. Vasiliev, *History of the Byzantine Empire 324–1453* (2nd English ed., Madison: University of Wisconsin Press, 1964), I: 312; George Ostrogorsky, *History of the Byzantine State*, translated by Joan Hussey (New Brunswick, New Jersey: Rutgers University Press, 1957), 278. Perhaps at this time of severe tension between Christian and Muslim in Italy, the Jews there were accused by the Christians of being in league with the Muslims. Was this why the Jew Kalonymus, in a famous episode, risked his life to save Emperor Otto II from the Arabs at Crotone, Calabria, circa 982, *i.e.*, to prove that the Jews were not in league with the Muslims against the Christians? Perhaps this is also why St. Simeon the Anchorite worked so zealously to convert the Jews of Lucca circa 985, *i.e.*, in order to weaken the Muslims by converting their Jewish allies living within Christian society away from the Judaeo/Islamic conspiracy and into the true faith. For the Jew Kalonymus (who would seem to have had close family ties with the Jews of Lucca, the very city of St. Simeon's missionary work) and Emperor Otto II, Margolis and Marx, *History of the Jewish People*, 299, 353; Baron, *Social and Religious History*, IV: 273, note 87; Blumenkranz, *Juifs et Chretiens*, 36 and note 25, and his *Auteurs*, 244–245; Attilio Milano, *Storia degli Ebrei in Italia* (Turin: Einaudi, 1963), 58 and note 1; Arthur Zuckerman, *Jewish Princedom in Feudal France 768–900* (New York: Columbia University Press, 1972), 66–67, note 35; 144, note 69.

There was an important Jewish revolt (led by Abu al-Faraj) in the Setif region of northeastern Algeria against the Muslim Zirid rulers of the country, which revolt was suppressed with great cruelty in 989. David Corcos, "Algeria," *Ency. Judaica* 2 (1971): 612–613. The Jewish revolt against the Zirids in northeastern Algeria could have helped contribute to the persecution of the Jews of Limoges, France, recorded by a Hebrew source as taking place circa 992. Western Christians may well have reasoned that the best time to attack the Jews, whom they considered Islamic fifth-columnists in Christian territory, was when there was a temporary falling-out between the two partners in the permanent Judaeo/Islamic conspiracy against the Christians, as, *e.g.*, during the Jewish revolt against the Zirids in northeastern Algeria circa 989. For the persecution of the Jews of Limoges circa 992, Baron, *Social and Religious History*, IV: 92, 283–284, note 2; Blumenkranz, *Juifs et Chretiens*, 103 and note 152, 363 and note 320; Schwarzfuchs, "France Under The Early Capets," in Roth, *Dark Ages*, 146–147, 410, note 6; Chazan, "The Persecution [at Limoges] of 992," *Revue des Etudes Juives* 129 (1970): 217–221.

There is no certainty with regard to the dating of the persecution of the Jews at Limoges circa 992. Baron, IV: 283–284, note 2, informs us that some have held that this persecution took place in 994, while it is also possible that it did not take place until 1010 and it was identical with the persecution that broke out at Limoges in connection with the alleged Jewish complicity in the anti-Christian persecution launched by Caliph Hakim of Egypt.

If we date the persecution in Limoges as taking place in 996, rather than 992, we can link it with the massacre of about 100 Christian merchants (from Amalfi) in Old Cairo which took place in 996, during the transition from the peaceful reign of Caliph al-Aziz (975–996) to the turbulent reign of Caliph Hakim (996–1021), only eleven years old when he came to power. Robert S. Lopez, *Birth of Europe* (New York and Philadelphia: Evans and Lippincott, 1967), 131; Armando O. Citarella, "The Relations of Amalfi with the Arab World before the Crusades," *Speculum* 42 (1967): 310–311; both relying on C. Cahen, "Un Texte peu Connu Relatif au Commerce Oriental d'Amalfi au Xe Siecle," *Archivio Storico per le Province Napoletane* 34 (1955): 61–67; Hitti, *History of the Arabs*, 619–621. Just as the Jews of Limoges were attacked circa 1010 for their alleged complicity in the anti-Christian persecution launched by Caliph Hakim of Egypt circa 1010, so perhaps the Jews of Limoges were earlier attacked circa 996 for the identical reason, their alleged complicity in the anti-Christian persecution which broke out in Cairo circa 996, the first year of Caliph Hakim's reign.

If we date the persecution of the Jews of Limoges in 996 (instead of 992), perhaps the Jews of Limoges were persecuted for alleged complicity in the Fatimid defeat of the Byzantines in northern Syria circa 994 which resulted in a serious threat to Christian control of Aleppo and especially of Antioch (for which, Ostrogorsky, *History of the Byzantine State*, 273).

If we date the persecution of the Jews of Limoges in 997 (instead of 992), it could also be linked with the devastation wrought upon the Christians of northern Spain by al-Mansur, the great vizier of the caliphs of Cordova, who took Zamora in 981, Barcelona in 985, Coimbra in 987, Leon in 988; defeated and captured Count Garcia Fernandez of Castile in 995; captured and devasted the great Christian pilgrimage shrine at Santiago de Compostela in Galicia in 997. Hitti, *History of the Arabs*, 533; Aguado-Bleye, *Manual*, I: 436–439. Perhaps the Jews of Limoges were persecuted in 997 for alleged complicity in al-Mansur's massive victories over the Christians of northern Spain circa 981 to 997, which struck terror into the hearts of the Christians of southern France as well.

Roth, "Economic Life and Population Movements," and "Italy," both in Roth, *Dark Ages*, 37 and 117 respectively, reports that in 992 the Byzantines pressured the Venetians into excluding Jews, Lombards, and Amalfitans from the lucrative Venetian trade with Byzantium. The Byzantine move may have been part of preparations for a major new offensive against the Arabs in northern Syria. The Byzantines may well have felt that the Jews and Amalfitans were allies of the Arabs and that allowing them to profit by the Venetian trade with Byzantium would indirectly help enrich Byzantium's Arab enemies. It is possible that the persecution of the Jews of Limoges, France, in the 990s was an attempt by the Christians of Limoges to curry favor with the Venetians and Byzantines in an attempt to gain and/or improve Limoges's share of the lucrative Venetian trade with Byzantium. Thus, just as the combined Byzantine and Venetian influence was decisive in the persecution of the Jews in Germany during the 930s (infra, note 25), so the combined Byzantine and Venetian influence would have been equally decisive in the persecution of the Jews at Limoges in the 990s. But just as the association of Jew with Muslim by medieval Christians played a major role in the Byzantine/Venetian-inspired persecution of the Jews of Germany in the 930s, so this same factor would also have played a major role in the Byzantine/Venetian-inspired persecution of the Jews at Limoges in the 990s.

12. Norman Cohn, *Pursuit of the Millennium: Revolutionary Messianism in Medieval and Reformation Europe and Its Bearing on Modern Totalitarian Movements* (2nd ed; New York: Harper Torchbooks/Academy Library, 1961), 58–74, in considering the causes of the great outburst of anti-Semitism in Western Europe during the High and Later Middle Ages (1000–1500), emphasizes Christian Messianic expectations, the association of the Jew with the demonic, and psychoanalytical factors, and deemphasizes Christian hatred of the Jews as moneylenders. Infra, note 16. However, Cohn also considers the association of Jew with Muslim a very important factor in the history of anti-Semitism, though he does not fully develop it in his book *Pursuit of the Millennium*. Thus, according to Cohn, 60: "[During the period of the Crusades against the Arabs and later against the Turks] Jews and Saracens were generally regarded as closely akin, if not identical." In his footnote at this point, p. 391, Cohn refers the reader to Marcel Bulard's monumental study, *Le Scorpion, Symbole du Peuple Juif dans l'Art Religieux des XIVe, XVe, XVIe Siecles* (Paris: Boccard, 1935), and states the following: "Bulard proves from iconographical evidence that Saracens were even believed to have taken part, along with Jews, in the Crucifixion." For Bulard's continuing scholarly validity, cf., e.g., B. Guidot, "L'Image du Juif dans la Geste de Guillaume d'Orange," *Revue des Etudes Juives* 137 (1978): 5 and note 7, 13 and note 44, 18 and note 74. Infra, text and notes 59–61, we reorganize Bulard's important artistic data and present it chronologically within the context of the association of Jew with Muslim by medieval Christians.

Synan, one of the leading Catholic authorities on the history of Christian-Jewish relations, agrees with Cohn when Synan states in his *The Popes and the Jews in the Middle Ages*, 52, that there is no need "to multiply texts to establish the existence of a conviction [*i.e.*, the conviction of Western Christians during the Middle Ages that the Jew was in league with the Muslim planning the destruction of the West] so evidently widespread as to require no proof."

Cf. also infra, note 17, for the views of Blumenkranz and Flannery on the association of Jew with Muslim by medieval Christians in the eleventh century, the century preceding the First Crusade, as well as for the views of Cantera Burgos and Baron that the Christians of Spain considered the Jews Islamic "fifth columnists" (the precise language used by both distinguished scholars) in Christian territory.

Cf. also infra, note 67, for Trachtenberg's view that the Jews of the sixteenth- and seventeenth-century Holy Roman Empire were considered to be in league with the Turks against the Christians, serving the Turks as spies and acting "in general as what we would call today 'fifth columnists' " (Trachtenberg's precise language).

13. The work of our teachers, Queller and Dales, is outlined immediately below: Donald Queller, *Early Venetian Legislation on Ambassadors* (Geneva: Droz, 1966); *The Office of the Ambassador in the Middle Ages* (Princeton: Princeton University Press, 1967); *The Latin Conquest of Constantinople* (New York: Wiley, 1971); ed. with Joseph R. Strayer, *Post Scripta: Essays on Medieval Law and the Emergence of the European State in Honor of Gaines Post* (Rome: Libreria Ateneo Salesiano, 1972); *The Fourth Crusade*

(Philadelphia: University of Pennsylvania Press, 1977); with Francis R. Swietek, *Two Studies on Venetian Government* (Geneva: Droz, 1977); *Medieval Diplomacy and the Fourth Crusade* (London: Variorum, 1980). Cf. *Directory of American Scholars* 1 (1982): 611.

Richard Dales, ed., *Robert Grosseteste's Commentarius in VIII Libros Physicorum Aristotelis* (Boulder: University of Colorado Press, 1964); *The Scientific Achievement of the Middle Ages* (Philadelphia: University of Pennsylvania Press, 1973); *Marius: On the Elements, a Critical Edition and Translation* (Berkeley and Los Angeles: University of California Press, 1976); *The Intellectual Life of Western Europe in the Middle Ages* (Washington, D.C.: University Press of America, 1980). Cf. *Directory of American Scholars* 1 (1982): 168.

James A. Brundage, an authority on medieval Western Christian canon law and the history of the Crusades, has also made many helpful suggestions to us over the years (infra, text and notes 16–18 to chapter 6). Cf. his five books, *The Chronicle of Henry of Livonia* (Madison: University of Wisconsin Press, 1961); *The Crusades: A Documentary Survey* (Milwaukee: Marquette University Press, 1962); *The Crusades: Motives and Achievements* (Boston: Heath, 1964); *Medieval Canon Law and the Crusader* (Madison: University of Wisconsin Press, 1969); *Richard Lion Heart* (New York: Scribner, 1974). Cf. *Directory of American Scholars* 1 (1982): 93.

14. For the massacre and the two libels, Trachtenberg, *Devil and the Jews*, 109–155; Baron, *Social and Religious History*, IV: 89–149. For the blood libel alone, articles by Hermann L. Strack and Joseph Jacobs, *Jewish Ency.* 3 (1902): 260–267; Haim Hillel Ben-Sasson and Yehuda Slutsky, *Ency. Judaica* 4 (1971): 1120–1131. For the desecration-of-the-host libel alone, articles by Max Schloessinger and Joseph Jacobs, *Jewish Ency.*, 6 (1904): 481–483; Cecil Roth, *Ency. Judaica* 8 (1971): 1040–1044.

In a future study we shall attempt to demonstrate the close correlation between the incidence of blood libel and desecration-of-the-host libel accusations against the Jews with outbreaks of war on the Christian-Islamic frontier. Was it mere coincidence that neither blood nor desecration-of-the-host libels were known in Western Europe before the Crusades? Was it sheer coincidence that the first known instance of the blood libel in Western Europe, at Norwich, England, 1144, occurred during the decade of the Second Crusade, while the first known instance of the desecration-of-the-host libel, at Belitz, near Berlin, 1243, occurred one year before the Christians lost Jerusalem to the Muslims (Steven Runciman, *History of the Crusades* [Harmondsworth, England: Penguin/Pelican, 1971], III: 224–225; Jerusalem was not to be recovered again until Allenby took it from the Turks in 1917). Christian anti-Muslimism may well have been a crucial factor in both the blood and desecration-of-the-host libels, two of the chief manifestations of Christian anti-Semitism in Europe since the Crusades.

Islamic antipathy toward the blood libel during the Middle Ages explains the relative paucity of blood libels in two Mediterranean Christian countries, both fairly heavily influenced by Islam: Spain and Italy. Cf. the map in Ben-Sasson and Slutsky, *Ency. Judaica*, IV: 1125–1126. For the blood libel in Spain, Baer, *Jews in Christian Spain*, II, index *s.v.* "Blood libels"; M. Despina, "Las Acusaciones de Crimen Ritual en Espanya," *El Olivo* 9 (1979): 48–70.

According to the article "Faisal Believed Jews Mix Christian Blood and Matzoh,"

B'nai B'rith Messenger (Los Angeles), April 4, 1975, 27, the late King Faisal of Saudi Arabia apparently accepted the Christian blood libel about the Jews, even though this libel is not one of the stock images of the Jew in traditional Islamic society. Our own thesis that Christian anti-Muslimism may well have been a crucial factor in the blood libel would help explain why this libel has not been one of the stock images of the Jew in traditional Islamic society. Cf. also infra, note 45, for Lynn White's views on this subject.

Of course, if we can ask how the advanced civilization of the High Middle Ages, which produced such giants of the human spirit as St. Francis of Assisi, could also have produced a revival of anti-Semitism, we can also ask how the advanced civilization of nineteenth- and early twentieth-century Germany which produced such giants of the human spirit as Goethe, could also have produced Nazism. Apparently, a high state of cultural achievement does not necessarily guarantee immunity from anti-Semitism (and anti-Muslimism)!

15. Cf. our articles in the field of the history of Christian-Islamic relations: "Who Was the 'Monk of France' and When Did He Write?: A Note on D.M. Dunlop's 'A Christian Mission To Muslim Spain in the 11th Century'," *Al-Andalus* 28 (1963): 249–269; "The Ninth-Century Spanish Martyrs' Movement and the Origins of Western Christian Missions to the Muslims," *The Muslim World* 55 (1965): 321–339; "The First Crusade and the Idea of 'Conversion'," ibid. 58 (1968): 57–71, 155–164; the four articles which form the bases of chapters 2–4 and 6 of this book (cf. the notes * of these chapters); and the Massignon book (supra, note 8 to chapter 1; infra, note 2 to chapter 9).

The first study in our series on medieval Christian-Islamic relations is completed. We refer to our *The Evolution of the Western Christian Mission to the Muslims to the End of the First Crusade*, a thorough revision and expansion of our 1963 dissertation under Professor Queller at the University of Southern California. The second is near completion, *St. Francis of Assisi and Islam, Revisionary Studies in the Early Franciscan Mission to the Muslims*, and is influenced by the work of Basetti-Sani, a leading authority on Franciscan-Islamic relations (supra, note 8 to chapter 1).

On Palestinian Jewish history during the Greco-Roman period we have published "Does the Simeon of Luke 2 Refer to Simeon the Son of Hillel?," *Journal of Bible and Religion* (since renamed *Journal of the American Academy of Religion*) 24 (1966): 29–35; "Symposium on the Pharisees," *Central Conference of American Rabbis Journal* 14 (June 1967): 32–47; "Third-Century Palestinian Rabbinic Attitudes towards the Prospect of the Fall of Rome," *Jewish Social Studies* 31 (1969): 275–285; "Do the Zugot Represent Opposing Left and Right Wing Factions Within the Pharisaic Party? A Critical Re-examination of Louis Ginzberg's Theory," in Mishael M. Caspi, ed., *Jewish Tradition in the Diaspora: Studies in Memory of Professor Walter J. Fischel* (Berkeley, California: Judah L. Magnes Memorial Museum, 1981), 61–81. Our book, *The Pharisaic Origins of Early Christianity: Judaism and the Non-Jewish World 300 B.C. to 300 A.D.*, which argues that Hillel the Elder's revolutionary Messianism crucially influenced Jesus and early Christianity, is near completion.

16. Factors in the history of anti-Semitism other than the anti-Islamic factor are:
Religious Factors
A.) It is often held that Christian theology was the primary factor in patristic anti-

Semitism (*e.g.*, supra, note 2). However, there is also the view which holds that the primary factor in patristic anti-Semitism was the legacy of Greco-Roman *pagan* anti-Semitism introduced into the church by its Gentile converts. Flannery, *Anguish of the Jews*, 3–24; Friedrich Heer, *God's First Love: Christians and Jews Over 2000 Years*, trans. G. Skelton (New York: Weybright and Talley, 1970), 15–21; B. Netanyahu, "Antishemiyyut: Mavo K'lali" [Anti-Semitism: General Introduction], and Isaac Heinemann and Joshua Gutmann, "Ha-Antishemiyyut Ba-Olam Ha-Atik" [Anti-Semitism in the Ancient (Greco-Roman Pagan) World], *Ency. Hebraica* 4 (1951–1952): 493–522; plus the English version of the Heinemann-Gutmann article, "Anti-Semitism: In Antiquity," *Ency. Judaica* 3 (1971): 87–96. Jerry L. Daniel, "Anti-Semitism in the Hellenistic-Roman Period," *Journal of Biblical Literature* 98 (1979): 45–65, concludes on p. 65 with the view that "anti-Semitism was more severe than usually realized" in the Greco-Roman world. If this view (supported by both Flannery and Neyanyahu) be correct, the main causes of Greco-Roman pagan anti-Semitism become the primary factors in patristic anti-Semitism. These causes were (1) religious (pagan insecurity vis-à-vis Jewish ethical monotheism); (2) ethnolinguistic (Indo-European Greco-Roman values at variance with those of the Semitic Jews); (3) political (the Diaspora Jews caught between the native Hamitic/Semitic populations of the Middle East and their Greco-Roman conquerors); and (4) the associative factor developed below.

To a certain extent premedieval Western anti-Semitism may have been partly due to the fear (at times well-founded) held by the Greco-Roman (both pagan as well as Christian) conquerors of the Middle East that the Jews of Palestine and the Middle East were conspiring with the Iranians (both pagan Parthian and Neo-Zoroastrian Sassanian) to end European domination of the Middle East. Thus, before there was an association of Jew with Muslim by medieval Christians (beginning with the seventh century A.D.), there may well have been an association of Jew with Iranian by Greco-Roman pagan and Christian (beginning with the third century B.C. and perhaps even earlier). However, the medieval Christian equation of Jew with Muslim was based on a much closer theological and ethnolinguistic affinity between the two equated groups than was the classical Greco-Roman equation of Jew with Iranian. The Iranians, unlike the Jews and Muslims, were neither Abrahamitic in faith nor Semitic in ethnolinguistic affiliation. Moreover, it was the medieval Christian equation of Jew with Muslim, rather than the classical Greco-Roman equation of Jew with Iranian, that helped revive anti-Semitism in Western Europe during the High Middle Ages (after its relative dormancy in the Carolingian-Ottonian period) and that has played such a major role in keeping anti-Semitism alive in Europe ever since.

B.) Undoubtedly the deicide charge (*i.e.*, the traditional Christian belief that the Jews and not the Romans killed Jesus, the Son of God, and the traditional Christian desire to punish the Jews everywhere, in each subsequent generation, for this horrendous crime supposedly committed by all the Jews of Palestine circa 30 A.D.) played an important role in the history of anti-Semitism. Hence, in the early 1960s Pope John XXIII and the Second Vatican Council attempted to discredit this charge. Supra, note 2 to chapter 1.

We suggest, however, that the deicide charge was not as heavily emphasized by Western Christian writers during the Carolingian-Ottonian period (circa 700–1000) as it was during the High Middle Ages (1000–1300) and thereafter. Therefore, it could well have been that the deicide charge was not the major cause of the great outburst of anti-Semitism in Western Europe during the High Middle Ages, which was caused instead primarily by Christian anti-Muslimism and the association of Jew with Muslim during the crusading period. Rather, the great outburst of anti-Semitism in Western Europe during the High Middle Ages was the major cause of the increasing emphasis on the deicide charge within Western Christendom from circa 1000.

Certainly, the deicide charge which played an important role in the massacre of the Jews of Central Europe circa 1096 was intimately bound up with anti-Muslimism and the association of Jew with Muslim. Thus, the Jewish chroniclers of the persecutions of the Jews during the First Crusade more or less agree in ascribing the following thoughts to the Christian masses participating in this Crusade:

> We [Christians] are marching a great distance [from Franco-Germany to Jerusalem] to seek our sanctuary [the Church of the Holy Sepulchre] and to take vengeance on the Muslims [anti-Muslimism]. Lo and behold, there live among us Jews whose forefathers slew him [Jesus] and crucified him for no cause [the deicide charge]. Let us revenge ourselves on them first [association of Jew with Muslim], and eliminate them from among the nations, so that the name of Israel no longer be remembered, or else let them be like ourselves and believe in the son of [Mary].

As quoted in Baron, *Social and Religious History*, IV: 102, 290, note 15. In this passage the deicide charge is clearly emphasized in the middle "Lo and behold" sentence. However, anti-Muslimism is mentioned in the preceding sentence, and the association of Jew with Muslim implied in the following sentence. Thus, the Jewish chronicles testify to the intimate link between the deicide charge and anti-Muslimism/association of Jew with Muslim in high medieval Western European anti-Semitism.

In reality, we would argue, anti-Muslimism/association of Jew with Muslim was the primary factor, while the deicide charge was only the secondary factor during the persecution of the Jews at the time of the First Crusade. In general, it was anti-Muslimism/association of Jew with Muslim, factors which assumed tremendous importance during the High Middle Ages, the period of the Crusades, that critically influenced and even helped revive the deicide charge in Western Europe after circa 1000. Infra, notes 17 and 28. Thus, our thesis about the crucial impact of anti-Muslimism upon the deicide charge parallels our similar thesis about the crucial impact of anti-Muslimism upon the blood and the desecration-of-the-host libels. Supra, note 14.

C.) *Christian Messianic Expectations.* The great clash between Christians and Jews during the First Crusade may have been in part the clash of two conflicting messianisms, for both groups expected the end in 1096. Cohn, *Pursuit of the Millennium*, 40–52; Baron, *Social and Religious History*, IV: 96–97; V: 199–200. The same thing was true in 1010. Lea Dasberg, *Untersuchungen ueber die Entwertung des Judenstatus im 11. Jahrhundert* (Paris and The Hague: Mouton, 1965), 180–182; A.H. Silver, *History of Messianic Speculation in Israel* (Boston: Beacon, 1959), 68–69.

D.) *Resentment at Jewish Proselytism.* For an introduction to medieval Jewish proselytism, David J. Seligson, "(Conversion to Judaism) in the Post-Talmudic Period," in David Max Eichhorn, ed., *Conversion to Judaism: A History and Analysis* (New York: K'tav, 1965), 67–95; Dasberg, *Untersuchungen*, 173–193; Ben Zion Wacholder, "The Halakah and the Proselytizing of Slaves during the Gaonic Period," *Historia Judaica* 18 (1956): 89–106, his "Attitudes toward Proselytizing in the Classical Halakah," ibid. 20 (1958): 77–96, and his "Cases of Proselytizing in the Tosafist Responsa," *Jewish Quarterly Review* 51 (1961): 288–315; Norman Golb, "Notes on the Conversion of European Christians to Judaism in the Eleventh Century," *Journal of Jewish Studies* 16 (1965): 69–74, and his "New Light on the Persecution of French Jews during the First Crusade," *Proceedings of the American Academy for Jewish Research* 34 (1966): 1–63. Conversion of a prominent Christian to Judaism could provoke a massacre of the Jews, and some scholars have suggested that the persecution of the Jews circa 1010 may have been due, at least in part, to the conversion of the Slovenian cleric Weceli- nus to Judaism circa 1005. Baron, *Social and Religious History*, IV: 66, 271–272, note 85; Blumenkranz, "The Roman Church and the Jews," and "Germany, 848–1096," in Roth, *Dark Ages*, 87–88, 173–174; supra, note 11. Wecelimus may have fled to Muslim Egypt. Golb, *Journal of Jewish Studies*, XVI: 69. If so, this could also help ex- plain why the Christians accused the Jews of Western Europe of being in league with the Muslims circa 1010.

Socio-Economic Factors

A). Dasberg, *Untersuchungen*, 1–111, deemphasizes the role of economic competi- tion between Jews and Christians as a factor in the persecution of the Jews during the First Crusade. Cf. our review of this book in *Speculum* 43 (1968): 701–702, as well as the review by Irving A. Agus, *American Historical Review* 72 (1966): 146–147. Agus' own important work has been criticized for overemphasizing the economic role of the Jews at this time. Cf. Agus' *Urban Civilization in Pre-Crusade Europe: A Study of Organized Town-Life in Northwestern Europe during the Tenth and Eleventh Centuries Based on the [Rabbinic] Responsa Literature* (New York: Yeshiva University Press, 1965), 2 vols., as reviewed by Archibald R. Lewis, *American Historical Review* 71 (1965): 135–136, and Robert S. Lopez, *Speculum* 42 (1967): 340–343; and Agus' *The Heroic Age of Franco-German Jewry: The Jews of Germany and France of the Tenth and Eleventh Centuries, the Pioneers and Builders of Town-Life, Town-Government, and Institutions* (New York: Yeshiva University Press, 1969), as reviewed by Robert Chazan, *Speculum* 46 (1971): 120–122, and J. Lee Shneidman, *American Historical Review* 77 (1972): 760–761.

B.) Wolfgang Seiferth attributes the great outburst of anti-Semitism in Western Europe during the High Middle Ages (1000–1300) primarily to Christian reaction against Jewish moneylending. Cf. Seiferth's *Synagogue and Church in the Middle Ages: Two Symbols in Art and Literature*, trans. L. Chadeayne and P. Gottwald (New York: Ungar, 1970), plus the reviews of the German original by Guido Kisch, *Speculum* 40 (1965): 753–754, and Joseph Gutmann, *Jewish Social Studies* 18 (1966): 174–175. See now also William C. Jordan, "Jews on Top: Women and the Availability of Consump- tion Loans in Northern France in the Mid-Thirteenth Century," *Journal of Jewish Studies* 29 (1978): 39–56. The Seiferth thesis may help explain thirteenth-century Western European anti-Semitism, for by this time a fairly large percentage of Jews were engaged in moneylending. However, this thesis cannot really explain the great outburst of anti-Semitism during the earlier portion of the High Middle Ages (*i.e.*, the great international persecutions of circa 1010, the 1060s and 1096), when few Jews were engaged in moneylending (with the overwhelming majority being merchants).

Gavin I. Langmuir agrees with Seiferth in stressing Jewish moneylending but also stresses psychological factors in his approach to medieval anti-Semitism. Cf. his "*Judei Nostri* and the Beginning of Capetian Legislation," *Traditio* 16 (1960): 203–239; his "The Jews and the Archives of Angevin England: Reflections on Medieval Anti-Semitism," ibid. 19 (1963): 183–244; his "Anti-Judaism as the Necessary Preparation for Anti-Semitism," *Viator* 2 (1971): 383–389; and his "The Knight's Tale of Young Hugh of Lincoln," *Speculum* 47 (1972): 459–482; "Prolegomena to Any Present Analysis of Hostility against Jews," *Social Science Information* 15 (1976): 689–727; "L'Absence d'Accusation de Meurtre Rituel a l'Ouest du Rhone," in M.H. Vicaire and B. Blumenkranz, eds., *Juifs et Judaisme de Languedoc: XIIIe Siecle—Debut XIVe Siecle* (Toulouse: Privat, 1977), 235–249; "From Ambrose of Milan to Emicho of Leiningen: The Transformation of Hostility against Jews in Northern Christendom," in *Gli Ebrei nell'Alto Medioevo* (Spoleto: Centro Italiano di Studi sull'Alto Medioevo, 1980), 313–373; "*Tanquam Servi*: The Change in Jewish Status in French Law about 1200," in Miriam Yardeni, ed., *Les Juifs dans l'Histoire de France* (Leiden: Brill, 1980), 24–54.

Lester A. Little seems to be in the same tradition as Langmuir. Cf. Little's "The Function of the Jews in the Commercial Revolution," in *Poverta e Ricchezza nella Spiritualita dei Secoli XI e XII* (Todi: Centro di Studi sulla Spiritualita Medievale, 1969), 271–287; and his *Religious Poverty and the Profit Economy in Medieval Europe* (Ithaca: Cornell University Press, 1978), 42–57.

C.) Henry Fischel, Indiana University, Bloomington, participated in an important research project 1963–1964, "Problems of Entrepreneurship and/or Alien-Pariah Entrepreneurship in Developing Countries," conducted under the auspices of his university's International Development Research Center, financed by the Ford Foundation, to investigate prejudice against minority groups throughout the world. Fischel's assignment was to analyze anti-Semitism in Europe, and his approach was primarily socio-psychological. He emphasized the fear which the peasant migrant to an urban situation (there were many of these in Western Europe during the High Middle Ages, the period of heavy urbanization and cathedral building) has of merchants and/or moneylenders, who live by their wits rather than from the soil, especially when these merchants and/or moneylenders are of an alien religioethnic group. According to Fischel, hatred for the Jew in medieval Western Europe arose out of the same socio-psychological source as hatred for overseas Chinese in contemporary Southeast Asia.

The following were among the participants in the Indiana project: (1) Henry Fischel, "Introductory Bibliographical Materials to the Political and Social History of the Jews in Eastern Europe," 41 pp. MS; (2) Fischel, "Related Phenomena concerning the Restriction and Control of Alien Entrepreneurship, Materials, Observations and Projects for Further Research, with Special Emphasis on the Histories of European Jews and Overseas Chinese," 59 pp. MS; (3) Norman Jacobs, "The Bahaii of Iran and Pariah Entrepreneurship, an Exploratory Paper," 20 pp. MS; (4) David Mozingo, "Obstacles to Alien Chinese Entrepreneurs in Indonesia," 9 pp. MS; (5) E.H. Valsan, "Preliminary Bibliography to Indians Overseas with Special Reference to Their Entrepreneurial Activities," 23 pp. MS; (6) R. Bayly Winder, "The Lebanese in West

Africa," based on his article of the same title in *Comparative Studies in Society and History* 4 (1962): 296–333; (7) Nicolas Spulber, "Development, Entrepreneurship and Discrimination: Antisemitic and Antisinitic [anti-Chinese] Aspects," 70 pp. MS, published in Spulber, *The State and Economic Development in Eastern Europe* (New York: Random, 1966), 89–141.

This important research project was based on the methodological principle that anti-Semitism must be studied by the comparative method, *i.e.*, that hatred of the Jew can only be understood by comparison with hatreds of other ethnoreligious groups, especially those who live as minorities scattered in diasporas relying upon the evanescent goodwill of host populations often in a lower stage of social and cultural development. Our own approach to the study of anti-Semitism has considerable affinity with the Indiana project. We share its emphasis upon the comparative method. However, its research methodology was primarily social-scientific, hence its heavy emphasis upon the twentieth century. Our own is primarily historical, hence its heavy emphasis upon the medieval roots of contemporary situations. The Indiana project compared hatred for the Jew with hatred for the overseas Chinese but, of course, could not argue a causal relationship between the two hatreds. In this book we compare hatred for the Jew in medieval Western Europe with hatred for the Muslims in the same society and argue a close causal relationship between the two hatreds, *i.e.*, that anti-Muslimism was the primary factor in medieval anti-Semitism.

D.) In private conversation with us during 1967–1968, Jaan Puhvel, UCLA's professor of Indo-European Studies, suggested that the primary factor in medieval Western European anti-Semitism may well have been the caste system. According to the researches of Georges Dumezil, the Indo-Europeans (the majority group in medieval Western Europe)—as opposed, for example, to the Semites (Jews, Arabs, etc.)—are characterized by their rigid tripartite (which can also be seen as quadripartite) conception of the universe, of society, and of the gods. H. Ringgren and A.V. Strom, *Religions of Mankind: Today and Yesterday*, ed. J.C.G. Greig and trans. N.L. Jensen (Philadelphia: Fortress, 1967), 68–73; Jacques Duchesne-Guillemin, *Symbols and Values in Zoroastrianism: Their Survival and Renewal* (New York: Harper and Row, 1970), 30, 33, 36, 67, 90, 128–129, 137; R.C. Zaehner, *Dawn and Twilight of Zoroastrianism* (New York: Putnam's, 1961), 49–50, 346; C. Scott Littleton, *The New Comparative Mythology: an Anthropological Assessment of the Theories of Georges Dumezil* (Berkeley: University of California Press, 1973).

The crucial factor in Puhvel's application of the Dumezil thesis to medieval anti-Semitism was not so much the progressive evolution of the socioeconomic system which saw Christians take over more and more of the socioeconomic opportunities which had previously been allowed to the Jews; nor Christian hatred of the money-lending function which the socioeconomic evolution of medieval Western European society had forced the Jews to assume. It was rather the rigid caste system, characteristic of the Indo-European peoples (as opposed to the Semites), which became the basis for Western European society during the Barbarian invasions circa 200–1000 A.D. when the center of gravity in Western Christian civilization shifted away from Italy and the Mediterranean to France and the North Sea. The Semitic Jews, despite no little effort on their part (and even some help from the Indo-European Christians themselves), could not understand this rigid caste system and could not fit into it. Hence, their persecution by it.

Psychological Factors

These have already been mentioned supra in part (Langmuir and Fischel). Cf. also Cohn, *Pursuit of the Millennium*, 69–74, for a Freudian (Oedipal) interpretation of medieval anti-Semitism influenced by a 1912 article of Ernest Jones. But cf. John J. Ray, "Is Antisemitism a Cognitive Simplification? Some Observations on Australian Neo-Nazis," *Jewish Journal of Sociology* 14 (1972): 207–213. He argues that the classical social-scientific account of anti-Semitism, developed by the California school (Adorno, Frenkel-Brunswik, Levinson, and Sanford circa 1950), in which the anti-Semite was presented as a sick, paranoid deviant, "is fundamentally mistaken" and has been "contradicted on many points by subsequent writers in the psychological literature."

17. Blumenkranz, "The Roman Church and the Jews," in Roth, *Dark Ages*, 98–99, holds that the association of Jew with Muslim by medieval Christians was the crucial factor in the great outburst of anti-Semitism in Western Europe during the High Middle Ages. Thus, he seems to feel that the association of Jew with Muslim by medieval Christians was caused by the crusading movement which only arose in the eleventh century. However, the association of Jew with Muslim was also a crucial factor in several important persecutions of the Jews even before the crusading movement (630s, Byzantine Empire, France, and Spain; 690s, Spain; 930s, Byzantine Empire, Italy, and Germany). Infra, notes 18ff.

Cf. also the views of Flannery, *Anguish of the Jews*, 89–90, who holds that "the Church's 'teaching of contempt' " is too superficial an explanation of the radical deterioration of the Jewish situation in Western Europe between 1000 and 1300 and that a much more important role was played by "renewed suspicions of Jewish complicity with Islam [which] heightened the sense of the Jews' alien and infidel character."

Is it extravagant to argue that the Jews were considered Islamic "fifth columnists" in Christian territory? Identical language is used by such eminent authorities as Francisco Cantera Burgos and Salo Baron. Cantera Burgos, "Christian Spain," in Roth, *Dark Ages*, 357, 450, note 1; Baron, *Social and Religious History*, V: 135–136. Whereas Cantera Burgos stresses the fact that the Jews were an actual Islamic "fifth column" in Spain in 711, Baron stresses the fact that from the time of the *Reconquista* (eleventh century) the Christians of Spain considered the Jews a potential Islamic "fifth column," perhaps in part because the Jews had been an actual Islamic "fifth column" in 711. Both Cantera Burgos and Baron focus on Spain, but, of course, both scholars were fully aware of the fact that the Christians of Franco-Germany also saw the Jews as a potential Islamic "fifth column" and at times persecuted the Jews very severely for this precise reason. Supra notes* and 11.

Cf. also supra, note 12, for the views of Cohn and Synan which parallel those of Blumenkranz and Flannery; infra, note 67, for the views of Trachtenberg which parallel those of Cantera Burgos and Baron.

18. On the Byzantine-French phase of the persecution of the 630s, Parkes, *Conflict of the Church and the Synagogue*, 261–263, 265 and note 5, 335 and note 2; Starr, *Jews in the Byzantine Empire*, 1–2, 149–157; his "St. Maximos and the Forced Baptism at

Carthage in 632," *Byzantinisch-Neugriechische Jahrbuecher* 16 (1940): 192–196; and his "Note on the Crisis of the Early Seventh Century C.E.," *Jewish Quarterly Review* 38 (1947): 97–99; Baron, *Social and Religious History*, III: 23–24, 40, 47, 53–54, 174–175, 220; Roth, "Economic Life and Population Movements," in Roth, *Dark Ages*, 16; Sharf, "Jews in Byzantium," ibid., 50–51, 53–57; Roth, "Italy," ibid., 104; Schwarzfuchs, "France and Germany under the Carolingians," ibid., 125ff; Blumenkranz, *Juifs et Chretiens*, 99–100 and notes 140–143; his *Auteurs*, 101–102, 217, 252, 259; Sharf, *Byzantine Jewry*, 94–102; and his "Heraclius," *Ency. Judaica* 8 (1971): 333–334; Zuckerman, *Jewish Princedom in Feudal France*, 7.

For the Spanish phase of this persecution, Margolis and Marx, *History of the Jewish People*, 305–306; Parkes, *Conflict of Church and Synagogue*, 356–358; Solomon Katz, *The Jews in the Visigothic and Frankish Kingdoms of Spain and Gaul* (Cambridge: Mediaeval Academy of America, 1937), 12–14, 17, 30, 50–51, 62, 71, 89, 99, 108, 110, 118; Baron, *Social and Religious History*, III: 39, 41–43, 53–54, 248; IV: 241; Blumenkranz, *Juifs et Chretiens*, 100–101, 109ff, 113ff, plus index, *s.v.* "Conciles: IVe Tolede" and "VIe Tolede"; E.A. Thompson, *The Goths in Spain* (Oxford: Clarendon, 1969), 112, 166ff, 178–179, 184–186, 188, 201, 315–316; Bernard S. Bachrach, "A Reassessment of Visigothic Jewish Policy, 589–711," *American Historical Review* 78 (1973): 20–22.

On Visigothic anti-Semitism cf. now Bachrach, *Early Medieval Jewish Policy in Western Europe* (Minneapolis: University of Minnesota Press, 1977), and as reviewed by S. Bowman, *Jewish Social Studies* 42 (1980): 93–94; and L. Garcia Iglesias, *Los Judios en la Espanya Antigua* (Madrid: Cristiandad, 1978), and as reviewed by E. Mitre Fernandez, *Hispania* 142 (1979): 485–487.

19. Margolis and Marx, *History of the Jewish People*, 306; Parkes, *Conflict of Church and Synagogue*, 368–369, 385; Katz, *Jews in the Visigothic and Frankish Kingdoms*, 21; Henri Pirenne, *Mohammed and Charlemagne*, trans. B. Miall (New York: Meridian, 1958), 155; Trachtenberg, *Devil and the Jews*, 184; Baron, *Social and Religious History*, III: 45–46; Blumenkranz, *Juifs et Chretiens*, 131–133, 381; Baer, *History of the Jews in Christian Spain*, I: 22; Synan, *Popes and the Jews in the Middle Ages*, 52; Thompson, *Goths in Spain*, 247, 315–316; Bachrach, *American Historical Review*, LXXVIII: 29–30; Ashtor, *Jews of Moslem Spain*, I: 13–14. Margolis and Marx, Parkes, Katz, Pirenne, Trachtenberg, Blumenkranz, and Synan interpret Egica's remarks at the Seventeenth Council of Toledo (November 694) as referring to alleged Spanish Jewish collaboration with the *Muslims* of North Africa.

According to Baron, *Social and Religious History*, III: 253–254, note 67, the *Life* of Bishop Ferreol of Uzes (Southern France) asserts that this ecclesiastic ate with Jews and Muslims, a patent impossibility since he flourished circa 550 and the Muslims did not invade southern France until circa 720. Baron suggests that the author of this *Life* (according to Blumenkranz, *Auteurs*, 131–132, he wrote in the early eighth century, *i.e.*, during the Islamic invasion of southern France) transformed the Syrian Christian merchants mentioned in his sixth-century source into Muslims. Perhaps he did so under the influence of King Egica's association of Jew with Muslim in Visigothic Spain circa 690, as well as the association of Jew with Muslim during the persecution of Byzantine Jews launched by Emperor Leo III the Isaurian circa 720 after fending off the massive Arab attack on Constantinople during the 710s. For Leo III's persecution of the Jews, Sharf, "Jews in Byzantium," in Roth, *Dark Ages*, 55, 394, note 29; Parkes, *Conflict of Church and Synagogue*, 225, 246, 265, 267, 271, 388; Starr, *Jews in the Byzantine Empire*, 2-3, 90-95; Baron *Social and Religious History*, III: 175-178; Sharf, *Byzantine Jewry*, 61-81; and his "Leo III," *Ency. Judaica* 11 (1971): 23; Paul J. Alexander, "Religious Persecution and Resistance in the Byzantine Empire of the Eighth and Ninth Centuries: Methods and Justifications," *Speculum* 52 (1977): 242 and note 6.

20. Cf. Baron's foreword to Zuckerman's *Jewish Princedom*, viii: "The author has definitely made a case for his alluring theory" that there was a semiautonomous Jewish state in southern France in the late eighth and during the ninth centuries. Roth, *Dark Ages*, 467, praises Zuckerman's command of the bibliography of Carolingian and Carolingian-Jewish history but states that Zuckerman's thesis, "in the *unlikely* [italics ours] event of its being substantiated would throw a sensational light on Jewish history in Western Europe" circa 711 to 1096. When Roth wrote that circa 1965, he had not yet had an opportunity to examine the full Zuckerman volume of almost 500 printed pages, but rather had only seen a challenging preliminary article, "The Nasi of Frankland in the Ninth Century and the *Colaphus Judaeorum* in Toulouse," *Proceedings of the American Academy for Jewish Research* 33 (1965): 51-82. Zuckerman's second major article published in advance of the full book was "The Political Uses of Theology: The Conflict of Bishop Agobard and the Jews of Lyons," in Sommerfeldt, *Studies in Medieval Culture*, III: 23-51. Had Roth been able to study the full Zuckerman volume (published in 1972), it is quite likely he would have spoken about "the *possible* event" or " the *probable* event" rather than "the unlikely event" of the Zuckerman thesis being substantiated.

On the Zuckerman thesis, also the following reviews of his book: Toni Oelsner, *The Reconstructionist* 38 (1972): 26-29; Mary Alfred Noble, *Review for Religious* 31 (1972): 887; I.M. Lask, *The Jewish Frontier* 40 (1973): 27-28; Robert Chazan, *Jewish Social Studies* 35 (1973): 163-165, to which Zuckerman has replied in a letter of April 28, 1974 (a copy of which he was kind enough to share with us in April 1975), published with Chazan's rejoinder, ibid., 37 (1975): 187-189; Daniel Jeremy Silver, *Central Conference of American Rabbis Journal* 20 (1973): 85-87; Frank J. Adler, *The Jewish Spectator* 38 (1973): 25-28; Bernard S. Bachrach, *American Historical Review* 78 (1973): 1440-1441, to which Zuckerman wrote a reply published ibid. 79 (1974): 1303-1304; Solomon Grayzel, *Jewish Quarterly Review* 65 (1975): 196-199; J. Cohen, "The Nasi of Narbonne: A Problem in Medieval Historiography," *Association for Jewish Studies Review* 2 (1977): 45-76.

21. For the conversion of Bodo-Elazar, Baron, *Social and Religious History*, IV: 52-53, 264, note 69; V: 126, 347, note 56; Blumenkranz, *Juifs et Chretiens*, index, *s.v.* "Bodo-Eleazar"; and his *Auteurs*, 182-191; 241, note 12; 249, note 12; Zuckerman, *Jewish Princedom*, index, *s.v.* "Bodo (Bodo-Eleazar)," especially 274-284; Cecil Roth, "Bodo," *Ency. Judaica* 4 (1971): 1164; Blumenkranz, "The Roman Church and the Jews," in Roth, *Dark Ages*, 84, 86-87, 89, 93, 96-97; Schwarzfuchs, "France and Germany under the Carolingians," ibid. 140-141; Cantera Burgos, "Christian Spain," ibid., 358; Synan, *Popes and the Jews*, 63-64; Ashtor, *Jews of Moslem Spain*, I: 70-81.

In the 840s the Muslims launched a major military offensive against Christendom with devastating results on three fronts: (1) northeastern Mediterranean (against

Byzantine Anatolia), (2) northcentral Mediterranean (against Sicily and Italy), and (3) northwestern Mediterranean (against northern Spain, the southern French coast and interior, as well as the French Atlantic coast). Ostrogorsky, *History of the Byzantine State*, 185, 196; Pirene, *Mohammed and Charlemagne*, 157–158, 161, 163; Hilmar C. Krueger, "The Italian Cities and the Arabs Before 1095," in Kenneth M. Setton, ed., *History of the Crusades* (Philadelphia: University of Pennsylvania Press, 1958), I: 44–48; Citarella, *Speculum*, XLII: 305–308; Imamuddin, *Political History of Muslim Spain*, 101–103. The Christians of Franco-Germany were well aware of the Islamic attack on fronts numbers 2 and 3 above because Italy and Spain were neighbors of Franco-Germany. However, the Christians of Franco-Germany were also equally aware of the Islamic attack on the Byzantines at this time (Ostrogorsky, 185 and note 3; F.L. Ganshof, *The Carolingians and the Frankish Monarchy: Studies in Carolingian History*, trans. J. Sondheimer [Ithaca: Cornell University Press, 1971], 166). Thus, Christendom was in a state of deep anxiety over the great Islamic offensive throughout the Mediterranean world during the 840s and this helps explain why there was a virulent renewal in France circa 850 of the Christian charge that the Jews were in league with the Muslims against the West (as per notes 21–24 of this chapter).

22. Pirenne, *Mohammed and Charlemagne*, 157, note 4.

23. According to the eleventh century *Life* of St. Theodard, archbishop of Narbonne (885–893), the Jews betrayed Toulouse to the Arabs led by Abd-ar-Rahman I, first Umayyad ruler of Muslim Spain (765–788). Zuckerman, *Proceedings of the American Academy for Jewish Research* 33 (1965): 58, note 7; 62–63 and note 15; 67; and his *Jewish Princedom*, 350–353. Most likely the earlier (ninth- or tenth-century) source of this *Life* accused the Jews of betraying Marseilles to the Arabs circa 848 (during the time of Emir Abd-ar-Rahman II of Cordova [822–852]), but the author of the eleventh-century *Life* preferred to transform Marseilles into Toulouse and to antedate the Arab attack in question about a century to the time of Abd-ar-Rahman I. Cf. also Parkes, *Jew in the Medieval Community*, 34 and notes 2–3, 43–44 and note 1; Katz, *Jews in the Visigothic and Frankish Kingdoms*, 117 and notes 5–6; Trachtenberg, *Devil and the Jews*, 184, 250, note 26; Baron, *Social and Religious History*, IV: 55–56, 265, note 72; Blumenkranz, *Juifs et Chretiens*, 382–383, note 1; and his *Auteurs*, 251–252 and note 11; Schwarzfuchs, "France and Germany under the Carolingians," in Roth, *Dark Ages*, 136, 409, note 21.

24. Parkes, *Jew in the Medieval Community*, 34 and note 1; Trachtenberg, *Devil and the Jews*, 184, 250, note 26; Baron, *Social and Religious History*, IV: 55; Blumenkranz, *Juifs et Chretiens*, 381 and note 11; and his *Auteurs*, 183; Dasberg, *Untersuchungen*, 164, note 1; Synan, *Popes and the Jews*, 52–53; Cantera Burgos, "Christian Spain," in Roth, *Dark Ages*, 359; Zuckerman, *Jewish Princedom*, 316–317, 324; Ashtor, *Jews of Moslem Spain*, I: 99–100, 338, 446, note 144.

According to Ashtor, I: 68–69, 92–93, 98–99, the Jews of ninth-century Muslim Spain firmly supported the Muslims against the Christian rebels (St. Eulogius, Umar ibn Hafsun, etc.) who attacked Muslim rule in Spain from within, and against the Christians of the north who attacked Muslim rule in Spain from without (especially King Alfonso III of Asturias circa 866–910). Jews even sat with Muslims in the Christian clerical Council of Cordova (863) to insure that this council did not encourage rebellion (so Ashtor, I: 92–93)! Cf. also Cantera Burgos, "Christian Spain," in Roth,

Dark Ages, 357–358, 450, notes 2–4. Jewish pro-Arab sentiments and actions within ninth-century Muslim Spain undoubtedly reinforced the association of Jew with Muslim by medieval Christians in ninth-century France and Italy.

Zuckerman, *Jewish Princedom*, 88, note 32, calls attention to page 140 of the Golden Psalter (MS 22) of St. Gall (circa 900), a highly probable artistic example of the association of Jew with Muslim by medieval Christians. According to Zuckerman the illustration on this page portrays King David's army riding out to do battle against the Arameans, carrying an Israelite battle standard whereon is depicted "a fire-spouting dragon (or serpent) narrowing into an arrowhead tail. . . . The dragon's head and tail are (Abbasid?) green, its body interlarded with red." As a matter of fact, the warriors' helmets also are green. Zuckerman cites as his source Johann Rudolf Rahn, *Das Psalterium Aureum von Sanct Gallen: Ein Beitrag zur Geschichte der Karolingischen Miniatur-Malerei* (St. Gall: Historischer Verein des Kantons St. Gallen, 1878), 33 and plate X. On the Golden Psalter of St. Gall, Beckwith, *Early Medieval Art*, figure no. 64, pp. 76 and 256; with description thereof, pp. 76, 233, note 66. Zuckerman's discovery of this probable example of the equation of Jew (King David's army) with Muslim (the Islamic green of the dragon in the army's battle standard and the army's helmets) by medieval Christians in the Golden Psalter of St. Gall may have pushed our knowledge of this phenomenon as represented in medieval Christian art back by several centuries (from circa 1200 to circa 900)! Infra. notes 57–72.

Three instances of the association of Jew with Muslim by Eastern Christians may have influenced the association of Jew with Muslim by Western Christians circa 850 (supra, notes 21–23). (1) Circa 800 the Eastern Christian legend of Jewish responsibility for the iconclastic movement clearly associated Jew with Muslim. Parkes, *Conflict*, 291; Baron, *Social and Religious History*, III: 178; Blumenkranz, *Juifs et Chretiens*, 59–60; Starr, "An Iconodulic Legend and Its Historical Basis," *Speculum* 8 (1933): 500–503; Sharf, "Jews in Byzantium," in Roth, *Dark Ages*, 57–58. The version of this legend reported by Theophanes could well have reached the Christians of Muslim Spain before 850; cf. d'Alverny's views infra, item number 3. (2) In 838, on the eve of Amorium's capture by the Arabs, fighting broke out in the city between Jews and Christians, perhaps because the Christians accused the Jews of being in league with the Arabs against them. Starr, *Jews in the Byzantine Empire*, 109; Sharf, "Jews in Byzantium," in Roth, *Dark Ages*, 57–58. For the possibility that news of this incident reached France, Ostrogorsky, *History of the Byzantine State*, 185 and note 3. (3) In his biography of Muhammad, Theophanes clearly associated Jew with Muslim. Schwabe, *Tarbiz*, II: 74–89. For the likelihood that Theophanes' biography of Muhammad influenced the Christians of Muslim Spain circa 850, and for the fact that Alvarus, the great Christian lay-theologian of midninth-century Muslim Spain, followed Theophanes in associating Jew with Muslim, d'Alverny, *Occidente e l'Islam*, II: 584–590.

Zuckerman, *Jewish Princedom*, 316–318, suggests that there was indeed a Judaeo/Islamic conspiracy to seize Barcelona circa 852 but that the Muslims involved favored the Abbasids of Iraq and not the Umayyads of Spain.

Emperor Louis II and the Council of Pavia decreed the expulsion of the Jews from Italy in 855. Roth, "Italy," in Roth, *Dark Ages*, 114. This decree may have been caused in part by the association of Jew with Muslim by medieval Christians. Since the Jews were considered Islamic fifth columnists in Christian territory, any Christian attack on the Jews in their midst was an indirect attack on the Muslims. In the 850s the Muslims ravaged southern Italy, and Emperor Louis II undoubtedly was infuriated at both the Muslims as well as at himself (for he had failed in his attempt to drive the Muslims from their two main south Italian bastions at this time, Bari and Taranto). Krueger, in Setton, *History of the Crusades*, I: 47–48. Could the expulsion of the Jews decreed in 855 have been part of an attempt to weaken the Muslims of southern Italy by attacking their alleged Jewish allies?

The association of Jew with Muslim was a crucial factor in the great persecution of the Jews within the Byzantine Empire (including southern Italy) launched by Emperor Basil I circa 874; for which, Starr, *Jews in the Byzantine Empire*, 3–7, 126–148; Baron, *Social and Religious History*, III: 179–181; Sharf, "Jews in Byzantium," in Roth, *Dark Ages*, 50–51, 57ff, 60–62; Roth, "Italy," ibid., 104–106; H.J. Zimmels, "Scholars and Scholarship in Byzantium and Italy," ibid., 188; J. Schirmann, "The Beginning of Hebrew Poetry in Italy and Northern Europe: Italy," ibid., 252–255, especially 255; Sharf, *Byzantine Jewry*, 82–94; and his "Basil I, " *Ency. Judaica* 4 (1971): 298–299.

In our monograph on the expulsion of the Jews from Sens circa 876 (infra, note 51) we argue that this expulsion, ordered by Archbishop Ansegise of Sens, primate of Franco-Germany, was really instigated by Pope John VIII, partly to curry favor with the Byzantine emperor, Basil I (who severely persecuted the Jews circa 874), because the pope desperately needed Byzantine help against the Arabs who were literally outside the gates of Rome circa 876. Vasiliev, *History of the Byzantine Empire*, I: 327; Ostrogorsky, *History of the Byzantine State*, 210–212; George Every, *The Byzantine Patriarchate 451–1204* (London: S.P.C.K., 1962), 124–126; Mann, *Lives of the Popes in the Middle Ages*, III: 296, 319–331; Krueger, in Setton, *History of the Crusades*, I: 48–49; Fred E. Engreen, "Pope John VIII and the Arabs," *Speculum* 20 (1945): 318–330, especially 319 and note 3, 323 with notes 3 and 5, 324 and note 3. It may also have been that because the Arabs were threatening Rome circa 876, the pope and the archbishop decided to expel the Jews from Sens on the theory that since the Jews were Islamic fifth columnists in Christian territory, any Christian attack on the Jews in their midst was an indirect attack on the Muslims.

25. Parkes, *Jew in the Medieval Community*, 26–27, 37, 315; Starr, *Jews in the Byzantine Empire*, 7–8, 148–166; Baron, *Social and Religious History*, III: 179, 182–183, 203, 317ff; IV: 6, 24–26, 66, 73ff, 241; Roth, "Economic Life and Population Movements," in Roth, *Dark Ages*, 28–29, 36–37; Sharf, "Jews in Byzantium," ibid., 60–63; Blumenkranz, "Roman Church and the Jews," ibid., 74–75, 78–79, 81; Roth, "Italy", ibid., 107–108, 115–119; Blumenkranz, "Germany 843–1096," ibid., 167–168; Zimmels, "Scholars and Scholarship in Byzantium and Italy," ibid., 180, 188; Schirmann, "The Beginning of Hebrew Poetry in Italy and Northern Europe: Italy," ibid., 259–261, 264–265; Blumenkranz, *Juifs et Chretiens*, 70, 95, 102, 135, 180, 206, 284ff, 319, 367, 374, 380; and his *Auteurs*, 218–221, 228–231; Synan, *Popes and the Jews*, 60; Sharf, *Byzantine Jewry*, 14, 95–100, 102, 202, 204, note 16; and his "Romanus I Lecapenus," *Ency. Judaica* 14 (1971): 239; Ashtor, *Jews of Moslem Spain*, I: 183–187.

In the 930s the Muslims launched another major military offensive against Christendom with serious results on three fronts: (1) northeastern Mediterranean/northern Fertile Crescent (against the Byzantines in the Upper Euphrates region), (2) north-central Mediterranean (Italy), and (3) northwestern Mediterranean (against the Christians of northern Spain and southern France). Ostrogorsky, *History of the Byzantine State*, 244–245; Citarella, *Speculum*, XLII: 310; Krueger, in Setton, *History of the Crusades* I: 51; Imamuddin, *Political History of Muslim Spain*, 140–145. The Christians of Franco-Germany were then well aware of the Islamic attack on fronts numbers 2 and 3 above because of Italian and Spanish proximity. However, the Christians of Franco-Germany were well aware of the Islamic attack on the Byzantines at this time through a papacy that was pro-Byzantine circa 928–964 (Every, *Byzantine Patriarchate*, 137, 197) and through Byzantine naval cooperation with the French Christians against the Arabs circa 930 (Krueger, 51). Thus, Christendom was again in a state of deep anxiety over the great Islamic offensive throughout the Mediterranean world during the 930s and this helps explain why there was in Byzantium, Italy, and Germany at this time a virulent renewal of the Christian charge that the Jews were in league with the Muslims against the West.

26. Supra, note 11; infra, note 27.

27. The two chief Christian accounts (both from the first half of the eleventh century) attribute the persecution of the Jews of France circa 1010 to their alleged treasonable relations with the Muslims of Egypt. Ralph Glaber, *Francorum Historiae Libri V*, 3:7, ed. Maurice Prou (Paris: Picard, 1886), 71–74; and Adhemar de Chabannes, *Chronicon Aquitanicum et Francicum . . . Libri III*, 3:47, ed. Jules Chavanon (Paris: Picard, 1897), 169–171, 205–206. The Jewish account of this persecution knows nothing of the Christian charge that the Jews were in league with the Muslims. Cf. the "Ma'aseh Nora Mi'Sh'nat D'Tashsaz" [A Terrible Story from the Year 4767 (= 1007 A.D.)], in A.M. Habermann, *Sefer G'zerot Ashk'naz V'Tzorfat* [Book of the Persecutions in Germany and France] (Jerusalem: Sifre Tarshish/Mosad Ha-Rav Kuk, 1945–1946), 19–21; and the French translation thereof by S. Schwarzfuchs, "Chroniques Hebraiques du XIe Siecle," *Evidences* 6 (1954): 33, 36–37. Undoubtedly the Christian writers (Ralph Glaber and Adhemar de Chabannes) were better informed about why the *Christians* persecuted the Jews of France circa 1010 than was the Jewish author of the *Ma'aseh Nora*. Apparently (judging by this Jewish account) the Jews of early eleventh-century France were much less willing to admit to themselves that the association of Jew with Muslim was the primary factor in Christian anti-Semitism than were the Jews of the late eleventh and early twelfth centuries (supra, note 16, Religious Factors, B).

28. Blumenkranz assumes the crucial influence of this factor upon the persecution of 1096. Supra, note 17. The Jewish chroniclers of the First Crusade were also well aware of its crucial influence. Supra, note 16, Religious Factors, B.

In support of the assumption that the association of Jew with Muslim was the crucial factor in the persecution of 1096 we note here several significant instances of this association around the time of the First Crusade: (1) Pope Gregory VII, *MPL*, CXLVIII: 400:B-C; (2) Abbot Hugh of Cluny, Dunlop, *Al-Andalus*, XVII: 265; (3) *Chanson de Roland*, line 3662, F. Whitehead, *La Chanson de Roland* (Oxford: Blackwell, 1942), 107; (4) Petrus Alphonsi, *Dialogi*, *MPL*, CLVII: 597:B and 600:A-C; (5) the association of Jew with Muslim by Theophanes and Alvarus (supra, note 24, para. 4) was known in France at the time of the First Crusade (*e.g.*, to Sigebert of Gembloux), d'Alverny, *Occidente e l'Islam*, II: 595 and note 31, 800; cf. also our article, *Muslim World*, LV: 334–336, and d'Alverny, 591 and note 26; (6) al'Kindi's great Christian anti-Islamic polemic written in ninth century Iraq associates Jew with Muslim (Kritzeck, *Peter the Venerable and Islam*, 103, 105) and was read by Christians in Spain circa 1100 (d'Alverny, *Occidente e l'Islam*, II: 592–594, especially 594); (7) the *Contrarietas Alpholica*, another great Christian anti-Islamic polemic probably written in eleventh-century Spain (which may have influenced Petrus Alphonsi), associates Jew with Muslim, Daniel, *Islam and the West*, 344, note 21; supra note 22 to chapter 2; (8) the Arabic original of the *Tractatus Rabbi Samuelis ad Rabbi Isaac de Adventu Messiae*, purportedly written in the 1070s, visits poetic justice on the two allies, Jews and Muslims, by using the doctrines of each to refute on the other, Daniel, *Islam and the West*, 54, 335, note 23; supra, note 21, para. 6, to chapter 3. Cf. also the equation of Jew with Muslim by King Roger I of Sicily circa 1095, as noted by Baron, *Social and Religious History*, IV: 243, note 22; infra, note 52.

The association of Jew with Muslim by medieval Christians was also a crucial factor in the great persecution of the Jews of Western Europe (Germany, France, Spain, and Italy) which raged during the 1060s, occasioned by an intensification of the crusading movement against the Muslims of Spain and Sicily during that decade. Flannery, *Anguish of the Jews*, 90; Synan, *Popes and the Jews in the Middle Ages*, 66–69. For the persecution of the Jews in Germany (at Trier) in this decade, A. Lewinsky, "Treves," *Jewish Ency.* 12 (1906): 242; Parkes, *Jew in the Medieval Community*, 39; Baron, *Social and Religious History*, IV: 92, 283, note 2; Blumenkranz, "The Roman Church and the Jews," in Roth, *Dark Ages*, 82; his "Germany 843–1096," ibid., 172; and his *Juifs et Chretiens*, 103–104; A. Shapiro and B.M. Ansbacher, "Trier," *Ency. Judaica* 15 (1971): 1390. For the persecutions in southern France, northern Spain, and southern Italy, Blumenkranz, *Auteurs*, 263–264; Schwarzfuchs, "France under the Early Capets," in Roth *Dark Ages*, 148, 410, note 8; Baron, V: 199, 383, note 63. For the persecutions in southern, central, and northern Italy, Roth, "Italy," in Roth, *Dark Ages*, 111, 404, note 40; 114, 405, note 50; 120, 405, note 46, and 406, notes 65–67. The Muslim massacre of the Jews of Granada in the 1060s (Perlmann, *Proceedings of the American Academy for Jewish Research*, XVIII: 269–290) may also have been related to the Christian persecutions of the Jews during that same decade.

For the association of Jew with Muslim by twelfth-century Western Christian writers, infra, notes 29 and 52; by Popes Innocent III and Gregory IX in the thirteenth-century, infra, notes 46–48, 54, and chapter 6 of this book *in toto* with its notes; by the Christians of France circa 1320, supra, note *; by medieval and modern Christians into the nineteenth century, infra, notes 51–72.

29. Three of these similarities between Jews and Muslims are specifically mentioned by Peter the Venerable, great abbot of Cluny (1094–1156). Kritzeck, *Peter the Venerable and Islam*, 192. The fourth, that Jews and Muslims both reject the Trinity, was undoubtedly understood by Peter the Venerable even though not specifically mentioned. It is highly possible that these same four similarities between Jews and Muslims were noted by Western Christians during the earlier Carolingian-Ottonian period as well. For futher examples of the association of Jew with Muslim by twelfth-century Western Christian writers (Otto of Freising, Giraldus Cambrensis, and Graindor of Douai), infra, note 52.

30. For the attitude of the seventh-century Middle Eastern Jews, Parkes, *Conflict*, 257–263; Starr, "Byzantine Jewry on the Eve of the Arab Conquest," *Journal of the*

Palestine Oriental Society 15 (1935): 280–293; Aldobrandino Malvezzi, *L'Islamismo e la Cultura Europea* (Florence: Sansoni, 1956), 47–52; Baron, *Social and Religious History*,III: 86–93; Sharf, "Jews in Byzantium," in Roth, *Dark Ages*, 54, 394, note 16; and Sharf's *Byzantine Jewry*, 42–60. For the attitude of the seventh-century Spanish Jews, supra, notes 18–19; infra, note 32.

31. M. Buttenweiser, "Apocalyptic Literature: Neo-Hebraic," *Jewish Ency.* 1 (1901): 675–685; Julius H. Greenstone, *The Messiah Idea in Jewish History* (Philadelphia: Jewish Publication Society of America, 1943), 114–155; Silver, *History of Messianic Speculation in Israel*, 36–57; Baron, *Social and Religious History*, IV: 138–208; Joseph Shapiro, *Bi-Sh'vile Ha-G'ulah: L'Tol'dot Ha'T'nuot Ha-M'shihiyyot* [In the Paths of Redemption, On the History of Jewish Messianic Movements] (Jerusalem: Levin-Epstein, 1947), I: 46–61; Aaron Z. Aescoly, *Ha-T'nuot Ha-M'shihiyyot B'Yisrael* [Jewish Messianic Movements], ed. J. Even-Sh'muel (Jerusalem: Mosad Bialik, 1956), 93–103; Ashtor, *Jews of Moslem Spain*, I: 34–38; Starr, "Le Mouvement Messianique au Debut du VIIIe Siecle," *Revue des Etudes Juives*, 102 (1937): 81–92; Sharf, "Jews in Byzantium," in Roth, *Dark Ages*, 56; and Sharf, *Byzantine Jewry*, 61–81.

32. Baron, *Social and Religious History*, III: 46; Baer, *Jews in Christian Spain*, I: 22–23; Ashtor, *Jews of Moslem Spain*, I: 3–42; Cantera Burgos, "Christian Spain," in Roth, *Dark Ages*, 357.

Norman Roth, "The Jews and the Muslim Conquest of Spain," *Jewish Social Studies* 38 (1976): 145–158, deemphasizes the Jewish role in the Islamic conquest of Spain during the 710s.

33. Blumenkranz, "The Roman Church and the Jews," in Roth, *Dark Ages*, 86–87; supra, note 21.

34. M. Kayserling, "Hasdai, Abu Yusuf . . . Ibn Shaprut," *Jewish Ency.* 6 (1904): 248–249; Jacob Mann, *Texts and Studies in Jewish History and Literature* (Cincinnati: Hebrew Union College Press, 1931), I: 3–30; Baron, *Social and Religious History*, III: 155–156; Starr, *Jews in the Byzantine Empire*, 7–8, 58, 153–155; Sharf, *Byzantine Jewry*, 99–101, 143, 166, 168; Baer, *Jews in Christian Spain*, I: 28–30, 382–383, note 7; Cantera Burgos, "Christian Spain," in Roth, *Dark Ages*, 362–364; Ashtor, *Jews of Moslem Spain*, I: 155–227; and his "Hisdai . . . Ibn Shaprut," *Ency. Judaica* 8 (1971): 533–534.

35. Baron, *Social and Religious History*, III: 154, 304–305, note 38; Roth, "Italy", in Roth, *Dark Ages*, 107, 403, note 25; Zimmels, "Aspects of Jewish Culture: Historiography," ibid., 276; Abraham David, "Paltiel," *Ency. Judaica* 13 (1971): 49–50.

36. There was even a legend of the Jewish origins of the Fatimid dynasty (Baron, *Social and Religious History*, III: 305, note 38), perhaps based in part on the prominent role played by Jews and Jewish converts to Islam in the Fatimid conquest of Egypt and Palestine circa 969 (Baron, III: 105). On Jewish officeholders in general in Islamic lands, Walter J. Fischel, *The Jews in the Political and Economic Life of Medieval Islam* (London: Royal Asiatic Society, 1937).

According to Baron, *Social and Religious History*, III: 103, Yahya of Antioch describes at some length an alleged joint attack by Jews and Muslims on both the Church of the Holy Sepulchre and the Zion Church in Jerusalem, May 966. News of this alleged Judaeo-Islamic anti-Christian collaboration in the Holy Land circa 966 could easily have reached Western Europe via pilgrims (Runciman, *History of the*

Crusades, I: 45) and via merchants like the Venetians (supra, note 25). It could have combined with news which may also have reached Western Europe about the alleged Jewish origin of the Fatimids, about the important role played by Jews and Jewish converts to Islam in the Fatimid conquest of Egypt and Palestine circa 969, and about high Jewish officeholders under the Fatimids in Egypt and Palestine (supra, note 35), to help provoke the persecution of the Jews of Limoges in the 990s (when the Fatimids persecuted the Amalfitan merchants in Egypt) and circa 1010 (when the Fatimids destroyed the Church of the Holy Sepulchre in Jerusalem). For these twin persecutions of the Jews of Limoges, supra, note 11.

37. Simon Dubnow, *Divre Y'me Am Olam* [World History of the Jewish People], trans. B. Krupnick (Tel Aviv: D'vir, 1933), IV: 59–60 = *History of the Jews*, trans. Moshe Spiegel (South Brunswick, New Jersey: Yoseloff, 1968), II: 539–541; Mark Wischnitzer, "Migrations of the Jews," *Univ. Jewish Ency.* 7 (1942): 544; Hirschel Revel, "Ashkenaz and Ashkenazim," ibid. 1 (1939): 543; Baron, *Social and Religious History*, IV: 3–5, 43ff, 57ff, 64ff; Roth, "Economic Life and Population Movements," in Roth, *Dark Ages*, 13–48.

Moses Shulvass, the distinguished authority on the history of the Jewish people in Europe at Chicago's Spertus College of Judaica, in personal conversation with us, concurred in the view that there was a heavy immigration of Jews from Arab lands into Franco-Germany from the Carolingian period through the First Crusade and will document this immigration movement as fully as sources allow in a comprehensive history of Jewish life and thought in medieval Germany through circa 1350 now in preparation. Among Professor Shulvass' many books are *Between the Rhine and the Bosporus: Studies and Essays in European Jewish History* (Chicago: College of Jewish Studies Press, 1964); *From East to West: the Westward Migration of Jews from Eastern Europe during the Seventeenth and Eighteenth Centuries* (Detroit: Wayne State University Press, 1971); *The Jews in the World of the Renaissance*, trans. Elvin A. Kose (Leiden: Brill and Spertus College of Judaica, 1973); and *Jewish Culture in Eastern Europe: The Classical Period* (New York: K'tav, 1975). For biographical data on Shulvass, Eisig Silberschlag, "Shulvass (Szulwas), Moses Avigdor," *Ency. Judaica* 14 (1971): 1479; *Who's Who in World Jewry* (1972), 833; *Directory of American Scholars* 1 (1982): 699.

Cf. also Armando O. Citarella, "A Puzzling Question concerning the Relations between the Jewish Communities of Christian Europe and Those Represented in the Geniza Documents," *Journal of the American Oriental Society* 91 (July-September 1971): 390–397, based on S.D. Goitein's monumental *A Mediterranean Society: The Jewish Communities of the Arab World as Portrayed in the Documents of the Cairo Geniza* [tenth through thirteenth centuries] (Berkeley and Los Angeles: University of California Press), I: *Economic Foundations* (1967); II: *The Community* (1971); and III: *The Family* (1978). Cf. also Goitein's *Letters of Medieval Jewish Traders* (Princeton: Princeton University Press, 1974). Cf. also the reviews of the Goitein volumes by N. Golb, *Journal of Near Eastern Studies* 38 (1979): 287–292; and by L. Nemoy, *Jewish Quarterly Review* 70 (1979): 50–56.

Cf. also Louis Isaac Rabinowitz, *Jewish Merchant Adventurers: A Study of the Radanites* (London: Goldston, 1948); Claude Cahen, "Y a-t-il eu des Rahdanites?" *Revue des Etudes Juives* 3 (1964): 499–505; Roth, "Economic Life and Population Movements," in Roth, *Dark Ages*, 23–29; Morris Epstein, *Tales of Sendebar* (Philadelphia:

Jewish Publication Society of America, 1967), 31-37; D.M. Dunlop, "Radaniya," *Ency. Judaica* 13 (1971): 1495.

There is an alternative view that the Jews of Franco-Germany during the period of circa 750 to 1096 were not primarily immigrants from Islamic lands but descendants of Jews who came to the Rhineland during the late Roman period before 300 A.D.; and during the Barbarian Invasions either remained there or fled to southern France and northern Italy only to return to the Franco-German area circa 750 with the rise of the Carolingian dynasty. Roth, "Economic Life and Population Movements," in Roth, *Dark Ages*, 16; Blumenkranz, "Germany 843-1096," ibid., 162, 413, note 1. Militating strongly in favor of the thesis that the Jews of Franco-Germany circa 750-1096 were primarily immigrants from Islamic lands is the fact that as late as the time of Rashi (the great Franco-Jewish Bible and Talmud commentator of the late eleventh and early twelfth centuries) the pulpit in the synagogue, from which the sacred Jewish prayers and the scripture passages were chanted in worship, was called the *almembra* by the Jews of Franco-Germany. This Hebrew word comes from the Arabic *al-minbar*! Kaufmann Kohler, "Almemar or Almemor," *Jewish Ency.* 1 (1901): 430-431; Rachel Wischnitzer, *The Architecture of the European Synagogue* (Philadelphia: Jewish Publication Society of America, 1964), 48, 284, note 11.

38. Palestine to Franco-Germany, Roth, "Economic Life and Population Movements," in Roth, *Dark Ages*, 41-42. Iraq to France, Roth, ibid.; plus supra, text at note 20 and note 20, the case of Natronai-Machir, from Arab Iraq to southern France circa 760.

39. From Palestine (Jerusalem) to Italy (Venosa), Zimmels, "Scholars and Scholarship in Byzantium and Italy," in Roth, *Dark Ages*, 179. From Iraq (Bagdad) to Italy (Lucca), cf. the case of Aaron the son of Samuel of Bagdad, a founder of the Jewish mystical tradition in Europe. J. Dan, "The Beginnings of Jewish Mysticism in Europe," in Roth, ibid., 283. From Italy (Lucca) to Franco-Germany (Mainz), cf. the case of Moses the son of Kalonymus of Lucca. I.A. Agus, "Rabbinic Scholarship in Northern Europe," ibid., 191-192.

40. For the case of Abraham of Saragossa circa 825, Baron, *Social and Religious History*, IV: 48ff; Roth, "Economic Life and Population Movements," in Roth, *Dark Ages*, 34, 41; Schwarzfuchs, "France and Germany under the Carolingians," ibid., 129-130, 134. For Ibrahim ibn Ya'qub circa 970, Ashtor, "Ibrahim ibn Ya'qub," ibid., 305-308.

41. Baron, *Social and Religious History*, IV: 43-53; Dasberg, *Untersuchungen*, 60-87, and in general throughout part one of the Dasberg book, 9-87; Schwarzfuchs, "France and Germany under the Carolingians," in Roth, *Dark Ages*, 122-142.

42. Likewise, Oliver Cromwell favored readmission of Jews into England in the 1650s partly in order to strengthen his country against its chief Protestant rival, The Netherlands (cf. the three Anglo-Dutch Wars circa 1650-1670; so Joseph Jacobs, "England," *Jewish Ency.* 5 (1903): 169; Albert M. Hyamson, *History of the Jews in England* (2nd ed.; London: Methuen, 1928), 151; Montagu Frank Modder, *The Jew in the Literature of England to the End of the 19th Century* (New York and Philadelphia: Meridian and Jewish Publication Society of America, 1960), 33-34; Cecil Roth, *History of the Jews in England* (2nd ed.; Oxford: Clarendon, 1949), 157-158; and his *History of the Marranos* (New York and Philadelphia: Meridian and the Jewish Publica-

tion Society of America, 1959), 260–261; Baron, *Social and Religious History of the Jews* (1st. ed.; New York: Columbia University Press, 1937), II: 186; Grayzel, *History of the Jews* (new revised ed.; New York and Toronto: New American Library/Mentor, 1968), 431.

43. The Jews were also accused of being in league with the Normans. However, to our knowledge, this charge appears in only one primary source, Prudence of Troyes (died 861), who alleges that the Jews helped the Normans capture Bordeaux circa 848. Parkes, *Jew in the Medieval Community*, 33 and note 3; Trachtenberg, *Devil and the Jews*, 184; Baron, *Social and Religious History*, IV: 55; Blumenkranz, *Juifs et Chretiens*, 381 and note 11; and his *Auteurs*, 183; Zuckerman, *Jewish Princedom*, 312–313 and notes 57–58. From Zuckerman's discussion it emerges that Duke William, the elder son of the former Franco-Jewish Nasi (Prince), Bernard of Septimania, was in charge of the defenses of Bordeaux against the Normans, though an opponent of King Charles the Bald. Failure of Duke William, the Jew, to prevent the Normans from taking Bordeaux, may well have given rise to Prudence of Troyes's charge that the Jews in general betrayed the town to the Normans. There is also the hypothesis that the "association of Jew with Norman" was the real reason for the expulsion of the Jews from Sens circa 876 (infra, note 51). For this view, Jacques Kahn, "Sens," *Jewish Ency.* 11 (1905): 196; Margolis and Marx, *History of the Jewish People*, 352. However, Prudence of Troyes, our only primary source for the accusation of Jewish collaboration with the Normans, also accuses the Jews of collaborating with the Muslims in betraying Barcelona circa 852. Supra, note 24. To our knowledge, the charge that the Jews were in league with the Muslims arose earlier than the charge that the Jews were in league with the Normans (seventh century versus ninth century); lasted longer than that charge (into the twentieth century versus restriction to the ninth century); had a much greater basis in actual fact (the Jews did feel considerable ethnolinguistic affinity for the Semitic Muslims from the Middle East but none whatsoever for the Indo-European Normans from Scandinavia); and triggered several major international persecutions between circa 632 and 1096 (whereas at most the charge that the Jews were in league with the Normans triggered only the expulsion of the Jews from Sens circa 876).

There was also a charge that the Jews were in league with the Mongols who invaded Central Europe circa 1240. Trachtenberg, *Devil and the Jews*, 185; Baron, *Social and Religious History*, IX: 218–219, 343, note 26.

The Jews were also accused of betraying Arles, then under Arian Visigothic control, to the Catholic Frank Clovis in 508; and Narbonne, then under Arab control, to the Catholic French Emperor Charlemagne circa 800. Trachtenberg, *Devil and the Jews*, 184; Baron, *Social and Religious History*, II: 179, 398, note 10; IV: 45–46, 258–259, notes 58–59. If precise memories of these two cases (betrayal of Arles and Narbonne) did survive into the Carolingian-Ottonian period, the damage to the Jews would not have been too great, for the external enemy with whom the Jews were accused of being in league were *Catholic Christians* in both instances!

The Albigensians were also accused of being in league with the Muslims, *e.g.*, by Joachim of Flora and Caesar of Heisterbach in the early thirteenth century. E.S. Gardner, "Joachim of Flora," in A.G. Little, ed., *Franciscan Essays* (Aberdeen: University Press, 1912), 60 and note 3; Mann, *Lives of the Popes in the Middle Ages*, XII: 178 and note 1. Also by Pope Gregory IX circa 1240. Elena Lourie, "Free Moslems in the Balearics under Christian Rule in the Thirteenth Century," *Speculum* 45 (1970): 628–629, note 21. In the 1250s, the Pastoureaux (led by Jacob the "Master of Hungary") who convulsed France (primarily attacking clerics and the Christian nobility but sometimes the Jews as well) were accused of being in league with the Muslims. Cohn, *Pursuit of the Millennium*, 82–87, especially 86, 395, note to p. 86.

In short, the charge that the Jews were in league with the Muslims was much more damaging to the group so accused than the charge that the Jews were in league with other external enemies (the Normans or Mongols). The charge that the Jews were in league with the Muslims seems to have been the prototypical or model charge upon which the other charges (Jews collaborating with Normans or Mongols; Albigensians collaborating with Muslims) were based.

44. We have expressed similar ideas supra, text between notes 8 and 9 to chapter 2.

45. Cf. the challenging researches of Lynn White, beginning with "Technology and Invention in the Middle Ages," *Speculum* 15 (1940): 141–159, which led to the revolutionary *Medieval Technology and Social Change* (New York: Oxford University Press, 1962); "What Accelerated Technological Progress in the Western Middle Ages?" in Alistair C. Crombie, ed., *Scientific Change* (New York: Basic Books, 1963), 272–291; "The Medieval Roots of Modern Technology and Science," in Katherine F. Drew and F.S. Lear, eds., *Perspectives in Medieval History* (Chicago: University of Chicago Press for Rice University, 1963), 19–34; "Conclusion: The Temple of Jupiter Revisited," in White, ed., *The Transformation of the Roman World: Gibbon's Problem after Two Centuries* (Berkeley and Los Angeles: University of California Press, 1966), 291–311; "The Life of the Silent Majority," in Robert S. Hoyt, ed., *Life and Thought in the Early Middle Ages* (Minneapolis: University of Minnesota Press, 1967), 85–100; "The Historical Roots of Our Ecological Crisis," *Science* 155:3767 (March 10, 1967): 1203–1207 = White's *Machina Ex Deo: Essays in the Dynamism of Western Culture* (Cambridge: Massachusetts Institute of Technology Press, 1968), 75–94; "The Iconography of *Temperantia* and the Virtuousness of Technology," in T.K. Rabb and J.E. Seigel, eds., *Action and Conviction in Early Modern Europe: Essays in Memory of E.H. Harbison* (Princeton: Princeton University Press, 1969), 197–219; "The Expansion of Technology 500–1500," in Carlo M. Cipolla, ed., *The Fontana Economic History of Europe* (London: Collins/Fontana Books, 1969) I: 143–174; "Cultural Climates and Technological Advance in the Middle Ages," *Viator* 2 (1971): 171–201; "Technology Assessment from the Stance of a Medieval Historian," *American Historical Review* 79 (1974): 1–13.

White has also published at least three articles that are superb examples of medieval cross-cultural studies: "Tibet, India and Malaya as Sources of Western Medieval Technology," *American Historical Review* 65 (1960): 515–526; "Medieval Borrowings from Further Asia," in O.B. Hardison Jr., ed., *Medieval and Renaissance Studies*, vol. 5, Proceedings of the Southeastern Institute of Medieval and Renaissance Studies, summer 1969 (Chapel Hill: University of North Carolina Press, 1971), 3–26; "Indic Elements in the Iconography of Petrach's *Trionfo della Morte*," *Speculum* 49 (1974): 201–221.

For further information on White's life and work, *Directory of American Scholars*

1 (1974): 674–675; 1 (1978): 734; 1 (1982): 823; *Repertoire International des Medievistes* (1965), 668, no. 3431; ibid. (1971), 828, no. 4635; ibid. (1979), 788, no. 5368. Cf. also Lynn Townsend White, Jr., *Medieval Religion and Technology: Collected Essays* (Berkeley, Los Angeles, and London: University of California Press, 1978); as well as Bert S. Hall and Delno C. West, eds., *On Pre-Modern Technology and Science: Studies in Honor of Lynn White, Jr.* (Malibu, California: Undena, 1976).

On the expansion of Western Europe circa 900–1100, also William Carroll Bark, *Origins of the Medieval World* (Garden City, New York: Doubleday/Anchor, 1960) and Hilmar C. Krueger, "Economic Aspects of Expanding Europe," in Marshall Clagett, Gaines Post, and Robert Reynolds, eds., *Twelfth Century Europe and the Foundations of Modern Society* (Madison: University of Wisconsin Press, 1961), 59–76.

With specific regard to Jewish matters, White's essay *A Jewish Option in Modern America* (Los Angeles: Hebrew Union College-Jewish Institute of Religion, 1964), 11 pp.; as well as his article "Death and the Devil," in Robert Kinsman, ed., *The Darker Vision of the Renaissance* (Berkeley: University of California Press, 1974), 25–46, wherein White attempts to correlate outbreaks of anti-Semitism and witch-hunting in the later Middle Ages/early modern times.

In private conversation with us at UCLA during 1967–1968, White expressed sympathy for the view that the association of Jew with Muslim by medieval Christians played an important role in medieval anti-Semitism. Those who reject this view might argue as follows. The association of Jew *with Muslims* was not an important factor because Jews were also associated with Normans and Mongols by medieval Christians, just as Jews have been associated with the Atlantic democracies by both Nazis and Russian Communists in the twentieth century. The association of Jew with Muslim by medieval Christians was nothing more than the equation of internal with external alien, a tendency found within every society.

However, White felt that those who denigrate thus the importance of the role played by the association of Jew with Muslim by medieval Christians in medieval anti-Semitism fail to take the following into account. If the association of Jew with Muslim by medieval Christians was no more than another example of the tendency of every society to equate internal with external alien, why did not the Muslims equate the Jews (internal aliens within medieval Islamic society) with the Christians (the external aliens who fought the Muslims of the Mediterranean on at least three fronts, Spain, Italy/Sicily, and the Middle East)? The general failure of medieval Muslims to equate Jew with Christian exalts the importance of the role which the tendency of medieval Christians to equate Jew with Muslim played within medieval anti-Semitism.

White also holds, however, that the deicide charge was an equally important factor in high medieval anti-Semitism. The High Middle Ages (1000–1300) saw a radical shift in Christian attitudes toward Jesus, which now emphasized Jesus the human rather than Jesus the God, Jesus the crucified savior rather than Jesus the resurrected judge. To this radical shift St. Francis of Assisi and his stigmata made a major contribution. Of course, the new emphasis on Jesus the crucified savior could not help but inflame latent anti-Jewish passions, since the Jews were generally held responsible for the crucifixion. However, we might add, the Muslims were also held responsible for the crucifixion. Infra, note 57. Moreover, anti-Muslimism and the equation of Jew with Muslim probably influenced the revival of the deicide charge in the High Middle Ages. Supra, note 16, Religious Factors, B.

46. Heinrich Graetz, *Geschichte der Juden*, ed. J. Guttmann (4th ed.; Leipzig: Leiner, no date [circa 1908]), VII: 17–18 = *History of the Jews*, trans. B. Loewy (Philadelphia: Jewish Publication Society of America, 1956), III: 512–513; Moritz Guedemann, *Geschichte des Erziehungswesens und der Cultur der Abendlaendischen Juden waehrend des Mittelalters* (Vienna: Hoelder, 1884), II: 89; Hermann Vogelstein and Paul Rieger, *Geschichte der Juden in Rom* (Berlin: Mayer & Mueller, 1896), I: 230; Vogelstein, *Jewish Communities Series: Rome*, trans. M. Hadas (Philadelphia: Jewish Publication Society of America, 1940), 164; Israel Abrahams, *Jewish Life in the Middle Ages* (Cleveland, New York, and Philadelphia: World/Meridian and Jewish Publication Society of America, 1961), 302; Joseph Jacobs, "Badge", *Jewish Ency.* 2 (1902): 425; I. Broyde, "Innocent III," ibid. 6 (1904): 586–587; Margolis and Marx, *History of the Jewish People*, 375; Dubnow, *Divre Y'me Am Olam*, V: 8–9 = *History of the Jews*, III: 26–28; A. Kober, "Jewish Badge," *Univ. Jewish Ency.* 6 (1942): 90; Grayzel, "Popes," ibid. 8 (1942): 509, and *The Church and the Jews in the XIIIth Century*, 59ff; G. Kisch, "The Yellow Badge in History," *Historia Judaica* 4 (1942): 101–102, 114; A. Shochat, "Ot Kalon" [Badge of Shame], *Ency. Hebraica* 2 (1955–1956): 338; Baron, *Social and Religious History*, IX: 27–28; Flannery, *Anguish of the Jews*, 103; Synan, *Popes and the Jews in the Middle Ages*, 104.

47. Cf. Pope Innocent III's well-known summation of the two chief aims of his pontificate, "the recovery . . . of the Holy Land and the reformation of the Universal Church," in his letter of April 19, 1213, *Vineam Domini Sabaoth*, summoning the Fourth Lateran Council. A. Potthast, *Regesta Pontificum Romanorum* (Graz: Akademische Druck-und Verlagsanstalt, 1957), I: 407–408, no. 4706; MPL, CCXVI: 824:A; Baron, *Social and Religious History*, IX: 27–28; Synan, *Popes and the Jews in the Middle Ages*, 83.

48. Infra, chapter 6; for Pope Innocent III's relative, Pope Gregory IX, infra, note 54 to this chapter.

49. In integrating the study of Jewish history into the study of world history in general, we must take into serious consideration the profoundly analytical and powerfully moving reconstructions by the late Marshall Hodgson, the brilliant Islamologist and historian of religious civilizations at the University of Chicago, a disciple of the late Gustave von Grunebaum of UCLA. We refer to Hodgson's history of Islamic civilization (with especial emphasis upon the period after 1200, which Hodgson, contrary to regnant opinion, considered as creative as the pre-1200 period), *The Venture of Islam: Conscience and History in a World Civilization*, 3 vols. (Chicago and London: University of Chicago Press, 1974). Unfortunately, the manuscript of several hundred pages which he left unfinished at his premature death, and which he tentatively had entitled *The Unity of World History*, will apparently never be published. Cf. ibid., I: viii. Hodgson's work has been influenced by Karl Jaspers, *Origin and Goal of History* (New Haven: Yale University Press, 1953), and has in turn influenced William H. McNeill, *The Rise of the West: A History of the Human Community* (New York and Toronto: New American Library/Mentor, 1965); cf. p. 483, note 31, of the McNeill work.

50. For Christian reconciliation with Islam, supra, note 8 to chapter 1.

For Jewish reconciliation with Islam, the powerful call for Jewish-Islamic dialogue issued by Trude Weiss-Rosmarin, editor of *The Jewish Spectator* magazine of New York City, which she published in her journal, 32 (September 1967): 2–18, after the June 1967 Six Day War in the Middle East; and the cogent reply thereto by R.J. Zwi Werblowsky, "The Futility of Dialogues," ibid. 33 (April 1968): 17–19. The entire fall 1968 issue (vol. 17, no. 4) of *Judaism: A Quarterly Journal of Jewish Life and Thought*, then edited by Steven Schwarzschild, was devoted to the Jewish-Islamic dialogue and included our article upon which the present fourth chapter of this book is based. Cf. also more recently Z.M. Schachter, "Bases and Boundaries of Jewish, Christian and Moslem Dialogue," *Journal of Ecumenical Studies* 14 (1977): 407–418; Trude Weiss-Rosmarin, "The Islamic Connection," *Judaism* 29 (1980): 272–278.

51. At this point we refer the reader to our monograph, completed spring 1975, *Why Did Pope John VIII (Acting Through Archbishop Ansegise, Primate of France and Germany) Order the Expulsion of the Jews of Sens Circa 876 A.D.?* For this expulsion, Parkes, *Jew in the Medieval Community*, 35; Baron, *Social and Religious History*, IV: 56, 61; Schwarzfuchs, "France Under the Early Capets," in Roth, *Dark Ages*, 146; Blumenkranz, *Auteurs*, 253; and his "Sens," *Ency. Judaica* 14 (1971): 1163. Our monograph on the expulsion is divided into nine chapters as follows: (1) Was the Expulsion to Punish the Jews for Real (or Imaginary) Sexual Misconduct with the Nuns of the Town? (2) Was It to Punish the Jews for Exerting Real (or Imaginary) Religious Influence upon the Nuns (and/or the People) of the Town? (3) Was It to Weaken the Power of the Franco-Jewish *Nasi* (or Prince), Bernard of Auvergne (following the Zuckerman thesis; supra, note 20); (4) Was It to Lend Credence to the Charge That the Jews Murdered Emperor Charles the Bald by Poison? (5) Was It to Punish the Jews for Alleged Collaboration with the Dreaded Norman Invaders (supra, note 43)? (6) Was It to Help Cement the New Papal-Byzantine Alliance by Imitating the Major Byzantine Persecution of the Jews Decreed by Emperor Basil I circa 874 (supra, note 24, concluding paragraph)? (7) Was It to Attack the Dreaded Arab Invaders through the Jews (Their Ethnoreligious Cousins) Who, Because of the Association of Jew with Muslim by Medieval Christians, Were Considered Islamic Fifth Columnists in Christian Territory, in League with the Muslims Planning the Destruction of Christendom (supra, note 24, concluding paragraph)? (8) The Historical Context and Import of the Expulsion of the Jews from Sens circa 876; and (9) The Expulsion of the Jews from Sens circa 876 and Western Christian Art circa 1000. In this monograph we consider factors (6) and (7), the pro-Byzantine and the anti-Islamic, the two chief causes for the expulsion.

52. Southern, *Western Views of Islam in the Middle Ages*, 28, note 25, citing Glaber, ed. Prou, 11–12 = MPL, CXLII: 619–620; also d'Alverny, *Occidente e l'Islam*, II: 595–596.

As pointed out in our article, *Al-Andalus*, XXVIII: 253–254, Glaber's statements that the Arabs believe the Old Testament prophecies were fulfilled in Muhammad and that the Arabs have genealogies tracing the descent of Muhammad from Ishmael may show a knowledge of the Arabic originals of the Islamic documents which were translated into Latin about a century later (in the 1140s as part of the Toletano-Cluniac corpus) under the titles (1) *Fabulae Saracenorum* or *Chronica Mendosa* (for which, Kritzeck, *Peter the Venerable and Islam*, 75–83), (2) *De Generatione Mahumet*

(Kritzeck, 84–88), and (3) *De Doctrina Mahumet* (Kritzeck, 89–96). The *Fabulae* and the *Generatione* contain the genealogy of Muhammad, while the *Generatione* and the *Doctrina* (both of which revolve around converts from Judaism to Islam—Kab al-Ahbar in the former and Abdallah ibn-Salam in the latter—and both of which heavily associate Jew with Muslim) seem to consider Muhammad the great prophet whose coming was allegedly foretold by the Old Testament. The Arabic originals of these Islamic documents were probably available in Spain already in the eleventh-century (though they were not translated into Latin until the twelfth century) and Petrus Alphonsi (brought up a Jew in Muslim Spain in the late eleventh century) may have known them. Alphonsi's *Dialogi* (circa 1110), MPL, CLVII: 600:B

For a late eleventh-century parallel to Glaber's equation of Jew with Muslim, we note that according to Baron, *Social and Religious History*, IV: 243, n. 22, King Roger I of Sicily "failed to distinguish clearly between Jews and Saracens." Circa 1095 "he transferred a large number of 'Saracens' to the control of the Church of Palermo," but included in this group were "several persons bearing indubitably Hebraic names."

For twelfth-century parallels to Glaber's equation of Jew with Muslim: the case of Peter the Venerable, supra, note 29, plus the following three additional examples. (1) Circa 1145 Otto of Freising, the great historian, wrote that the Muslims "receive the Old Testament law [which is incorrect] and the [Jewish] rite of circumcision [which is correct]." Southern, *Western Views of Islam*, 36 and note 4. (2) In the late twelfth century, Giraldus Cambrensis, the noted English writer, reported that the educated people of his day were beginning to attribute Islamic abstinence from pork to Judaic influence. Southern, *Making of the Middle Ages*, 41. The *Doctrina Mahumet* in the Toletano-Cluniac corpus of the 1140s had already equated Jew with Muslim by making this same point. Kritzeck, *Peter the Venerable and Islam*, 95. (3) In the late twelfth century Graindor of Douai, the great French epic poet, in his *Conquete de Jerusalem*, claimed that the Jewish custom of abstaining from pork stemmed from the fact that Muhammad (apparently here considered the prophet of the Jews as well as the Muslims), in a fit of drunkenness, was devoured by pigs on a dungheap, and when Muhammad's body was taken to Mecca for his last rites, the body was entrusted to a Jewish sorcerer for burial. Gerald Herman, "A Note on Medieval Anti-Judaism as Reflected in the *Chansons de Geste*," *Annuale Mediaevale* 14 (1973): 68–69.

53. Baron, *Social and Religious History*, V: 124–125, 347, note 55, citing Munyoz Sendino, *Miscellanea Comillas*, XI–XII: 411, lines 5–7: "*Sicut de Iudeo proverbium dicit, Iudeus nisi postquam efficitur Sarracenus Iudeus non est, vix aliquis suam legem, nisi prius aliam acceperit, diligat.*" On al-Kindi's *Risalah*, Monneret de Villard, *Lo Studio dell'Islam in Europa*, 13–14; Kritzeck, *Peter the Venerable and Islam*, 101–107.

54. Grayzel *The Church and the Jews in the XIIIth Century*, 203.

Cf. Grayzel, ibid., 159, for Pope Honorius III's letter of November 4, 1220, to the kings of Aragon, Navarre, Castile, and Leon, as well as the archbishop of Toledo, and the bishops of Burgos, Palencia, Leon, and Zamora, in which the pope accused the Jews of "exposing to him [the Almohade Sultan of Morocco] the plans and the state of the Christians and revealing their secrets [i.e., the secrets of the Christians]." We have here a clear papal subscription to the thesis that the Jew was an Islamic fifth columnist in Christian territory, in league with the Muslims planning the destruction of the West.

Cf. also the equation of Jew with Muslim in the thirteenth-century French epic poem, *Les Enfances Garin de Monglane*, in Guidot, *Revue des Etudes Juives*, CXXXVII: 16–17 and note 63.

Without realizing it, Nahmanides, the greatest thirteenth- century rabbinic figure in Aragon, fanned the flames of the Christian equation of Jew with Muslim at the famous Barcelona disputation of 1263 by seeming to express a preference for the Muslims over the Christians. He did this by asserting that the Islamic empire was "greater" in might but less violent and bloodthirsty than the Christian. H. Beinart, "Barcelona, Disputation of," *Ency. Judaica* 4 (1971): 214. For the similar fanning of the flames by Barfat, Nahmanides's fourteenth-century successor, infra, note 56; on the extent to which Jewish literature equated Jew with Muslim to circa 1200, the fifth chapter of this book, supra.

55. Teddy Kollek and Moshe Pearlman, *Pilgrims to the Holy Land: The Story of Pilgrimage through the Ages* (New York and Evanston: Harper and Row, 1970), 154.

56. Baron, *Social and Religious History*, XI: 169, 346, note 11; also 368–369, note 60; citing the "Miracle de Sainte-Gudule," in C.G.N. de Vooy, *Middelnederlandse Legenden en Exemplen* (The Hague: Nijhoff, 1900), 199ff, especially 216 and note 2; as well as J. Stengers, *Les Juifs dans les Pays-Bas au Moyen Age* (Brussels: Palais des Academies, 1950), 24ff, 54, 134ff, note 169.

According to Bulard, *Le Scorpion: Symbole du Peuple Juif*, 226, note 1, the Italian Passion of Ravello makes the Jewish King Herod swear "by our god Muhammad," and the Jewish High Priest Annas swear "by the faith which I place in Muhammad," while the Passion of Arnoul Greban has the Jewish King Herod cry out "Muhammad, my infinite god!" Infra, notes 65 and 68, for additional examples (from as late as the sixteenth century) of the Christian belief that the Jews considered Muhammad their god. For the Christian belief that Muhammad was the god of the Muslims, just as Jesus was the God of the Christians, Southern, *Western Views of Islam*, 32–36; William Wistar Comfort, "The Literary Role of the Saracens in the French Epic," *Publications of the Modern Language Association of America* 55 (1940): 628–659; and C. Meredith Jones, "The Conventional Saracen of the Songs of Geste," *Speculum* 17 (1942): 201–225.

Without realizing it, Isaac the son of Sheshet Barfat (1326–1408, Gerona to Valencia to Algiers), one of the greatest rabbinic authorities in fourteenth-century Aragon, followed Nahmanides in fanning the flames of the Christian equation of Jew with Muslim. He did this when, agreeing with Maimonides (who, of course, wrote in an Islamic environment where expressing this idea posed no problems for Jews), he concluded that Muslims were less defiling than Christians, i.e., Jews could neither use nor sell Christian wine, but they could at least sell Muslim wine. Cf. Netanyahu, *Marranos*, 27, note 67 (Barfat and Maimonides); Septimus, *Speculum*, LVI: 519 and note 10 (Maimonides); supra, note 54 (Nahmanides); supra, chapter five (Jewish equation of Jew with Muslim to circa 1200).

Cf. also the poem "La Dance de la Muerte," circa 1400, in which a Jewish rabbi and a Muslim legist, among others, dance with death. J.M. Sola Sole, "El Rabi y el Alfaqui en la Dance General de la Muerte," *Romance Philology* 18 (1965): 272–283; Baron, *Social and Religious History*, XI: 347, note 12; Kenneth R. Scholberg, "Spanish and Portuguese Literature," *Ency. Judaica* 15 (1971): 249.

For the Valencian Holy Cross Altarpiece of circa 1409, infra, note 65.

Cf. also the following examples of the Christian equation of Marrano (Jewish convert to Christianity) with Muslim in fifteenth-century Spain.

Don Diego Arias de Avila, the Marrano secretary and auditor of King Henry IV of Castile (1454–1474), was accused of rising to power with the help of the peasants with whom he had ingratiated himself by singing Muslim songs to them. Baer, *Jews in Christian Spain*, II: 283, 488, note 27.

In 1486 the Inquisition executed Juan de Pineda, a commander of the Order of the Knights of Santiago and its former emissary to the papal court in Rome. A Marrano from Cordova, Juan was accused of sympathizing with the Turks who had reached the Adriatic by conquering Albania in 1468. He was alleged to have considered the Turks the Jewish Messiah and to have predicted a Turkish conquest of Spain between 1464 and 1473. Baer, *Jews in Christian Spain*, II: 347–349, 495, note 21.

An anti-Marrano treatise written circa 1488 by a close associate of the grand inquisitor Thomas de Torquemada presents a detailed comparison of the Marranos with Buraq, the mythical beast upon which the Prophet Muhammad, the lawgiver of Islam, rode in his journey from Jerusalem to heaven. On this treatise cf. Isadore Loeb, "Polemistes Chretiens et Juifs en France et en Espagne," *Revue des Etudes Juives* 18 (1889): 238–242; Trachtenberg, *Devil and the Jews*, 223, note 35; Baer, *Jews in Christian Spain*, II: 390–391, 394–398. This same author accuses the Marranos of emigrating to Turkey so that they could help the Ottomans against the Christians (Baer: II, 395) as well as of introducing homosexuality into Christendom through the Muslims (Baer, II: 397).

The great late-fifteenth-century Spanish chronicler, Andres Bernaldez, a strong supporter of the Inquisition and an archenemy of the Marranos, listed the Islamic lands first among the lands to which the Marranos fled. Netanyahu, *Marranos*, 216.

Finally, news of the following episode would have confirmed the Christian view that the Jews were in league with the Muslims. In 1498 some Jews fleeing expulsion from Navarre were arrested in Almeria, southeastern Spain, on their way to North Africa. They sought to escape arrest for being Jews (it was a crime to be a Jew in Spain after 1492) by claiming to be Muslims and reciting Muslim prayers in faultless Arabic. Maurice Kriegel, *Les Juifs a la fin du Moyen Age dans l'Europe Mediterraneene* (Paris: Hachette, 1979), 83, 259 and note 51; and as reviewed by E. Roditi, *Judaism* 29 (1980): 244.

57. Francesco Gabrieli, ed., *Arab Historians of the Crusades*, trans. E.J. Costello (Berkeley: University of California Press, 1969), 182–183; and our review of this book, *Journal of Ecumenical Studies* 9 (1972): 366–369. C.J. Bishko, "The Spanish and Portuguese Reconquest, 1095–1492," in Setton, *History of the Crusades*, III: 420, states that the thirteenth-century Spanish poet Gonzalo of Berceo "could depict the Moors as responsible for the Crucifixion." Gonzalo may have been influenced by the Crusade propaganda at the time of the Third Crusade described by Ibn al-Athir.

The Muslims were portrayed in the French epic poems (*chansons de geste*) as glorying in and relying upon the alleged Jewish crucifixion of Christ to vindicate theologically the Islamic faith against the Christian. Cf. *Les Enfances Renier*, circa 1300, wherein the Muslim king Brunamon forbids his daughter to convert to Christianity in order to marry the Christian Renier and argues, against said proposed conversion, that the Christian God cannot be a true god because the Jews crucified him. Guidot, *Revue des Etudes Juives*, CXXXVII: 10–11 and notes 35–36. Of course, the Muslims did not in reality glory in the alleged Jewish crucifixion of Christ because the Muslims do not believe that Christ was crucified (a phantom died on the cross in his stead—Islamic docetism). Be that as it may, evidently French Christians circa 1300 imagined that Muslims gloried in the alleged Jewish crucifixion of Christ. Assuming this same French Christian view existed around 1150, the next step was to imagine (as shown in the Gabrieli text and by Gonzalo of Berceo) that the Muslims participated in the crucifixion along with the Jews.

58. Martin Blindheim, *De Malte Antemensaler i Norge*, Sartryck ur Nationalmusei Arsbok 1968; Smaskrift, 1, Universitetets Oldsakssamling 1969 (Stockholm: Victor Pettersons Bokindustri AB, 1969), 23, black-and-white photo. Cf. also Blindheim's *The Stave Church Paintings: Mediaeval Art from Norway* (no place: Collins and UNESCO, 1965), 18 and plate XV; as well as *Norway: Paintings from the Stave Churches*, preface by R. Hauglid and introduction by L. Grodecki (New York: New York Graphic Society and UNESCO, 1955), 15 and plate XXXI. In both cases the plates offer a color photo of another panel from the same Roldal altar frontal, "Christ at the Gates of Hell."

We express sincerest thanks to Per Gjaerder, curator of folk art, Historical Museum of Bergen, who extended every possible courtesy to us during our visit to his museum, September 1971, and gave us a copy of his magnificent book, *Norske Pryd-Dorer Fra Middelalderen*, Universitetet i Bergen Skrifter, 24 (Bergen: Grieg, 1952), 273 folio size pages with English summary and 252 illustrations.

There was a Mediterranean and Catalan influence on medieval Norwegian altar painting. *Norway: Paintings from the Stave Churches*, 18. Thus, the image of Islamic participation in the crucifixion of Christ could have come north from the Mediterranean and Catalonia (see note 57 above) to Norway and into the Roldal altar frontal.

59. Baron, *Social and Religious History*, XI: 346, note 11, citing Bulard, *Scorpion*, 227ff. Actually, Bulard's entire thirteenth chapter, "A Quelles Representations Est Associe Le Scorpion Symbolique? II. Emblemes Divers," 223–239, is very relevant.

60. Bulard, *Scorpion*, 251, note 2, calls attention to the association of Jew with Muslim in Piero della Francesca's "Battle of Constantine and Maxentius" (from "The Legend of the True Cross Cycle"), a fresco in the Church of St. Francis, Arezzo, painted circa 1453–1454. However in this case the Judaeo/Islamic conspiracy is not linked with Christ's passion but rather with Maxentius, the pagan Roman emperor defeated by Constantine, the Christian Roman hero. Maxentius's troops, fleeing in disarray on the right side of the fresco, carry two primary banners: one on the far right bears a black Muslim head; another, to the left of this banner, bears a Basilisk (a Greek mythological dragon which like the scorpion, was a Jewish symbol). For a color reproduction of this fresco, Frederick Hartt, *History of Italian Renaissance Art: Painting, Sculpture, Architecture* (Englewood Cliffs, New Jersey and New York City: Prentice-Hall and Abrams, 1969), colorplate 30, facing p. 231.

Bulard, *Scorpion*, 233 and plate XLVI:1, also calls attention to della Francesca's fresco, "Battle of Heraclius and Chosroes" (in the same "True Cross Cycle"), wherein the Persians under King Chosroes carry a banner bearing a black Muslim. Cf. Hartt, *History of Italian Renaissance Art*, 239, figure 285, for a black-and-white reproduction of this fresco. Could the lion on the banner in the center of the fresco be a Jewish symbol (the "lion of Judah")? See in general Louis Isaac Rabinowitz, "Lion: In Folklore and Art," *Ency. Judaica* 11 (1971): 275–276. If so, here too we would have an association of Jew with Muslim.

61. Hartt, *History of Italian Renaissance Art*, 244–245 and colorplate 31, facing p. 231. Supra, note 56 for the Italian Passion of Ravello which makes King Herod a Muslim. Cf. also Creighton Gilbert, "Piero della Francesca's *Flagellation*: The Figures in the [Right] Foreground," *Art Bulletin* 53 (September 1971): 41–51, discussing in detail the important earlier article by M. Lavin, "Piero della Francesca's *Flagellation*: The Triumph of Christian Glory," ibid. 50 (1968): 321–342. Gilbert identifies the bald and brocaded male figure on the far right of della Francesca's "Flagellation" (outside of the flagellation scene proper) as the Jew, Joseph of Arimathea. Hartt also seems to consider him a Jew. One might be tempted to identify the male figure with the strange headgear and the short but forked beard (standing two figures to the left of the bald, brocaded Joseph of Arimathea) as a Jew, but both Hartt and Gilbert insist he is a Greek. (Hartt: the Byzantine emperor John Paleologus).

62. Baron, *Social and Religious History*, XI: 131, citing Bulard, *Scorpion*, 227.

For the Italian original we have used Lodovico Magugliani, ed., *Dante Alighieri: La Divina Commedia: Inferno* (Milan: Rizzoli, 1949), 150 and notes; our English translation follows that of John Ciardi, *Dante Alighieri: The Inferno, a Verse Rendering for the Modern Reader* (New York and Toronto: New American Library/Mentor, 1954), 230 and notes thereto on p. 233.

For Dante and the Jews, articles on Dante by H. Vogelstein, *Jewish Ency.* 4 (1903): 435–436; *Univ. Jewish Ency.* 3 (1941): 468; J.B. Sermoneta, *Ency. Judaica* 5 (1971): 1296–1297; Cecil Roth, *Jews in the Renaissance* (Philadelphia: Jewish Publication Society of America, 1959), 86–110, 347–348; Shulvass, *Jews in the World of the Renaissance*, 220–222; H. Rheinfelder, "Dante und die Hebraeische Sprache," in Paul Wilpert and Willehad Paul Eckert, eds., *Judentum im Mittelalter: Beitraege zum Christlich-Juedischen Gespraech* (Berlin: Gruyter, 1966), 442–457.

For Dante and Islam, Enrico Cerulli, *Il "Libro della Scala" e la Questione 'delle Fonti Arabo-Spagnole della Divina Commedia*; his "Dante e Islam," *Al-Andalus* 21 (1956): 229–253; and his *Nuove Ricerche sul "Libro della Scala" e la Conoscenza dell'Islam in Occidente*; Giorgio Levi della Vida, "Nuova Luce sulle Fonti Islamiche della Divina Commedia," *Al-Andalus* 14 (1949): 377–407; Maxime Rodinson, "Dante et l'Islam d'apres les Travaux Recents," *Revue d'Histoire des Religions* 140 (1951): 203–236; Umberto Rizzitano, "Dante e il Mondo Arabo," in Vittore Branca and Ettore Caccia, *Dante nel Mondo* (Florence: Olschki, 1965), 1–17; Vincent Cantarino, "Dante and Islam: Theory of Light in the Paradiso," *Kentucky Romance Quarterly* 15 (1968): 3–36; R.W. Southern, "Dante and Islam," in Derek Baker, ed., *Relations between East and West in the Middle Ages* (Edinburgh: University of Edinburgh Press, 1973), 133–145.

It is now recognized that Dante was more heavily influenced by Islamic than by Jewish literature (Roth, *Jew in the Renaissance*, 86–89, 347, note to pp. 86–89). However, it is more likely that Dante (and/or his colleagues and friends) was personally acquainted (and/or in correspondence) with Jewish writers (like Immanuel of Rome and Hillel of Verona; Sermoneta, *Ency. Judaica*, V: 1296) than with their Islamic counterparts. There were more Jewish than Muslim writers living in Italy circa

1300, and the Jews would have been better able than the Muslims to communicate with Dante in the languages he knew well (Latin and Italian; he does not seem to have known Hebrew or Arabic well).

63. For the black Muslim in Giotto's Arena Chapel frescoes, Mario Bucci, *Giotto: I Diamanti dell'Arte* (Florence: Sadea/Sansoni, 1966), figure 51 and p. 38; James Stubblebine, ed., *Giotto: The Arena Chapel Frescoes* (New York: Norton, 1969), figure 44 and p. 87.

For the black Muslim in the frescoes of the Chapel of St. Mary Magdalen, Assisi, Walter Goetz, *Assisi: Mit 118 Abbildungen* (Leipzig: Seemann, 1909), figure 74, p. 113; Francis Newton, *S. Francis and His Basilica* (Assisi: Casa Editrice Francescana, 1926), 37; Giovanni Previtali, "Le Cappelle di San Nicola e di S. Maria Maddalena nella Chiesa Inferiore di San Francesco," in Giuseppe Palumbo, ed., *Giotto ed i Giotteschi in Assisi* (Rome: Canesi, 1969), figures 93a, 93b, and 94, pp. 112–113. On this chapel in general and its frescoes, Sandro Chierichetti, *Assisi: An Illustrated Guide Book, With the Plan of the Monuments* (Milan: Moneta, no date [after 1962]), 42; Touring Club Italiano, *Guida d'Italia: Umbria* (4th ed.; Milan: T.C.I, 1966), 200.

For the black Muslim in the Bardi Chapel frescoes, Florence, Hartt, *History of Italian Renaissance Art*, 65–66; in the Taddeo Gaddi panel, Bulard, *Scorpion*, 233 and note 1, plus plate XLVI: 2; in the Pentecost scene of Andrea di Buonaiuto's Spanish Chapel frescoes (circa 1350), the discussion in the text infra, figure III:B:4.

Cf. Burns, *American Historical Review*, LXXVI: 1406–1407, 1413–1432, for numerous depictions of black Muslims in the illuminations to two great thirteenth-century Spanish literary works produced for King Alfonso X el Sabio of Castile, the *Libro de Ajedrez* (1283) and the *Cantigas de Santa Maria* (circa 1259), especially the latter. Burns, p. 1406, cautions that not all blacks who were depicted in the aforementioned illuminations were Muslims because there were also black Christians in thirteenth-century Spain. However, the overwhelming majority of the blacks depicted therein were Muslims. The depiction of black Muslims in thirteenth-century Spanish art may have influenced the depiction of black Muslims in Italian art circa 1300 and thereafter.

Cf. also the black Muslim in the twelfth-century Byzantine manuscript of the homilies of Gregory Nazianzen (Florence, Laurentian Library MS Plut. 7.32, fol. 18v), Friedman, *The Monstrous Races*, 63–65, and figure 25, p. 63.

64. Alexander Altmann, "Judaism and World Philosophy," in Louis Finkelstein, ed., *The Jews: Their History, Culture and Religion* (2nd ed.; Philadelphia: Jewish Publication Society of America, 1949), I: 645, 669, note 41; citing C. and D.W. Singer, "The Jewish Factor in Medieval Thought," in Edwyn R. Bevan and Charles Singer, eds., *The Legacy of Israel* (Oxford: Clarendon, 1948), 265.

65. Hartt, *History of Italian Renaissance Art*, 95–97, and colorplate 12, facing p. 101; Touring Club Italiano, *Guida d'Italia: Firenze e Dintorni* (5th ed.; Milan: T.C.I, 1964), 294–295; Raimond van Marle, *Development of the Italian Schools of Painting* (The Hague: Nijhoff, 1924), III: 425–453; J. Wood-Brown, *The Dominican Church of S. Maria Novella at Florence* (Edinburgh: Schulze, 1902), 137ff; Piero Bargellini, *Il Cappellone degli Spagnoli* (Florence: Del Turco, 1950); W. and E. Paatz, *Die Kirchen von Florenz* (Frankfurt a. M.: Klostermann, 1952), III: 720ff; Evelyn Sandberg-Vavala, *Studies in the Florentine Churches: Part I, Pre-Renaissance Period* (Florence: Olschki,

1959), 182–196; Alberto Lucchi, *Santa Maria Novella: Firenze, Tesori d'Arte Cristiana* (Bologna: Officine Grafiche Poligrafici il Resto del Carlino, 1967), 26–28; S. Orlandi, *S. Maria Novella and the Monumental Cloisters: Short Historic-Artistic Guide*, trans. A.M. Greathed (2nd ed.; Florence: Convento S. Maria Novella, 1966), 44–57.

In October 1981 we had an opportunity to study the equation of Jew with Muslim in the Holy Cross Altarpiece of circa 1409 by the Maestro de Gil y de Pujades, no. 254 in the Museo Provincial de Bellas Artes, Valencia, Spain. There is a tall, rectangular crucifixion scene at the center of this altarpiece, similar to that on the front or altar wall in the Spanish Chapel, Santa Maria Novella, Florence, Italy, which antedates it by about half a century. In the crucifixion of the Maestro de Gil the figure standing on the immediate left of Christ's cross, partly hidden by it, with a dark face, wearing a beard and low or tight-fitting turban, seems to be a Muslim; as does the figure to the immediate right of the Bad Thief's cross (itself on the right side of the total crucifixion scene), who wears a tall conical hat and bears a shield.

66. Seiferth, *Synagogue and Church in the Middle Ages*, 148, 170, and figure 60. Bulard, *Scorpion*, 230–231, had already called attention to the Burgkmair woodcut in the 1930s.

67. Trachtenberg, *Devil and the Jews*, 185.

68. Trachtenburg, *Devil and the Jews*, 185–186; 250, note 29; 251, note 31, citing the following works: (1) For Crete in 1538, Joshua Starr, "Jewish Life in Crete under the Rule of Venice," *Proceedings of the American Academy for Jewish Research* 12 (1942): (on this episode, also Simon Marcus, "Crete," *Ency. Judaica* 5 (1971): 1089–1090); (2) Bohemia in 1541, Gottlieb Bondy and Franz Dworsky, *Zur Geschichte der Juden in Boehmen, Maehren und Schlesien* (Prague: G. Bondy, 1906), I: 336ff, 447, note; and II: 567; (3) Austria 1544–1602, A.F. Pribram, *Urkunden und Akten zur Geschichte der Juden in Wien* (Vienna and Leipzig: Braumueller, 1918), I: 8, 32, 45; and Johann Jakob Schudt, *Juedische Merckwuerdigkeiten* (Frankfort and Leipzig: Nocker, 1714), I: 89, 344; (4) the Spanish ambassador to England in 1566, Jacob R. Marcus, "Notes on Sephardic Jewish History of the Sixteenth Century," in David Philipson et al., eds., *Hebrew Union College Jubilee Volume* (Cincinnati: Hebrew Union College, 1925), 380; (5) Buda and Italy in 1684, Adolf Buechler, "Buda, Purim of," *Jewish Ency.* 3 (1902): 416.

In 1532 the Jewish Messianic figures, David Reuveni and Solomon Molcho, were arrested by the Holy Roman Emperor Charles V at Regensburg and taken to Mantua. The emperor probably arrested them because he considered them Turkish double-agents who pretended to want to help the Christians but who in reality were attempting to gain the confidence of the Christians in order to betray them to the Turks at a decisive moment later in time. Selma Stern, *Josel of Rosheim: Commander of Jewry in the Holy Roman Empire of the German Nation*, trans. G. Hirschler (Philadelphia: Jewish Publication Society of America, 1965), 135. On Reuveni and Molcho and the Christian-Islamic struggle as the background for their arrest in 1532, Margolis and Marx, *History of the Jewish People*, 506–507; Samuel Ettinger, "Reuveni, David," *Ency. Judaica* 14 (1971): 114–116; Joseph Shochetman, "Molcho, Solomon," ibid. 12 (1971): 225–227; Brockelmann, *History of the Islamic Peoples*, 291.

Throwing light on the expulsion of the Jews of Austria circa 1572 for alleged collaboration with the Turks is the statement in Margolis and Marx, *History of the Jewish*

People, 509–510, that the Venetians blamed their loss of Cyprus to the Turks in 1570 on the Sultan's Jewish advisor, Don Joseph Nasi; hence, when the Christians defeated the Turks at Lepanto in 1571, the Jews of Venice narrowly escaped expulsion. Cf. also Brockelmann, *History of the Islamic Peoples*, 327–328; Cecil Roth, "Nasi, Joseph," *Ency. Judaica* 12 (1971): 839.

Throwing light on the Italian attack on the Jews as alleged Turkish collaborators in 1684, we have the fact that the Jews of the Ukraine, during the terrible Cossack persecutions of circa 1650, preferred to fall into the kinder hands of the *Muslim* Tatars (allies of the Cossacks), who shipped them to Istanbul (the Turkish capital) where they were sold back to their fellow Jews, than into the crueler hands of the Eastern Orthodox *Christian* Cossacks, who massacred them with savage barbarity. Margolis and Marx, *History of the Jewish People*, 552. Italian Jews helped ransom these captives in Istanbul, and Italian Christians who learnt about how the Jews of the Ukraine were saved by the *Muslim* Tatars might have seen therein additional confirmation of the alleged Judaeo/Islamic conspiracy. Likewise, in 1666 Shabbetai Tzvi, who led a worldwide Jewish messianic movement that created a considerable stir even among many Christians in both Western and Eastern Europe, converted to Islam. Margolis and Marx, *History of the Jewish People*, 562–565; Gershom Scholem, "Shabbetai Zevi," *Ency. Judaica* 14 (1971): 1219–1254. Might not Italian Christians who learnt of Shabbetai Tzvi's conversion to Islam have seen therein additional confirmation of the alleged Judaeo/Islamic conspiracy?

Cf. the frontispiece of the second printed edition of Raymond Martin's *Pugio Fidei* ("Dagger of Faith"), a great thirteenth-century Spanish Christian polemic against Judaism and Islam, published at Leipzig by F. Lanckisi in 1687 with preface by J.B. Carpzov. It is reproduced in *Ency. Judaica* 4 (1971): 215. On Raymond Martin, cf. the article by B. Suler and the editor, ibid. 11 (1971): 1065–1066.

In this frontispiece the Jews and Muslims are depicted as allies. The "dagger of the Christian faith" (the *pugio fidei*) points ominously at the Jewish rabbi (lower right-hand corner) who sits in terror at a table upon which lie copies of the Old Testament and the Talmud, books that can offer him no help against the truth of Christianity

The Jew's Muslim ally lies sprawling on the ground, with the top of his turbaned head facing us directly and not allowing us to see his dejected face. The Muslim is undoubtedly dejected in part because the Christians won a great victory over the Turks besieging Vienna in September 1683; the papacy launched a great anti-Turkish Crusade in March 1684, in which the Germans, Poles, and Venetians joined; and the Germans captured Buda in 1686, a city which had been the bulwark of Turkish domination over Hungary for 145 years. The dejected Muslim attempts to find shelter from the power of the "dagger of the Christian faith" beneath the legs of the Jewish rabbi and the Jew's table but to no avail.

In 1821 the Jews of Odessa were massacred for alleged complicity in the Turkish execution the same year of the Greek Orthodox patriarch of Constantinople. Josef Meisl, "Odessa," *Univ. Jewish Ency.* 18 (1942): 283.

69. Trachtenberg, *Devil and the Jews*, 185–186, 251, note 30 citing the following works: (1) Martin Luther: Reinhold Lewin, *Luthers Stellung zu den Juden* (Berlin: Trowitzsch, 1911), 74; (2) The miracle play: David Strumpf, *Die Juden in der Mittelalterlichen Mysterien-, Mirakel- und Moralitaeten-Dichtung Frankreichs*, Heidelberg Thesis

of 1919 (Ladenburg a. N., 1920), 29, 39, note 17: (3) French Besancon Antichrist play, as well as the *Mystere de la Sainte Hostie*, and Wilson's *Three Ladies of London*: Manya Lifschitz-Golden, *Les Juifs dans la Litterature Francaise du Moyen Age* (New York: Columbia University, 1935), 97, and H. Michelson, *The Jew in Early English Literature* (Amsterdam: H.J. Paris, 1926), 77; (4) Marlowe's *Jew of Malta*: Michelson, *Jew in Early English Literature*, 79, and Hiram Haydn and Edmund Fuller, eds., *Thesaurus of Book Digests* (New York: Crown, 1949), 381–382; (5) Ayrer's *Comoedie von Nikolaus*: Oskar Frankl, *Der Jude in den Deutschen Dichtungen des 15., 16. und 17. Jahrhundertes* (Maehrisch-Ostrau and Leipzig: Papuscheck and Hoffmann, 1905), 107.

70. Roger B. Merriman, *Six Contemporaneous Revolutions* (Hamden, Conn.: Archon, 1963), 93–94. For additional references to the alleged Jewish take-over of St. Paul's Cathedral in London, Baron, *The Jewish Community: Its History and Structure to the American Revolution* (Philadelphia: Jewish Publication Society of America, 1948), I: 257; Modder, *Jew in the Literature of England*, 370.

71. Robert Hughes, "Painter Possessed," *Time*, March 3, 1975, 50–51, with one black-and-white and three color illustrations, on the occasion of the great exhibition at London's Tate Gallery of over 200 Fuselis (oils, engravings, and drawings) to commemorate the 150th anniversary of the artist's death in 1825. Cf. also Harold H. Fisch, "Blake, William," *Ency. Judaica* 4 (1971): 1070–1071, describing Blake's ambivalence toward the Jews.

For the equation of Jew with Muslim by Edmund Burke, Frederick Dreyer, "Burke's Religion," *Studies in Burke and His Time* 17 (1976): 203 and note 21.

For the equation of Jew with Muslim (Turk) by the great English poet Lord Byron, in his *Age of Bronze* (1823), "Byron, George Gordon, Lord," *Ency. Judaica* 4 (1971): 1549.

For the equation of Jew with Turk in the New York State Constitutional Convention of 1777, David Lefkowitz, "Church and State," *Univ. Jewish Ency.* 3 (1941): 198. For the equation of Jew with Turk (and Jacobin) by a Federalist supporter of the Alien and Sedition Acts during the late 1790s, Leo Pfeffer, *This Honorable Court: A History of the United States Supreme Court* (Boston: Beacon, 1965), 62. For the equation of Jew with Arab in a letter of February 1, 1863, sent from New Orleans by George S. Denison, to his superior, Salmon P. Chase, secretary of the Treasury (later chief justice) in Washington, D.C., *Diary and Correspondence of Salmon P. Chase* = Annual Report of the American Historical Association for the Year 1902 (Washington, D.C.: United States Government Printing Office, 1903). II: 353.

72. Mira Gavrilovich, "Oscar Gavrilovich's World Press in a Nutshell," *B'nai B'rith Messenger* (Los Angeles), April 11, 1975, 38.

For Disraeli's statement that "Arabs are only Jews on horseback," Robert Blake, *Disraeli* (Garden City, New York: Doubleday/Anchor, 1968), 196.

Apropos of recent efforts to sell Mentmore Towers, in Buckinghamshire, England, the $8 million mansion (with over 200 guest rooms) of Baron Meyer de Rothschild, the British press was "saying that, ironically, only an *Arab oil sheik* can afford to buy the monumental symbol of the Jewish family's wealth." *Los Angeles Times*, May 9, 1977, part 1, 7.

5. The Association of Jew with Muslim by Medieval Jews

* Chapter five is based on two separate but closely related papers: (1) "Conflicting Jewish Attitudes toward Arabs circa 600–1100 A.D.," Fifth Biennial Conference on Medieval Studies, Western Michigan University, Kalamazoo, Michigan, May 20, 1970; and (2) "Jewish Attitudes toward Arabs in the Chronicle of Ahima'atz (Eleventh-Century, Italy)," annual spring meeting, Southeastern Region, American Academy of Religion, University of Tennesse, Knoxville, March 19, 1971. We thank Robert Burns, Joseph O'Callaghan, and Victor Reichert for their encouragement of our work after the delivery of the paper at the Fifth Biennial Conference.

1. Cf. Trachtenberg's *Devil and the Jews*, iv and ix, for his acknowledgment of the influence of such distinguished Jewish historians and philosophers as Jacob Mann, Morris Raphael Cohen, Salo W. Baron, Guido Kisch, and Solomon Grayzel. This Trachtenberg classic grew out of work on his earlier volume, *Jewish Magic and Superstition: A Study in Folk Religion* (New York: Behrman House, 1939). Cf. the articles on Trachtenberg, *Univ. Jewish Ency.* 10 (1943): 286, and Sefton D. Temkin, *Ency. Judaica* 15 (1971): 1293.

2. Cf. Cohn's important subsequent books, *Warrant for Genocide: The Myth of the Jewish World Conspiracy, the Protocols of the Elders of Zion* (New York: Harper and Row, 1967) and *Europe's Inner Demons: An Enquiry Inspired by the Great Witch-Hunt* (New York: Basic Books, 1975).

3. Supra, notes 12 and 67ff to chapter 4.

4. Herman Rosenthal, "Poland," *Jewish Ency.* 10 (1905): 572; and his "Cossacks' Uprising," ibid. 4 (1903): 286; Margolis and Marx, *History of the Jewish People*, 556; Solomon Grayzel, *History of the Jews from the Babylonian Exile to the Present 1968* (2nd ed.; New York and Toronto: New American Library/Mentor, 1968), 442; two articles on Stefan Czarniecki, by J.G. Lipman, *Jewish Ency.* 4 (1903): 406, and *Ency. Judaica* 5 (1971): 1187; two articles on Cracow, by M.S. Balaban, *Univ. Jewish Ency.* 3 (1941): 392 and A. Cygielman, *Ency. Judaica* 5 (1971): 1030.

5. Supra, notes 67-69 to chapter 4.

6. Supra, note 56 to chapter 4.

7. Supra, note 43 to chapter 4; John L. LaMonte, *World of the Middle Ages: A Reorientation of Medieval History* (New York: Appleton-Century-Crofts, 1949), 534ff.

8. Supra, note 16, Religious Factors, A, to chapter 4.

9. Genesis 37:28 equates Midianites with Ishmaelites (Arabs). Exodus 3:1 (and 18:1) says that Jethro was a Midianite (= Ishmaelite = Arab). Exodus 3:1 (cf. 2:15–22) says that Jethro was Moses's father-in-law. Exodus chapter 18 makes Jethro an important religiopolitical advisor of Moses. Medieval students of the Bible, whether Jews, Latins, Greeks, or Muslims, would not have had much difficulty putting the aforementioned Pentateuchal passages together, thereby equating Jews with Arabs. For Jewish-Arab relations before Islam, Gerson B. Levi, Hartwig Hirschfeld, and Louis Ginzberg, "Arabic," *Jewish Ency.* 2 (1902): 40–44; Richard J.H. Gottheil, "Arabia," and Julian Morgenstern, "Arab: Biblical Period," *Univ. Jewish Ency.*. 1 (1939): 438–441, 443; H.Z. Hirschberg, "Arabia," *Ency. Judaica* 3 (1971): 232–237; Baron, *Social and Religious History*, III: 60–74; S.D. Goitein, *Jews and Arabs: Their Contacts through the Ages* (New York: Schocken, 1967), 3–61; Abraham I. Katsh, *Judaism and the Koran: Biblical and*

Talmudic Backgrounds of the Koran and Its Commentaries (New York: Barnes/Perpetua, 1962), i–xiii; Theophile J. Meek, *Hebrew Origins* (New York: Harper Torchbooks/ Cloister Library, 1960), 82–118.

10. Cf. three articles on Bustanai, Louis Ginzberg, *Jewish Ency.* 3 (1902): 330–331; *Univ. Jewish Ency.* 2 (1940): 480; Simha Assaf, *Ency. Judaica* 4 (1971): 1537. Cf. also F. Lazarus, "Die Haeupter der Vertriebenen," *Bruell's Jahrbuecher fuer Juedische Geschichte und Litteratur* 10 (1890): 24–25, 174; Solomon Schechter, "Geniza Specimens: Saadyana, Part 2," *Jewish Quarterly Review* 14 (1902): 242–246; G. Margoliouth, "Some British Museum Genizah Texts," ibid., 303–307; E.J. Worman, "The Exilarch Bustanai," ibid. 20 (1908): 211–215; H. Tykocinski (with important notes by J.N. Epstein), "Bustanai Rosh Ha-Golah" [Bustanai the Exilarch]," *D'vir* (Berlin) 1 (1923): 145–179; Alexander Marx, "Der Arabische Bustanai-Bericht und Nathan Ha-Babli," in A. Freimann, M. Schorr, and D. Simonsen, eds., *Livre de'Hommage a la Memoire du Dr. Samuel Poznanski (1864–1921)* (Warsaw and Leipzig: Great Synagogue and Harrassowitz, 1927), 76–81; Jacob Mann, *Texts and Studies in Jewish History and Literature* (Cincinnati: Hebrew Union College Press, 1931), I: 334ff; Alexander D. Goode, "The Exilarchate in the Eastern Caliphate 637–1258," *Jewish Quarterly Review* 31 (1940–1941): 154, 157, 169; Ben-Zion Dinur, *Yisrael Ba-Golah* [The Jewish People in the Diaspora] (2nd ed.; Tel Aviv: D'vir, 1958–1961), I:1: 15, 23–24; I:2: 88–91, 143–145, 315; Salo W. Baron, *The Jewish Community: Its History and Structure to the American Revolution* (Philadelphia: Jewish Publication Society of American, 1948), I: 177; III: 39–40, 46; and his *Social and Religious History*, III: 89, 270; V: 8ff, 141ff, 294–295, 354–355; VI: 11, 19, 200, 214–215; Cohen, *Book of Tradition*, 45, 126; Zuckerman, *Jewish Princedom*, 4, 61, 77–79, 81, 103–104, 118, 128.

11. Cf. three articles on Eldad the Danite, I. Broyde, *Jewish Ency.* 5 (1903): 90–92; *Univ. Jewish Ency.* 4 (1941): 46; Azriel Shochat, *Ency. Judaica* 6 (1971): 576–578. Cf. also A. Neubauer, "Where Are the Ten Tribes," *Jewish Quarterly Review* 1 (1888–1889): 95–114; Abraham Epstein, "La Lettre d'Eldad sur les Dix Tribus," *Revue des Etudes Juives* 25 (1892): 30–43; Max Schloessinger, *The Ritual of Eldad Ha-Dani* (Leipzig and New York: Haupt, 1908); Samuel Krauss, "Or Hadash Al Elu Y'diot Giografiyyot Etzel Eldad Ha-Dani U'Vinyamin Mi-Tudela" [New Light on Some Geographic Data in Eldad the Danite and Benjamin of Tudela], *Tarbitz* 8 (1936–1937): 208–232; Starr, *Jews in the Byzantine Empire*, 38, 118, 219; Franciszek Kupfer and Stefan Strelcyn, "Un Nouveau Manuscript Concernant Eldad Haddani," *Rocznik Orientalistyczny* 19 (1954): 125–143; Meyer Waxman, *History of Jewish Literature* (New York and London: Yoseloff, 1960), I: 432–434; Baron, *Social and Religious History*, III: 116–117, 208, 286–287, 329; VI: 122, 220–221, 433–434; VIII: 179, 228; H.Z. Hirschberg, *Tol'dot Ha-Y'hudim B'Afrikah Ha-Tz'fonit* [History of the Jews in North Africa] (Jerusalem: Bialik Institute, 1965), I: 72, 208, 230; II: 24; Ashtor, *Jews of Moslem Spain*, I: 140–154, 194, 212–213.

For the Hebrew original of Eldad's narrative, Adolf Jellinek, *Bet Ha-Midrasch: Sammlung Kleiner Midraschim und Vermischter Abhandlungen aus der Aeltern Juedischen Literatur* (3rd ed.; Jerusalem: Wahrmann, 1967), II: 102–113; III: 6–11; V: 17–21; Abraham Epstein, *Eldad Ha-Dani, Seine Berichte ueber die X Staemme und Deren Ritus* (Pressburg: Alkalay, 1891); D.H. Mueller, *Die Recensionen und Versionen des Eldad Had-Dani*, Denkschriften der Kaiserlichen Akademie der Wissenschaften, Philosophisch-Historische Classe, 41 (Vienna: Tempsky, 1892), 1–80; Benzion Halper, *Post-Biblical Hebrew Literature: An Anthology of Texts with Notes and Glossary* (Philadelphia: Jewish Publication Society of America, 1946), 25–29, 214–215; Abraham Kahana, *Sifrut Ha-Historiyya Ha-Yisr'elit* [The Literature of Jewish History] (Jerusalem: Hotza'-at Makor, 1968–1969), I: 21–29; Dinur, *Yisrael Ba-Golah*, I:2: 5, 9–13, 82.

For the English translation, Elkan Nathan Adler, *Jewish Travelers: A Treasury of Travelogues from Nine Centuries* (2nd ed.; New York: Hermon, 1966), 4–21; Leo W. Schwarz, ed., *The Jewish Caravan: Great Stories of Twenty-Five Centuries* (Revised and enlarged ed.; New York: Holt, Rinehart and Winston, 1965), 193–196; Curt Leviant, *Masterpieces of Hebrew Literature: A Treasury of 2000 Years of Jewish Creativity* (New York: K'tav, 1969), 146–153.

12. Cf. two articles on Nathan the Babylonian, *Univ. Jewish Ency.* 8 (1942): 106; Abraham David, *Ency. Judaica* 12 (1971): 858–859. Cf. also A.E. Harkavy, "Netira und Seine Soehne: Eine Angesehene Juedische Familie in Bagdad am Anfang des X. Jahrhunderts," in A. Freimann and M. Hildesheimer, ed., *Festschrift zum Siebzigsten Geburtstage A. Berliners* (Frankfurt a. M.: Kauffmann, 1903), 34–43; Sigmund Fraenkel, "Juedisch-Arabisches," *Jewish Quarterly Review* 17 (1904–1905): 386–388; I. Friedlaender, "The Arabic Original of the Report of R. Nathan Hababli," ibid. 17 (1904–1905): 747–761; Abraham Epstein, "M'korot L'Tol'dot Ha-G'onim Viyshivot Bavel" [Sources for the History of the G'onim and the Babylonian Academies], in D. von Guenzburg and I. Markon, eds., *Festschrift zu Ehren des Dr. A. Harkavy* (St. Petersburg: Itzkovsky, 1908), Hebrew section, 169–172; Louis Ginzberg, *Geonica, I: The Geonim and Their Halakic Writings* (New York: Hermon, 1968), 22–37, 55–66; H. Malter, *Saadia Gaon: his Life and Works* (Philadelphia: Jewish Publication Society of America, 1921), 89–134; Marx, in Freimann, Schorr, and Simonsen, *Livre d'Hommage . . . Samuel Poznanski*, 76–81; M. Auerbach, "Die Streit Zwischen Saadia Gaon und den Exilarchen David ben Sakkai," in *Juedische Studien Josef Wohlgemuth zu Seinem Sechzigsten Geburtstage von Freunden und Schuelern Gewidmet* (Frankfurt a. M.: Kauffmann, 1928), 1–30; Jacob Mann, "Inyanim Shonim L'Heker T'kufat Ha-G'onim" [Various Topics in the Study of the Period of the G'onim], *Tarbitz* 5 (1933–1934): 148–179; Salo W. Baron, "Saadia's Communal Activities,"in B. Cohen, ed., *Saadia Anniversary Volume* (New York and Philadelphia: American Academy for Jewish Research and Jewish Publication Society of America, 1943), 9–74; Alexander Marx, "Rab Saadia Gaon," in Louis Finkelstein, ed., *Rab Saadia Gaon: Studies in His Honor* (New York: Jewish Theological Seminary of America, 1944), 53–95; A. N. Tzvi Roth, "K'tav Yad L'Mavo Ha-Talmud" [A Manuscript of Samuel Ha-Nagid's Introduction to the Talmud], *Kirjath Sepher* 30 (1954–1955): 254–266; Ellis Rivkin, "The Saadia-David ben Zakkai Controversy: A Structural Analysis," in Meir Ben-Horin et al., eds., *Studies and Essays in Honor of Abraham A. Neuman* (Leiden: Brill, 1962), 388–423; Waxman, *History of Jewish Literature*, I: 422–423; Baron, *Jewish Community*, I: 175, 182, 202; III: 38–39, 42–43, 50; and his *Social and Religious History*, V: 6–7, 50–51, 293–294, 314; VI: 36, 213–214, 336, 430–431; VII: 284; Cohen, *Book of Tradition*, 54ff; 130ff; Zuckerman, *Jewish Princedom*, 2, 91, 163.

For the Arabic original and medieval Hebrew translation fragments of Nathan's chronicle, Adoph Neubauer, *Anecdota Oxoniensia: Medieval Jewish Chronicles and Chronological Notes* (Oxford: Clarendon, 1895), II: 77–88; Kahana, *Sifrut Ha-*

Historiyya Ha-Yisr'elit, I: 57–72; Halper, *Post-Biblical Hebrew Literature: Texts*, 37–40, 218–220; Dinur, *Yisrael Ba-Golah*, I:1: 293; I:2: 91–101, 185, 204, 384–387.

For English translations of three different portions of Nathan's chronicle, Friedlaender, *Jewish Quarterly Review*, XVII: 755–761; Jacob Rader Marcus, *The Jew in the Medieval World: A Source Book 315–1791* (Cleveland, New York, and Philadelphia: World/Meridian and Jewish Publication Society of America, 1961), 287–292; Leviant, *Masterpieces of Hebrew Literature*, 154–157.

13. Cf. three articles on Hasdai the son of Shaprut, M. Kayserling, *Jewish Ency.* 6 (1904): 248–250; *Univ. Jewish Ency.* 5 (1941): 236; E. Ashtor, *Ency. Judaica* 8 (1971): 533–534. Cf. also Umberto Cassuto, "Una Lettera Ebraica del Secolo X," *Giornale della Societa Asiatica Italiana* 29 (1918–1920): 97–110; Margolis and Marx, *History of the Jewish People*, 308–314; S. Dubnow, "Maskanot Aharonot Bi-Sh'elat Ha-Kuzarim" [Latest Conclusions about the Khazar Question], in Freimann, Schorr, Simonsen, *Livre d'Hommage Samuel Poznanski*, Hebrew section, 1–4; Jacob Mann, "Gaonic Studies," in Philipson, *Hebrew Union College Jubilee Volume*, 252–257; and his *Texts and Studies*, I: 3–30; S. Krauss, "Zu Dr. Mann's Neuen Historischen Texten," *Hebrew Union College Annual* 10 (1935): 265–296, 307–308; Mann's "Rejoinder," ibid., 297–307; Maximilian Landau, "Der Brief Hasdai ibn Sapruts an den Chazarenkoenig Joseph," in H. Levy, ed., *Festschrift Dr. Jakob Freimann* (Berlin: Rabbiner-Seminar fuer das Orthodoxe Judentum, 1937), 125–143; his *Beitraege zum Chazarenproblem* (Breslau: Muenz, 1938); and his "Ma'amadah Ha-Noh'hi Shel Ba'ayat Ha-Kuzarim" [The Present State of the Khazar Problem], *Zion* 8 (1942–1943): 94–106; Abraham N. Poliak, "Hitgayy'rut Ha-Kuzarim" [The Conversion of the Khazars to Judaism], ibid. 6 (1940–1941): 106–112, 160–180; and his *Kazariyyah: Tol'dot Mamlahah Y'hudit B'Eropah* [Khazariah: History of a Jewish Kingdom in Europe] (3rd ed.; Tel Aviv: Bialik/Masadah, 1951), 17–21; S.M. Stern, "Sh'te Y'di'ot Hadashot Al Hasdai Ibn Shaprut" [Two New Data about Hasdai ibn Shaprut], *Zion* 11 (1945–1946): 141–146; J. H. Schirmann, *Ha-Shirah Ha-Ivrit Bi'S'farad U'Vi-Provence* [Hebrew Poetry in Spain and Southern France] (Jerusalem and Tel Aviv: Bialik/D'vir, 1954), I: 3–48; Waxman, *History of Jewish Literature*, I: 434–436; Baron, *Jewish Community*, I: 189; and his *Social and Religious History*, III: 155ff, 183, 198, 201, 204ff, 210, 217, 305–306, 324–325; IV 29; V: 44, 47, 161, 378; VI: 27, 195, 219ff; VII: 20, 22, 146, 273, 433; VIII: 65, 245ff; Cohen, *Book of Tradition*, 57, 67, 70, 93, 102, 136, 164, 200, 269, 271ff, 276, 279, 281, 287, 289; Zuckerman, *Jewish Princedom*, 60, 256–257, 351; and his article, *Proceedings of the American Academy for Jewish Research*, XXXIII: 51–82; Baer, *Jews in Christian Spain*, I: 28–30, 46, 382–383; Ashtor, *Jews of Moslem Spain*, I: 155–263, 319, 344, 361, 363–364, 419–434; Starr, *Jews in the Byzantine Empire*, 7–8, 58, 153–156; Sharf, *Byzantine Jewry*, 99–101, 143, 166, 168; D.M. Dunlop, *History of the Jewish Khazars* (Princeton: Princeton University Press, 1954), 116–170; and his "Khazars," *Ency. Judaica* 10 (1971): 950–951; plus the following articles in Roth, *Dark Ages*: Roth, "Economic Life and Population Movements," 46; Sharf, "Jews in Byzantium," 63; Roth, "Italy," 108; Zimmels, "Aspects of Jewish Culture: Historiography," 280; Ashtor, "Early Jewish Settlement in Central and Eastern Europe," 306–307; A. Scheiber, "Hungary," 315; Dunlop, "Khazars," 331–333, 336, 340; Cantera Burgos, "Christian Spain," 362–364.

Baer, following Poliak, considers the entire Hasdai/Joseph correspondence an eleventh-century product. Ashtor, following Jost and Steinschneider, considers the Hasdai letter genuine tenth century, but the Joseph reply an eleventh-century product. Dunlop considers the entire Hasdai/Joseph correspondence genuine tenth century.

For the Hebrew original of the Hasdai/Joseph correspondence, A. Zifrinowitsch, ed., *Judah Ha-levi: Das Buch Kusari* (Warsaw: "Tuschijah," 1911), supplement, 25ff, 33ff; Kahana, *Sifrut Ha-Historiyya Ha-Yisr'elit*, I: 30–56; P.P. Kokovtzov, *Evreisko-Khazarskaia Perepiska v X Veke* [Jewish-Khazar Correspondence in the Tenth Century] (Leningrad: Izdatelstvo Akademii Nauk SSR, 1932).

For English translations of the Hasdai/Joseph correspondence, S. Davidson, "The Epistle of R. Chisdai . . . The Answer of Joseph, etc.," in S. Davidson and A. Loewy, eds., *Miscellany of Hebrew Literature* (London: Truebner, 1872), I: 92–112; Adler, *Jewish Travelers*, 22–36, 369–370; Schwartz, *Jewish Caravan*, 197ff; Marcus, *Jew in the Medieval World*, 227–232; Franz Kobler, *Treasury of Jewish Letters* (Philadelphia: Jewish Publication Society of America, 1954), I: 97–115; Leviant, *Masterpieces of Hebrew Literature*, 158–169.

14. Cf. three articles on Ahima'atz, Richard Gottheil, *Jewish Ency.* 1 (1901): 290–291; *Univ. Jewish Ency.* 1 (1939): 139–140; J.H. Schirmann, *Ency. Judaica* 2 (1971): 463. Cf. also A. Neubauer, 'Abou Ahron le Babylonien," *Revue des Etudes Juives* 23 (1891): 230–232; and his "The Early Settlement of the Jews in Italy," *Jewish Quarterly Review* 4 (1892): 606ff; David Kaufmann, "Die Chronik des Achimaaz von Oria," *Monatsschrift fuer Geschichte und Wissenschaft des Judentums* 40 (1896): 462–473, 496–509, 529–554; and his "Beitraege zur Geschichte Aegyptens aus Juedischen Quellen," *Zeitschrift der Deutschen Morgenlaendischen Gesellschaft* 51 (1897): 436–442; M.J. de Goeje, "Paltiel-Djauhar," ibid. 52 (1898): 75–80; A. Marx, "Studies in Gaonic History and Literature: Paltiel-Jauhar," *Jewish Quarterly Review* 1 (1910–1911): 78–85; N. Ferorelli, *Gli Ebrei nell'Italia Meridionale dall' Eta Romana al Secolo XVIII* (Turin: Il Vessillo Israelitico, 1915), 23–35; Jacob Mann, *The Jews in Egypt and in Palestine under the Fatimid Caliphs* (Oxford: Clarendon, 1920), I: 13–19, 49, 64, 72; J.H. Schirmann, "Zur Geschichte der Hebraeischen Poesie in Apulien und Sizilien," *Mitteilungen des Forschungsinstituts fuer Hebraeische Dichtung* 1 (1933): 96–120; Joseph Marcus, "Studies in the Chronicle of Ahima'atz," *Proceedings of the American Academy for Jewish Research* 5 (1933–1934): 85–93; Fischel, *Jews in the Economic and Political Life of Medieval Islam*, 64–68; D. Neustadt, "Inyane N'gidut B'Mitzrayyim Bime Ha-Benayyim" [Some Problems Concerning the *N'gidut* in Egypt during the Middle Ages], *Zion* 4 (1938–1939): 135–143; Benjamin Klar, "S'lihah L'Ta'anit Ester L'Rabbi Ahima'atz B'Rabbi Paltiel" [A Penitential Hymn for the Fast of Esther by Rabbi Ahima'atz the Son of Rabbi Paltiel], *Sinai* 22 (1947–1948): 243–248; Waxman, *History of Jewish Literature*, I: 425–427; Baron, *Jewish Community*, I: 190; II: 75–76; III: 43, 121, 134; and his *Social and Religious History*, III: 154–155, 180; IV: 23, 157, 243; V: 40–41, 309–310; VIII: 44; Zuckerman, *Jewish Princedom*, 201–202; the following articles in Roth, *Dark Ages*: "Introduction," 10; Roth, "Economic Life and Population Movements," 31; Sharf, "Jews in Byzantium," 61; Roth, "Italy," 102–110, 115, 407; Zimmels, "Scholars and Scholarship in Byzantium and Italy," 179–180; Schirmann, "The Beginning of Hebrew Poetry in Italy," 250ff, 258; Zimmels, "Historiography," 275–276; Dan, "The Beginnings of Jewish Mysticism in Europe," 283, 289: Star, *Jews in the Byzantine Empire*, 4–5, 30, 37, 39, 52, 56–59,

70-72, 114-119, 123-126, 128-131, 133, 139-143, 159-160, 199; Sharf, *Byzantine Jewry*, 87-89, 91-94, 123, 134, 164-172, 175, 205; Hirschberg, *Tol'dot Ha-Y'hudim B'Afrikah Ha-Tz'fonit*, I: 152-154; Bernard Lewis, "Paltiel: A Note," *Bulletin of the School of Oriental and African Studies* 30 (1967): 177-181; Abraham David, "Paltiel," *Ency. Judaica* 13 (1971): 49-50; Attilio Milano, *Storia degli Ebrei in Italia* (Turin: Einaudi, 1963), 28, 60-64, 84, 109.

For the Hebrew original of the chronicle of Ahima'atz, Neubauer, *Anecdota Oxoniensia: Medieval Jewish Chronicles*, II: 111-132; Kahana, *Sifrut Ha-Historiyya Hayisr'elit*, I: 113-140; Marcus Salzman, *The Chronicle of Ahimaaz* (New York: AMS Press, 1966), Hebrew section, 1-24; Benjamin Klar, *M'gillat Ahima'atz* [The Scroll of Ahima'atz] (Jerusalem: Sifre Tarshish and Mosad Ha-Rav Kuk, 1944), 11-52, 123-127, 159-174.

For English translations of the chronicle of Ahima'atz, Salzman, *Chronicle of Ahimaaz*, English section, 60-102; Marcus, *Jew in the Medieval World*, 241-243, 293-296; Leo W. Schwarz, ed., *Memoirs of My People through a Thousand Years* (Philadelphia: Jewish Publication Society of America, 1955), 3-14; Leviant, *Masterpieces of Hebrew Literature*, 241-263.

15. Schechter, *Jewish Quarterly Review*, XIV: 242-245; Tykocinski, *D'vir*, I: 146-147; Dinur, *Yisrael Ba-Golah*, I:2: 88, para. 2.

16. Margoliouth, *Jewish Quarterly Review*, XIV: 304-307; Tykocinski, *D'vir*, I: 152-154; Dinur, *Yisrael Ba-Golah*, I:2: 89-90.

17. Tykocinski assigns the present form of the similar versions 5 and 7 to thirteenth-century Iraq (*D'vir*, I: 154-156, 161-162) and their common source to ninth-century Iraq (ibid., 162-163). Margoliouth, *Jewish Quarterly Review*, XIV: 303; and Worman, ibid., XX: 211, assign the British Museum and Cambridge texts of version 5 to the twelfth century. In the late twelfth century Benjamin of Tudela reports that he was shown the alleged Tomb of Bustanai near Pumpedita, Iraq. Ginzberg, *Jewish Ency.*, III: 331. Tykocinski, *D'vir*, I: 148, 151, assigns the present forms of versions 1 to 3 respectively to the late tenth century, circa 1000, and the tenth century in general, and their sources to circa 650-750 Iraq.

18. Each of the two great heads of the talmudical seminary at Pumpedita, *i.e.*, Sherira (circa 968-998) and Hai (circa 998-1038), stressed that they were not descendants of Bustanai's Persian wife. Ginzberg, *Jewish Ency.*, III: 330; Tykocinski, *D'vir*, I: 155 and note 3; Baron, *Social and Religious History*, V: 9, 294-295, note 5.

19. In Judaeo-Arabic the insect here is called *ba'ūdatun*, gnat or mosquito" = Hebrew *z'vūv*, "fly." Margoliouth, *Jewish Quarterly Review*, XIV: 305 and note 4, translates "insect" in the text and "apparently a wasp" in the note. Ginzberg, *Jewish Ency.*, III: 331, translates "wasp." The wasp appears only in the closely related versions 5 and 7: version 5, Tykocinski, *D'vir*, I: 153, lines 4-6 (Judaeo-Arabic), and 154, lines 8-10 (Hebrew); version 7, ibid., 160, lines 9-13, 19-20 (Hebrew only).

20. Tykocinski, *D'vir*, I: 158; Cohen, *Book of Tradition*, Hebrew text, 34-35; English translation, 44-45, plus supplementary notes to chapter 5, lines 35-37, found on p. 126. Ibn Daud's version mentions both caliphs Umar and Ali. Umar is the only caliph mentioned in four other versions (nos. 1-3 and 5); Ali is the only caliph mentioned in two versions (nos. 7-8); one version (no. 4, thirteenth-century Italy) mentions no caliph by name. Infra, note 31.

For Ibn Daud's relationship with Christian scholars, Cohen, *Book of Tradition*, xxvi–xxvii; d'Alverny, "Avendauth?" in *Homenaje a Millas-Vallicrosa* (Barcelona: Consejo Superior de Investigaciones Cientificas, 1954), I: 19–43; Ilona Opelt, "Zur Uebersetzungstechnik des Gerhard von Cremona," *Glotta* 38 (1959): 135–170; supra, note 36 to chapter 3; Millas-Vallicrosa, *Journal of World History*, II, 417–421; Lemay, *Abu Ma'shar and Latin Aristotelianism*, 9ff; Kritzeck, *Peter the Venerable and Islam*, 51–55.

21. Margoliouth, *Jewish Quarterly Review*, XIV: 305, line 4 (Arabic of version 5); 306, lines 15–16 (English); Tykocinski, *D'vir*, 153, lines 11–12 (Arabic of version 5); 154, line 16 (Hebrew); cf. discussion, *ibid.*, 154–155, 155, note 1; Cohen, *Book of Tradition*, Hebrew, 44–45; English, 60–62, plus supplementary notes, 132–133; supra, note 21, para. 3, and notes 43–44 to chapter 3.

22. Zuckerman, *Jewish Princedom*, 77–83, 118ff. Natronai was his Aramaic name; Machir his Hebrew name; Theodoric his Frankish name.

23. Katz, *Jews in the Visigothic and Frankish Kingdoms of Spain and Gaul*, 63, 133, 163; Baron, *Social and Religious History*, IV: 45, 174, 257–258, 322–323; Blumenkranz, *Juifs et Chretiens*, 14, 41, 182ff; plus the following articles in Roth, *Dark Ages*: Roth, "Economic Life and Population Movements," 41; Schwarzfuchs, "France and Germany under the Carolingians," 127; R. Kestenberg-Gladstein, "Bohemia," 310–311; Zuckerman, *Jewish Princedom*, 138, 172, 186–190. According to Zuckerman this Isaac = Count William of Toulouse = son of Natronai/Machir/Theodoric (supra, note 22). Therefore, this Isaac was the second ruler of the semi-independent Jewish state in southern France. When he went to Bagdad, he visited the city that was the birthplace of his father (the first ruler of the semi-independent Jewish state in southern France).

24. Zuckerman, in Sommerfeldt, *Studies in Medieval Culture*, III: 34 and note 36; and Zuckerman's *Jewish Princedom*, 211 and note 91; Katz, *Jews in the Visigothic and Frankish Kingdoms*, 61 and notes 4–6, 65 and note 10; Blumenkranz, *Juifs et Chretiens*, 50 and note 300, 309 and note 60; and his *Auteurs*, 161 and notes 40–42.

25. Katz, *Jews in the Visigothic and Frankish Kingdoms*, 66–68; Baron, *Social and Religious History*, VIII: 26; Blumenkranz, *Juifs et Chretiens*, 50–51, 51, notes 301–304; his *Auteurs*, 164–165 and notes 62–65; J. Dan, "The Beginnings of Jewish Mysticism in Europe," in Roth, *Dark Ages*, 289; Zuckerman, in Sommerfeldt, *Studies in Medieval Culture*, III: 35 and note 44. According to Katz, 68 and note 5, Hai Gaon, head of the talmudical seminary at Pumpedita (near Bagdad) in the early eleventh century, reported that the Jews of France already possessed (Iraqi?) Jewish mystical treatises in the early ninth century. The same may have been true for Italian Jewry. Dan, in Roth, *Dark Ages*, 283–284. For the important Jewish mystical tradition of Arab Iraq circa 650–1050, Baron, *Social and Religious History*, VIII: 3–54; Gershom G. Scholem, *Major Trends in Jewish Mysticism* (3rd ed.; New York: Schocken, 1965), 40–79.

26. Katz, *Jews in the Visigothic and Frankish Kingdoms*, 76–78; Baron, *Social and Religious History*, III: 205, 329, note 41; V: 130–131, 349, note 61; Blumenkranz, *Juifs et Chretiens*, 230–231, 236–237; his *Auteurs*, 192–193, 211; and his "Roman Church and the Jews," in Roth, *Dark Ages*, 96; Zuckerman, *Jewish Princedom*, 94–95.

Agobard had Jews and converts from Judaism as informants. Blumenkranz, *Juifs et Chretiens*, 48 and note 284, 49 and note 291. He was also quite interested in the Judaeo-Islamic alliance. Thus, he pointed out that the Saracens [Arabs] and Africans

[Berbers] were as much physical descendants of Abraham as the Jews. Blumenkranz, *Auteurs*, 166 and note 70. He charged the Jewish slave-merchants of France with kidnapping French Christian children for sale to the Muslims of Spain. Roth, "Economic Life and Population Movements," in Roth, *Dark Ages*, 27–28, 33–34; Blumenkranz, *Juifs et Chretiens*, 194 and note 141; and his *Auteurs*, 163 and note 53. If Agobard was interested in the Judaeo-Islamic alliance, he may well have also been interested in the Bustanai story, a good example of that alliance. He could have learnt the Bustanai story from his informants who were Jews or converts from Judaism, though he might not have felt it necessary to mention this story explicitly in his extant writings.

Likewise, Florus of Lyons (died circa 860), Agobard's colleague, had some knowledge of Hebrew, perhaps acquired from the Jews of Lyons. Katz, 69 and note 3. Rabanus Maurus (died circa 856) had a Jewish informant. Katz, 69–70; Baron, *Social and Religious History*, IV: 44, 256, note 56; Blumenkranz, *Juifs et Chretiens*, 48 and notes 285–287; and his *Auteurs*, 174–175. Paschasius Radbertus (died circa 865) claims to have had a Jewish informant. Blumenkranz, *Juifs et Chretiens*, 49 and notes 292–293; and his *Auteurs*, 193 and notes 9–12. Amolo of Lyons (died circa 852), Agobard's successor as bishop of Lyons, had converts from Judaism as informants. Katz, 68; Blumenkranz, *Juifs et Chretiens*, 143 and note 283; and his *Auteurs*, 199; Zuckerman, *Jewish Princedom*, 304. In the ninth century Remigius of Auxerre, Theodulf of Orleans, and Pseudo-Jerome all seem to have had "the assistance of learned Jews." Baron, *Social and Religious History*, IV: 257, note 56; Blumenkranz, *Juifs et Chretiens*, 48 and note 286, 49 and note 295; and his *Auteurs*, 174 and note 1, 215ff. From their informants, whether Jews or converts from Judaism, Florus of Lyons, Rabanus Maurus, Paschasius Radbertus, Amolo of Lyons, Remigius of Auxerre, Theodulf of Orleans, and Pseudo-Jerome, especially Paschasius and Amolo, could all have learnt the Bustanai story. This story was a good example of the Judaeo-Islamic alliance. Paschasius Radbertus was interested in Islam. Southern, *Western Views of Islam in the Middle Ages*, 27 and note 24. Amolo was quite concerned about the Judaeo-Islamic alliance. Zuckerman, *Jewish Princedom*, 276–277 and notes 46–47; Blumenkranz, *Auteurs*, 199 and notes 25–27; supra, note 21 to chapter 4.

Finally, Emperor Charles the Bald's Jewish physician, Zedekiah, could well have informed the emperor (plus other nobles and clerics at court) of the Bustanai story. On Zedekiah, Blumenkranz, *Auteurs*, 209 and note 5, 217 and note 3; Roth, "Economic Life and Population Movements," in Roth, *Dark Ages*, 392; Zuckerman, *Jewish Princedom*, 314 and note 67. Charles the Bald may well have been especially interested in Bustanai because Charles' grandfather Charlemagne was considered by Christian tradition a new King David (Zuckerman, 120 and note 15) and Bustanai, as exilarch, was considered by Jewish tradition a descendant of King David.

27. Zuckerman, *Jewish Princedom*, 211. For intellectual relations between the Jews of Barcelona and those of Arab Iraq after circa 850, Baer, *Jews in Christian Spain*, I: 24, 382, note 5; Cantera Burgos, "Christian Spain," in Roth, *Dark Ages*, 359, 450, note 6; Zuckerman, *Jewish Princedom*, 211, 317–322.

28. According to Zuckerman, *Jewish Princedom*, 316ff, 339, 341ff, Barcelona was an independent Jewish and Abbasid-Arab city circa 852–877, after which period it was incorporated into Carolingian France through the efforts of the Jewish Prince, Bernard of Auvergne.

29. Roth, "Economic Life and Population Movements," in Roth, *Dark Ages*, 24. One Radanite route went from Aix-la-Chapelle to China via southern France, the Mediterranean, Suez, the Red Sea, and India. Another went from Aix-la-Chapelle to Bagdad via southern France, the Mediterranean, and Antioch. Another from Aix-la-Chapelle to Bagdad via southern France, Spain, North Africa, Egypt, Palestine, and Syria.

30. Morris Epstein, *Mishle Sendebar* (Philadelphia: Jewish Publication Society of America, 1967), 5–7, 31–37, 383–386, notes 1–38. Epstein, 37, 386, note 35, cites Rabinowitz, *Jewish Merchant Adventurers: A Study of the Radanites*, 197, to the effect that "the Jews of the Early Middle Ages were carriers not only of goods but also of the learning of the Arab world to the Christian." The most radical position would be to suggest that, in addition to goods, the Radanites transmitted books of a highly technical nature (theology, philosophy, science, medicine). Epstein's position is more moderate than that, *i.e.*, that the Radanites transmitted books of a popular nature (*e.g.*, the Hebrew original of the later Latin *Seven Sages of Rome*). Our position is even more moderate than that, *i.e.*, that the Radanites may have transmitted oral materials (not books) of a popular nature (*e.g.*, the Bustanai story).

31. Supra, note 20; Schechter, *Jewish Quarterly Review*, XIV: 243 and note 2; Tykocinski, *D'vir*, I: 151–152; two articles on Isaiah ben Mali di Trani the Elder, M. Schloessinger, *Jewish Ency.* 6 (1904): 644–645, and I.M. Ta-Shma, *Ency. Judaica* 9 (1971): 73–74. Isaiah di Trani's failure to mention the Muslims and the caliph in his version of the Bustanai story may reflect an attempt by south Italian Jewry in the early thirteenth century to dissociate itself as much as possible from the Muslims at a time of profound Christian anti-Islamic feeling in Sicily/southern Italy. This anti-Islamic feeling resulted from the great Arab revolt against Emperor Frederick II in Sicily circa 1212–1223, upon the defeat of which Frederick forcibly relocated thousands of Sicilian Arabs to Lucera, northern Apulia, not too far from Rabbi Isaiah's home in Trani. Steven Runciman, *Sicilian Vespers: A History of the Mediterranean World in the Later Thirteenth Century* (Baltimore: Penguin, 1960), 28. Emperor Frederick II tended to equate Jew with Muslim. Baron, *Social and Religion History* IX: 142–143. Christian anti-Islamic feeling in southern Italy at this time was also the result of the Islamic reconquest of Jerusalem (1187), the failure of the Third and Fifth Crusades to retake Jerusalem (1192 and 1221), and the Islamic reconquest of Jerusalem (1244) after Emperor Frederick II had retaken it by diplomacy (1229).

32. Salzman, *Chronicle of Ahimaaz*, Hebrew, 3; English, 62–63; Klar, *M'gillat Ahima'atz*, 13.

Thirteenth-century German Jewish tradition (*e.g.*, Rabbi Elazar of Worms) held that Aaron's father was named Samuel and that this Samuel was a *Nasi* [= Prince]. Klar, *M'gillat Ahima'atz*, 57, line 7; Louis Ginzberg, "Aaron Ben Samuel Ha-Nasi," *Jewish Ency.* 1 (1901): 20; Baron, *Social and Religious History*, V: 56–57, 316–317; Schirmann, "The Beginning of Hebrew Poetry in Italy and Northern Europe," in Roth, *Dark Ages*, 264; Dan, "The Beginnings of Jewish Mysticism in Europe," ibid., 283. The Hebrew term *Nasi* [= Prince] was used by the exilarchs themselves during the Arab period as a synonym for the more technical Aramaic term for exilarch, *Resh Galuta* = Hebrew *Rosh Galut* = Arabic *Ras al-Jalut* = English "the head of the exile." E. Bashan, "Exilarch," *Ency. Judaica* 6 (1971): 1032. The chronicle of Ahima'atz does not mention Aaron's father, Samuel the *Nasi*, but it does call Aaron himself a *"head and father."* The word "head" here may be an abbreviation for "head of the exile," or exilarch, and may be hinting at the fact that Aaron's father and/or Aaron himself was an exilarch or a pretender to the exilarchate.

Neubauer, *Revue des Etudes Juives*, XXIII: 230ff—followed by Salzman, *Chronicle of Ahimaaz*, 63, note 3; Starr, *Jews in the Byzantine Empire*, 117, note to no. 50; and apparently also Roth, "Italy," in Roth, *Dark Ages*, 102, 402, note 7—had suggested that Aaron's father Samuel was the Exilarch Samuel who reigned circa 773–816. However, Aaron himself flourished circa 850–870. Hence, from a chronological perspective it is more likely that Aaron and his father should be linked with the chaotic period in the history of the Exilarchate circa 820–850. This period began when Exilarch Isaac Iskoi ben Moses died circa 820 and was succeeded by two rival exilarchs, David ben Judah and Daniel, who were allowed to set up rival administrations by Caliph al-Ma'mun in 825. It ended when Caliph al-Mutawakkil recognized David ben Judah as legitimate exilarch and suppressed the rival administration of Daniel. Bashan, *Ency. Judaica*, VI: 1028. Perhaps Aaron's father's name was not Samuel (as thirteenth-century German Jewish tradition held) but Daniel, the same Daniel who was rival exilarch circa 820–850; or Aaron's father was named Samuel but this Samuel was a brother or son of exilarch Daniel. When Mutawakkil suppressed Daniel's exilarchate circa 850 and in general persecuted the Jews (infra, note 81), Aaron may have considered it wise to go into Italian exile. When Mutawakkil was assassinated in 861, Aaron could consider returning home from Italy.

The Bustanai story may have been involved in the struggle between rival exilarchs David ben Judah and Daniel circa 820–850, for it was involved in the struggle between rival candidates for the exilarchate, Natronai/Machir and Judah/Baboi Zakkai b. Ahunai in the 760s. Natronai/Machir was a descendant of Bustanai through his Jewish wife; Judah/Baboi Zakkai b. Ahunai, a descendant of Bustanai through his Persian wife. Zuckerman, *Jewish Princedom*, 79 and note 13. In the 760s Bustanai's descendants by his Jewish wife lost out, and Natronai Machir had to go into exile to the West (southern France). Perhaps the same thing happened again circa 850. Possibly the Exilarch Daniel lost the struggle partly because he was of the purely Jewish line of descent from Bustanai. If Aaron was related to Exilarch Daniel, Aaron may also have been a descendant of Bustanai via his Jewish wife. If so, Aaron could certainly have brought the Bustanai story to southern Italy circa 850.

Because Jewish religious courts rarely had power to impose the death penalty during the Middle Ages, scholars are surprised by the statement in the chronicle of Ahima'atz that Aaron of Bagdad imposed the death penalty. Salzman, *Chronicle of Ahimaaz*, Hebrew, 5; English 66–67; Klar, *M'gillat Ahima'atz*, 17–18; Starr, *Jews in the Byzantine Empire*, 117–118; Baron, *Social and Religious History*, V: 56–57, 316–317; Sharf, *Byzantine Jewry*, 164–166. We suggest that, by stressing Aaron's imposition of the death penalty, our chronicler may well have been saying that Aaron's authority was even greater than that of the exilarch. The exilarch could only impose such punishments as excommunication, fines, imprisonment, and flogging. Bashan, *Ency. Judaica*, VI: 1031.

33. Roth, "Economic Life and Population Movements," in Roth, *Dark Ages*, 44, 389, note 51; Irving A. Agus, "Rabbinic Scholarship in Northern Europe," ibid., 191,

419, note 17; and Dan, "The Beginnings of Jewish Mysticism in Europe," ibid., 283, notes 6–8. Dan, 282–283, cites two additional German Jewish traditions about the transmission of Jewish mystical ideas to Germany during the Carolingian-Ottonian periods (circa 800–1000): (1) tracing the medieval German Jewish mystical movement back through Italy to Palestine and giving the agent of transmission the name Joseph Ma'on; (2) tracing the medieval Geman Jewish mystical movement back only to Italy and giving the agent of transmission the name Rabbi Todros of Rome. Cf. in general also Dan, 283–284.

34. Blumenkranz, *Juifs et Chretiens*, 279ff, especially 279; and his "Roman Church and the Jews," in Roth, *Dark Ages*, 96, 401, note 55. Cf. also Samuel Krauss, "Nathan Ben Joseph 'Official'," *Jewish Ency.* 9 (1905): 183; Isaac Broyde, "Joseph Ben Nathan Official," ibid. 8 (1904): 269–270; Judah M. Rosenthal, "Official, Nathan Ben Joseph and Joseph," *Ency. Judaica* 12 (1971): 1338–1339; Chazan, *Medieval Jewry in Northern France*, 145; Blumenkranz, "Les Origines et le Moyen Age," in Blumenkranz, ed., *Histoire des Juifs en France* (Toulouse: Privat, 1972), 35, 68, note 53.

35. Supra, note 37 to chapter 4.

36. The Arabs, attacking Byantium from the east, fell heir to the role played by the Sassanian Persians circa 225–625. Hitti, *History of the Arabs*, 142. For the equation of Arab with Sassanian Persian by Western Christians at the time of the First Crusade and into the twelfth century, Dana C. Munro, "The Western Attitude toward Islam during the Period of the Crusades," *Speculum* 6 (1931): 330; Runciman, *History of the Crusades*, I: 11. "Emperor Heraclius Recovers the Holy Cross from the Persians under King Chosroes," an altar frontal from the Nedstryn Stave Church, Nordfjord, Norway, circa 1300 (now in the Historical Museum, Bergen), also equates Arab with Sassanian Persian. Blindheim, *De Malte Antemensaler i Norge*, 20–21; and his *The Stave Church Paintings: Medieval Art from Norway*, 16–17 and plate VIII; *Guide to the Historical Museum Bergen* (Bergen: Historical Museum, 1971), 16–17; Signe Nordhagen, *Maleri Publikumskatalog* (typescript) (Bergen: Historical Museum, no date), 68–75, 91–92.

37. Dunlop, *History of the Jewish Khazars*, 140–142; and his "The Khazars," in Roth, *Dark Ages*, 348, 448, note 79.

38. In citing the Eldad material infra, we first cite version B (which Epstein considered the most authentic; cf. *Revue des Etudes Juives*, XXV: 31) in the original Hebrew of Epstein's edition (1891); then cite the same English translation of version B as found in both Adler and Leviant; then cite version B plus all other versions in Mueller's edition (1892). Thus, for the Zoroastrians in Eldad the Danite, Epstein, *Eldad Ha-Dani*, paras. 4–5, pp. 23–24; Adler, *Jewish Travelers*, 7; Leviant, *Masterpieces*, 149; Mueller, *Die Recensionen*, 72–75. All versions refer to Zoroastrian fireworship and incest.

39. Epstein, *Eldad Ha-Dani*, paras. 1–2, p. 23; Adler, *Jewish Travelers*, 6; Leviant, *Masterpieces*, 148; Mueller, *Die Recensionen*, 70–73. All versions refer to black cannibalism.

40. Epstein, *Eldad Ha-Dani*, para. 8, p. 25; Adler, *Jewish Travelers*, 8; Leviant, *Masterpieces*, 149; Mueller, *Die Recensionen*, 76–77. From Mueller it emerges that five of the six main versions refer to the mountains surrounding Mecca; two of the six refer to Mecca by name; one of the six (version B) refers to Mecca as the $ta^c\bar{u}t$ of the

Ishmaelites; four of the six refer to the Prophet Muhammad's alleged madness or insanity. Infra, note 42, for another attack by Eldad on Islamic "idolatry."

Mueller, 76, note 9 to Recension B, holds that the reference to Mecca as the $ta^c\bar{u}t$ of the Ishamelites is a later interpolation and was not part of Eldad's original narrative, because it is too harshly anti-Islamic and is found in only one version, B. We believe that Mueller is being hypercritical. Mueller does not question the authenticity of Eldad's reference to the Prophet Muhammad's alleged madness or insanity, and that is just as harshly anti-Islamic as the pejorative reference to Mecca. What is more, Epstein had considered version B the most authentic of the several versions.

With regard to the meaning of Eldad's attack on Mecca as the $ta^c\bar{u}t$ of the Ishmaelites, Schwarz, Jewish Caravan, 194, relying on Halper, Post-Biblical Hebrew Literature: Texts, 281, translates it as "idolatry." For additional information on this Semitic term and its reference to "idolatry," in Hebrew, Aramaic, Ethiopic, and Arabic, Marcus Jastrow, Dictionary of the Targumim, the Talmud Babli and Yerushalmi, and the Midrashic Literature (New York: Pardes, 1950), I: 542, left-hand column, second meaning; F. Brown, S.R. Driver, and C.A. Briggs, Hebrew and English Lexicon of the Old Testament (Oxford: Clarendon, 1957), 380, right-hand column, bottom; L. Koehler and W. Baumgartner, Lexicon in Veteris Testamenti Libros (Leiden, Holland, and Grand Rapids, Michigan: Brill and Eerdmans, 1958), 354, right-hand column, bottom; Hans Wehr, Dictionary of Modern Written Arabic ed. by J. Milton Cowan (Ithaca: Cornell University Press, 1961), 561, left-hand column. In the Quran, 4:51 and 60, the Arabic word $\overline{ta}g\bar{u}t$ (cognate of Hebrew $ta^c\bar{u}t$) is translated as "false deities" by M.M Pickthall, Meaning of the Glorious Koran (New York: New American Library/Mentor, 1960), 84–85; cf. also A. Yusuf Ali, The Holy Qur-an: Text, Translation and Commentary (Beirut: Dar al-Arabia, 1968), 196, note 573.

The Arabic root ḍ-l-l is also used in the Quran to refer to "idolatry." Quran 4:116, in Pickthall, 90; Yusuf Ali, 217. What is the Hebrew translation of ḍ-l-l here? T-^{c}-h = ṭ-^{c}-h. Joseph J. Rivlin, Alkoran [Hebrew translation of the Quran] (Tel Aviv: D'vir, 1962–1963), I: 94, bottom.

For the medieval Jewish charge of idolatry against Mecca and the Islamic pilgrimage thereto, Steinschneider, Polemische und Apologetische Literatur in Arabischer Sprache, Zwischen Muslimen, Christen und Juden (Leipzig: Brockhaus, 1877), 310–313 (wherein we learn that Eldad's attack on alleged Meccan idolatry was one of the earliest such attacks in Jewish literature); Septimus, Speculum, LVI: 517–533. For the medieval Christian version (East and West) of this same charge, Eichner, Der Islam, XXIII: 158–162, 233–241; Meyendorff, Dumbarton Oaks Papers, XVIII: 115–125; Daniel, Islam and the West, 217–220, 309–315; Kritzeck, Peter the Venerable and Islam, 105; Henri Gregoire, "Des Dieux Cahu, Baraton, Tervagant . . . et de Maints Autres Dieux non Moins Extravagants," Annuaire de l'Institut de Philologie et d'Histoire Orientales et Slaves 7 (1939–1944): 451–472. For the medieval Jewish and Christian charges that the Prophet Muhammad was "mad" or "insane," Steinschneider, 302–303; Perlmann, Samau'al Al-Maghribi, English section, 62, 99, note B66; Daniel, Islam and the West, 28–31, 69–81, 90, 104–105, 239, 246, 280, 287, 327–328, 339, 344.

41. Epstein, Eldad Ha-Dani, para. 9, p. 25; Adler, Jewish Travelers, 8–9; Leviant, Masterpieces, 149–150; Mueller, Die Recensionen, 76–77. All six versions agree that the Ishmaelites pay tribute to these one and one-half Jewish tribes. Four of the six versions

read "Khazaria" as the land wherein these one and one-half Jewish tribes dwell; two of the six versions read "Chaldea"=Iraq. All six versions agree that the full tribe residing in Khazaria was Simeon. Four of the six hold that the one-half tribe was Manasseh; two of the six versions hold that it was Judah.

42. Epstein, *Eldad Ha-Dani*, para. 10, p. 25; Adler, *Jewish Travelers*, 9; Leviant, *Masterpieces*, 150; Mueller, *Die Recensionen*, 78, note 2 to Recension B. This statement appears only in version B. However, its affinity with Qumran (infra, note 43) seems to militate against Mueller's view that it is a later interpolation.

43. A. Dupont-Sommer, *The Essene Writings from Qumran*, trans. G. Vermes (Cleveland and New York: World/Meridian, 1962), 273; G. Vermes, *The Dead Sea Scrolls in English* (Baltimore: Penguin, 1962), 243. Psalm 37:15 is not commented on in the Mishnah (which comments on some thirty-nine other Psalm passages), or in the Tosefta (which comments on some ninty-four other Psalm passages). Herbert Danby, *The Mishnah* (Oxford: Oxford University Press, 1954), 810; M.S. Zuckermandel, *Tosephta* (Jersualem: Wahrmann, 1963), xxx.

44. Epstein, *Eldad Ha-Dani*, paras. 16-18, pp. 27-28; Adler, *Jewish Travelers*, 12-13; Leviant, *Masterpieces*, 152; Mueller, *Die Recensionen*, 62-67. The particular about the absence of slaves is found in five of the six versions.

45. For the great revolt of the black slaves in southern Iraq circa 869-883, Th. Noeldeke, *Sketches from Eastern History*, trans. J.S. Black (London and Edinburgh: A&C. Black, 1892), 174; Brockelmann, *History of the Islamic Peoples*, 133-137; Hitti, *History of the Arabs*, 467-468; Reuben Levy, *Social Structure of Islam* (Cambridge: Cambridge University Press, 1965), 420, 422, 438, 441-442; Bernard Lewis, *Race and Color in Islam* (New York: Harper and Row/Torchbooks, 1971), 65-66.

According to Lewis, 66, even such "left-wing" (and/or anarchistic) Islamic sects as the Carmathians "accepted slavery of the Black man as natural." Thus, the eleventh-century Carmathian republic in Bahrain, while launching a fierce attack on traditional concepts of property, "had a force of 30,000 Black slaves to do the rough work." This is probably what Eldad the Danite was protesting against. If the Islamic "utopia" was built upon black slavery, the Jewish "utopia" would not be.

Could Eldad have known about the black slave revolt in Iraq circa 869-883? According to Ashtor, *Jews of Moslem Spain*, I: 142, 145-146, Eldad was born in Iraq, left for southern Arabia to engage in international commerce, but returned to Iraq circa 880, before going on to Tunisia and Spain. If Eldad returned to Iraq circa 880, he would have been in the country during the final turbulent years of the black slave revolt, and it is difficult to imagine that he was unaware of it since it was a major cataclysm in the history of the country. If Eldad was engaged in international commerce in southern Arabia circa 850-880, he almost certainly was aware of the trade in black slaves, for, as Ashtor points out (142), "these ports [of southern Arabia and the Red Sea] served as important way stations for the slave trade," wherein blacks were captured in Ethiopia, transported to Iraq, and sold to plantation owners.

Jellinek, *Bet Ha-Midrasch*, III: xiv, followed by Steinschneider, *Polemische und Apologetische Literatur*, 312, point out a fifth anti-Islamic statement in Eldad the Danite, *i.e.*, that Moses was the "true prophet" and, by implication, that Muhammad was a "false prophet." This statement appears only in version B. Epstein, *Eldad Ha-Dani*, introductory para., p. 22; Adler, *Jewish Travelers*, 5; Leviant, *Masterpieces*, 148;

Mueller, *Die Recensionen*, 52, footnote 1 to Recension B.

46. Our general account of Eldad's description of the threefold location of the Lost Ten Tribes (Persia/Caucasus; Arabia; Ethiopia) follows version B. For Eldad's description of the fierceness of the Jewish tribes living in Arabia, Epstein, *Eldad Ha-Dani*, para. 8, p. 25; Adler, *Jewish Travelers*, 8; Leviant, *Masterpieces*, 149; Mueller, *Die Recensionen*, 76–77. Five of the six versions read *z'ᶜume nefesh* and *k'huye lev*. All six versions agree that the Arabian Jewish tribesmen are excellent horsemen. Five of the six versions agree that these Jewish tribesmen "show no mercy." All six versions agree that these tribesmen take booty, but only five go so far as to say that booty is their *only* means of livelihood. Five of the six versions agree that each of these Jewish tribesmen is worth 1,000 of his enemies, but one version holds that each of these Jewish tribesmen is only worth 100 of his enemies.

Schloessinger, *Ritual of Eldad Ha-Dani*, 9, 107, followed by Krauss, *Tarbitz*, VIII: 230 and note 1, adopted the extreme view that "the only authentic account of Eldad and the [Lost] Tribes is the Kairawan Epistle to Gaon Zemah [ben Hayyim; late ninth century]." Scholoessinger, 4 and note 17, stresses the fact that the Kairawan Epistle to Gaon Zemah mentions only four tribes, instead of the ten Lost Tribes mentioned in the traditional narrative ascribed to Eldad (and utilized here). We do not accept the Schloessinger and Krauss view; it was refuted by Kupfer and Strelcyn, *Rocznik Orientalistyczny*, XIX: 125–143, especially 126–127 and 141. However, even if for the sake of argument we assume it to be correct, according to this Kairawan Epistle to Gaon Zemah, all four Lost Tribes are said to be residing in Ethiopia, which is still on the fringe of *Arab* territory. For the reference to Ethiopia as the land wherein the four Lost Tribes reside according to the Kairawan Epistle to Gaon Zemah, Epstein, *Eldad Ha-Dani*, para. 3, p. 4; Mueller, *Die Recensionen*, para. 2, p. 16; Neubauer, *Jewish Quarterly Review*, I: 104; Adler, *Jewish Travelers*, 15. For the reference to Ethiopia as the land where the Lost Tribes dwell according to Gaon Zemah's reply to the Kairawan Epistle, Epstein, *Eldad Ha-Dani*, paras. 11–12, pp. 6–7; Mueller, *Die Recensionen*, paras. 11–12, p. 19; Neubauer, *Jewish Quarterly Review*, I: 106–107; Adler, *Jewish Travelers*, 19.

Whether one accepts the authenticity of the traditional narrative ascribed to Eldad, or only of the Kairawan Epistle to Gaon Zemah (with Schloessinger), in either case Western Christians who heard the story of Eldad the Danite circa 900–1100 would have been tempted to conclude that at least four lost Jewish tribes, who were quite warlike (even according to the Kairawan Epistle to Gaon Zemah) and resided in Ethiopia (next door to their cousins, the Arabs), must be in league with the Muslims planning the destruction of the West. Joseph Jacobs, "Tribes, Lost Ten," *Jewish Ency*. 12 (1906): 249: "[According to Eldad the Danite] the 10 Tribes were settled in parts of Southern Arabia, or perhaps Abyssinia. . . . *The connection of this view with that of the Jewish origin of Islam is obvious* [and would have seemed so to Western Christians! italics ours]." Jacobs goes on to point out that David Reuveni, early sixteenth century, revived this view when he claimed to be related to the tribe of Reuben situated in Khaibar in northern Arabia. Cf. supra, note 68 to chapter 4, for the important extent to which David Reuveni reinforced the Christian belief that the Jew was in league with the Muslim against the West.

47. Daniel, *Islam and the West*, 123–127.

48. Eldad the Danite's travel narrative seems to have influenced the development of the Western Christian "Prester John" legend which first emerged in the twelfth century, for which, Henry Yule, "Prester John," *Ency. Brit.* 22 (1926): 304–307; Runciman, *History of the Crusaders*, II: 247, 422; III: 163, 240, 254; Southern, *Making of the Middle Ages*, 71–73; A.N. Poliak, "Armenia," and L.I. Rabinowitz, "Ten Lost Tribes," *Ency. Judaica* 3 (1971): 475, and 15 (1971): 1005, respectively.

Those who argue that the Eldad material did influence the Prester John legend assume (correctly, in our view) that the travel narrative traditionally ascribed to Eldad is genuine and therefore that it antedates the birth of the Prester John legend in the twelfth century. Among the scholars who accept and/or argue the influence of the Eldad material on the Prester John legend are Epstein, *Eldad Ha-Dani*, xxiii–xxiv; Mueller, *Die Recensionen*, 4–8 (a detailed point-by-point comparison of Latin and Hebrew texts); Broyde, *Jewish Ency.*, V: 91; Jacob S. Raisin, *Gentile Reactions to Jewish Ideals with Special Reference to Proselytes*, ed. H. Hailperin (New York: Philosophical Library, 1953), 409; Silver, *History of Messianic Speculation in Israel*, 57. The particular in the Prester John legend that the Prester allegedly ruled over some Jewish tribes as well as his own Christian people is considered a telling argument that the Prester John story developed (at least partly) under the influence of, and/or as a reaction against, the Eldad material.

Krauss, *Tarbitz*, VIII: 228–232, rejected the Epstein/Mueller thesis about the influence of the Eldad material upon the Prester John legend, with Krauss arguing vice versa that the Prester John legend influenced the Eldad material (and therefore that the Eldad material was later than the twelfth century). However, Krauss's case is flawed by the severe weakness of one of his key arguments, *i.e.*, that there was no communication whatsoever between Jewish and Christian scholars in twelfth-century Western Europe, and therefore that the Eldad material could not possibly have influenced the Prester John legend. Krauss denies that the Eldad material could have been transmitted orally because "in the twelfth century we find no social and intellectual contacts between Christians and Judaism," far too hasty a statement. Krauss also denies that the Eldad material could have been transmitted in writing, because we know of no Latin translation of the Eldad material until the sixteenth century and because Christian intellectuals of the twelfth century could not read Hebrew. But Krauss apparently forgot completely about converts from Judaism to Christianity.

There were enough such converts who knew Hebrew and could easily have transmitted the Eldad material to the Christian intellectuals. What about Petrus Alphonsi (for whose Jewish knowledge, supra, note 10 to chapter 3)? What about the converts who served as Peter the Venerable's informants? Baron, *Social and Religious History*, V: 341, note 41; Lieberman, *Shkiin*, iv: 27–42; Kritzeck, *Peter the Venerable and Islam*, 26–27. What about Herman of Scheda (circa 1107–1198)? Baron, *Social and Religious History*, V: 112–113, 340–341, note 39; Grayzel, "The Confession of a Medieval Jewish Convert," *Historia Judaica* 17 (1955): 89–120; Gerlinde Niemeyer, *Hermanus Quondam Judaeus: Opusculum de Conversione Sua* (Weimar: Boehlau, 1963), and Grayzel's review thereof, *Jewish Social Studies* 18 (1966): 170–171; M. Lamed, "Hermanus Quondam Judaeus," *Ency. Judaica* 8 (1971): 365–366. What about Chretien of Troyes (circa 1170), the great writer of Arthurian romances, who was a convert from Judaism according to Urban Tigner Holmes and Mary Amelia Klenke, *Chretien*,

Troyes and the Grail (Chapel Hill: University of North Carolina Press, 1959)? For discussion of the Holmes-Klenke thesis, J. Frappier, "Le 'Conte du Graal' est Il une Allegorie Judaeo-Chretienne?" *Romance Philology* 16 (1962–1963): 179–213; 20 (1966): 1–31. What about Rabbi Micah and the Jewish physician, Joshua, two converts in late eleventh- and early twelfth- century Trier? Lewinsky, *Jewish Ency.*, XII: 242; Margolis and Marx, *History of the Jewish People*, 362; Shapiro and Ansbacher, *Ency. Judaica*, XV: 1390.

The Eldad material could also have been transmitted to twelfth-century Franco-German Christians by loyal Jews, because Krauss is mistaken in arguing that there were no social contacts between twelfth century Christians and loyal Jews.

We can document knowledge of the Eldad material by the following Jewish intellectuals in Franco-Germany circa 1050–1300: (1) Rashi (1040–1105; Troyes in Champagne); (2) Abraham ibn Ezra (1092–1167; Spain, Italy, France, England); (3) Jacob Tam (circa 1100–1171; Ramerupt in Champagne); (4) Meir of Rothenburg (1220–1293; Germany). We can also document knowledge of this material by Abraham ben David of Posquieres in twelfth-century southern France and by Abraham ben Maimon in thirteenth-century Egypt. Epstein, *Eldad Ha-Dani*, xxiii–xxiv; Broyde, *Jewish Ency.* V: 91; Baron, *Social and Religious History*, VI: 434, note 86. Of these six Jewish intellectuals who knew the Eldad material, three were favorable to it (Rashi, Abraham ben David, and Abraham ben Maimon) and three antagonistic to it (Abraham ibn Ezra, Jacob Tam, and Meir of Rothenburg). The key factor here apparently was the description of the Judaeo/Islamic alliance by Eldad. Abraham ben Maimon in Islamic Egypt, and Abraham ben David in Islamic- and Albigensian-influenced twelfth-century southern France, were untroubled by the description of that alliance. Rashi, who lived primarily before the especially heavy emphasis upon the Jew as ally of the Muslim during and after the First Crusade, was also untroubled by the description of the Judaeo/Islamic alliance in Eldad. But Abraham ibn Ezra, Jacob Tam, and Meir of Rothenburg, all of whom lived in Christian Europe after the First Crusade, were probably deeply troubled by the description of the Judaeo/Islamic alliance in Eldad, holding that it gave Jewish support to the Christian charge that the Jew was an ally of the Muslim, a charge that in the twelfth and thirteenth centuries was responsible for many massacres of the Jews in Franco-Germany.

How could information about Eldad the Danite have been transmitted by these Jewish intellectuals (and/or their relatives, colleagues, and disciples) to Franco-German Christians? Perhaps by the Jew from Mainz who debated Gilbert Crispin in London in the early 1090s. Supra, note 26, para. 2, to chapter 3. Perhaps by Rashi's grandson, Rabbi Samuel ben Meir (called the Rashbam) of Ramerupt (circa 1080–1184), a pupil of his grandfather, for the Rashbam knew French and Latin and participated in discussions with Christians. Cf. two articles on the Rashbam, S. Ochser, *Jewish Ency.* 11 (1905): 23; A. Grossman, *Ency. Judaica* 14 (1971): 811. Perhaps by the anonymous rabbi whom Abelard consulted on the meaning of an obscure passage in the Book of Kings. Kraus, *The Living Theatre of Medieval Art*, 147, 232, note 27, citing J.G. Sikes, *Peter Abailard* (Cambridge: Cambridge University Press, 1932), 30; also supra, notes 25 to chapter 2, and 3 to chapter 3. Perhaps by the father and son team of Jewish debaters, Nathan ben Joseph and Joseph ben Nathan Official, both of Sens, mid to late thirteenth-century France. Supra, note 34.

Thus, Krauss is incorrect. The Eldad material could well have been transmitted to twelfth-century Franco-German Christians by both loyal Jews and Jewish converts to Christianity. Therefore, the Eldad material could have influenced the development of the Prester John legend in twelfth-century Western Europe. If so, the description of the Judaeo/Islamic alliance in the Eldad material could have helped reinforce the Western Christian conviction that the Jew was in league with the Muslim during the twelfth century, when Western Christian crusading enthusiasm and corresponding anti-Muslimism was at a peak.

However, Blumenkranz suggests that the Eldad material influenced Western Christians as early as circa 1000, *e.g.*, Fulbert of Chartres, who preached three anti-Jewish sermons circa 1009 (at the time of the great persecution of the Jews of Franco-Germany, for which, supra, note 11 to chapter 4). Blumenkranz, *Juifs et Chretiens*, 232–233, especially 233 and notes 90–91; his *Auteurs*, 237–243, especially 242 and note 15; and his "Roman Church and the Jews," in Roth, *Dark Ages*, 96. Who could have informed Fulbert of Chartres about the Eldad material? Most likely, his friend, Herbert, a convert from Judaism. Blumenkranz, *Auteurs*, 237–238, note 1. Fulbert of Chartres was also quite interested in refuting the Muslims. Blumenkranz, *Auteurs*, 239 and note 8; Southern, *Making of the Middle Ages*, 198, 201–202. If Fulbert of Chartres was interested in both Islam and Judaism, it is highly likely that Fulbert would have been impressed by the description of the Judaeo/Islamic alliance within the Eldad material, a description serving as evidence from Jewish sources themselves of the truth of the long-standing Christian belief that the Jews were in league with the Muslims. Was it mere coincidence that Western Christian intellectuals (Fulbert of Chartres and his important circle) seem to have been aware of the description of the Judaeo/Islamic alliance within the Eldad material at the very time of a great persecution of the Jews (circa 1010) occasioned largely by the charge that the Jews were in league with the Muslims?

Fulbert of Chartres's early eleventh-century knowledge of the Eldad material comes only a generation after the life and work of Hasdai ibn Shaprut. Infra, notes 66–78, we suggest several ways by which information in the Hasdai/Joseph correspondence (as well as the related Bustanai, Eldad, and Nathan materials) could have been transmitted to Franco-German Christians during Hasdai's lifetime. Fulbert of Chartres's knowledge of the Eldad material and its description of the Judaeo/Islamic alliance confirms our suggestion that Jewish historical materials depicting that Judaeo/Islamic alliance did reach the Christians of Franco-Germany by one or more of the various transmission routes developed infra that were so intimately related to the life and work of Hasdai ibn Shaprut.

Finally, Baron, *Social and Religious History*, III: 205; VI: 434, note 86, suggests that the shift in the Prester John legend (which occurred in the fourteenth century), tranferring the Prester from Central Asia to Ethiopia, may have been due partly to the Eldad material. However, according to Baron the Eldad material did not influence the actual emergence of the Prester John legend in twelfth-century Western Europe. With all due respect to Baron, because of the case developed by Epstein, *Eldad Ha-Dani*, xxiii–xxiv, and Mueller, *Die Recensionen*, 4–8, and because of Blumenkranz's argument that the Eldad material was known to and influential upon Fulbert of Chartres circa 1009, we would suggest that Baron has been too hasty in dismissing the view that the Eldad material was influential upon the Prester John legend as early as its twelfth-century origin. Cf. in general infra, note 122.

49. The Arabic version: Friedlaender, *Jewish Quarterly Review*, XVII: 753–754; for the Hebrew version, Neubauer, *Medieval Jewish Chronicles*, II: 78–79; Kahana, *Sifrut Ha-Historiyya Ha-Yisr'elit*, I: 60–61; Dinur, *Yisrael Ba-Golah*, I:2: 384–386; for the English translation, Friedlaender, 755–759. On the historical incidents involved, two articles on Mar Uqba, by S. Ochser, *Jewish Ency.* 12 (1906): 339, and A. David, *Ency. Judaica* 15 (1971): 1512; Baron, *Jewish Community*, I: 183; and his *Social and Religious History*, V: 10–11. In the generation after that of Mar Uqba, when a quarrel broke out between Saadia Gaon=the "church" and Exilarch David the son of Zakkai=the "state," Nathan the Babylonian reports that "all the weathly [Jews] of Bagdad . . . sided with Saadia and were ready to help him by means of their money and influence with the king [Caliph]." Cf. the Hebrew text in Neubauer, II: 80–83; Kahana, I: 62–65; English translation in Marcus, *Jew in the Medieval World*, 287–292; commentary in the writings of Malter, Auerbach, Baron, Marx, and Rivkin citied supra, note 12. This story about Saadia repeats the theme of the Mar Uqba story, *i.e.*, the influence of the Jewish bankers at the caliphal court.

50. For the Hebrew version, Harkavy, in Freimann and Hildesheimer, *Festschrift Berliner*, 34–43; Kahana, *Sifrut Ha-Historiyya Ha-Yisr'-elit*, I: 70–71. On the historical incidents involved, Baron, *Jewish Community*, I: 160, 188–189, 211; III: 34; and his *Social and Religious History*, III: 152–153; A. David, "Netira," *Ency. Judaica* 12 (1971): 999–1000.

51. For this portion of the Hebrew original of Hasdai's letter, Kahana, *Sifrut Ha-Historiyya Ha-Yisr'elit*, I: 36–37; Kokovtzov, *Evreisko-Khazarskaia Perepiska*, 11–13. For the English translation, Adler, *Jewish Travelers*, 24–26; Leviant, *Masterpieces*, 159–160.

52. Kahana, *Sifrut Ha-Historiyya Ha-Yisr'elit*, I: 36; Kokovtzov, *Evreisko-Khazarskaia Perepiska*, 10–11; Adler, *Jewish Travelers*, 24; Leviant, *Masterpieces*, 159.

53. Kahana, *Sifrut Ha-Historiyya Ha-Yisr'elit*, I: 37–38; Kokovtzov, *Evreisko-Khazarkaia Perepiska*, 13–14 (cf. p. 14, lines 1–2, for merchants coming to Muslim Spain not only from Egypt but from Iraq, Khurasan [northeastern Iran], and India [via the Red Sea] as well); Adler, *Jewish Travelers*, 26; Leviant, *Masterpieces*, 160–161.

According to the "Story of the Four Captives" in Abraham ibn Daud's mid-twelfth-century Toledan *Book of Tradition*, Spanish Muslim shipping linked southern Italy, Palestine, Egypt, and Tunisia with Cordova. Cohen, *Book of Tradition*, Hebrew, 46–48; English, 63–66; Zimmels, "Scholars and Scholarship in Byzantium and Italy," in Roth, *Dark Ages*, 178–179; Sharf, *Byzantine Jewry*, 167–168; Ashtor, *Jews of Moslem Spain*, I: 234–236, 429–431. According to the chronicle of Ahima'atz, tenth-century south Italian Christian shipping linked Tunisia, Spain, southern France, and Constantinople, with Ancona and Amalfi. Salzman, *Chronicle Of Ahimaaz*, Hebrew, 19; English, 93; Klar, *M'gillat Ahima'atz*, Hebrew only, 43.

54. Kahana, *Sifrut Ha-Historiyya Ha-Yisr'elit*, I: 38 and line 9; Kokovtzov, *Evreisko-Khazarskaia Perepiska*, 14 and line 11; Adler, *Jewish Travelers*, 26–27; Leviant, *Masterpieces*, 161. For Khurasan as an important Christian anti-Islamic symbol during the crusading period, Runciman, *History of the Crusades*, I: 60, 130, 202; II: 13, 120, 147–148; III: 245, 250, 397; Daniel, *Islam and the West*, index, *s.v.* "Corozan story."

For Khurasan in Hasdai's letter, supra, note 53 (Kokovtzov's edition); in Nathan the Babylonian's account of Mar Uqba, supra, note 49, especially Friedlaender, *Jewish Quarterly Review*, XVII: Arabic, 753–754; English, 756. Dunlop, *History of the Jewish Khazars*, 135, note 55, 138–139, suggests that these Khurasanian merchants were Radanites.

55. Kahana, *Sifrut Ha-Historiyya Ha-Yisr'elit*, I: 40, line 20; Kokovtzov, *Evreisko-Khazarskaia Perepiska*, 18, line 9; Adler, *Jewish Travelers*, 31; Leviant, *Masterpieces*, 163.

56. Kahana, *Sifrut Ha-Historiyya Ha-Yisr'elit*, I: 38; Kokovtzov, *Evreisko-Khazarskaia Perepiska*, 15; Adler, *Jewish Travelers*, 27–28; Leviant, *Masterpieces*, 161–162.

57. For this portion of Khan Joseph's reply, version A (= Dunlop's short version of 134 lines, the traditional version printed by Isaac Akrish in the sixteenth century = Christ Church College Oxford MS 193 = the version whose *incipit* reads *Hineh 'Odi^{c}aha*), Hebrew original, Kahana, *Sifrut Ha-Historiyya Ha-Yisr'elit*, I: 43, lines 17–25; and Kokovtzov, *Evreisko-Khazarskaia Perepiska*, 23, lines 5–12; English translation, Kobler, *Treasury of Jewish Letters*, I: 110–111; and Leviant, *Masterpieces*, 167. Cf. also version B (= Dunlop's long version of 152 lines, the version discovered by Harkavy in 1874 = Lenigrad MS Hebrew 157 of the second Firkovich Collection = the version whose *incipit* reads *Shalom Rav*), Hebrew original only, Kokovtzov, 30, lines 10–18. On version B in general, Dunlop, *History of the Jewish Khazars*, 130–132, 151–153; and his "Khazars," in Roth, *Dark Ages*, 331–333; and his "Khazars," *Ency. Judaica*, X: 951. According to Dunlop, version B, the longer version, is probably closer to the original version.

58. Joseph's reply, version A, Kahana, *Sifrut Ha-Historiyya Ha-Yisr'elit*, I: 43, lines 2–17; Kokovtzov, *Evreisko-Khazarskaia Perepiska*, 22, line 12, to 23, line 5: Kobler, *Treasury of Jewish Letters*, I: 109–110; Leviant, *Masterpieces*, 166–167. Version B, Kokovtzov, 29, line 16, to 30, line 10.

59. Joseph's reply, version A, Kahana, *Sifrut Ha-Historiyya Ha-Yisr'elit*, I: 43, lines 4–5, 10–11; Kokovtzov, *Evreisko-Khazarskaia Perepiska*, 22, lines 14–15, 20; Kobler, *Treasury of Jewish Letters*, I: 109–110; Leviant, *Masterpieces*, 166–167. Version B, Kokovtzov, 29, lines 19–20, 26.

60. Joseph's reply, version A, Kahana, *Sifrut Ha-Historiyya Ha-Yisr'elit*, I: 43, lines 13–14; Kokovtzov, *Evreisko-Khazarskaia Perepiska*, 23, lines 1–2; Kobler, *Treasury of Jewish Letters*, I: 110; *Leviant*, Masterpieces, 167. Version B, Kokovtzov, 30, lines 6–7. In both versions A and B the Khan asks both Christian and Muslim if Judaism is "better." In both A and B the Christian answers "no religion can be compared to Judaism." In A the Muslim answers that "Judaism is better and all of it is true." In B the Muslim simply answers that "Judaism is true."

61. Joseph's reply, version A, Kahana, *Sifrut Ha-Historiyya Ha-Yisr'elit*, I: 43, lines 5–11; Kokovtzov, *Evreisko-Khazarskaia Perepiska*, 22, lines 15–22; Kobler, *Treasury of Jewish Letters*, I: 109–110; Leviant, *Masterpieces*, 166–167. Version B, Kokovtzov, 29, line 19, to 30, line 3.

Our account here follows the traditional Hebrew text (Kahana; Kobler; Leviant). In Kokovtzov's edition of both version A (22, lines 20–22) and B (30, lines 1–3), the Christian priest *does* attack Islam. The following is a comparison of eleven particulars in the priest's attack on Islam in Kokovtzov's edition. (1) Muslims do not keep the

Jewish Sabbath. Both versions A and B. (2) Muslims do not keep the Jewish festivals. Both versions A and B. (3) Muslims do not accept the entire Old Testament as revelation—version A. Muslims do not obey those Old Testament commandments which can be accepted on the basis of reason alone—version B. (4) The Muslims never had an Israelite priesthood that wore Urim on their breastplates—version A. Muslims do not obey those Old Testament commandments which can only be accepted on the basis of faith—version B. (5) Muslims eat unclean animals in general. Both versions A and B. (6) Muslims eat camel meat, considered unclean by Jews. Found only in version B. (7) Muslims eat horse meat, considered unclean by Jews. Found only in version B. (8) Muslims eat dog meat, considered unclean by Jews. Found only in version B. (9) Muslims eat *sheretz* (insects and/or reptiles), considered unclean by Jews—version A. Muslims eat *sheketz* (abominations, unclean animals in general)—version B. (10) Muslims eat *remes* (creeping things, reptiles, worms), considered unclean by Jews. Both version A and B. (11) "The Islamic religion is not a [true monotheistic] religion but is rather like unto the religions of the pagans [the *goye ha-aratzot*, 'the peoples of the lands' = pagans, heathens, idolaters]." This concluding sentence is found only in version B. Kokovtzov's version A is not as harshly anti-Islamic as his version B.

62. Joseph's reply, version A, Kahana, *Sifrut Ha-Historiyya Ha-Yisr'elit*, I: 43, lines 14–16; Kokovtzov, *Evreisko-Khazarskaia Perepiska*, 23, lines 2–4; Kobler, *Treasury of Jewish Letters*, I: 110; Leviant, *Masterpieces*, 167. Version B, Kokovtzov, 30, lines 6–9. The following is a comparison of five particulars in the qadi's attack on Christianity in Kokovtzov's edition (version A, 23, lines 3–4; version B, 30, lines 8–9). (1) "Christianity is not a [true monotheistic] religion." Found only in version B. (2) "Christians eat pig meat," considered unclean by Jews. Found only in version B. (3) Christians eat unclean animals in general. Both versions A and B. (4) Christians "bow down to the work of their hands," *i.e.*, worship icons and crucifixes, *i.e.*, "worship idols." Both versions A and B. (5) "Christians have no [true Messianic] hope [or no hope for salvation in the afterlife]." Found only in version B. Just as Kokovtzov's version A was not as harshly anti-Islamic as his version B (supra, note 61), so his version A is not as harshly anti-Christian as his version B. Thus, Kokovtzov's version B is harsher on both Muslims and Christians. It may well be the original version of Khan Joseph's reply, reflecting the fearless viewpoint of the independent Jewish kingdom, which felt free to attack both Muslims and Christians with equal fervor. Kokovtzov's version A may be an edition of version B prepared in a land where Jews were less independent (and thus where Jews could not be as free in their attacks on other religions), perhaps in Muslim Spain (Dunlop, *History of the Jewish Khazars*, 151–153, and his "Khazars," in Roth, *Dark Ages*, 332–333). Rabbi Judah ben Barzillay of Barcelona (circa 1100), however, seems to have known version B (the longer, more original and more intolerant version), not version A (the shorter, edited Spanish version that was more tolerant of other religions). Dunlop, *History*, 132, and "Khazars," in Roth, 332.

63. Joseph's reply, version A, Kahana, *Sifrut Ha-Historiyya Ha-Yisr'elit*, I: 43, line 11; Kokovtzov, *Evreisko-Khazarskaia Perepiska*, 22, line 22; Kobler, *Treasury of Jewish Letters*, 110; Leviant, *Masterpieces*, 167. Version B, Kokovtzov, 30, lines 3–4. Our account in the text here follows version A, according to which the Khan's full reply to the priest is as follows: "Thus you have spoken your words [*i.e.*, you have only told

me your opinion which may or may not be the truth]; know of a truth that I shall honor you." The Khan's full reply to the priest in version B is as follows: "You have told these your words in truth and I will show mercy unto you and send you back with honor to the King of Edom [the King of the Christians, the Byzantine Emperor]." The key difference is that version A applies the term "truth" to the Khan's promise to honor the priest, whereas version B applies the term "truth" to the priest's words.

64. Joseph's reply, version A, Kahana, *Sifrut Ha-Historiyya Ha-Yisr'elit*, I: 43, line 17; Kokovtzov, *Evreisko-Khazarskaia Perepiska*, 23, lines 4–5; Kobler, *Treasury of Jewish Letters*, I: 110; Leviant, *Masterpieces*, 167. Version B, Kokovtzov, 30, lines 9–10. Our account in the text here follows version A, according to which the Khan's full reply to the qadi is as follows: "You have *already* spoken the truth unto me; and verily I shall honor you." Notice the word "already" here (Hebrew *k'var* = Arabic *qad*), which lends added emphasis to the word "truth" as applied to the words of the qadi. The Khan's full reply to the qadi in version B is as follows: "Truthfully have you spoken; and I shall show mercy unto you." Thus, comparing the Khan's reaction to the words of the priest (in both versions A and B) and the Khan's reaction to the words of the qadi (again in both versions), we find that the Khan applies the term "truth" to the priest's words in *at most* one version (version B), while he applies the term "truth" to the qadi's words in both versions (A and B), adding the emphatic term "already" to the "truth" of the qadi's words in one version (A). Khan Joseph's reply seems to feel that Islam is a "truer" religion than Christianity!

65. Joseph's reply, version A, Kahana, *Sifrut Ha-Historiyya Ha-Yisr'elit*, I: 44, lines 12–15; Kokovtzov, *Evreisko-Khazarskaia Perepiska*, 24, lines 18–21; Adler, *Jewish Travelers*, 35; Leviant, *Masterpieces*, 168. Version B, Kokovtzov, 32, lines 4–7.

66. Hasdai's letter, Kahana, *Sifrut Ha-Historiyya Ha-Yisr'elit*, I: 40, lines 23–26; Kokovtzov, *Evreisko-Khazarskaia Perepiska*, 18, lines 11–15; Adler, *Jewish Travelers*, 31–32; Leviant, *Masterpieces*, 164. According to the conclusion of Eldad's narrative he sent a copy thereof to Spain circa 883. Epstein, *Eldad Ha-Dani*, version B, para. 20, pp. 29, 41, notes 30–31, and version D, para. 16, pp. 53, 54, note 8; Adler, *Jewish Travelers*, 15; Leviant, *Masterpieces*, 153. It is also possible that Eldad himself visited Spain circa 883. For at the conclusion of his letter, where Hasdai mentions Eldad the Danite, he uses language that could be interpreted to mean that Eldad himself actually visited Spain in addition to sending a copy of his narrative there. Hasdai states that "during the days of our fathers" [*i.e.*, circa 883, for Hasdai himself was writing in the 950s] Eldad the Danite *nafal etzlenu*. This Hebrew expression, which translates literally as "he fell near us," is probably an Arabism = Arabic *nazala 'indanā* = "he stayed at our home or lived with us," or = Arabic *waqa'a/saqata 'ilā* = "to reach or arrive at." Hasdai, thus, seems to be saying that circa 883 Eldad the Danite "stayed at our home" or "lived with us" or "reached us" in Spain, *i.e.*, came to Spain. Ashtor, *Jews of Moslem Spain*, I: 152–153, 419, notes 70–73, holds that Eldad did visit Spain. Eldad's travel narrative could, thus, have been transmitted from Kairawan to Spain; thence to Franco-Germany the same way material from the Hasdai/Joseph correspondence was transmitted. Or, it could have been transmitted from Kairawan to southern Italy, thence through northern Italy to Franco-Germany. Cf. infra, note 69, for links between Kairawan and southern Italy; supra, notes 32–33, for links between southern Italy and Franco-Germany. For Eldad's messianism, Ashtor, I: 140ff, and for

Hasdai's messianism, Ashtor, I: 193–194, 214–215, 427, notes 85–87.

67. Hasdai's letter, Kahana, *Sifrut Ha-Historiyya Ha-Yisr'elit*, I: 40–41; Kokovtzov, *Evreisko-Khazarskaia Perepiska*, 18, line 15, to 19, line 13; Adler, *Jewish Travelers*, 32; Leviant, *Masterpieces*, 164.

68. According to Baron, *Social and Religious History*, VI: 213–214, 431, notes 76–77, Nathan the Babylonian's chronicle was written in Kairawan in the 960s, though the latest incident described therein took place in the early 940s. However, Ginzberg, *Geonica*, I: 61, assigned the date of circa 947 to Nathan's chronicle. If it was written circa 947, it could have reached Spain around the time Hasdai sent his letter to Joseph in the 950s. The Shii Buwayhid take-over of the caliphate of Bagdad and the capital city in 945 may have occasioned Nathan the Babylonian's emigration to Kairawan, as well as the writing of his chronicle circa 947 to recall Jewish glory in Bagdad under the old Sunni regime, before the Shii Buwayhid coup. On the Buwayhid take-over, Brockelmann, *History of the Islamic Peoples*, 155; Hitti, *History of the Arabs*, 470–471. For Nathan the Babylonian's description of the installation of the exilarch, Neubauer, *Medieval Jewish Chronicles*, II: 83–85; Kahana, *Sifrut Ha-Historiyya Ha-Yisr'elit*, I: 65–67; Halper, *Post-Biblical Hebrew Literature: Texts*, 37–40; Leviant, *Masterpieces*, 154–157; Baron, *Social and Religious History*, VI: 214, 431, note 77; and his *Jewish Community*, III: 39, note 13.

Saadia Gaon's son Dosa sent Hasdai a copy of Dosa's biography of his famous father. Mann, *Texts and Studies*, I: 6–7 and notes 7–9a; Cohen, *Book of Tradition*, English section, 57 and note to line 159; Ashtor, *Jews of Moslem Spain*, I: 183, 423, note 28. Hasdai was undoubtedly interested in Saadia's life and work because of Saadia's quarrel with the Exilarch David ben Zakkai. But this quarrel was also described by Nathan the Babylonian. Neubauer, *Medieval Jewish Chronicles*, II: 80–83; Kahana, *Sifrut Ha-Historiyya Ha-Yisr'elit*, I: 62–65. If Hasdai was interested in reading Dosa's account of that quarrel, he would also have been interested in reading Nathan the Babylonian's account of that same quarrel. Perhaps Hasdai wrote to Dunash ibn Tamin in Kairawan for a copy of Nathan's chronicle; infra, note 69.

The *Sefer Yosippon*, the medieval Hebrew version of Josephus, treats the history of the Jewish people in Palestine during the second Temple period, *ancient* history from Hasdai's perspective. Yet, virtually at the very time it was being completed in southern Italy circa 953 (David Flusser, "Josippon," *Ency. Judaica* 10 [1971]: 296–298), Hasdai ordered a copy from Samuel of Otranto. Starr, *Jews in the Byzantine Empire*, 154; Baron, *Social and Religious History*, VI: 195; Zimmels, "Historiography," in Roth, *Dark Ages*, 280; Sharf, *Byzantine Jewry*, 170; Ashtor, *Jews of Moslem Spain*, I: 229–230; infra, note 75, for Hasdai and the Jews of southern Italy in general. The chronicle of Nathan the Babylonian treats the history of the Jewish people in Iraq (then the most important Jewish center in the world, demographically and culturally) more or less during Hasdai's own lifetime, *recent* history from Hasdai's perspective. Would not it have been just as likely that virtually at the same time as it was being completed in Kairawan (circa 947; the Yosippon was completed circa 953 in nearby southern Italy) Hasdai would also order a copy of Nathan's chronicle for himself?

69. Nathan the Babylonian's material could have been transmitted from Kairawan to Franco-Germany either via (1) Spain or (2) Italy.

1. FROM KAIRAWAN TO *SPAIN* TO FRANCO-GERMANY.

A. It could have reached Spain directly from Kairawan.

B. Or it could have gone from Kairawan to southern Italy and thence

C. from southern Italy to Spain.

Once in Spain (either via route A, directly from Kairawan, or via routes B and C, indirectly via southern Italy) the Nathan material could have been transmitted over the Pyrenees by one of the routes associated with Hasdai the son of Shaprut (infra, notes 70–78).

2. FROM KAIRAWAN TO ITALY TO FRANCO-GERMANY.

Once in southern Italy (via route B, Kairawan to southern Italy), the Nathan material could have been transmitted over the Alps by the same Kalonymid route which took Jewish mystical ideas from Italy to Franco-Germany (supra, notes 32–33).

A. Jewish cultural transmission between Kairawan and Spain

Supra, note 66; Ashtor, Jews of Moselm Spain, I: 45, 61–62, 66, 111–112, 127–128, 134–135, 224–226, 238, 278, 380, 411, 416, 428, 431, 436, 451; Cohen, Book of Tradition, English section, 64, note 30; 66, lines 60–61; 138, note to line 270.

Cf. also Joshua Blau, "Ibn Quraysh, Judah," Ency. Judaica 8 (1971): 1192–1193; Starr, Jews in the Byzantine Empire, 55; Georges Vajda, "Dunash Ibn Tamim," Ency. Judaica 6 (1971): 271–272; Zimmels, "Historiography," in Roth, Dark Ages, 280; J.H. Schirmann, "Ibn Abitur, Joseph Ben Isaac," Ency. Judaica 8 (1971): 1152–1153; Chaim M. Rabin, "Dunash Ben Labrat," ibid., 6 (1971): 270–271; Samuel Ha-Nagid and Kairawan: Y. Horowitz, "Hushiel Ben Elhanan," ibid. 8 (1971): 1130; Cohen, Book of Tradition, English, 77; "Ibn Khalfun, Isaac," Ency. Judaica 8 (1971): 1187–1188; "Gabirol, Solomon Ben Judah, Ibn," ibid. 7 (1971): 236; Daniel Carpi, "Kairouwan," ibid. 10 (1971): 698; Alexander Altmann, "Israeli, Isaac Ben Solomon," ibid. 9 (1971): 1065; and Cohen, Book of Tradition, English section, 136, note to line 73.

B. Jewish cultural transmission between Kairawan and southern Italy.

Infra, note 96; Zimmels, "Historiography," in Roth, Dark Ages, 280; Baron, Social and Religious History, VIII: 395–396, note 31 (the views of S. Fried); Zimmels, "Scholars and Scholarship in Byzantium and Italy," in Roth, Dark Ages, 178–179; Horowitz, Ency. Judaica, VIII: 1129–1130; infra, note 107; Salzman, Chronicle of Ahimaaz, Hebrew, 18; English, 92–93; Klar, M'gillat Ahima'atz, Hebrew, 42; Salzman, Hebrew, 18–19; English, 92–93; Klar, Hebrew, 42–43; Ashtor, Jews of Moslem Spain, I: 225, 428, note 107.

C. Jewish cultural transmission between southern Italy and Spain.

Salzman, Chronicle of Ahimaaz, Hebrew, 3–4; English, 63–64; Klar, M'gillat Ahima'atz, Hebrew, 14; infra, note 75; supra, note 68, conclusion; Ashtor, Jews of Moslem Spain, I: 234–237; and his article "Moses Ben Hanokh," Ency. Judaica 12 (1971): 417–418; the "Story of the Four Captives" and the chronicle of Ahima'atz, both on tenth-century Mediterranean commerce, supra, note 53.

70. Kayserling, "Hasdai, Abu Yusuf . . . Ibn Shaprut," Jewish Ency. 6 (1904): 249; Margolis and Marx, History of the Jewish People, 308; Hitti, History of the Arabs, 524; Baron, Social and Religious History, III: 155–156; Baer, Jews in Christian Spain, I: 29; Cantera Burgos, "Christian Spain," in Roth, Dark Ages, 362–364: Ashtor, Jews of Moslem Spain, I: 176–181; and his article "Hisdai (Hasdai) Ibn Shaprut," Ency. Judaica 8 (1971): 533.

71. For links between the Christians of France and Spain during the first half of

the tenth century, Colbert, *Martyrs of Cordoba*, 382; Aguado-Bleye, *Manual*, I: 488, col. b.

72. Kayserling, *Jewish Ency.*, VI: 249; Margolis and Marx, *History of the Jewish People*, 308–309; Hitti, *History of the Arabs*, 590 and note 1; Baer, *Jews in Christian Spain*, I: 29; Blumenkranz, *Auteurs*, 232–233; Ashtor, *Jews of Moslem Spain*, I: 169–176; and his article, *Ency. Judaica*, VIII: 533. Cf. also Baron's view infra, note 73, that Ibrahim ibn Ya'qub was also an emissary of Hasdai to Germany.

73. Kahana, *Sifrut Ha-Historiyya Ha-Yisr'elit*, I: Saul and Joseph in Hasdai's letter, p. 39, lines 2–3 and 29; Jacob b. Eliezer in Joseph's reply, version A, p. 41, line 10; Kokovtzov, *Evreisko-Khazarskaia Perepiska*, Saul and Joseph in Hasdai's letter, p. 16, line 2, and p. 17, line 9; Jacob b. Eliezer in Joseph's reply, version A, p. 19, line 17; called Isaac b. Eliezer in Joseph's reply version B, p. 26, line 14; Adler, *Jewish Travelers*, 28, 30, 32; Leviant, *Masterpieces*, 162–164; Dunlop, *History of the Jewish Khazars*, 136; Ashtor, *Jews of Moslem Spain*, I: 171, 192, 209, 211, 216.

Additional Jewish travelers going from Spain to Franco-Germany mentioned in Hasdai's letter are (1) the learned team of Rabbi Judah the son of Meir (the son of Nathan) and Rabbi Joseph Haggaris, who went from Spain to Khazaria via Franco-Germany; and (2) the messengers Hasdai sent on an unsuccessful mission to find the blind Mar Amram, a Jew who moved to Germany from Khazaria. They too, in addition to Saul, Joseph, and Jacob (or Isaac) the son of Eliezer, could have transmitted information from Eldad and Nathan to the Christians of Franco-Germany. For Rabbi Judah the son of Meir (the son of Nathan) and Rabbi Joseph Haggaris, Hasdai's letter, Kahana, *Sifrut Ha-Historiyya Ha-Yisr'elit*, I: 37, lines 11–12; Kokovtzov, *Evreisko-Khazarskaia Perepiska*, 12, lines 10–11; Adler, *Jewish Travelers*, 25; Leviant, *Masterpieces*, 160; Dunlop, *History*, 134; Roth, "Economic Life and Population Movements," in Roth *Dark Ages*, 46. For the messengers Hasdai sent on an unsuccessful mission to find the blind Mar Amram, Hasdai's letter, Kahana, I: 39, line 29, to 40, line 3; Kokovtzov, 17, lines 9–13; Adler, 30; Leviant, 163; Dunlop, *History*, 137 and note 64.

The Jewish traveler Ibrahim ibn Ya'qub, who left Muslim Spain to visit Central Europe circa 970, could also have transmitted information about Eldad, Nathan, and the Hasdai/Joseph correspondence to the Christians of Franco-Germany. For Ibrahim ibn Ya'qub, Ashtor, "Ibrahim Ibn Ya'qub," in Roth, *Dark Ages*, 305–308; his *Jews of Moslem Spain*, I: 344–349; and his "Ibrahim Ibn Ya'qub of Tortosa," *Ency. Judaica* 8 (1971): 1214. Ashtor, in Roth, 306–307, too hastily dismisses Baron's suggestion (*Social and Religious History*, III: 217) that Ibrahim was an emissary of Hasdai to Otto I of Germany.

74. Hasdai's letter, Kahana, *Sifrut Ha-Historiyya Ha-Yisr'elit*, I: 38, lines 1–9; Kokovtzov, *Evreisko-Khazarskaia Perepiska*, 14, lines 4–11; Adler, *Jewish Travelers*, 26–27; Leviant, *Masterpieces*, 161.

75. Baron, *Social and Religious History*, III: 156, 305–306; VI: 195; Mann, *Texts and Studies*, I: 10–16; Starr, *Jews in the Byzantine Empire*, 7–8, 58, 152–156; Sharf, *Byzantine Jewry*, 99–101, 166, 170; and his "Jews in Byzantium," in Roth, *Dark Ages*, 62–63; Roth, "Italy," ibid., 108; Zimmels, "Historiography," ibid., 280; Ashtor, *Jews of Moslem Spain*, I: 183–191, 229–230.

76. Ashtor, *Jews of Moslem Spain*, I: 199–200, 211; supra, note 56.

77. Kayserling, *Jewish Ency.*, VI: 249; Margolis and Marx, *History of the Jewish People*, 309 (following Steinschneider, dating it too late, circa 959–963); Mann, *Texts and Studies*, I: 12 and note 16; Hitti, *History of the Arabs*, 577 and note 3; Baron *Social and Religious History*, VIII: 65, 245–246; Ashtor, *Jews of Moslem Spain*, I: 164–169; and his article, *Ency. Judaica*, VIII: 533.

78. Ashtor, *Jews of Moslem Spain*, I: 165, for the eunuch Salemon, whom the Byzantine emperor sent to Muslim Spain and Christian Germany circa 947 to negotiate a Byzantine-Umayyad and Byzantine-Ottonian alliance against the Fatimid threat in southern Italy. The eunuch Salemon could also have helped transmit information (received from Hasdai with whom Salemon probably met in Cordova) about the Judaeo/Islamic alliance. For Byzantine influence on the persecution of the Jews of Germany in the 930s, supra, note 25 to chapter 4. There was major Byzantine influence upon Ottonian Germany circa 972–1002. Vasiliev, *History of the Byzantine Empire*, I: 308–312, 327–329, 336; Ostrogorsky, *History of the Byzantine State*, 188, 250, 258ff, 263, 269, 278; Every, *Byzantine Patriarchate*, 139–142. If information about the Hasdai/Joseph correspondence (and/or the Eldad and Nathan material) had not been transmitted from Byzantium to Germany during Hasdai's lifetime, *i.e.*, the 950s and 960s, it could perhaps even more easily have been transmitted from Byzantium to Germany circa 972–1002.

79. Salzman, *Chronicle of Ahimaaz*, Hebrew, 3; English, 62–63; Klar, *M'gillat Ahima'atz*, Hebrew, 13.

On Aaron of Bagdad, Louis Ginzberg, "Aaron Ben Samuel Ha-Nasi," *Jewish Ency.* 1(1901): 20–21; Margolis and Marx, *History of the Jewish People*, 299–300; Starr, *Jews in the Byzantine Empire*, 39, 70, 115, 117, 124; Baron, *Social and Religious History*, V: 56–57; VIII: 44; Sharf, *Byzantine Jewry*, 164–165, 169–170; Joseph Dan, "Aaron of Baghdad," *Ency. Judaica* 2 (1971): 21; plus the following articles in Roth, *Dark Ages*: Roth, "Italy," 102, 104, 106–107, 109–110; Agus, "Rabbinic Scholarship in Northern Europe," 192; Agus, "Rashi and His School," 247; Schirmann, "The Beginning of Hebrew Poetry in Italy and Northern Europe: Italy," 264; Zimmels, "Historiography," 276; Dan, "The Beginnings of Jewish Mysticism in Europe," 283–284, 289.

80. On Aaron's father, supra, note 32. Why did Aaron leave Bagdad? Our suggestion is that Aaron's flight was related to the suppression of Daniel's exilarchate by Caliph Mutawakkil circa 850. Supra, note 32; infra, note 81. Ginzberg, *Jewish Ency.*, I: 20, states that Aaron fled because of "disagreements between father and son." Sharf, *Byzantine Jewry*, 169, suggests that Aaron fled because he was suspected of practicing black magic.

81. Baron, *Social and Religious History of the Jews*, III: 135, 139ff, 148; Brockelmann, *History of the Islamic Peoples*, 132–133.

82. Salzman, *Chronicle of Ahimaaz*, Hebrew, 3–4; English, 63–64; Klar, *M'gillat Ahima'atz*, Hebrew, 13–14.

83. Gaeta was under heavy Arab attack and possibly a temporary occupation circa 844–848, shortly before Aaron's arrival. Krueger, in Setton, *History of the Crusades*, I: 46. Arab occupation, however, did not necessarily mean a cessation of travel and trade with the Christians of Italy and Franco-Germany. Pirenne, *Mohammed and Charlemagne*, 180 and note 3; Fred E. Engreen, "Pope John the Eighth and the Arabs," *Speculum* 20 (1945): 321 and note 8. For Gaetan collaboration with the Arabs

circa 876, 882, and 915, Krueger, 49–50; Engreen, 329; Pirenne, 182 and notes 4–5. If Aaron arrived in Gaeta when it was under Arab control (circa 844–848), this would help explain why he found a Jew from Spain (presumably Arab Spain) resident there at the time. Supra, note 69, route C, first item.

84. Salzman, *Chronicle of Ahimaaz*, Hebrew, 4–5; English, 64–66; Klar, *M'gillat Ahima'atz*, Hebrew, 15–17.

85. Salzman, *Chronicle of Ahimaaz*, English, 66, note 2; Joseph Jacobs, "Wandering Jew," *Jewish Ency*. 12 (1906): 462–463; Baron, *Social and Religious History of the Jews* (1st ed.; New York: Columbia University Press, 1937), II: 27–32, 84–85, 162–163; III: 58, 102, 105; Baron, *Social and Religious History*, XI: 177–182, 373–375, notes 73–81; Y. Glikson, "Wandering Jew," *Ency. Judaica* 16 (1971): 259–263.

86. For the Christian conception of the Muslim as sorcerer, Daniel, *Islam and the West*, index, *s.v.* "Muhammad, presented as magician"; for the Christian conception of the Jew as sorcerer, Trachtenberg, *Devil and the Jews*, 57ff; for the Christian equation of Jewish sorcery with Islam, Herman, *Annuale Mediaevale*, XIV: 68–69.

87. Salzman, *Chronicle of Ahimaaz*, Hebrew, 5; English, 66–67; Klar, *M'gillat Ahima'atz*, Hebrew, 17–18.

88. Baron, *Social and Religious History*, V: 56–57, 316–317, note 69, suggests that Aaron was acting here under Islamic influence in a south Italian city then under Islamic domination. The chronicle of Ahima'atz, however, says that the imposition of capital punishment took place in Oria and leaves the impression that at that time Oria was not under Islamic domination. Salzman, *Chronicle of Ahimaaz*, Hebrew, 9; English, 74–76; Klar, *M'gillat Ahima'atz*, Hebrew, 24–25. Perhaps the capital punishment was imposed in Bari or Taranto, which were under Islamic domination circa 840–880. Cf. also Starr, *Jews in the Byzantine Empire*, 38–39, 117–119; Sharf, *Byzantine Jewry*, 165–166, 184–185, notes 2–6. For the Jewish right to impose the death penalty in Muslim Spain, Schirmann, "Ibn Abitur, Joseph Ben Isaac," *Ency. Judaica* 8 (1971): 1152. Cf. also Kayserling, "Moser," *Jewish Ency*. 9 (1905): 42–44; S. Mendelsohn, "Capital Punishment," ibid. 3 (1902): 554–558; Jacob Klatzkin and Haim H. Cohn, "Informer," *Ency. Judaica* 8 (1971): 1364–1367, 1370–1373; Cohn and L.I. Rabinowitz, "Capital Punishment," *Ency. Judaica* 5 (1971): 142–147. For our own suggestion about Aaron of Bagdad's imposition of the death penalty, supra, note 32. For the ability to impose the death penalty in the travel narrative of Eldad the Danite as well as in the exchange of correspondence about Eldad between Kairawan and Iraq, Epstein, *Eldad Ha-Dani*, para. 5, p. 24, as well as para. 2, p. 4, and para. 13, p. 7; Mueller, *Die Recensionen*, 74–75, as well as 16 and 19; Adler, *Jewish Travelers*, 7–8, as well as 15, 19–20.

89. Engreen, *Speculum*, XX: 327 and notes 4–11; Krueger, in Setton, *History of the Crusades*, I: 47; Salzman, *Chronicle of Ahimaaz*, Hebrew, 9, lines 1–4, 20–21; English, 74–75; Klar, *M'gillat Ahima'atz*, Hebrew, 24, lines 6–11, and 25, lines 8–10.

90. Salzman, *Chronicle of Ahimaaz*, Hebrew, 9–10; English, 74, 76–77; Klar, *M'gillat Ahima'atz*, Hebrew, 24, 26–27. Cf. also Salzman, English, 20; Michele Amari, *Storia dei Musulmani di Sicilia*, ed. C.A. Nallino (Catania: Prampolini, 1933), I: 513–525; Hitti, *History of the Arabs*, 604–605; J. Gay, *L'Italie Meridionale et l'Empire Byzantin 867–1071* (Paris: Fontemoing, 1904), 52, 66, 74–76, 96ff; Vasiliev, *History of the Byzantine Empire*, I: 280, 303, 326; Ostrogorsky, *History of the Byzantine State*,

210–211; Mann, *Lives of the Popes in the Early Middle Ages*, III: 187, 320, 329; Pirenne, *Mohammed and Charlemagne*, 163, 178–180; Krueger, in Setton, *History of the Crusades*, I: 46–49; and, in general, Giosue Musca, *L'Emirato di Bari 847–871* (Bari: Dedalo, 1964).

91. Salzman, *Chronicle of Ahimaaz*, Hebrew, 6–8; English, 69–74; Klar, *M'gillat Ahima'atz*, Hebrew, 20–24. On Sh'fatyah the son of Amittai, Margolis and Marx, *History of the Jewish People*, 300; Starr, *Jews in the Byzantine Empire*, 4–5, 30, 37, 58, 70–72, 115, 117, 123–126, 128–131, 133, 139, 159; Baron, *Social and Religious History*, III: 180; VIII: 60; Sharf, *Byzantine Jewry*, 87–89, 91, 164, 169–172; Y. David, "Shephatiah Ben Amittai," *Ency. Judaica* 14 (1971): 1380; plus the following articles in Roth, *Dark Ages*: Roth, "Italy," 104–107; Schirmann, "Beginning of Hebrew Poetry in Italy and Northern Europe: Italy," 251–252; Zimmels, "Historiography," 275–276.

92. Starr, "An Eastern Christian Sect: The Athinganoi," *Harvard Theological Review* 29 (1936): 93–106; Baron, *Social and Religious History*, III: 178–179; Sharf, "Jews in Byzantium," in Roth, *Dark Ages*, 60–61; and his *Byzantine Jewry*, 74–77, 80–81, notes 73–81; supra, note 24, paras. 4 and 7, to chapter 4.

93. Engreen, *Speculum*, XX: 323; Ostrogorsky, *History of the Byzantine State*, 317.

94. Salzman, *Chronicle of Ahimaaz*, Hebrew, 9; English, 74–76: Klar, *M'gillat Ahima'atz*, Hebrew, 24–25.

95. Cf. 1 Maccabees 2:29–38, in Sidney Tedesche and Solomon Zeitlin, eds., *The First Book of Maccabees* (New York: Harper for Dropsie College, 1950), pp. 82–85, for the view that Jews should not fight in self-defense on the Sabbath but should die as martyrs instead. Eldad the Danite, however, urged the Jews to fight in self-defense on the Sabbath. Epstein, *Eldad Ha-Dani*, para. 4, p. 4; Mueller, *Die Recensionen*, 17; Adler, *Jewish Travelers*, 16. Hence, Hasdai asked Joseph if the Khazars fought in self-defense on the Sabbath. Kahana, *Sifrut Ha-Historiyya Ha-Yisr'elit*, I: 40, lines 14, 17–18; Kokovtzov, *Evreisko-Khazarskaia Perepiska*, 18, lines 3, 6–8; Adler, 31; Leviant, *Masterpieces*, 163.

96. Salzman, *Chronicle of Ahimaaz*, Hebrew, 18; English, 91–92; Klar, *M'gillat Ahima'atz*, Hebrew, 41–42; Starr, *Jews in the Byzantine Empire*, 168–169. There were two great Arab raids on Oria circa 900–960. 1. Circa 925: (a) wherein Shabbethai Donnolo was taken captive (to be ransomed at Taranto) = Starr, *Jews in the Byzantine Empire*, 149, and (b) Hananel II son of Paltiel I was also taken captive (to Tunisia, thence back to Bari via Constantinople) = supra, beginning of this footnote and Starr, 168–169. The latter's captivity is dated too late by Starr as circa 985: there was no Hananel son of Paltiel in Ahima'atz's family tree circa 985 (cf. Gottheil, "Ahimaaz," *Jewish Ency.* 1 [1901]: 290, and Roth, "Italy," in Roth, *Dark Ages*, 407). On Hananel II son of Paltiel I, also Baron, *Social and Religious History*, V: 317, note 70; Roth, "Italy," in Roth, ibid., 109, 404, note 32; Sharf, *Byzantine Jewry*, 116, 166. 2. Circa 952 wherein Paltiel II was taken captive to Sicily = Starr, 159–160; Roth, "Italy," in Roth, ibid., 107, 403, notes 24–25.

97. Salzman, *Chronicle of Ahimaaz*, Hebrew, 16–21; English, 88–97; Klar, *M'gillat Ahima'atz*, Hebrew, 38–47. On Paltiel II, the numerous references cited supra, note 14. De Goeje (1898) and Marx (1910–1911) equated Paltiel with the great Fatimid general, Jawhar, born in southern Italy/Sicily and taken captive by the Fatimids.

Hitti, *History of the Arabs*, 619. Kaufmann (1897) and Fischel (1937) equated Paltiel with the well-known Fatimid Vizier, Ya'qub ibn Killis (Hitti, 627), who, however, is said by other sources to have been born in Bagdad, not southern Italy/Sicily. What is more, both the De Goeje/Marx and the Kaufmann/Fischel theses were weakened by the fact that Jawhar and ibn Killis were both described by other sources as converts to Islam, whereas Paltiel II, at least as described by the chronicle of Ahima'atz, was a loyal Jew. Bernard Lewis, *Bulletin of the School of Oriental and African Studies*, XXX: 177–181, solved the problem by equating Paltiel II with Musa b. Elazar, described by other sources as having been born in Oria and captured during a Fatimid raid. He became physician to the Fatimid Caliph al-Muizz and moved with him to Egypt. As far as we know, Musa remained a loyal Jew though enjoying the friendship of ibn Killis, the Jewish convert to Islam. Cf. also David, *Ency. Judaica*, XIII: 49–50; Mark R. Cohen, *Jewish Self-Government in Medieval Egypt: The Origins of the Office of Head of the Jews circa 1065-1126* (Princeton: Princeton University Press, 1980), index *s.v.* "Paltiel b. Shephatiah."

98. Salzman, *Chronicle of Ahimaaz*, Hebrew, 16, lines 24–30; English, 88; Klar, *M'gillat Ahima'atz*, Hebrew, 38, lines 13–22; Starr, *Jews in the Byzantine Empire*, 159–160.

99. Salzman, *Chronicle of Ahimaaz*, Hebrew, 16–17; English, 88–89; Klar, *M'gillat Ahima'atz*, Hebrew, 38–39.

100. Salzman, *Chronicle of Ahimaaz*, introduction, 23; Hitti, *History of the Arabs*, 605, 617–619.

101. Salzman, *Chronicle of Ahimaaz*, Hebrew, 17, line 6, to 18, line 12; English, 89–91; Klar, *M'gillat Ahima'atz*, Hebrew, 39, line 9, to 41, line 17.

102. Salzman, *Chronicle of Ahimaaz*, Hebrew, 19, lines 8–26; English, 93–94; Klar, *M'gillat Ahima'atz*, Hebrew, 43, line 7, to 44, line 7.

103. Salzman, *Chronicle of Ahimaaz*, Hebrew, 19, line 27, to 20, line 8; 22, lines 1–15; English, 94–95, 98–99; Klar, *M'gillat Ahima'atz*, Hebrew, 44, line 9, to 45, line 3; 48, line 11, to 49, line 10.

104. Salzman, *Chronicle of Ahimaaz*, Hebrew, 20, line 9, to 21, line 2; English, 95–96; Klar, *M'gillat Ahima'atz*, Hebrew, 45, line 4, to 46, line 16.

105. Salzman, *Chronicle of Ahimaaz*, Hebrew, 21, lines 3–8; English, 96–97; Klar, *M'gillat Ahima'atz*, Hebrew, 46, lines 17–26.

106. Salzman, *Chronicle of Ahimaaz*, introduction, 28, states that the unnamed "King of Bagdad in the North" here refers to "Rokn, the *Caliph* of Bagdad." Klar, *M'gillat Ahima'atz*, 173, note to p. 46, line 2, states that the "King of Bagdad" here refers to "Sultan Rukn al-Dawlah who also died in the year 976." Salzman is correct when he states that the word "king" here refers to the caliph but incorrect when he makes Rukn caliph (he was only the Buwayhid sultan, the protector of the caliph; Hitti, *History of the Arabs*, 470–471). Klar is incorrect when he states that the word "king" here refers to the Buwayhid sultan but is correct when he states that Rukn was indeed sultan and not caliph. Most likely the word "king" here refers to the caliph himself, al-Muti (Hitti, 473), who died in 974 and was succeeded by al-Tai.

107. Salzman, *Chronicle of Ahimaaz*, Hebrew, 21, lines 9–12, then 19, line 27, to 20, line 8; English, 97, then 94–95; Klar, *M'gillat Ahima'atz*, Hebrew, 46, line 26, to 47, line 5; then 44, line 8, to 45, line 3.

108. Salzman, *Chronicle of Ahimaaz*, Hebrew, 21, lines 13–21; English, 97; Klar, *M'gillat Ahima'atz*, Hebrew, 47, lines 6–18.

109. There are at least four key numismatic references in the chronicle of Ahima'atz: (1) circa 850, Salzman, *Chronicle of Ahimaaz*, Hebrew, 4, line 21; English, 65 and note 2; Klar, *M'gillat Ahima'atz*, Hebrew, 16, line 1; (2) circa 875, Salzman, Hebrew, 11, lines 19–20; and 12, lines 12–13; English, 79–80; Klar, Hebrew, 28, lines 24–25; and 30, lines 10–11; and infra, note 115; (3) circa 975, Paltiel II, supra, note 107; (4) circa 1000 Samuel the son of Paltiel II, supra, note 108 . After consulting the following works on Byzantine, Arab, and Jewish coinage from the ninth through the twelfth centuries—Steven Runciman, *Byzantine Civilization* (New York: Meridian, 1956) 141; Hitti, *History of the Arabs*, 172, note 4; and especially Starr, *Jews in the Byzantine Empire*, 111, 182–184, 186–191, 194, 220–221; and Sharf, *Byzantine Jewry*, 114; 119–121; 128, note 3; 129, notes 45 and 48; 178–179, 191–192, 194—we have come to the following conclusion. Though Samuel gave 20,000 units of money while his father Paltiel gave only 5,000 units, because Samuel's donation was in silver coinage while his father Paltiel's was in gold, the value of Samuel's donation was not as great as that of his father. It could have ransomed at most 30 to 60 male captives while his father's donation could have ransomed about 150 male captives. Samuel was either less generous or less wealthy. Since he presumably inherited much of his father's money (while his father began with nothing), Samuel may not have had as lucrative a post in Fatimid Egypt as that of his father.

110. For Samuel and Joseph Ha-Nagid, three articles on Samuel, by I. Broyde, *Jewish Ency.* 11 (1905): 24–25, Joseph Marcus, *Univ. Jewish Ency.* 9 (1943): 348–349, and A.M. Habermann, *Ency. Judaica* 14 (1971): 816–818; two articles on Joseph Ha-Nagid, Kayserling, *Jewish Ency.* 9 (1905): 142, and Ashtor, *Ency. Judaica* 9 (1971): 1324–1325; Margolis and Marx, *History of the Jewish People*, 313–321; Baron, *Social and Religious History*, index to vols. 1–8, p. 68; Cohen, *Book of Tradition*, index, both *s.v.* "Ibn Nagrela, Joseph" and "Ibn Nagrela, Samuel"; Ashtor, *Jews of Moslem Spain*, II: 41–189.

111. Supra, note 33. According to Elazar Rokeach of Worms (early thirteenth century) "King Charles" brought Rabbi Moses ben Rabbi Kalonymus ben Rabbi Judah and his sons (along with other relatives and notables) from Lucca to Mainz. Klar, *M'gillat Ahima'atz*, 57, 174–175; Dan, "Beginnings of Jewish Mysticism in Europe," in Roth, *Dark Ages*, 283, 435, notes 6–8; and his "Kalonymus," *Ency. Judaica* 10 (1971): 719–720. The "King Charles" here would seem to refer to Charlemagne. It was so understood by the great sixteenth-century Jewish historian Joseph Ha-Kohen, as well as by M. Wiener, writing in 1854 (Katz, *Jews in the Visigothic and Frankish Kingdoms*, 161, note 2), and Cecil Roth, writing in 1966 (Roth, "Economic Life and Population Movements," in Roth, *Dark Ages*, 44, 389, note 51). However, Agus, "Rabbinic Scholarship in Northern Europe," in Roth, *Dark Ages*, 191, 419, note 17, also relying upon sixteenth-century Jewish tradition, holds that the Kalonymids crossed the Alps in 877, and therefore the "King Charles" in question was Charles the Bald (Agus says "Charles the Fat" when he should say "Charles the Bald," for Charles the Fat did not come to power until 881).

112. Supra, notes 33 and 111. Harry Bresslau, the distinguished nineteenth-century paleographer, writing in 1887, was among the first to argue that Elazar

Rokeach's early thirteenth-century tradition that it was Charlemagne who brought Moses ben Kalonymus from Lucca to Mainz was based on faulty recollection. In reality, the Kalonymus in question was the Kalonymus who, according to a reliable Christian chronicle (Dietmar of Mersebourg) rescued Emperor Otto II at the Battle of Crotona in southern Italy, July 982. In gratitude for saving his life, Emperor Otto brought this Kalonymus from Italy to Mainz, the first Kalonymus to cross the Alps. Bresslau's view is accepted by Margolis and Marx, *History of the Jewish People*, 299, 353. Meir ben Simon of Narbonne, writing in the 1240s, apparently transformed Dietmar of Mersebourg's story as follows: the emperor in question became a Carolingian not Otto II; the Jew in question was not declared to have been a Kalonymid nor an Italian; the Jew who rescued the emperor was declared to have lost his own life in the process and hence the emperor could only reward his relatives; the emperor brought his relatives to Narbonne, not Mainz, in the ninth, not the tenth, century. Katz, *Jews in the Visigothic and Frankish Kingdoms*, 160-161; Blumenkranz, *Juifs et Chretiens*, 36 and note 225; and his *Auteurs*, 244-245 and notes 2-3; Zuckerman, *Jewish Princedom*, 64-67.

The history of the Kalonymid family in Western Europe (Italy, southern France, and Germany) circa 711 to 1096 is an extremely complicated problem. Supra, notes 33, 111-112; plus two articles on the Kalonymids, by Broyde, *Jewish Ency.* 7 (1904): 424-426; and Dan, *Ency. Judaica* 10 (1971), 718-722; Baron, *Social and Religious History*, IV: 46, 273; V: 60ff; VI: 117; VII: 181; VIII: 44, 50; and Roth, *Dark Ages*, index, *s.v.* "Kalonymus (name)" and "Kalonymus, Family of," and 407 for a Kalonymid family tree.

113. Supra, note 91 to this chapter; supra, notes 18-25 and 51 to chapter 4 and notes 75-78 to this chapter.

114. Supra, notes 94 and 113.

115. Salzman, *Chronicle of Ahimaaz*, Hebrew, 11, line 7, to 12, line 15; English, 78-80 (and 78, note 1); Klar, *M'gillat Ahima'atz*, Hebrew, 28, line 6, to 30, line 14; Starr, *Jews in the Byzantine Empire*, 49, 132-133; Sharf, *Byzantine Jewry*, 87, 103, note 7; supra, notes 113-114.

116. Salzman, *Chronicle of Ahimaaz*, Hebrew, 15, line 27, to 16, line 9; English, 86-87 (and 87, note 1); Klar, *M'gillat Ahima'atz*, Hebrew, 36, line 18, to 37, line 16; two articles on Moses of Pavia, by I. Elbogen, *Jewish Ency.* 9 (1905): 92; and U. Cassuto, *Ency. Judaica* 12 (1971): 434; Baron, *Social and Religious History*, V: 105, 292-293, note 20, plus the following articles in Roth, *Dark Ages*: Roth, "Italy," 109, 113-114; Zimmels, "Scholars and Scholarship in Byzantium and Italy," 180; and Schirmann, "Beginning of Hebrew Poetry in Italy and Northern Europe: Italy," 253; supra, notes 111-112; Roth, "Economic Life and Population Movements," in Roth, ibid., 43-44.

117. Supra, notes 96, 113-115. Information about Aaron and Sh'fatyah could have reached Hasdai in midtenth-century Cordova, for Hasdai was vitally interested in ancient (*Yosippon*) and recent (Saadia Gaon) Jewish history and was in close touch with south Italian Jewry (supra, notes 68-69, especially route C, southern Italy to Spain). Via Hasdai, information about Aaron and Sh'fatyah could have reached the Christians of Franco-Germany (supra, notes 70-78). Thus, we would have three channels of cultural transmission: (1) Italian Jews directly to Franco-Germany (supra, notes

111-112, 116); and/or (2) south Italian Jews to Byzantium and thence to the Christians of France-Germany (notes 113–115, 117–118 to this chapter), and/or (3) south Italian Jews to Hasdai in Cordova and thence to the Christians of Franco-Germany (supra, notes 70–78).

118. Supra, notes 101, 113-115, 117.

119. Salzman, *Chronicle of Ahimaaz*, Hebrew, 18–19; English, 93; Klar, *M'gillat Ahima'atz*, Hebrew 42–43. Before the First Crusade, when Amalfitan policy was basically pro-Arab (Citarella, *Speculum*, XLII: 229–312), the data on the Judaeo/ Islamic alliance in the chronicle of Ahim'atz would have been relatively harmless. However, in the twelfth century, after the Crusades had begun (for Amalfitan participation therein, Runciman, *History of the Crusades*, I: 37, 48, 54, 154; II: 156, 294), such data could well have led some Amalfitans to detest the Jews as potential collaborators with the Muslims. On Amalfi and the Jews, Roth, "Economic Life and Population Movements," in Roth, *Dark Ages*, 36ff, 44, 392; and his "Italy," ibid., 108, 110, 117; "Amalfi," *Ency. Judaica* 2 (1971): 791–792.

120. Cf. two articles on Donollo, R. Gottheil, *Jewish Ency.* 4 (1903): 639–640; and J. Dan, *Ency. Judaica* 6 (1971): 168–170; also Starr, *Jews in the Byzantine Empire*, 28, 48, 51–56, 59, 149, 156–159, 162–164, 166–167; Baron, *Social and Religious History*, IV: 44; VI: 470; VIII: 30, 60, 103, 171, 185, 243ff, 253, 258; Milano, *Storia degli Ebrei in Italia*, 55, 65–66; the following articles in Roth, *Dark Ages*: Sharf, "Jews in Byzantium," 65; Zimmels, "Scholars and Scholarship in Byzantium and Italy," 179; Schirmann, "Beginning of Hebrew Poetry in Italy and Northern Europe: Italy," 257; Zimmels "Historiography," 276; Dan, "Beginnings of Jewish Mysticism in Europe," 284, 290; Sharf, *Byzantine Jewry*, 108, 169–170, 181–182.

Cf. Also Andrew Sharf, *The Universe of Shabbetai Donnolo* (Warminster: Aris and Phillips, 1976).

121. For St. Nilus (who had major influence with the papacy and the Holy Roman emperors in the late tenth century), Every, *Byzantine Patriarchate*, 141 and note 6; plus three articles on St. Nilus, by T. Minisci, *Encic. Catt.* 8 (1952): 1884; G. Giovanelli, *Bib. Sanct.* 9 (1967): 995–1008; and B.J. Comanskey, *New Cath. Ency.* 10 (1967): 470. For St. Nilus and the Jews, Starr, *Jews in the Byzantine Empire*, 20, 48, 161–163; Sharf, *Byzantine Jewry*, 77–78, 182.

122. Supra, note 48. Rashi (late eleventh-century France) knew the Eldad material (and its description of the Judaeo/Islamic alliance). Supra note 48. Rashi probably also knew the Hasdai/Joseph correspondence (with its description of the same alliance), for he knew the work of Menahem ben Saruk (Hasdai's Hebrew secretary who prepared Hasdai's letter to Joseph). Agus, "Rashi and His School," in Roth, *Dark Ages*, 226–227. Rashi possibly also knew the chronicle of Ahima'atz material (with its description of the same alliance) since he knew the work of the south Italian Donnolo. Gottheil, *Jewish Ency.*, IV; 640; Starr, *Jews in the Byzantine Empire*, 167; supra, note 120. Jacob Tam, Rashi's grandson, knew the Eldad material. Supra, note 48. He probably knew the Hasdai/Joseph correspondence since he knew the work of Menahem ben Saruk. Cf. two articles on Jacob Tam, by M. Schloessinger, *Jewish Ency.*, VII: 38; and I. Ta-Shma and N. Netzer, *Ency. Judaica*, XV: 781. Jacob Tam possibly also knew the chronicle of Ahima'atz material since he had such high regard for the Jews of southern

Italy. Agus, "Rabbinic Scholarship in Northern Europe," in Roth, *Dark Ages*, 191, 419, note 15; Sharf, *Byzantine Jewry*, 168, 185, note 20.

The two great German Jewish mystics, Judah the Pious and Elazar Rokeach, late twelfth and early thirteenth centuries respectively, both Kalonymids from Worms, probably knew the chronicle of Ahima'atz material (with its description of the Judaeo/Islamic alliance). Starr, *Jews in the Byzantine Empire*, 149, 160, 167; David, *Ency. Judaica*, XIII: 49; supra, notes 33, 111-112; Gottheil, *Jewish Ency.*, IV: 640; Sharf, *Byzantine Jewry*, 170, 185, note 27. Judah the Pious and Elazar Rokeach were in close touch with German Christian religious circles. Scholem, *Major Trends in Jewish Mysticism*, 83–84, 370, notes 7–8, citing Yitzhak Fritz Baer, "Ha-M'gammah Ha-Datit Ha-Hevratit Shel *Sefer Hasidim*" [The Religious-Social Tendency of the *Book of the Pious*], *Zion* 3 (1938): 1–50. Perhaps these same German Christian religious circles acquired some information about the Judaeo/Islamic alliance as developed in the chronicle of Ahima'atz from Judah the Pious and Elazar Rokeach (and/or their relatives, friends, disciples, business and literary contacts).

Many Jews and converts from Judaism have been cited supra, note 48, as possible transmitters of information about the Judaeo/Islamic alliance in the Eldad material to the Christians of twelfth-century Franco-Germany in time to influence the emergence of the Prester John legend. Some of them could have transmitted information about the Judaeo/Islamic alliance in the Hasdai/Joseph and chronicle of Ahima'atz material in time to reinforce the Christian equation of Jew with Muslim during the Second and Third Crusades.

Herbert, the convert from Judaism, who probably transmitted information about the Judaeo/Islamic alliance in the Eldad material to Fulbert of Chartres in the early eleventh century (supra, note 48), could also have transmitted information about the Judaeo/Islamic alliance in the Bustanai, Nathan, Hasdai/Joseph, and Ahima'atz materials to Fulbert and other French Christian religious and political leaders. This would have been in time to influence the equation of Jew with Muslim that played such an important role in the great persecutions of the Jews of Western Europe circa 1010, the 1060s, and the First Crusade.

In addition to Herbert there were at least five other converts from Judaism in tenth-century France (or northern Spain), plus twelve possible informants (many of them converts from Judaism) in eleventh-century (or late tenth-century) Franco-Germany and Central Europe. Some could have transmitted information about the Judaeo/Islamic alliance in the Bustanai, Eldad, Nathan, Hasdai/Joseph, and Ahima'atz materials to Christian religious and political leaders in time to influence the great persecutions of the Jews during the eleventh century in which the equation of Jew with Muslim played such a crucial role.

First the five converts in tenth-century France (or northern Spain): (1) Habaz of Leon, Blumenkranz, *Juifs et Chretiens*, 143 and note 285; (2) Gautier of Orleans, Blumenkranz, 143, note 286; (3) Guillaume of Chalon-sur-Saone, Blumenkranz, 143 and notes 287–288; (4) Tz'hok ben Esther Israeli of Blois, Baron, *Social and Religious History*, IV: 92, 283–284, note 2; Schwarzfuchs, "France under the Early Capets," in Roth, *Dark Ages*, 146–147, 410, note 6; Blumenkranz, "Limoges," *Ency. Judaica* 11 (1971): 254; Chazan, *Medieval Jewry in Northern France*, 12; and his "The Persecution of 992," *Revue des Etudes Juives* 129 (1970): 217–221; (5) Theodelinus of Maillezais, Blumenkranz, *Juifs et Chretiens*, 143 and note 289.

Then the twelve possible informants in eleventh- (or late tenth-) century Franco-Germany and Central Europe: (1) The Hebrew teachers of Bishop Reginald of Eichstaedt, Blumenkranz, 49–50 and notes 297–298; (2) the Jerusalemite Jewish convert informant of Ekkehard IV of St. Gaul, Blumenkranz, 52 and note 312; (3) Emperor Conrad II's Jewish physician who debated Wazo, later bishop of Liege, Blumenkranz, *Juifs et Chretiens*, 46ff, 71, 74, 182, note 99, 221; his *Auteurs*, 260; and his "Roman Church and the Jews," in Roth, *Dark Ages*, 89; (4) the Jews of Regensburg who debated the monastic colleagues of Arnold de Vohburg, monk of St. Emmeran, Blumenkranz, *Juifs et Chretiens*, 46, note 279; and his *Auteurs*, 253–254; (5) the Hebrew teachers of Bernon of Reichenau, Blumenkranz, *Juifs et Chretiens*, 49 and note 296; and his *Auteurs*, 255 and note 2; (6) the Jew, Abraham of Regensburg, who dialogued with Othlo of St. Emmeran, Blumenkranz, *Juifs et Chretiens*, 45 and note 275; and his *Auteurs*, 261; (7) the Jewish convert, Benedict of Fecamp, Blumenkranz, *Juifs et Chretiens*, 50 and note 299; (8) the Hebrew teachers of Sigebert of Gembloux (and the Jews of Metz who dialogued with him), Blumenkranz, 50 and note 299; (9) the Jewish convert Podiva of southern Moravia, Blumenkranz, *Juifs et Chretiens*, 144 and note 293; and his *Auteurs*, 277–278 and note 2; (10) the Jewish convert Paul in the entourage of Archbishop Adalbert of Hamburg, Blumenkranz, *Juifs et Chretiens*, 144–145 and note 295; and his *Auteurs*, 276; (11) the Jew who converted after hearing Gilbert Crispin debate the Jew from Mainz in London in the early 1090s, Blumenkranz, *Juifs et Chretiens*, 144 and note 296; (12) the Jewish convert Henry of Regensburg, Blumenkranz, 144 and note 294.

123. For the persecution of the Jewish community of Zirid Tunisia (1016–1062), Broyde, "Tunis," *Jewish Ency.* 12 (1906): 272; D. Corcos, "Tunis, Tunisia," *Ency. Judaica* 15 (1971): 1436; and his "Kairouan," ibid. 10 (1971): 698–699; E. Bashan, "Nagid," ibid. 12 (1971): 760; Goitein, *Mediterranean Society*, II: 24–25, 352. The massacre of the Jews of Zirid Granada circa 1066 (infra, note 125) could have been related to the contemporary persecution of the Jewish community of Zirid Tunisia. Supra, note 69, route B, for cultural transmission between Kairawan and southern Italy.

124. Bernard Lewis demonstrated (supra, note 97) that the figure of Paltiel II in the chronicle of Ahima'atz was probably based on Musa b. Elazar, the Jewish physician (of southern Italian origin) who served the Fatimid Caliph al-Muizz. Ahima'atz transformed Musa, who was only a physician, into Paltiel, vizier and foreign minister. Was this transformation partly an attempt to create a south Italian Jewish hero of a stature great enough to challenge that of both illustrious Spanish Jewish heroes, Hasdai the son of Shaprut of tenth-century Cordova, a Jewish foreign minister (Paltiel's second area of distinction) and Samuel Ha-Nagid of eleventh-century Granada, a Jewish vizier (Paltiel's first area of distinction)? Was Ahima'atz motivated by intense Italian Jewish patriotism, and equally intense Italian Jewish jealousy of the achievements of the rival Spanish Jews, to inflate Musa b. Elazar's life and work and to immortalize him as Paltiel II, Jewish vizier and foreign minister of North Africa and Egypt?

For Hasdai the son of Shaprut's relations with south Italian Jewry and for cultural transmission between southern Italy and Spain, supra, notes 68, para. 3; note 69, route

C; and note 75. There assuredly was deep awareness of Hasdai the son of Shaprut and his achievements among south Italian Jews circa 950 (and presumably until circa 1055 when Ahima'atz wrote his chronicle). Hasdai helped save south Italian Jewry from Byzantine persecution and was interested in south Italian Jewish cultural accomplishments (*Yosippon*). Undoubtedly, south Italian Jews were grateful to Hasdai for his help and interest in them. But resentment is the other side of gratitude. In the ninth century south Italian Jews had their own local heroes (*e.g.*, Sh'fatyah the son of Amittai) of sufficient stature to intercede successfully with the Byzantine authorities to stop persecutions. They did not have to humiliate themselves by turning for help to the Jews of *Spain*. In the tenth century, however, south Italian Jews apparently no longer had such local heroes. They had to humiliate themselves by turning for help to the Jews of *Spain*. Humiliation breeds resentment which breeds jealousy which breeds contempt. For Samuel Ha-Nagid's accomplishments, supra, note 110. Hasdai the son of Shaprut's influence was felt practically everywhere in the Western civilization area (Muslim Spain united under the caliph of Cordova, Christian Spain, Germany and the Slavic lands, Jewish Khazaria, Arab Iraq, Palestine, Kairawan, Christian Byzantium, and Byzantine southern Italy). Samuel Ha-Nagid's influence was felt in a more circumscribed sphere (a portion of Muslim Spain, *i.e.*, Granada, plus Arab Iraq, Palestine, Kairawan, and Sicily). Nevertheless, even Samuel Ha-Nagid's more circumscribed sphere of influence would have been wide enough to produce significant jealousy among the Jews of southern Italy.

Ahima'atz's description of the large donations to Jewish charities made by Paltiel II (5,000 gold dinars) and his son Samuel (20,000 silver drachmae) may well have been colored by his desire to make the donations of the Jewish leaders in Fatimid Egypt (who were of south Italian extraction) match the lavish donations to Jewish charities which our sources tell us were made all over the Mediterranean by both Hasdai ibn Shaprut and Samuel Ha-Nagid. Likewise, Samuel Ha-Nagid was famous for the olive oil which he donated every year from his own orchards to light the lamps of the synagogues of Jerusalem. Cohen, *Book of Tradition*, Hebrew, 56; English, 75 and note to line 245, plus 138, supplementary note to line 245. The chronicle of Ahima'atz also depicts both Paltiel II and his son Samuel as making generous donations to help pay for oil to light the lamps of the synagogues of Jerusalem. Supra, notes 107-108.

Ahima'atz's application of the exalted Hebrew term *Nagid* (= leader, ruler, prince) to Paltiel II may well have been colored by his desire to grant Paltiel the same exalted title and status as that enjoyed by both Hasdai the son of Shaprut in Cordova and Samuel Ha-Nagid in Granada. Cohen, *Book of Tradition*, supplementary notes, 136, note to line 73, for the fact that the title *Nagid* was applied to Hasdai in Cordova; Baron, *Social and Religious History*, V; 45, for the fact that this titled was applied to Samuel in Granada. For the application of this title to Paltiel II at least twice in the chronicle of Ahima'atz, Salzman, *Chronicle of Ahimaaz*, Hebrew, 20, line 15; 21, line 9 and note 4; and 22, line 8; English, 95, 97, and 99 with note 1; Klar, *M'gillat Ahima'atz*, Hebrew, 45, line 13; 46, line 26; and 48, line 25. Baron, *Social and Religious History* V: 310, note 48, seems to be engaging in hypercriticism when he denies that the term *Nagid* is used in the chronicle of Ahima'atz in the same sense that it was used to apply to Hasdai in Cordova and Samuel in Granada. Cf. in general Cohen, *Book of Tradition*, English, 74, notes to line 234; Baron, *Jewish Community*, III, index, *s.v.* *"Nagid"* and *"n'gidim"*; and his *Social and Religious History*, V: 39ff, 51, 56, 308ff; Bashan, "Nagid," *Ency. Judaica* 12 (1971): 758–764.

The chronicle of Ahima'atz's jealousy of Hasdai and Samuel, the two great heroes of Spanish Jewry, may also have been influenced by the strongly pro-Fatimid bias of the chronicle of Ahima'atz. For the Shii Fatimids were strongly opposed to the Sunni Umayyads of Spain. Hitti, *History of the Arabs*, 618–619; Imamuddin, *Political History of Muslim Spain*, 148–150; Ashtor, *Jews of Moslem Spain*, I: 165–166, 235–236. A pro-Fatimid bias would assuredly have helped turn the chronicle of Ahima'atz strongly against Hasdai the son of Shaprut who served the Umayyads of Cordova. Admittedly, Samuel Ha-Nagid did not serve the Umayyads of Cordova but rather the Zirids of Granada. However, the cousins of the Zirids of Granada, the Zirids of Tunisia (who may have persecuted the Jews during the first half of the eleventh century; supra, note 123), rebelled against the Fatimids of Egypt in the early eleventh century. G. Marcais, "Zirids [of North Africa]," *Ency. of Islam* 4 (1934): 1229; H.R. Idris, "Hilal," ibid. 3 (1971): 385. Thus, the chronicle of Ahima'atz's pro-Fatimid bias might have generated contempt for the rebellious Zirids of Tunisia strong enough to encompass their cousins as well, the Zirids of Granada, including their Jewish vizier, Samuel Ha-Nagid.

Shulvass, *Between the Rhine and the Bosporus*, 158–163, and *Jews in the World of the Renaissance*, 56ff, points out that sixteenth-century native Italian Jews admired the German Jewish immigrants but despised the Spanish Jewish immigrants to Italy, even though the Italian and Spanish Jews were equally Mediterranean and Latin, while the German Jews differed from both by being northern European and Teutonic! One reason may have been that the Jews of Spain received their rabbinic traditions primarily from the Jews of Arab Iraq circa 600–1000 A. D. (and thus did not know the Palestinian Talmud, only the Babylonian), whereas the Jews of Italy and Germany both received their rabbinic traditions primarily from the Jews of Arab Palestine circa 600–1000 A. D. (and thus knew the Palestinian Talmud as well as they Babylonian). Since the Jewries of Iraq and Palestine were rivals circa 600–1000 A. D. (as well as in the previous period circa 200–600 A. D.), they transmitted their rivalry to the Jewries of Spain (the successor of Iraq) and Italy/Germany (the successor of Palestine). This would also have affected Italian Jewish attitudes toward Spanish Jews in the eleventh century, when the chronicle of Ahima'atz was written. Did Ahima'atz share the same contempt for Spanish Jews that the Jews of Italy felt in the sixteenth century and for the same reason?

125. For the massacre of the Jews of Granada circa 1066, supra, note 28 to chapter 4, and notes 110 and 123 to this chapter. Cf. also two articles on Granada, by Kayserling, *Jewish Ency.* 6 (1904): 80; and H. Beinart, *Ency. Judaica.* 7 (1971): 852.

Cf. also Isidro de las Cagigas, *Los Mozarabes* (Madrid: Instituto de Estudios Africanos, 1947), II: 454, for the important suggestion that the Islamic massacre of the Jews of Granada in 1066 was influenced by the Islamic massacre of the Christians of Saragossa in 1065, itself in retaliation for the massacre of the Muslims of Barbastro by French Crusaders in 1064.

126. Were the persecutions of the Jews of southern Italy in the 1060s (Benevento and Aterno; supra, note 28 to chapter 4) influenced, at least in part, by the description of the Judaeo/Islamic alliance in the chronicle of Ahima'atz?

The Byzantines are said to have burnt the Jewish quarter of Bari in 1051. Starr, *Jews in the Byzantine Empire*, 198–199; Sharf, *Byzantine Jewry*, 123, 130, note 62. Did that persecution represent Byzantine retaliation against the Jews of Bari for alleged collaboration with the Normans who from circa 1040 represented a serious threat to Byzantine domination of southern Italy and who would eventually take Bari from the Byzantines in 1067? If so, perhaps Ahima'atz wrote his chronicle in part to demonstrate that the Jews were not allies of the Normans but rather of the Fatimids (with whom the Byzantines were generally on friendly terms during the eleventh century).

6. Why Did Pope Innocent III Want the Fourth Lateran Council (1215) to Impose a Distinction in Clothing on Muslims and Jews?

* Chapter six goes back ultimately to the middle portion of the paper, "The Franciscan Moroccan Martyrs of 1220 and the Fifth Crusade in Spain (1218-1219)," delivered at the fourth annual meeting, Mid-West Medieval History Conference, Chicago, October 23, 1965. An earlier version of the chapter was delivered as a paper at the subsequent Third Biennial Conference on Medieval Studies, Western Michigan University, Kalamazoo, Michigan, March 18, 1966. We express our gratitude to the late Judah Rosenthal and to Seymour Feldman for their reactions to the Kalamazoo paper. We also thank James Brundage for criticisms and suggestions regarding both the Chicago and the Kalamazoo papers. An earlier version of this chapter appeared in John R. Sommerfeldt, ed., *Studies in Medieval Culture* (Kalamazoo, Michigan: Western Michigan University Press for the Medieval Institute, 1970), III: 92–116. With his permission, it is reproduced here after further revisions.

1. Potthast, *Regesta Pontificum Romanorum*, I: 410, no. 4725; *MPL*, CCXVI: 818: A–B. The *signum in bonum* mentioned here may refer to the great Christian victory over the Almohades at Las Navas de Tolosa in Spain, July 16, 1212, which Innocent helped achieve (infra, notes 16 and 19). An-Nasir, the Almohade caliph defeated at Las Navas, was depicted by contemporary Christians (in Germany and Italy) as proclaiming his intention to stable his horses in the portico of St. Peter's at Rome and to impose the Islamic faith on all of Western Europe. Mann, *Lives of the Popes in the Middle Ages*, XII: 178 and note 2. Hence, the Papacy could easily have considered his defeat an event of eschatological importance.

For this crucial passage from Innocent III's letter of April 19, 1213, cf. the following fourteen scholars: Basetti-Sani, *Per un Dialogo Cristiano-Musulmano*, 257–262; and his *L'Islam e Francesco d'Assisi*, 20–22; Burns, *American Historical Review*, LXXVI: 1390–1391 and note 18; Cohen, *Friars and the Jews*, 247 and note 12; J.P. Donovan, *Pelagius and the Fifth Crusade* (Philadelphia and London: University of Pennsylvania Press and Geoffrey Camberlege/Oxford University Press, 1950), 27 and note 5; Richard Kenneth Emmerson, *Antichrist in the Middle Ages: A Study of Medieval Apocalypticism, Art and Literature* (Seattle: University of Washington Press, 1981), 67, 261, note 90; Robert E. Lerner, "Joachim of Fiore as a Link between St. Bernard and Innocent III on the Figural Significance of Melchisedech," *Mediaeval Studies* 42 (1980): 475–476 and note 19; W. Nigg, *Das Ewige Reich: Geschichte einer Sehnsucht und einer Enttaeuschung* (Erlenbach and Zurich: Rentsch, 1944), 156; Ray C. Petry, *Christian Eschatology and Social Thought: A Historical Essay on the Social Implications of Some Selected Aspects*

in Christian Eschatology to A.D. 500 (New York and Nashville: Abingdon, 1956), 318
and note 20; H. Preuss, *Die Vorstellungen vom Antichrist im Spaeteren Mittelalter bei
Luther und in die Konfessionellen Polemik* (Leipzig: Hinrichs, 1906), 81; Helmut Roscher,
Papst Innocenz III und die Kreuzzuege (Goettingen: Vandenhock and Ruprecht, 1969),
143–144, 158ff, 288–291; Runciman, *History of the Crusades*, III: 145 and note 2;
Southern, *Western Views of Islam in the Middle Ages*, 42 and note 10; F. Saxl, "A
Spiritual Encyclopaedia of the Later Middle Ages," *Journal of the Warburg and Cour-
tauld Institutes* 5 (1942): 86 and note 1; E. Wadstein, *Die Eschatologische Ideengruppe:
Antichrist, Weltsabbat, Weltende und Weltgericht* (Leipzig: Reisland, 1896), 125.

The mere fact that Innocent III's millenarianism is not noted nor commented
upon by the following two works does not negate its very existence, accepted by the
fourteen scholars cited immediately above: Sylvia Thrupp, ed., *Millenial Dreams in Action: Essays in Comparative Study* (The Hague: Mouton, 1962); and Bernard McGinn,
Visions of the End: Apocalyptic Traditions in the Middle Ages (New York: Columbia
University Press, 1979).

We agree with Southern's use of the term "apocalyptic" to describe the view that
Pope Innocent III expresses in this letter, but disagree with Southern when he states
that it is "surprising" to find such views being expressed by this pope. Infra, notes
24ff, on Innocent III's spirituality.

Roscher also calls attention to two other important documents of Pope Innocent
III's apocalyptic, a letter of January 21, 1205, and his sermon at the opening of the
Fourth Lateran Council in November 1215, which make us much less "surprised" by
the apocalyptic ideas expressed by Innocent in his crusade appeal of April 19, 1213.
Far from holding that there was a decline in Innocent's apocalptic enthusiasm between 1205 and 1215, Roscher considers Innocent's sermon at the Fourth Lateran
Council the climax of his apocalyptic. However, we believe that Roscher has over-
stated the difference between Pope Innocent III's more "sober" apocalyptic and the
more "fantastic" apocalyptic of Joachim of Flora and three important participants in
the Fifth Crusade: St. Francis of Assisi, Cardinal Pelagius (the papal legate to the
crusade), and Jacques of Vitry (who had profound sympathy for the early Franciscan
movement). Roscher apparently did not fully appreciate the probable influence of the
ninth-century Spanish martyrs' movement and the "Letter of Toledo" upon Pope Innocent III via Archbishop Rodrigo Jimenez de Rada of Toledo (infra, note 3 and notes
7ff). Cf. also infra, notes 37–50, as well as notes 38 and 54.

2. Southern, *Western Views*, 42 and note 10; also Basetti-Sani, *Per Un Dialogo*,
260–261.

3. Southern, *Western Views*, 24; Colbert, *Martyrs of Cordoba*, 335–336.

4. For the siege of Damietta in 1218, Donovan, *Pelagius*, 38ff; Runciman, *History
of the Crusades*, III: 151ff; T.C. Van Cleve, "The Fifth Crusade," in Setton, *History
of the Crusades*, II: 396ff; infra, note 58. Two important ecclesiastical leaders of the
Fifth Crusade, Cardinal Pelagius and Jacques of Vitry, were profoundly influenced by
Christian anti–Islamic Messianic expectations circa 1220. Roscher, *Papst Innocenz III*,
291, note 99; Burns, *American Historical Review*, LXXVI: 1390–1391 and note 19. For
1218 as a year of redemption in Jewish messianism, Silver, *History of Messianic Speculation in Israel*, 65–66; for 1216 as a similar year of redemption, ibid., 47, 75; infra, note
20.

5. New Testament, Book of Revelation (Apocalypse of John), chapters 13–20 in general, plus 19:19–21 and 20:4–6 in particular. Cf. also P. Alphandery, "Mahomet-Antichrist dans le Moyen Age Latin," in *Melanges Hartwig Derenbourg* (Paris: Leroux, 1909), 261–277; Daniel, *Islam and the West*, 184–185, 187, 193, 200, 225, 280–281, 316, 382–383; Southern, *Western Views*, 22–25; Kritzeck, *Peter the Venerable and Islam*, 152.

6. For further light on the year 1284 as a year of Christian messianic redemption, Cohn, *Pursuit of the Millenium*, 107, 398–399, notes to p. 107: three pseudo-Frederick II (infra, note 47) revolutionary messianic pretenders of the early 1280s, the "hermits" of Worms and Luebeck and the "monarch" of Neuss, the two "hermits" expressly associated with the year 1284. Cf. also Southern, *Western Views*, 62–63, for the statement of William of Tripoli, writing in Acre circa 1273, that the Muslims expected the end of their faith "soon" (*i.e.*, in 1284?); Marjorie Reeves, *The Influence of Prophecy in the Later Middle Ages: A Study in Joachimism* (Oxford: Clarendon, 1969), 248 and note 3, 249 and notes 1–4, for the Joachite prophetess Guglielma of Milan circa 1277, whose disciples claimed that she was the Holy Spirit incarnate through whom Jews, Muslims, and all other infidels would be converted; Reeves, 52–53 and 53, note 1, for the Joachite prophet Asdente of Parma, who arose in 1282; Reeves, 313–314, for Alexander von Roes, who expected the second coming of Charlemagne circa 1281 as well as the revival of the Holy Roman Empire, the recovery of Jerusalem, and a new golden age circa 1288; Reeves, 59 and note 5, for the fact that when the Joachite messianic year 1260 passed without cosmic cataclysm, the Joachites revised their computations so that Joachim's 1260 became 1290.

For parallels from Jewish Messianism, Silver, *Messianic Speculation*, 87, for the precise year 1284 as a crucial one for the Spanish Jewish mystic Abraham Abulafia, and Scholem, *Major Trends in Jewish Mysticism*, 128–129, for Abulafia's close links with Christian mystics, probably in southern Italy/Sicily in the early 1280s; Silver, 90 and note 32, for the German Rabbi Meir of Rothenburg's expectation of the messianic redemption in 1286; Schloessinger, *Ritual of Eldad Ha-Dani*, 109, note 3, for the Iranian Jewish magician Jacob Ha-Nasi's expectation of the messianic redemption in 1276.

7. Southern, *Western Views*, 42 and note 10.

8. Southern, *Western Views*, 19–26; Basetti-Sani, *Per Un Dialogo*, 257–262; and his *L'Islam e Francesco d' Assisi*, 20–22.

9. Southern, *Western Views*, 24. The 3 1/2 "times" of the Book of Daniel, chapter 7, verse 25 = for the ninth-century Spanish martyrs' movement (*i.e.*, for Eulogius, infra) three periods of seventy years each and one half-period of thirty-five years. 70 + 70 + 70 + 35 = 245 years. 618 (the beginning of Islam; supra, note 3) + 245 = 863.

Southern is not quite correct here when he states that *Alvarus* expected the Second Coming in 863. More likely it was Eulogius who expected the Second Coming in 863, whereas Alvarus expected it in 870. Colbert, *Martyrs of Cordoba*, 96, note 15, and 288; Waltz, *Muslim World*, LX: 231, note 63. We would suggest that the agreements of Eulogius and Alvarus as well as their difference over the question of the apocalyptic significance of Islam can be explained as follows. Both Eulogius and Alvarus agreed that (1) the number of years assigned to the reign of Antichrist was 245 (3 1/2 multiplied by 70, in accordance with Daniel 7:25); (2) the reign of Antichrist = the reign of Islam; and (3) the reign of Islam began with Muhammad's *Hijrah* (exodus from Mecca to Medina; not his birth or death). But Eulogius and Alvarus differed over the date of the *Hijrah*. Eulogius, following the view which prevailed among the Christians of eighth- and ninth-century Spain (the view in the chronicles of 741 and 754 as well as the Leyre life of Muhammad), held that the *Hijrah* took place in 618. Supra, note 3. Alvarus, following his own unique view, held that the *Hijrah* took place in 625. Hence, for Eulogius the 245-year reign of Antichrist = Islam began with the *Hijrah* in 618 and ended in 863; whereas for Alvarus the same 245-year reign of Antichrist = Islam began with the *Hijrah* in 625 and ended in 870. What is more, Eulogius's year 863 *Anno Domini* in the Christian calendar = the year 250 *Anno Hegirae* in the Muslim calendar. By predicting the end of Islam for 863 A.D. = 250 A.H., Eulogius would have been predicting Islam's end after five *jubilees* of years (or five periods of 50 years each) in the Islamic calendar, a neatly divisible scheme of years and an auspicious one since the jubilee number (50) had important redemptive and messianic connotations in the Old Testament. We suggest that it was Eulogius's years, 618 and 863, rather than Alvarus's years, 625 and 870, that were more influential upon Pope Innocent III writing in 1213, for Eulogius was a saint and a former archbishop of Toledo, whereas Alvarus was neither a saint nor a cleric.

Eulogius's year of 863 as the year of the end of Islam coincides fairly closely with the assassination of the fanatical Caliph al-Mutawakkil (who persecuted Shiis, Christians, and Jews), poisoned in 861 by his own son Muntasir (Brockelmann, *History of the Islamic Peoples*, 133; Hitti, *History of the Arabs*, 467); with the Byzantine general Petronas's massive victory over an Arab army led by Emir Umar of Melitene in 863, during which the emir was slain (Ostrogorsky, *History of the Byzatine State*, 202 and note 1); with the mission of Saints Cyril and Methodius to Moravia and the beginning of the conversion of the Slavic peoples to Christianity in 863, which relieved some of the pressure on Byzantium from the north and allowed it a freer hand to expand against Islam in the south (Every, *Byzantine Patriarchate*, 112ff); and with the great Viking raid on Muslim Spain circa 859–862 (Johannes Brondsted, *The Vikings*, trans. K. Skov [Baltimore: Penguin, 1967], 59–60).

10. L. Vazquez de Parga, "Cronica Profetica," *Diccionario de Historia de Espanya* 1 (1952): 814; Diaz y Diaz, *Index Scriptorum Latinorum Medii Aevi Hispanorum*, I: 132, no. 522; Aguado-Bleye, *Manual*, I: 321; Colbert, *Martyrs of Cordoba*, 88, 92, 95–98; O'Callaghan, *History of Medieval Spain*, 113; *Chronicon Albeldense*, paras. 77–86, in Florez, *Espanya Sagrada*, XIII: 459–463. The unknown author of the *Cronica Prophetica* may have added 6 years to each of Eulogius's three periods of 70 years, to obtain three periods of 76 years each, and 3 years to Eulogius's half-period of 35 years, to obtain a half-period of 38 years. 76 + 76 + 76 + 38 = 266 years. 618 (the beginning of Islam) + 266 = 884.

The messianic expectations of the Christians of Spain circa 884 may have been encouraged by the Christian reconquest of southeastern Italy (Bari and Taranto) from the Arabs circa 870–880 (Hitti, *History of Arabs*, 605) and the temporary Byzantine reconquest and occupation of Cyprus for 7 years about this same time (Ostrogorsky, *History of the Byzantine State*, 211 and note 2); by the decisive victory of King Alfred the Great of Wessex over the Vikings at Edington in Wiltshire in 878 and the important victory of King Louis III of France over the Vikings at Saucourt in 881 (Brondsted,

Vikings, 50–51); and by the visit to Spain circa 884 of the Jewish messianic figure Eldad the Danite (supra, note 66 to chapter 5).

11. Cf. our article on the ninth-century Spanish martyrs' movement, *Muslim World*, LV: 333–339, especially 334 and notes 59–62, 335 and note 70, 336 and notes 71–73.

12. Diaz y Diaz, *Index*, I: 132, no. 521; Colbert, *Martyrs of Cordoba*, 88. Both list one twelfth-century MS of the *Cronica*.

13. Cohn, *Pursuit of the Millennium*, 75–76, 393, notes to pp. 75–76; H. von Grauert, "Meister Johann von Toledo," *Sitzungsberichte der Muenchener Akademie der Wissenschaften, Philosophisch-Historische Klasse* 42 (1901): 111–325; M. Gaster, "The Letter of Toledo," *Folk-Lore* 13 (1902): 115–134; Y. Baer, "Eine Juedische Messias Prophetie auf das Jahr 1186 und der Dritte Kreuzzug," *Monatsschrift fuer Geschichte und Wissenschaft des Judentums* 70 (1926): 113–122, 155–165; and his *Jews in Christian Spain*, I: 59; 66; 389, note 33; 391, note 47; Baron, *Social and Religious History*, IV: 302, note 45; V: 386, note 70; Basetti-Sani, *Per Un Dialogo*, 260; Emmerson, *Antichrist in the Middle Ages*, 54, 257, note 54; Nigg, *Das Ewige Reich*, 156. Abraham bar Hiyya (died circa 1136), the great Spanish Jewish intellectual, saw 1186 as a crucial year in the preparation for the messianic redemption and 1206 as the year of the beginning of the downfall of Islam. Silver, *Messianic Speculation*, 74.

14. Gaster, *Folk-Lore*, XIII: 115, and Cohn, *Pursuit of the Millennium*, 75, point out that the letter had been circulating in England from 1184. 1184 was exactly 300 years after 884. Perhaps the "Letter of Toledo" added 86 years to each of the *Cronica Prophetica's* three periods of 76 years, to obtain three periods of 162 years each, and 43 years to the *Cronica Prophetica's* half-period of 38 years, to obtain a half-period of 81 years. 162 + 162 + 162 + 81 = 567 years. 618 (the beginning of Islam) + 567 = 1185. If you have difficulty believing that medieval people made such messianic computations, Silver, *Messianic Speculations*, passim!

15. Gaster, *Folk-Lore*, XIII: 121–126. Perhaps these Toledan apocalypticists added 28 years to each of their three former periods of 162 years, to obtain three periods of 190 years each, and 14 years to their former half-period of 81 years, to obtain a half-period of 95 years. 190 + 190 + 190 + 95 = 665 years. 618 (the beginning of Islam) + 665 = 1283.

16. Nigg, *Das Ewige Reich*, 156, also suggests that the "Letter of Toledo" influenced Pope Innocent III but does not suggest the possible link between the pope and the letter. For the relationship between Innocent and Rodrigo circa 1213, J. Gorosterratzu, *Don Rodrigo Jimenez de Rada* (Pamplona: Bescansa, 1925), 414–418; Mann, *Lives of the Popes*, XII: 177–179; H. Tillmann, *Papst Innocenz III* (Bonn: Roehrscheid, 1954), 221; Demetrio Mansilla Reoyo, *La Documentacion Pontificia Hasta Inocencio III (965–1216)* (Rome: Instituto Espanyol de Estudios Eclesiasticos, 1955), index, *s.v.* Rodericus .. Archiep. Toletanus"; A. Huici-Miranda, *Historia Politica del Imperio Almohade* (Tetuan: Marroqui, 1957), II: 422–428; J. Gonyi Gaztambide, *Historia de la Bula de la Cruzada en Espanya* (Vitoria: Editorial del Seminario, 1958), 102–134; J. Gonzalez, *El Reino de Castilla en la Epoca de Alfonso VIII* (Madrid: Consejo Superior de Investigaciones Cientificas, Escuela de Estudios Medievales, 1960), index, *s.v.* "Inocencio III." Rodrigo became archbishop of Toledo in 1209, only about twenty-five years after apocalyptic circles in the same city had produced the "Letter of

Toledo." The archbishop was well informed about contemporary events and well read in the history of Spain and the Christian-Islamic struggle in the Iberian peninsula. Rodrigo's canon, Mark of Toledo, knew the writings of Eulogius and Alvarus, the leaders of the ninth-century Spanish martyrs' movement. D'Alverny and Vajda, *Al-Andalus*, XVI: 118 and note 1; our own article, *Muslim World*, LV: 336 and note 72; 337–338 and notes 86–87. It is highly possible that both Archbishop Rodrigo and Canon Mark of Toledo knew the "Letter of Toledo" and/or the Toledan apocalyptic circles which had produced the letter in the 1180s.

17. On the official correspondence of Pope Innocent III, C.R. Cheney,"The Letters of Pope Innocent III," *Bulletin of the John Rylands Library* 35 (1952): 23–43; F. Bock, "Studien zur den Originalregistern Innocenz' III," *Archivalische Zeitschrift* 51 (1955): 329–364; 54 (1958): 206–210; F. Kempf, "Zu den Originalregistern Innocenz' III: eine Kritische Auseinandersetzung mit F. Bock," *Quellen und Forschungen aus Italienischen Archiven und Bibliotheken* 36 (1956): 86–137; O. Hageneder, "Studien und Vorarbeiten zur Edition der Register Papst Innocenz' III: die Aeusseren Merkmale der Originalregister Innocenz' III," *Mitteilungen des Instituts fuer Oesterreichische Geschichtsforschung* 65 (1957): 296–339; and his "Quellenkritisches zu den Originalregistern Innozenz' III," ibid. 68 (1960): 128–139; A. Haidacher, "Beitraege zur Kenntnis der Verlorenen Registerbaende Innozenz' III: Die Jahrgaenge 3–4 und 17–19 der Hauptregisterreihe und die Urspruengliche Gestalt des Thronstreitregisters," *Roemische Historische Mitteilungen* 4 (1960–1961): 37–62; P. Herde, *Beitraege zum Paepstlichen Kanzlei- und Urkundwesen im 13. Jahrhundert* (2nd. ed.; Kallmeunz: Lassleben, 1967), index, *s.v.* "Innocenz III."

18. The secondary authorities who cite this passage (supra, note 1) do not seem to consider it an interpolation. Lerner, *Mediaeval Studies*, XLII, 476, note 19, argues against viewing it as an interpolation. Nor did Brundage seem to consider it an interpolation in personal conversation with us. Militating against the view that this passage is a later interpolation is the fact that it cites the New Testament Book of Revelation (Apocalypse of John), which is also cited very frequently in Innocent's unquestionably genuine prepapal work the *De Miseria Humanae Conditionis*. Infra, notes 37–39.

19. Tillmann, *Papst Innocenz III*, 256 = J.M. Powell, ed., *Innocent III: Vicar of Christ or Lord of the World* (Boston: Heath, 1963), 71: "No real decision could be made by the chancery without his [Pope Innocent III's] knowledge. He drew up his own letters, insofar as they were not purely formal, either completely or for the most part." How much the more so would this have been true of a great Crusade appeal, addressed to every part of Western Europe except one (Spain)! The list of Western European territories to which copies of the letter were sent between April 19 and 29, 1213, as given by Potthast, *Regesta*, I: 410, no. 4725, is as follows: Mainz, Magdeburg, Bremen, Cologne, Sardinia, Salzburg, Dalmatia, Trier, Ravenna, Poland, Milan, Genoa, Sweden, Ancona, Lund, Hungary, England, Prague, Bohemia, Tuscany, Norway, Ireland, Calabria, Scotland, and France. Presumably Spain was excluded because the pope knew that it was already deeply involved with its own continuing struggle against the Muslims (the aftermath of the Crusade of 1212, to which Innocent significantly contributed, culminating in the great victory over the Almohades at Las Navas). Roscher, *Papst Innocenz III*, 142 and note 11. Supra, notes 1 and 16. On the overwhelming im-

portance of the Crusading movement to Pope Innocent III circa 1213, supra, note 47 to chapter 4.

20. Silver, *Messianic Speculation*, 75. Admittedly, several earlier authorities did consider the passage wherein Maimonides predicts the return of prophecy for 1216 as an interpolation. A. Cohen, *The Teachings of Maimonides* (London: Routledge, 1927), 229–230, 331, note 19; D. Yellin and I. Abrahams, *Maimonides* (Philadelphia: Jewish Publication Society of America, 1944), 102, 225, note 36. Jacob I. Dienstag, ed., *Eschatology in Maimonidean Thought: Messianism, Resurrection and the World to Come* (New York: K'tav, 1983), 190, reprints Cohen's skepticism. However, more recent authorities defend the authenticity of the passage. S. Zeitlin, *Maimonides: A Biography* (2nd ed.; New York: Bloch, 1955), 51-52, 219, note 6-7; Baron, *Social and Religious History*, V: 164, 365, note 25. How far apart were Maimonides' 1216 and Innocent's 1218 as years of the beginning of the end? In 1211 about 300 leading Jews of France and England, some of whom had corresponded with Maimonides, departed from Jerusalem in expectation of the messianic coming. Graetz, *Geschichte*, VII: 11 = *History*, III: 505; Silver, *Messianic Speculation*, 76. Christian messianic hopes were also quite fervent at this time. A Christian prophet at Paris foresaw the end circa 1209–1214. Cohn, *Pursuit of the Millennium*, 65. The early followers of Amalric of Bene expected the millennium to occur shortly after 1210. Infra, note 24. The German Children's Crusade with significant apocalyptic overtones occurred in 1212 and could have influenced Pope Innocent III to some extent during the interview which the youthful leaders of this Crusade had with the pope in Rome. Runciman, *History of the Crusades*, III: 141; A. Waas, *Geschichte der Kreuzzuege* (Freiburg: Herder, 1956), I: 255; II: 71; N.P. Zacour, "The Children's Crusade," in Setton, *History of the Crusades*, II: 325–342. Jewish and Christian messianic speculations coincided in 1186 and 1284. Supra, notes 6 and 13. Could they also have coincided circa 1212 and 1218?

21. The messianism of Abraham bar Hiyya, a contemporary of Maimonides's grandfather and father in Spain, has links with that of the Toledan apocalypticists of the 1180s, who, we have suggested, may have influenced Pope Innocent III. Supra, notes 13–16.

22. For St. Francis' Portiuncula conversion experience, February 24, 1208, which revolved around Matthew 10:7, "The Kingdom of Heaven Is at Hand," J. Joergensen, *St. Francis of Assisi*, trans. T.O. Sloane (Garden City, New York: Doubleday/Image, 1955), 57–58; Englebert, *St. Francis of Assisi*, 84–86.

On St. Francis's eschatology, also Van der Vat, *Die Anfaenge der Franziskanermissionen*, 5, note 20; R.C. Petry, *Francis of Assisi: Apostle of Poverty* (Durham, North Carolina: Duke University Press, 1941), 86–102; Nigg, *Das Ewige Reich*, 175; K. Esser, "Homo Alterius Saeculi: Endzeitliche Heilswirklichkeit im Leben des Hl. Franz von Assisi," *Wissenschaft und Weisheit* 20 (1957): 180–197 = Esser, *Repair My House*, trans. M.D. Meilach (Chicago: Franciscan Herald Press, 1963), 15–45, 175–184.

For the possible influence of Joachim of Flora on St. Francis of Assisi, Paul Sabatier, *Life of St. Francis of Assisi*, trans. L.S. Houghton (New York: Scribner's, 1895), 46ff; Father Cuthbert, *Life of St. Francis of Assisi* (3rd ed.; London: Longmans, Green, 1960), 10–13; Englebert, *St. Francis of Assisi*, 111; E. Buonaiuti, *Gioacchino da Fiore: I Tempi, La Vita, Il Messagio* (Rome: Collezione Meridionale, 1931), v–x; F. Foberti, *Gioacchino da Fiore: Nuovi Studi Critici sulla Mistica e la Religione in Calabria* (Florence:

Sansoni, 1934), index, *s.v.* "Francesco di Assisi"; L. Tondelli, *Il Libro delle Figure dell'Abate Gioachino da Fiore* (2nd ed.; Turin: Societa Editrice Internazionale, 1953), I: 183ff, 256ff, 338ff; F. Russo, "Francescanesimo e Gioacchino da Fiore," *Archivio Storico per la Calabria e la Lucania* 7 (1937): 79-90; his "Gioachismo e Francescanesimo," *Miscellanea Francescana* 41 (1941): 61–73 = Delno C. West, ed., *Joachim of Fiore in Christian Thought: Essays on the Influence of the Calabrian Prophet* (New York: Burt Franklin, 1975), I: 129–141; Russo's "Spiritualita Gioachimita e Spiritualita Francescana," *Bollettino degli Istituti Comunali di Cultura di Pinerolo* 7 (1961): 3–12; and his *Gioacchino da Fiore e le Fondazioni Florensi in Calabria* (Naples: Fausto Fiorentino, 1958), index, *s.v.* "Francesco d'Assisi"; L. Salvatorelli, "Movimento Francescano e Gioachimismo: Francesco d'Assisi e il Francescanesimo nel Primo Secolo dell'Ordine," Comitato Internazionale de Scienze Storiche, *X Congresso Internazionale di Scienze Storiche (Roma, 4–11 Settembre, 1955): Relazioni* (Florence: Sansoni, 1955), III: 403-448; P. Ilarino da Milano, "L'Incentive Escatologico nel Riformismo dell'Ordine Francescano," in *L'Attesa dell'Eta Nuova nella Spiritualita della Fine del Medio Evo* (Todi: Accademia Tudertina, 1962), 283–337; H. Grundmann, *Studien ueber Joachim von Floris* (Leipzig and Berlin: Treubner, 1927), 188ff; C.H. Lyttle, "The Stigmata of St. Francis Considered in the Light of Possible Joachimite Influence upon Thomas of Celano," *American Society of Church History Papers* 4 (1914): 79–85; M.W. Bloomfield, "Joachim of Fiora," *Traditio* 13 (1957): 298 and note 217; Reeves, *Influence of Prophecy in the Later Middle Ages*, index, *s.v.* "Francis, St."; E.R. Daniel, *The Franciscan Concept of Mission in the High Middle Ages* (Lexington: University Press of Kentucky, 1975), 29ff.

Geoffrey of Auxerre, a friend of St. Bernard of Clairvaux, claimed that Joachim of Flora was a convert from Judaism. Hirsch-Reich, in Wilpert and Eckert, *Judentum im Mittelalter*, 239-243, rejects this idea. Baer, *Jews in Christian Spain*, I:438, note 25, and Reeves, *Influence of Prophecy in the Later Middle Ages*, 14-15 and notes 1-2, are both willing to keep an open mind on this question.

There is also a view that St. Francis of Assisi was of Jewish descent. Cf. G. Fortini, "Una Nuova Ipotesi sulle Origini della Famiglia di S. Francesco," *Analecta Tertii Ordinis Regularis Sancti Francisci* 13 (1976): 817-841. Ariel Toaff, *The Jews in Medieval Assisi, 1305-1487* (Florence: Olschki, 1979), v, 4 and note 2, is skeptical. Cohen, in his otherwise very thorough work, *Friars and the Jews*, inadvertently omits this issue. With Baer and Reeves regarding Joachim of Flora, an open mind on this question would be the most fruitful for further research. Indeed, St. Francis's Jewish descent might help explain his intense interest in the conversion of the Muslims—which was unique in its time and place; i.e., his mission to the Muslims would have arisen, consciously or subconsciously, out of the desire of Jews (and converts from Judaism—supra, note 56 to chapter 4) to refute the charge that they were in league with the Muslims.

The antipope Anacletus II (Peter Pierleone, circa 1090-1137) was of actual Jewish descent. S. Grayzel, "Anacletus II," *Ency. Judaica* 2 (1971): 916-917. His actual Jewish descent may be relevent to the question of the possible Jewish descent of Joachim and Francis.

23. Joergensen, *St. Francis*, 61, 190–191; Englebert, *St. Francis*, 180, 433, 438.

24. Ferdinand Schevill's one-sided view of Pope Innocent III prevails among many American medieval historians. Schevill, *Medieval and Renaissance Florence* (New York:

Harper and Row/Torchbooks and Academy Library, 1965), I: 95: "Like all the great medieval popes, practically without exception, far from falling under the type of mystic and dreamer, he [Pope Innocent III] was primarily an administrator, a jurist, and a statesman." Schevill neglects to mention that *before* Innocent studied law at Bologna he studied theology at Paris. Michele Maccarrone," Innocent III," *Dict. de Spiritualite* 7:2 (1971): 1768. Also, though Innocent wrote no treatises on law before becoming pope in 1198, he did write at least three religious treatises. Infra, note 25. Cf. also A. Fliche, "La Reforme de l'Eglise," in Fliche, ed., *Histoire de l'Eglise Depuis les Origines a Nos Jours* (Paris: Bloud and Gay, 1950), X: 167 = Powell, *Innocent III*, 36, who warned against the view that Pope Innocent III was merely "a narrow jurist." Cf. the similar warnings against this view by Hans Wolter as well as Father Cuthbert, infra, notes 25 and 36.

The best corrective of the Schevill view can be found in the writings of Michele Maccarrone. We refer to his *Chiesa e Stato nella Dottrina di Papa Innocenzo III* (Rome: Facultas Theologica Pontificii Athenaei Lateranensis, 1940); "Innocenzo III Prima del Pontificato," *Archivo della Regia Deputazione Romana de Storia Patria* 66 (1943): 59–134; *Vicarius Christi: Storia del Titolo Papale* (Rome: Facultas Theologica Pontificii Athenaei Lateranensis, 1952), 109–119; his edition of *Innocentius III: De Miseria Humanae Conditionis* (Lugano: Thesaurus Mundi, 1955); "Innocenzo III e la Famiglia di San Tommaso d'Aquino," *Rivista di Storia della Chiesa in Italia* 10 (1956): 165–192; "Il IV Concilio Lateranense," *Divinitas* 3 (1961): 270–298; "Riforma e Sviluppo della Vita Religiosa con Innocenzo III," *Rivista di Storia della Chiesa in Italia* 16 (1962): 29–72; "La Ricerca dell'Unione con la Chiesa Greca Sotto Innocenzo III," *Unitas: Rivista Internazionale* (Associazione Unitas, Roma) 19 (1964): 251–267; "Innocenzo III Teologo dell'Eucaristia," *Divinitas* 10 (1966): 362–412; "Orvieto e La Predicazione della Crociata," in Maccarrone's *Studi su Innocenzo III* (Padua: Antenore 1972), 3ff. In addition to this previously unpublished Orvieto essay, Maccarrone's *Studi* include revisions of three of his previously published articles on Pope Innocent III listed supra: "La Famiglia d'Aquino (1956), 167ff; "Riforma e Sviluppo" (1962), 223ff; and "Teologo dell'Eucarestia" (1966), 341ff.

On Maccarrone's life and work, *Repertoire des Medievistes Europeens* (1960), 146, no. 945; *Repertoire International des Medievistes* (1965), 390, no. 2007; ibid. (1971), 477, no. 2659; ibid. (1979), 466, no. 3188.

Cf. also four doctoral dissertations at the Pontificia Universita Lateranense listed in Maccarrone, *Dict. de Spiritualite*, VII: 2: 1773: B. Devlin, *The Concept of Poverty and Preaching in the Writings of Pope Innocent III* (1956); G. Scuppa, *I Sermoni di Innocenzo III* (1961); L. Monti, *Il "Commentarium in Septem Psalmos Poenitentiales" di Innocenzo III* (1961); and C. Petraccini, *L' Ordinario dell'Ufficio di Innocenzo III* (1962).

Cf. also the following additional works in what we would call the "Italian School of Innocentian Studies": A. Serafini, "I Precedenti Storici del Concilio Lateranense IV, ossia Innocenzo III e la Riforma Religiosa agli Inizi del Secolo XIII," *L'Arcadia* 1 (1917): 91–122; Salvatore Sibilia, *Innocenzo III (1198–1216)* (Rome: Edizioni Paoline, 1951); G. Martini, *Il Pontificato d'Innocenzo III* (Milan: Cooperativa Editoriale Universitaria Milanese, 1952); G. Barbero, *La Dottrina Eucaristica negli Scritti di Papa Innocenzo III* (Rome: Edizioni Paoline, 1953); Cosimo Damiano Fonseca, *Aspetti della Politica Anglo-Franco-Pontificia tra il XII ed il XIII Secolo* (Milan: C.E.L.U.C., 1968).

Among those who view Innocent III more as a theologian than a canon lawyer are K. Pennington, "Legal Education of Pope Innocent III," *Bulletin of the Institute of Medieval Canon Law* 4 (1974): 70-77; and his "Pope Innocent III's Views on Church and State: A Gloss to *Per Venerabilem*," in Pennington and R. Sommerville, eds., *Law, Church and Society: Essays in Honor of Stephan Kuttner* (Philadelphia: University of Pennsylvania Press, 1977), 49-67; and R. Lerner, *Mediaeval Studies*, XLII: 475-476.

During Innocent's student days in Paris, was he influenced by the millenarianism of Amalric of Bene and/or his circle? On Amalric and his followers, Cohn, *Pursuit of the Millennium*, 156-157, 401–402, notes to pp. 156–157; plus articles by F. Vernet, *Dict. de Spiritualite* 1 (1937): 422–425; E. Chiettini, *Encic. Catt.* 1 (1949): 967–968; L. Baur and E. Hammerschmidt, *Lexikon fuer Theologie und Kirche* 1 (1957): 415–416; M.A. Schmidt, *Die Religion in Geschichte und Gegenwart* 1 (1957): 302–303; B. Chudoba, *New Cath. Ency.* 1 (1967): 364–365. Amalric was interviewed by Innocent in Rome in 1204 and condemned posthumously by Innocent at the Fourth Lateran Council in 1215. The condemnation, however, does not preclude the possibility that at some earlier date (while Amalric was still alive) Innocent may have been more favorably inclined toward Amalric's millenarianism.

25. For brief summaries of these three important prepapal Innocentian treatises, A. Luchaire, *Innocent III* (Paris: Hachette, 1905), I: 7–12 = Powell, *Innocent III*, 7–8; Maccarrone, *Dict. de Spiritualite*, VII: 2: 1768–1771. Hans Wolter, "The Papacy at the Height of Its Power, 1198 to 1216," in Hubert Jedin and John Dolan, eds., *Handbook of Church History*, trans. A. Biggs (New York: Herder and Herder, 1970), IV: 138–139, note 6, holds that these three prepapal Innocentian treatises are more in accord with the Bernardine-Victorine mystical than with the Parisian dialectical tradition.

Maccarrone published the critical edition of Pope Innocent III's *De Miseria* in 1955 (supra, note 24). For an English summary of this treatise, Frank N. Magill, ed., *Masterpieces of Catholic Literature in Summary Form* (New York: Harper, 1965), 342–345. For an English translation, Donald R. Howard, ed., *Lothario Dei Segni (Pope Innocent III): On the Misery of the Human Condition—De Miseria Humanae Conditionis*, trans. M.M. Dietz (Indianapolis and New York: Bobbs-Merrill, 1969). For discussion of the *De Miseria*, Howard, "Hamlet and the Contempt of the World," *South Atlantic Quarterly* 58 (1959): 167–175; and his *The Three Temptations: Medieval Man in Search of the World* (Princeton: Princeton University Press, 1966), index, *s.v.* "Innocent III"; F.F. Reinlein, *Papst Innocenz der Dritte und Seine Schrift: De Contemptu Mundi* (Erlangen: Deichert, 1871); M. Florin, "Innocenz III. als Schriftsteller und als Papst," *Zeitschrift fuer Kirchengeschichte* 45 (1926): 344–358; Antonio Viscardi, *Saggio sulla Letteratura Religiosa del Medio Evo Romanzo* (Padua: CEDAM, 1932), 63–76; A. Nagy, *De Tractatu de Miseria Humanae Conditionis Innocentii III* (Budapest, 1943); W. Will, "Innocenz III. und sein Werk 'Ueber das Elend des Menschlichen Daseins'," in J. Koch, ed., *Humanismus, Mystik und Kunst in der Welt des Mittelalters* (Leiden: Brill, 1953), 125–136; M. di Pinto, "Il *De Miseria Conditionis Humanae* di Innocenzo III," in *Studi Medievali in Onore di A. de Stefano* (Palermo: Societa Siciliana per la Storia Patria, 1956), 177–201; Robert Bultot, "Mepris du Monde, Misere et Dignite de l'Homme dans la Pensee d'Innocent III," *Cahiers de Civilisation Medievale* 4 (1961): 441–456; Robert E. Lewis, "Chaucer's Artistic Use of Pope Innocent III's *De Miseria Humanae Conditionis* in the 'Man of Law's' Prologue and Tale," *Publications of the Modern Language Associa-*

tion 81 (1966): 485-492; and his "Glosses to the 'Man of Law's' Tale from Pope Innocent III's *De Miseria Humanae Conditionis*," *Studies in Philology* 64 (1967): 1-16.

For an English summary of Pope Innocent III's *De Sacro Altaris Mysterio*, Magill, *Masterpieces of Catholic Literature*, 345-348. Cf. also David F. Wright, "A Medieval Commentary on the Mass: *Particulae* 2-3 and 5-6 of the *De Missarium Mysteriis* (circa 1195) of Cardinal Lothar of Segni (Pope Innocent III)," *Dissertation Abstracts International* A 38:6 (1977): 3571-3572.

On Innocent's *De Quadripartita Specie Nuptiarum*, M. Wilks, "Chaucer and the Mystical Marriage in Medieval Political Thought," *Bulletin of the John Rylands Library* 44 (1961): 489-530; Connie M. Munk, "A Study of Pope Innocent III's Treatise: *De Quadripartita Specie Nuptiarum*," *Dissertation Abstracts International* A 37 (1976): 509-510.

26. Luchaire, *Innocent III*, I: 32-33 = Powell, *Innocent III*, 15.

27. Pope Innocent III's religious writings (both before and after becoming pope in 1198) can all be found in *MPL*, CCXVII. On these writings in general, Tillmann, *Papst Innocenz III*, 247ff, 251ff; Sibilia, *Innocenzo III*, 365-379; the four dissertations by Devlin, Scuppa, Monti, and Petraccini and the book by Barbero listed supra, note 24; the article by Florin listed supra, note 25. Cf. also James M. Powell, "*Pastor Bonus*: Some Evidence of Honorius III's Use of the Sermons of Pope Innocent III," *Speculum* 52 (1977): 522-537. At p. 536, n.59, Powell mistakenly assumes that Pope Innocent III was reluctant to recognize the new Franciscan movement. Langmuir, in *Gli Ebrei nell 'Alto Medioevo*, 365, realizes that there was no such reluctance on Innocent III's part.

28. Cohn, *Pursuit of the Millennium*, 76; plus Mann, *Lives of the Popes*, XI: 235-236, 236, note 1; M.R. Gutsch, "A Twelfth Century Preacher—Fulk of Neuilly," in L.J. Paetow, ed., *The Crusades and Other Historical Essays Presented to Dana C. Munro* (New York: Crofts, 1928), 200-204; Runciman, *History of the Crusades*, III: 109; E.H. McNeal, "The Fourth Crusade," in Setton, *History of the Crusades*, II: 157-158, 158, note 15; Roscher, *Papst Innocenz III*, 65ff, 78. There is direct evidence that Pope Urban II commissioned Robert of Arbrissel to preach the First Crusade, but none that he commissioned Peter the Hermit to do the same. Runciman, I: 113-115.

29. Sabatier, *Life of St. Francis*, 75-76, 88-89; Joergensen, *St. Francis*, 72-76, 84-85; Culthbert, *Life of St. Francis*, 90-108; Englebert, *St. Francis*, 100-116; John Moorman, *History of the Franciscan Order from Its Origins to the Year 1517* (Oxford: Clarendon 1968), 10-19.

30. On Joachim of Flora's vision of a new order of monks, Cohn, *Pursuit of the Millennium*, 102; E.R. Daniel, "Apocalyptic Conversion: The Joachite Alternative to the Crusades," *Traditio* 25 (1969): 137-139; Reeves, *Influence of Prophecy in the Later Middle Ages*, 135ff; infra, note 54. On the millenarian ingredient in the early Franciscan movement, supra, note 22.

31. Sabatier, *Life of St. Francis*, 99-101; Joergensen, *St. Francis*, 87; Cuthbert, *Life of St. Francis*, 100; Englebert, *St. Francis*, 115; Moorman, *History of the Franciscan Order*, 19; Maccarrone, *Rivista di Storia della Chiesa in Italia*, XVI: 56-59. St. Francis himself may not really have wanted *written* approval for his plans. He may have been quite satisfied with oral approval. Cuthbert, 288-289.

32. Sabatier, *Life of St. Francis*, 161; and his "Le Privilege de la Pauvrete," *Revue*

d'Histoire Franciscaine 1 (1924): 1–54; Joergensen, *St. Francis*, 116–117; Cuthbert, *Life of St. Francis*, 171; Englebert, *St. Francis*, 172; Moorman, *History of the Franciscan Order*, 35, 205; Francesco Salvatore Attal, *San Francesco d'Assisi* (2nd ed.; Padua: Messaggero di S. Antonio, Basilica del Santo, 1947), 211; Arnaldo Fortini, *Nova Vita di San Francesco* (2nd ed.; Assisi: Edizioni Assisi, n.d. [1959 and thereafter]), I:1: 447ff; L. Elliott-Binns, *Innocent III* (London: Methuen, 1931), 190; Tillmann, *Papst Innocenz III*, 183; Maccarrone, *Rivista di Storia della Chiesa in Italia*, XVI: 71, note 90.

33. Sabatier, *Life of St. Francis*, 199–200; Joergensen, *St. Francis*, 142–143; Cuthbert, *Life of St. Francis*, 209–210; Englebert, *St. Francis*, 196; Moorman, *History of the Franciscan Order*, 29–30; Mann, *Lives of the Popes*, XII: 280–284; Tillmann, *Papst Innocenz III*, 183–184; Maccarrone, *Rivista di Storia della Chiesa in Italia*, XVI: 59–72.

34. Sabatier, *Life of St. Francis*, 199–200; Joergensen, *St. Francis*, 160–161; Cuthbert, *Life of St. Francis*, 209, 216–217; Englebert, *St. Francis*, 196; Moorman, *History of the Franciscan Order*, 29; A. Matanic, "Papa Innocenzo III di Fronte a San Domenico e San Francesco," *Antonianum* 35 (1960): 508–527; B. Jarrett, *Life of St. Dominic* (Garden City, New York: Doubleday/Image, 1964), 60–65; M.H. Vicaire, "St. Dominic and the Pope in 1215," appendix 5 of Pierre Mandonnet, *St. Dominic and His Work*, trans. M.B. Larkin (St. Louis and London: Herder, 1948), 422–446; Mann, *Lives of the Popes*, XII: 284–285; Tillmann, *Papst Innocenz III*, 183–185.

35. For the influence of St. Francis on St. Dominic, Sabatier, *Life of St. Francis*, 199–200, 215ff; Joergensen, *St. Francis*, 133, 160–161, 165–166; Cuthbert, *Life of St. Francis*, 213–222; Englebert, *St. Francis*, 56, 111, 196, 198–214; Moorman, *History of the Franciscan Order*, 29, 295–296. Cf. also M. Faloci Pulignani, "San Francesco e San Domenico," *Miscellanea Francescana* 9 (1902): 13–15; Hermann Fischer, *Der Hl. Franz von Assisi Waehrend der Jahre 1219–1221* (Freiburg, Switzerland: Gschwend, 1907), 83–108; Berthold Altaner, "Die 'Beziehungen des Hl. Dominikus zum Hl. Franz von Assisi," *Franziskanische Studien* 9 (1922): 1–28; Luis de Sarasola, *San Francisco de Asis* (1st ed.; Madrid: Espasa-Calpe, 1929), cv–cvii; the Matanic article cited supra, note 34; William A. Hinnebusch, "Poverty in the Order of Preachers," *Catholic Historical Review* 45 (1960): 450–452; Vicaire, *St. Dominic and His Times*, trans. K. Pond (New York: McGraw-Hill, 1964), index, *s.v.* "Francis, St."

36. Cuthbert, *Life of St. Francis*, 93–94, 107–108, 205–206, 212, note 1, calls Pope Innocent III "a deeply religious man," whose "sermons breathe a spirit of burning piety," a person "in whom the mysticism of religion blended curiously with the statemanship of the world"; who had "intense sympathy with the penitential spirit which gave rise to the penitent fraternities of the time" like the early Franciscans.

Cf. the work of Maccarrone, his disciples, and the Italian school, as well as of Pennington, supra, note 24.

37. Maccarrone, *De Miseria*, 112. By contrast, Innocent cited the Gospel of Luke only twenty times. Maccarrone, 110.

38. Maccarrone, *De Miseria*, 78, line 17. Another reference to the Second Coming of Christ, in this case described as being preceded by the conversion of the Jews (who, however, were generally equated with the Muslims) is found in Innocent's *Commentarium in Septem Psalmos Poenitentiales*, 5 (on Psalm 101), MPL, CCXVII, 1096–1097. L. Lucas, "Innocent III et les Juifs," *Revue des Etudes Juives* 35 (1897): 250 and note 6; and his "Judentaufen und Judaismus zur Zeit des Papstes Innocenz III," in *Beitraege*

zur Geschichte der Deutschen Juden: Festshrift zum Seibzigsten Geburtstage Martin Philipp-sons (Leipzig: Fock, 1916), 25.

For a similar reference in Joachim of Flora, Cohen, *Friars and the Jews*, 247 and note 11.

Cf. also supra, note 1; infra, note 54.

39. Maccarrone, *De Miseria*, 91–98.

40. Mansi, *Sacrorum Conciliorum Nova et Amplissima Collectio*, XXII: 986, lines 29–32; C.J. Hefele and H. Leclercq, *Histoire des Conciles* (Paris: Letouzey et Ane, 1913), V:2: 1329, lines 5–7; Mann, *Lives of the Popes*, XII: 297–298, note 3; Reeves, *Influence of Prophecy in the Later Middle Ages*, 28–36, especially 32; for Innocent and Amalric, supra, note 24.

41. Pope Innocent III and the Fourth Lateran Council condemned Joachim of Flora's treatise on the Trinity. However, the papacy and the church as a whole have never condemned any of Joachim's other writings (especially his apocalyptic writings). Rather, they have expressly declared that Joachim was a *virum catholicum* and have showed so much respect for the Florensian Order which he founded that in 1346 an attempt was made to open canonization proceedings on Joachim's behalf. Tillmann, *Papst Innocenz III*, 203 and note 92; Maccarrone, *Divinitas*, III: 287–288; Bloomfield, *Traditio*, XIII: 256–257; Reeves, *Influence of Prophecy in the Later Middle Ages*, 28-36, 126-132; Lerner, *Mediaeval Studies*, XLII: 474-476.

42. Infra, notes 51 and 54.

43. Cf. Reeves, *Influence of Prophecy in the Later Middle Ages*, 28–29 and notes 1–3, for the facts that Joachim had been encouraged to write by three popes, Lucius III, Urban III, and Clement III (1181–1191), and had been especially befriended by Pope Celestine III (1191–1198). Assuredly, Pope Innocent III could not have escaped being influenced by the positive attitudes toward Joachim of his four papal predecessors, especially Clement III, Innocent III's own uncle. Cohn, *Pursuit of the Millennium*, 101, speaks of the papacy as having "sponsored" Joachim, though without realizing that by so doing it was undermining the entire foundation of organized Christianity. If, however, Pope Innocent III did support Joachim's apocalyptic theology of history, he would have done so knowing full well what he was and was not undermining. Perhaps Innocent would have been willing to sacrifice "organized" Christianity for what he considered even more important, *i.e.*, the true Gospel message, including its apocalyptic emphasis, if he was the deeply religious Christian we think he was. Cf. also infra, notes 44–45, especially note 45, and H. Grundmann, "Joachim von Fiore," *Die Religion in Geschichte und Gegenwart* 3 (1959): 799.

44. J. Ratzinger, "Joachim von Fiore," *Lexikon fuer Theologie und Kirche* 5 (1957): 975; Bloomfield, *Traditio*, XIII: 266–267; B.D. Dupuy, "Joachim, de Flore," *Catholicisme: Hier, Aujourd'hui, Demain* 6 (1965): 884–885; Reeves, *Influence of Prophecy in the Later Middle Ages*, 139–140.

45. Tillmann, *Papst Innocenz III*, 240 = Powell, *Innocent III*, 70, referring to Innocent's favorable reception of Gerald of Wales's *Gemma Ecclesiastica* which attacked church bureaucracy. On Innocent the church reformer, Serafini, *L'Arcadia*, I: 91–122; Fliche, "La Reforme de l'Eglise," in Fliche, *Histoire de l'Eglise*, X: 146ff = in part Powell, *Innocent III*, 29ff; C.E. Smith, *Innocent III, Church Defender* (Baton Rouge: Louisiana State University Press, 1951); Tillmann, *Papst Innocenz III*, 152–185; Mac-

carrone, "Riforma e Sviluppo etc.," *Rivista di Storia della Chiesa in Italia*, XVI: 29–72 = his *Studi su Innocenzo III*, 223ff. For Innocent's well-known summation of the two chief aims of his pontificate as Crusade and church reform, supra note 47 to chapter 4.

46. Pope Gregory IX's letter of February 15, 1233, *Caelestis Altitudo*, to five Islamic rulers (Damascus, Egypt, Aleppo, Iconium and Morocco), Potthast, *Regesta*, I: 779, no. 9093; L. Wadding, *Annales Minorum* (Quaracchi: College of St. Bonaventure, 1931), II: 358, line 13; *Monumenta Germaniae Historica . . . Epistolae Saeculi XIII*, I: 412, line 40. Cf. also Van der Vat, *Anfaenge*, 137, note 4; 138, note 10; 187-188; 188, note 10; R. Streit and J. Dindinger, *Bibliotheca Missionum* (Freiburg: Herder, 1951), XV: 43, nos. 82–83. Van der Vat, an extremely sensitive critic of primary sources, does not question the authenticity or the sincerity of Pope Gregory IX's millenarianism, though he is surprised by it and does not know its origin. Cf. also Pope Gregory IX's two letters of February 15, 1235, *Cum Hora Undecima* (Potthast, *Regesta* I: 838, nos. 9845–9846; Streit-Dindinger, *Bibliotheca Missionum*, XV: 46, nos. 92–93) and one letter of June 11, 1239, with the same title (Potthast, I: 911, no. 10763; Streit-Dindinger, XV: 49–50, no. 105). The question of Pope Gregory IX's millenarianism deserves further study. Perhaps he was influenced by a revised version of the "Letter of Toledo" that circulated in Western Europe circa 1230, for which, Gaster, *Folk-Lore*, XIII: 123–125, and Palmer Throop, *Criticism of the Crusade* (Amsterdam: Swets and Zeitlinger, 1940), 134–135.

47. Cohn, *Pursuit of the Millenium*, 104, 398, note to p. 104; Reeves, *Influence of Prophecy in the Later Middles Ages*, 309–310.

48. T.L. Kington-Oliphant, *History of Frederick the Second, Emperor of the Romans* (Cambridge and London: Macmillan, 1862), I: 130ff; Friedrich Baethgen, *Die Regentschaft Papst Innocenz III im Koenigreich Sizilien* (Heidelberg: Winter, 1914); Mann, *Lives of the Popes*, XI: 219–220; XII: 261; E. Kantorowicz, *Frederick the Second 1194–1250*, trans. E.O. Lorimer (London: Constable, 1931), 55–56; Tillmann, *Papst Innocenz III*, 139ff; Thomas C. Van Cleve, *Emperor Frederick II of Hohenstaufen: Immutator Mundi* (Oxford: Clarendon, 1972), index, *s.v.* "Innocent III, Pope."

49. Kington-Oliphant, *Frederick the Second*, I: 155; Mann, *Lives of the Popes*, XI: 219, 271; Kantorowicz, *Frederick the Second*, 73–74; Tillmann, *Papst Innocenz III*, 232 and note 57; Roscher, *Papst Innocenz III*, index, *s.v.* "Friedrich II"; Runciman, *History of the Crusades*, III: 163–164; Van Cleve, "The Crusade of Frederick II," in Setton, *History of Crusades*, II: 430–431. Emperor Frederick II was also among the first to adopt a Jewish badge. Infra, note 59, item no. 5.

50. It is possible that Innocent did not influence Gregory and Frederick but rather that all three drew independent but common millenial inspiration from Joachim of Flora. However, Joachim could not have been the *sole* millenial influence on Pope Innocent III (supra, notes 2–16) because (1) to our knowledge, the number 666 was not of major importance to Joachim (Reeves, *Influence of Prophecy in the Later Middle Ages*, index, s.v. "Number Patterns"), whereas it was of crucial importance to Innocent; and (2) Innocent foresaw the end as coming in the 1280s, whereas Joachim (and/or disciples) foresaw it as coming circa 1260 (Bloomfield, *Traditio*, XIII: 264–265; Daniel, ibid., XXV: 137–138, 140; Reeves, *Influence of Prophecy in the Later Middle*

Ages, 48), after 1260 revised as circa 1290 (supra, note 6). Cf. Lerner, *Mediaeval Studies*, XLII: 476 and note 20.

51. In Joachim of Flora's apocalyptic theology of history, mankind most certainly does play a role in bringing about the end. During a 60-year period, circa 1200–1260, the new order of monks will prepare the way for the age of the Holy Spirit. Cohn, *Pursuit of the Millennium*, 102; infra, note 54. We have argued in our article, *Muslim World*, LV: 329ff, that the ninth-century Spanish martys' movement also held that mankind had a crucial role to play in bringing about the end. In his Crusade appeal of April 19, 1213 (Potthast, *Regesta*, I: 410, no. 4725; MPL, CCXVI: 817:B; supra, note 1), Innocent "declared that he was crying out as did Christ on the Cross and that God could easily liberate the Holy Land from the enemies of Christianity, *but He imposed this task on the faithful* [italics ours] so that their devotion could be proved as gold in the furnace." Smith, *Innocent III*, 182–183.

52. Potthast, *Regesta*, I: 409, no. 4719; MPL, CCXVI: 831–832; R. Roehricht, "Zur Korrespondenz der Paepste mit den Sultanen und Mongolenchanen des Morgenlandes im Zeitalter der Kreuzzuege," *Theologische Studien und Kritiken* 64 (1981): 361–362; Runciman, *History of the Crusades*, III: 145; Daniel, *Islam and the West*, 113, 348, note 2, 349, note 14; Basetti-Sani, *Per Un Dialogo*, 255–256; and his *L'Islam e Francesco d'Assisi*, 17–20, 84; Roscher, *Papst Innocenz III*, 286–287 and note 86.

53. Daniel, *Islam and the West*, 113–114, 349, note 14. D'Alverny had indicated her intention of publishing an edition of the *Liber Nicholay* from the Paris, Bibliotheque Nationale, Latin MS 14503, ff. 352–354. To our knowledge, her edition has not yet appeared. Kritzeck, *Peter the Venerable and Islam*, 124, note 47, speaks of two Vatican MSS of the same work. On the *Liber Nicholay*, d'Alverny, *AHDLMA*, XVI: 111, note 1; plus H. Prutz, *Kulturgeschichte der Kreuzzuege* (Hildesheim: Olms, 1964), 517; D'Ancona, *Giornale Storico della Letteratura Italiana*, XIII: 248, note 4; A. Mancini, "Per lo Studio della Leggenda di Maometto in Occidente," *Rendiconti della Regia Accademia Nazionale dei Lincei, Classe di Scienze Morali, Storiche e Filologiche*, 6th series, 10 (1934): 327–328, note 4; Daniel, *Islam and the West*, 83, 233, 374, note 63, 397, 408.

For parallels to the relatively tolerant attitude toward Islam of Pope Innocent III and the *Liber Nicholay*, cf. Innocent's contemporary and critic Walther von der Vogelweide, in C. von Kraus, *Die Gedichte Walthers von der Volgelweide* (12th ed.; Berlin: de Gruyter, 1962), 28, no. 22, line 16; and W.A. Phillips, *Selected Poems of Walther von der Volgelweide, The Minnesinger* (London: Smith, Elder, 1896), 81. Cf. also an anonymous late twelfth-century Spanish Christian treatise discussed by Gilson, *History of Christian Philosophy in the Middle Ages*, 243, 654, note 10, relying upon d'Alverny, "Les Peregrinations de l'Ame dans l'Autre Monde d'apres un Anonyme de la Fin du XIIe Siecle," *AHDLMA* 13 (1940-1942): 239–299. Cf. also the view of the Benedictine Uthred of Boldon at Oxford in the 1360s discussed by Southern, *Western Views of Islam in the Middle Ages*, 76 and note 18, relying upon M.D. Knowles, "The Censured Opinions of Uthred of Boldon," *Proceedings of the British Academy* 38 (1953): 315. Cf. also the view which Columbus expressed in a letter to Ferdinand and Isabella as discussed in Friedrich Heer, *God's First Love: Christians and Jews over 2000 Years*, trans. G. Skelton (New York: Weybright and Talley, 1970), 105.

Cf. also the story of "the Three Rings" (one version of which appears in Boccaccio's *The Decameron*, First Day, Novel III), a major document in the history of religious tolerance, as discussed in detail by Mario Penna, *Parabola dei Tre Anelli e la Tolleranza nel Medio Evo* (Turin: Gheroni, 1952). Cf. also the reverse of this story, the story of "the Three Imposters," as discussed by Louis Massignon, in Y. Moubarac, ed., *Louis Massignon: Opera Minora* (Paris: Presses Universitaires de France, 1969), I: 82–85; Jacob Presser, *Das Buch 'De Tribus Impostoribus'* (Amsterdam: H. J. Paris, 1926); M. Esposito, "Una Manifestazione d'Incredulita Religiosa nel Medioevo," *Archivio Storico Italiano*, 7th series, 16 (1931): 3–48; Gilson, *History of Christian Philosophy in the Middle Ages*, 523–524, 797, note 64; Southern, *Western Views of Islam in the Middle Ages*, 75; Baron, *Social and Religious History*, V: 103–104, 336–337, note 29.

For the tolerant twelfth-century Jewish attitudes toward Christianity and Islam of Maimonides and Judah Ha-Levi, infra, note 3 to chapter 9.

54. In Joachim of Flora's apocalyptic theology of history, the new order of monks will help bring about the end by preaching the true Gospel throughout the world, one of the results of which will be the conversion of the Muslims and the Jews. Cohn, *Pursuit of the Millennium*, 102; G. Bondati, *Gioachinismo e Francescanesimo nel Dugento* (Santa Maria degli Angeli: Porziuncola, 1924), 24ff; Van der Vat, *Anfaenge*, 36 and note 41; Bloomfield, *Traditio*, XIII: 264; and his "Joachim," *Ency. Brittanica* 13 (1964): 71; Daniel, *Traditio*, XXV: 137–139, especially 138 and notes 56–57; Reeves, *Influence of Prophecy in the Later Middle Ages*, 140–141.

Roscher, *Papst Innocenz III*, 290 and note 96, calls attention to Pope Innocent III's apocalyptic letter of January 21, 1205, in which the pope subscribes to the view (shared with Joachim of Flora, supra, this note; and with the "Letter of Toledo," supra, note 13) that the Second Coming of Christ would be preceded by the conversion of the Muslims and Jews. Supra, notes 1 and 38.

55. Streit-Dindinger, *Bibliotheca Missionum*, XV: 9, no. 9; Mann, *Lives of the Popes*, XI: 232; Grayzel, *Church and the Jews*, 88–91, 97 and bottom note 1, 110–113, 119, 309; Fliche, "La Reforme de l'Eglise," in Fliche, *Histoire de l'Eglise*, X: 170 and note 3; 171 and note 4 = Powell, *Innocent III*, 38–39; Vicaire, in Mandonnet, *St. Dominic*, 411; Runciman, *History of the Crusades*, III: 141; Waas, *Geschichte der Kreuzzuege*, I: 255; II: 71, 238 and note 255; Roscher, *Papst Innocenz III*, 174, 285–287, 290; Joergensen, *St. Francis*, 133; H. Felder, *The Ideals of St. Francis of Assisi*, trans. B. Bittle (New York: Benziger, 1925), 335; Van der Vat, *Anfaenge*, 3, note 11; 39–40; 203–204; M. Roncaglia, *St. Francis of Assisi and the Middle East*, trans. S. Janto (3rd ed.; Cairo: Franciscan Center of Oriental Studies, 1957), 19ff, 26ff; Basetti-Sani, *L'Islam e Francesco d'Assisi*, 1-113 and index, *s.v.* "Innocenzo III, Papa."

Roscher holds that Pope Innocent III had both a theoretical and a practical interest in the conversion of the Muslims of Spain but only a theoretical interest in the conversion of the Muslims of the Middle East. However, Roscher seems to have been unaware of the fact that Pope Innocent III approved of St. Francis of Assisi's desire to go as a missionary to the Muslims of the Middle East in 1212. Roscher, index, *s.v.* "Franz von Assisi." Infra, note 65.

56. The Islamic mind makes relatively little provision for the possibility that large numbers of Muslims may have to live under non-Muslim rule. This may be true in part because fewer Muslims have had to live under Christian or Hindu rule than

Christians or Hindus under Islamic rule. Gustave E. von Grunebaum, *Medieval Islam: A Study in Cultural Orientation* (2nd ed.; Chicago: University of Chicago Press/ Phoenix Books, 1962), 1–63; Cagigas, *Los Mudejares* (Madrid: Instituto de Estudios Africanos, 1948), I: 65ff. The authors of the eleventh- and twelfth-century French *chansons de geste* clearly believed that by defeating the Muslims in battle the Christians could shake their faith in Islam to its very foundations and induce them to accept baptism voluntarily. A.J. Dickman, *Le Role du Surnaturel dans les Chansons de Geste* (Paris: Champion, 1926), 188ff; M. Skidmore, *Moral Traits of Christian and Saracen as Portrayed by the Chansons de Geste* (Colorado Springs: Colorado College, 1935); U.T. Holmes, *History of Old French Literature* (2nd ed.; New York: Russell and Russell, 1962), excellent short summaries of the plots of the *chansons*; W.W. Comfort, "The Literary Role of the Saracens in the French Epic," *Publications of the Modern Language Association* 55 (1940): 628–659; C.M. Jones, "The Conventional Saracen of the Songs of Geste," *Speculum* 17 (1942): 201–225; J. Crossland, *Old French Epic* (Oxford: Blackwell 1951), 138–166.

57. E. Sachau, *Muhammedanisches Recht nach Schafiitischer Lehre* (Stuttgart: Spemann, 1897), 843–846; Th. W. Juynboll, "Apostasy (Muhammadan)," *Hastings's Ency. of Religion and Ethics* 1 (1926): 625–626; S.M. Zwemer, *The Law of Apostasy from Islam* (London: Marshall, 1924); W. Heffening, *Das Islamische Fremdenrecht bis zu den Islamisch-Fraenkischen Stattsvertraegen: eine Rechtshistorische Studie zum Fiqh* (Hannover: Lafaire, 1925), 32; and his "Murtadd," *Ency. of Islam* 3 (1926): 736–738; D. Santillana, *Istituzioni di Diritto Musulmano Malichita con Riguardo anche al Sistema Sciafiita* (Rome: Instituto per l'Oriente, 1926), 118, 167–170; A.S. Tritton, *The Caliphs and Their Non-Muslim Subjects* (London: Oxford University Press, 1930), 5ff, 178ff; Laurence E. Browne, *Eclipse of Christianity in Asia* (Cambridge: Cambridge University Press, 1933), 63; Van der Vat, *Anfaenge*, 7 and note 27; Roncaglia, *St. Francis of Assisi and the Middle East*, 16 and note 19; Runciman, *History of the Crusades*, I:22; Baron, *Social and Religious History*, III: 129, 132–133, 293, note 10, 295, note 15; Goitein, *Mediterranean Society*, II: 303–311; A. Fattal, *Le Statut Legal des Non-Musulmans en Pays d'Islam* (Beirut: Imprimerie Catholique, 1958), 163–168; S.A. Rahman, *Punishment of Apostasy in Islam* (Lahore: Institute of Islamic Culture, 1972); Bat Ye'or, *Le Dhimmi: Profil de l'Opprime en Orient et en Afrique du Nord depuis la Conquete Arabe* (Paris: Anthropos, 1980).

58. Cf. Van Cleve, in Setton, *History of the Crusades*, II: 382–383, for the following decrees of the Fourth Lateran Council (November 1215) relative to the new Crusade. The clergy were to donate one-twentieth of their income to the support of the Crusade, and there were to be no tournaments *for three years*. Christian maritime trade with the Muslims and a general intra-Christian peace was to prevail *for four years*. Apparently Pope Innocent III and/or the Fourth Lateran Council believed that the great (Fifth) Crusade would take no more than three to four years (from November 1215) to succeed. Supra, note 4.

59. Precisely what kind of distinction in clothing Pope Innocent III had in mind is a problem. Canon 68 of the Fourth Lateran Council is not specific. It merely speaks of a distinction in the *qualitas* of the *habitus*. Mansi, *Amplissima Collectio*, XXII: 1055, lines 41–42; Hefele-Leclercq, *Histoire des Conciles*, V:2: 1387, line 6; Grayzel, *Church and the Jews*, 68, 308; Synan, *Popes and the Jews in the Middle Ages*, 233. Innocent's

letter of 1215–1216 to the archbishops and bishops of France (Potthast, *Regesta*, I: 459, no. 5302; *MPL*, CCXVI: 994; Grayzel, 140–141) speaks of "*portare habitus per quem inter Christianos decerni possint.*" These references could mean merely that Jews and Muslims were to wear only old and worn, cheap or soiled clothing. Cf. Canon 68's dislike of Jews dressing too ornately (*ornatius*) during Easter week. Mansi, XXII: 1055, line 48; Hefele-Lerclercq, V:2: 1387, line 11; Grayzel, 308; Synan, 233. Cf. also Grayzel, 62 and note 102; Kisch, *Historia Judaica*, IV: 112. However, if the Islamic example was crucial here (infra, note 60) and Innocent was imitating the practice of the contemporary Almohade Caliph an-Nasir, all Innocent would have had in mind was that the outer garment and the headgear of the Jews and Muslims should be distinquished by a special color (an-Nasir used yellow; cf. also infra, item no. 9) which Christians would henceforth avoid.

However, militating in favor of the view that the distinction in clothing Pope Innocent III had in mind was a special badge are the following considerations (which are by no means conclusive).

(1) In a crucial letter of January 17,1208, to the count of Nevers (Potthast, *Regesta*, I: 280, no. 3274; *MPL*, CCXV: 1291:C; Grayzel, 126–127; Synan, 96, 224, 226) Innocent equates Cain with the Jews and speaks of God's setting a *signum* upon Cain. This word *signum*, "sign," was later used in referring to the Jewish badge. Infra, item no. 6 and note 72. However, perhaps interpreting *signum* to mean "badge" here may be reading too much into the word in view of Innocent's love of analogy and Maccarrone's warning against interpreting Innocent's rhetorical language too literally. Maccarrone's *Chiesa e Stato nella Dottrina di Innocenzo III*, 26–31, 37–42 = in part Powell, *Innocent III*, 43–46 (cf. also Powell, x–xi, 29).

(2) According to the *Chronicon Rotomagense* (*i.e.*, of Rouen), *ad annum* 1215, the Fourth Lateran Council "*Judaeis indixit signum circulare* (infra, item no. 7) *in pectoribus bajulare ut inter ipsos et Christianos discretio seu divisio vestium haberetur.*" Bouquet's *Recueil des Historiens des Gaules et de la France* 18 (1879): 361, lines 19–20. It is problematical how much credence should be given to this report inasmuch as the chronicle in question was probably edited circa 1280, about three generations after the Fourth Lateran Council, though, of course, it could have been relying upon earlier documents. Potthast, *Bibliotheca Historica Medii Aevi* (2nd ed.; Berlin: Weber, 1896), I: 288.

(3) The Jewish chronicler Solomon ibn Verga (circa 1500, Spain and Turkey), relying upon earlier documents no longer extant, reported that in 1215–1216, the year of the Fourth Lateran Council, Christians imposed a badge (*hotam*) upon all Jews twelve years of age and over. The men had to wear this badge on their hats, the women on their veils. Ibn Verga's *Shevet Y'hudah* [Judah's Rod], ed. M. Wiener (Hannover: Lafaire, 1924), I (Hebrew): 114, lines 3-5; II (German translation): 233; ed. A. Shochat (Jerusalem: Bialik Institute, 1946–1947), 148, lines 1–2; 223, notes to p. 148, lines 1–4; Graetz, *Geschichte*, VII: 16 = *History*, III: 511; Dubnow, *divre Y'me Am Olam*, V: 10 and note 1 = *History*, III: 29 and note 3; Grayzel, 67 and note 115a; Baron, *Social and Religious History*, IX: 253–254, note 30. In view of the lateness of Ibn Verga's chronicle, it is problematical how far we can trust it with regard to the question of the Jewish badge in the early thirteenth century.

(4) England was among the first Christian lands to enforce a distinction in clothing upon Jews (as early as 1217–1218). The distinction in clothing King Henry III

decided to impose was a badge consisting of "two white tablets on the chest made of linen cloth or parchment" (infra, items nos. 8 and 9). Grayzel, 67 and note 115; Kisch, *Historia Judaica*, IV: 105, 127–128; C. Roth, *History of the Jews in England* (3rd ed.; Oxford: Clarendon, 1964), 40 and note 1; H.G. Richardson, *The English Jewry under Angevin Kings* (London: Methuen, 1960), 178 and note 1. Since England was a papal fief during the latter part of Innocent's reign, its action with regard to the distinction in clothing may represent the pope's mind. Baron, IX: 19.

(5) Emperor Frederick II, a protege of Pope Innocent III (supra notes 48–49), enforced the distinction in clothing upon Jews at an early date (1221–1222). The distinction in clothing he decided to impose was a blue badge in the form of the Greek letter Tau (T), so A. Shochat, *Ency. Hebraica*, II: 338. Cf. also Graetz, *Geschichte*, VII: 88–90 = *History*, III: 567–569; U. Robert, *Les Signes d'Infamie au Moyen Age* (Paris: Champion, 1891), 72 and note 4; H.C. Lea, *History of the Inquisition of Spain* (New York and London: Macmillan, 1922), I: 68–69, note 2; R. Straus, *Die Juden im Koenigreich Sizilien unter Normannen und Staufern* (Heidelberg: Winter, 1910), 104ff; L.I.Newman, *Jewish Influence on Christian Reform Movements* (New York: Columbia University Press, 1925), 291 and note 4; Kantorowicz, *Frederick the Second*, 268; Van Cleve, *Emperor Frederick II*, 144 and note 2; Grayzel, 67, note 114, 68, note 120, 70, note 127; Baron, IX: 142–143, 311, note 9. Since Frederick was a protege of Pope Innocent III, his action in this regard may represent the pope's mind. Regarding the importance of the Tau in Innocent's sermon at the Fourth Lateran Council and its possible influence on St. Francis of Assissi, Cuthbert, *Life of St. Francis*, 212 and note 1, affirms, and Basetti-Sani, *L'Islam e Francesco d'Assisi*, 102–105, denies its influence.

(6) Pope Honorius III (1216–1227), upon whom it was presumably incumbent to carry out the unfinished work of his predecessor Innocent III and to enforce the decrees of the Fourth Lateran Council, already spoke about Jews having to wear *signa*, "signs," *i.e.*, "badges." Cf. Honorius's letter of March 20, 1219, to the archbishop of Toledo, Grayzel, 150–151; and his letter of September 3, 1220, to the archbishop of Tarragona and his suffragans, Grayzel, 156–157. Supra, item no. 1.

(7) According to Ibn Verga (supra, item no. 3), in 1216–1217 the papal legate in southern France (perhaps Bertrand Savelli, cardinal-priest of Saints John and Paul; Mann, *Lives of the Popes*, XIII: 158 and note 5; A.P. Evans, "The Albigensian Crusade," in Setton, *History of the Crusades*, II: 312, 807) decreed that the Jews should be distinguished from the Christians by a circle (supra, item no. 2) on their upper garment. However, after a few days the decree was revoked. Ibn Verga's *Shevet Y'hudah*, ed. Wiener, I:114, lines 15–16; II: 234; ed. Shochat, 148, lines 12–13; 223, notes to p. 148, lines 5 and 11. Did the legate's action in this regard represent the mind of Innocent III or only that of Honorius III? According to L. Jadin, "57. Bertrand," *Dict. Hist. Geog. Eccles.* 8 (1935): 1078, Bertrand may have served under both Innocent and Honorius. Cf. also H. Zimmerman, *Die Paepstliche Legation in der Ersten Haelfte des XIII Jahrhunderts (1198–1241)* (Paderborn: Schoeningh, 1913), 72ff, 284, 305.

(8) Rabbi Isaac ben Moses of Vienna reported that in Paris circa 1217 the Jews were required "to wear round signs (wheels) [supra, items nos. 2 and 7] upon the clothes, for thus it was decreed against the Jews at that time . . . Some used to sew them into the garment. . . . Others used to make a circle from parchment [supra, item no. 4] and attach it to the garment by means of a needle." Grayzel, 65, note 112,

68, note 120; Kisch, *Historia Judaica*, IV: 106.

(9) Pope Gregory IX (1227–1241), a nephew of Pope Innocent III who had worked closely with his uncle, in a letter of 1234 to the King of Navarre spoke of "one round patch [supra, items nos. 2, 7, and 8] of yellow cloth or linen [supra, item no. 4] . . . worn on the uppermost garment stitched in front of and in back of the heart." Grayzel, 188–189.

Does Canon 68's vague language with regard to the kind of distinction in clothing mean that Pope Innocent III was content to let each territory decide for itself? This is apparently the view of Abrahams, *Jewish Life in the Middle Ages*, 296; Grayzel, 67 and note 115a; Kisch, *Historia Judaica*, IV: 110; L. Poliakov, *History of Anti-Semitism*, trans. R. Howard (New York: Vanguard, 1965), I: 65. However, in view of Pope Innocent III's centralizing propensity (cf. also infra, text accompanying notes 83–85), it is difficult to imagine that he would a priori have favored such a chaotic situation as would have prevailed if each territory decided for itself in this matter. Our hypothesis is that what Frederick II imposed circa 1221–1222 was what had been favored by his guardian Innocent III a priori in 1215: a blue badge in the form of the Greek letter Tau. Supra, item no. 5. This is the kind of badge that Pope Innocent III wanted to impose primarily upon the Muslims he hoped to conquer in the Middle East and secondarily upon the Jews (and the few Muslims) already living under Christian control in Western Europe. However, a posteriori, because the various rulers, both ecclesiastical and political, of Western Europe insisted upon the right to determine what kind of badge the Jews and relatively few Muslims) in their own particular territory would be required to wear, Pope Innocent III was forced to abandon his original intention in this matter and to leave Canon 68 purposefully vague enough to allow local variations. For bibliography on the highly complex question of the Jewish badge in Christian lands, Grayzel, 61–70, notes 97–127; Kisch, *Historia Judaica*, IV: 140–144; Baron, IX: 253, note 28, 255, note 33; Blumenkranz and B.M. Ansbacher, "Badge, Jewish," *Ency. Judaica* 4 (1971): 73.

60. Several scholars have suggested that Innocent's desire to impose a distinction in clothing upon Jews (and Muslims) may have been influenced by the Almohade practice. Graetz, *Geschichte*, VII: 16–17 = *History*, III: 511–512; Abrahams, *Jewish Life in the Middle Ages*, 296; Jacobs, *Jewish Ency.*, II: 425; Kisch, *Historia Judaica*, IV: 105; Baron, *Social and Religious History*, III: 298, note 22; IX: 27. During the reign of the Almohade Caliph al-Mansur (1184–1199) Jews (and Christians as well?), most of whom had been forcibly converted to Islam at least on the surface, were required to wear "dark blue garments with sleeves reaching down to their feet, and vile skullcaps covering their ears," *i.e.*, a special color and a special form of both the outer garment and the headgear. During the reign of al-Mansur's son and successor, an-Nasir (1199–1214), Jews (and Christians?) were required to wear a yellow cloak and a yellow turban, *i.e.*, a special color but no special form of the outer garment and the headgear. So Baron, III: 141, 298, note 22. Cf. also Graetz, *Geschichte*, VII: 16–17 = *History*, III: 511–512; E. Fagnan, "Le Signe Distinctif des Juifs au Maghreb," *Revue des Etudes Juives* 28 (1894): 295; Grayzel, *Church and the Jews*, 61; A.S. Halkin, "L'Tol'dot Ha-Sh'mad Bime Ha-Almohadin" [On the History of the Forced Apostasy at the Time of the Almohades], in A.G. Duker et al., eds., *The Joshua Starr Memorial Volume* (New York: Conference on Jewish Relations, 1953), 101–110, especially 109, notes 66–70

NOTES TO PAGES 194-195

and 74; Shochat, *Ency. Hebraica*, II: 338; Fattal, *Le Statut Legal des Non-Musulmans*, 105. After circa 1224 the Almohades may have changed their distinction in clothing requirement to a simple badge of yellow or black. Fagnan, *Revue des Etudes Juives*, XXVIII: 296; Grayzel, 61, note 97. Pope Innocent III was definitely in contact with the Muslims and the Christians of Almohade Morocco circa 1200 and again circa 1212 (Streit-Dindinger, *Bibliotheca Missionum*, XV: 9, no. 9: 10, no. 12; Mann, *Lives of the Popes*, XII: 178 and note 2) and seems to have known about the harsh Almohade treatment of the Jews at least. Cf. his letter of July 15, 1205, to the archbishop of Sens and the bishop of Paris, Potthast, *Regesta*, I: 220, no. 2565; *MPL*, CCXV: 694:B; Grayzel, 115 and note 3; M. Elias, "Die Roemische Kurie, Besonders Innozenz III., und die Juden," *Jahrbuch der Juedisch-Literarischen Gesellschaft* 12 (1918): 40 and note 3; Baron, IX: 137-138; Synan, *Popes and the Jews*, 92, 196, note, 39. The Almohades imposed a distinction in clothing upon Jews (and Christians?) who had been forcibly converted to Islam but who secretly maintained their old faith. Thus, the Almohade distinction in clothing requirement was closely related to their attempt to make genuine Muslims out of the forced Jewish (and Christian?) converts. It was a result of an intense desire to proselytize. In his letter of January 17, 1208 (supra, note 59, item no. 1; infra, note 61), Innocent links *signum*, "sign," possibly "badge," with *ignominia*, "shame," and *ignominia* with conversion to Christiantity.

61. For the view that the distinction in clothing requirement meant social degradation, cf. the literature cited supra, note 46 to chapter 4. Certainly distinction in clothing implied social degradation in Islamic and Almohade society (whence Pope Innocent III may have derived the idea for a badge; supra, note 60). For the "badge" in Islamic society, Grayzel, *Church and the Jews*, 61, note 97; Baron, *Social and Religious History*, III: 126-127, 139-141, 298, note 22, and the literature they cite, especially I. Lichtenstadter, "The Distinctive Dress of Non-Muslims in Islamic Countries," *Historia Judaica* 5 (1943): 35-52. In his letter of January 17, 1208, to the count of Nevers (supra, note 59, item no. 1), Innocent does say that Jews should be allowed to live dispersed over the earth as wanderers (*vagi*) *"until their countenance be filled with shame [ignominia*, italics ours] and they seek the name of Jesus Christ, the Lord"* (Grayzel's translation; supra, note 59, item no. 1). Notice how dispersion, shame, and conversion to Christianity are all intimately linked here. Immediately preceding this passage the same letter makes mention of God as putting a *signum*, "sign" possibly "badge," on Cain, who is a figure of the Jews. Thus, we have *signum*, "sign," possibly "badge," linked with *ignominia*, "shame," in Innocent's own writing. Pope Gregory IX, Innocent's nephew who worked closely with his uncle for many years, clearly links his "badge" with the degradation of the Jews. Cf. Gregory's letter of May 18, 1233, to the archbishop of Compostella and his suffragans, Grayzel, 204-207.

62. For the situation in Palestine, Prutz, *Kulturgeschichte der Kreuzzuege*, 139ff; Arnold, *Preaching in Islam*, 2nd ed., 88-96; F. Duncalf, "Some Influences of Oriental Environment in the Kingdom of Jerusalem," *Annual Report of the American Historical Association* 1 (1916): 135-145; J. Longnon, *Les Francais d'Outre-Mer au Moyen Age* (Paris: Perrin, 1929), 102ff; D.C. Munro, *The Kingdom of the Crusaders* (New York: Appleton-Century, 1935), 105-128; Hitti, *History of the Arabs*, 643-644; Runciman, *History of the Crusades*, II: 318-320; Waas, *Geschichte der Kreuzzuege*, I: 368ff; II: 208ff, 239ff; Van Cleve, in Setton, *History of the Crusades*, II: 381-382; Aharon Ben-Ami,

Social Change in a Hostile Environment: The Crusaders' Kingdom of Jerusalem (Princeton: Princeton University Press, 1969), especially 118ff.

For the situation in Sicily, M. Amari, *Storia dei Musulmani di Sicilia*, ed. C.A. Nallino (Catania: Prampolini, 1939), III: 2–3, 447ff, 671–922; S.P. Scott, *History of the Moorish Empire in Europe* (Philadelphia and London: Lippincott, 1904), II: 63ff; E. Curtis, *Roger of Sicily (1116–1154)* (New York and London: Putnam's, 1912), 94–95, 417–425; Longnon, 35ff; Lynn T. White, Jr., *Latin Monasticism in Norman Sicily* (Cambridge: Mediaeval Academy of America, 1938), 58; Hitti, 606ff; F. Gabrieli, "Frederick II and Moslem Culture," *East and West* 9 (1958): 53–61; L.R. Menager, *Amiratus: l'Emirat et les Origines de l'Amiraute (XIe–XIIIe Siecles)* (Paris: S.E.V.P.E.N., 1960); H. Wieruszowski, "The Norman Kingdom of Sicily and the Crusades," in Setton, *History of the Crusades*, II: 25–28, 33–34; Aziz Ahmad, *History of Islamic Sicily* (Edinburgh: Edinburgh University Press, 1975), 63–106; infra, notes 141ff to chapter 8.

For the situation in Spain, Lea, *Inquisition of Spain*, I: 58–59; Longnon, 78ff; Hitti, 543; A. Gonzalez-Palencia, *Historia de la Espanya Musulmana* (4th ed.; Barcelona: Editorial Labor, 1945), 191–210; Cagigas, *Mudejares*, I: 145ff, 283–284; Waas, II: 213 and note 103; infra., notes 82ff to chapter 8.

Cf. also Daniel, *Arabs and Mediaeval Europe*, 167ff and 192ff for the situation in Palestine, 140ff for the situation in Sicily, and 80ff for the situation in Spain.

63. Innocent was willing to condone a posteriori the forced baptism of Jews if they did not protest until the very last moment. Only Jews who protested to the end could thereafter revert to their former faith. Cf. Innocent's letter of September-October 1201 to the archbishop of Arles (Potthast, *Regesta* I: 131, no. 1479; Grayzel, *Church and the Jews*, 15 and note 15; 100–103). If Innocent was willing to condone a posteriori forced baptism, he certainly would have been willing to use a priori the less brutal and more subtle social pressure of a distinction in clothing as an aid to proselytism.

64. Innocent may also have thought that his misssionaries would be assisted by the Muslim belief that Christian baptism was an aid to health. For this Muslim belief in the late twelfth and early thirteenth century, Speros J. Vryonis, Jr., *The Decline of Medieval Hellenism in Asia Minor and the Process of Islamization* [Eleventh through Fifteenth centuries] (Berkeley: University of California Press, 1971), 442 and note 124; 487–489; Munro, *Kingdom of the Crusaders*, 124; Throop, *Criticism of the Crusade*, 143 and notes 125–126. Vryonis cites especially the Byzantine canonist Balsamon, while Munro and Throop both cite Jacques of Vitry. Both Balsamon and Vitry were contemporaries of Pope Innocent III.

65. For Innocent's extremely favorable attitude toward the early Franciscans, supra, notes 29ff. For his probable involvement in St. Francis's two early missions to the Muslims, *i.e.*, to those of the Middle East in 1212 and to those of Spain 1213–1215, Joergensen, *St. Francis*, 133; Felder, *Ideals of St. Francis*, 335; supra, note 55. For the rather large-scale early Franciscan attempt to convert the Muslims of Egypt as well as Spain/North Africa circa 1217–1227, Vat, *Anfaenge*, 1–28, 39–59, 194–197, 201–210; Roncaglia, *St. Francis of Assisi and the Middle East*, 26–34; Basetti-Sani, *Per Un Dialogo*, 225–464; and his *L'Islam e Francesco d'Assisi*, 114–267.

66. Supra, chapter 4.

67. In Canon 68, the distinction in clothing canon of the Fourth Lateran Council, the word *eis* (Mansi, *Amplissima Collectio*, XXII: 1055, line 44; Hefele-Leclercq, *His-*

toire des Conciles, V:2: 1387, line 8; Grayzel, *Church and the Jews*, 308, line 22; Synan, *Popes and the Jews*, 233, line 13) in the clause *"cum etiam per Mosen hoc ipsum legatur eis injunctum,"* refers back to the word *tales* (Mansi, line 39; Hefele-Leclercq, line 5; Grayzel, line 20: Synan, line 11) in the clause *"statuimus ut tales utriusque sexus etc.,"* and the word *tales* refers to both Jews and Muslims. Grayzel, 61, note 98; 309. Kisch, *Historia Judaica*, IV:109, and Synan, 104, have missed this point. Therefore, Canon 68 considered Moses the lawgiver of both Jews and Muslims, which is in perfect accord with what we know about the medieval Christian tendency to equate Jew with Muslim as discussed supra, chapter 4.

There is a difference of opinion with regard to which Mosaic commandment Cannon 68 refers. Abrahams, *Jewish Life in the Middle Age*, 296; Kisch, *Historia Judaica*, IV: 109 and Flannery, *Anguish of the Jews*, 102, 298, note 67, hold that the reference is to Numbers 15:38, the commandment to attach fringes to the corners of one's garment. However, Mansi, XXII: 1055, marginal note to lines 43–44; Synan, 233; and Blumenkranz, "Badge, Jewish," *Ency. Judaica* 4 (1971): 4, hold that the reference is to Leviticus 19:19, the prohibition against wearing a garment woven of a mixture of linen and wool. The assumption of a reference here to Numbers 15:38 seems to make more sense because Numbers 15:38 is a positive command and involves a clearly visible distinction in clothing, whereas Leviticus 19:19 is a negative command and only involves a far less obvious distinction in clothing.

68. In Canon 69 of the Fourth Lateran Council, Mansi, *Amplissima Collectio*, XXII: 1058; Hefele-Leclercq, *Histoire des Conciles*, V:2: 1387–1388; Grayzel, *Church and the Jews*, 311; Synan, *Popes and the Jews*, 233–236, "pagans" = Muslims. So Daniel, *Islam and the West*, 116. Cf. in general, Daniel, index, *s.v.* "Idolatry" and "Idols." Cf. also Roques, *Structures Theologiques de la "Gnose" a Richard de Saint-Victor*, 258–268, who argues that the "pagans" in St. Anselm's *Cur Deus Homo* = the Muslims, and who cites parallels to this usage from the *Chanson de Roland*, Abelard, Peter the Venerable, and Alan of Lille. Cf. the similar usage of the term "pagan" in Joachim of Flora's *Adversus Judeos*, ed. A. Frugoni (Rome: Istituto Storico per Il Medio Evo, 1957), 92, line 17. Cf. also the similar usage in Canon 11 of the Council of Montpellier (December 1195), Mansi, XX: 669: E; Hefele-Leclercq, V:2: 1171; Grayzel, 298–299. Finally, cf. the similar usage of the term "pagan" to mean Muslim by Pope Innocent III himself, *e.g.*, letter of May 1, 1199, to the bishop of Ferrara, Potthast, *Regesta*, I: 65, no. 684 = *MPL*, CCXVI: 1267 = Grayzel, 91; letter of June 4, 1205, to all the people of Viterbo, Potthast, I: 217, no. 2532 = *MPL*, CCXV: 654–655 = Luchaire, *Innocent III*, I: 93–94 = Grayzel, 25, note 19; letter of January 21, 1205, to the bishops, abbots, and other clergy of Constantinople, Potthast, I: 205, no. 2382 = *MPL*, CCXV: 514 = Grayzel, 110–111.

69. Supra, note 13.

70. Supra, note 54.

71. For Muslims in Christian Palestine, Prutz, *Kulturgeschichte der Kreuzzuege*, 144–146; C.R. Conder, *The Latin Kingdom of Jerusalem 1099–1291 A.D.* (London: Palestine Exploration Fund, 1897), 225–242; J.L. La Monte, *Feudal Monarchy in the Latin Kingdom of Jerusalem 1100–1291* (Cambridge: Mediaeval Academy of America, 1932), 175, 181; Grayzel, *Church and the Jews*, 88–89; Munro, *Kingdom of the Crusaders*, 105–128; J. Richard, *Le Royaume Latin de Jerusalem* (Paris: Presses Univer-

sitaries de France, 1953), 122–124; Runciman, *History of the Crusades*, II: 295; Waas, *Geschichte der Kreuzzuege*, II: 185ff; J. Prawer, *Histoire du Royaume Latin de Jerusalem*, trans. G. Nahon (Paris: Centre National de la Recherche Scientifique, 1969), I: 505ff; and his *The Latin Kingdom of Jerusalem: European Colonialism in the Middle Ages* (London: Weidenfeld and Nicolson, 1972), index, *s.v.* "Moslems" and "Natives"; J. Riley-Smith, *The Feudal Nobility and the Kingdom of Jerusalem 1174–1277* (Hamden, Connecticut: Shoe String/Archon, 1973), index, *s.v.* "Muslims."

For Muslims in Christian Sicily, Kington-Oliphant, *Frederick the Second*, I: 97–99, 218–220; Amari, *Storia dei Musulmani di Sicilia*, III:2–3: 578ff; Baethgen, *Die Regentschaft Papst Innozenz III. im Koenigreich Sizilien*, index, *s.v.* "Sarazenen"; White, *Latin Monasticism in Norman Sicily*, index, *s.v.* "Saracens"; Kantorowicz, *Frederick the Second*, index, *s.v.* "Saracens in Sicily"; Van Cleve, *Emperor Frederick II*, 151–155, 276, 304–306, 501; Ahmad, *History of Islamic Sicily*, 68ff.

For Muslims in Christian Spain, Lea, *Moriscos*, 4; and his *Inquisition of Spain*, I: 57ff; Cagigas, *Mudejares*, vols. I and II; Grayzel, 112–113, 118–119, 192–195, 254–257, 286–287, 320–321, 324–325; Maria Riansares Prieto Paniagua, *La Arquitectura Romanico–Mudejar en la Provincia de Salamanca* (Salamanca: Centro de Estudios Salmantinos, 1980), especially 15-23; supra, chapters 2 and 3.

For Muslims in northern Italy, Grayzel, 25 and 91. For Muslims in southern France, Grayzel, 43, note 11; 298–299. For Muslims in Hungary, Grayzel, 172–173, 184–185, 206–211, 244–245. For Muslims in Christian territory in general, Canon 26 of the Third Lateran Council (March 1179), in Mansi, *Amplissima Collectio*, XXII: 231; Hefele-Leclercq, *Histoire des Conciles*, V:2: 1105–1106; Grayzel, 296–297; Canon 69 of the Fourth Lateran Council, supra, note 68; Pope Honorius III's letter of September 5, 1219, to the Almohade Caliph Abu Ya'kub, Streit-Dindinger, *Bibliotheca Missionum*, XV: 14, no. 24; Mann, *Lives of the Popes*, XIII: 157–158.

For Islamic influence in late medieval Spain, infra, text and notes 82–87 to chapter 8; for Islamic influence in late medieval Italy, infra, text and notes 141–161 to chapter 8.

72. The original purpose of the distinction in clothing requirement was by no means to set the Jews apart for physical abuse and/or massacre, against the implication of Graetz, *Geschichte*, VII: 27 = *History*, III: 512; Broyde, *Jewish Ency.*, VI: 586; Dubnow, *Divre Y'me Am Olam*, V:9 = *History*, III: 27–28; Flannery, *Anguish of the Jews*, 103. Innocent's letter of January 17, 1208, to the count of Nevers (supra note 59, item no. 1) does equate Cain with the Jews and speak of God's having set a *signum*, "sign," possibly "badge," upon Cain. However, we must not forget that Innocent thought of the "sign" as protecting Cain "lest any finding him should slay him," according to the words of this letter to the count of Nevers. Synan, *Popes and the Jews*, 96. Peter the Venerable similarly interpreted the "sign of Cain" as protection in his letter to King Louis VII of France circa 1146, for which, *MPL*, CLXXXIX: 367:B–C; Grayzel, *Church and the Jews*, 126, note 3; Kritzeck, *Peter the Venerable the Islam*, 21–22. Innocent definitely wanted to keep the Jews alive, at least physically, because dead Jews could not be converted to Christianity en masse; and if the Jews could not be converted to Christianity en masse, the Second Coming of Christ might not take place circa 1284. For Innocents's attempts to protect the Jews, cf. his edict in their favor, *Sicut Judaeis*, September 15, 1199, Potthast, *Regesta*, I: 79, no. 834 = *MPL*, CCXIV:

864–865 = Grayzel, 92–95 = Synan, 97–98, 229–232; and Innocent's two letters of 1215–1216 to the archbishop and bishops of France, letters whose rubrics alone are known (the contents apparently having been lost), Potthast, I: 456, 459, nos. 5257, 5302 = MPL, CCXVI: 994 = Grayzel, 140–143. Cf. in general Grayzel, 76–82.

There is no concrete evidence that Innocent contemplated a "Jewish badge" before 1213, the year of his crucial Crusade appeal with its important millenarian passage (supra, note 1). Several scholars—e.g., Kisch, Historia Judaica, IV: 104; Shochat, Ency. Hebraica, II: 338; Baron, Social and Religious History, IX: 27—have indeed assumed that Innocent contemplated imposing the "badge" as early as 1204, apparently following J.E. Scherer, Die Rechtsverhaeltnisse der Juden in der Deutsch-Oesterreichischen Laendern (Leipzig: Duncker and Humblot, 1901), 43. However, Grayzel, 61, note 98, has expressed his inability to trace Scherer's source and knows of no document by Innocent from the year 1204 which deals with the Jews. Perhaps Scherer was thinking of Innocent's letter of January 17, 1208, to the Count of Nevers (supra, note 59, item no. 1) but misdated it to 1204. Grayzel, 61, note 98; 301, note 4, rejects the view of U. Robert, "Etude Historique et Archaeologique sur la Roue des Juifs Depuis le XIIe Siecle," Revue des Etudes Juives 6 (1882): 82 and note 2 = Robert's Les Signes d'Infamie, 11 and note 1, oft repeated, that the "badge" is already referred to by the word rota in the synodical rules of Odo of Sully, bishop of Paris, circa 1198–1208. According to Grayzel the word rota here probably means "pulpits," not badges.

Did Article 55 of the southern French Charte d'Allais of 1200 directly influence Canon 68 of the Fourth Lateran Council? This article is quoted in full in S. Kahn, "Documents Inedits sur les Juifs de Montpellier," Revue des Etudes Juives 19 (1889): 267 and note 2; cf. Robert, Les Signes d'Infamie, 7, note 1; Lea, Inquisition of Spain, I: 68, note 2; Grayzel, 62, note 98. Article 55 of the Charte d'Allais and Canon 68 of the Fourth Lateran Council each contains regulations dealing (1) with two, and only two, subjects and (2) with the same two subjects, i.e., Jews should be distinguished in clothing (but neither document speaks of a signum, "sign," or "badge") and remain indoors during Holy Week. The southern French Council of Montpellier (December 1195) would seem to have influenced the Fourth Lateran Council's treatment of Jews and Muslims. Canon 9 of this council, forbidding Jews and Muslims to hold office in Christian lands (Mansi, Amplissima Collectio, XXII: 669; Hefele-Leclercq, Histoire des Conciles, V:2: 1171–1172; Grayzel, 298–299), may have influenced Canon 69 of the Fourth Lateran Council containing the same prohibition upon Jews and Muslims (supra, note 68). Canon 9 of the Council of Montpellier's prohibition against Jews employing Christians as servants in their homes also influenced Innocent. Grayzel, 25, 104–111.

73. For medieval Jewish proselytism, supra, note 16, Religious Factors, D, to chapter 4.

Several scholars have suggested that the real reason why Innocent wanted to degrade the Jews was not so much because he feared their proselytizing activities but rather because he thought they were encouraging heresy in southern France and that by degrading them in the eyes of Christians he could stop such encouragement. Graetz, Geschichte, VII: 7–8 = History, III: 501; Broyde, Jewish Ency., VI: 586; J. Regne, Etude sur la Condition des Juifs de Narbonne du Ve au XIVe Siecle (Narbonne: Caillard, 1912), 96–97; Dubnow, Divre Y'me Am Olam, V: 6 = History, III: 24;

Grayzel, *Church and the Jews*, 25–26, note 19; Kisch, *Historia Judaica*, IV: 104. This suggestion, as well as the general question of the possible link between the Jews and the heretical movements of the late twelfth and early thirteenth century, and the Church's attitude toward this possible link, deserve further study. Preliminary data can be found in Newman, *Jewish Influence on Christian Reform Movements*, 131–330, and Trachtenberg, *Devil and the Jews*, 174ff. Cf. also the view of Chazan regarding the persecution of 1010, supra, note 11 to chapter 4. According to David Berger, "Christian Heresy and Jewish Polemic in the Twelfth and Thirteenth Centuries," *Harvard Theological Review* 68 (1975): 287–303, the heretics may have used *anti-Jewish polemic* as a cover for efforts to undermine the traditional Christian faith. Nevertheless, Luke of Tuy, the thirteenth-century Spanish historian, equated Jew with Albigensian; so N. Roth, *Jewish Social Studies*, XXXVIII: 158 and note 60. Contemporaries of Pope Innocent III (*e.g.*, Joachim of Flora and Caesar of Heisterbach) charged the Albigensian heretics with being in league with the Muslims. Supra, note 43 to chapter 4. Cf. also now S. Shahar, "The Relationship between Kabbalism and Catharism in the South of France," in Miriam Yardeni, ed., *Les Juifs dans l'Histoire de France* (Leiden: Brill, 1980), 55-62, N. Roth, "Jews and Albigensians in the Middle Ages: Lucas of Tuy on Heretics in Leon," *Sefarad* 41 (1981): 71ff.

74. Supra, text and note 62; infra, text and notes 76ff.

75. Supra, note 63.

76. Abrahams, *Jewish Life in the Middle Ages*, 296; Lea, *Inquisition of Spain*, I: 68; Scherer, *Rechtsverhaeltnisse der Juden*, 42–43; Jacobs, *Jewish Ency.*, II: 425; Dubnow, *Divre Y'me Am Olam*, V: 9 = *History*, III: 27; Grayzel, *Church and the Jews*, 62, note 101; Shochat, *Ency. Hebraica*, II: 338.

77. Grayzel, *Church and the Jews*, 59–60 and note 92; Baron, *Social and Religious History*, IX: 32.

78. Grayzel, *Church and the Jews*, 65–68 and notes 112–116; Kisch, *Historia Judaica*, IV: 97–99, 110; Blumenkranz, "Badge, Jewish," *Ency. Judaica* 4 (1971): 63–64.

79. Grayzel, *Church and the Jews*, 41ff, and index, *s.v.* "Usury"; Baron, *Social and Religious History*, IV: 202ff.

80. Supra, note 34 to chapter 5; Newman, *Jewish Influence on Christian Reform Movements*, 330ff; Grayzel, *Church and the Jews*, 26–27, 29–30. Cf. also Innocent's letter of July 15, 1205, to the archbishop of Sens and the bishop of Paris, Potthast, *Regesta*, I: 220, no. 2565 = MPL, CCXV: 694–695 = Grayzel, 114–117 = Synan, *Popes and the Jews*, 95, 219–224; paras. 2–3 of Canon 68 of the Fourth Lateran Council, Mansi, *Amplissima Collectio*, XXII: 1055, lines 45–61 = Hefele-Leclercq, *Histoire des Conciles*, V:2: 1387, lines 9–19 = Grayzel, 34 and note 70; 308–309 = Synan, 105, 233, 235.

81. Against Kober, *Univ. Jewish Ency.*, V: 89, who implies that Jews could pass for non-Jews, thinking, in all likelihood, more of the situation in late nineteenth- and early twentieth-century Germany than of that in Western Europe circa 1215.

82. Cf. Innocent's letter to the archbishop and bishops of France, 1215–1216, Potthast, *Regesta*, I: 459, no. 5302 = MPL, CCXVI: 994 = Grayzel, *Church and the Jews*, 140–141. Cf. also Grayzel, 69 and notes 122–123; Kisch, *Historia Judaica*, IV: 111–112; Baron, *Social and Religious History*, IX: 29, 253, note 29.

83. Supra, note 78.

84. Against Grayzel, *Church and the Jews*, 67–68.

85. Supra, note 59, item no. 5, and conclusion of that note.

86. Kisch, *Historia Judaica*, IV: 110–111.

87. Newman, *Jewish Influence on Christian Reform Movements*, 291 and note 5. Cf. also supra, note 73.

88. For some limited data on such intermarriages in the Middle Ages, K. Kohler, "Intermarriage," *Jewish Ency.* 6 (1904): 610–612; N. Cohn, "Mischehe," *Juedisches Lexikon* IV: 1 (1930): 212–215; Grayzel, *Church and the Jews,* index, *s.v.* "Intermarriage"; Baron, *Social and Religious History,* index volume to vols. I–VIII, *s.v.* "Marriage, Interfaith." Regrettably, E. Rosenthal and B.Z. Schereschewsky, "Mixed Marriage, Intermarriage," *Ency. Judaica* 12 (1971): 164–169, deal only with the twentieth century.

89. Blumenkranz, "Badge, Jewish," *Ency. Judaica* 4 (1971): 64.

90. Supra, note 67.

91. Ibid.

92. For the term "pagan" as applying to the Muslims, supra, note 68.

93. Supra, note 47 to chapter four.

94. Supra, note 26, paragraph 3, to chapter three.

7. The Netanyahu Thesis on the Marranos

* Earlier versions of chapter seven appeared in *The Jewish Spectator* 32 (October 1967): 16–18 (reprinted by *The Jewish Digest* 13 [March 1968]: 67–70) and in the *Journal of Ecumenical Studies* 4 (1967): 734–739. With the permission of Trude Weiss-Rosmarin, editor of *The Jewish Spectator*, and the Swidler's, editors of the *Journal of Ecumenical Studies*, it is reproduced here after further revisions. We acknowledge Netanyahu's and Weiss-Rosmarin's criticisms of the earlier version of this chapter prior to its appearance in *The Jewish Spectator*.

1. For Netanyahu's life and work, *Directory of American Scholars* 4 (1969): 267; *Repertoire International des Medievistes* (1971), 556, no. 3091; Martin A. Cohen, "Netanyahu, Benzion," *Ency. Judaica* 12 (1971): 970-971; *Who's Who in World Jewry* (1978), 647; *Who's Who in Israel* (1980-1981), 236.

On some of Netanyahu's early publications, *Hebrew Union College–Jewish Institute of Religion: Dictionary Catalogue of the Klau Library, Cincinnati* (Boston: Hall, 1964), XIX: 32-33; *New York Public Library, Reference Department, Jewish Collection Catalog* (Boston: Hall, 1960), VIII: 6538; and especially for the six volumes published between 1935 and 1938, *Kiryat Sefer* 13 (1936-1937): 157, no. 569, and 430, no. 1510; 14 (1937-1938): 295-296, no. 1070; 15 (1938-1939): 410-411, no. 1556.

The compelling analysis of modern anti-Semitism made in the late nineteenth and early twentieth centuries by the fathers of political Zionism (Pinsker, Herzl, Nordau, Zangwill, and Jabotinsky) has influenced Netanyahu's approach to the study of the Marranos.

The following is a list of some of the main reviews of Netanyahu's *Marranos:* Jose Maria Millas-Vallicrosa, *Sefarad* 26 (1966): 152-153; Albert A. Sicroff, *Midstream* 12 (1966): 72-75; Georges Vajda, *Revue des Etudes Juives: Historia Judaica* 126 (1967): 317-319; Ellis Rivkin, *American Historical Review* 72 (1967): 1408–1409; Thomas F. Glick, *Speculum* 42 (1967): 401-403; Gerson D. Cohen, *Jewish Social Studies* 29 (1967): 178-184; Vincent Cantarino, *Hispanic American Historical Review* 47 (1967): 256ff; Michael A. Meyer, *The Reconstructionist* 34 (April 5, 1968): 25-29; Frank Talmage, *Judaism* 17 (summer 1968): 366-376; Leon Poliakov, *Rivista Storica Italiana* 81 (1969): 376-378; Paul J. Hauben, ed., *The Spanish Inquisition* (New York: Wiley, 1969), 40-41, 48-49; Baron, *Social and Religious History,* XIII: 348-351; Yerushalmi, *From Spanish Court to Italian Ghetto,* 21ff; David Berger, *American Historical Review* 78 (1973): 1163-1164; C. Carrete Parrondo, *Sefarad* 35 (1975): 213-215; Gerard Nahon, *Revue des Etudes Juives* 136 (1977): 202-205; and his "Les Marranes Espagnols et Portugais et les Communautes Juives Issues du Marranisme dans l'Historiographie Recente (1960-1975)," ibid., 308-309 and note 37; J.C. Boyajian, "The New Christians Reconsidered: Evidence from Lisbon's Portuguese Bankers, 1497-1647," *Studia Rosenthaliana* 13 (1979): 129-131.

Netanyahu responds to three of the above reviewers, Sicroff, Cohen, and Cantarino, in "On the Historical Meaning of the Hebrew Sources Related to the Marranos (A Reply to Critics)," in Joseph M. Sola-Sole, Samuel G. Armistead, and Joseph H. Silverman, eds., *Hispania Judaica: Studies on the History, Language, and Literature of the Jews of the Hispanic World* (Barcelona: Puvill, 1980), I: 79-102.

Two forerunners of Netanyahu's more realistic approach to the Marranos and the Inquistion were Antonio Vieira (1608–1697) and Baruch Braunstein. A. Lichtenstein, "Vieira, Antonio," *Ency. Judaica* 16 (1971): 121–122; A.J. Saraiva, "Antonio Vieira, Menasseh Ben Israel et le Cinquieme Empire," *Studia Rosenthaliana* 6 (January 1972): 25–56. Baruch Braunstein, *The Chuetas of Majorca: Conversos and the Inquisition of Majorca* (2nd ed.; New York: K'tav, 1972). For more recent work on the Chuetas, Juan Riera, *Carlos III y los Chuetas Mallorquines* (Valladolid: Cuadernos Simancas de Investigaciones Historicas, 1975); and Kenneth Moore, *Those of the Street: The Catholic-Jews of Mallorca* (Notre Dame: University of Notre Dame Press, 1976); and both as reviewed by Thomas F. Glick, *Jewish Social Studies* 40 (1978): 323–324.

The late Cecil Roth (1899–1970) (England and Israel) adopted the Netanyahu approach in the mid- and late-1960s, after having been one of the main exponents of the romantic approach which viewed the Marranos as secret Jews.

For the life and work of Roth, V.D. Lipman, "Roth, Cecil," *Ency. Judaica* 14 (1971): 326–328. Salomon, in the fourth edition of Roth's *History of the Marranos,* viii–ix, reports that in later life Roth acknowledged the "high romanticism" of his writings on the Marranos and the Inquisition produced during the 1930s and the 1940s (the period of the Nazi attack on the Jews) and "lamented that he had not sufficiently stressed the possibility that the New Christian [Marrano] problem was one of caste, rather than of religion."

Professor Netanyahu himself, in personal conversation with us, reports that in the Spring of 1966, when the first edition of his book on the Marranos appeared, Roth publicly disowned his previous writings on this subject and accepted the Netanyahu thesis at a meeting of the Israel Historical Society; thereafter wrote Professor Netanyahu a letter, had many conversations with him, and published an article about this change of mind.

Other contemporaries of Netanyahu who share his approach are (1) Ellis Rivkin, "The Utilization of Non-Jewish Sources for the Reconstruction of Jewish History," *Jewish Quarterly Review* 48 (1957-1958): 183-203; his *The Shaping of Jewish History: A Radical New Interpretation* (New York: Scribner's 1971), 140-158; and his "How Jewish Were the New Christians," in Sole, Armistead, and Silverman, *Hispania Judaica*, I:105-115; (2) Herman P. Salomon, "Introduction" to Cecil Roth, *History of the Marranos* (4th ed.; New York: Hermon, 1974), vii-xix; and his articles, "New Light on the Portuguese Inquisition: The Second Reply to the Archbishop of Cranganor," *Studia Rosenthaliana* 5 (July 1971): 178-186; and his "Review Essay" on Y.H. Yerushalmi's "Prolegomenon" to the second edition of A. Herculano, *History of the Origin and Establishment of the Inquisition in Portugal*, trans. J.C. Branner (New York: K'tav, 1972), published in the *Journal of the American Portuguese Cultural Society* 6-7 (1972-1973): 59-65, 69-75; (3) the great Portuguese scholar, Antonio Jose Saraiva, for whose work, Salomon, in the fourth edition of Roth's *History of the Marranos*, xii-xiii; Salomon, "The Portuguese Inquisition and Its Victims in the Light of Recent Polemics," *Journal of the American Portuguese Cultural Society* 5 (summer-fall 1971): 19-28, 50-55; and Edouard Roditi, "The Making of Jews, or the Inquisition in Portugal," *Judaism* 19 (fall 1970): 435-443.

Boyajian, *Studia Rosenthaliana*, XIII: 129-156, shares the Netanyahu, Roth, Rivkin, Salomon, Saraiva approach.

Cf. also Martin A. Cohen, "Toward a New Comprehension of the Marranos," in Sole, Armistead, and Silverman, *Hispania Judaica*, I: 23-35.

The chief scholarly spokespersons for the romantic approach to the study of the Marranos and the Inquisition are Yitzhak Baer (born 1888); his disciple Haim Beinart (born 1917) (both of the Hebrew University, Jerusalem); and the late Israel Salvator Revah (1917-1973) (France).

For the life and work of Baer, Benzion Dinur, "Baer, Yitzhak," *Judaica* 4 (1971): 82–83; Beinart's two bibliographies of Baer's writings, in Salo W. Baron et al., eds., *Sefer Ha-Yovel L'Yitzhak Baer* [Yitzhak Baer Jubilee Volume] (Jerusalem: Historical Society of Israel, 1960), 474–484, and *Zion* 34 (1970): 226–228. The Baer book in question, of course, is his *History of the Jews in Christian Spain*, 2 volumes.

For the life and work of Beinart, "Beinart, Haim," *Ency. Judaica* 1 (1971): 28. Cf. also his two articles "The *Converso* Community in 15th Century Spain" and "The *Converso* Community in 16th and 17th Century Spain," in R.D. Barnett, ed., *The Sephardi Heritage* (London: Valentine, Mitchell, 1971), I: 425–478; and his book, *Records of the Trials of the Spanish Inquisition in Ciudad Real*, vol 1. (Jerusalem: The Israel National Academy of Sciences and Humanities, 1974) (with three more volumes announced). Volume 2 appeared in 1977. Cf. the reviews of this work by J.L. Lacave, *Sefarad* 38 (1978): 171-174: T.L. Ryan de Heredia and H.P. Salomon, *The American Sephardi* 9 (1978): 156-157; Martin Cohen, *Jewish Quarterly Review* 70 (1979): 119-120.

Also by Beinart are *Trujillo: A Jewish Community in Extremadura on the Eve of the Expulsion from Spain* (Jerusalem: Magnes Press, 1980); and *Conversos on Trial: The In-*

quisition in Ciudad Real, trans Y. Giluadi (Jerusalem: Magnes Press, 1981).

For the life and work of Revah, "Revah, Israel Salvator," *Ency. Judaica* 14 (1971): 116; and G. Nahon, "Les Sephardim, Les Marranes, Les Inquisitions Peninsulaires de Leurs Archives dans les Travaux Recents de I.S. Revah: a la Memoire de Mon Maitre," *Revue des Etudes Juives* 132 (1973): 30–48. Salomon, in the fourth edition of Roth's *History of the Marranos*, xii, points out that Revah eventually "admitted to some doubt as to whether the entire Inquisitorial procedure was not 'a tragic hoax perpetrated by a bureaucracy which had invented *marranic judaizing* in order to condemn it and to enrich itself with the spoils.' "

Baron and Yerushalmi as cited supra in this note, in dismissing the Netanyahu thesis, demonstrate basic sympathy with the more romantic Baer-Beinart-Revah school of thought.

Cf. in general G. Nahon, "La Conference sur les Juifs et les *Conversos* dans l'Espagne du Bas Moyen Age (Universite de Toronto, 30 Avril-ler Mai 1979)," *Revue des Etudes Juives* 138 (1979): 517-520.

2. Margolis and Marx, *History of the Jewish People*, 440–458; Baer, *Jews in Christian Spain*, I: 375–378; II: 95–243; Baron, *Social and Religious History*, X: 139–187.

For the possible impact of Christian messianic expectations on the Spanish Christians (led by Ferrand Martinez of Seville) who massacred the Jews in the 1390s, Peter E. Russell, *English Intervention in Spain and Portugal in the Time of Edward III and Richard II* (Oxford: Clarendon, 1955), 280, 496–498, 501; Reeves, *Influence of Prophecy*, 222ff, 324ff. For the definite impact of Christian messianic expectations on the Spanish Christians (led by San Vicente Ferrer) who put intense pressure for conversion on the Jews during the 1410s, Cohn, *Pursuit of the Millenium*, 146, 307; Reeves, *Influence of Prophecy*, index, *s.v.* "Vincent Ferrer, St., Dominican." For the impact of messianism upon Pope Paul IV's anti-Jewish policy of the mid-sixteenth century, Stow, *Catholic Thought and Papal Jewry Policy*, 225–227.

By the same token, the mass conversion of Spanish Jews to Christianity in the 1390s may in part have been a delayed reaction of disillusionment over the failure of the intense Jewish messianic expectation of the 1350s (for which, Silver, *History of Messianic Speculation in Israel*, 102); just as the mass conversion of Spanish Jews in the 1410s may in part have been an immediate reaction of disillusionment over the failure of the intense Jewish messianic expectation of the early fiteenth century (for which, Silver, 103, 108–109, 220–221; Baer, *Jews in Christian Spain*, II: 159–162). Supra, note 21, para. 4, to chapter 3.

During the discussions following Mr. Cutler's lecture on the topic of this book to Professer Robert Ignatius Burns' Seminar on Medieval Spain at UCLA, November 13, 1979, it was emphasized that the Black Plague had a much more devastating impact on Spain in general and Castile in particular than had previously been believed. If so, the concept of the Jews as causing the plague by well-poisoning which prevailed north of the Pyrenees when the disease first struck circa 1350 may also have been entertained in Spain, fanning the flames of anti-Semitism there. For the impact of the plague on anti-Semitism north of the Pyrenees and in Aragon circa 1350, Baron, *Social and Religious History*, XI: 160–164; S. Rowan, "The *Grand Peur* of 1348–49: The Shock Wave of the Black Death in the German Southwest," *Journal of the Rocky*

Mountain Medieval and Renaissance Association 5 (January 1984): 19–30. Moreover, the plague devastated the Spanish economy, heightening tensions between rich and poor. The Jews, allied more with the former, were all the more detested by the latter. Finally, the plague also strongly encouraged eschatological ideas among the populace, especially the lower class. Cohn, *Pursuit of the Millennium*, 127–138. Such ideas often led to anti-Semitic outbursts. Supra, this note. Thus, the Black Plague could have been a major factor in the anti-Semitism which broke out in Castile during the Civil War (circa 1350–1370) and, since the plague kept recurring throughout the second half of the fourteenth century, a major factor in the anti-Jewish massacres which spread from Seville to the rest of Castile and Aragon during the 1390s. The plague (along with anti-Semitic excesses) recurred in Thuringia circa 1391. Cohn, 145–146. It also recurred in the Middle East (Syria and Egypt) circa 1388–1393 (though not necessarily with similar anti-Semitic excesses). Michael W. Dols, *The Black Death in the Middle East* (Princeton: Princeton University Press, 1977), 180–181, 190, note 16 The plague not only struck Spain circa 1348–1352 but recurred in 1358, 1361–1363, 1371, 1375, 1381, 1383–1387 (especially striking Seville at this time), and 1394–1397. Jean-Noel Biraben, *Les Hommes et la Peste en France et dans les Pays Europeens et Mediterraneans* (Paris and the Hague: Mouton, 1975), I: 389.

For the impact of the Black Plague on fourteenth-century Spain in general and on anti-Semitism therein in particular, in addition to the Baron reference from the previous paragraph, Jaime Vicens Vives, *Approaches to the History of Spain*, trans. Joan C. Ullmann (Berkeley and Los Angeles: University of California Press, 1967), 72, 75-77; George Deaux, *The Black Death 1347* (London: Hamilton, 1969), 114-115; Philip Ziegler, *The Black Death* (New York: Day, 1969), 33, 63, 97-98, 107-108, 113-115, 133; Geoffrey Marks, *The Medieval Plague: The Black Death of the Middle Ages* (Garden City, New York: Doubleday, 1971), 47, 67, 108-109, 116; Gabriel Jackson, *The Making of Medieval Spain* (New York: Harcourt, Brace and Jovanovich, 1972), 146-147; Stanley G. Payne, *History of Spain and Portugal* (Madison: University of Wisconsin Press, 1973), I, 104-105, 126, 138, 144-145, 160; Angus MacKay, *Spain in the Middle Ages: From Frontier to Empire 1000-1500* (London: Macmillan, 1977), 71-72, 117, 165, 168, 174-177, 190-191; Dols, *Black Death in the Middle East*, 54ff, 65ff, 98ff, 200ff (in Spain); 66 (in Castile); 66, 82, 100, note 57, 320-324 (in Granada); Charles Verlinden, "Le Grande Peste de 1348 en Espagne," *Revue Belge de Philologie et d'Histoire* 17 (1938): 103-146; Nicolas Cabrillana, "La Crisis del Siglo XIV en Castille: La Peste Negra en el Obispado de Palencia," *Hispania* 109 (1968): 245-258; Jaime Sobreques Callico, "La Peste Negra en la Peninsula Iberica," *Annuario de Estudios Medievales* 7 (1970-1971): 67–102; Pilar Leon Tello, "Judios Toledanos Victimas de la Peste Negra," *Sefarad* 37 (1977): 333–337; M. V. Shirk, "Violence and the Plague in Aragon, 1348–1351," *Journal of the Rocky Mountain Medieval and Renaissance Association* 5 (January 1984): 31–39.

3. Netanyahu, *Marranos*, 1-4. For the work of Baer, Beinart, Roth, and Revah, the romantic school, supra, note 1. For the views of the two Spanish scholars in question, Bernardino Llorca, *La Inquisicion Espanyola: Estudio Critico* (Comillas: Universidad Pontificia, 1953), 18; B. Lopez Martinez, *Los Judaizantes Castellanos y la Inquisicion en Tiempo de Isabel la Catolica* (Burgos: Seminario Metropolitano, 1954), 52–56.

4. A comparison with the south Italian/Sicilian situation may be instructive, for Spain and southern Italy/Sicily were the only two Western European regions wherein the following two crucial events transpired during the Middle Ages and early modern times: (1) a major interreligio-civilizational dialogue between Christians, Muslims, and Jews and (2) mass conversion of Jews and Muslims to Christianity. Infra, text and notes 103ff to chapter 8.

5. In the early fifteenth century at least two Spanish Jewish writers, Solomon Alami and Shem Tov the son of Shem Tov, and at the end of the fifteenth century at least one other, Isaac Arama, blamed philosophy for the collapse of Spanish Jewry. Netanyahu, *Marranos* 103–104, 110–111, 139. Infra, text and notes 40ff to chapter 8.

Cf. also Netanyahu, *Abravanel*, 3rd ed., and his *Marranos*, 2nd ed., both index, *s.v.* "Averroes"; Baer, *Jews in Christian Spain*, II, index, *s.v.* "Averroism"; Julius Guttman, *Philosophies of Judaism: The History of Jewish Philosophy from Biblical Times to Franz Rosenzweig*, trans. D.W. Silverman (Philadelphia and New York: Jewish Publication Society of America and Holt, Rinehart and Winston, 1964), 134–256; S. Pines, B. Suler, and S. Muntner, "Averroes," *Ency. Judaica* 3 (1971): 949–953.

6. We need a history of Jewish and Hebraic studies in Spain to match the history of Islamic and Arabic studies in Spain written by James T. Monroe, *Islam and the Arabs in Spanish Scholarship (Sixteenth Century to the Present)* (Leiden: Brill, 1970). For a general introduction to the history of Christian Hebraism, three articles on this subject, R. Gottheil, *Jewish Ency.* 6 (1904): 300–304; M. Lehrer, *Universal Jewish Ency.* 5 (1941): 270–275; and R. Loewe, *Ency. Judaica* 8 (1971): 9–71. For an introduction to Christian Hebraism in sixteenth-century Spain, H. Peri, "Arias Montano, Benito," *Ency. Judaica* 3 (1971): 434–435; and K.R. Scholberg, "Leon, Luis De," ibid. 11 (1971): 27; F. Cantera Burgos, "Bartolome Valverde y su Desconocido Lexico Hebraico," in L. Alvarez Verdes and E.J. Alonso Hernandez, eds., *Homenaje a Juan Prado: Miscelanea de Estudios Biblicos y Hebraicos* (Madrid: Consejo Superior de investigaciones Cientificas, 1975), 607-643.

The realism of Netanyahu's future book on the history of the Inquisition will parallel that of Henry Kamen, *Spanish Inquisition* (New York: New American Library/ Mentor, 1968). On both the Spanish and Portuguese Inquisitions, Baron, *Social and Religious History*, XIII: 3–158; XV: 161–373.

7. For an introduction to the history of Christian-Jewish religious polemics, I. Broyde, "Polemics," *Jewish Ency.* 10 (1905): 102-109; H.H. Ben Sasson, "Disputations and Polemics," *Ency. Judaica* 6 (1971): 82-94; Oliver S. Rankin, *Jewish Religious Polemics of Earlier and Later Centuries* (Edinburgh: Edinburgh University Press, 1956); Talmadge, *Joseph Kimhi's Book of the Covenant*; Yehuda Shamir, *Rabbi Moses Ha-Kohen of Tordesillas and His Book Ezer Ha-Emunah: A Chapter in the History of the Judeo-Christian Controversy* (Leiden: Brill, 1975); David Berger, *The Jewish-Christian Debate in the High Middle Ages: A Critical Edition of the Nizzahon Vetus* (Philadelphia: Jewish Publication Society of America, 1979); J. Rembaum, "Medieval Jewish Criticism of the Christian Doctrine of Original Sin," *Association for Jewish Studies Review* 7-8 (1982-1983): 353–382.

For an introduction to the history of the medieval status of the Jews as *servi camerae*, G. Deutsch, "Kammerknechtschaft," *Jewish Ency.* 7 (1904): 431; Cecil Roth,

"Servi Camerae Regis," *Ency. Judaica* 14 (1971): 1188; Baron, *Jewish Community*, III, index, *s.v.* " 'Serfdom', Jewish, Medieval"; and his *Social and Religious History*, IV: 70ff; V: 128ff; IX: 135ff, 234ff; XI: 3ff.

8. Cf. the following articles on these distinguished scholars in the *Ency. Judaica* of 1971: on Amador de los Rios, K.R. Scholberg, II: 787; on Katz, I.L. Merker, X: 827; on Ashtor, S.D. Goitein, III: 737; on Kayserling, Cecil Roth, X: 855–856; on Neuman, S. Grayzel, XII: 1009–1010; on Baer, B. Dinur, IV: 82–83; on Millas-Vallicrosa, H. Beinart, XI: 1578–1579; on Cantera Burgos, V: 127; on Castro, Scholberg, V: 246.

Cf. also Julio Caro Baroja, *Los Judios en la Espanya Moderna y Contemporanea*, 3 vols (Madrid: Arion, 1962); *La Sociedad Criptojudia en la Corte de Felipe IV* (Madrid: Maestre, 1963); and *Inquisicion, Brujeria y Criptojudaismo* (Barcelona: Ariel, 1970).

The late great Americo Castro forcefully defended the highly controversial scholarly thesis of maximal Jewish influence in Medieval and Renaissance Spain. His thesis of maximal Jewish influence on the creation of the Spanish Inquisition circa 1480 scandalized many Jewish scholars. Baer, *Jews in Christian Spain*, II: 444ff. Yet his theory of maximal Jewish influence on the intellectual and cultural achievements of the sixteenth-century Spanish golden age scandalized as many Spanish non-Jewish scholars. A.A. Sicroff, "Americo Castro and His Critics: Eugenio Asensio," and the reply thereto by Asensio, "En Torno a Americo Castro: Polemica con Albert A. Sicroff," *Hispanic Review*, 40 (winter and autumn 1972): 1–30, 365–385. Cf. also in general Thomas F. Glick and Oriol Pi-Sunyer, "Acculturation As an Explanatory Concept in Spanish History," *Comparative Studies in Society and History* 11 (1969): 136–154; E.M. Gerli, "History, Medieval Spanish Literature and the Lessons of Americo Castro," *Kentucky Romance Quarterly* 26 (1979): 169–179.

Robert Ignatius Burns, professor of history, UCLA, is critical of both Castro and the latter's great opponent, Sanchez-Albornoz, who de-emphasized Jewish and Islamic influence upon Spain. Cf. the article which Burns published in *Thought*, LIV: 239-240. "Of the two, Castro did the greater service and forced a confrontation with the more essential questions." Ibid., 240.

Netanyahu attempts to refute the Castro view that the Spanish concept of "purity of blood" (*limpieza de sangre*), a concept closely allied with inquisitorial persecution of the Marranos, was derived from Jewish sources in general and the Marranos themselves in particular. Cf. Netanyahu, "Americo Castro and His View of the Origins of the *Pureza de Sangre*," *Proceedings of the American Academy for Jewish Research* (Jubilee Volume) 46-47 (1979–1980): 397-457.

Castro also argued maximal Jewish influence in the Spanish and Portuguese movement to explore and colonize Latin America. For the debate over the question of Columbus's Jewish origin, Kayserling, "Columbus, Christopher and the Jews," *Jewish Ency.* 4 (1903): 180; and his "America, The Discovery of," ibid 1. (1901): 511–512; A.A. Neuman, "Columbus, Christopher," *Universal Jewish Ency.* 3 (1941): 306–310; S. Cohen, "American Continent: I. Participation of Jews in the Discovery," ibid. 1 (1939): 225–228; Cecil Roth, "Columbus, Christopher," *Ency Judaica* 5 (1971): 756–757. Cf. also Baron, *Social and Religious History*, XIII: 132ff, 376ff, who lists six authorities favoring Columbus' Jewish (and Spanish) origin, including Madariaga; seven authorities favoring Columbus' Christian (and Italian) origin, including Morison and Menendez Pidal; and five authorities who take an intermediate postition, including Cecil Roth, Millas-Vallicrosa, and Cantera Burgos.

Cf. also now Abbas Hamdani, "Columbus and the Recovery of Jerusalem," *Journal of the American Oriental Society* 99 (1979): 39-48.

For an introduction to the history of the Jews in colonial Latin America, C. Adler, "America," *Jewish Ency.* 1 (1901): 492–495; S. Cohen, "American Continent," *Univ. Jewish Ency.* 1 (1939): 225–230, 235; Cecil Roth, "America," *Ency. Judaica* 2 (1971): 808–809; and Martin Cohen et al., "Latin America," *ibid.* 19 (1971): 1448–1457; Baron, *Social and Religious History*, XV: 259-373; Seymour B. Liebman, *New World Jewry 1493-1825: Requiem for the Forgotten* (New York: K'tav, 1983).

On Millas-Vallicrosa, Castro and Caro Baroja, also infra, note 28.

9. Cf. Netanyahu, *Marranos*, 133 and note 17, for the observation by the anonymous author of the *Sefer Ha-Kanah* (the early fifteenth-century Jewish mystical treatise) that if the Marranos had really been secret Jews, they would have intermarried only among themselves (the Marranos could not marry other unconverted Jews, because by law Christians could not marry unconverted Jews). They would never have married Old Christians. Yet the latter is precisely what happened. The Marranos did indeed marry Old Christians (often of distinguished families) and thereby demonstrated that they were not secret Jews, because secret Judaism would be much more difficult, if not impossible, to maintain in a marriage to an Old Christian than in a marriage to a fellow Marrano.

Cf. also Netanyahu, *Marranos*, 186, for Abravanel's observation (late fifteenth century) that if the Marranos had really been secret Jews, they would not only have refrained from marrying Old Christians (restating the argument of the *Sefer Ha-Kanah*) but would also have lived in compact communities, where they could physically and psychologically reinforce one another. However, Abravanel noted, the Marranos behaved in precisely the opposite fashion. They repeatedly married Old Christians and lived scattered throughout the land, which proved to Abravanel that the Marranos as a group were not secret Jews but rather *Gentiles both in private as well as public.*

10. Spanish Jewish hatred for the Marranos probably arose out of jealousy of the fact that the Marranos were much more successful economically, socially, and politically within fifteenth-century Spanish Christian society than the unconverted Jews, because the Marranos were no longer subject to those laws which made Jews second-class citizens within Western European society at that time.

Jewish hatred for the Marranos is well represented by the harshly anti-Marrano statements of the following fifteenth-century Spanish Jewish writers: first half of the fifteenth century—Matityahu Ha-Yitzhari (Netanyahu, *Marranos*, 127–128); second half of the fifteenth century—Isaac Arama (Netanyahu, 146–149), Isaac Caro (Netanyahu, 167–169), Abraham Saba (Netanyahu, 169–172), Joel ibn Shuaib (Netanyahu, 172–175), Joseph Jabez (Netanyahu, 175–176), and Isaac Abravanel (Netanyahu, 180–181).

Baer, *History of the Jews in Christian Spain*, II: 319, also notes that during the reign of Ferdinand and Isabella, "many Jews were no doubt persuaded that . . . persecution of the *conversos* [Marranos] was a necessary political expedient for which there was even a certain justification." Baer considers Rabbi Judah ibn Verga an exception in that he attempted to help the Marranos partly in order to win them back to Judaism. Baer, II: 317.

Animosity between Jews and Marranos in Spain during the last third of the fifteenth century is also documented by Tarsicio de Azcona, *Isabel la Catolica: Estudio Critico de su Vida y su Reinado* (Madrid: Editorial Catolica, 1964), 372; and C. Carrete Parrondo, "Fraternization between Jews and Christians in Spain before 1492," *The American Sephardi* 9 (1978): 18, 20-21, note 19.

Cf. also the behavior of the Jews of Cobenya, a small town in the province of Madrid, who denounced a Marrano to the Inquisition in 1491, i.e., Juan de Cobenya. C. Carrete Parrondo, "Cobenya, Aljama Castellana en los Albores de la Expulsion," in *Proceedings of the Sixth World Congress of Jewish Studies* (Jerusalem: World Union of Jewish Studies, 1975), II: 71-76.

Cf. also the behavior of the Jews of Cuenca and Huete who, in March 1492, upon the issuance of the expulsion decree, rioted and threatened revenge against the Marranos, whom they blamed for the expulsion. H. Beinart, "Cuenca," *Ency. Judaica* 5 (1971): 1153.

11. Marrano hatred for the unconverted Jews probably arose in part by way of reaction against the hatred which the unconverted Jews felt for the Marranos (supra, note 10). In addition, the Marranos may well have hated the unconverted Jews because the unconverted Jews, by their mere existence and presence in Iberia, continually reminded both the Old Christians and the Marranos themselves that the Marranos were not Christian by ethnic origin. Simon Wiesenthal, *Sails of Hope: The Secret Mission of Christopher Columbus*, trans. R. and C. Winston (New York: Macmillan, 1973), 21. Further, it is possible that Marrano hatred for the unconverted Jews was partly an attempt to curry favor with the Old Christians, who the Marranos believed (correctly or incorrectly) were prejudiced against the Jews. Moreover, when the Old Christians began to turn against the Marranos circa 1450 (primarily because of Christian fear of Jewish assimilation as developed infra in the text of this chapter between notes 19 and 28), the Marranos probably began to hate *themselves* since they had been rejected because of their Jewish origins. The Marranos assuredly could not allow themselves to hate the Old Christians for rejecting them, because the Marranos, despite their rejection, never gave up hope of eventually becoming an equal partner in Spanish Christian society. However, if the Marranos began circa 1450 to hate themselves because of their *Jewish origin*, how much the more so would the Marranos now hate the unconverted Jews, who were Jews not only in origin but in public practice as well. Finally, just as the unconverted Jews were jealous of the Marranos (because the Marranos were theoretically free of the burdens of Jewish second-class citizenship), so the Marranos now may have become jealous of the unconverted Jews for the following reasons. At least the unconverted Jews knew why they were persecuted—their adherence to Jewish religious law—while the Marranos could not understand why they were rejected—for they did not adhere to Jewish religious law. Moreover, the unconverted Jews had always been rejected by Christian society, but the Marranos had first been accepted and only thereafter rejected, which made their rejection twice as humiliating to them as consistent rejection was to the unconverted Jews.

For the feeling among the unconverted Jews of fifteenth-century Spain that the Marranos hated the unconverted Jews, Netanyahu, *Marranos*, 125, 128, 147, 149, 173–176, 180, 220, 228 (or 231 in the 2nd edition).

Stephen H. Haliczer, "The Castilian Urban Patriciate and the Jewish Expulsions of 1480–1492," *American Historical Review* 78 (1973): 35–58, argues that the prime movers behind the expulsion of the unconverted Jews from Spain in the late fifteenth century were the Marranos, who applied pressure on the crown through their influence with the town councils. Cf. the discussion of this article (replies by Peggy K. Liss, David Berger, and Teofilo F. Ruiz, with rejoinder by Haliczer), ibid. 78 (1973): 1163–1166; by Martin A. Cohen, *The American Sephardi* 7–8 (autumn 1975): 148; and by Stow, *Catholic Thought and Papal Jewry Policy*, 230–231 and note 18. Though he does not seem to cite Netanyahu, Haliczer's thesis seems plausible in view of the data developed by Netanyahu from Jewish sources which testify to *intense Marrano hatred* for the unconverted Jews of Spain in the late fifteenth century.

Cf. also Carrette Parrondo, *The American Sephardi*, IX: 18, 20-21, note 19; Beinart, *Ency. Judaica*, V: 1153.

The Old Christians began to persecute the Marranos beginning about the middle of the fifteenth century, *i.e.*, during the civil war between Marranos and Old Christians in Toledo circa 1450, when Pedro Sarmiento, Old Christian alcalde of Toledo, forbade the appointment of Marranos to civil or ecclesiastical office in Toledo. Baer, *Jews in Christian Spain*, II: 277–283; Netanyahu, "Did the Toledans in 1449 Rely on a Real Royal Privilege? A Privilege Issued by Alfonso VII and the Toledans' Judgement on the Conversos," *Proceedings of the American Academy for Jewish Research* 44 (1977): 93-125.

Cf. the contemporaneous Christian attack on the Jews of Lisbon in 1449. H.C. Baquero Moreno, "O Assalto a Judiaria Grande de Lisboa em Dezembro de 1449," *Revista de Ciencias do Homem da Universidade de Lourenco Marques* 3 (1970): 5-51.

Netanyahu, *Marranos*, 144-145, 187-188, 207, 235-236, recognizes the likelihood of a crypto-Jewish awakening, a revival of Jewish consciousness, among some of the Marranos prior to the establishment of the Inquisition circa 1480. Netanyahu, 145, traces this revival of Jewish consciousness among some of the Marranos to the persecution of Marranos by Old Christians which began circa 1450. This revival, however, affected only a small portion of the Marranos, perhaps no more than 25 percent. It is quite possible, nevertheless, that despite its relative numerical weakness, this movement for return to Judaism among some Marranos even before the establishment of the Inquisition created a sense of panic among the rest of the Marranos who were sincere Christians, who probably believed that this movement would taint the entire group even more than it was already tainted and encourage even more severe persecution of the Marranos as a whole by the Old Christians.

Thus, the movement for a return to Judaism among some of the Marranos between circa 1450 and 1480, despite its numerical weakness, could well have driven the rest of the Marranos, who remained fiercely loyal to Christianity despite their apparent rejection by the Old Christians, to encourage the introduction of the Inquisition circa 1480 to destroy the pro-Jewish Marranos and thus make it easier for the pro-Christian Marranos to assimilate successfully. This calculation, if present, misfired tragically. Once established the Inquisition attacked all Marranos, pro-Christian Marranos perhaps even more than pro-Jewish Marranos. Since the basic motive behind the Inquisition was Christian fear of Jewish assimilation in general, the Inquisition probably saw pro-Christian Marranos as an even more dangerous threat than the pro-Jewish Marranos.

12. In view of Jewish hatred for the Marranos (note 10) and rejoicing at the sufferings inflicted by the Inquisition upon the Marranos (cf. especially the rejoicing thereover by ibn Shuaib, Netanyahu; *Marranos*, 174), it is highly possible that the unconverted Jews of Spain actually encouraged the introduction of the Inquisition circa 1480 on the assumption that it would attack only the Marranos and not the unconverted Jews. Just as some unconverted Jews (though, of course, for reasons far different from those obtaining in fifteenth-century Spain) encouraged similar twentieth-century tyrannies, *e.g.*, Trotsky, who encouraged Bolshevism in Russia; or those Jews who encouraged Fascism, both in its less anti-Semitic form under Mussolini (H. Bieber, "Mussolini, Benito," *Univ. Jewish Ency.* 8 [1942]: 68-69; Michael A. Ledeen, "Italian Jews and Fascism," *Judaism* 18 [summer 1969]: 277-298) and even in its more anti-Semitic form under Hitler (H. Wasserman, "[Max Naumann and the] Verband Nationaldeutscher Juden," *Ency. Judaica* 16 [1971]: 106-107).

The irony was that if the unconverted Jews of Spain betrayed the Marranos by encouraging the Inquisition circa 1480 to punish the Marranos, the Inquisition engineered the expulsion of the unconverted Jews from Spain in 1492. This was so that it could have a freer hand to attack the Marranos by falsely charging them with crypto-Judaism. The false charge could not succeed as long as unconverted Jews were present in Spain because they gave the charge the lie by vociferously condemning the Marranos as non-Jews!

Cf. also Netanyahu, *Marranos*, 68–72, 158, 215, for additional information on the Jewish attitude toward the Marranos at the time of the Inquisition (circa 1480).

13. For the rabbinic view that the Marranos who "returned to Judaism" after 1480 should be considered converts to Judaism from another religion, Netanyahu, *Marranos*, 45, 53, 55, 57, 61, 64, 71–72, 152–154, 191. For rabbinic objections to this view and for the counterview that the Marranos who "returned to Judaism" after 1480 should merely be considered penitent Jewish sinners, Netanyahu, 45, 53, 55, 58, 62–66, 71–72.

14. Netanyahu, *Marranos*, 2nd ed., 216–220, 251–254.

15. Timothy Ware, *The [Eastern] Orthodox Church* (Baltimore: Penguin, 1969), 9, citing a Khomiakov letter printed in W.J. Birkbeck, *Russia and the English Church* (London: Rivington, Percival, 1895), 67. Cf. also Ware, ibid., index, *s.v.* "Khomiakov," for many further references to this great nineteenth-century Eastern Orthodox thinker. Cf. also Nicholas Zernov, *Eastern Christendom: A Study of the Origin and Development of the Eastern Orthodox Church* (New York: Putnam's, 1961), 187 for this specific Khomiakov idea and 185ff for Khomiakov's views in general. Cf. also D.S. Mirsky, *History of Russian Literature from Its Beginnings to 1900*, ed. F.J. Whitfield (New York: Knopf/Vintage, 1958), 170-171, for the view that all Russian Orthodox thought after Khomiakov has followed his general lead.

16. Cf. three articles on Christian Judaizers, by Herman Rosenthal, *Jewish Ency.* 7 (1904): 369–370; Baruch Braunstein, *Univ. Jewish Ency.* 6 (1942): 246–248; *Ency. Judaica* 10 (1971): 397–402.

17. For Jacob Frank and the Frankist movement he led, three articles, by S.M. Dubnow and Herman Rosenthal, *Jewish Ency.* 5 (1903): 475–478; Josef Meisl, *Univ. Jewish Ency.* 4 (1941): 390–393; G. Scholem, *Ency. Judaica* 7 (1971): 55–72.

For the waves of Jewish conversion to Christianity in Germany and England circa 1800, Kaufmann Kohler, "Conversion to Christianity," *Jewish Ency.* 4 (1903): 250–252; Kohler and I. Broyde, "Converts to Christianity: Modern," ibid., 253; Felix Goldmann, "Converts," *Univ. Jewish Ency.* 3 (1941): 341–346; H.H. Ben Sasson, "Apostasy," *Ency. Judaica* 3 (1971): 205–211.

18. Supra, note 17. The Italian Jewish assimilationist movement circa 1870 to 1938 (reversed when Mussolini adopted Hitler's racial laws) was at least as intense as the similar drive among the Jews of Germany at this same time. As Ledeen points out, *Judaism*, XVIII: 279 and note 5, between 1930 and 1937 30 percent of the Italian Jews who married married non-Jews, while the figure for Germany during this same period was only 11 percent.

19. Netanyahu, *Marranos*, 184 and note 114.

Cf. also the following parallels from modern times to what Abravanel said about fifteenth-century Spain, *i.e.*, the more the Jews try to be like the Christians, the more the Christians will persecute them for being Jews. (1) Moshe Catane, "Dreyfus, Alfred," *Ency. Judaica* 6 (1971): 229: "Jews everywhere were shocked that the [Dreyfus] affair could take place in France . . . in particular when the Jewish victim [Dreyfus] was completely assimilated. This seemed to prove clearly that assimilation was no defense against anti-Semitism." (2) Morin, *Rumour in Orleans*, 65–66, 105 (supra, notes 9–11 to chapter 4), points out that the prime target of anti-Semitism in Orleans in May–June 1969 were the most highly assimilated Jews, not the more religiously traditional Jews of the community, the recent repatriates from Algeria. (3) In early twentieth-century Russia, Mendel Beilis, whom a decaying Czarist regime chose as its Jewish scapegoat upon whom to fasten a ritual murder accusation, 1911–1913, was far more an assimilated than a religiously traditional Jew. Cf. two articles on Beilis, by I. Lewin, *Univ. Jewish Ency.* 2 (1940): 139–141; and C. Turtel, *Ency. Judaica* 4 (1971): 399–400. (4) Jewish Communist leaders whom Stalin and disciples chose to liquidate after putting them through show trials in the 1930s and circa 1950 were far more assimilated than religiously traditional Jews. Cf. the following articles in the 1971 *Ency. Judaica*: B. Eliav, "Kamenev, Lev Borisovich," X: 726–727; "Radek, Karl," XIII: 1496–1497; "Trotsky, Lev Davidovich," XV: 1404–1406; W. Korey, "Zinoviev, Grigory Yevseyevich," XVI: 1029–1030; Y. Slutsky, "Anti-Fascist Committee, Jewish," III: 62–65; B. Pinkus, "Cosmopolitans," V: 984–985; J. Frankel, "Doctors' Plot," VI: 144–145; B. Eliav and J. Leftwich, "Mikhoels, Solomon," XI: 1530–1531; A. Dagan, "Slansky Trial," XIV: 1653–1654; E. Kulka, "London, Artur," XI: 482–483. (5) Jayant P. Parekh, "Letter to the Editor," *New York Times*, August 30, 1972, part 1, 32, protesting the expulsion of the Asians from Uganda by General Idi Amin: "It is ironical that the Asian community of South Africa, although living in segregated units, are better off living among themselves than the persecuted Asians of East Africa," because the less assimilated Asians of South Africa were not expelled when the more assimilated Asians of Uganda were. Cf. also supra, note 16 to chapter 4, Economic Factors, C. Professor Henry Fischel and the Indiana University, Bloomington, project.

20. For the circa 98 percent survival rate of Danish Jewry during World War II, L. Yahil, "Denmark: Holocaust Period," *Ency. Judaica* 5 (1971): 1538–1540. For a similar almost 100 percent survival rate in Finland, Y. Gaulan, "Finland," ibid. 6 (1971): 1298.

In addition to Denmark and Finland, does moderate Jewish assimilation help explain the survival of the following Jewries during World War II? (1) Algeria, circa 100 percent survival (D. Corcos, "Algeria: Holocaust Period," ibid. 2 [1971]: 616–617); (2) Bulgaria, circa 90 percent survival (N. Oren, "Bulgaria in World War II," ibid. 4 [1971]: 1485–1489); (3) Rumania, circa 57 percent survival (T. Lavi, "Rumania, Holocaust Period," ibid. 14 [1971]: 399–410); (4) Budapest, circa 50 percent survival (B.A. Vago, "Budapest: Holocaust Period," ibid. 4 [1971]: 1453–1454).

Cf. also in general on Jewish survival in these areas during World War II, J. Robinson, "Holocaust: The Geography of the Second Period," ibid. 8 (1971): 851–852.

21. Eugene Mason, ed., *Aucassin and Nicolette and Other Medieval Romances and Legends* (New York: Dutton, 1958), 6–7; R.S. and L.H. Loomis, eds., *Medieval Romances* (New York: Random House/Modern Library, 1957), 251; Holmes, *History of Old French Literature*, 9, 147, 150, 250–251; Robert Griffin, "Aucassin et Nicolette and the Albigensian Crusade," *Modern Language Quarterly* 26 (June 1965): 243–256.

22. Supra, note 16 to chapter 4, Economic Factors, D, the Puhvel thesis, for the role of the Jews in rigidly stratified Indo-European society.

23. Ware, *Orthodox Church*, 26–43; also Zernov, *Eastern Christendom*, 58ff; Alexander Schmemann, *Historical Road of Eastern Orthodoxy*, trans. L.W. Kesich (New York: Holt, Rinehart and Winston, 1963), 113ff; Henri Gregoire, "Byzantine Church," in Baynes and Moss, *Byzantium*, 94ff; Vasiliev, *History of the Byzantine Empire*, index, *s.v.* "Monophysitism"; Ostrogorsky, *History of the Byzantine State*, 54–55, 59, 62, 71, 96ff, 135, 142, 153.

24. W.D. Davies, *Introduction to Pharisaism* (Philadelphia: Fortress, 1967), 27 and note 45, citing James Parkes, *Judaism and Christianity* (Chicago: University of Chicago Press, 1948) and his *Foundations of Judaism and Christianity* (London: Valentine, Mitchell, 1960). Cf. also John Pawlikowski, "The Church and Judaism: The Thought of James Parkes," *Journal of Ecumenical Studies* 6 (1969): 573–597.

25. Samuel Hugo Bergman, *Faith and Reason: An Introduction to Modern Jewish Thought*, trans. and ed. Alfred Jospe (New York: Schocken, 1963), 60–65; also Steven Schwarzschild, "Rosenzweig, Franz," *Ency. Judaica* 14 (1971): 301; Nahum N. Glatzer, *Franz Rosenzweig: His Life and Thought* (2nd ed.; New York: Schocken, 1967), 336–349; Guttman, *Philosophies of Judaism*, 388–398; Nathan Rotenstreich, *Jewish Philosophies in Modern Times: From Mendlessohn to Rosenzweig* (New York: Holt, Rinehart and Winston, 1968), 204–215; Richard Rubenstein, "On Death in Life: Reflections on Franz Rosenzweig," *Soundings: An Interdisciplinary Journal* 55 (summer 1972): 216–235; Milton Himmelfarb, "The State of Jewish Belief: A Symposium," *Commentary* 42 (August 1966): 72, for Rosenzweig's influence.

26. The German original of these four lectures can also be found in Renate Albrecht, ed., *Paul Tillich: Gesammelte Werke* (Stuttgart: Evangelisches Verlagswerk, 1965), III: 128–170. An English translation of most of the German original, prepared by Professor and Mrs. Wilhelm Pauck (Tillich's long-time friends and official biographers), appeared in *Jewish Social Studies* 33 (1971): 253–271. Davies, *Introduction*

to Pharisaism, 28 and note 47, cites Tillich's *Die Judenfrage* as having an approach similar to that of Parkes (supra, note 24) and to Davies' own approach.

27. The tripartite nature of Christianity as a cultural system can perhaps most easily be seen in and through the work of the greatest Christian artists, *e.g.*, Michelangelo (Catholicism) and Rembrandt (Protestantism). In Michelangelo's case the Judaic heritage can be seen in and through his "Moses" (circa 1515, S. Pietro in Vincoli, Rome); the Greco-Roman heritage, "Bacchus" (circa 1496–1497, Bargello, Florence); and the purely Christian, "Last Judgement" (circa 1536–1541, Sistine Chapel, Vatican, Rome). In Rembrandt's case the Judaic heritage can be seen in and through his many sympathetic portraits of Jews; the Greco-Roman heritage, "Danae" (1636, in Leningrad); the purely Christian, "Pilgrims at Emmaus" (1648, at the Louvre).

For Michelangelo and Judaism, Ruth Mellinkoff, *The Horned Moses in Medieval Art and Thought* (Berkeley: University of California Press, 1970). For Rembrandt and Judaism, three articles on Rembrandt, by F.T. Haneman, *Jewish Ency.* 10 (1905): 371–375; *Univ. Jewish Ency.* 9 (1943): 132–133; A. Werner, *Ency. Judaica* 14 (1971): 66–69; plus Franz Landsberger, *Rembrandt, the Jews and the Bible*, trans. F.N. Gerson (2nd ed.; Philadelphia: Jewish Publication Society of America, 1972).

28. Those who advocate the comparative approach to the history of Spanish Jewry can cite the work of Americo Castro, as well as that of Don Francisco Fernandez y Gonzalez, Henry Charles Lea, Julio Caro Baroja, and Jose Maria Millas-Vallicrosa.

Thus, Castro's books—*Structure of Spanish History*, trans. E.L. King (Princeton: Princeton University Press, 1954) and *The Spaniards: An Introduction to Their History*, trans. W.F. King and S. Margaretten (Berkeley: University of California Press, 1971) —deal simultaneously with both Christian-Islamic and Christian-Jewish relations; whereas his *Santiago de Espanya* (Buenos Aires: Emece, 1958) tends to stress Christian-Islamic relations, and his *De la Edad Conflictiva: El Drama de la Honra en Espanya y en su Literatura* (Madrid: Taurus, 1961), his *"La Celestina" como Contienda Literaria: Castas y Casticismos* (Madrid: Revista de Occidente, 1965), and his *Cervantes y los Casticismos Espanyoles* (Madrid: Alfaguara, 1967) all tend to stress Christian-Jewish relations.

Fernandez y Gonzalez produced one book on the Muslims in Christian Spain, *Estado Social y Politico de los Mudejares de Castilla* (Madrid: Munyoz, 1866), and two books on the Jews in Christian Spain, *Institutiones Juridicas del Pueblo de Israel en los Diferentes Estados de la Peninsula Iberica* (Madrid: Revista de Legislacion, 1881) and *Ordenamiento Formado por los Procuradores de las Aljamas Hebreas Pertenecientes al Territoria de los Estados de Castilla, en la Asemblea Celebrada en Valladolid el Anyo 1432* (Madrid: Fortanet, 1886).

Lea's *History of the Inquisition of Spain*, 4 vols. (New York and London: Macmillan, 1906–1907), dealt with both Christian-Jewish and Christian-Islamic relations, though more with the former than the latter; whereas his *Moriscos of Spain: Their Conversion and Expulsion* (Philadelphia: Lea Brothers, 1901) stressed Christian-Islamic relations, and his *Inquisition in the Spanish Dependencies* (New York and London: Macmillan, 1908) stressed Christian-Jewish relations.

Caro Baroja has devoted individual books to the problems of four different minority groups in Spanish history: (1) Jews, (2) Muslims, (3) Basques, and (4) witches. For his work on the Jews, supra, note 8. On the Muslims, *e.g.* his *Los Moriscos del Reino de Granada: Ensayo de Historia Social* (Madrid: Instituto de Estudios Politicos, 1957); on the Basques, *e.g.*, his *Los Vascos* (3rd ed.; Madrid: Istmo, 1972); on the witches, *e.g.*, his *World of the Witches*, trans. N. Glendinning (Chicago: University of Chicago Press, 1964).

In including the problem of the witches within his purview, Caro Baroja follows the example of Lea, whose *Materials toward a History of Witchcraft*, ed. G.L. Burr,[3] vols. (Philadelphia: Univeristy of Pennsylvania Press, 1939), was published posthumously. Lynn White and Norman Cohn are also aware of the similarities between persecution of Jews and witches. Supra, note 45, para. 5, to chapter 4; note 2 to chapter 5; Adolf Leschnitzer, *The Magic Background of Modern Anti-Semitism: An Analysis of the German-Jewish Relationship* (New York: International Universities Press, 1956), 139–149; Kamen, *Spanish Inquisition*, 202–209.

Millas-Vallicrosa's two books, *Estudios sobre Historia de la Ciencia Espanyola* as well as *Nuevos Estudios sobre Historia de la Ciencia Espanyola* (Barcelona: Consejo Superior de Investigaciones Cientificas, Instituto Luis Vives, 1949 and 1960), deal with both Christian-Islamic and Christian-Jewish relations simultaneously. Many of his other books deal exclusively with the Jewish contribution to Spanish culture, *e.g.*, *Selomo Ibn Gabirol como Poeta y Filosofo* (Madrid and Barcelona: Consejo Superior de Investigaciones Cientificas, Instituto Arias Montano, 1945), or with the Islamic contribution thereto, *e.g.*, *Estudios sobre Azarquiel* (Madrid: Consejo Superior de Investigaciones Cientificas, Instituto Miguel Asin, 1950). Cf. Millas-Vallicrosa's article, "Arab and Hebrew Contributions to Spanish Culture," *Journal of World History* 6 (1961): 732–751.

Other Spanish scholars who are sympathetic to the comparative approach include I. de las Cagigas, author of two separate two-volume works, one on the Mozarabs, the Christian minority in Islamic Spain, and the other on the Mudejars, the Muslim minority in Christian Spain (infra, notes 29–30); and Cantera Burgos, who has specialized in Jewish Studies (supra, note 8) but also published a book on the Mozarabs in 1957 (infra, note 29).

Cf. also the works of Alberto I. Bagby, Jr.: "Alfonso X, el Sabio, Compara Moros y Judios," *Romanische Forschungen* 82 (1970): 578–583; "The Jew in the Cantigas of Alfonso X, el Sabio," *Speculum* 46 (October 1971): 670–688; "The Moslem in the Cantigas of Alfonso X, el Sabio," *Kentucky Romance Quarterly* 20 (1973): 173–207.

Robert Ignatius Burns, a leading authority on the Muslims in Christian Spain (infra, note 30), is by no means oblivious to comparative data from the history of the Christian-Jewish encounter in Spain. Cf. Burns, "Jaume I and the Jews of the Kingdom of Valencia," in *Jaime I y su Epoca*, X Congreso de Historia de la Corona de Aragon (Saragossa: Institucion "Fernando el Catolica," 1980), 245–322; supra, note 1 to chapter 2.

Two other commendable recent examples of the comparative method are A. Ivory, "Juan Latino: The Struggle of Blacks, Jews and Moors in Golden Age Spain," *Hispania* 62 (1979): 613–618; and H. Goldberg, "Two Parallel Medieval Commonplaces: Antifeminism and Antisemitism in the Hispanic Literary Tradition," in Szarmach, *Aspects of Jewish Culture in the Middle Ages*, 85–119.

29. For the Mozarabs, supra, note 30 to chapter 2, and infra, note 84 to chapter 8. Cf. also F.J. Simonet, *Historia de los Mozarabes de Espanya* (Madrid: Tello,

1897–1903); Angel Gonzalez Palencia, *Los Mozarabes de Toledo en los Siglos XII y XIII*, 3 vols. (Madrid: Instituto de Valencia de Don Juan, 1926–1928); I. de las Cagigas, *Los Mozarabes*, 2 vols. (Madrid: Consejo Superior de Investigaciones Cientificas, Instituto de Estudios Africanos, 1947–1948); Francisco Cantera Burgos, *La Cancion Mozarabe* (Santander: Universidad Internacional "Menendez Pelayo," 1957); Juan Francisco Rivera Recio, *Estudios sobre la Liturgia Mozarabe* (Toledo: Diputacion Provincial, 1965); Giorgio Levi della Vida, "I Mozarabi tra Occidente e Islam," *L'Occidente e l'Islam nell Alto Medioevo*, II: 667–696; Miguel de Epalza, "Trois Siecles d'Histoire Mozarabe," *Travaux et Jours* 20 (1966): 25–40; J.F. Rollan Ortiz, *Iglesias Mozarabes Leonesas* (Leon: Everest, 1976); Henri Stierlin, *Die Visionen der Apokalypse: Mozarabische Kunst in Spanien* (Zurich: Atlantis, 1978); *I Congreso Internacional de Estudios Mozarabes*, 2 vols. (Toledo: Instituto de Estudios Visigothico-Mozarabes, de San Eugenio, 1978); Thomas F. Glick, *Islamic and Christian Spain in the Early Middle Ages* (Princeton, New Jersey: Princeton University Press, 1979); University of British Columbia, Committee for Medieval Studies, *The Mozarabs and the Interaction of Muslims, Christians and Jews in Medieval Spain, Programme and Abstracts* (Carr Hall and St. Mark's College, 18–20 November, 1982), the Twelfth Medieval Workshop (Vancouver, British Columbia: University of British Columbia, 1982), 23 pp.—this international symposium featured a total of at least eleven papers on the Mozarabs (the rest of the papers dealt with the Mudejars, Moriscos, and Jews): (1) John W. Williams, Univ. of Pittsburgh; (2) Dolores A. Reventlow, Univ. of Victoria; (3) Alvaro Galmes de Fuentes, Univ. of Oviedo; (4) Richard Hitchcock, Univ. of Exeter; (5) Vicente Cantarino, Univ. of Texas; (6) Dr. Norman Daniel; (7) Rosa Guerreiro, Univ. of Geneva; (8) James Kritzeck, Univ. of Utah; (9) Rosa Maria Pia Garrido, Trent University; (10) James T. Monroe, Univ. of California, Berkeley; and (11) Harold Livermore; Paul Merritt Bassett, Nazarene Theological Seminary, Kansas City, Missouri, forthcoming book on Christian theology in Islamic Spain, anticipated by his paper on "A Ninth Century Mozarabic Theological Squabble: Bishop Hostegesis vs. Abbot Samson," delivered at the One Hundred Thirty-Third Meeting, American Society of Church History, Washington, D.C., December 29, 1982, a copy of which he was kind enough to send us.

30. For the Mudejars, Cagigas, *Los Mudejares*, 2 vols. (Madrid: Consejo Superior de Investigaciones Cientificas, Instituto de Estudios Africanos, 1948–1949); Robert Ignatius Burns, supra, note 1 to chapter 2; John Boswell, *The Royal Treasure: Muslim Communities under the Crown of Aragon in the Fourteenth Century* (New Haven: Yale University Press, 1977); Miguel Angel Ladero Quesada, *Los Mudejars de Castilla en Tiempos de Isabel I* (Valladolid: Universidad de Valladolid, 1968); Juan Contreras Marques de Lozoya, *La Moreria de Segovia* (Madrid: Consejo Superior de Investigaciones Cientificas, 1967); supra, note 71 to chapter 6; infra, note 86 to chapter 8.

On the independent Muslims of Spain, thirteenth through fifteenth centuries, Miguel Angel Ladero Quesada, *Granada: Historia de Un Pais Islamico (1232-1571)* (Madrid: Gredos, 1969); Rachel Arie, *L'Espagne Musulmane au Temps des Nasrides (1232-1492)* (Paris: Boccard, 1973).

On the conquest of Granada, Ladero Quesada, *Castilla y la Conquista del Reino de Granada* (Valladolid: Universidad de Valladolid, 1967).

31. Louis Massignon, the great French Islamologist and prophet of reconciliation between Judaism, Christianity, and Islam, lamented the fate of *both the Muslims and the Jews* in late medieval/early modern Spain. Basetti-Sani, *Louis Massignon (1883–1962): Christian Ecumenist*, 124. In this passage Massignon also cites J. Cantineau, "Lettre d'un Moufti d'Oran aux Musulmans d'Andalousie," *Journal Asiatique* 210 (1927): 1–17, who publishes a letter from the Mufti of Oran, sent by secret messenger to the persecuted Moriscos, explaining how to expiate the sin of their public acceptance of Christianity. Baron, *Social and Religious History*, XIII: 147–148, 385, note 91, calls attention to this same Cantineau article and states that there is "no Jewish parallel to the casuistry of Ahmad ibn Ali Jumu'a, a Muslim teacher of Oran who in 1503 gave his former coreligionists [the Moriscos] of Andalusia detailed advice on how to reconcile outward Christian worship with continued faith in the teachings of Mohammed." But why do we not find any Jewish parallel to this Islamic letter? Was it, perhaps, because the Jewish rabbinic authorities in North Africa knew that it was a complete waste of time to give such detailed instructions to the Marranos because the Marranos by and large, even after the introduction of the Inquisition circa 1480, were uninterested in crypto-Judaism?

Leon Poliakov is among the few Jewish scholars who also discuss in some detail, in a book otherwise devoted to Christian-Jewish relations, the treatment which the Muslims received in Renaissance Spain. Cf. Poliakov's *History of Anti-Semitism*, trans. N. Gerardi (New York: Vanguard, 1973), II: appendix B, "The Moors and Their Expulsion," 328–357.

For the Moriscos, Lea, *Moriscos of Spain*; Caro Baroja, *Moriscos del Reino de Granada*; H. Lapeyre, *Geographie de l'Espagne Morisque* (Paris: S.E.V.P.E.N., 1959); Dario Cabanelas Rodriguez, *El Morisco Granadino Alonso del Castillo* (Granada: Patronato de la Alhambra, 1965); Antonio Gallego Burin and Alfonso Gamir Sandoval, *Los Moriscos del Reino de Granada segun el Sinodo de Guadix de 1554* (Granada: Universidad de Granada, 1968); James T. Monroe, "A Curious Morisco Appeal to the Ottoman Empire," *Al-Andalus* 31 (1966): 281–303; Andrew C. Hess, "The Moriscos: An Ottoman Fifth Column in Sixteenth-Century Spain," *American Historical Review* 74 (October 1968): 1–25 and his *The Forgotten Frontier: A History of the Sixteenth Century Ibero-African Frontier* (Chicago: University of Chicago Press, 1978), index, *s.v.* "Moriscos"; Kamen, *Spanish Inquisition*, 109–120; Imamuddin, *Political History of Muslim Spain*, 303–320; Anwar G. Chejne, *Muslim Spain: Its History and Culture* (Minneapolis: University of Minnesota Press, 1974), 375–396; Juan Regla Campistol, *Estudios sobre los Moriscos* (3rd ed.; Barcelona: Editorial Ariel, 1974); Mercedes Garcia-Arenal, *Los Moriscos* (Madrid: Editora Nacional, n.d. [1975]); L. Garcia Ballester, "The Minority of Morisco Physicians in the Spain of the Sixteenth Century and Their Conflicts in a Dominant Christian Society," *Sudhoffs Archiv* 60 (1976): 209–234; Louis Cardaillac, "Morisques et Protestants," *Al-Andalus* 36 (1971): 29–55; his *Morisques e Chretiens, Un Affrontement Polemique (1492–1640)* (Paris: Klincksieck, 1977); and his "Un Aspecto de la Relaciones entre Moriscos y Cristianos: Polemica y *Taqiyya*," in *Actas Coloquio Internacional sobre Literatura Aljamiada y Morisca* (Madrid: Gredos, 1978), 107–122; Antonio Dominguez Ortiz and Bernard Vincent, *Historia de los Moriscos: Vida y Tragedia de una Minoria* (Madrid: Biblioteca de la

Revista de Occidente, 1978); Antonio Garrido Aranda, *Moriscos e Indios: Precedentes Hispanicos de la Evangelizacion en Mexico* (Mexico: Universidad Nacional Autonoma de Mexico, 1980).

For sixteenth-century Spanish Protestantism, Marcel Bataillon, *Erasmo y Espanya*, 2 vols., trans. A. Alatorre (Mexico City: Fondo de Cultura Economica, 1950); Paul J. Hauben, *Three Spanish Heretics and the Reformation: Antonio del Corro, Cassiodoro de Reina, Cypriano de Valera* (Geneva: Droz, 1967); J.E. Longhurst, *Erasmus and the Spanish Inquisition: The Case of Juan de Valdes* (Albuquerque: University of New Mexico Press, 1950); his *Luther and the Spanish Inquisition: The Case of Diego de Uceda, 1528-1529* (Albuquerque: University of New Mexico Press, 1953); and his *Luther's Ghost in Spain (1517-1546)* (Lawrence, Kansas: Coronado Press, 1969).

32. For the history of the Jewish people in Portugal, the following three articles on Portugal, by Kayserling and G. Deutsch, *Jewish Ency.* 10 (1905): 136–141; Baer, *Univ. Jewish Ency.* 8 (1942): 606–607; A. Lichtenstein, R. Nall, H. Avni, and S. Amir, *Ency. Judaica* 13 (1971): 919–926; Manual Viegas Guerreiro, "Judeus," *Dicionario de Historia de Portugal* 2 (1965): 633–638; Maria Jose Pimenta Ferro, *Os Judeus em Portugal no Seculo XIV* (Lisbon: Instituto de Alta Cultura, Centro de Estudios Historicos, 1970); Gabrielle Sed-Rajna, *Manuscrits Hebreux de Lisbonne: Un Atelier de Copistes et d'Enlumineurs au XVe Siecle* (Paris: Editions du Centre National de la Recherche Scientifique, 1970); A. Paulo, "A Comuna Judaica do Porto na Idade Media," *Miscelanea de Estudios Arabes y Hebraicos* 23 (1974): 93–102.

For the history of the Muslims in Portugal, Jose D. Garcia Domingues, *Historia Luso-Arabe: Episodios e Figuras Meridionais* (Lisbon: Pro Domo, 1945); A. Huici-Miranda, "Los Almohades en Portugal," *Academia Portuguesa da Historia: Anais* 5 (1954): 11–51; and his "Gharb al-Andalus, Algarve," *Ency. of Islam* 2 (1965): 1009; D.M. Dunlop, "Burtukal," ibid. 1 (1960): 1338–1339; and Jose Pedro Machado, "Arabe: Lingua (em Portugal)" and "Arabes na Peninsula," *Dicionario de Historia de Portugal* 1 (1963): 165–167.

33. Cf. Graetz, *Geschichte der Juden*, VIII: 59 = *History of the Jews*, IV: 170, plus Baer, *Jews in Christian Spain*, II: 100, for the facts that the Christians of Seville and Valencia who massacred the Jews in the summer of 1391 also wanted to massacre the Muslims of these two cities (and in Valencia actually began to do so). However, they basically refrained from so doing because they feared reprisal from the armed Muslims who lived in the rural areas of Christian Spain and/or from the independent Muslims of Granada and North Africa, and/or that the Muslims of North Africa would massacre the Christians thereof in retaliation.

The military prowess of the Muslims who remained in Christian Spain can be seen from the fact that toward the end of the fourteenth century there were Muslim-Christian "brotherhoods" against bandit raiders in southeastern Spain. Burns, *Thought*, LIV: 249, note 10; citing J.B. Vilar, *Los Siglos XIV y XV en Orihuela* (Orihuela: Caja de Ahorros de Alicante y Murcia, 1977), 55.

The Jews of Spain apparently still had some military prowess in the late thirteenth century as seen from Elena Lourie, "A Jewish Mercenary in the Service of the King of Aragon," *Revue des Etudes Juives* 137 (1978): 367–373 (on "Abrahim el Jenet" circa 1290 whom the author considers "undoubtedly a Jew," cf. p. 368). They also fought on Pedro the Cruel's side in the great midfourteenth-century Spanish Civil War but had apparently lost the will to fight by circa 1391. Infra, note 9 to chapter 8.

We would suggest that it was the Muslims, rather than the Jews, whom the Christians considered the real enemy in Spain circa 1391 because they were strong militarily; but it was the Jews, rather than the Muslims, who were massacred (or converted) because they were weak militarily. Indeed, throughout the period of mass Jewish conversion to Christianity in Castile and Aragon circa 1390 to 1420, major Castilian and Portuguese attacks on the Muslims of Granada and Morocco were both contemplated and carried out, though the preceding twenty-year period of circa 1370 to 1390 was one of relative peace on the frontier between Christian and Muslim in southern Iberia. For the revival of the Christian Crusade against the Muslims of Spain/Morocco circa 1390 to 1420, Roger Bigelow Merriman, *Rise of the Spanish Empire in the Old World and the New* (New York: Cooper Square, 1962), I: 130–131; Imamuddin, *Political History of Muslim Spain*, 293–296; Aguado-Bleye, *Manual de Historia de Espanya*, I: 781–782, 808–809; Ladero Quesada, *Granada: Historia de un Pais Islamico*, 94–118; Arie, *L'Espagne Musulmane au Temps des Nasrides*, 121ff; Bishko, "Spanish and Portuguese Reconquest, 1095–1492," in Setton, *History of the Crusades*, III: 439ff.

34. For Abner of Burgos (Alfonso of Valladolid), Z. Avneri, "Abner of Burgos," *Ency. Judaica* 2 (1971): 88–89; Baer, *Jews in Christian Spain*, I: 327–354, 357ff, 446ff; II: 171ff. For Paul of Burgos (Solomon Ha-Levi), Joseph Kaplan, "Pablo de Santa Maria," *Ency. Judaica* 13 (1971): 3–4; Baer, II: 139–151, 154ff, 473ff. For Geronimo de Santa Fe (Joshua Ha-Lorki), H. Beinart, "Lorki, Joshua," *Ency. Judaica* 11 (1971): 494–495; Baer, II: 175–229, 479–483. For Franciscus de Sant Jordi/Dios Carne (Astruc Rimoch), "Rimoch, Astruc," *Ency. Judaica* 14 (1971): 187; Baer, II: 131, 218ff, 484, 500; Netanyahu, *Marranos*, 119, 132; F. Talmadge, "The Francesc de Sant Jordi—Solomon Bonafed Letters," in I. Twersky, ed., *Studies in Medieval Jewish History and Literature* (Cambridge, Massachusetts: Harvard University Press, 1979), 231–257. For Pedro Ferrus, K. Kohler and R. Gottheil, "Apostasy and Apostates from Judaism," *Jewish Ency.* 2 (1902): 15; I. Broyde, "Ferrus, Peter," ibid. 5 (1903): 373–374. For Diego de Valencia, Juan Alfonso de Baena (the compiler of the *Cancionero*), and Francisco de Baena (his brother), Kohler and Gottheil, ibid., II: 15. For Maestro Juan de Espanya El Viejo of Toledo, "Juan de Espanya," *Ency. Judaica* 10 (1971): 322; Baer, II: 159ff, 476.

To our knowledge there was at least one major fifteenth-century Spanish Muslim convert to Christianity who wrote against his former coreligionists: Juan Andres, a Muslim faqih who was converted circa 1487 and joined the Castilian royal court. Daniel, *Islam and the West*, 278; 284; 329, note 63; 410; Cerulli, *Nuove Ricerche sul "Libro della Scala,"* 121ff.

If, indeed, there were more Jewish than Muslim converts to Christianity who wrote against their former religion, this would seem to indicate that in general the Marranos were more sincere in their conversion to Christianity than were the Moriscos.

We also have an instance of a fifteenth-century convert from Christianity to Islam who wrote against his former religion: the Catalan Franciscan Anselm of Turmeda. Basetti-Sani, *Louis Massignon (1883–1962): Christian Ecumenist*, 65; Miguel de Epalza,

La Tuhfa, Autobiografia y Polemica Islamica contra el Christianismo de Abdallah al-Tarjuman (Fray Anselmo Turmeda) (Rome: Accademia Nazionale dei Lincei, 1971); O'Callaghan, *History of Medieval Spain*, 637–638.

The great fifteenth-century religious debate between Christians, Muslims, and Jews in Spain was foreshadowed by the equally great thirteenth-century religious debate between thse same three faiths. Recent studies of the thirteenth-century Christian-Jewish debate include: Robert Chazan, "The Barcelona Disputation of 1263: Christian Missionizing and Jewish Response," *Speculum* 52 (1977): 824–842; M. Orfali Levi, "R. Selomoh ibn Aderet y la Controversia Judeo Cristiana," *Sefarad* 39 (1979): 111–120; Jeremy Cohen, "The Christian Adversary of Solomon ibn Adret," *Jewish Quarterly Review* 71 (1980): 48–55. For the thirteenth-century Christian-Islamic debate, Fernando de la Granja, "Una Polemica Religiosa en Murcia en Tiempos de Alfonso el Sabio," *Al-Andalus* 31 (1966): 47–72.

35. For the apocalyptic motive of San Vicente Ferrer's campaign to convert the Jews of Spain the the 1410s, supra, note 2. On this campaign, also Francisca Vendrell, "La Actividad Proselitista de San Vicente Ferrer durante el Reinado de Fernando I de Aragon," *Sefarad* 13 (1953): 87–104; B. Llorca, "San Vicente Ferrer y su Labor en la Conversion de los Judios," *Razon y Fe* 152 (1955): 277–296; Millas-Vallicrosa, "En Torno a la Predicacion Judaica de San Vicente Ferrer," *Boletin de la Real Academia de la Historia* 142 (1958): 189–198.

However, we would suggest that for San Vicente Ferrer the problem of Islam (and the conversion of the Muslims) was as important as (if not more important than) the problem of Judaism (and the conversion of the Jews) in preparation for the Second Coming. O'Callaghan, *History of Medieval Spain*, 634, points out that San Vicente was just as interested in the conversion of the Muslims as the conversion of the Jews, though perhaps not as successful in the conversion of the former as in the conversion of the latter. The following scholars also stress San Vicente's vital interest in the conversion of the Muslims of Spain: A. Reinhart, "Vincent Ferrer, Saint," *Catholic Ency.* 15 (1912): 438; Browe, *Judenmission*, 25–26; M.M Gorce, "Vincent Ferrier (Saint)," *Dict. Theol. Cath.* 15 (1946): 3038; A. Redigonda, "Vincenzo Ferreri," *Encic. Catt.* 12 (1954): 1444; H. Thurston and D. Attwater, eds., *Butler's Lives of the Saints* (London: Burns and Oates, 1956), II: 33; Antonio Macia Serrano, *San Vicente Ferrer en su Vida, Actos y Obras* (Madrid: Publicaciones Espanyoles, 1971), 41. Baer, *Jews in Christian Spain*, II: 167, realizes that the harsh Castilian anti-Jewish legislation of circa 1412, inspired by San Vicente Ferrer, was directed against the Muslims as well as the Jews.

36. Beinart, "Tortosa, Disputation of," *Ency. Judaica* 15 (1971): 1268–1272; Baer, *Jews in Christian Spain*, II: 170–243; Baron, *Social and Religious History*, IX: 87–94; Pacios Lopez, *Disputa de Tortosa*, 2 vols.

37. Beinart, "Cavalleria (Caballeria), De La, 10. Pedro," *Ency. Judaica* 5 (1971): 264: Baer, *Jews in Christian Spain*, II: 276–277; Cerulli, *Nuove Ricerche sul "Libro della Scala*," 275–276.

38. On Alphonso de Spina, three articles, Kayserling, *Jewish Ency.* 11 (1905): 510; *Univ. Jewish Ency.* 10 (1943): 4; and Beinart, *Ency. Judaica* 2 (1971): 605–606; plus Baer, *Jews in Christian Spain*, II: 283–292, 403–404, 486, 488, 500; Daniel, *Islam and the West*, 276, 278, 383; Cerulli, *Nuove Ricerche sul "Libro della Scala*," 97ff.

Cf. also Netanyahu, "Alonso de Espina: Was He a New Christian?" *Proceedings of the American Academy for Jewish Research* 43 (1976): 107–165, replying very force-fully in the negative to this question. In this article Netanyahu also demonstrates major dependence of Alphonso de Spina upon Petrus Alphonsi among others. Ibid., 156–165.

For the relationship between witch-hunting and persecution of Jews, supra, note 28.

39. On Juan de Torquemada, Roth, *Marranos*, 24; Daniel, *Islam and the West*, 276, 278, 383, 421; Cerulli, *Nuove Ricerche sul "Libro della Scala,"* 78ff, 87ff; plus articles, A. d'Amato, *Encic. Catt.* 12 (1954): 330–331; F. Courtney, *New Cath. Ency.* 14 (1967): 204–205; and Justa de la Villa, *Diccionario de Historia de Espanya* 3 (1969): 788.

In his article on Juan de Torquemada, *Dict. Theol. Cath.* 14 (1946): 1235–1239, especially 1238, no. 15 of Torquemada's writings, A. Michel suggests that the mistaken notion that Juan de Torquemada was of Jewish origin has arisen from the fact that Torquemada's *Tractatus contra Madianitas et Ismaelitas, Adversarios et Detractores Illorum Qui de Populo Israelitico Originem Traxerunt*, which in 1946 was still in manuscript (Vatican 5606), represented a plea for toleration of Marranos. But is the notion that Juan de Torquemada was of Jewish origin such a mistaken notion? How many high Spanish ecclesiastics of the midfifteenth century who wrote actively against Muslims and Jews (as did Juan de Torquemada) also pleaded for toleration of Marranos (again as did Juan de Torquemada) when they themselves were not of Jewish background? Cf. Nicolas Lopez Martinez and Vicente Gil, eds., *Juan de Torquemada: Tractatus contra Madianitas et Ismaelitas* (Burgos: Seminario Metropolitano, 1957).

For another fifteenth-century literary defense of the Marranos, Manuel Alonso, ed., *D. Alonso de Cartagena: Obispo de Burgos: Defensorium Unitatis Christianae (Tratado en Favor de los Judios Conversos)* (Madrid: Consejo Superior de Investigaciones Cientificas, Instituto Arias Montano, 1943). Alonso de Cartagena was definitely of Jewish background. Luciano Serrano, *Los Conversos D. Pablo de Santa Maria y D. Alfonso de Cartagena: Obispos de Burgos, Governantes, Diplomaticos y Escritores* (Madrid: Bermejo, 1942).

40. Just as we have suggested that the Marranos may have played an important role in the introduction of the Inquisition circa 1480 (supra, note 11), as did the un-converted Jews (supra, note 12); so we would suggest that the Marranos may have played an important role in the three closely interrelated events of 1492: Granada, expulsion, and Columbus.

Why would the Marranos have wanted Granada conquered? Several reasons can be suggested: (1) to repay the Muslims for persecuting the Jews of Andalusia and Morocco (infra, notes 13–27 to chapter 8); (2) to defend themselves against the charge that the Jews (and by extension the Marranos) were in league with the Muslims conspiring to overthrow Christendom (supra, note 56 to chapter 4; infra, notes 28–30 to chapter 8); (3) to defend themselves against the Inquisition by demonstrating through their enthusiastic support of the Crusade against the infidel Muslims that they were just as loyal to Christianity as were the Inquisitors; (4) to prepare the groundwork for the expulsion of the unconverted Jews (supra, note 11). The Marranos may have believed that perhaps the primary reason why the Christians allowed the unconverted Jews to remain in the Iberian peninsula was because they accepted the argument that the help of the unconverted Jews was crucial in the defense of Spain against the

Muslims. However, if Granada was to be conquered, it could no longer be persuasively argued that the presence of the unconverted Jews was required in Iberia if the Christians were to defend themselves against the Muslims. See infra, note 90 to chapter 8.

If the Marranos helped engineer the downfall of Granada, they could also have helped engineer the expulsion of the unconverted Jews whom they despised (supra, note 11).

At the same time the Marranos may well have played a major role in Columbus's expedition and in general have encouraged the exploration and colonization of the New World (supra, note 8; Baer, *Jews in Christian Spain*, II: 321–322) for several reasons. (1) Since the exploration/colonization movement was in many senses an extension of the Crusades, by supporting this movement the Marranos could demonstrate their Christian zeal to the population as a whole and thereby refute inquisitorial charges of disloyalty to Christianity. (2) By encouraging development of Latin America the Marranos could also win vast fortunes that could be put to use in defending themselves against the Inquisition (buying support at court, etc.). (3) By encouraging the exploration and colonization of the New World the Marranos, should every other means of defeating the Inquisition fail, could find new places of refuge on the frontier, far from the main center of the Inquisition's power and close to the Indians to whom, as an absolute last resort, they could always flee. For the Marrano defense of the Indians, Castro, *Structure of Spanish History*, 58, 590–591; and his *The Spaniards*, 51, 84, 96, 139, 170, 320, 567–568. Cf. also Lewis Hanke, *All Mankind Is One: A Study of the Disputation between Bartolome de Las Casas and Juan Gines de Sepulveda on the Religious and Intellectual Capacity of the American Indians* (DeKalb: Northern Illinois University Press, 1971); Las Casas, Bartolome de, *In Defense of the Indians: The Defense of . . . Bartolome de Las Casas* etc., ed. and trans. Stafford Poole (DeKalb: Northern Illinois University Press, 1974). Cf. also Elisabeth Levi de Montezinos, "The Narrative of Aharon Levi, Alias Antonio de Montezinos," *The American Sephardi* 7–8 (autumn 1975): 60–83.

The edict expelling the Jews from Spain was promulgated from the *Alhambra in Granada*, not from Seville, Toledo, or Burgos, in March 1492. Margolis and Marx, *History of the Jewish People*, 470–471. Was there some kind of poetic significance therein? There is a thesis that the first Alhambra was constructed for the Muslims by the Jews (Joseph Ha-Nagid, the Jewish vizier of the mideleventh century). Frederick Bargebuhr, *The Alhambra: A Cycle of Studies on the Eleventh Century in Moorish Spain* (Berlin: De Gruyter, 1968); and the review thereof by D.M. Dunlop, *Speculum* 45 (October 1970): 652–656. If the unconverted Jews were expelled from Spain in 1492 partly because their services were no longer needed in the struggle against the Muslims of the south (which struggle ended with the fall of Granada in 1492), what better place from which to expel the Jews than from the very building whose first form they constructed for their Muslim cousins and allies in the eleventh century?

41. There were at least two major Morisco armed revolts during the sixteenth century, *i.e.*, in Valencia circa 1525 and in Andalusia circa 1570. Supra, note 31, especially the Monroe, Hess, Kamen, and Imamuddin references.

To our knowledge there were no similar Marrano revolts during the sixteenth century. The closest the Marranos came to such a revolt was their support of messianic pretenders (like the "Maid of Herrera"; Luis Diaz, the "Messiah of Setubal"; Reuveni and Molcho [supra, note 68 to chapter 4]). However, again to our knowledge, none of these messianic pretenders ever led an actual armed revolt against the Spanish crown. For Marrano messianism, Roth, *History of the Marranos*, 4th ed., 81, 146ff, 171–172, 214, 249–251, 261ff, 326; infra, note 51 to chapter 8.

Why did the Moriscos at times offer violent resistance to forced conversion and/or the Inquisition, whereas the Marranos offered no more than nonviolent resistance thereto? Was it because the Moriscos were more numerous than the Marranos (partly because they had a much higher birth rate, perhaps because many more Moriscos than Marranos were poor rural agriculturalists who traditionally have had a higher birth rate than middle-class city dwellers) and thus felt that they had a better chance to win an armed struggle than did the Marranos? Or was it because far more Moriscos than Marranos lived in the countryside, further away from the main center of royal and Inquisitorial power based in the cities? Or was it because the Moriscos, who were primarily a depressed peasant class, were the mainstays of Spanish agriculture and thus were defended by important elements of the landed aristocracy, who were not as eager to defend the largely urban-based Marranos? Or was it that the Moriscos, as Muslims, could hope for aid from their coreligionists in North Africa and Turkey (indeed, the Ottomans did raid the eastern Spanish coast in the 1560s, the same decade in which the Ottomans unsuccessfully attacked Malta in the central Mediterranean, relieved by the Spanish), and from France, Spain's chief Christian enemy and an ally of Turkey?

However, another important factor in the apparent greater willingness of the Moriscos than of the Marranos to organize armed resistance against forced conversion and/or the Inquisition was the fact that the Marranos were the first to suffer. The Moriscos could learn from the Marranos' tragedy. Thus, the Christians of Spain applied tremendous conversionist pressure to the Jews with great success in the fifteenth century but could not do the same to the Muslims (who still had an independent kingdom, Granada, to 1492) until the sixteenth century. The Jews by and large accepted conversion to Christianity sincerely but nevertheless were eventually rejected by Christian society and tortured by the Inquisition, all in the same fifteenth century. The Muslims could see what had happened to the Jews. Should they in the following century become involved in the same fate? The only way the Moriscos could avoid this was by doing what the Marranos had not done, *i.e.*, offer as much armed resistance to forced conversion and/or the Inquisition as possible in the sixteenth century. The eventual result was that the Moriscos were *expelled* in the beginning of the seventeenth century, whereas the Marranos were not. The Moriscos suffered the tragedy of expulsion in order to avoid the tragedy of torture at the hands of the Inquisition. The Marranos, on the other hand, avoided the tragedy of expulsion (in the early seventeenth century) but suffered the tragedy of torture at the hands of the Inquisition into the seventeenth and eighteenth centuries. The Jewish tragedy came first. The Jews had no group from whose mistakes they could learn, while the Moriscos did!

Does not the greater reluctance of the Marranos, as compared to the Moriscos, to rise up in armed revolt against forced conversion and/or the Inquisition also indicate the greater sincerity of the Marrano than the Morisco conversion to Christianity?

42. Most of the Moriscos expelled from Spain in the early seventeenth century went to North Africa (Morocco and Tunisia), but some went to the Mediterranean

islands and others as far east as Ottoman Turkey. Imamuddin, *Political History of Muslim Spain*, 318. Some (perhaps as many as 50,000 out of circa 275,000, or no more than 20 percent at most) found refuge in southern France at least for a while. Poliakov, *History of Anti-Semitism*, II: 352.

The question of the extent to which Moriscos emigrated to the Americas requires further investigation. Baron, *Social and Religious History*, XV: 300, cites a decree of King Philip III forbidding both "Moors and Jews" from settling in Latin America. Would the king have attempted to forbid something that was not in fact actually taking place, *i.e.*, the emigration of some Moriscos to Latin America? C. Rodriguez Eguia, "Mudejar," *Enciclopedia de la Cultura Espanyola* 4 (1963): 411, considers it probable that some Moriscos, expelled from Granada circa 1613 by King Philip III, went to America and helped develop the Mudejar style in the New World, described by Manuel Toussaint, *Arte Mudejar en America* (Mexico City: Porrua, 1946). Cf. also Castro, *The Spaniards*, 216–217 and note 7; L. Cardaillac, "Le Probleme Morisque en Amerique," *Melanges de la Casa de Velazquez* 12 (1976), 283–303; P. Dressendoerfer, "Crypto-Musulmanes en la Inquisicion de la Nueva Espanya," in *Actas Coloquio Internacional sobre Literatura Aljamiada y Morisca*, 475–494.

43. Cf. supra, note 4 to the introduction, for the views of Blumenkranz. For the views of Yerushalmi and Flusser, which have some similarity with those of Netanyahu and Blumenkranz, *i.e.*, that Christian theology was not the primary factor in the history of anti-Semitism, supra, text with notes 3 and 5 to chapter 4.

44. As do Blumenkranz, Netanyahu, Yerushalmi, and Flusser (supra, note 43), Arthur Hertzberg deemphasizes the role of Christian theology in the history of anti-Semitism. His *The French Enlightenment and the Jews* (New York and Philadelphia: Columbia University Press and the Jewish Publication Society of America, 1968) argues that twentieth-century anti-Semitism owes more to the secularist philosophies of eighteenth-century France (*e.g.*, Voltaire) and the Jacobin social radicals than to Christian theology. Cf. however Zosa Szajkowski, *Jews and the French Revolutions of 1789, 1830 and 1848* (New York: K'tav, 1970), ix–lv, for a refutation of this view. L. Poliakov apparently agrees with Hertzberg in "Voltaire," *Ency. Judaica* 16 (1971): 220–221. Jacob Katz seems to agree with Szajkowski. Cf. Katz's *From Prejudice to Destruction: Anti-Semitism 1700–1933* (Cambridge, Massachusetts: Harvard University Press, 1980), according to which the new "racialist" anti-Semitism which appeared in Europe in the 1870s merely echoed the "old" anti-Semitism prior thereto which was based on Christian theology.

8. The Critical Influence of Islam upon the Collapse of the Jewish Community of Spain (circa 1400) and the Jewish Community of Southern Italy (circa 1300)

* Chapter eight is based upon a paper delivered at the annual spring meeting, American Society of Sephardic [Mediterranean Jewish] Studies, Yeshiva University, New York City, May 2, 1971. We thank Moses Shulvass for his suggestions regarding this paper prior to its delivery (infra, note 71) and Herman P. Salomon for his remarks about the paper at the meeting itself (infra, note 2).

1. Margolis and Marx, *History of the Jewish People*, 410–414; Baron, *Social and Religious History*, IX: 197–198, 201–202; plus the following articles in the 1971 *Ency. Judaica*: J. Herman and C. Yahil, "Prague," XIII: 965; A. David, "Kara (Cara), Avigdor Ben Isaac," X: 758–759; I.M. Ta-Shma, "Muehlhausen, Yom Tov Lipmann," XII: 499–502; Y.L. Bato, "Vienna," XVI: 122; B.M. Ansbacher, "Wiener Gesera," XVI: 502–503; and S. Katz, "Isserlein, Israel Ben Pethahiah," IX: 1080–1081.

2. We now feel that reason no. 12, the Semiticization of Spanish Christian culture in advance of the mass Jewish conversion, was probably the most important reason for the collapse of Spanish Jewry circa 1390–1420. However, we had earlier believed that reason no. 11, the constant shifting of the majority culture within the Iberian peninsula, was probably the most important reason, and were reinforced in this belief by Herman P. Salomon (supra, note 1 to chapter 7 and footnote* to the present chapter). After considerable further research and reflection, we came to the conclusion we now hold, *i.e.*, that reason no. 12 probably was the most important. It sets the Spanish situation more graphically into the context of world religions and reflects the ideas of the late, great Americo Castro (supra, note 8 to chapter 7), on which, Stanley Payne, *History of Spain and Portugal* (Madison: University of Wisconsin Press, 1973), I: 136. We would agree with Payne that Castro's thesis of heavy Semitic influence upon Spanish Christian culture in general is more plausible than Castro's attempt to explain Spanish Christian religious fanaticism and intolerance as being a product of the same Semitic influence.

3. Cf. Lewis Way, *Adler's Place in Psychology: An Exposition of Individual Psychology* (New York: Collier, 1962), 351, for Alfred Alder's view that the power drive is an "over-compensation for insecurity" arising out of a feeling of weakness rather than strength. Adler's view could be applied to the power drive of medieval Spanish Jewry.

4. Supra, note 88 to chapter 5. Cf. also the following articles in the *Jewish Ency.*: S. Mendelsohn, "Capital Punishment," 3 (1902): 554–558; L.N. Dembitz, "Crimes," 4 (1903): 357–358; M. Kayserling, "Moser," 9 (1905): 42–44, Dembitz, "Punishment," 10 (1905): 273. Cf. the following articles in the *Univ. Jewish Ency.*: H. Revel, "Capital Punishment," 3 (1941): 25–27; S. Cohen, "Informers," 5 (1941): 564-565; and Cohen, "Law, Criminal," 6 (1942): 554. Cf. the following articles in the 1971 *Ency. Judaica*: H.H. Cohn and L.I. Rabinowitz, "Capital Punishment," V: 142–147; J. Klatzkin and Cohn, "Informers," VIII: 1364–1367, 1370–1373; Cohn, "Penal Law," XIII: 222–228; and Cohn and I. Levitatz, "Punishment," XIII: 1386–1390. Cf. also Abraham A. Neuman, *Jews in Spain: Their Social, Political and Cultural Life during the Middle Ages* (Philadelphia: Jewish Publication Society of America, 1948), index, *s.v.* "Courts, General," "Courts, Jewish," "Informers," and "Jurisdiction." Baer, *Jews in Christian Spain*, index, *s.v.* "Criminal Jurisdiction of Jewish Community," "Informers," and "Juridical Relations." Baron, *Jewish Community*," index, *s.v.* "Capital Punishment," "Crime and Punishment," "Crimes," "Criminal Law," "Informing and Informers," and "Penalties, Jewish." Baron, *Social and Religious History*, index vol. to vols. 1–8, *s.v.* "Capital Punishment," "Crime," "Informers among Jews," and "Punishments."

Cf. especially Baron, *Social and Religious History*, V: 45–46, for a discussion of the Visigothic and Islamic influence upon Spanish Jewry's time immemorial right to exercise capital jurisdiction, "a right invariably denied to its coreligionists in other lands"; and Baron, XI: 61, for the fact that Isaac b. Sheshet Perfet, the great Catalan rabbi of the late fourteenth century, the generation before the Jewish collapse of circa 1390–1420, held that a Jew who even *threatened* to inform could legally be executed by his fellow Jews *without trial*.

5. Netanyahu, *Marranos*, 133 and note 117. On the *Sefer Ha-Kanah* in general, J. Dan, "Kanah, Book of," *Ency. Judaica* 10 (1971): 733–734; Baer, *Jews in Christian Spain*, I: 369ff, 450ff; Netanyahu, "L'Verur Z'man Hibburam Shel Sifre *Ha-Kanah V'Ha-P'liah*" [Toward a Clarification of the Time of the Composition of the Books *Kanah* and *P'liah*], in S. Lieberman and A. Hyman, eds., *Salo Wittmayer Baron Jubilee Volume on the Occasion of His Eightieth Birthday* (New York: Columbia University Press, 1974), III (Hebrew Section): 247–267.

6. Netanyahu, *Marranos*, 103–104; plus three articles on Solomon Alami: S. Baech, *Jewish Ency.* 1 (1901): 316–317; *Univ. Jewish Ency.* 1 (1939): 154; and A. Shochat, *Ency. Judaica* 2 (1971): 509–510; plus Baer, *Jews in Christian Spain*, II: 239–242, 484.

7. Supra, note 6; infra, note 75.

8. On the life and work of Samuel Abravanel (Juan Sanchez de Sevilla), two articles, Kayserling, *Jewish Ency.* 1 (1901): 129; and Roth, *Ency. Judaica* 2 (1971): 102–103; plus Neuman, *Jews in Spain*, II: 257; Baer, *Jews in Christian Spain*, I: 366, 378, 450ff; II: 93, 354ff, 468, 474, 496; Netanyahu, *Don Isaac Abravanel*, 3–6, 265–270. The older scholarly view (Kayserling, Neuman, Roth) was that Samuel Abravanel converted to Christianity during the massacres of 1391. We follow the more recent view (Baer, Netanyahu) that he converted in the 1380s.

For the life and work of Asher the son of Yehiel, three articles: G. Deutsch, *Jewish Ency.* 2 (1902): 182–183; H. Revel, *Univ. Jewish Ency.* 1 (1939): 538–539; and *Ency. Judaica* 3 (1971): 706–708; plus Neuman and Baer, both index, *s.v.* "Asher ben Yehiel." For the life and work of Menaham the son of Zerah of Toledo, three articles: L. Ginzberg, *Jewish Ency.* 8 (1904): 466; *Univ. Jewish Ency.* 7 (1942): 465; and S. Eidelberg, *Ency. Judaica* 11 (1971): 1303–1304. Thus, Asher the son of Yehiel forbade the Jewish courtiers to practice concubinage (Neuman, II: 39), while Menaham the son of Zerah permitted the practice (Baer, I: 451).

Cf. also the life and work of Rabbi Hayyim Galipappa of Pamplona, on which, two articles, Kayserling, *Jewish Ency.* 5 (1903). 555; and J.S. Levinger, *Ency. Judaica* 7 (1971): 271–272; plus Baer, II: 75, 465.

9. Cf. two articles on Spain: J. Jacobs, *Jewish Ency.* 11 (1905): 493–495; and S. Schwarzfuchs, *Ency. Judaica* 15 (1971): 233: plus Margolis and Marx, *History of the Jewish People*, 440–443; and Baer, *Jews in Christian Spain*, I: 362–375. Cf. also three articles on Samuel Abulafia: Kayserling, *Jewish Ency.* 1 (1901): 143; *Univ. Jewish Ency.* 1 (1939): 62: and Z. Avneri, *Ency. Judaica* 2 (1971): 193. Cf. also two articles on Burgos: *Univ. Jewish Ency.* 2 (1940): 592; and Avneri, *Ency. Judaica* 4 (1971): 1513. Cf. also three articles on Toledo: J. Jacobs, *Jewish Ency.* 12 (1906): 180–181; M. Freier, *Univ. Jewish Ency.* 10 (1943): 261–262; and H. Beinart, *Ency. Judaica* 15 (1971): 1203–1204. Cf. also three articles on the Jewish badge: Jacobs, *Jewish Ency.* 2 (1902): 426; Kober, *Univ. Jewish Ency.* 6 (1942): 89–90; and Blumenkranz, *Ency. Judaica* 4 (1971): 65–67.

10. Baer, *Jews in Christian Spain*, I: 366.

11. Baer, ibid. II: 98.

12. Merriman, *Rise of the Spanish Empire*, I: 127–128; Aguado-Bleye, *Manual*, I: 713–715; Ladero Quesada, *Granada*, 91–93; Inamuddin, *Political History of Muslim Spain*, 291; Chejne, *Muslim Spain*, 100; Baer, *Jews in Christian Spain*, I: 354–360.

13. D. Corcos, "Fez," *Ency. Judaica* 6 (1971): 1256; and his "Morocco," ibid. 12 (1971): 329; Baron, *Social and Religious History*, III: 108.

14. Supra, note 28 to chapter 4; notes 110 and 125 to chapter 5.

15. H. Beinart, "Lucena," *Ency. Judaica* 11 (1971): 550; Baron, *Social and Religious History*, III: 170.

16. Cf. two articles on Lucena: Kayserling, *Jewish Ency.* 8 (1904): 204; and Beinart, *Ency. Judaica*, XI: 550; plus Baron, *Social and Religious History*, III: 124.

17. Cf. two articles on Cordova: Kayserling, *Jewish Ency.* 4 (1903): 266; and Beinart, *Ency. Judaica* 5 (1971): 964; plus Silver, *History of Messianic Speculation*, 79 and note 81; Baron, *Social and Religious History*, V: 200–201; and Baer, *Jews in Christian Spain*, I: 65.

18. Silver, *History of Messianic Speculation*, 79 and note 79; Baron, *Social and Religious History*, V: 201–202; Baer, *Jews in Christian Spain*, I: 65–66; Corcos, "Fez," *Ency. Judaica*, VI: 1256.

19. Corcos, "Almoravides, "*Ency. Judaica* 2 (1971): 667; and his "Marrakesh," *ibid.* 11 (1971): 1015; Baron, *Social and Religious History*, III: 145.

20. Kayserling, "Lucena," *Jewish Ency.*, VIII: 204; Corcos, "Almohads," *Ency. Judaica* 2 (1971): 662; Beinart, "Cordoba" and "Lucena," ibid., V: 964, and XI: 550; Baron, *Social and Religious History*, III: 124–126.

21. Corcos, "Almohads, "Fez," and "Morocco," *Ency. Judaica* II: 662–663, VI: 1256, and XII: 330; Baron, *Social and Religious History*, III: 124–126.

22. Corcos, "Almohads" and "Morocco," *Ency. Judaica*, II: 663, and XII: 330; Baron, *Social and Religious History*, III: 126–127, 141.

23. Corcos, "Almohads," *Ency. Judaica*, II: 663; Baron, *Social and Religious History*, III: 298, note 22.

24. Corcos, "Marrakesh" and "Morroco," *Ency. Judaica*, XI: 1015, and XII: 330.

25. M. Schloessinger, "Fez," *Jewish Ency.*. 5 (1903): 380; Corcos, "Fez" and "Morocco," *Ency. Judaica*, VI: 1256, and XII: 330.

26. For the imposition of the Jewish badge in Granada circa 1320, Jacobs, "Badge," *Jewish Ency.*, II: 426: Kayserling, "Granada," ibid. 6 (1904): 80; Arie, *L'Espagne Musulmane au Temps des Nasrides*, 330.

The Portuguese imposed the Jewish badge circa 1325, around the same time as the Granadans. Kober, "Jew-Badge," *Univ. Jewish Ency.*, VI: 90; Blumenkranz, "Badge," *Ency. Judaica*, IV: 66. There may have been a connection between the simultaneous imposition of the badge in both Granada and Portugal in the first quarter of the fourteenth century.

The badge was not prevalent in either Castile or Aragon in the first quarter of the fourteenth century. There had been a serious papal effort to impose the badge in Castile circa 1220, but the Jews were able to lobby effectively against it. Blumenkranz, 65–66. Alfonso X of Castile theoretically required the badge in his *Siete Partidas* of 1263 (Kober, 89; Blumenkranz, 66), but it apparently was not effectively and permanently enforced (as was lamented by the Council of Zamora in 1313; Jacobs, *Jewish Ency.*, II: 426) until circa 1370.

The badge was required in Aragon in 1228 and in Navarre in 1234 (Blumenkranz, 66), but King James I of Aragon disfavored it in 1268 (Blumenkranz, 66), and apparently the badge was not effectively and permanently imposed in Aragon until the period of crisis circa 1390 to 1420 (Blumenkranz, 66–67).

27. Margolis and Marx, *History of the Jewish People*, 442; Baer, *Jews in Christian Spain*, I: 366; Beinart, "Jaen," *Ency. Judaica* 9 (1971): 1248; Arie, *L'Espagne Musulmane au Temps des Nasrides*, 114, 330.

For general background on the alliance between Pedro the Cruel and Muhammad V of Granada, Merriman, *Rise of the Spanish Empire*, I: 130; Aguado-Bleye, *Manual*, I: 761–763; Ladero Quesada, *Granada*, 94ff; Brockelmann, *History of the Islamic Peoples*, 215; Imamuddin, *Political History of Muslim Spain*, 293–294; Russell, *English Intervention in Spain and Portugal*, 138, 147, 153.

According to Payne, *History of Spain and Portugal*, I: 208, the Jews dominated moneylending and suffered several massacres in fourteenth- and fifteenth-century Granada. According to Baer, II: 349, the Muslims of fifteenth-century Granada hated the Jews. By contrast, according to E. Spivakovsky, "The Jewish Presence in Granada," *Journal of Medieval History* 2 (1976): 229-234, the Jews of Nasrid Granada were heavily Islamicized and virtually indistinguishable from the Muslims.

The Granadan Muslim treatment of the Jews may help explain in part the financial encouragement which the Jews of Castile (led by Isaac Abravanel) lent to the movement to conquer Granada; on which financial encouragement, Baer, II: 319; and Miguel Angel Ladero Quesada, "Un Prestamo de los Judios de Segovia y Avila para la Guerra de Granada en el Anyo 1483," *Sefarad* 35 (1975) : 151-157.

28. Supra, note * to chapter 4.

29. Supra, note 12.

30. Cf. O'Callaghan, *History of Medieval Spain*, 540, for the view that the growing Ottoman Turkish threat to the Balkans and Eastern Europe circa 1396–1404 also demanded the attention of Enrique III of Castile and that when the Ottoman Turks resumed their offensive against the Balkans and Eastern Europe in the first third of the fifteenth century, the Spanish Christians had to consider a possible response. The Mediterranean world was a unity. Any Islamic advance in the East was also considered a threat to the Christians of the West.

For the Ottoman advance of the 1380s, Brockelmann, *History of the Islamic Peoples*, 268–270, Vasiliev, *History of the Byzantine Empire*, II: 621ff, 629ff; Ostrogorsky, *History of the Byzantine State*, 479–491; Runciman, *History of the Crusades*, III: 454ff.

In the late fourteenth and early fifteenth century the Spanish, though at the other end of the Mediterranean, were seriously interested in and deeply involved in the eastern Mediterranean. That was especially true for the Catalans, Aragonese, and Navarrese. Merriman, *Rise of the Spanish Empire*, I: 363–382; Payne, *History of Spain and Portugal*, I: 102, 110; Vasiliev, *History of the Byzantine Empire*, II: 604–608, 680, 689; Ostrogorsky, *History of the Byzantine State*, 415, 438ff, 441ff, 488; Kenneth M. Setton, *Catalan Domination of Athens 1311–1388* (Cambridge: Harvard University Press, 1948); his "The Latins in Greece and the Aegean from the Fourth Crusade to the End of the Middle Ages," *Cambridge Medieval History* 4 (1966): 388–430, 908–

938; as well as his "The Catalans in Greece, 1311-1380" and his "The Catalans and Florentines in Greece, 1380-1462," in Setton, *History of the Crusades*, III: 167-277; Aziz Atiya, *Egypt and Aragon: Embassies and Diplomatic Correspondence 1300-1330* (Leipzig: Brockhaus, 1938); Francesco Giunta, *Aragonesi e Catalani nel Mediterraneo*, 2 vols. (Palermo: Manfredi, 1953-1959); J.F. Cabestany, *Expansio Catalana per la Mediterrania* (Barcelona: Bruguera, 1967).

Castile was also involved in the eastern Mediterranean, especially through its close link with the Genoese, for which, Aguado-Bleye, *Manual*, I: 927; Russell, *English Intervention*, 14, 31, 212, 228-229, 237; R.B. Tate, "Medieval Kingdoms of the Iberian Peninsula (to 1474)," in P.E. Russell, ed., *Spain: A Companion to Spanish Studies* (London: Methuen, 1973), 99; Payne, I: 103. For the Genoese in the eastern Mediterranean, Vasiliev and Ostrogorsky, both index, *s.v.* "Genoa." Circa 1389-1399 the Genoese persuaded the French that the Turkish advance into the Balkans was a threat to Western Europe. Tuchman, *Distant Mirror: The Calamitous Fourteenth Century*, 463; Runciman, *History of the Crusades*, III: 455 and note 3; 457; 462 and note 2. Perhaps the Genoese also attempted to persuade the Spanish to the same effect. Cf. also the Castilian negotiations with the Turkish Sultan Bayezid and with the Tartar Tamerlane, Merriman, I: 159-164; Aguado-Bleye, I: 781; O'Callaghan, 540.

31. Merriman, *Rise of the Spanish Empire*, I: 34-41; Payne, *History of Spain and Portugal*, I: 1; Aguado-Bleye, *Manual*, I: 53-63.

32. The Jews of France had two chief rabbis in the fourteenth century: Mattathias the son of Joseph and his son Johanan. The Jews of thirteenth-century England had a chief rabbi, the *Presbyter Judeorum*. Germany had a chief rabbi in the thirteenth century, Meir the son of Baruch of Rothenburg, as well as several chief rabbis in the fifteenth century, including Israel of Krems, Anselm of Cologne, and Seligmann Oppenheim of Bingen. Turkey had a chief rabbi from 1453, called the Haham Bashi, the first of which was Moses Capsali. However, in Iberia there were five chief rabbis, one for each of the five kingdoms (Portugal; the *arraby moor*; Castile, the *rab de la corte*; Granada, title unknown to us; Aragon, title unclear, perhaps the same as Navarre, which was *rabi mayor*). For the chief rabbis of the various independent Iberian kingdoms in general, I. Levitats, "Chief Rabbi, Chief Rabbinate," *Ency. Judaica* 5 (1971): 418-420; Baron, *Jewish Community*, I: 283-303.

The Jews of Poland in the sixteenth century were united by the famed Council of Four Lands, for which, three articles, S.M. Dubnow, *Jewish Ency.* 4 (1903): 304-308; M.S. Balaban, *Univ. Jewish Ency.* 3 (1941): 382-383; and H.H. Ben Sasson, *Ency. Judaica* 5 (1971): 995-1003; also Baron, *Jewish Community*, I: 323-337. However, there was no such council in Iberia, despite the fact that Iberia was a peninsula, relatively cut off from the rest of the world, while Poland was open to Germany on the west and Russia on the east; and we would normally expect that Jews in a more isolated situation (Iberia) would feel greater cohesiveness than those in a more accessible situation (Poland).

Thus, a great council of the Jewish communities which met in Barcelona in 1354 (under the general spiritual direction of Rabbi Nissim the son of Reuben Gerondi) attempted unsuccessfully to set up a permanent executive committee for the Jews of eastern Iberia (two representatives each from Catalonia and Aragon, one each from Valencia and Majorca). Despite the importance of this council, apparently no representatives of the Jewries of Portugal, Castile, Granada, or Navarre attended. Baer, *Jews in Christian Spain*, II: 24–28.

Likewise, the great Tortosa disputation (1413–1414), the most spectacular theological debate between Jewish and Christian theologians during the Middle Ages, involved only the Jews of Aragon and Catalonia. Baer compares the Tortosa disputation to the contemporaneous Council of Constance, which was a great international meeting of profound significance in the history of the papacy and the church. Yet, despite the tremendous importance of the Tortosa disputation, which lasted more than a year, apparently no representatives of the Jewries of Portugal, Castile, Granada, or Navarre were present to encourage their beleaguered brethren of Aragon. Baer, II: 170–174.

Further, when Abraham Bienveniste reorganized the Jewish communities of Castile by convoking the great Jewish council of Valladolid in 1432, apparently no representatives of the Jewish communities of Portugal, Granada, Aragon, and Navarre were present, despite the fact that this council attempted with relative success the monumentally important task of restoring to the Jewish communities of Castile (the largest of the five Iberian kingdoms, whose Jewish population was greater than that of any of the other four kingdoms) the same power and influence which they had enjoyed before the crisis of circa 1390 to 1420. Baer, II: 259–270.

By contrast, the Jews of medieval France had synods which drew delegates from all (or most) of the major regions of the country. Baron, *Jewish Community*, I: 309–323.

Thus, when the time of troubles came upon the Jewries of Castile and Aragon circa 1390–1420, perhaps they converted in part because they knew that they would receive no help from each other or the independent-minded Jewries of Portugal, Granada, and Navarre.

The Jewries of Portugal, Granada, and Navarre were more or less able to escape attack and collapse during the time of troubles circa 1390 to 1420. Kayserling, "Portugal," *Jewish Ency.* 10 (1905): 138; his "Granada, ibid., VI: 80; and his "Navarre," ibid. 9 (1905): 192. Hence, they were theoretically able to offer psychological and material support to the Jewries of Castile and Aragon during the time of troubles, but it is unclear how much support, if any, they *actually* did offer.

33. Romans 15:24 and 28. Cf. also three articles on Spain: Kayserling and Jacobs, *Jewish Ency.* 11 (1905): 484; Baer, *Univ. Jewish Ency.* 9 (1943): 686; and Schwarzfuchs, *Ency. Judaica* 15 (1971): 220; plus Katz, *Jews in the Visigothic and Frankish Kingdoms*, 3–5; Baer, *Jews in Christian Spain*, I: 15–17; and Baron, *Social and Religious History*, I: 169–170, 176; II: 188, 210.

34. Thus, Menahem the son of Saruk was born in Tortosa. Cf. two articles on Menahem, by W. Bacher, *Jewish Ency.* 7 (1904): 470; and J. Blau, *Ency. Judaica* 11 (1971): 1305. He was thus a native of northeastern Spain, but not Andalusia or Cordova where he entered into Hasdai ibn Shaprut's service. Hasdai ibn Shaprut's familial roots, by contrast, were purely Andalusian. His grandfather resided in Jaen, while his father moved from Jaen to Cordova, where Hasdai was born. Ashtor, "Hisdai Ibn Shaprut," *Ency. Judaica* 8 (1971): 533; and his *Jews of Moslem Spain*, I: 159. Dunash ibn Labrat's familial roots were in Bagdad, Iraq, and Fez, Morocco, whence he came to Cordova. Cf. two articles on Dunash, Bacher, *Jewish Ency.* 5 (1903): 11; and C.M. Rabin, *Ency. Judaica* 6 (1971): 270; plus Ashtor, *Jews of Moslem Spain*, I: 252. Hasdai's decision to support Dunash instead of Menahem may have

reflected in part an alliance of the more heavily Islamicized Jews of southern Spain against the Jews of northern Spain who were more open to Christian influence.

35. Ibn Abitur was a native of Merida (Guadiana River Valley). *northwest* of Cordova (Guadalquivir River Valley). His family had long been resident in Spain. J.H. Schirmann, "Ibn Abitur, Joseph Ben Isaac," *Ency. Judaica* 8 (1971): 1152; Ashtor, *Jews of Moslem Spain*, I: 356. Enoch ben Moses, like his father, Moses ben Enoch, was an immigrant to Andalusia and Cordova from southern Italy. Ashtor, "Moses Ben Hanokh," *Ency. Judaica* 12 (1971): 417; his "Hanokh Ben Moses," *ibid.* 7 (1971): 1226; and his *Jews of Moslem Spain*, I: 234–235, 355–356. Thus, when Hasdai ibn Shaprut supported Enoch ben Moses against Joseph ibn Abitur (Ashtor, *Jews of Moslem Spain* I: 364), he was again supporting a foreign immigrant to Spain (as was Dunash ibn Labrat) over a more native Jew, from a region of Spain north of Cordova (as was Menahem ben Saruk).

Ashtor, *Jews of Moslem Spain*, I: 365, argues that the Jewish upper class of Cordova supported ibn Abitur while the Jewish middle class thereof supported Enoch ben Moses. Yet Ashtor, 364, also points out that the Jewish upper class of Cordova that supported ibn Abitur was composed of "old families," *i.e.*, families with deeper historical roots in Spain (like ibn Abitur himself). The ibn Jau brothers, Jacob and Joseph, were apparently born in Cordova, like Hasdai ibn Shaprut ("Ibn Jau, Jacob," *Ency. Judaica* 8 [1971]: 1186; Ashtor, 376); yet they supported ibn Abitur, not Enoch ben Moses, perhaps because they favored Jews with deeper historical roots in Spain and/or needed the support of the Jewish upper class of Cordova, the "old families."

36. Ibn Janah was born in either Cordova or nearby Lucena but spent most of his creative life in Saragossa, northeastern Spain. Cf. two articles on ibn Janah, Bacher, *Jewish Ency.* 6 (1904): 534; and D. Tene, *Ency. Judaica* 8 (1971): 1182. Samuel Ha-Nagid was born in Cordova (to a family which, like that of ibn Abitur, was originally form Merida) but spent most of his creative life in Granada. Cf. two articles on Samuel Ha-Nagid, I. Broyde, *Jewish Ency..* 11 (1905): 24; and *Ency. Judaica* 14 (1971): 816.

Samuel's literary quarrel with ibn Janah may have been caused in part by Samuel's resentment over the following fact. When the Jewish community of Cordova scattered upon the collapse of the caliphate circa 1013, ibn Janah went to live and work in the north, an area exposed to constant Christian attack and influence, while he, Samuel, remained in the more heavily Islamicized south. Samuel, thus, could have seen ibn Janah as a betrayer of the pure Andalusian Jewish tradition. Samuel's enmity toward ibn Janah would thus have had much in common with Hasdai ibn Shaprut's enmity toward Menahem ben Saruk (supra, note 34).

37. For the northern Abulafias of Burgos, two articles on the Abulafia family, Kayserling et al., *Jewish Ency.* 1 (1901): 140–144; and Roth et al., *Ency. Judaica.* 2 (1971): 184–196; plus Baer, *Jews in Christian Spain*, II, index, *s.v.* "Abulafia family." For Samuel ibn Wakar of Toledo, an ally of the Abulafia's against the southern Joseph of Ecija, Z. Avneri, "Ibn Wakar [Family]," *Ency. Judaica* 8 (1971): 1205–1206; Baer, I: 327, 354–356. For the northern Paul of Burgos, supra, notes 2 and 34 to chapter 7.

For the southern Abravanels of Seville, two articles on the Abravanel family, Kayserling and L. Ginzberg, *Jewish Ency.* I (1901): 126-129; and Roth, *Ency. Judaica* 2 (1971); 102–111; plus Baer, 1, index, *s.v.* "Abravanel." For the southern Joseph of Ecija (near Seville), two articles on Joseph, I. Broyde, *Jewish Ency.* 3 (1902): 40; and

Beinart, *Ency. Judaica* 6 (1971): 356; plus Baer, I: 325–327, 355, 359, 445. For the southern Joseph Pichon of Seville, two articles on Pichon, Kayserling, *Jewish Ency.* 10 (1905): 30–31; and *Ency. Judaica* 13 (1971): 498–499; plus Baer, I: 336, 367, 376, 450.

38. For the Karaites in Algeria, Baron, *Social and Religious History*, VII: 17–18, 225–227, notes 17–18. For the Karaites in Italy between circa 800 and 1000, J. Schirmann, "Beginning of Hebrew Poetry in Italy," in Roth, *Dark Ages*, 251; Zimmels, "Scholars and Scholarship in Byzantium and Italy," ibid., 182, 186–188. For the Karaites in Spain, infra, note 39. Cf. also in general Judah Rosenthal, "Kara'im V'Kara'ut B'Eropa Ha-Ma'aravit" [Karaites and Karaism in Western Europe], in *Sefer Ha-Yovel L'Rabbi Hanoh Albeck* [Jubilee Volume for Rabbi Hanoh Albeck] (Jerusalem: Mosad Ha-Rav Kuk, 1963), 425–442.

39. Cantera Burgos, "Christian Spain," in Roth, *Dark Ages*, 377–378; Leon Nemoy, *Karaite Anthology* (New Haven: Yale University Press, 1955), xxi, 4, 124, 133, 254, 382, 393; Baron, *Social and Religious History*, VII: 21–22, 228, note 21; Zukerman, *Jewish Princedom*, 211 and note 91; Cohen, *Book of Tradition*, index, *s.v.* "Karaites"; Baer, *Jews in Christian Spain*, I: 26, 51, 65, 77, 95, 104, 151, 350, 390; II: 456.

40. Supra, note 5 to chapter 7. Cf also Meyer Waxman, *History of Jewish Literature* (2nd.; New York: Yoseloff, 1960), II: 197–271; Isaac Husik, *History of Medieval Jewish Philosophy* (New York and Philadelphia: Meridian and Jewish Publication Society of American, 1958, (index, *s.v.* "Aristotelians," "Aristotle," and "Averroes"; Guttmann, *Philosophies of Judaism*, index, *s.v.* "Aristotelianism," "Aristotle," and "Averroes"; A. Hyman, "Philosophy, Jewish," *Ency. Judaica* 13 (1971): 440–452. Cf also four articles on Averroes/Averroism, A. Loewenthal, *Jewish Ency.* 2 (1902): 346–347; I. Broyde, ibid., II: 347–348; *Univ. Jewish Ency. 1* (1939): 643; and Pines, Suler, and Muntner, *Ency. Judaica*, III: 949–953.

For reasons that are worthy of further study, the Averroist threat to orthodoxy was neutralized in Western Christendom (it never existed in Eastern Christendom) and Islam during the thirteenth century, though it continued to pose a major threat in Judaism for at least two centuries thereafter.

41. Cf. two articles on Moses of Narbonne, I. Broyde, *Jewish Ency.* 9 (1905): 71–72; and Alfred L. Ivry, *Ency. Judaica* 12 (1971): 422–424; Hyman, "Philosophy, Jewish," ibid., XIII: 446; Husik, *History of Medieval Jewish Philosophy*, 309–310, 328, 430, 451, note 403a; Guttman, *Philosophies of Judaism*, 206–208, 225; Baer, *Jews in Christian Spain*, I: 332, 373, 446, 449; Waxman, *History of Jewish Literature*, II 208–210, 542; Israel Zinberg, *History of Jewish Literature*, trans. and ed. Bernard Martin (Cleveland and London: Case Western Reserve University Press, 1973), III: 125–128.

Cf. also C. Touati, "Dieu et le Monde selon Moise Narboni," *Archives d'Histoire Doctrinale et Litteraire du Moyen Age* 21 (1954): 193–205; G. Vajda, *Recherches sur la Philosophie et la Kabbale dans le Pensee Juive du Moyen Age* (Paris and The Hauge: Mouton, 1962), 396–403; Colette Sirat, "Moise de Narbonne et l'Astrologie," *Proceedings of the Fifth World Congress of Jewish Studies* (Jerusalem: World Union of Jewish Studies, 1972), III: 61ff; and her *"Pirke Mosheh l'Moshe Narboni"* [Moses of Narbonne's *Chapters of Moses*], *Tarbitz* 39 (April 1970): 287–306; Alexander Altmann,

"Moses Narboni's Epistle on Shiur Quoma," in Altmann's *Studies in Religious Philosophy and Mysticism* (Ithaca: Cornell University Press, 1969), 180–209; Alfred L. Ivry, "Moses of Narbonne's 'Treatise on the Perfection of the Soul'," *Jewish Quarterly Review* 57 (1967): 271-297; E.I.J. Rosenthal, "Political Ideas in Moshe Narboni's Commentary on Ibn Tufayl's *Hayy b. Yaqzan*," in G. Nahon and C. Touati, eds., *Hommage a Georges Vajda: Etudes d'Histoire et de Pensee Juives* (Louvain: E. Peeters, 1980), 227-234; Maurice Hayoun, "Moise de Narbonne, Commentateur du *Guides des Egares de Egares* de Maimonide," *Revue des Etudes Juives* 137 (1978): 467-468; and his "L'Epitre du Libre Arbitre de Moise de Narbonne (c. 1360-1362)," ibid. 141 (1982): 139-167; Kalman P. Bland, *Epistle on the Possibility of Conjunction with the Active Intellect by ibn Rushd with the Commentary of Moses Narboni, a Critical Edition and Annotated Translation* (New York: K'tav, 1983).

The ultra-Averroism of Moses of Narbonne reinforced, and was reinforced by, the Averroism of the following other Jewish philosophers who flourished in Spain (and/or nearby southern France) circa 1200–1391: (1) ibn Matkah, (2) Falaquera, (3) Albalag, (4) Kaspi, and (5) Gersonides.

For ibn Matkah of Toledo (circa 1200–1250), Pines, Suler, and Muntner, "Averroes," *Ency. Judaica*, III: 952: "Matkah (Ibn), Judah Ben Solomon Ha-Kohen," ibid. 11 (1971): 1126–1127.

For Falaquera (circa 1225–1295), Pines, Suler, and Muntner, *Ency. Judaica*, III: 951–952; Hyman, "Philosophy, Jewish," ibid., XIII: 444; M.N. Zobel, "Fallaquera Shem Tov Ben Joseph," ibid. 6 (1971): 1140–1143.

For Albalag (second half of the thirteenth century), Altmann, "Judaism and World Philosophy," in Finkelstein, *The Jews: Their History, Culture and Religion*, I: 645; Hyman, "Philosophy, Jewish," *Ency. Judaica*, XIII: 445; G. Vajda, "Albalag, Isaac," ibid. 2 (1971): 520–521.

For Kaspi (circa 1279–1340), Altmann, in Finkelstein, *The Jews*, I: 645; Pines, Suler, and Muntner, *Ency. Judaica*, III: 952; Hyman, ibid., XIII; 444; E. Kupfer, "Kaspi, Joseph Ben Abba Mari Ibn," ibid. 10 (1971): 809-811; I. Twersky, "Joseph ibn Kaspi: Portrait of a Medieval Jewish Intellectual," in Twersky, *Studies in Medieval Jewish History and Literature*, 231-257; Basil Herring, *Joseph Ibn Kaspi's Gevia^c Kesef: A Study of Medieval Jewish Philosophic Bible Commentary* (New York: K'tav, 1983).

For Gersonides (1288–1344), Altmann, in Finkelstein, *The Jews*, I: 645; Pines, Suler, and Muntner, *Ency. Judaica*, III: 951; Hyman, ibid., XIII: 446–447; B.R. Goldstein, "Levi Ben Gershom," ibid. 11 (1971): 92–98; Seymour Feldman, "Gersonides on Creation," *Proceedings of the American Academy for Jewish Research* 35 (1967): 113–137; B.R. Goldstein, "Preliminary Remarks on Levi ben Gerson's Contributions to Astronomy;" *Proceedings of the Israel Academy of Sciences and Humanities* 3 (1969): 239–254; Norbert Samuelson, "Gersonides's Account of God's Knowledge of Particulars," *Journal of the History of Philosophy* 10 (1972): 399–416; Menachem Marc Kellner, "Gersonides, Providence and the Rabbinic Tradition," *Journal of the American Academy of Religion* 42 (1974): 673-685; and his "Gersonides on Miracles, the Messiah and Resurrection," *Daat* 4 (1980): 5-34; T.M. Rudavsky, "Individuals and the Doctrine of Individuation in Gersonides," *New Scholasticism* 56 (1982): 30-50; Seymour Feldman, ed. and trans., *Wars of the Lord: Levi Ben Gershom (Gersonides)* (Philadelphia: Jewish Publication Society of America, 1983).

513

According to Davidson, Maimonides denied the eternity of the universe and believed either in creation from preexisting matter or in creation *ex nihilo*. H. Davidson, "Maimonides' Secret Position on Creation," in Twersky, *Studies in Medieval Jewish History and Literature*, 16-40

According to Marc Angel and H.P., Salomon, "Nahmanides' Approach to Midrash in the Disputation of Barcelona," *The American Sephardi* 6 (Winter 1973): 41-51, Nahmanides (thirteenth-century Catalonia), though a towering mystical figure, encouraged the development of an ultrarationalist attitude toward the *midrash* (the non-legal portions of rabbinic literature), thereby unintentionally, though significantly, contributing to the impact of philosophy upon the collapse of Spanish Jewry.

The following Jewish theologians of fourteenth-century Spain (and Morocco, ibn Malkah) attempted unsuccessfully to stem the Averroist tide but were overwhelmed by the superior brilliance of Moses of Narbonne and the other extreme Aristotelian thinkers listed immediately above: (1) Abudarham (Seville, early fourteenth century), (2) Ibn Waqar (Toledo, midcentury), (3) Ibn Malkah (Morocco, midcentury), (4) Ibn Motot (Guadalajara, midcentury), (5) Isaac Aboab (Toledo?, late fourteenth century), (6) Al-Nakawa (Toledo, late fourteenth century). Cf. the following articles in the 1971 *Ency. Judaica*: Z. Avneri, "Abudarham, David Ben Joseph," II: 181-182; G. Vajda, "Ibn Waqar, Joseph Ben Abraham," VIII: 1206-1207; his "Malkah, Judah Ben Nissim Ibn," XI: 827-828; and his "Ibn Motot, Samuel Ben Saadiah," VIII: 1189-1190; "Aboab, Isaac, I," II: 90-93; M.N. Zobel, "Al-Nakawa, Israel B. Joseph," II: 672-673.

Daniel J. Lasker, "Averroistic Trends in Jewish-Christian Polemics in the Late Middle Ages," *Speculum* 55 (1980): 294-304, de-emphasizes the Averroist influence on the collapse of Spanish Jewry circa 1390-1415, but in the article he does not seem to take any account of Moses of Narbonne, the ultra-Averroist of the generation immediately preceding the collapse. Lasker does refer to Moses of Narbonne all too briefly in his book *Jewish Philosophical Polemics against Christianity in the Middle Ages* (New York: K'tav, 1977), 65, 79-81, as refuting the Trinity. The fact that the Jewish Averroists used Averroism in an attempt to defend Judaism and attack Christianity by no means militates against the likelihood that their encouragement of Averroism unwittingly undermined the very religion they were attempting to defend. Similar ironies are known to the history of civilization in general and the Jewish people in particular!

Cf. also in general M. Kellner, "Jewish Dogmatics after the Spanish Expulsion: Rabbis Isaac Abravanel and Joseph Ya'bes on Belief in Creation as an Article of Faith," *Jewish Quarterly Review* 72 (1982): 178-187.

42. Baer, *Jews in Christian Spain*, II, index *s.v.* "Averroism"; Netanyahu, *Abravanel*, 3rd ed., and his *Marranos*, 2nd ed., both index, *s.v.* "Averroes."

43. For Crescas, three articles, E.G. Hirsch, *Jewish Ency.* 4 (1903): 350-353; A. Kaminka, *Univ. Jewish Ency.* 3 (1941): 408-409; and W. Harvey, *Ency. Judaica* 5 (1971): 1079-1085; Baer, *Jews in Christian Spain*, II, index, *s.v.* "Hasdai Crescas"; Netanyahu, *Abravanel*, 3rd ed., and *Marranos*, 2nd ed., both index, *s.v..* "Crescas, Hasdai." For Spinoza, infra, note 97.

44. Netanyahu, *Marranos*, 103-106. For Alami, supra, note 6.

45. Netanyahu, *Marranos*, 98, 110-111, 116. Cf. also two articles on Shem Tov ibn Shem Tov, M. Schloessinger, *Jewish Ency.* 6 (1904): 541-542; and W. Harvey, *Ency. Judaica* 8 (1971): 1198-1199; Baer, *Jews in Christian Spain*, II: 234-239, 426, 484.

46. Netanyahu, *Marranos*, 135–137, 139–140, 163–165. Cf. also two articles on Arama, L. Ginzberg, *Jewish Ency.* 2 (1902): 66–67; and S.O. Heller-Wilensky, *Ency. Judaica* 3 (1971): 256–259; Baer, *Jews in Christian Spain*, I: 395, 432; II: 254–258, 286, 426, 486, 488, 507. Cf. also supra, note 10 to chapter 7.

47. Netanyahu, *Marranos*, 172–173. Cf. also two articles on Ibn Shuaib, I. Broyde, *Jewish Ency.* 6 (1904): 543; and A. David, *Ency. Judaica* 8 (1971): 1201; Baer, *Jews in Christian Spain*, II: 507. Cf also supra, notes 10 and 12 to chapter 7.

48. Gershom G. Scholem, *Major Trends in Jewish Mysticism* (3rd ed.; New York: Schocken, 1965), 1–39; and his *On the Kabbalah and Its Symbolism*, trans. R. Manheim (New York: Schocken, 1965), 1–31. Cf. also Scholem, *Major Trends* and *On the Kabbalah*, both index, *s.v.* "Unio Mystica."

Kriegel, *Juifs a la Fin du Moyen Age*, 145-179, shares our view that it was the combined effect of both philosophy and mysticism that undermined Judaism in fourteenth-century Spain. Cf. Roditi, *Judaism*, XXIX: 246.

49. Scholem, *On the Kabbalah*, 92–93. On the *Sefer Bahir*, Scholem, *On the Kabbalah* and *Major Trends*, both index, *s.v.* "Bahir." Cf. also Scholem's article, "Bahir, Sefer Ha-,"*Ency. Judaica* 4 (1971): 96–101.

Cf. J. Dan, "Samael, Lilith, and the Concept of Evil in Early Kabbalah," *Association for Jewish Studies Review* 5 (1980): 17-40.

50. Scholem, *Major Trends*, 238–239.

51. Scholem, *Major Trends*, chapter 8, "Sabbatianism and Mystical Heresy," 287–324. In the table of contents to this book, xiii–xiv, Scholem lists the topics he treats in this chapter. They include "Quasi Sacramental Character of Anti-nomian Actions," "Influence of *Marranic* Psychology on Sabbatianism," "Doctrine of the Necessary Apostasy of the Messiah," "The Problem of Antinomianism," "Mystical Nihilism and the Doctrine of the Holiness of Sin." Cf. also Scholem, "Shabbetai Zevi," *Ency. Judaica* 14 (1971): 1219–1254; and his *Sabbatai Sevi: The Mystical Messiah 1626–1676*, trans. R.J. Zwi Werblowsky (Princeton: Princeton University Press, 1973).

Indeed, Herman P. Salomon argues that Scholem's monumental *Sabbatai Sevi* has been superseded by Yerushalmi's *From Spanish Court to Italian Ghetto* (for which, supra, note 3 to chapter 4), because Yerushalmi helps demonstrate something of which Scholem was apparently unaware, *i.e.*, that "the true focus of 'Sabbatianism' . . . [was] the overwhelming ex-Marrano participation therein," under the influence of the seventeenth-century Portuguese Christian messianic movement known as Sebastianism, whose leading representative was the Christian pro-Marrano figure Antonio Vieira (for whom, supra, note 1 to chapter 7). Cf. Salomon's review of Scholem's *Sabbatai Sevi*, in *The American Sephardi* 7–8 (autumn 1975): 130–132.

52. Supra, note 17 to chapter 7 and note 51 to the present chapter.

53. Scholem, *Major Trends*, 296, 299, 302, 306–311, 321.

54. For Shabbatianism and Hasidism, Scholem, *Major Trends*, 325–334. Cf. also S.M. Dubnow, "Hasidism," *Jewish Ency.* 6 (1904): 251–252. For Shabbatianism and Zionism, two articles on Zionism, R. Gottheil, *Jewish Ency.* 12 (1906): 666–668; and L. Lipsky, *Univ. Jewish Ency.* 10 (1943): 646; Scholem, "Judah Hasid (Segal) Ha-Levi," *Ency. Judaica* 10 (1971): 373.

55. Scholem, *Major Trends*, 304.

56. John B. Noss, *Man's Religion* (3rd ed.; New York: Macmillan, 1963), 145ff, 150,

298; Ringgren and Strom, *Religons of Mankind*, 320–324; A.L. Basham, *The Wonder That Was India: A Survey of the Culture of the Indian Sub-Continent before the Coming of the Muslims* (New York: Grove, 1959), 242–243, 322–323, 333, 340; Swami Prabhavananda and Frederick Manchester, *The Spiritual Heritage of India* (Garden City, New York:: Doubleday/Anchor, 1964), 5, 57–62, 225.

57. For the doctrine of reincarnation in Buddhism, Noss, *Man's Religions*, 181–183; Ringgren and Strom, *Religions of Mankind*, 365–370; Basham, *Wonder That Was India*, 271, 278; Prabhavananda and Manchester, *Spiritual Heritage of India*, 1–98, 202. Cf. also Steven Runciman, *The Medieval Manichee: A Study of the Christian Dualist Heresy* (Cambridge: Cambridge University Press, 1969), 186.

For the doctrine of reincarnation in Jainism, Noss, 158ff; Ringgren and Strom, 333; Basham, 291; Prabhavananda and Manchester, 169.

58. Noss, *Man's Religions*, 89, Ringgren and Strom, *Religions of Mankind*, 230; B.A.G. Fuller and S.M. McMurrin, *History of Philosophy* (3rd ed.; New York: Holt, 1955), I: 41–42; John Burnet, *Early Greek Philosophy* (4th ed.; New York: Meridian, 1960), 84–85, 93; Martin P. Nilsson, *History of Greek Religion*, trans. F.J. Fielden (2nd ed.; New York: Norton, 1964), 201–202; Runciman, *Medieval Manichee*, 186.

59. George Widengren, *Mani and Manichaeism*, trans. C. Kessler (New York:: Holt, Rinehart and Winston, 1965), 65; Runciman, *Medieval Manichee*, 186. For the doctrine of reincarnation among the Druzes, D.G. Hogarth and G.M.L. Bell, "Druses," *Ency. Brit.* 8 (1926): 604. This doctrine was also linked with the Byzantine philosopher John Italus (circa 1081–1118). Runciman, *Medieval Manichee*, 70. For Italus in general, Vasiliev, *History of the Byzantine Empire*, II: 473–475, 497, 699; Ostrogorsky, *History of the Byzantine State*, 331–332.

60. Cf. Runciman, *Medieval Manichee*, 150, for the doctrine of reincarnation among the Cathars of southern France, and Runciman, 129, 174, 186, for possible Cathar influence on St. Francis of Assisi. Cf. also Lynn White's essay, "The Historical Roots of Our Ecological Crisis," *Science* 155 (March 10, 1967): 1206–1207 = White's *Machina Ex Deo: Essays in the Dynamism of Western Culture* (Cambridge: Massachusetts Institute of Technology Press, 1968), 91–95. Cf. also Kajetan Esser, "Franz von Assisi und die Katharer seiner Zeit," *Archivum Franciscanum Historicum* 51 (1958): 225–264; Ilarino da Milano, "Il Dualismo Cataro in Umbria al Tempo di San Francesco d'Assisi," in *Filosofia e Cultura in Umbria tra Medioevo e Rinascimento, Atti del IV Convegno di Studi Umbri, Gubbio, 22-26 Maggio, 1966* (Perugia: Facolta di Lettere e Filosofia dell'Universita degli Studi di Perugia, 1967), 175–216.

61. Scholem, *Major Trends*, 242–243, 250, 278, 281–284, 402, 406–407, 409, 413–414, 418; plus three articles on transmigration of souls (called *gilgul n'fashot* in Hebrew), I. Broyde, *Jewish Ency.* 12 (1906): 213–214; *Univ. Jewish Ency.* 9 (1943): 654–655; and Scholem, *Ency. Judaica* 7 (1971): 573–577.

62. According to Scholem, "Gilgul," *Ency. Judaica*, VII: 574–575, the *Sefer Bahir* (late twelfth-century southern France) held that reincarnation could continue for *as many as 1,000 generations*. On the other hand, the prevailing view among Spanish Jewish mystics from the thirteenth century was that sinners are reincarnated only three more times, whereas the righteous are reincarnated *forever* for the benefit of the sinners. However, there was a minority opinion among Spanish Jewish mystics which held vice

versa, *i.e.*, that the righteous are reincarnated only three times, whereas the sinners are reincarnated *forever*. According to Scholem there was also a view among Spanish Jewish mystics (as evidenced by the *Sefer Ha-P'liah* written circa 1375 to 1425; for which, supra, notes 1 to chapter 7 and 5 to the present chapter) that a Jewish soul could pass into the body of a Gentile in the next reincarnation. It is quite conceivable, then, that there was also a belief among Spanish Jewish mystics at the time of the crisis that if a Jew converted to Christianity *with sincerity*, his soul would be permanently reincarnated in Christian bodies throughout all succeeding generations!

63. Supra, note 60; Scholem, *Major Trends*, 242–243; and his "Gilgul," *Ency. Judaica*, VII: 574. Abraham bar Hiyya (Catalonia and southern France, early twelfth century) accepted the doctrine of reincarnation in his treatise *Hegyon Ha-Nefesh* but rejected it in his treatise *M'gillat Ha-M'galleh*. Hyman, "Philosophy," *Ency. Judaica*, XIII: 436. Abraham ibn Daud (Toledo, mid twelfth century) also rejected the doctrine of reincarnation. Broyde, "Transmigration of Souls," *Jewish Ency.*, XII: 232; Scholem, "Gilgul," *Ency. Judaica*, VII: 573. These two rejections (Abraham bar Hiyya and Abraham ibn Daud) indicate that the doctrine of reincarnation was accepted in twelfth-century Spain by a number of Jews large enough to be noticed by the rejectors.

64. Scholem, *Major Trends*, 242; supra, notes 49 and 62.

65. Scholem, *Major Trends*, 415, note 122; and his "Gilgul," *Ency. Judaica*, VII: 574; E.Z. Liebes, "Isaac the Blind," ibid. 9 (1971): 35.

66. Scholem, *Major Trends*, 242–243; and his "Gilgul," *Ency. Judaica*, VII: 574–575.

67. Scholem, *Major Trends*, 281, 414, note 116. On Ibn Latif in general, S.O. Heller-Wilensky, "Latif, Isaac Ben Abraham Ibn," *Ency. Judaica* 10 (1971): 1446–1448. Other thirteenth-century Spanish Jewish writers who favored the doctrine of reincarnation were as follows: (1) Nahmanides (Scholem, "Gilgul," *Ency. Judaica*, VII: 574; T. Preschel, "Nahmanides: As Biblical Commentator," ibid. 12 [1971]: 778); (2) *Sefer Ha-T'munah* (Scholem, *Ency. Judaica*, VII: 574–575; E. Gottlieb, "Temunah, The Book of," ibid. 15 [1971]: 999–1000); (3) Bahya b. Asher (Scholem, *Ency. Judaica*, VII: 575; Gottlieb, "Bahya Ben Asher Ben Hlava," ibid. 4 [1971]: 104–105); (4) David b. Abraham Ha-Lavan (Scholem, *Ency. Judaica*, VII: 576; and his "David Ben Abraham Ha-Lavan, ibid. 5 [1971]: 1347); (5) *Ta'ame Ha-Mitzvot* (Scholem, *Ency. Judaica*, VII: 575). Jedaiah Bedersi rejected the doctrine of reincarnation in a letter to Solomon ibn Adret of Barcelona (Broyde, "Transmigration," *Jewish Ency.* XII: 232).

68. Scholem, *Major Trends*, 243, 407, note 137; and his "Gilgul," *Ency. Judaica*, VII: 575–576; M. Hallamish, "Joseph Ben Shalom Ashkenazi," ibid. 10 (1971): 237. Other fourteenth-century Spanish Jewish writers who favored the doctrine of reincarnation include (1) Judah ben Asher (Broyde, "Transmigration," *Jewish Ency.*., XII: 232; Y. Horowitz, "Judah Ben Asher," *Ency. Judaica* 10 [1971]: 341); (2) Joseph of Hamadan (Scholem, "Gilgul," ibid., VII: 575). Cf. also infra, notes 131 and 135, for Menahem Recanati and reincarnation.

69. Netanyahu, *Marranos*, 116 and note 83; supra, note 45. Cf. supra, note 62, for reincarnation in the *Sefer Ha-P'liah* circa 1375–1425. Other fifteenth-century Spanish Jewish writers who discuss reincarnation include (1) Crescas (who opposed it;

Broyde, "Transmigration," *Jewish Ency.* XII: 232); (2) Albo (who opposed it; Broyde, 232; Scholem, "Gilgul," *Ency. Judaica*, VII: 573); (3) Abravanel (who favored it; Broyde, 232; Netanyahu, *Abravanel*, 117–118, 297).

70. Scholem, *Major Trends*, 80–118; three articles on Judah He-Hasid, M. Schloessinger, *Jewish Ency.* 7 (1904): 356–358; W. Ducat, *Univ. Jewish Ency.* 6 (1942): 224; and J. Dan, *Ency. Judaica* 10 (1971): 352; three articles on Elazar of Worms, I. Broyde, *Jewish Ency.* 5 (1903): 100–101; J. Lerner, *Univ. Jewish Ency.* 4 (1941): 61–62; and J. Dan, *Ency. Judaica* 6 (1971): 592–594; J. Dan, "Hasidei Ashkenaz" and "Hasidim, Sefer," ibid. 7 (1971): 1377–1383, 1388–1390.

71. We owe the basic idea behind reason no. 10 to Professor Moses A. Shulvass, Spertus College of Judaica, Chicago (for whose work, supra, note 37 to chapter 4), who conveyed it to us in a private conversation; however, he bears no responsibility for the detailed development of this basic idea as presented here. Supra, footnote * to the present chapter.

72. For agriculture as the main occupation of Christian Spain, O'Callaghan, *History of Medieval Spain.* 300, 615. For agriculture as the main occupation of the Muslims in Christian Spain (the Mudejars), O'Callaghan, 605. However, the Jewish situation was different. While most of the Christians and Muslims of Spain were farmers, only "some" of the Jews of Spain were farmers, and many of the Jews who farmed did so only as a sideline to some other urban-based business or craft. Baron, *Social and Religious History*, XII: 37; and his "Economic History," *Ency. Judaica* 16 (1971): 1284–1286.

Cf. also Baer, *Jews in Christian Spain*, II, index, *s.v.* "Farmers, Jewish," wherein we note that there are references to only eight discussions of Jewish farming in Baer's two volumes (though Baer, index, *s.v.* "Land ownership," refers to twenty-three discussions of this subject in the two volumes, while Baer, index, *s.v.* "Artisans (city-dwellers)," refers to fifty discussions of this subject in both volumes.

Cf., however, Justiniano Rodriguez Fernandez, *La Juderia de la Ciudad de Leon* (Leon: Centro de Estudios e Investigacion "San Isidoro," 1969), as reviewed by Herman P. Salomon, *The American Sephardi* 7–8 (autumn 1975): 129–130, for the fact that most Jews in the province of Leon tilled the soil, which Salomon calls "surprising." It assuredly is an exception that proves the rule that most Spanish Jews engaged in urban-oriented economic activities in the later Middle Ages (1300–1500).

73. O'Callaghan, *History of Medieval Spain*, 464, 466; Payne, *History of Spain and Portugal*, I: 207; Baron, *Social and Religious History*, XII: 91, 153–154; Baer, *Jews in Christian Spain*, II, index, *s.v.* the following: "Physicians," "Astronomers, Jewish," "Translators," "Tax Farming," and "Moneylending."

74. Baer, *Jews in Christian Spain*, I: 369–373; supra, note 1 to chapter 7 and notes 40 and 62 to the present chapter.

75. Graetz, *Geschichte der Juden*, VIII: 37–38 = *History of the Jews*, IV: 154–155; supra, note 6.

76. Netanyahu, *Marranos*, 138; supra, note 46.

77. Netanyahu, *Marranos*, 160–161, 163–165; supra, note 10 to chapter 7.

78. On the Almohade invasion of the midtwelfth century, Brockelmann, *History of the Islamic Peoples*, 202, 207ff; Hitti, *History of the Arabs*, 545–549; Imamuddin, *Political History of Muslim Spain*, 265–271; Chejne, *Muslim Spain*, 79–89; Richard Hitch-

cock, "Muslim Spain," in Russell, *Spain: A Companion to Spanish Studies*, 55–56; Payne, *History of Spain and Portugal*, I: 70–72; O'Callaghan, *History of Medieval Spain*, 227–229; Aguado-Bleye, *Manual*, I: 589–591.

79. According to the great American historian of immigration, Marcus Lee Hansen, "What the son [second generation immigrant] wishes to forget, the grandson [third generation immigrant] wishes to remember." *Newsweek Magazine* 90:1 (July 4, 1977): 26. For the second generation, Hansen's *The Immigrant in American History*, ed. Arthur M. Schlesinger (New York: Harper and Row/Torchbooks, 1964), 92–95, 141, 145–146, 202–203; for the third generation, 153. Cf. also on the third generation, Philip Taylor, *The Distant Magnet: European Emigration to the United States of America* (London: Eyre and Spottiswoode, 1971), 274–278.

Jewish scholars who agree with Hansen about the return of the third generation include Will Herberg, *Protestant, Catholic and Jew* (New York: Doubleday/Anchor, 1960), 186–191; Nathan Glazer, *American Judaism* (Chicago: University of Chicago Press, 1960), 106–126, 172; Jacob Neusner, *American Judaism: Adventure in Modernity* (Englewood Cliffs, New Jersey: Prentice-Hall, 1972), 68–71.

80. Merriman, *Rise of the Spanish Empire*, I: 6–9; Payne, *History of Spain and Portugal*, I: 1–3; Aguado-Bleye, *Manual*, I: 154–157; Baron, *Social and Religious History*, I: 175–176, 374–375, note 13.

Cf. also W.F. Albright, "Phoenicians," *Univ. Jewish Ency.* 8(1942): 517–518; A.S. Kapelrud, "Phoenicia," *Interpreter's Dictionary of the Bible* 3 (1962): 802–803; A. Blanco Freijeiro, "Cartagineses" and "Fenicios," *Diccionario de Historia de Espanya* (1968), I: 741–742; II: 42; H.J. Katzenstein, "Phoenicia, Phoenicians," *Ency. Judaica* 13 (1971): 478–479; R.D. Barnett, "Phoenicia," *Ency. Brit.* 17 (1972): 888; H.V. Livermore, "Spain: History," ibid. 20 (1972): 1084; A. Garcia y Bellido, "Spain: History," *Ency. Brit. Macropaedia* 17 (1976): 402; Rhys Carpenter, "The Phoenicians in the West," *American Journal of Archeology* 62 (1958): 48–53; W. Culican, "Aspects of Phoenician Settlement in the Western Mediterranean," *Abr-Nahrain* 1 (1959–1960): 36–55; Garcia y Bellido, H. Schubart, and H.G. Niemeyer, "Espagne," in S. Moscati, ed., *L'Espansione Fenicia nel Mediterraneo, Relazioni del Colloquio in Rome, 4–5 Maggio 1970* (Rome: Consiglio Nazionale delle Ricerche, 1971), 145–160; the four following: Dimitri Baramki, *Phoenicia and the Phoenicians* (Beirut: Khayats, 1961), Donald Harden, *The Phoenicians* (New York: Praeger, 1962), B.H. Warmington, *Carthage* (2nd ed.; London: Hale, 1969), and Gerhard Herm, *Die Phoenizier: das Purpurreich der Antike* (Duesseldorf and Vienna: Econ, 1973)—all index, *s.v.* "Spain/Spanien"; Moscati, *The World of the Phoenicians*, trans. A. Hamilton (London: Weidenfeld and Nicolson, 1968), 230ff.

81. For Byzantine influence in Visigothic Spain, Vasiliev, *History of the Byzantine Empire*, I: 137–138, 196; Ostrogorsky, *History of the Byzantine State*, 65, 72; Aguado-Bleye, *Manual*, I: 348–349, 352; E.A. Thompson, *The Goths in Spain* (Oxford: Clarendon, 1969), index, *s.v.* "Byzantines."

82. Castro, *Structure of Spanish History*, chapter 7, "Three Christian-Islamic Institutions: Military Orders, Holy War, Tolerance," 202–229 = *The Spaniards*, 471–508.

Cf. O'Callaghan, *History of Medieval Spain*, 456–457, for the nine Christian military orders in medieval Spain. Cf. also O'Callaghan, *The Spanish Military Order* of *Calatrava and Its Affiliates* (London: Variorum, 1975); Derek W. Lomax, *La Orden de Santiago (1170-1275)* (Madrid: Consejo Superior de Investigaciones Cientificas, Escuela de Estudios Medievales, 1965); J. M. Lacarra, "Les Villes-Frontieres dans l'Espagne des XIe et XIIe Siecles," *Le Moyen Age* 69 (1963): 205-222; Elena Lourie, "A Society Organized for War: Medieval Spain," *Past and Present* 35 (December 1966): 54-76; J.F. Powers, "Townsmen and Soldiers: The Interaction of Urban and Military Organization in the Militias of Medieval Castile," *Speculum* 46 (1971): 641-655.

During the discussion following Mr. Cutler's lecture on the topic of this book to Professor Robert Ignatius Burns' Seminar on Medieval Spain at UCLA, November 13, 1979, Professor Burns acknowledged that there might well have been an Islamic influence upon the Castilian war machine, since the light cavalry was its most prominent feature. In a letter to Mr. Cutler dated the following day, November 14, 1979, Professor Burns stated that he had "come to have a very different view" from that of Americo Castro about the Islamic influence upon two of the three Spanish Christian institutions stressed by Castro, *i.e.*, the military orders and the holy war. As Professor Burns further stated in this letter: "I think his [Castro's] principle is correct; but the institutions now seem to me mutually independent yet ultimately mutually 'osmotic,' especially the Holy War development." For Burns on Castro and Sanchez-Albornoz, supra, note 8 to chapter 7.

83. Brockelmann, *History of the Islamic Peoples*, 205; Hitti, *History of the Arabs*, 544-545; Imamuddin, *Political History of Muslim Spain*, 262-263; Chejne, *Muslim Spain*, 53, 123. Cf. also R.B. Tate, "Medieval Kingdoms of the Iberian Peninsula (to 1474)," in Russell, *Spain*, 74-75; Ian Michael, "Spanish Literature and Learning to 1474," ibid., 201-203; Payne, *History of Spain and Portugal*, I: 63-64; O'Callaghan, *History of Medieval Spain*, 205-206, 211-212, 314-317; Aguado-Bleye, *Manual*, I: 605-618.

For the Cid and the Jews, Baron, *Social and Religious History*, IV: 29, 246; Baer, *Jews in Christian Spain*, I: 52, 58-59, 80, 386-389; Cantera Burgos, "Christian Spain," in Roth, *Dark Ages*, 374-375, 452, notes 42-44.

84. For the Mozarabs in general, supra, note 30 to chapter 2 and note 29 to chapter 7. Cf. also Brockelmann, *History of the Islamic Peoples*, 206; Hitti, *History of the Arabs*, 515, 543-544, 559, 597; Imamuddin, *Political History of Muslim Spain*, 211-212; Chejne, *Muslim Spain*, 118-120; R. Hitchcock, "Muslim Spain," in Russell, *Spain*, 46-48, 56, 58; Payne, *History of Spain and Portugal*, I: 22, 33, 37, 47-48, 53, 114, 116, 123, 131; O'Callaghan, *History of Medieval Spain*, 107-115, 150-153, 176-177, 185-190, 285-286; Aguado-Bleye, *Manual*, I: 412-413, 415-423, 461-462, 468-469, 527-533; Castro, *Structure of Spanish History*, 317-321; and his *Spaniards*, 22-23, 54-55, 227-228.

On Gundissalinus, Chejne, 322, 358, 403; Michael, "Spanish Literature and Learning to 1474," in Russell, 197; O'Callaghan, 313-314, 326; Aguado-Bleye, I: 933-934; Castro, *Structure of Spanish History*, 301, 324; and his *Spaniards*, 519-521; Gilson, *History of Christian Philosophy in the Middle Ages*, 237-240, 652-653; d'Alverny, "Avendauth?" in *Homenaje a Millas-Vallicrosa*, I: 19-43; and her "Dominic Gundisalvi," *New Cath. Ency.* 4 (1967): 966-967; M. Alonso, *Temas Filosoficos Medievales (Ibn Daud y Gundisalvo)* (Comillas: Universidad Pontificia, 1959).

85. On the contribution of Arabic science and technology, the work of Millas-Vallicrosa, supra, notes 8 and 28 to chapter 7.

For Alfonso X, Brockelmann, *History of the Islamic Peoples*, 214; Hitti, *History of the Arabs*, 559, 570–571, 600; Imamuddin, *Political History of Muslim Spain*, 286–288; Chejne, *Muslim Spain*, index, s.v. "Alfonso X"; Merriman, *Rise of the Spanish Empire*, I: 98–115; Michael, "Spanish Literature and Learning to 1474," in Russell, *Spain*, 212, 216–219; Payne, *History of Spain and Portugal*, I: 76–77, 80–81, 153–154; O'Callaghan, *History of Medieval Spain*, 358–381, 479–481, 509–517; Aguado-Bleye, *Manual*, I: 681–696, 935–936, 947; Castro, *Structure of Spanish History and Spaniards*, both index, s.v. "Alphonso X the Learned"; Baer, *Jews in Christian Spain*, I: 111–130, 402ff, 437ff.

Cf. also Antonio Ballesteros y Beretta, *Alfonso X el Sabio* (Barcelona: Salvat, 1963); John E. Keller, *Alfonso X el Sabio* (New York: Twayne, 1967); articles by Albert Bagby, supra, note 28 to chapter 7.

For Ramon Lull, Hitti, 587, 663; Chejne, 403; P. Russell-Gebbett, "Medieval Catalan Literature," in Russell, *Spain*, 249–252, 261; Payne, I: 107, 137, 139; O'Callaghan, 504–506; Aguado-Bleye, I: 938–941; Castro, *Structure of Spanish History*, 309–314; and his *Spaniards*, 45, 191, 279, 503–505, 519, 529; Baer, I: 183ff, 417ff; II: 6, 208.

Cf. also Juan Saiz Barbera, *Raimundo Lullo: Genio de la Filosofia y Mistica Espanyola* (Madrid: Ediciones y Publicaciones Espanyolas, 1963); A. Llinares, *Raymond Lulle: Philosophe de l'Action* (Paris: Presses Universitaires de France, 1963); Erhard W. Platzeck, *Raimund Lull: Sein Leben, Sein Werke, die Grundlagen Seines Denkens*, 2 vols. (Duesseldorf: Schwann, 1962–1964); Jocelyn Hillgarth, *Ramon Lull and Lullism in Fourteenth-Century France* (Oxford: Clarendon Press, 1971).

For Don Juan Manuel, Chejne, 408; Michael, "Spanish Literature and Learning to 1474," in Russell, *Spain*, 223–225; O'Callaghan, 510–512; Aguado-Bleye, I: 947–948; Castro, *Structure of Spanish History*, 219–221, 241–242, 383–387; and his *Spaniards*, 76, 495–498, 501, 504, 556–559; Baer, I: 121ff, 136ff; K.R. Scholberg, "Spanish and Portuguese Literature," *Ency. Judaica* 15 (1971): 249.

Cf. also A. Gimenez Soler, *Don Juan Manuel: Biografia y Estudio Critico* (Saragossa: Academia Espanyola e F. Martinez, 1932).

For Juan Ruiz, Chejne, 245, 259; Michael, in Russell, *Spain*, 222–223; O'Callaghan, 478, 492, 497, 514, 643; Aguado-Bleye, I: 948; Castro, *Structure of Spanish History* 392–465; and his *Spaniards*, 559, 586; Scholberg, "Spanish and Portuguese Literature," *Ency. Judaica*, XV: 249.

Cf. also M.R. Lida de Malkiel, *Two Spanish Masterpieces: The "Book of Good Love" and the "Celestina"* (Urbana: University of Illinois Press, 1961); A.N. Zahareas, *Art of Juan Ruiz: Archpriest of Hita* (Madrid: Estudios de Leteratura Espanyola, 1965); G.B. Gybbon-Monypenny, ed., *"Libro de Buen Amor" Studies* (London: Grant and Cutler, 1970).

86. For Islamic influence on Spanish music, J. Ribera, *Historia de la Musica Arabe Medieval y su Influencia en la Espanyola* (Madrid: Voluntad, 1927) and his *Music in Ancient Arabia and Spain*, trans. and ed. E. Hague and M. Leffingwell (London and Palo Alto: H. Milford, Oxford University Press and Stanford University Press, 1929); Hitti, *History of the Arabs*, 598–601; Chejne, *Muslim Spain*, 368–374; R. Stevenson,

"Spanish Music," in Russell, *Spain*, 547–549; Gustave Reese, *Music in the Middle Ages* (New York: Norton, 1940), 245ff.

For Mudejar architecture, Hitti, 593–597: Chejne, 359–368; O.N.V. Glendinning, "Visual Arts in Spain," in Russell, *Spain*, 474–475; Aguado-Bleye, *Manual*, I: 1004–1011.

Cf. also Rodriguez Eguia, "Mudejar," *Enciclopedia de la Cultura Espanyola*, IV: 407–412; G. Marcais, "Moorish Style," *Encyclopedia of World Art* 10 (1965): 320–321; J. Gudiol and S. Alcolea, "Spanish and Portuguese Art," ibid. 13 (1967): 316–317; Georgiana G. King, *Mudejar* (Bryn Mawr and London: Bryn Mawr College and Longmans, Green, 1927); L. Torres Balbas, *Arte Almohade, Arte Nazari, Arte Mudejar* (Madrid: Editorial Plus-Ultra, 1949); Basilio Pavon Maldonado, *Tudela, Ciudad Medieval: Arte Islamico y Mudejar* (Madrid: Institute Hispano-Arabe de Cultura, 1978); Paniagua, *La Arquitectura Romanico-Mudejar en la Provincia de Salamanca*.

87. For Pedro the Cruel and ibn Khaldun, Brockelmann, *History of the Islamic Peoples*, 215. For the predominance of Mudejar in royal buildings circa 1250–1400, Aguado-Bleye, *Manual*, I: 1006.

During the discussion following Mr. Culter's lecture on the topic of this book to Professor Robert Ignatius Burns' Seminar on Medieval Spain at UCLA, November 13, 1979, Professor Burns suggested that Islamic influence on Christian Spain became stronger in the fourteenth century as the spirit of the thirteenth-century *Reconquista* waned, and that one additional example of this influence is Castilian courtly life heavily Arabicized in the fourteenth century. For strong Islamic influence on the mid-thirteenth-century Aragonese monarchy, Burns, "The Spiritual Life of James the Conqueror, King of Arago-Catalonia, 1208–1276: Portrait and Self-Portrait," *Catholic Historical Review* 62 (1976): 1–35.

88. Cf. three articles on the Marranos, Kayserling, *Jewish Ency.* 8 (1904): 318–322; Baer, P. Goodman, N. Sargologos, and J. Brawer, *Univ. Jewish Ency.* 7 (1942): 366–369; and Martin Cohen, *Ency. Judaica* 11 (1971): 1019–1025; plus Roth, *Marranos*, 195–295; Baron, *Social and Religious History*, XIII: 64–158; XV: 3–73, 259–373; Netanyahu, *Marranos*, 2nd ed., 216ff, 251ff. The greatest center of the Marrano diaspora was Amsterdam. Cf. also infra, note 89.

89. Cf. three articles on the Sephardim, Kayserling, *Jewish Ency.* 11 (1905): 197–198; Neuman, *Univ. Jewish Ency.* 9 (1943): 477–478; A.D. Corre, Cecil Roth, and H.J. Campeas, *Ency. Judaica* 14 (1971): 1164–1177. The greatest center of the Sephardi diaspora was Istanbul. Cf. also supra note 88.

90. Supra, note 40 to chapter 7. For Marrano influence in the highest echelons of government in late fifteenth-century Spain (those echelons which planned and successfully executed the conquest of Granada in 1492), Roth, *Marranos*, 24–25; Caro Baroja, *Los Judios en la Espanya Moderna y Contemporanea*, II: 14ff; Kamen, *Spanish Inquisition*, 36–37; Haliczer, *American Historical Review*, LXXVIII: 41; Castro, *The Spaniards*, 147–164, especially 149–150, 156, 157 and note 19, 158 and note 50.

91. Richard H. Popkin, "Philosophy," *Ency. Judaica* 13 (1971): 416–417; and his "The Historical Significance of Sephardic Judaism in Seventeenth-Century Amsterdam," *American Sephardi* 5 (autumn 1971): 18–27. Cf. also in general Roth, *Marranos*, 195–251; Jacob S. Raisin, *Gentile Reactions to Jewish Ideals, with Special Reference to*

Proselytes, ed. Herman Hailperin (New York: Philosophical Library, 1953), 528–670; Baron, *Social and Religious History*, XIII: 3–158; XV: 3–160.

92. Popkin, "Philosophy," *Ency. Judaica*, XIII: 416; Roth, "Vitoria, Francisco de," ibid. 16 (1971): 195; Roth, *Marranos*, 303, 396, note 3; Baron, *Social and Religious History*, XIII: 80.

93. Popkin, "Philosophy," *Ency. Judaica*, XIII: 416; and his "Vives, Juan Luis," ibid. 16 (1971): 197–198; K.R. Scholberg, "Spanish and Portuguese Literature," ibid. 15 (1971): 253; Baron, *Social and Religious History*, XIII: 77. Juan Valdes (died 1541), the great Spanish Erasmian, and his brother Alfonso (died 1532) were also Marranos. Baron, XIII: 78–79.

94. A. Yarmolinsky, "Montaigne, Michel de," *Univ. Jewish Ency.* 7 (1942): 626–627; D.R. Goitein, "French Literature," *Ency. Judaica* 7 (1971): 146; Roth, *Marranos*, 227; and his "The Jewish Ancestry of Michel de Montaigne," in Roth's *Personalities and Events in Jewish History* (Philadelphia: Jewish Publication Society of America, 1953), 212–225; Raisin, *Gentile Reactions*, 595, 603; Baron, *Social and Religious History*, XIII: 118–119; R.A. Mentzner, "Marranos of Southern France in the Early Sixteenth Century," *Jewish Quarterly Review* 72 (1982): 304 and note 3.

95. Popkin, "Philosophy," *Ency. Judaica*, XIII: 416–417; and his "La Boetie, Etienne De," ibid. 10 (1971): 1319.

96. Cf. two articles on Bodin, *Univ. Jewish Ency.* 2 (1940): 436; and Blumenkranz, *Ency. Judaica* 4 (1971): 1161–1162; also H.H. Ben-Sasson, "History," ibid. 8 (1971): 701; Raisin, *Gentile Reactions*, 595, 603; Baron, *Social and Religious History*, XV: 94–96. Blumenkranz holds that Bodin definitely was not of Marrano descent, while Raisin, Baron, and Ben-Sasson consider it possible that he was.

97. Cf. three articles on Spinoza, Jacobs, *Jewish Ency.* 11 (1905): 511–520; Max Joseph, *Univ. Jewish Ency.* 10 (1943): 5–8; and Popkin and R. Smend, *Ency. Judaica* 15 (1971): 275–284; also Popkin, "Philosophy," ibid., XIII: 417; Roth, *Marranos*, 157, 247, 250, 288, 300, 318; Raisin, *Gentile Reactions*, 614–615, 665; Baron, *Social and Religious History*, 1st ed., index, *s.v.* "Spinoza, Baruch"; Baron, *Social and Religious History*, 2nd ed., XV: 65.

98. Cf. three articles on Uriel da Costa, F. de Sola Mendez, *Jewish Ency.* 1 (1901): 167–168; Sol Bernstein, *Univ. Jewish Ency.* 1 (1939): 72–74; and Popkin and B. Bayer, *Ency. Judaica* 5 (1971): 987–989; also Popkin, "Philosophy," ibid., XIII: 417; Roth, *Marranos*, 231, 247, 298, 397; Baron, *Social and Religious History*, 1st ed., II: 208–210; III: 140.

99. Cf. two articles on Isaac la Peyrere, *Univ. Jewish Ency.* 8 (1942): 472; and Popkin, *Ency. Judaica* 10 (1971): 1425–1426; also Popkin, "Philosophy," ibid., XIII: 417; Roth, *Marranos*, 227; Raisin, *Gentile Reactions*, 602; Baron, *Social and Religious History*, XV: 90–91. Cf. also Popkin, "The Marrano Theology of Isaac La Peyrere," *Studi Internazionali di Filosofia* 5 (1973): 97–126; and his "Menasseh Ben Israel and Isaac La Peyrere," *Studia Rosenthaliana* 8 (January 1974): 59–63; Ira Robinson, "Isaac de la Peyrere and the Recall of the Jews," *Jewish Social Studies* 40 (1978): 117–130.

100. Popkin, "Philosophy," *Ency. Judaica*, XIII: 417; "Prado, Juan De," ibid. 13 (1971): 962–963; Roth, *Marranos*, 300; Baron, *Social and Religious History*, XV: 65, 407–408.

101. Netanyahu, *Marranos*, 2nd ed., 227–237.

102. Netanyahu, *Marranos*, 2nd ed., 238–248, assumes an approximate 50 percent increase in the number of Spanish Marranos between circa 1400 and 1480. He considers but rejects the possibility of a 100 percent increase in the number of Marranos during this same period as being "most unlikely for the Middle Ages" (p. 245). However, Netanyahu may be *too* cautious here! Thus, Vicens Vives held that the population of Spain increased by 100 percent between circa 1130 and 1340. O'Callaghan, *History of Medieval Spain*, 459. The population of Iberia increased by about 100 percent between circa 1380 and 1480, *i.e.*, from around 5 million people in 1380 to around 10 million people in 1480. Infra, notes 107-108. The population of northern Europe increased by about 200 percent circa 1250 to 1482. O'Callaghan, 604. Likewise, Vicens Vives estimated that the number of unconverted Jews in Castile increased by 100 percent between circa 1391 and 1492. O'Callaghan, 606. Infra, note 109, for our estimates of an average 160 percent increase for Marranos and unconverted Jews in Iberia circa 1400 to 1480.

103. On Roman Spain, D. Gifford, "Spain and the Spanish Language," in Russell, *Spain*, 7–12; Tate, "Medieval Kingdoms of the Iberian Peninsula (to 1474)," ibid., 65–67; Payne, *History of Spain and Portugal*, I: 5–8; Aguado-Bleye, *Manual*, I: 194–314; C.H.V. Sutherland, *The Romans in Spain 217 B.C - A.D. 117* (London: Methuen, 1939); F.J. Wiseman, *Roman Spain: An Introduction to the Roman Antiquities of Spain and Portugal* (London: Bell, 1956).

On Spanish imperial domination within Italy circa 1300–1700, Merriman, *Rise of the Spanish Empire*, IV, index, *s.v.* "Italy"; Payne, I: 248–252, 273–280; P. Trevor Davies, *The Golden Century of Spain 1501–1621* (London and New York: Macmillan and St. Martin's, 1961), and his *Spain in Decline 1621–1700* (London and New York: Macmillan and St. Martin's, 1961), both index, *s.v.* "Italy"; J.H. Elliott, *Imperial Spain 1469–1716* (New York: St. Martin's 1964), index, *s.v.* "Italy"; John Lynch, *Spain under the Hapsburgs* (Oxford: Blackwell, 1964–1969), I, index, *s.v.* "Italy"; C.M. Ady, "Italy: History," *Ency. Brit.* 12 (1972): 754–755; E. Pontieri, "Italy and Sicily: History," *Ency. Brit. Macropaedia* 9 (1976): 1148–1151; L. Salvatorelli, *Concise History of Italy*, trans. B. Miall (New York: Oxford University Press, 1940), 396–457; G. Procacci, *History of the Italian People*, trans. A. Paul (New York and Evanston: Harper and Row, 1968), 111–114, 118–124, 152–155, 160–164, 171.

104. For the Jewish fate in southern Italy circa 1300 we rely primarily on Baron, *Social and Religious History*, X: 220–231, 253; also ibid., XIII: 54–61.

Cf. also Attilio Milano, *Storia degli Ebrei in Italia* (Turin: Einaudi, 1963), 99–104; Cecil Roth, *History of the Jews of Italy* (Philadelphia: Jewish Publication Society of America, 1946), 100–102; his *Jews in the Renaissance* (Philadelphia: Jewish Publication Society of America, 1959), 5–6; and his *Marranos*, 5; Yerushalmi, *Spanish Court to Italian Ghetto*, 16 and note 21; Joshua Starr, "The Mass Conversion of Jews in Southern Italy (1290–1293)," *Speculum* 21 (1946): 203–211; and his "Johanna II and the Jews," *Jewish Quarterly Review* 31 (1940): 67–78; Ferorelli, *Gli Ebrei nell'Italia Meridionale*, 53ff; O. Dito, *La Storia Calabrese e la Dimora degli Ebrei in Calabria dal Secolo V alla Seconda Meta del Secolo XVI* (Rocca San Casciano: Cappelli, 1916), 161ff; A. Parisi, "Gli Ebrei in Reggio Calabria fino al XIII Secolo," *Historica* 20 (1967): 1–12; G. Sumo, *Gli Ebrei in Puglia dall XI al XVI Secolo* (Bari: Cressati, 1939), 48ff; L.

Amabile, *Il Santo Ufficio della Inquisizione in Napoli* (Castello: Lapi, 1892), I: 50ff; E. Munkacsi, *Der Jude von Neapel* (Zuerich: "Die Liga," 1940), 67ff; Umberto Cassuto, "Sulla Storia degli Ebrei Italiani nell'Italia Meridionale nell'Eta Angioina," *Vessilo Israelitico* 59 (1911): 338–341, 422–424; his "Un Ignoto Capitolo di Storia Ebraica," in *Judaica: Festschrift zu Hermann Cohens 70stem Geburtstage* (Berlin: Bruno Cassirer, 1912), 389–404; his "Iscrizioni Ebraiche a Trani," *Rivista degli Studi Orientali* 13 (1932): 172–180; his "Iscrizioni Ebraiche a Bari," ibid. 15 (1934): 316–322; and his "Hurban Ha-Y'shivot B'Italiyah Ha-D'romit Ba-Meah Ha-Sh'losh Esreh" [The Destruction of the Jewish Academies in Southern Italy in the Thirteenth Century], in S. Asaf and G. Scholem, eds., *Sefer Zikkaron L'Asher Gulak UliSh'muel Klein* [Memorial Volume for Asher Gulak and Samuel Klein] (Jerusalem: Hebrew University Press, 1942), 139–152; V. Vitale, "Un Particolare Ignorato di Storia Pugliese: Neofiti e Mercanti," in *Studi di Storia Napoletana in Onore di M. Schipa* (Naples: I.T.E.A., 1926), 233–246; plus the following articles in the 1971 *Ency Judaica:* "Amalfi," II: 791–792, U. Cassuto, "Apulia," III: 226–228; A. Milano, "Bari," IV: 223–224; Milano, "Brindisi," 1375–1376; A. Toaff, "Calabria," V: 33; Toaff, "Catanzaro," V: 252–253; Milano, "Cosenza," V: 977–978; Toaff, "Lecce," X: 1554; Taoff, "Naples," XII: 822; Roth, "Oria," XII: 1460; Toaff, "Otranto," XII: 1521; Toaff, "Salerno," XIV: 683; Toaff, "Taranto," XV: 806–807; Toaff, "Trani," XV: 1313–1314.

105. Baron, *Social and Religious History*, XII: 23, holds that in late medieval Germany and Spain we should multiply the number of Jewish families (or households) "by 7 or even 7.7" to arrive at a total population figure. We have multiplied by 8 in southern Italy circa 1300 (Baron's higher figure of 7.7 rounded off).

Netanyahu, *Marranos*, 2nd ed., 240 and note 3, prefers to multiply the number of Jewish households in Seville circa 1390 (6–7,000 households) by 5 to arrive at the total Jewish population of the town but allows that others have suggested multiples of 6 and even 7.

We suggest a multiple of 8 for southern Italian Jewry circa 1280: circa 2,600 Jewish families (= circa 20,000 Jews); 1,300 families (= circa 10,000 Jews) convert to Christianity and 1,300 families (= circa 10,000 Jews) survive as Jews.

A. Milano, "Italy," *Ency. Judaica* 9 (1971): 1121, estimates a total Jewish population in southern Italy circa 1290 of around 13,500 (too low a figure in our view; perhaps Milano counts only 5 people per family [2,600 families multiplied by 5 = 13,000], whereas we count about 8 people per family [2,600 families multiplied by 8 = around 20,000]). According to Milano, half of the Jews of southern Italy converted to Christianity circa 1290. This seems a reasonable estimate and one which we would agree with.

106. Cf. Starr, *Speculum*, XXI: 208, for a contemporary Christian estimate (circa 1304) of the total number of southern Italian Jewish converts at circa 8,000. We have estimated the total number of such converts at the higher figure of circa 10,000.

Cf. Starr for a population statistic of circa 2,750 Jews in Calabria in 1276. We have estimated the number of Calabrian Jews circa 1280 higher, at around 4,000. We have then estimated the Jewish population of both the Campanian and Apulian coasts each at about 75 percent greater than that of Calabria (or 7,000 each for Campania and Apulia) and the Jewish population of the interior at only 50 percent of that of Calabria (or 2,000 Jews in the interior).

525

107. Cf. O'Callaghan, *History of Medieval Spain*, 604–605, for the following Iberian population figures circa 1480: Castile, 7.5 million; Aragon, 1.0 million; Portugal, 1.0 million; Granada, 0.3 million; Navarre, 0.1 million. Total Iberian population circa 1480: 9.9 million.

How many Muslims were there in Iberia circa 1480? Hitti, *History of the Arabs*, 556, speaks of about 3 million Muslims in the sixteenth century. Would this mean about 2 million Muslims in the previous fifteenth century? Payne, *History of Spain and Portugal*, I: 213, considers the Muslims only about 5 percent of the total Iberian population circa 1500 (500,000 out of 10 million) and the Marranos about another 5 percent (500,000) This seems too low for both minority groups. We estimate that circa 1480 the Muslims were about 20 percent of the population, or 2 million, and the Jews (both Marranos and unconverted Jews together) were about 10 percent of the population, or 1 million.

We follow Netanyahu, *Marranos*, 2nd ed., 245, who estimates the number of Marranos circa 1480 at 7 percent of the total Iberian population (which was 10 million), *i.e.* circa 700,000 people, and the number of unconverted Jews at 3 percent of the total Iberian population, *i.e.*, circa 300,000 people.

Baron, *Social and Religious History*, XII: 25, estimates the total Iberian population circa 1490 at 8 million, too low by 2 million, and the total number of unconverted Jews in Iberia at that time at circa 330,000, quite close to Netanyahu's figure of 300,000.

Vicens Vives's figure of unconverted Jews in Iberia circa 1490 at around 200,000 (O'Callaghan, 606) seems too low.

108. Cf. O'Callaghan, *History of Medieval Spain*, 460–461, for a total Iberian population of about 6.7 million circa 1350. However, the Black Plague decimated the population, which dropped by about 25 percent in Catalonia between circa 1325 and 1375. Assuming a similar 25 percent population drop for all Iberia between circa 1325 and 1375, we obtain a total Iberian population of about 5 million circa 1380.

We estimate the total number of Iberian Jews circa 1380 at about 10 percent of this 5 million = 500,000. Vicens Vives's figure (O'Callaghan, 606) of only about 250,000 Iberian Jews circa 1380 seems too low again (supra, note 107, conclusion).

109. We have assumed that about 50 percent of the Jews of Castile and Aragon converted to Christianity circa 1390–1420. For similar assumptions, Payne, *History of Spain and Portugal*, I: 208; O'Callaghan, *History of Medieval Spain*, 606, both following Vicen Vives. For a similar assumption by Milano about south Italian Jewry circa 1300, supra, note 105.

However, Vicens Vives (O'Callaghan) assumes that only 12.5 percent of the Jews were massacred while 37.5 percent survived as Jews. We assume a higher percentage massacred, *i.e.*, 25 percent, and a correspondingly lower percentage who survived as Jews, again 25 percent.

Thus, circa 1380–1420

	VICENS VIVES		CUTLER	
total Jews in Iberia		250,000		500,000
total converts to Christianity	50%	125,000	50%	250,000
total massacred	12.5%	31,250	25%	125,000
total survived as Jews	37.5%	93,750	25%	125,000

Netanyahu, *Marranos*, 2nd ed., 238–243, points out that three well-informed Jewish chroniclers—Joseph ben Tzaddik of Arevalo (writing circa 1487), Abraham Zacuto (writing circa 1504), and Abraham ben Solomon of Torrutiel (writing circa 1510)—estimate the total number of Jewish converts to Christianity in Castile and Aragon circa 1390 to 1420 at about 400,000. This figure is probably too high. Our own figure is more conservative. We have estimated about 250,000 Jewish converts to Christianity in Spain circa 1390–1420.

Thus, according to our estimate, the Marrano population jumped from around 250,000 circa 1400 to around 700,000 circa 1480, an increase of about 180 percent within a century or less; whereas the population of unconverted Jews jumped from around 125,000 circa 1400 to around 300,000 circa 1480, an increase of about 140 percent within a century or less.

Hence, the total number of both Marranos and unconverted Jews increased by an average of about 160 percent between 1400 and 1480, while the total number of Christians in Iberia increased by only about 100 percent during this same period (from circa 5 million to circa 10 million; supra, notes 107–108. Why did the total number of Marranos and unconverted Jews increase by a greater percentage than the total number of Iberians in general? Perhaps because both minority groups felt considerably beleaguered. The Marranos could not gain full acceptance from the Old Christians and were hated by the unconverted Jews; the unconverted Jews were hated by both the Old Christians and the Marranos. Both groups (Marranos and unconverted Jews) thought (whether consciously or unconsciously) that they had vastly to increase their total numbers if they were to have any hope of increasing their political and social power, thereby of defeating their enemies and surviving.

110. Cf. supra, note 88 to chapter 5, for Aaron of Bagdad and the imposition of the death penalty in the south Italian Jewish community during the midninth century, the exception that proves the rule.

111. For the end of the Muslim colony of Lucera circa 1300, Starr, *Speculum*, XXI: 206–209, who cites especially R. Bevere, "Ancora sulla Causa della Distruzione della Colonia Saracena di Lucera," *Archivio Storico per le Province Napoletane* 60 (1936): 222–228; F. Gabrieli, "La Colonia Saracena di Lucera e la sua Fine," *Archivio Storico Pugliese* 30 (1977): 169-176.

112. Blumenkranz, "Badge, Jewish," *Ency, Judaica*, IV: 62–63; S.J. Siera, "Sicily," ibid. 14 (1971): 1493; supra, note 96 to chapter 5.

113. For the Arab threat to Italy and Rome circa 800 to 1100, Engreen, *Speculum*, XX: 318–330; Krueger, in Setton, *History of the Crusades*, I: 40–53. For the North African Islamic threat to Norman Sicily circa 1125, Brockelmann, *History of the Islamic Peoples*, 208. For the same threat to Italy circa 1212, Brockelmann, 211; supra, note 1 to chapter 6. For the North African Islamic threat to Sicily circa 1270, Runciman, *Sicilian Vespers: A History of the Mediterranean World in the Later Thirteenth Century* (Baltimore: Penguin, 1960), 157–163; and his *History of the Crusades*, III: 290–292.

114. Starr recognized the close link between the twin persecutions of the Muslims and Jews in southern Italy circa 1300. Supra, note 111.

For the association of Jew with Muslim by Pope Innocent III in the early thirteenth century, supra, chapter 6 of this book. For the same association by Dante in the late thirteenth century, supra, note 62 to chapter 4. For the same association by other thirteenth-fourteenth–century Italian Christians, supra, notes 54, 57, 59–65 to chapter 4.

For the association of Jew with Muslim in the great persecution of the Jews of France, Iberia, and Italy circa 1320, supra, note * to chapter 4. Thus, according to the testimony of Jacob ben Hananel Sikili (Kupfer, *Ency. Judaica*, XIV: 1530), Pope John XXII circa 1320 ordered the Portuguese fleet "to plunder and rob any Jew or Muslim they met on the sea." If Pope John XXII's association of Jew with Muslim was a factor in the Portuguese persecution of the Jews circa 1320 (for the Portuguese imposition of the "badge of shame" on the Jews circa 1325, supra, note 26), it was probably also a factor in the expulsion of the Jews from Rome which the pope very seriously contemplated circa 1321–1322 (but did not carry out thanks to an intervention in favor of the Jews by King Robert of Naples). Baron, *Social and Religious History*, XI: 250–252. From Baron's account it seems that there were riots against the Jews in Rome for three days circa 1321–1322 (during which 15,000 Jews are said to have been converted to Christianity), and there were similar disturbances in Naples around the same time. These disturbances almost certainly were occasioned by the association of Jew with Muslim, the same factor which occasioned the similar and contemporaneous riots against the Jews in France and northeastern Spain circa 1320.

What we seem to have had circa 1320 was a major persecution of the Jews of the northwestern Mediterranean (involving Portugal [but apparently not Castile], Aragon and Navarre, France, the Papal States and Campania/Naples) occasioned by the association of Jew with Muslim and the Christian belief that the Jew was in league with the Muslim planning the destruction of the West. What event so greatly intensified the Christian fear of a Judaeo/Islamic alliance circa 1320? We would suggest that it was the major Granadan victory over the Castilian army circa 1319, in which two of the highest-placed nobles in Castile were slain, Pedro and the Infante Juan (the son and the brother-in-law respectively of Maria de Molina, regent of Castile for the seven-year-old ruler Alfonso XI). O'Callaghan, *History of Medieval Spain*, 403; Imamuddin, *Political History of Muslim Spain*, 290: Bishko, "Spanish and Portuguese Reconquest," in Setton, *History of the Crusades*, III: 436–437. This spectacular Muslim victory over the Castilians would seem to have generated a powerful anti-Islamic crusading response among the Christians of the northwestern Mediterranean circa 1320, which, because of the preexisting equation of Jew with Muslim, spilled over onto the Jews who were severely persecuted in Spain, France, and Italy at this same time.

115. Thus, according to Gerson Cohen, Abraham ibn Daud's great Hispano-Jewish chronicle of the midtwelfth century was directed primarily against the Karaites. Supra, note 39. On the other hand, we know of no scholar who would interpret the greatest Italian-Jewish chronicle of the Middle Ages (the mideleventh-century chronicle of Ahima'atz) against the backdrop of the struggle against the Karaites. For whatever meager evidence we have of the Karaite presence in Italy circa 800–1000, supra, note 38.

116. Hartt, *History of Italian Renaissance Art*, 36–47, especially 36–37; also the Jansons, *History of Art*, 262, 264, 272, 306; Helen Gardner, *Art through the Ages*, ed. Sumner McK. Crosby (4th ed.; New York: Harcourt, Brace, 1959), 272–273; E.H.

Gombrich, *The Story of Art* (8th ed.; New York: Phaidon and Garden City, 1957), 143; Bernard S. Myers, *Art and Civilization* (New York: McGraw-Hill, 1957), 275, 322, 335, 338, 366, 373.

117. H. Hearder and D.P. Waley, *Short History of Italy from Classical Times to the Present Day* (Cambridge: Cambridge University Press, 1966), 55–58; Walter Ullman, *History of Political Thought: The Middle Ages* (Harmondsworth, England: Penguin, 1965), 189ff; A.P. d'Entreves, *Dante as a Political Thinker* (Oxford: Clarendon Press, 1952); and Charles T. Davis, *Dante and the Idea of Rome* (Oxford: Clarendon Press, 1957).

For the Spiritual Franciscan and Joachite link between Dante, William of Ockham, and Wycliffe, Moorman, *History of the Franciscan Order*, index, *s.v.* "Dante Alighieri," "Hussites," "John Wyclif," and "William of Ockham"; Reeves, *Influence of Prophecy*, index, *s.v.* "Dante," "Hus, J.," and "Wycliffe, J."

118. Supra, the discussion of the seventh, the geriatric, factor in the collapse of Spanish Jewry.

119. According to T. Ashby, "Lucera," *Ency. Brit.* 17 (1926): 96, Emperor Frederick II deported around 20,000 Arabs to Lucera circa 1223. To assume a 100 percent rate of increase between circa 1223 and 1300 for this initial group of Arab settlers at Lucera (*i.e.*, from 20,000 to 40,000) seems reasonable. However, it is likely that Frederick II deported many additional Arabs from Sicily to Lucera in the 1230s and 1240s. Supra, note 71 to chapter 6, for the Muslims in Christian Sicily, especially the Kantorowicz, Van Cleve, and Ahmad references. Cf. also supra, note 111.

120. Starr, *Speculum*, XXI: 209 and notes 38–39; supra, note 113.

121. Altmann, in Finkelstein, *The Jews*, I: 645; Pines, Suler, and Muntner, "Averroes," *Ency. Judaica*, III: 952; Hyman, "Philosophy, Jewish," ibid., XIII: 444–445; plus three articles on Hillel ben Samuel, A. Peiginsky, *Jewish Ency.* 6 (1904): 401–402; *Univ. Jewish Ency.* 5 (1941): 363; and J.B. Sermoneta, *Ency. Judaica* 8 (1971): 488–490.

122. U. Cassuto, "Gracian (Hen), Zerahiah Ben Isaac Ben Shealtiel," *Ency. Judaica* 7 (1971): 842–843.

Cf. also "Abbasi, Jacob Ben Moses Ibn," ibid. 2 (1971): 41, where we learn that Abbasi, though born in southern France, lived in Huesca, Aragon, in the second half of the thirteenth century. In Huesca circa 1297–1298 he translated Maimonides's commentary on the third order of the Mishnah from Arabic into Hebrew at the request of the Jews of Rome, Italy, who sent an emissary, one Rabbi Simhah, to Huesca via Rabbi Solomon ibn Adret at Barcelona.

123. Cf. three articles on Immanuel of Rome, I. Elbogen, *Jewish Ency.* 6 (1904): 563–564; S. Meisels, *Univ. Jewish Ency.* 5 (1941): 544; and U. Cassuto, *Ency. Judaica* 8 (1971): 1295–1298.

124. Altmann, in Finkelstein, *The Jews*, I: 645; Hyman, "Philosophy, Jewish," *Ency. Judaica*, XIII: 444; plus three articles on Jacob Anatoli, H.G. Enelow, *Jewish Ency.* 1 (1901): 562–564; J. Marcus, *Univ. Jewish Ency.* 1 (1939): 296–297; and U. Cassuto, *Ency. Judaica* 2 (1971): 927–929.

Judah ben Solomon Ha-Kohen ibn Matkah of Toledo, first half of the thirteenth century, the Hispano-Jewish Averroist philosopher (supra, note 41), was in correspondence with Emperor Frederick II and traveled to southern Italy to participate in translation projects sponsored by him. On this occasion ibn Matkah could well have met Anatoli.

Cf. also on Anatoli and ibn Matkah, Van Cleve, *Emperor Frederick II of Hohenstaufen*, 312–313.

125. Cassuto, "Anatoli," *Ency. Judaica* II: 929.

126. For Moses of Salerno (and his son Isaiah, who carried on his father's philosophical tradition), J.S. Raisin, "Moses Ben Solomon of Salerno," *Jewish Ency.* 9 (1905): 94; Cassuto, on Anatoli, supra, note 124; Milano, on Faraj, infra, note 127.

127. For Faraj (Ferragut) ben Solomon of Agrigento, two articles, I. Broyde, *Jewish Ency.* 5 (1903): 342–343; and A. Milano, *Ency. Judaica* 6 (1971): 1179–1180.

For Ahitub of Palermo, two articles, J. Marcus, *Univ. Jewish Ency.* 1 (1939): 140; and U. Cassuto, *Ency. Judaica* 2 (1971): 466–467.

For Moses of Palermo, two articles, I. Broyde, *Jewish Ency.* 9 (1905): 92; and J.B. Sermoneta, *Ency. Judaica* 12 (1971): 433–434.

Cf. also four important Jewish Averroists in Renaissance Italy (fifteenth through midsixteenth century): U. Cassuto, "Judah Ben Jehiel [Messer Leon]," *Ency. Judaica* 10 (1971): 347–348; J.S. Levinger, "Delmedigo, Elijah Ben Moses Abba," ibid. 5 (1971): 1477–1478; A. Toaff, "Sforno, Obadiah Ben Jacob," ibid. 14 (1971): 1209–1211; and A. Milano, "Mantino, Jacob Ben Samuel," ibid. 11 (1971): 895.

128. I. Broyde, "Translations," *Jewish Ency.* 12 (1906): 222; Broyde and I. Elbogen, "Meati, ha [Family]," ibid. 8 (1904): 398; Broyde, "Kalonymus Ben Kalonymus Ben Meir (Maestro Calo)," ibid. 7 (1904): 426–429; U. Cassuto, "Romano, Judah Ben Moses Ben Daniel," *Ency. Judaica* 14 (1971): 237.

129. Cf. Cassuto on Anatoli, supra, note 124; also ibn Matkah's Spanish link with southern Italy circa 1200–1250, supra, note 124; and Jacob Abbasi's Spanish link via ibn Adret of Barcelona with Rome circa 1297–1298, supra, note 122.

130. Cf. two articles on Isaiah di Trani the Younger, M. Schloessinger, *Jewish Ency.* 6 (1904): 644; and I.M. Ta-Shma, *Ency. Judaica* 9 (1971): 73. Normally the principle of the return of the third generation (supra, note 79) would have meant that Isaiah di Trani the Younger would have been as strongly prophilosophical as his distinguished grandfather, Isaiah di Trani the Elder. However, this was not the case. The deleterious effects of the philosophical movement on south Italian Jewry circa 1280 must have been truly great for the younger Trani to violate the principle of the return of the third generation.

131. Cf. two articles on Menahem Recanati, U. Cassuto, *Jewish Ency.* 10 (1905): 340; and E. Gottlieb, *Ency. Judaica* 13 (1971): 1608; plus Scholem, *Major Trends*, 243; 392–393; 407, note 137; 415, note 122; and his "Gilgul," *Ency. Judaica*, VII: 575.

132. Infra, note 133, references to Abraham Abulafia; supra, notes 121 and 127, references to Hillel of Verona and Ahitub of Palermo.

133. Supra, note 132. Cf. also Scholem, *Major Trends*, 126–130; plus three articles on Abraham Abulafia, P. Bloch, *Jewish Ency.* 1 (1901): 141–142; J. Marcus, *Univ. Jewish Ency.* 1 (1939): 60–62; and Scholem, *Ency. Judaica* 2 (1971): 185–186; supra note 6, para. 2, to chapter 6.

134. Cf. two articles on Isaac of Acre, M. Seligsohn, *Jewish Ency.* 6 (1904): 629–630; and E. Gottlieb, *Ency. Judaica* 9 (1971): 29–30.

135. Supra, notes 66–68, 131.

136. On Amalfi and the Arabs, supra, note 119 to chapter 5; on Italian Jews as intermediaries between Christians and Arabs circa 800–1100, supra, notes 79-110, 123-126, to chapter 5.

137. Cf. the references cited supra, notes 73, 104, 121-128.

138. E.A. Freeman and T. Ashby, "Sicily: History," *Ency. Brit.* 25 (1926): 25–30; Barnett, "Phoenicia," *Ency. Brit.* 17 (1972): 888; T.J. Dunbabin, "Sicily: History," ibid. 20 (1972): 467–469; Carpenter, *American Journal of Archeology,* LXII: 42–48; V. Tusa, "Sicilia," in Moscati, *Espansione Fenicia nel Mediterraneo,* 175–191; the four following: Baramki, *Phoenicia and the Phoenicians;* Harden, *Phoenicians;* Warmington, *Carthage;* Herm, *Phoenizier*—all index, *s.v.* "Sicily/Sizilien"; Moscati, *World of the Phoenicians,* 187ff; E.A. Freeman, *The Story of Sicily: Phoenician, Greek and Roman* (New York and London: Putnam's and T. Fisher Unwin, 1892); G. Cavallaro, *Panormos Preromana* (Palermo: Societa Siciliana per la Storia Patria, 1951); Margaret Guido, *Sicily: An Archaeological Guide* (London: Faber and Faber, 1967), index, *s.v.* "Carthage," "Carthaginians," and "Phoenicians."

139. Cf. Waverly Root, *The Food of Italy,* introduction by Samuel Chamberlain (New York: Atheneum, 1971), 551, for *caldariello* (lamb or kid cooked in sheep or goat milk), a specialty of the town of Gravina, in southern Italy. For possible Near Eastern links (via Crete) of the Iapigi, the main tribal group in Apulia in pre-Roman times, A. Pagliaro, "Iapigi," *Enciclopedia Italiana* 18 (1933): 655; Touring Club Italiano, *Guida d'Italia: Puglia* (3rd ed.; Milan: Touring Club Italiano, 1962), 27 and 271. For the Phoenician background of boiling a kid in milk, C. Virolleaud, "La Naissance des Dieux Gracieux et Beaux, Poeme Phenician de Ras-Shamra," *Syria* 14 (1933): 128–130, 133, 140; H.L. Ginsberg, "Notes on 'The Birth of the Gracious and Beautiful Gods'," *Journal of the Royal Asiatic Society* (1935): 65, 72; U. Cassuto, "G'di B'Halav Imo" [A Kid in Its Mother's Milk]," *Antziklopediyyah Mikrait* [Biblical Encyclopedia] 2 (1954): 435–437.

140. Steven Runciman, *Byzantine Civilization* (New York: Meridian, 1956), 211–213, 216–217; Ware, *Orthodox Church,* 38–43; Zernov, *Eastern Christendom,* 77, 86ff, 91, 93, 290; Schmemann, *Historical Roots of Eastern Orthodoxy,* 198–214; Vasiliev, *History of the Byzantine Empire,* index, *s.v.* "Iconoclasm"; Ostrogorsky, *History of the Byzantine State,* index, s.v. "Iconoclasm" and "Icon Veneration"; Gerhart Ladner, "Origin and Significance of the Byzantine Iconoclastic Controversy," *Mediaeval Studies* 2 (1940): 127–149. Cf. also Baron, *Social and Religious History* III: 178, 193; VIII: 26, 31; Parkes, *Conflict of Church and Synagogue,* 291–294; Starr, *Jews in the Byzantine Empire,* 3, 48, 76, 83, 89–90, 103; Sharf, *Byzantine Jewry.* 61–81.

For opposition to sculpture in Jainism, Noss, *Man's Religions,* 165; in Manicheanism, Runciman, *Medieval Manichee,* 33, 38, 51; Ringgren and Strom, *Religions of Mankind,* 286, 293; in Islam, Vasiliev, "The Iconoclastic Edict of the Caliph Yazid II, A.D. 721," *Dumbarton Oaks Papers* 9-10 (1956): 23–47; Gustave von Grunebaum, "Byzantine Iconoclasm and the Influence of the Islamic Environment," *History of Religions* 2 (1962-1963): 1–11; Marshall Hodgson, "Islam and Image," ibid. 3 (1963-1964): 220–260.

141. Hitti, *History of the Arabs,* 606–609; Runciman, *Sicilian Vespers,* 47, 50, 73, 113, 122–123, 126, 141, 147, 164, 269.

142. Joergensen, *St. Francis,* 121; Englebert, *St. Francis,* 169–172, 472, note 15a;

Moorman, *History of the Franciscan Order*, 207, Antonio Cristofani, *Delle Storie d'Assisi Libri Sei* (2nd ed.; Assisi: Sensi, 1875), 155ff; Lina Duff Gordon, *The Story of Assisi* (London and New York: Dent and Dutton, 1925), 267–269; Arnaldo Fortini, *Assisi nel Medio Evo: Leggende, Avventure, Battaglie* (Rome: Edizioni Roma, 1940), 157–212; Ezio Franceschini, "I Due Assalti dei Saraceni a San Damiano e ad Assisi, " *Aevum* 27 (1953): 289–306.

143. Hitti, *History of the Arabs*, 609-613; Haskins, *Studies in the History of Mediaeval Science*, 242-299; F. Gabrieli, "Frederick II and Moslem Culture," *East and West* (Instituto Italiano per il Medio ed Estremo Oriente) 9 (1958): 53-61; Ahmad, *History of Islamic Sicily*, 82ff; U. Rizzitano, "Cultura Araba nella Sicilia Normanna," *Atti del Congresso Internazionale di Studi sulla Sicilia Normanna* (Palermo: Istituto di Storia Medievale, Universita di Palermo, 1973), 279-297; Giuseppe de Pasquale, *L'Islam in Sicilia* (Palermo: Flaccovio, 1980).

144. Hitti, *History of the Arabs*, 608–609, 613; Ahmad, *History of Islamic Sicily*, 97ff; D. Serradifalco, *Del Duomo di Monreale e di Altre Chiese Siculo-Normanne* (Palermo: Roberti, 1838); G.U. Arata, *Architettura Arabo-Normanna e il Rinascimento in Sicilia* (Milan: Bestetti and Tumminelli, 1914); Perry B. Cott, *Siculo-Arabic Ivories* (Princeton: Princeton University Press, 1939); U. Monneret de Villard, *Le Pitture Musulmane al Soffitto della Cappella Palatina in Palermo* (Rome: Libreria dello Stato, 1950).

145. Ettore Li Gotti, *Il Teatro dei Pupi* (Florence: Sansoni, 1957); Felice Cammarata, *Pupi e Carretti* (Palermo: Palma, 1969); G. Vapito, *Il Carretto Siciliano* (Milan: Valcarenghi, 1923); and S. Lo Presti, *Il Carretto* (Palermo: Flaccovio, 1959).

146. Supra, notes 83 and 119 to chapter 5.

147. On Amalfi, "Italy: Amalfi," *Ency. of World Art* 8 (1963): 694; R.F. di Candida, "Amalfi," *Enric. Ital.* 2 (1929): 746; Touring Club Italiano, *Guida d'Italia: Campania* (3rd ed.; Milan: Touring Club Italiano, 1963), 413–414; Pietro Pirri, *Il Duomo di Amalfi ed il Chiostro del Paradiso* (Rome: Luigi Guanella, 1941); Robert Gathorne-Hardy, *Amalfi: Aspects of the City and Her Ancient Territories* (London: Faber and Faber, 1968), 43, 59.

For Islamic influence at Salerno, Baron, *Social and Religious History*, VIII: 245; Zimmels, "Science," in Roth, *Dark Ages*, 297; plus the following articles on Constantine the African, Charles Singer and I. Veith, *Ency. Brit.* 6 (1973): 389; F. Tinivella, *Enric. Catt.* 4 (1950): 716; R. Dagorn, *Dict. Hist. Geog. Eccles.* 13 (1956): 621–623; O.J. Blum, *New Cath. Ency.* 4 (1967): 230; M. Meyerhoff, *Ency. of Islam*, Supplement (1938): 48–49; and B. Ben Yahia, *Ency. of Islam* 2 (1965): 59–60.

148. M. Hamidullah, "Embassy of Queen Bertha to Caliph al-Muktafi billah in Baghdad 293/906," *Journal of the Pakistan Historical Society* 1 (1953): 272–300; G. Levi della Vida, "La Corrispondenza di Berta di Toscana col Califfo Muktafi," *Rivista Storica Italiana* 66 (1954): 21–38; Baron, *Social and Religious History* IV: 245, note 28; Bernard Lewis, "The Muslim Discovery of Europe," *Bulletin of the School of Oriental and African Studies* 20 (1957): 412 and note 3.

For comparative data from Spain, A. Ali El-Hajji, "Intermarriage between Andalusia and Northern Spain in the Umayyad Period," *Islamic Quarterly* 11 (1967): 3–7. Cf. also El-Hajji's "Diplomatic Relations between Andalusia and Italy during the

Umayyad Period," ibid. 12 (1968): 140–145; and his "Ibrahim b. Yaqub at-Turtushi and His Diplomatic Activity," ibid. 14 (1970): 22–40.

149. Hitti, *History of the Arabs*, 613–614; Beckwith, *Early Medieval Art*, 165, 245, note 27–29; Daniel, *Arabs and Mediaeval Europe*, 219–220.

150. Joergensen, *St. Francis*, 261, 341, note 5; Englebert, *St. Francis*, 318; Marion A. Habig, ed., *St. Francis of Assisi: Writings and Early Biographies: English Omnibus of the Sources for the Life of St. Francis* (Chicago: Franciscan Herald Press, 1973), 1001, 1094, note 48.

151. For Brother Berardo and St. Francis' visit to the Sultan, Sabatier, *Life of St. Francis*, 223–238; Joergensen, *St. Francis*, 167–170; Cuthbert, *Life of St. Francis*, 273–286; Englebert, *St. Francis*, 229–241. For St. Francis' visit to the Sultan alone, A. Ghinato, "Sanctus Franciscus in Oriente Missionarius ac Peregrinus," *Acta Ordinis Fratrum Minorum* 83 (1964): 164–181. Supra, note 24 to chapter 2.

152. Van der Vat, *Anfaenge der Franziskanermissionen*, 1ff, 9ff, 39ff, 51ff; Roncaglia, *St. Francis of Assisi and the Middle East*, 19–30; Oktavian von Rieden, "Die Sehnsucht des Hl. Franz nach dem Martyrium," *Collectanea Franciscana* 30 (1960): 365–372.

153. Basetti-Sani, *Mohammed et St. Francois*; his *Per Un Dialogo Cristiano-Musulmano*; and his *L'Islam e Francesco d'Assisi*, all cited supra, note 8 to chapter 1.

154. For Islamic influence on the troubadours, cf. the alleged link between the Albigensians and the Muslims, supra, note 43 to chapter 4. Cf. also A.R. Nykl, *Hispano-Arabic Poetry and Its Relations with the Old Provencal Troubadours* (Baltimore: Furst, 1946); Frederick B. Artz, *Mind of the Middle Ages: An Historical Survey A.D. 200–1500* (3rd ed.; New York; Knopf, 1962), 334–337, 340–341; Hitti, *History of the Arabs*, 562, 600, 611, 643; Chejne, *Muslim Spain*, 244–246; Denomy, *Mediaeval Studies*, XV: 147–158.

155. Supra, note 62 to chapter 4.

156. F. Gabrieli, "Petrarca e gli Arabi," *Atti e Memorie della Accademia Petrarca di Lettere, Arti e Scienze* (Arezzo) 38 (1965–1967; published in 1968): 109–118; K. Dannenfeldt, "The Renaissance Humanist and the Knowledge of Arabic," *Studies in the Renaissance* 2 (1955): 96–117.

157. Supra, note 53 to chapter 6.

158. Ibid.

159. Supra, notes 155-157. Cf. also John Addington Symonds, *Renaissance in Italy* (New York: Modern Library, 1935), II: 114ff, 154ff, 171, 718ff, 755ff; Jefferson Butler Fletcher, *Literature of the Italian Renaissance* (New York: Macmillan, 1934), 142ff, 150ff, 228ff, 301ff; Will Durant, *Story of Civilization* (New York: Simon and Schuster, 1953), V (The Renaissance): 125–128, 270–278, 602, 696, 712; Artz, *Mind of the Middle Ages*, 353–354; Wallace K. Ferguson, *Europe in Transition 1300–1520* (Boston: Houghton Mifflin, 1962), 522–524; S. Harrison Thomson, *Europe in Renaissance and Reformation* (New York: Harcourt, Brace and World, 1963), 680–682; Robert A. Hall, *Short History of Italian Literature* (Ithaca, New York: Linguistica, 1951), 168ff, 244ff, 273ff; Ernest H. Wilkins, *History of Italian Literature* (Cambridge: Harvard University Press, 1954), 158ff, 172ff, 184ff, 268ff; Francesco de Sanctis, *History of Italian Literature*, trans. J. Redfern (New York: Basic Books, 1959), I: 403ff, 406ff, 432ff; II:

469ff, 621ff; E.W. Edwards, *Orlando Furioso and Its Predecessor* (Cambridge: Cambridge University Press, 1924); Giacomo Grillo, *Two Aspects of Chivalry: Pulci and Boiardo* (Boston: Excelsior, 1942); and his *Poets at the Court of Ferrara: Ariosto, Tasso and Guarini* (Boston: Excelsior, 1943).

160. Gilson, *History of Christian Philosophy in the Middle Ages*, 521-527; F. Copleston, *History of Philosophy* (Garden City, New York: Doubleday/Image, 1963), III: 2: 26-33; E. Cassirer, P.O. Kristeller, and J.H. Randall, Jr., *Renaissance Philosophy of Man* (Chicago: University of Chicago Press, 1959), 1-20, 257-279; Randall, "The Development of Scientific Method in the School of Padua," *Journal of the History of Ideas* 1 (1940): 177-206; E. Troilo, *Averroismo e Aristotelismo Padovano* (Padua: C.E.D.A.M., 1939); Z. Kuksewicz, *Averroisme Bolonais au XIVe Siecle* (Wroclaw and Warsaw: Ossolineum, 1965).

161. Root, *Food of Italy*, passim. Cf. also by way of summary and conclusion, Alessandro Bausani, "Islamic Influences on Italian Culture," *Pakistan Quarterly* (Karachi) 14 (summer 1966): 45-53.

162. On Italian immigration to Latin America, Salvatore Saladino, *Italy from Unification to 1919: Growth and Decay of a Liberal Regime* (New York: Crowell, 1970), 60; Robert F. Foerster, *The Italian Emigration of Our Times* (New York: Russell and Russell, 1968), 223-319. For the Italian role in the discovery of the Americas, Roberto Almagia, *Gli Italiani: Primi Esploratori dell'America* (Rome: Libreria dello Stato, 1937).

163. The list also includes Marsilio Ficino (1433-1499) and Giovanni Pico della Mirandola (1463-1494), who both led a (Neoplatonist) revolt against Aristotle which ultimately paved the way for Descartes and the birth of modern philosophy; Agostino Nifo (1473-1546), the Averroist philosopher who joined the movement against Ptolemaic astronomy; Niccolo Machiavelli (1469-1527), who carried Marsilio of Padua's liberalization of political theory to its logical conclusion; Pietro Pomponazzi (1462-1525), the Averroist philosopher who advanced the cause of naturalism; Girolamo Cardano (1501-1576), who stressed the role of mathematics in philosophy; Bernardino Telesio (1508-1588), who rebelled against Aristotle in favor of the pre-Socratic and Stoic philosophers; Fausto Sozzini (1539-1604), the great Unitarian liberalizer of theology and religion; Giordano Bruno (1548-1600), the Italian Spinoza whose advocacy of pantheism, naturalism, and the Copernican theory contributed to his martyrdom; Jacopo Zabarella (1532-1589), the Aristotelian thinker who deepened Pomponazzi's naturalism; Francisco Patrizzi (1529-1597) and Tommaso Campanella (1568-1639), two forerunners of Cartesian dualism and intuitionism; Galileo Galilei (1564-1642), who greatly liberalized science by devastating Aristotelian physics and Ptolemaic astronomy; Giambattista Vico (1668-1744), the liberalizer of historical thought.

164. When the Jews of Provence were expelled between 1498 and 1501, a number remained behind as converts to Christianity. The number was about 164 families, or about 1300 people (given a multiple of eight per family—see note 105 to chapter 8). B. Blumenkranz, "Provence," *Ency. Judaica* 13 (1971): 1262; Baron, *Social and Religious History* XI: 224-225, 395, note 41. What percentage of the total number of Jews of Provence converted at this time? At Marseilles, the largest Provencal Jewish community, "great numbers" converted, though apparently not a majority. Blumenkranz, "Marseilles," *Ency. Judaica* 11 (1971): 1057. However, at Arles, a relatively small

number (only "certain Jews") converted. Blumenkranz, "Arles," *Ency. Judaica* 3 (1971): 469. We would suggest that the Arles situation was more typical than that of Marseilles. The Provencal Jewish converts of *circa* 1500 continued to exist as a separate caste within the Christianity community and suffered social discrimination for several centuries thereafter. See Blumenkranz on "Provence" and "Arles" as well as Baron as cited immediately above. In Provence also (circa 1500), as in southern Italy (circa 1300) and Spain (circa 1400), the Christianity to which the Jews were converting was an Islamicized one. There was heavy Islamic influence upon Marseilles, from, among other things, this city's active participation in the trade with the Islamic Mediterranean (North Africa, Egypt, etc.). For this trade in the Later Middle Ages, and the Jewish role therein, Baron, *Social and Religious History* X: 87-88, 341, note 39.

9. Louis Massignon (1883-1962) and the Contemporary Ramifications of the Thesis about the Anti-Islamic Origins of Modern Anti-Semitism

* Chapter nine, "The Profound Contemporary Ramifications of the Thesis about the Anti-Islamic Origins of Modern Anti-Semitism," was written in the summer of 1975, on the basis of remarks delivered at the conclusion of our Solomon Goldman Memorial Lecture, "Further Reflections on the Association of Jew with Muslim by Medieval Christians, a New Comparative Approach to the Origins of Modern Anti-Semitism," Spertus College of Judaica, Chicago, January 5, 1975. The remarks themselves grew out of our work editing and translating Basetti-Sani's *Louis Massignon*, supra, note 8 to chapter 1. They also grew out of our translation of Massignon's crucial 1949 essay "The Three Prayers of Abraham" (French original in his *Opera Minora*, ed. Y. Moubarac [Paris: Presses Universitaires de France, 1969], III: 804–816), which we submitted in September of 1975 to Herbert Mason, of Boston University, Massignon's leading American disciple and his official English language translator.

  1. Supra, text and notes 1-3 of chapter 5.

  2. Supra, notes 2 and 8 to chapter 1.

  3. On Massignon's life and work, the Basetti-Sani book cited supra, notes 1 to the Introduction and 8 to chapter 1, the first book-length volume available in English on this subject; with the reviews by Quitslund and Speight.

  Cf. also Vincent Monteil, "Introduction," to Massignon, *Parole Donee* (Paris: Julliard, 1962), 9-60; Jean Morillon, *Massignon* (Paris: Editions Universitaires, 1964); Waardenburg, *L'Islam dans le Miroir de l'Occident*, passim; and his "L. Massignon's Study of Religion and Islam: An Essay a Propos of His *Opera Minora*," *Oriens* 21-22 (1968-1969): 136-158; Jean Francois Six, ed., *Cahier Louis Massignon* (Paris: Editions de l'Herne, 1970); Y. Moubarac, *Pentalogie Islamo-Chretienne* (Beirut: Editions du Cenacle Libanais, 1972), vol. 1; Hodgson, *Venture of Islam*, I: 28-29; Louis Massignon, *The Passion of Al-Hallaj: Mystic and Martyr of Islam*, 4 vols., trans. Herbert Mason (Princeton: Princeton University Press, 1981), as well as the definitive biography of Massignon upon which Mason is currently at work.

  More popular recent discussions of Massignon's contribution are J.M. Sola-Sole, "Massignon, Louis," *New Catholic Ency.* 9 (1967): 435; Richard Griffiths, *The Reactionary Revolution: The Catholic Revival in French Literature 1870-1914* (New York: Ungar, 1965), 244-257; Anne Fremantle, *Pilgrimage to People* (New York: David

McKay, 1968), 108-132; Basetti-Sani, "Christian Witness to Islam [Louis Massignon]," *The Cord* 17 (1967): 332–343.

Massignon held that the Holy Land "is the fatherland of the soul . . . and it is certain that one day all of the bishops, and even the bishop of bishops, the pope, will return again to Jerusalem." In a private audience with Pope Pius XII he urged the Supreme Pontiff to go on pilgrimage to the Holy Land, an ideal which was realized not by Popes Pius or John but rather by Pope Paul in 1964. Basetti-Sani, *Louis Massignon*, 76, 240, note 62. What may well be needed in the future is not a temporary visit of the pope to the Holy Land but rather a permanent resettlement of the papacy in Jerusalem, as the representative not of Christendom alone but rather of all three Abrahamitic faiths: Judaism, Christianity, and Islam.

4. For the Maimonidean view on the positive role of Christianity and Islam in the salvation history of mankind, as well as the anticipation of this view by Maimonides's older contemporary, Judah Ha-levi (who, like Maimonides, was born in Muslim Spain and died in Muslim Egypt), Abrahams, *Jewish Life in the Middle Ages*, 413–414; Kaufmann Kohler, "Christianity," *Jewish Ency.* 4 (1903): 56; Baron, *Social and Religious History*, V: 163-164, 365, note 24; H. Bamberger, "Some Difficulties in Dialogue," *Judaism* 32 (1983): 177-178 and notes 1-2.

5. Henry Kamm, "Pope, at Lourdes, Seeks to Console the Suffering," *New York Times*, August 16, 1983, part 1, 3; supra, note 2 to Introduction.

6. "Pope, in Vienna, Stresses Christian Heritage," *New York Times*, September 11, 1983, part 1, 9; supra, note 3 to Introduction.

Bibliography

For the extensive bibliography herein we have followed the format used by Norman Daniel in *The Arabs and Mediaeval Europe* (2nd ed.; London and New York: Longman and Librairie du Liban, 1979), 365-8. In accordance with this format the first references to all books and articles cited in the footnotes are set forth below as follows: Author, Chapter Number in Roman Numerals: footnote number (page number). For example, Burns, R. I., II: 1(347) = Chapter 2: footnote 1(page 347), wherein first references to eight books and six articles appear. For first references which appear in the text see the Index. The first references provide full bibliographical information.

Abrahams, I., IV: 46 (409)

Adler, C., VII: 8(488)

Adler, E. N., V: 11(422)

Adler, F. J., IV: 20(397)

Ady, C. M., VIII: 103(524)

Aescoly, A. Z., IV: 31(403)

Aguado Bleye, P., III: 21(364)

Agus, I. A., IV: 16(392), 39(405); V: 79(444)

Ahmad, A., VI: 62(476)

Albrecht, R., VII: 26(493)

Albright, W. F., VIII: 80(519)

Alexander, P. J., IV: 19(397)

Algerny, A. d', and Narducci, G., II: 24(353)

Ali, A. Y., V: 40(431)

Almagia, R., VIII: 162(534)

Alonso, M., VII: 39(501); VIII: 84(52)

Alphandery, P., VI: 5(457)

Altaner, B., VI: 35(466)

Altmann, A., IV: 64(416); V: 69(442); VIII: 41(512-3)

Alvarez Verdes, L., and Alonso Hernandez, E. J., VII: 6(486)

Alverny, M.-T. d', II: 4(349), 5(349), 22(352-3), 33(355); III: 33(370); V: 20(469); V: 20(426); VI: 53(469); VIII: 84(52)

Alverny, M.-T. d', and Vajda, G., II: 22(353)

Amabile, L., VIII: 104(524-5)

Amari, M., V: 90(445); VI: 62(476)

Amato, A. d', VII: 39(501)

Anawati, G., I: 8(345)

Ancona, A. d', III: 55(376)

Angel, M., and Salomon, H. P., VIII: 41(514)

Ansbacher, B. M., VIII: 1(505)

Arata, G. U., VIII: 144(532)

Arendonk, C. van, II: 27(354)

Arie, R., VII: 30(496)

Arnaldez, R., II: 27(354)

Arnold, T., II: 16(351)

Artz, F. B., VIII: 154(533)

Asaf, S., and Scholem, G., VIII: 104(525)

Ascensio, E., VII: 8(487)

Ashby, T., VIII: 119(529)

Ashtor, E., III: 12(361); IV: 34(403), 40(405); V: 13(423), 69(442), 73(443), 110(448); VIII: 34(510), 35(511)

Asin Palacios, M., II: 27(354)

Assaf, S., V: 10(421)

Atiya, A., VIII: 30(509)

Attal, F. S., VI: 32(466)

Auerbach, M., V: 12(422)

Avneri, Z., VII: 34(499); VIII: 9(506),

37(511), 41(514)

Azcona, T. de, VII: 10(489)

Aziza, C., IV: 2(382)

Bacher, W., VIII: 34(510), 36(511)

Bachrach, B. S., IV: 18(396), 20(397)

Baech, S., VIII: 6(506)

Baer, Y., III 3(358), 21(364); V: 122(451);
VI: 13(459); VII: 32(498); VIII: 33(510)

Baer, Y., Goodman, P., Sargologos, N., and
Brawer, J., VIII: 88(522)

Baethgen, F., VI: 48(468)

Bagby, A. I., VII: 28(495)

Baker, D., II: 33(355); IV: 62(415)

Balaban, M. S., V: 4(420); VIII: 32(509)

Ballesteros y Beretta, A., VIII: 85(521)

Bamberger, H., IX: 4(536)

Baneth, D. T., III: 59(377)

Baquero Moreno, H. C., VII: 11(490)

Baramki, D., VIII: 80(519)

Barbero, G., VI: 24(463)

Bargebuhr, F., VII: 40(502)

Bargellini, P., IV: 65(416)

Baring Gould, S., IV: 1(384)

Bark, W. C., IV: 45(408)

Barnett, R. D., VII: 1(483); VIII: 80(519)

Baron, S. W., II: 14(351); IV: 20(397),
42(406), 70(419); V: 12(422); VIII:
72(518)

Baron, S. W., et al., VII: 1(483)

Basham, A. L., VIII: 56(516)

Bashan, E., V: 32(428), 123(452)

Basetti Sani, G., Intro.: 1(343); I: 8(346);
IX: 3(536)

Bassett, Paul Merritt, VII: 29(496)

Bataillon, M., VII: 31(498)

Bato, Y. L., VIII: 1(505)

Bat Ye'or, VI: 57(471)

Baum, G., IV: 1(381)

Baur, L., and Hammerschmidt, E., VI:
24(464)

Bausani, A., VIII: 161(534)

Baynes, N. H., and Moss, H. St. L. B., IV:
11(384)

Beaujouan, G., III: 6(359)

Beck, H., II: 8(350)

Beck, H. G., II: 8(350)

Beckwith, J., II: 34 & 41(355)

Beinart, H., IV: 54(412); V: 125(454); VII:
1(483-4), 10(489), 34(499), 36, 37 &
38(500); VIII: 9(506), 15 & 17(507),

27(508), 37(511-2)

Ben Ami, A., VI: 62(475-6)

Ben Horin, M., et al., V: 12(422)

Ben Sasson, H. H., VII: 7(486), 17(492);
VIII: 32(509), 96(523)

Ben Yahia, B., VIII: 147(532)

Berger, D., I: 9(346); II: 33(355); III: 3(359);
IV: 11(384); VII: 1(482), 7(486), 11(490)

Bergman, S. H., VII: 25(493)

Bernstein, S., VIII: 98(523)

Bevan, E. R., and Singer, C., IV: 64(416)

Bevere, R., VIII: 111(527)

Bieber, H., VII: 12(491)

Biraben, J. N., VII: 2(485)

Birge, J. K., II: 19(352)

Birkbeck, W. J., VII: 15(491)

Bishko, C. J., IV: 57(413)

Blake, R., IV: 72(419)

Blanco Freijeiro, A., VIII: 80(519)

Bland, K., VIII: 41(513)

Blau, J., V: 69(442); VIII: 34(510)

Blindheim, M., IV: 58(414)

Block, P., VIII: 133(530)

Bloomfield, M. W., III: 3(358); VI: 54(480)

Blum, O. J., VIII: 147(532)

Blumenkranz, B., Intro.: 4(343); I: 6(345);
III: 9(393), 11(384), 16(393), 52(410);
V: 122(451); VIII: 164(534-5)

Blumenkranz, B., and Ansbacher, B. M.,
VI: 59(474)

Bober, H., II: 41(355)

Bock, F., VI: 17(460)

Boissonnade, P., III: 26(368)

Bondati, G., VI: 54(470)

Bondy, G., and Dworsky, F., IV: 68(417)

Bosch Vila, J., II: 7(349)

Boswell, J., VII: 30(496)

Bowman, S., IV: 18(396)

Boyajian, J. C., VII: 1(482)

Brady, I., and Brown, R., Intro.: 6(343)

Branca, V., and Caccia, F., IV: 62(415)

Braunstein, B., VII: 1(482), 16(491)

Brockelmann, C., II: 17(351)

Brondsted, J., VI: 10(458)

Browe, P., III: 3(358)

Brown, F., Driver, S. P., and Briggs, C. A.,
V: 40(431)

Browne, L. E., VI: 57(471)

Broyde, I., III: 21(364-5); IV: 46(409); V:
11(421), 34(430), 110(448), 112(449),

123(452); VII: 7(486), 34(499), 36 &
  37(511), 40 & 41(512), 47(515), 61(516),
  70(518), 127 & 128(530)
Broyde, I., and Elbogen, I., VIII: 128(530)
Brundage, J. A., IV: 13(388)
Bucci, M., IV: 63(416)
Buechler, A., IV: 68(417)
Bulard, M., IV: 12(387)
Bulliet, R., II: 16(351)
Bultot, R., VI: 25(464)
Bunim, I. M., I: 3(344)
Buonaiuti, E., VI: 22(461)
Burnet, J., VIII: 58(516)
Burnett, C. F., III: 35(371)
Burns, R. I., II: 1(347); III: 21(364); VII:
  28(495); VIII: 87(522)
Busard, H. L. L., III: 35(371)
Buttenweiser, M., IV: 31(403)
Buytaert, E. M., II: 25(353)

Cabanelas Rodriguez, D., II: 1(348); VII:
  31(497)
Cabestany, J. F., VIII: 30(509)
Cabrillana, N., VII: 2(485)
Cagigas, I. de las, V: 125(454) VII: 29 & 30
  (496)
Cahen, C., IV: 11(386), 37(404)
Cammarata, F., VIII: 145(532)
Canard, M., IV: 11(384)
Candida, R. F. di, VIII: 147(532)
Cantarino, V., IV: 62(415); VII: 1(482)
Cantera Burgos, F., III: 4(359), 35(371); VII:
  6(486), 29(496)
Cantineau, J., VII: 31(497)
Caraffa, F., IV: 11(384)
Cardaillac, L., VII: 31(497), 42(504)
Carmondy, F. J., III: 32(370)
Caro Baroja, J., VII: 8(487), 28(494-5)
Carpenter, R., VIII: 80(519)
Capri, D., V: 69(442)
Carrete Parrondo, C., VII: 1(482), 10(489)
Caspi, M. M., IV: 15(389)
Cassirer, E., Kristeller, P.O., and Randall, J.
  H., VIII: 160(534)
Cassuto, U., V: 13(423), 116(449); VIII:
  104(525), 122, 123 & 124(529), 127,
  128 & 131(530), 139(531)
Castro, A., VII: 28(494)
Catane, M., VII: 19(492)
Cavallaro, G., VIII: 138(531)

Cerulli, E., II: 1(347); IV: 62(415)
Chakmakjian, H., II: 8(350)
Chavanon, J., IV: 27(401)
Chazan, R., II: 25(353); IV: 11(384), 11
  (385), 16(392), 20(397); V: 122(451-2);
  VII: 34(500)
Chejne, A. G., VII: 31(497)
Cheney, C. R., VI: 17(460)
Chew, S. C., III: 55(376)
Chierichetti, S., IV: 63(416)
Chiettini, E., VI: 24(464)
Chudoba, B., VI: 24(464)
Ciardi, J., IV: 62(415)
Cipolla, C. M., IV: 45(407)
Citarella, A. O., IV: 11(386), 37(404)
Clagett, M., III: 35(370)
Clagett, M., Post, G., and Reynolds, R., IV:
  45(408)
Cohen, A., VI: 20(461)
Cohen, B., III: 59(377); V: 12(422)
Cohen, G. D., III: 10 & 12(361); VII: 1
  (481-3)
Cohen, J., III: 10(361); IV: 20(397); VII:
  34(500)
Cohen, M. A., VII: 1(481), 1(483), 11(490);
  VIII: 88(522)
Cohen, M., et al., VII: 8(488)
Cohen, M. R., V: 97(447)
Cohen, S., VII: 8(488); VIII: 4(505)
Cohn, H. H., VIII: 4(505)
Cohn, H. H., and Levitatz, I., VIII: 4(505)
Cohn, H. H., and Rabinowitz, L. I., V:
  88(445)
Cohn, N., IV: 12(387); V: 2(420)
Colbert, E. P., II: 30(354)
Colish, M., III: 61(377)
Comanskey, B. J., V: 121(450)
Comfort, W. W., IV: 56(412)
Conder, C. R., VI: 71(477)
Constable, G., and Kritzeck, J., II: 2(348)
Constantelos, D., II: 8(350)
Contreras, J., M. de Lozoya, VII: 30(496)
Copleston, F., VIII: 160(534)
Corcos, D., IV: 11(385); V: 123(452); VII:
  20(493)
Corre, A. D., Roth, C., and Campeas, H.
  J., VIII: 89(522)
Cott, P. B., VIII: 144(532)
Courtney, F., VII: 39(501)
Courtois, C., II: 24(353)

Cowan, J. M., V: 40(431)
Cristofani, A., VIII: 142(532)
Crombie, A. C., IV: 45(407)
Crossland, J., IV: 56(471)
Culican, W., VIII: 80(519)
Curtis, E., VI: 62(476)
Cuthbert, Father, VI: 22(461)
Cutler, A. H. and H. E., Intro.: 1(343); I:
    *(343-4); II: *(346), 3(348-9), 6 &
    7(349), 12 & 13 (351), 21(352); III:
    *(356-7), 50(375); IV: *(379-80), 15(389),
    16(392), 51(410), 57(413); V: *(420);
    VI: *(455); VII: *(481); VIII: *(504); IX:
    *(535)
Cygielman, A., V: 4(420)

Dagan, A., VII: 19(492)
Dagon, R., VIII: 147(532)
Dajani Shaked, H., II: 12(351)
Dales, R., IV: 13(388)
Dan, J., IV: 39(405); V: 79(444), 111(448),
    112(449), 120(450); VIII: 5(506), 49
    (515), 70(518)
Danby, H., V: 43(432)
Daniel, E. R., VI: 22(462), 30(465)
Daniel, J. L., IV: 16(390)
Daniel, N., II: 1(347), 6(349)
Dannenfeldt, K., VIII: 156(533)
Dasberg, L., IV: 16(391)
David, A., IV: 35(403); V: 12(422), 49 &
    50(437); VIII: 1(505), 47(515)
David, J., V: 91(446)
Davidson, H., VIII: 41(514)
Davidson, S., V: 13(424)
Davidson, S., and Loewy, A., V: 13(424)
Davies, A. T., IV: 2(381)
Davies, P. T., VIII: 103(524)
Davies, W. D., VII: 24(493)
Davis, C. T., VIII: 117(529)
Deaux, G., VII: 2(485)
Defourneaux, M., III: 28(369)
Dembitz, L. N., VIII: 4(505)
Denomy, A. J., II: 38(355)
Despina, M., IV: 14(388)
Deutsch, G., VII: 7(486)'; VIII: 8(506)
Devic, M., II: 5(349)
Devlin, B., VI: 24(463)
Diaz y Diaz, M. C., II: 4(349)
Dickman, A. J., VI: 56(471)
Dienstag, J. I., VI: 20(461)

Dinur, B. Z., V: 10(421); VII: 1(483)
Dito, O., VIII: 104(524)
Dols, M. W., VII: 2(485)
Dominguez Ortiz, A., and Vincent, B., VII:
    31(497-8)
Donovan, J. P., VI: 1(455)
Douglas, D. C., III: 26(368)
Dressendoerfer, P., VII: 42(504)
Drew, K. F., and Lear, F. S., IV: 45(407)
Dreyer, F., IV: 71(419)
Dubnow, S. M., IV: 37(404); V: 13(423);
    VIII: 32(509), 54(515)
Dubnow, S. M., and Rosenthal, H., VII:
    17(492)
Ducat, W., VIII: 70(518)
Ducay, E., III: 1(357)
Duchesne Guillemin, J., IV: 16(394)
Duhem, P., III: 33(370)
Duker, A. G., et al., VI: 60(474)
Dunbabin, T. J., VIII: 138(531)
Duncalf, F., VI: 62(475)
Dunlop, D. M., II: 7(349); III: 35(371); IV:
    37(405); V: 13(423); VII: 32(498), 40
    (502)
Dunn, M., IV: 11(384)
Dupont Sommer, A., V: 43(432)
Dupuy, B. D., VI: 44(467)
Durant, W., VIII: 159(533)

Eckardt, A. R., I: 3(344)
Edwards, E. W., VIII: 159(534)
Eichhorn, D. M., IV: 16(392)
Eichner, W., II: 8(350)
Eidelberg, S., VIII: 8(506)
Elbogen, I., V: 116(449); VIII: 123(529)
Elias, M., VI: 60(475)
Eliav, B., VII: 19(492)
Eliav, B., and Leftwich, J., VII: 19(492)
Elliot Binns, L., VI: 32(466)
Elliott, J. H., VIII: 103(524)
Emmerson, K., VI: 1(455)
Enelow, H. G., VIII: 124(529)
England, J., III: 46(374)
Englebert, O., Intro.: 6(343)
Engreen, F. E., IV: 24(400)
Entreves, A. P. d', VIII: 117(529)
Epalza, M. de, VII: 29(496), 34(499-500)
Epstein, A., V: 11(421), 12(422)
Epstein, J. N., V: 10(421)
Epstein, M., IV: 37(404-5)

Esposito, M., VI: 53(470)
Esser, K., VI: 22(461); VIII: 60(516)
Ettinger, S., IV: 68(417)
Evans, A. P., VI: 59(473)
Evans, G. R., III: 26(367)
Evans, J., II; 38(355)
Every, G., IV: 24(400)

Fagnan, E., VI: 60(474)
Fattal, A., VI: 57(471)
Federici, T., I: 2(344), 8(345)
Felder, H., VI: 55(470)
Feldman, S., VIII: 41(513)
Ferguson, W. K., VIII: 159(533)
Fernandez y Gonzalez, F., VII: 28(494)
Ferorelli, N., V: 14(424)
Finkelstein, L., IV: 64(416); V: 12(422)
Fisch, H. H., IV: 70(419)
Fischel, H., IV: 16(393)
Fischel, W. J., IV: 36(403)
Fischer, H., VI: 35(466)
Flannery, E., I: 4(344)
Fleischner, E., IV: 1(381)
Fleming, L., I: 8(345)
Fletcher, J. B., VIII: 159(533)
Fliche, A., VI: 24(463)
Florin, M., VI: 25(464)
Flusser, D., V: 68(441)
Foberti, F., VI: 22(461-2)
Foerster, R. F., VIII: 162(534)
Fonseça, C. D., VI: 24(463)
Fortini, A., VI: 32(466): VIII: 142(532)
Fortini, G., VI: 22(462)
Fournier, P., III: 17(362)
Fraenkel, S., V: 12(422)
France, J., II: 12(351)
Franceschini, E., VIII: 142(532)
Franke, F. R., II: 30(354)
Frankl, O., IV: 69(419)
Frappier, J., V: 48(435)
Freeman, E. A., VIII: 138(531)
Freeman, E. A., and Ashby, T., VIII:
    138(531)
Freimann, A., and Hildesheimer, M., V:
    12(422)
Freimann, A., and Schorr, M., and Simon-
    sen, D., V: 10(421)
Fremantle, A., IX: 3(535-6)
Friedlaender, I., V: 12(422)
Friedman, J. B., II: 42(356)

Friedman, Y., II: 14(351)
Frugoni, A., VI: 68(477)
Fueck, J., II: 1(348), 19(352)
Fuller, B. A. G., and McMurrin, S. M.,
    VIII: 58(516)
Funkenstein, A., II: 33(355); III: 10(361)

Gabrieli, F., IV: 57(413); VI: 62(476); VIII:
    111(527), 143(532), 156(533)
Gallego Burin, A., and Gamir Sandoval,
    A., VII: 31(497)
Gandz, S., III: 59(377)
Ganshof, F. L., IV: 21(398)
Garcia Arenal, M., VII: 31(497)
Garcia Ballester, L., VII: 31(497)
Garcia Dominguez, J. D., VII: 32(498)
Garcia Gomez, E., III: 15(361), 30(369)
Garcia Iglesias, L., IV: 18(396)
Garcia y Bellido, A., VIII: 80(519)
Garcia y Bellido, A., Schubart, H., and
    Niemeyer, H. G., VIII: 80(519)
Gardner, E. S., IV: 43(406)
Gardner, H., VIII: 116(528)
Garofalo, S., and Federici, T., I: 2(344),
    8(345)
Garrido Aranda, A., VII: 31(498)
Gaster, M., VI: 13(459)
Gathorne Hardy, R., VIII: 147(532)
Gaulan, Y., VII: 20(493)
Gauss, J., II: 8(350); III: 26(367)
Gay, J., V: 90(445)
Gayangos, P. de, III: 21(364)
Gerli, E. M., VII: 8(487)
Ghinato, A., VIII: 151(533)
Gifford, D., VIII: 103(524)
Gilbert, C., IV: 61(415)
Gilson, E., II: 5(349)
Gimenez Soler, A., VIII: 85(521)
Ginzberg, H. L., VIII: 139(531)
Ginzberg, L., V: 10(421), 12(422), 32(428);
    VIII: 8(506), 40(515)
Giovanelli, G., V: 121(450)
Giunta, F., VIII: 30(509)
Gjaerder, P., IV: 58(414)
Glatzer, N. N., VII: 25(493)
Glazer, N., VIII: 79(519)
Glendinning, O. N. V., VIII: 86(522)
Glick, T. F., VII: 1(481-2), 1(482), 29(496)
Glick, T. F., and Pi Sunyer, O., VII: 8(487)
Glickson, Y., V: 85(445)

Goeje, M. J. de, V: 14(424)

Goetz, W., IV: 63(416)

Goitein, S. D., IV: 37(404); V: 9(420); VIII: 94(523)

Golb, N., IV: 16(392), 37(404)

Goldberg, H., VII: 28(495)

Goldin, J., I: 3(344)

Goldman, F., VII: 17(492)

Goldstein, B. R., VIII: 41(513)

Gombrich, E. H., VIII: 116(529-30)

Gonyi Gaztambide, J., VI: 16(459)

Gonzalez, J., VI: 16(459)

Gonzalez Palencia, A., III: 1(357), 33(370): VI: 62(476); VII: 29(496)

Goode, A. D., V: 10(421)

Gorce, M. M., VII: 35(500)

Gordon, L. D., VIII: 142(532)

Gorosterratzu, J., VI: 16(459)

Gottheil, R. J. H., V: 9(420), 14(424), 120(450); VII: 6(486); VIII: 54(515)

Gotti, E. Li, VIII: 145(532)

Gottlieb, E., VIII: 67(517), 131 & 134(530)

Graefe, E., IV: 11(384)

Graetz, H., IV: 46(409)

Granja, F. de la, VII: 34(500)

Grauert, H. von, VI: 13(459)

Grayzel, S., I: 1(344), 9(346); IV: 20(397), 42(406), 46(409); V: 4(420), 48(434); VI: 22(462)

Greenstone, J. H., IV: 31(403)

Gregoire, H., V: 40(431); VII: 23(493)

Greig, J. C. G., IV: 16(394)

Griffin, R., VII: 21(493)

Griffiths, R., IX: 3(535)

Grillo, G., VIII: 159(534)

Grivot, D., and Zarnecki, G., II: 42(356)

Grossman, A., V: 48(435)

Grundmann, H., VI: 22(462), 43(467)

Grunebaum, G. E. von, VI: 56(471); VIII: 140(531)

Gudiol, J., and Alcolea, S., VIII: 86(522)

Guedemann, M., IV: 46(409)

Guenzburg, D. von, and Markon, I., V: 12(422)

Gueterbock, K. E., II: 8(350)

Guido, M., VIII: 138(531)

Guidot, B., IV: 12(387)

Gutmann, J., IV: 16(392)

Gutsch, M. R., VI: 28(465)

Guttman, J., IV: 46(409); VII: 5(486)

Guzman, G. C., II: 31(354)

Gybbon Monypenny, G. B., VIII: 85(521)

Habermann, A. M., IV: 27(401); V: 110(448)

Habig, M. A., VIII: 150(533)

Hageneder, O., VI: 17(460)

Hagerty, M. J., II: 30(354)

Haidacher, A., VI: 17(460)

Hailperin, H., V: 48(434)

Hajji, A. el, VIII: 148 (532-3)

Haliczer, S. H., VII: 11(490)

Halkin, A. S., VI: 60(474)

Hall, B. S. and West, D. C., IV: 45(408)

Hall, R. A., VIII: 159(533)

Hallamish, M., VIII: 68(517)

Halper, B., V: 11(422)

Hamdani, A., VII: 8(488)

Hamidullah, M., VIII: 148(532)

Haneman, F. T., VII: 27(494)

Hanke, L., VII: 40(502)

Hansen, M. L., VIII: 79(519)

Harden, D., VIII: 80(519)

Hardison, O. B., IV: 45(407)

Harkavy, A. E., V: 12(422)

Hartt, F., IV: 60(414)

Harvey, W., VIII: 43 & 45(514)

Haskins, C. H., IIII: 3(358), 6(359), 29(369)

Hasson, S., IV: 7(383)

Hauben, P. J., VII: 1(482), 31(498)

Haydn, H., and Fuller, E., IV: 69(419)

Hayoun, M., VIII: 41(513)

Hearder, H., and Waley, D. P., VIII: 117(529)

Heer, F., IV: 16(390)

Hefele, C. J., and Leclercq, H., VI: 40(467)

Heffening, W., VI: 57(471)

Heinemann, I., and Gutmann, J., IV: 16(390)

Hell, V. and H., II: 41(355)

Heller Wilensky, S. O., VIII: 46(515), 67(517)

Herberg, W., VIII: 79(519)

Herculano, A., VII: 1(483)

Herde, P., VI: 17(460)

Heredia, T. L. R. de, and Salomon, H. P., VII: 1(483)

Herm, G., VIII: 80(519)

Herman, G., IV: 52(411)

Herman, J., and Yahil, C., VIII: 1(505)

542

Hermes, E., III: 1(357)

Herring, B., VIII: 41(513)

Hertzberg, A., VII: 44(504)

Hess, A. C., VII: 31(497)

Hilka, A., and Soederhjelm, W., III: 1(357)

Hillgarth, J., VIII: 85(521)

Himmelfarb, M., VII: 25(493)

Hinnebusch, A., VI: 35(466)

Hirsch, E. G., VIII: 43(514)

Hirschberg, H. Z., III: 10(360), 59(377); V: 9(420), 11(421)

Hirsch Reich, B., III: 3(358)

Hitchcock, R., II: 17(352)

Hitti, P. K., II: 17(351)

Hodgson, M. G. S., I: 8(346); IV: 49(409); VIII: 140(531)

Hoffman, P., IV: 4(383)

Hogarth, D. G., and Bell, G. M. L., VIII: 59(516)

Holmes, U. T., VI: 56(471)

Holmes, U. T., and Klenke, M. A., V: 48(434-5)

Horovitz, J., III: 59(377)

Horowitz, Y., V: 69(442); VIII: 68(517)

Howard, D. R., VI: 25(464)

Hoyt, R. S., IV: 45(407)

Hughes, R., IV: 71(419)

Huici Miranda, A., VI: 16(459); VII: 32(498)

Hunt, R. W., III: 3(358)

Hurwitz, B. P., III: 2(357)

Husik, I., VIII: 40(512)

Hyamson, A. M., IV: 42(405)

Hyman, A., VIII: 40(512)

Idinopulos, T. A., and Ward, R. B., IV: 2(381)

Idris, H. R., V: 124(454)

Imamuddin, S. M., II: 17(352)

Ivory, A., VII: 28(495)

Ivry, A. L., III: 31(370); VIII: 41(512-3)

Jackson, G., VII: 2(485)

Jacobs, J., IV: 42(405), 46(409); V: 46(433), 85(445); VIII: 9(506), 97(523)

Jacobs, N., IV: 16(393)

Jadin, L., VI: 59(473)

Janson, D. J., II: 41(355)

Jarrett, B., VI: 34(466)

Jaspers, K., IV: 49(409)

Jastrow, M., V: 40(430)

Jeaneau, E., II: 25(353-4)

Jedin, H., and Dolan, J., VI: 25(464)

Jellinek, A., V: 11(421)

Joergensen, J., VI: 22(461)

Jolivet, J., II: 25(354)

Jones, C. M., IV: 56(412)

Jones, J. R., and Keller, J. E., I: 5(345); III: 1(357)

Jordan, W. C., IV: 16(392)

Joseph, M., VIII: 97(523)

Juynboll, Th. W., VI: 57(471)

Kaegi, W. E., II: 8(350)

Kahana, A., V: 11(422)

Kahn, J., IV: 43(406)

Kahn, M. H., II: 19(352)

Kamen, H., VII: 6(486)

Kaminka, A., VIII: 43(514)

Kamm, H., Intro.: 2(343)

Kantorowicz, E., VI: 48(468)

Kapelrud, A. S., VIII: 80(519)

Kaplan, J., VII: 34(499)

Katsh, A. I., V: 9(420-1)

Katz, J., VII: 44(504)

Katz, S., IV: 18(396); VIII: 1(505)

Katzenellenbogen, A., II: 42(356)

Katzenstein, H. J., VIII: 80(519)

Kaufmann, D., V: 14(424)

Kayserling, M., IV: 34(403); V: 13(423), 88(445), 110(448), 125(454); VII: 8(487), 38(500); VIII: 4(505), 8(506), 9(506), 16, 17 & 26(507), 32(510), 37(512), 88 & 89(522)

Kayserling, M., et al., VIII: 37(511)

Kayserling, M., and Deutsch, G., VII: 32(498)

Kayserling, M., and Ginzberg, L., VIII: 37(511)

Kayserling, M., and Jacobs, J., VIII: 33(510)

Keller, H. E., II: 47(356)

Keller, J. E., VIII: 85(521)

Kellner, M. M., VIII: 41(513), 41(514)

Kempf, F., VI: 17(460)

Kestenberg Gladstein, R., V: 23(426)

Khoury, A. T., III: 8(350)

King, G. G., VIII: 86(522)

Kington Oliphant, T. L., VI: 48(468)

Kinsman, R., IV: 45(408)

Kisch, G., IV: 16(392), 46(409)

Klar, B., V: 14(424), 14(425)

Klatzkin, J., and Cohn, H. H., V: 88(445)
Kniewasser, M., III: 10(361)
Knowles, M. D., VI: 53(469)
Kober, A, IV: 46(409)
Kobler, F., V: 13(424)
Koch, J., VI: 25(464)
Koehler, L., and Baumgartner, W., V: 40(431)
Kohler, K., IV: 37(405); VII: 17(492); IX: 4(536)
Kohler, K., and Broyde, I., VII: 17(492)
Kohler, K., and Gottheil, R., VII: 34(499)
Kohut, G. A., III: 16(362)
Kokovtzov, P. P., V: 13(424)
Kollek, T., and Pearlman, M., IV: 55(412)
Korey, W., VII: 19(492)
Kraus, C. von, VI: 53(469)
Kraus, H., II: 41(355)
Krauss, S., IV: 2(382); V: 11(421), 13(423), 34(430)
Kriegel, M., IV: 56(413)
Kristeller, P. O., III: 7(360)
Kritzeck, J., I: 8(346); II: 2(348), 6(349), 25(354)
Krueger, H. C., IV: 21 (398), 45(408)
Kuksewicz, Z., VIII: 160(534)
Kulka, E., VII: 19(492)
Kupfer, E., IV: *(381); VIII: 41(513)
Kupfer, F., and Strelcyn, S., V: 11(421)
Kurdzialek, M., II: 25(353)
Kurzman, D., IV: 6(383)

Lacarra, J. M., III: 28(369); VIII: 82(520)
Lacave, J. L., VII: 1(483)
Ladero Quesada, M. A., VII: 30(496); VIII: 27(508)
Ladner, G., VIII: 140(531)
Ladner, G., von Grunebaum, Funkenstein, Langmuir, and Leschnitzer, IV: *(380)
Lage, G. R. de, II: 33(355)
Lamed, M., V: 48(434)
LaMonte, J. L., V: 7(420); VI: 71(477)
Landau, M., V: 13(423)
Landsberger, F., VII: 27(494)
Lange, N. de, IV: 2(382)
Langmuir, G. I., IV: 16(393)
Leon Tello, P., VII: 2(485)
Lapeyre, H., VII: 31(497)
Lask, I. M., IV: 20(397)
Lasker, D. J., VIII: 41(514)

Lavi, T., VII: 20(493)
Lavin, M., IV: 61(415)
Lazarus, F., V: 10(521)
Lazenby, F. D., IV: 11(384)
Lea, H. C., VI: 59(473); VII: 28(494-5)
Ledeen, M. A., VII: 12(491)
Lefkowitz, D., IV: 71(419)
Lehrer, M., VII: 6(486)
Lemay, R., III: 33(370)
Lerner, J., VIII: 70(518)
Lerner, R. E., VI: 1(455)
Lesarte, A. de, III: 4(359)
Leschnitzer, A., VII: 28(495)
Leveen, J., III: 59(377)
Levey, M., III: 35(371)
Levi, G. B., V: 9(420)
Levi, G. B., Hirschfeld, H., and Ginzberg, L., V: 9(420)
Leviant, C., V: 11(422)
Levi della Vida, G., IV: 62(415); VII: 29(496); VIII: 148(532)
Levinger, J. S., VIII: 9(506), 127(530)
Levitats, I., VIII: 32(509)
Levtzion, N., II: 16(351)
Levy, H., V: 13(423)
Levy, R., V: 45(432)
Lewin, I., VII: 19(492)
Lewin, R., IV: 69(418)
Lewinsky, A., IV: 28(402)
Lewis, A. R., IV: 16(392)
Lewis, B., V: 14(425), 45(432); VIII: 148(532)
Lewis, R. E., VI: 25(464-5)
Lewis, W., II: 2(348)
Lichtenstadter, I., VI: 61(475)
Lichtenstein, A., VII: 1(482)
Lichtenstein, A., Nall, R., Avni, H., and Amir, S., VII: 32(498)
Lida de Malkiel, M. R., VIII: 85(521)
Lieberman, S., III: 10(361)
Lieberman, S., and Hyman, A., VIII: 5(506)
Liebes, E. Z., VIII: 65(517)
Liebeschutz, H., II: 25(353)
Liebman, S. B., VII: 8(488)
Lifschitz Golden, M., IV: 69(419)
Lipman, J. G., V: 4(420)
Lipman, V. D., VII: 1(482)
Lipsky, L., VIII: 54(515)
Liss, P. K., VII: 11(490)
Little, A. G., IV: 43(406)

Little, L., IV: 16(393)
Littleton, C. S., IV: 16(394)
Livermore, H. V., VIII: 80(519)
Llinares, A., VIII: 85(521)
Llorca, B., VII: 3(485), 35(500)
Loeb, I., IV: 56(413)
Loewe, R., III: 3(358); VII: 6(486)
Loewenthal, A., VIII: 40(512)
Lomax, D. W., VIII: 82(520)
Longhurst, J. E., VII: 31(498)
Longnon, J., VI: 62(475)
Loomis, R. S., and L. H., VII: 21(493)
Lopez, R. S., II: 24(353); IV: 11(386), 16(392)
Lopez Martinez, B., VII: 3(485)
Lopez Martinez, N., and Gil, V., VII: 39(501)
Lourie, E., IV: 43(407); VII: 33(498); VIII: 82(520)
Lucas, L., VI: 38(466-7)
Lucchi, A., IV: 65(417)
Luchaire, A., VI: 25(464)
Lynch, J., VIII: 103(524)
Lyttle, C. H., VI: 22(462)

Maccarrone, M., VI: 24(463)
Machado, J. P., VII: 32(498)
Macia Serrano, A., VII: 35(500)
MacKay, A., VII: 2(485)
Magill, F., VI: 25(464)
Magugliani, L., IV: 62(415)
Makdisi, G., II: 25(354)
Male, E., II: 38(355)
Malter, H., V: 12(422)
Malvezzi, A., II: 1(348)
Mancini, A., VI: 53(469)
Mandel, A., IV: (383)
Mandonnet, P., VI: 34(466)
Mann, H. K., II: 24(353)
Mann, J., III: 59(377); IV: 34(403); V: 12(422), 13(423), 14(424)
Mansilla Reoyo, D., VI: 16(459)
Marcais, G., V: 124(454); VIII: 86(522)
Marcus, J., V: 14(424), 110(448): VIII: 124(529), 127 & 133(530)
Marcus, J. R., IV: 68(417); V: 12(423)
Marcus, S., IV: 68(417)
Mareto, F. da, IV: 11(384)
Margoliouth, G., V: 10(421)
Margolis, M. L., and Marx, A., III: 19(363)

Marks, G., VII: 2(485)
Marle, R. van, IV: 65(416)
Marshall, F. H., IV: 11(384)
Martin, B., VIII: 41(512)
Martini, G., VI: 24(463)
Martins, M., III: 4(359)
Marx, A., III: 16(362); V: 10(421), 12(422), 14(424)
Mason, E., VII: 21(493)
Mason, H., IX: 3(535)
Massignon, L., IX: *(535), 3(535)
Matanic, A., VI: 34(466)
Matteo, I. di, II: 27(354)
McGinn, B., VI: 1(456)
McNeal, E. H., VI: 28(465)
McNeill, W. H., IV: 49(409)
Meek, T. J., V: 9(421)
Meisels, S., VIII: 123(529)
Meisl, J., IV: 68(418); VII: 17(492)
Mellinkoff, R., VII: 27(494)
Menager, L. R., VI: 62(476)
Mendelsohn, S., V: 88(445)
Mendez, F. de Sola, VIII: 98(523)
Mentzner, R. A., VIII: 94(523)
Meredith Owens, G. M., II: 19(352)
Merhavya, H. M., III: 10(361)
Merriman, R. B., IV: 70(419); VII: 33(499)
Metlitzki, D., III: 26(366)
Meyendorff, J., II: 8(350)
Meyer, M. A., VII: 1(482)
Meyerhoff, M., VIII: 147(532)
Michael, I., VIII: 83(520)
Michel, A., VII: 39(501)
Michelson, H., IV: 69(419)
Milano, A., IV: 11(385); VIII: 104(525), 127(530)
Milano, I. da, VI: 22(462); VIII: 60(516)
Millas Vallicrosa, J. M., III: 6(359), 19(362); VII: 1(481), 28(495), 35(500)
Minisci, T., V: 121(450)
Mirsky, D. S., VII: 15(491)
Mitre Fernandez, E., IV: 18(396)
Modder, M. F., IV: 42(405)
Montgomery, E. D., III: 1(357)
Moorhead, J., II: 8(350)
Moorman, J., VI: 29(465)
Monneret de Villard, U., II: 1(348); VIII: 144(532)
Monroe, J.T., II: 1(348); VII: 6(486), 31(497)

Monteil, V., IX: 3(535)
Montezinos, E. L. de, VII: 40(502)
Monti, L., VI: 24(463)
Moore, K., VII: 1(482)
Moreno, M. M., II: 19(352)
Morgenstern, J., V: 9(420)
Morillon, J, IX: 3(535)
Morin, E., IV: 9(383)
Moscati, S., VIII: 80(519)
Moubarac, Y., VI: 53(470); IX: 3(535)
Mozingo, D., IV: 16(393)
Mueller, D. H., V: 11(421-2)
Munk, C. M., VI: 25(465)
Munkacsi, E., VIII: 104(525)
Munro, D. C., V: 36(430); VI: 62(475)
Munyoz Sendino, J., II: 1(348), 21(352)
Musca, G., V: 90(446)
Myers, B. S., VIII: 116(529)

Nagy, A., VI: 25(464)
Nahon, G., VII: 1(482), 1(484)
Nahon, G., and Touati, C., VIII: 41(513)
Nallino, C. A., VI: 62(476)
Nedelcou, C., II: 18(352)
Nemoy, L., IV: 37(404); VIII: 39(512)
Nepaulsingh, C. I., III: 46(374)
Netanyahu, B., IV: 16(390); VII: 8(487),
    11(490), 38(500-1); VIII: 5(506)
Neubauer, A., V: 11(421), 12(422), 14(424)
Neuman, A. A., VII: 8(487); VIII: 4(505),
    89(522)
Neusner, J., VIII: 79(519)
Neustadt, D., V: 14(424)
Newman, A. H., II: 25(353)
Newman, L. I., VI: 59(473)
Newton, F., IV: 63(416)
Niemeyer, G., V: 48(434)
Nigg, W., VI: 1(455)
Nilsson, M. P., VIII: 58(516)
Noble, M. A., IV: 20(397)
Noeldeke, Th., V: 45(432)
Nordhagen, S., V: 36(430)
Noss, J. B., VIII: 56(515-6)
Nykl, A. R., VIII: 154(533)

O'Callaghan, J. F., II: 17(351); VIII: 82(519)
Ochser, S., V: 48(435), 49(437)
O'Donnel, J. R., I: 5(345)
Oelsner, T., IV: 20(397)
Oesterreicher, J., III: 10(361)

Oesterreicher, J. M., I: 1(344), 2(344),
    5(345)
O'Malley, A., III: 17(362)
Opelt, I., V: 20(426)
Oren, N., VII: 20(493)
Orfali Levi, M., VII: 34(500)
Orlandi, S., IV: 65(417)
Ostrogorsky, G., IV: 11(385)
Otte, J., III: 36(371)

Paatz, W. and E., IV: 65(416)
Pacios Lopez, A., III: 4(359)
Paetow, L. J., VI: 28(465)
Pagliaro, A., VIII: 139(531)
Palol, P. de, and Hirmer, M., III: 26(368)
Palumbo, G., IV: 63(416)
Parekh, J. P., VII: 19(492)
Parel, A., I: 5(344)
Parkes, J., I: 1(344); IV: *(381), 2(382); VII:
    24(493)
Parisi, A., VIII: 104(524)
Pasquale, G. de, VIII: 144(532)
Pauck, W. and M., VII: 26(493)
Paulo, A., VII: 32(498)
Pavon Maldonado, B., VIII: 86(522)
Pawlikowski, J., VII: 24(493)
Payne, S. G., VII: 2(485); VIII: 2(505)
Pearson, J. D., II: 19(352)
Peiginsky, A., VIII: 121(529)
Penna, M., VI: 53(470)
Pennington, K., VI: 24(464)
Pennington, K., and Sommerville, R., VI:
    24(464)
Perez Castro, F., III: 4(359)
Peri, H., VII: 6(486)
Perlmann, M., II: 27(354); III: 59(377)
Petraccini, C., VI: 22(463)
Petry, R. C., VI: 1(455-6), 22(461)
Pfeffer, L., IV: 71(419)
Philipson, D., et al., IV: 68(417)
Phillips, W. A., VI: 53(469)
Pickthall, M. M., V: 40(431)
Pimenta Ferro, M. J., VII: 32(498)
Pines, S., II: 27(354)
Pines, S., Suler, B., and Muntner, S., VII:
    5(486)
Pinkus, B., VII: 19(492)
Pinto, M. di, VI: 25(464)
Pirenne, H., IV: 19(396)
Pirri, P., VIII: 147(532)

Plaas, P. G. van der, III: 26(367)
Platzeck, E. W., VIII: 85(521)
Poliak, A. N., V: 13(423), 48(434)
Poliakov, L., VI: 59(474); VII: 1(482),
    31(497), 44(504)
Pontieri, E., VIII: 103(524)
Poole, S., VII: 40(502)
Popkin, R. H., VIII: 91(522), 93, 95, &
    99(523)
Popkin, R. H., and Bayer, B., VIII: 98(523)
Popkin, R. H., and Smend, R., VIII:
    97(523)
Porcher, J., II: 42(356)
Potthast, A., IV: 47(409); VI: 59(472)
Powell, J. M., I: 5(344); VI: 19(460),
    27(465)
Powers, J. F., VIII: 82(520)
Prabhavananda, S., and Manchester, F.,
    VIII: 56(516)
Prawer, J., VI: 71(478)
Preschel, T., III: 23(366); VIII: 67(517)
Presser, J., VI: 53(470)
Presti, S. Lo, VIII: 145(532)
Preuss, H., VI: 1(456)
Previtali, G., IV: 63(416)
Pribram, A. F., IV: 68(417)
Prieto Paniagua, M. R., VI: 71(478)
Procacci, G., VIII: 103(524)
Prou, M., IV: 27(401)
Prutz, H., VI: 53(469)
Puhvel, J., IV: 16(394)
Pulignani, M. F., VI: 35(466)

Quarrie, P. R., III: 1(357)
Queller, D., IV: 13(387-8)
Quitslund, S. A., I: 8(346)

Rabb, T. K., and Seigel, J. E., IV: 45(407)
Rabin, C. M., V: 69(442); VIII: 34(510)
Rabinowitz, L. I., IV: 37(404), 60(415); V:
    48(434)
Rahman, S. A., VI: 57(471)
Rahn, J. R., IV: 24(399)
Raisin, J. S., V: 48(434); VIII: 91(522),
    26(530)
Rankin, O. S., VII: 7(486)
Randall, J. H., VIII: 160(534)
Ratzinger, J., VI: 44(467)
Ray, J. J., IV: 16(395)
Redigonda, A., VII: 35(500)

Reese, G., VIII: 86(522)
Reeves, M., VI: 6(457)
Regla Campistol, J., VII: 31(497)
Regne, J., VI: 73(479)
Reilly, B., III: 26(368)
Reinhart, A., VII: 35(500)
Reinlein, F. F., VI: 25(464)
Rembaum, J., III: 3(358); VII: 7(486)
Revel, H., IV: 37(404); VIII: 4(505), 8(506)
Rheinfelder, H., IV: 62(415)
Ribera, J., VIII: 86(521)
Richard, J., VI: 71(477-8)
Richardson, H. G., VI: 59(473)
Rieden, O. von, VIII: 152(533)
Riera, J., VII: 1(482)
Riley Smith, J., VI: 71(478)
Ringgren, H., and Strom, A. V., IV:
    16(394)
Rivera Recio, J. F., VII: 29(496)
Rivkin, E., V: 12(422); VII: 1(481), 1(482-3)
Rivlin, J. J., V: 40(431)
Rizzitano, U., IV: 62(415); VIII: 143(532)
Robert, U., VI: 59(473)
Robinson, I., VIII: 99(523)
Robinson, J., VII: 20(493)
Rodinson, M., IV: 62(415)
Roditi, E., IV: 56(413); VII: 1(483)
Rodriguez Eguia, C., VII: 42(504)
Rodriguez Fernandez, J., VIII: 72(518)
Roehricht, R., VI: 52(469)
Rollan Ortiz, J. F., VII: 29(496)
Roncaglia, M., VI: 55(470)
Root, W., VIII: 139(531)
Roques, R., II: 25(353)
Roscher, H., VI: 1(456)
Rosenthal, E. I. J., VIII: 41(513)
Rosenthal, F., III: 21(363)
Rosenthal, H., V: 4(420); VII: 16(491)
Rosenthal, J. M., V: 34(430); VIII: 38(512)
Rotenstreich, N., VII: 25(493)
Roth, A. N. T., V: 12(422)
Roth, C., I: 1(344); III: 26(367); IV:
    11(383), 11(386), 21(397), 42(405-6),
    62(415), 68(418); VI: 59(473); VII:
    7(486-7), 8(487), 8(488); VIII: 8(506),
    37(511), 92 & 94(523), 104(524),
    104(525)
Roth, C., et al., VIII: 37(511)
Roth, N., IV: 32(403)
Rowan, S., VII: 2(484-5)

Rubenstein, R., VII: 25(493)

Rudavsky, T. M., VIII: 41(513)

Ruether, R., IV: 2(381-2)

Ruiz, T. F., VII: 11(490)

Runciman, S., IV: 14(388); V: 31(428), 109(448); VIII: 57(516)

Russell, J. C., III: 36(371)

Russell, P. E., II: 17(352); VII: 2(484); VIII: 30(509)

Russell Gebbett, P., VIII: 85(521)

Russo, F., VI: 22(462)

Sabatier, P., VI: 22(461), 32(465-6)

Sachau, E., VI: 57(471)

Sahas, D., II: 8(350)

Saiz Barbera, J., VIII: 85(521)

Saladino, S., VIII; 162(534)

Saliba, J. A., I: 8(346)

Salmon, P., II: 8(350)

Salomon, H. P., VII: 1(483); VIII: 51(515), 72(518)

Salvador Miguel, N., III: 46(374)

Salvatorelli, L., VI: 22(462); VIII: 103(524)

Salzman, M., V: 14(425)

Samuelson, N., VIII: 41(513)

Sancris, F. de, VIII: 159(533-4)

Sandberg Vavala, E., IV: 65(416)

Santamaria, Mariano, III: 8(360), 44(373)

Santillana, D., VI: 57(471)

Saraiva, A. J., VIII: 1(482-3)

Sarasola, L. de, VI: 35(466)

Sarton, G., III: 6(359)

Saxl, F., VI: 1(456)

Schacht, J., and Bosworth, C. E., III: 21(363)

Schachter, Z. M., IV: 50(410)

Schapiro, M., II: 41(355)

Schechter, S., V: 10(421)

Scheiber, A., V: 13(423)

Scherer, J. E., VI: 72(479)

Schevill, F., VI: 24(462-3)

Schirmann, J. H., III: 30(370); IV: 24(400); V: 13(423), 14(424), 69(442)

Schlesinger, A. M., VIII: 79(519)

Schloessinger, M., V: 11(421), 31(428), 122(450); VIII: 45(514), 130(530)

Schmemann, A., VII: 23(493)

Schmidt, M. A., VI: 24(464)

Schmitt, F. A., III: 26(368)

Scholberg, K. R. III: 17(362); IV: 56(412); VII: 6(486), 8(487); VIII: 85(521)

Scholem, G., IV: 68(418); V: 25(426); VII: 17(492); VIII: 48, 49, 51 & 54(515), 61 & 62(516), 67(517), 131 & 133(530)

Schudt, J. J., IV: 68(417)

Schwabe, M., III: 59(377)

Schwartz, L. W., V: 11(422), 14(425)

Schwarzbaum, H., III: 1(357)

Schwarzfuchs, S., IV: 11(384), 18(396), 27(401); VIII: 9(506)

Schwarzschild, S., VII: 25(493)

Schwoebel, R., II: 3(348-9)

Schott, S. P., VI: 62(476)

Scuppa, G., VI: 24(463)

Sed Rajna, G., VII: 32(498)

Seiferth, W., IV: 16(392)

Seligsohn, M., VIII: 134(530)

Seligson, D. J., IV: 16(391-2)

Septimus, B., III: 10(361)

Serafini, A., VI: 24(463)

Sermoneta, J. B., IV: 62(415); VIII: 121(529), 127(530)

Serradifalco, D., VIII: 144(532)

Serrano, L., VII: 39(501)

Setton, K. M., IV: 21(398); VIII: 30(508-9)

Shakir, M., II: 19(352)

Shamir, Y., VII: 7(486)

Shapiro, A., and Ansbacher, B. M., IV: 28(402)

Shapiro, J., IV: 31(403)

Sharf, A., IV: 11(384), 18(396), 19(397), 24(399), 25(400); V: 120(450)

Shellabear, W. G., II: 19(352)

Shirk, M. V., VII: 2(485)

Shneidman, J. L., IV: 16(392)

Shochat, A., IV: 46(409); V: 11(421); VI: 59(472); VIII: 6(506)

Shochetman, J., IV: 68(417)

Shulavass, M., IV: 37(404)

Sibilia, S., VI: 24(463)

Sicroff, A. A., VII: 1(481), 8(487)

Siera, S. J., VIII: 112(527)

Sikes, J. G., V: 48(435)

Silberschlag, E., IV: 37(404)

Silver, A. H., III: 21(364); IV: 16(391)

Silver, D. J., IV: 20(397)

Simon, M., IV: 2(382)

Simonet, F. J., VII: 29(495-6)

Singer, C., III: 36(371); IV: 64(416)

Singer, C., and D. W., IV: 64(416)

548

Singer, C. and Veith, I., VIII: 147(532)
Sirat, C., Intro.: 4(343); VIII: 41(512)
Six, J. F. IX: 3(535)
Skidmore, M., VI: 56(471)
Slomp, J., III: 26(367)
Slutsky, Y., VII: 19(492)
Smith, C. E., VI: 45(467)
Sobreques Callico, J., VII: 2(485)
Soederhjelm, W., III: 4(359)
Sola Sole, J. M., IV: 56(412); IX: 3(535)
Sola Sole, J. M., Armistead, S. G., and
    Silverman, J. H., VII: 1(482)
Sommerfeldt, J., II: 15(351); VI: *(455)
Southern, R. W., II: 1(348); III: 26(367),
    63(378); IV: 62(415)
Speight, R. M., I: 8(346)
Spivakovsky, E., VIII: 27(508)
Spulber, N., IV: 16(394)
Starr, J., IV: 11(384), 18(395-6), 24(399),
    30(402-3), 31(403), 68(417); V: 92(446);
    VIII: 104(524)
Steinschneider, M., V: 40(431)
Stengers, J., IV: 56(412)
Stern, S., IV: 68(417)
Stern, S. M., V: 13(423)
Stevenson, R., VIII: 86(521-2)
Stierlin, H., VII: 29(496)
Stitskin, D., III: 35(371)
Stow, K., I: 9(346)
Straus, R., VI: 59(473)
Streit, R., and Dindinger, J., VI: 46(468)
Strumpf, D., IV: 69(418-9)
Stubblebine, J., IV: 63(416)
Suler, B., IV: 68(418)
Sumo, G., VIII: 104(524)
Sutherland, C. H. V., VIII: 103(524)
Sweetman, J. W., II: 1(348)
Symonds, J. A., VIII: 159(533)
Synan, E., I: 1(344), 5(344-5)
Szajkowski, Z., VII: 44(504)
Szarmach, P. E., IV: 2(381)

Talmadge, F., I: 5(345); VII: 1(482), 34(499)
Ta Shma, I. M., V: 31(428); VIII: 1(505),
    130(530)
Ta Shma, I. M., and Netzer, N., V:
    122(450)
Tate, R. B., VIII: 30(509)
Tatlock, J. S. P., III: 55(376)
Taton, R., III: 6(359)

Taylor, A. J. P., II: 3(348)
Taylor, P., VIII: 79(519)
Tedesche, S., and Zeitlin, S., V: 95(446)
Tee, G., III: 35(371)
Temkin, S. D., V: 1(420)
Tene, D., VIII: 36(511)
Thery, P. G., III: 29(369)
Thomas, R., II: 25(353)
Thompson, E. A., IV: 18(396); VIII:
    81(519)
Thompson, J. W., III: 26(368)
Thomson, S. H., VIII: 159(533)
Thorndike, L., III: 6(359)
Thorndike, L., and Kibre, P., III: 6(359)
Throop, P., VI: 46(468)
Thrupp, S., VI: 1(456)
Thurston, H., and Attwater, D., IV: 11(384)
Tibawi, A. L., II: 19(352)
Tillmann, H., VI: 16(459)
Tinivella, F., VIII: 147(532)
Toaff, A., VI: 22(462); VIII: 104(525),
    127(530)
Tondelli, L., VI: 22(462)
Torres Balbas, L., VIII: 86(522)
Touati, C., VIII: 41(512)
Touring Club Italiano, IV: 63 & 65(416);
    VIII: 139(531), 147(532)
Toussaint, M., VII: 42(504)
Trachtenberg, J., IV: *(381); V: 1(420)
Tritton, A. S., VI: 57(471)
Troilo, E., VIII: 160(534)
Tuchman, B., IV: *(380-1)
Turki, A. M., II: 7(349)
Turtel, C., VII: 19(492)
Tusa, V., VIII: 138(531)
Twersky, I., VII: 34(499); VIII: 41(513)
Tykocinski, H., V: 10(421)

Ullman, W., VIII: 117(529)
Unterman, I., I: 3(344)

Vago, B. A., VII: 20(493)
Vajda, G., V: 69(442); VII: 1(481-2),
    41(512), 41(513), 41(514)
Valsan, E. H., IV: 16(393)
Van Cleve, T., VI: 4(456), 48 & 49(468)
Vapito, G., VIII: 145(532)
Vasiliev, A. A., IV: 11(385); VIII: 140(531)
Vat, O. van der, II: 24(353)
Vazquez de Parga, L., VI: 10(458)

Vendrell, F., VII: 35(500)
Vera, F., III: 6(359)
Verlinden, C., VII: 2(485)
Vermes, G., V: 43(432)
Vernet, F., VI: 24(464)
Vicaire, M. H., VI: 34 & 35(466)
Vicaire, M. H., and Blumenkranz, B., IV: 16(393)
Vicens Vives, J., VII: 2(485)
Viegas Gueireiro, M., VII: 32(498)
Vilar, J. B., VII: 33(498)
Villa, J., de la, VII: 39(501)
Vincke, J., III: 17(362)
Virolleaud, C., VIII: 139(531)
Viscardi, A., VI: 25(464)
Vitale, V., VIII: 104(525)
Vogelstein, H., IV: 46(409), 62(415)
Vogelstein, H., and Rieger, H., IV: 46(409)
Vooy, C. G. N. de, IV: 56(412)
Vorgrimler, H., I: 2(344), 8(345)
Voulgarakis, E., IV: 11(384-5)
Vryonis, S. J., II: 8(350); VI: 64(476)

Waardenburg, J. J., II: 1(348); IX: 3(535)
Waas, A., VI: 20(461)
Wacholder, B. Z., IV: 16(392)
Wadding, L., VI: 46(468)
Wadstein, E., VI: 1(456)
Walsh, P. G., II: 33(355)
Waltz, J. C., II: 12(351), 30(354), 47(356)
Ware, T., VII: 15(491)
Warmington, B. H., VIII: 80(519)
Wasserman, H., VII: 12(491)
Waxman, M., V: 11(421); VIII: 40(512)
Way, L., VIII: 3(505)
Weakland, J. E., IV: *(381)
Wehr, H., V: 40(431)
Weinstein, M., III: 59(377)
Weiss Rosmarin, T., IV: 50(410)
Welborn, M. C., III: 26(368)
Werblowsky, R. J. Z., IV: 50(410)
Werner, A., VII: 27(494)
West, D. C., VI: 22(462)
Whartman, E., IV: 5(383)
White, L. T., Jr., III: 26(368); IV: 45(407-8); VI: 62(476); VIII: 60(516)
Whitehead, F., IV: 28(401)

Whitfield, F. J., VII: 15(491)
Whitmarsh, G., II: 3(348)
Widengren, G., VIII: 59(516)
Wiener, M., VI: 59(471)
Wieruszowski, H., VI: 62(476)
Wiesenthal, S., VII: 11(489)
Wigoder, G., III: 35(371)
Wilken, R., IV: 2(381-2)
Wilkins, E. H., VIII: 159(533)
Wilks, M., II: 33(355); VI: 25(465)
Will, W., VI: 25(464)
Williams, A. L., III: 10(361)
Wilpert, P., and Eckert, W., III: 3(358)
Winder, R. B., II: 2(348); IV: 16(393-4)
Winegarten, R., IV: 9(383)
Wischnitzer, M. IV: 37(404)
Wischnitzer, R., IV: 37(405)
Wiseman, F. J., VIII: 103(524)
Wolter, H., VI: 25(464)
Wood Brown, J., IV: 65(416)
Worman, E. J., V: 10(421)
Wright, D. F., VI: 25(465)

Yahil, L., VII: 20(493)
Yardeni, M., IV: 16(393)
Yarmolinsky, A., VIII: 94(523)
Yellin, D., and Abrahams, I., VI: 22(461)
Yerushalmi, Y., IV: 3(382-3)
Yule, H., V: 48(434)

Zacour, N. P., VI: 20(461)
Zaehner, R. C., IV: 16(394)
Zahareas, A. N., VIII: 85(521)
Zeitlin, S., VI: 20(461)
Zernov, N., VII: 15(491)
Ziegler, P., VIII: 2(485)
Zifrinowitsch, A., V: 13(424)
Zimmels, H. J., IV: 24(400), 35(403); VIII: 147(532)
Zimmerman, A., IV: 11(384)
Zimmerman, H., VI: 59(473)
Zinberg, I., VIII: 41(512)
Zobel, M. N., VIII: 41(513), 41(514)
Zuckerman, A., IV: 11(385), 20(397)
Zuckermandel, M. S., V: 43(432)
Zwemer, S. M., VI: 57(471)

Index

B'ne Mosheh, 133–4
Boccaccio, 330, 470
Bodin, Jean, 300, 532
Bodo-Elazar, 90–1, 93
Boetie, Etienne de la, 299
Bogomils, 26, 280
Bohemia, 116, 267, 417, 460
Boiardo, 330
Bologna, 188
Boniface IV, Pope, 345
Boniface VIII, Pope, 108, 118
Book of Common Prayer, 118
Book of Memoirs (of the exilarchate), 124
Bordeaux, 406
Bosh-Vila, J., 349
Bosnia, 280
Bramimonde, 356
B'ratzon (voluntary conversion), 207
Brazil, 247, 332
Bremen, 460
Breslau, Harry, 448
Bretons, 263
Bribes, 303–4, 307
Brindisi, 305
British Isles (see also England), 226
Brockelmann, C., 349
Brunamon, King, 413
Brundage, James, 186, 460
Bruno, Giordano, 534
Brussels, 100
Budapest, 417–8, 493
Buddhism, Buddha, 17, 280, 516
Buenhombre, Alfonso, 364
al-Buhari, 36
Bulan, Khan of the Khazars, 142–3
Bulard, Marcel, 103–7, 108–10
Bulgaria, 261, 344
Bulgars, 146
Buonaiuto, Andrea di (or da Firenze), artist, 110-4, 416
Buraq, 413
Burgkmair, Hans, artist, 114–6, 417
Burgo de Osma, 60–61, 363, 370
Burgos, 255, 266, 316, 374–5, 411
Burgundy, 49
Burke, Edmund, 419
Burns, Robert Ignatius, S.J., 2, 416, 420, 484, 487, 520, 522
Bustanai, 6, 124, 126–32, 173–7, 179-

80, 421, 425–30, 436
Bustanai, tomb of, 425
Buwayhid Sultans (see also al-Dawlah), 447
Byron, George Gordon, Lord, 419
Byzantium, Byzantine Empire, 25, 36, 90–3, 95, 124, 133, 139, 141–2, 144, 147–51, 155–67, 170, 174, 180, 227–8, 237, 312, 318, 324–5, 386–7, 395–7, 398, 400, 410, 416, 430, 444, 453, 455, 519
Byzantine Greek Orthodox Christians, 16, 25, 27, 37, 90, 116, 122, 292, 312, 317, 325, 328, 331, 352, 418

Cabanelas Rodriquez, 34
Cadiz, 256
Caesar of Heisterbach, 406, 480
Cahorsins, 302
Cain, 472, 475, 478
Cairo, 163, 169, 386
Cairo Genizah, 127–8
Calabria, 152, 164, 176, 305, 316, 385, 460
Caliphs, 33, 90, 126, 228, 259
Calvet, Melanie, of La Salette, 338
Calvinists, 16, 118, 238
Camaldoli, 25
Cambio, Arnolfo di, artist, 88
Campanella, Tommaso, 534
Campania, 303, 316, 329, 528
Canavesi, Giovanni, artist, 105
Candia, 116
Canon 68, Fourth Lateran Council (see also Badge of shame), 96, 196, 198-204, 471–2, 474, 479
Canon 69, Fourth Lateran Council, 196, 477
Canon law, 285
Cantera-Burgos, Francisco, 116, 216, 374, 387, 395
Cantigas de Santa Maria, 416
Capetians, 289
Capital (see also Wealth), 252
Capitula, 31, 38–9, 45
Capsali, Moses, chief rabbi, 509
Captives, 40, 97, 418, 448